BELLIGERENT REPRISALS

SCIENTIFIC COLLECTION
OF THE HENRY DUNANT INSTITUTE
Volume I

BELLIGERENT REPRISALS

by

FRITS KALSHOVEN

*Reader in International Law
in the University of Leyden*

Preface by
JEAN PICTET
*Member of the International Committee
of the Red Cross*

A. W. SIJTHOFF—LEYDEN

1971

ISBN 90 218 9051 8

Library of Congress Catalog Card Number: 76-147067
© A. W. Sijthoff's Uitgeversmaatschappij N.V., 1971

Printed in the Netherlands by A. W. Sijthoff, Printing Division, Leyden

"Saeva res bellum est, inquit Plutarchus, cumulum-
que secum trahit et injuriarum et insolentiae."

Grotius, *De iure belli ac pacis*, Lib. II Cap.
XXIV, § X.

"Les représailles ... sont ... un moyen d'empêcher
la guerre de devenir tout-à-fait barbare."

Henri Brocher, "Les principes naturels du droit
de la guerre", in *Revue de droit international et
de législation comparée*, Vol. V, 1873, p. 349.

Préface

Les actes de violence, commis en négation du droit humanitaire—terrorisme, représailles, prises d'otages, torture—se multiplient aujourd'hui dans le monde de façon inquiétante et laissent présager une redoutable escalade. On constate que plus les conflits prennent un caractère passionnel, moins le droit y est respecté. Des formes nouvelles de lutte, que l'on prétend justifiées par les nécessités de la guerre, se répandent, en violation des principes d'humanité les plus élémentaires, et tendent à abaisser, jusqu'à la barbarie, le niveau des affrontements. Veillons à ne pas leur donner trop de respectabilité. Il y a des comportements qui ne seront jamais des actes de guerre, mais qui resteront, toujours et seulement, des crimes. Loin d'être inéluctables, ces méthodes sont plutôt des solutions de facilité, qui, à la longue, ne sont pas "payantes" et feront du tort à la cause de ceux qui les emploient.

Depuis plus d'un demi-siècle, la Croix-Rouge s'est élevée contre les mesures de rigueur que l'on prétend infliger à des innocents, sous prétexte de nécessités militaires ou politiques. C'est ainsi qu'en 1916 le Comité international de la Croix-Rouge avait lancé un mémorable appel contre les représailles, proposant d'y renoncer totalement envers les personnes protégées par les Conventions de Genève. A cette époque encore, la majorité de la doctrine admettait les représailles comme moyen de coercition à l'encontre d'un adversaire qui ne tenait pas ses engagements, témoignant du caractère inorganique du droit international, puisqu'ainsi chaque Etat se faisait justice à lui-même. En 1943, le Comité international adjura les gouvernements de "respecter, même en face de considérations militaires, le droit naturel qu'a l'homme d'être traité sans arbitraire et sans lui imputer la responsabilité d'actes qu'il n'a pas commis."

Le Comité international de la Croix-Rouge fut entendu, puisque les Conventions de Genève, révisées et développées en 1949, ont interdit toutes représailles à l'égard des victimes soumises au droit de Genève, consacrant ainsi le principe de la responsabilité personnelle, l'un des fondements du droit. Ce fut certainement là une grande victoire de l'humanité, qu'ont saluée avec ferveur tous les hommes épris de justice et d'idéal. Car les représailles non seulement créent de grandes souffrances, mais aussi—et l'ouvrage de M. Kalshoven le montre à l'évidence—manquent presque toujours leur but, qui est la restauration du droit. Dans la tension extrême des esprits, qui accompagne les hostilités, elles risquent de provoquer des contre-mesures et, par un enchaînement fatal, de conduire aux plus graves abus. Une telle prohibition va dans le sens de l'évolution moderne du droit international: c'est un coup de plus porté au principe de la souveraineté absolue de l'Etat, déjà bien ébranlé.

L'interdiction des représailles ainsi établie a un caractère absolu. Elle vaut même si la violation à laquelle on prétend répondre s'est produite dans le champ des Conventions de Genève. Ainsi s'affirme le caractère inconditionnel de l'engagement contracté par les Puissances lorsqu'elles ont mis leur griffe au bas du parchemin.

Si les Conventions de Genève ont pu exclure les représailles, c'est parce qu'elles leur ont substitué d'autres moyens, plus propres à asseoir le respect du droit, notamment un système de contrôle et quelques mesures, encore embryonnaires, de sanction. Les dispositions relatives aux représailles rejoignent donc celles qui, en assurant l'application des Conventions en toutes circonstances, lui donnent le caractère d'un ordre supérieur fondé essentiellement sur la protection de la personne humaine.

Certes, la victoire remportée en 1949 n'est pas complète. Il reste à proscrire les représailles d'un vaste domaine—les lois et coutumes de la guerre, ou droit de La Haye—et c'est là, estime M. Kalshoven, qu'elles pourraient être le plus dangereuses. On sait que le Comité international de la Croix-Rouge a entrepris de nouveaux travaux tendant à réaffirmer et à développer les règles applicables dans les conflits armés. Il ne manquera pas d'appeler très sérieusement, sur ce point, l'attention des experts. Espérons qu'il en sortira une solution conforme aux expoirs légitimes des peuples.

Par les quelques réflexions qui précèdent, je crois avoir montré l'importance du problème des représailles, qui, loin d'être un sujet purement académique, recouvre aussi une brûlante actualité, puisqu'il doit, dans un proche avenir, faire l'objet de discussions approfondies en vue d'une extension du droit conventionnel. Le monumental ouvrage de M. Kalshoven apportera à cette entreprise une contribution de première valeur.

On sait aujourd'hui que le droit suit les faits plus qu'il ne les précède. On peut affirmer aussi qu'un de ses éléments fondamentaux est la stabilité. C'est pour cela—et sans que l'on en soit toujours conscient—que l'histoire tient une si large place dans l'étude des disciplines juridiques. Pour approcher un problème tel que celui des représailles, il est nécessaire d'en connaître les bases historiques et doctrinales, ainsi que les expériences faites. M. Kalshoven n'y a pas manqué et l'on doit lui en savoir gré.

Je tiens enfin à féliciter l'auteur d'avoir fait oeuvre scientifique et objective. Le livre qu'il nous apporte témoigne de solides recherches, d'un réel effort d'analyse et de synthèse, ainsi que d'une grande clarté de pensée. Cette somme, qui vient à son heure, constituera une source précieuse pour

PRÉFACE

quiconque s'intéresse non seulement à la question des représailles, mais également au développement du droit humanitaire dans son ensemble. Je suis heureux qu'on la doive à un citoyen des Pays-Bas, une nation qui a tant fait pour que la guerre soit moins inhumaine.

JEAN PICTET
*Membre du Comité international
de la Croix-Rouge
Membre du Conseil de l'Institut Henry-Dunant
Chargé de cours à l'Université de Genève*

12 novembre 1970

IX

Introduction

One of the methods used by States to protect their legal interests against unlawful encroachments by another State consists in recourse to reprisals, *i.e.*, an equally unlawful retort destined to make the opponent mend his ways. Nowadays, States are no longer completely free in selecting measures of reprisal: an obvious restriction is implied in their obligation, contained in Article 2, paragraph 4, of the Charter of the United Nations, to "refrain in their international relations from the threat or use of force against the territorial integrity or political independence of any state, or in any other manner inconsistent with the Purposes of the United Nations". The Special Committee which the General Assembly of the United Nations set up in 1964 to study the "Principles of International Law concerning Friendly Relations and Co-operation among States" found no difficulty whatsoever in concluding from this general obligation that States have, in particular, a duty to refrain from acts of reprisal involving the use of armed force.[1]

While the above applies in normal times, one can equally envisage that States (or, more generally, belligerent parties) involved in an armed conflict resort to reprisals consisting in an intentional infringement of the law of armed conflict,[2] with a view to making the opposing party abandon an unlawful practice of warfare. The purpose of this study is to examine whether, and to what extent, belligerents are free, as a matter of law, to have recourse to such belligerent reprisals.

The importance of this subject is evident when it is realized that the law of armed conflict is itself a marginal law, in that it deals for the most part with situations where the behaviour of the human species verges on the brink of what could still be considered human, and, at any rate, can only be justified by an appeal to military necessity. The act of setting aside, by way of belligerent reprisals, such marginal norms involves, therefore, the perplexing question of how far one may go in using inhumanity as a means of enforcing the law of armed conflict, that is, in the interests of humanity.

[1] See the 1969 report of the Special Committee on Principles of International Law concerning Friendly Relations and Co-operation among States (Doc. A/7619), paras. 26(4) and 69-72.

[2] As regards this terminology, see: G. Schwarzenberger, *The Law of Armed Conflict*, 1968, p. 1.

The paradoxical nature of this question, combined with a certain fatalistic acceptance of the phenomenon of belligerent reprisals as something unavoidable, have more than once in the past led to the idea that they had better be left undiscussed, so as to avoid even the semblance of attributing legality to so odious a concept.[3] It need hardly be emphasized that the present writer does not share that feeling. Indeed, I am firmly convinced that it is vastly preferable to bring the concept into the open and so to create the possibility of its ultimate control, where otherwise it might remain a sort of bogey tormenting the minds of those engaged in the codification and further development of the law of armed conflict.

The enquiry is organized along the following lines. In a first Chapter, the concept of belligerent reprisals is placed, both historically and from a systematic point of view, in the context of the general notion of reprisals and, even wider, of international law and the sanctions processes forming part of it. The second and third Chapters are devoted to an examination of the attitudes taken, and the rules developed, with respect to belligerent reprisals by the various Conferences and other international bodies involved, in the periods prior to the First and Second World Wars, respectively. The fourth Chapter deals with the complicated matter of the British measures of reprisal taken in the Second World War, in 1939 and 1940, in the context of economic warfare against Germany and her allies. Other reprisals, or alleged reprisals, taken by belligerents in that war and involving such matters as indiscriminate bombardment of the enemy population, the killing of prisoners of war and the taking and killing of hostages, are examined in Chapter V.

The developments after the Second World War are dealt with in Chapter VI: war crimes trials involving the plea of belligerent reprisals, achievements and so far unsuccessful attempts in the field of the codification and development of the law of armed conflict and, in that context, of the law as to belligerent reprisals, and instances of (alleged) belligerent reprisals in recent armed conflicts. Chapter VII, finally, summarizes the results of these enquiries; it sets out the present state of the law with respect to belligerent reprisals, applies this to certain topical and so far unsolved issues such as nuclear retaliation, and points out some developments of the law which will be necessary in order ultimately to achieve the complete prohibition of all forms of belligerent reprisals.

While the subject of enquiry of the present study is wide and in fact covers the whole field of the law of armed conflict, the author has found it necessary to apply certain limitations in order to avoid the work becoming unduly extended. Firstly, the impact of belligerent reprisals on the rights of

[3] See in particular the record of the debates at the Brussels Conference of 1874, *infra*, Chapter II, § 2.1.

neutrals has not been discussed separately. It is felt that the crucial issues of belligerent reprisals lie not so much in that connection as in their effects on the belligerents and, in particular, on the human beings on the two opposing sides. Even the British reprisals taken in 1939 and 1940 in the context of economic warfare, although directly interfering with neutral interests, are therefore discussed first and foremost from the point of view of their legality or illegality as against Germany and her allies.

Secondly, the author has refrained from making the earlier State practice, *i.e.*, the practice preceding the Second World War, the subject of separate discussion. The reason for this limitation is purely economical: this practice has been described in the literature several times, and any new description could hardly add much to what already has been written. The outcomes of these earlier writings have been used where necessary, such as, for instance, in the concluding section of Chapter III where the state of the law as to belligerent reprisals before the outbreak of the Second World War is summarized. One might in addition remark that evidently much of the older State practice has been familiar to, and has been taken into account by, those taking part in the drafting process of the various conventions and other international instruments bearing on the law of armed conflict that were brought about in that period.

A third limitation concerns the more recent literature. There is a vast amount of literature dealing with the law of armed conflict in general or with specific aspects thereof. As the subject of the present study touches upon many of these general and specific issues, the idea of completeness in referring to those other writings has been abandoned as both impracticable and for present purposes unnecessary. After all, the intention was not to write another book over the law of armed conflict in its entirety, but merely on the specific subject of belligerent reprisals as one of its means of enforcement.

There remains the agreeable task of expressing my gratitude to all those who in one way or another have contributed to the success of my undertaking. First of all, I thank the Henri Dunant Institute for their willingness to include this book in their scientific series. Then, I thank the personnel of the Peace Palace Library, and Miss A. Belinfante in particular, for their invaluable help in finding the many, often well-hidden publications and documents necessary for my investigations. Again, I owe a debt of gratitude to Mrs. M. van Leeuwen Boomkamp, Mrs. E. Kettner and my son Erik, who have taken upon themselves the task of reading the proofs, and Mr. J. G. Lammers who has helped me in composing the index. Lastly, I thank Mr. G. Wittenberg, barrister-at-law, who began the task of correcting my Dutchman's English, and Mr. S. Kahn, barrister-at-law, who has finished this task and, in fact, has borne by far the greater part of it.

Contents

III. THE PERIOD BETWEEN THE FIRST AND SECOND WORLD WARS

IV. REPRISALS IN THE SECOND WORLD WAR-I: BRITISH REPRISALS ORDERS, 1939-1940

V. REPRISALS IN THE SECOND WORLD WAR-II

CONTENTS

VI. DEVELOPMENTS AFTER THE SECOND WORLD WAR

VII. RESULTS AND PERSPECTIVES

CONTENTS

XVIII

Abbreviations

AJIL	American Journal of International law
Annuaire	Annuaire de l'Institut de droit international
Annual Digest	Annual Digest and Reports of Public International Law Cases
BYIL	British Yearbook of International Law
Cmd.	(British) Command Papers
ICRC	International Committee of the Red Cross
I.C.J.	International Court of Justice
I.M.T.	International Military Tribunal, Nuremberg
I.M.T. Vol. ...	Trial of the Major War Criminals before the International Military Tribunal, Nuremberg, 14 November 1945-1 October 1946; official text in the English language, published at Nuremberg, Germany, by the Secretariat of the Tribunal, Vols. I-XLII
IRRC	International Review of the Red Cross
N.R.G.	De Martens, Nouveau Recueil Général
Off. J.	League of Nations Official Journal
POW	Prisoner(s) of War
R.d.C.	Académie de droit international, Recueil des Cours
RDILC	Revue de droit international et de législation comparée
RGDIP	Revue générale de droit international public
RICR	Revue internationale de la Croix-Rouge
U.N.T.S.	United Nations Treaty Series
U.N.W.C.C.	United Nations War Crimes Commission

CHAPTER I

General Aspects of Reprisals

1.1. HISTORICAL OUTLINE

Belligerent reprisals are not an isolated notion: they are a species of the genus reprisals. Consequently, before the specific notion of belligerent reprisals can be adequately discussed, it is necessary to give the main lines of the general concept of reprisals, from both the historical and the theoretical points of view.

The evolution through the centuries of the concept of reprisals in its broadest sense has more than once been the subject of apt and detailed description,[1] when it was duly emphasized that reprisals have had a place in all primitive legal orders. As one author has put it: "The simple idea of retaliation is as old as the customs underlying the *lex talionis*."[2] On the other hand, reprisals gained particular importance in the context of international relations, where they came to embrace such divergent notions as private reprisals, taken against foreigners by or on behalf of private persons, and, at a later stage, the public reprisals of State against State.

For present purposes, a mere outline of this historical development will suffice, taking as our starting-point the disintegration of the Roman Empire and the attendant dissolution of centralized authority in Europe. Among the effects thereof was the revival of private reprisals. These "had as their aim the compensation of specific individuals in cash terms of loss plus damage",[3] in cases where the "loss plus damage" resulted from dealings with a foreigner[4] and compensation could not be obtained (or was not even sought) with the aid of regular judicial proceedings before a competent foreign court. Compensation was then sought by the simple method of

---

[1] See, *e.g.*, Evelyn Speyer Colbert, *Retaliation in International Law*, 1948; Yves de la Brière, "Evolution de la doctrine et de la pratique en matière de représailles", *R.d.C.* 1928, Vol. II, p. 241; H. A. Schütze, *Die Repressalie unter besonderer Berücksichtigung der Kriegsverbrecherprozesse*, 1950.

[2] Colbert, *op. cit.* n. 1, p. 10.

[3] *Loc. cit.* n. 2.

[4] That private reprisals developed in particular in relation to foreigners and thus serve "to illuminate the significance of citizenship in earlier stages of the development of international law", is emphasized by H. F. van Panhuys, *The Rôle of Nationality in International Law*, 1959, p. 106.

1

taking possession, on the high seas or in the territory of the creditor, of a certain quantity of goods belonging either to the debtor or to his compatriots, and the seizure was effected either by the creditor himself or by the public authorities.

The practice of private reprisals, largely unregulated at the outset, gradually became subject to norms locally regulating both its substantive and its procedural aspects, and extending even to judicial supervision in the territory of the creditor. It was bound to disappear sooner or later, however, with the "... development of alternative practices. One of the most important of these was the development of legal procedures expediting the settlement of disputes in which foreigners were involved."[5] After a gradual decline, the practice finally died out in the second half of the 17th century.

This practice of claiming and collecting external debts by laying hands on any goods of the foreign debtor or of his compatriots within reach was obviously an abnormal one, motivated and justified by the apparent impracticability of collecting the debt in question by normal means (*e.g.*, a voluntary payment by the debtor, perhaps under the stimulus of a summons, or the normal enforcement of a legal title). In the decentralized situation resulting from the disintegration of the Roman Empire, private reprisals were applied in Europe as an expedient for the unilateral enforcement of external claims, where there were no reasonably effective, publicly organized procedures of judicial settlement available to the creditor in the country of the debtor. The practice, however, though irregular, was not arbitrary: the reprisals were kept in check by regulations,—at least so long as they were resorted to and carried out in the exclusive interest of the individual creditors. For the increasing practice of executing private reprisals with the aid of the local authorities carried the danger that "they could so easily become a tool of state policy as distinct from a legal remedy for certain well-understood wrongs",[6] that is, when Governments for political reasons decided to stage a resort to so-called private reprisals in circumstances where these were not justified. This danger became manifest in complete "wars of reprisals" in the 16th and 17th centuries. With this development, however, the field of private reprisals proper had already become entangled with that of public reprisals.

The initial absence of a concept of public reprisals is explained by the fact that in early European practice no distinction was made between the several more or less limited modes of using force in interstate relations: all of these were indiscriminately brought under the heading of war.[7] A separate

---

[5] Colbert, *op. cit.* n. 1, p. 13.

[6] *Ibid.*, p. 47.

[7] *E.g.*, N. Politis, preliminary report on reprisals in time of peace, composed for the Commission of the *Institut de Droit International* charged with preparing a resolution on that subject; in: *Annuaire*, 1934, p. 27.

2

category of public reprisals developed in Europe from the 16th century. Not unlike private reprisals, early public reprisals as applied from the 16th to 18th centuries took the form of the seizure in port or on the high seas, by public or private ships, of ships and goods of the opposing State or its nationals. The most characteristic feature of public, as opposed to private, reprisals was that the former "... authorized unlimited seizures as a sort of punishment of the offending state. In other words, compensation ceased to be the object of reprisals when they became public; retaliatory seizures became instead a sanction, a weapon to enforce a change in the opponent's policy." [8]

Like private reprisals, public reprisals also developed in a period characterized by the disappearance of centralized authority, in this case that of the Holy Roman Emperor and the Pope, and by the almost complete decentralization of the international community which resulted. The situation leading to the practice of public reprisals was, however, characterized by other factors that had not played a part in the early stages of private reprisals. It may suffice to mention two: the fact that under the dual reign of Emperor and Pope, the princes had resorted to war as frequently as to other less violent, more or less centrally controlled methods of resolving disputes; and the development of the personal principalities into territorial entities (States). Whereas in the case of private reprisals the disappearance of centralized authority had left the actors and the nature of their claims unchanged and it was the unilateral use of force that emerged as an unprecedented, irregular practice, public reprisals developed among actors differing significantly from their predecessors in the international arena but who had inherited from them a practice of resorting to force that could be regarded as a customary form of irregular conduct. While it is therefore correct to observe that both private and public reprisals emerged in a situation characterized by the lack of an authority capable of ensuring the normal enforcement of legitimate claims and thus of removing the urge towards the unilateral execution of justice where it was not administered, this cannot provide a completely satisfactory explanation of the emergence of public reprisals: that can only be attained when one takes into account that in the emerging situation of international decentralization the leaders of the newly independent territorial entities came to perceive that it was sometimes to their advantage, as well as feasible, to make an express distinction in their international relations between the employment of armed force limited to a single form and the comprehensive use of armed force amounting to war.

Another parallel with private reprisals may be discerned: like the resort to private reprisals in the early stages of their development, the recourse to public reprisals was not at the outset subject to any particular limitations.

[8] Colbert, *op. cit.* n. 1, p. 55.

The parallel is not, however, complete. Private reprisals, being a mode of obtaining compensation for a private external claim, usually a readily ascertainable sum, could be said to possess an intrinsic limit and, both therefore and because of the position of the claimant as a member of an organized territorial community, were not opposed to regulations of that community intended to ensure the observance of that limit. These aspects were somewhat different in the case of early public reprisals: usually, neither the size of the State's claim nor the severity of the reprisal, as a "punishment of the offending state" inflicted "to enforce a change in the opponent's policy", would be easily ascertainable. Furthermore, neither the claimant nor the opponent were subject to any higher authority, as both were sovereign members of the decentralized international community. Hence, apart from the obvious limitation implicit in the seizure of ships as the sole mode of force applied, no special characteristics gave impetus to the idea of regulation and limitation of recourse to public reprisals.

The further history of public reprisals shows first of all a gradual widening of their scope, as more and more specific actions were removed from the general concept of war and brought under the specific heading of reprisals. In the 19th century, peacetime reprisals came to embrace such measures of force short of war as pacific blockade and military occupation. This type of reprisals involving the use of armed force came to an end, as far as the period before the Second World War is concerned, with the Italian bombardment and occupation of Corfu, in 1923.[9]

A further extension of the category of public reprisals resulted from the gradual realization that the characteristic features of armed reprisals could equally be discerned in certain retaliatory acts of a non-violent nature involving economic or financial, diplomatic or cultural relations. This rather less violent manifestation of reprisals, the rise of which is connected with the gradual increase in the areas of State activity governed by international law, appears to subsist to the present day.

A final field of application of public reprisals opened with the rapid development, since the 19th century, of the general law of war, both as customary law and in the form of multilateral treaties. An infringement of one or other rule of the law of war would usually entail some form of damage for the enemy, and the offended belligerent might, in the absence of more adequate means of redress, feel entitled to resort to reprisals in order to compel the offender to comply with the rules of warfare. Initially,

---

[9] Instances of armed reprisals have probably occurred in the period after the Second World War, *e.g.*, in the relations between Israel and the Arab countries, and between the U.S.A. and North Viet Nam. However, these events cannot simply be classed as peacetime reprisals as they occurred in the context of situations bearing many characteristics of war. See also hereafter, Ch. VI, § 6.3.1.

some authors defended the view that such belligerent reprisals were inconceivable, in view of the, indeed blatant, impracticability of recourse to measures short of war whilst a war is being waged. It was soon realized, however, that this was a false argument and that the law of war itself offered ample room for a recourse to measures violating one or other of its norms, but which might operate—and, it was hoped, find justification—in a way similar to that of the measures short of war applied in more peaceful times. The wars of the 19th and 20th centuries abound in instances of this practice, e.g. refusing quarter to the enemy, maltreatment and killing of prisoners of war, etcetera.

Another aspect of the development of public reprisals was the gradual recognition, by theorists and States alike, of norms limiting their legitimate use. It was observed in the foregoing that early public reprisals had actually possessed some limits of sorts: viz., the requirement of a previous infringement of law on the part of the other State, and the restriction of the actions to the seizure of ships and goods. The latter limitation in particular was of a political rather than a legal nature: the recourse to reprisals was an indication that no intention of war was present on the part of the retaliating State. The further development emphasizes this point: the disengagement of specific coercive actions from the general concept of war served to create the possibility of a resort to limited force without starting a war.

Other limits, of a legal character, became manifest only at a relatively late stage. Confining the discussion for the moment to peacetime reprisals, one of the first questions was whether a resort to armed force could constitute a legitimate reprisal. This question was broached (though in a far from satisfactory manner) in the debate which arose after the abovementioned Italian bombardment and occupation of Corfu, in September 1923; an action which had resulted in some fifteen dead and numerous wounded among the population of the island. The action had clearly been intended as a coercive measure, motivated by the refusal of the Greek Government to concede to the strong demands of the Italian Government to remedy the wrong caused by the assassination on Greek territory, on 27 August of that year, of the Italian members of an international commission for the delimitation of the southern boundary of Albania. Indeed, in the course of the ensuing debate in the Council of the League of Nations the Italian representative characterized the action as a legitimate reprisal.[10]

After the parties had reached agreement on the settlement of the dispute, the League Council submitted the delicate problems that had arisen concerning, *inter alia*, the relation between the Covenant and an institution of classical international law like reprisals, to a Special Committee of Jurists

---

[10] Off. J. 1923: Minutes of the Council's 26th Meeting held at Geneva from 31 August to 29 September 1923.

composed of ten jurists from all parts of the world.[11] This Committee produced the following, wonderfully non-committal reply: [12]

"Coercive measures which are not intended to constitute acts of war may or may not be consistent with the provisions of Articles 12 to 15 of the Covenant, and it is for the Council, when the dispute has been submitted to it, to decide immediately, having due regard to all the circumstances of the case and to the nature of the measures adopted, whether it should recommend the maintenance or the withdrawal of such measures."

This reply, to be sure, can be interpreted as an acknowledgment that measures of coercion, reprisals not excluded, might be inconsistent with the Covenant. It may even have been the intention of the Committee (as has been stated by one of its members) to convey the idea that a coercive use of military force like this by Italy was forbidden under its terms.[13] The reply pointedly refrained, however, from giving even the slightest indication of the circumstances that would render coercive measures inconsistent with the Covenant. When at a later stage, at the instigation of the Netherlands Government, the Council invited the Governments which might so desire to comment on the Committee's reply, eleven out of the twenty-one Governments who responded expressed the opinion that the Committee should have given such an indication.[14]

It should be added that under the Charter of the United Nations this question has gained greater clarity. For, while it is saying too much that the coming into force of the Charter has removed any uncertainty concerning the legitimacy or illegitimacy of reprisals involving the use of armed force

---

[11] It was even managed to avoid prejudicing the question of the legitimacy of coercive measures under classical international law. The question ran as follows (Off. J. 1923, p. 1351): "Are measures of coercion which are not meant to constitute acts of war consistent with the terms of Articles 12 to 15 of the Covenant when they are taken by one Member of the League of Nations against another Member of the League without prior recourse to the procedure laid down in these Articles?"

[12] Off. J. 1924, p. 524.

[13] In 1924, Ch. de Visscher wrote that "en déclarant en termes généraux qu'il y a des mesures de coercition incompatibles avec [les obligations du Pacte], [la réponse] réprouve au moins implicitement les plus graves d'entre elles, notamment les occupations de territoire, les bombardements, etc. Quoi qu'il en soit, la légitimité des représailles armées, sous l'empire du Pacte, est à nos yeux une question de principe et non une question d'espèce: estimant que le Pacte a condamné d'une façon absolue et a priori le recours à des mesures de cette nature, nous ne pourrions reconnaître au Conseil le pouvoir d'en admettre, dans un cas donné, la légitimité"; "L'Interprétation du Pacte au lendemain du différend italo-grec", in RDILC, 1924, p. 213, at p. 387.

[14] League of Nations Document C. 212, M. 72, 1936. V.—As for the history of the Corfu incident, see, e.g., G. P. Pink, The Conference of Ambassadors (1920-1931), Geneva Studies Vol. XII, 1942, Nos. 4-5; J. Barros, The Corfu Incident of 1923. Mussolini and the League of Nations, 1965.

in time of peace, it cannot be denied that the Principles laid down in Article 2, sections 3 and 4, point strongly towards the prohibition of such use.[15]

Other aspects of the limits to reprisals were examined by arbitrators in the Naulilaa case.[16] The facts, as far as here relevant, may be summarized as follows. In October 1914, at a time when Portugal was still neutral in the First World War, three German officials of the German colony of South-West Africa were killed by Portuguese soldiers at Naulilaa, a Portuguese station near the boundary between Portuguese Angola and the German colony. The incident was the result of a series of misunderstandings coupled with a certain imprudence and an unfortunate gesture on the part of one of the Germans. Afterwards, it was held by the arbitrators that the incident did not amount to an illegal act either on the part of Germany or Portugal. The German authorities in the colony had, however, at the time and without much inquiry taken the view that it constituted an international wrong by Portugal which justified a resort to reprisals, and, after the news of the incident had for several consecutive nights been transmitted in clear from the German colony to all German radio stations, the Germans carried out several military actions against Portuguese stations in the region across the border, causing the Portuguese to retreat in a northerly direction. This in turn gave the natives an opportunity to rise in the whole region south-west of the new front and Portugal had to send a major expeditionary force to restore its authority.

After due consideration, the arbitrators gave a negative answer to the question as to whether this sequence of violent actions constituted a legitimate reprisal, on the grounds that: (1) no illegal action on the part of Portugal had warranted recourse to reprisals, (2) such recourse ought to have been preceded by a request to remedy the alleged injury (a requirement that, as the arbitrators expressly pointed out, had not been met by the nocturnal transmissions to German radio stations outside the colony), and (3) the actions chosen were disproportionate to the alleged wrong. With regard to the last requirement the arbitrators placed on record that an earlier consensus of opinion among authors, to the effect that proportionality must be observed in recourse to reprisals, had recently lost some ground; but, as they said, the tendency of the developing international law

[15] See also the report of the Special Committee on Principles of International Law concerning Friendly Relations and Co-operation among States, United Nations Document A/6799, 26 Sept. 1967, § 107: "There was agreement that every State has the duty to refrain from acts of armed reprisal, but agreement was not reached on whether a statement to this effect should refer as well to acts of this nature not involving the use of armed force."
[16] Arbitration between Portugal and Germany, Award of 31 July 1928; Reports of International Arbitral Awards, Vol. II, p. 1011.

7

was certainly "à restreindre la notion de représaille légitime et à prohiber l'excès".[17] And they added the following important observation: [18, 19]

> "Même si l'on admettait que le droit des gens n'exige pas que la représaille se mesure approximativement à l'offense, on devrait certainement considérer, comme excessives et partant illicites, des représailles hors de toute proportion avec l'acte qui les a motivées. Or, en l'espèce, ... il y a eu disproportion évidente entre l'incident de Naulilaa et les 6 actes de représailles qui l'ont suivi."

The issue of the limitations on peacetime reprisals was finally dealt with in its entirety by the *Institut de Droit International* in a resolution adopted in 1934, which contained a complete set of rules, both of a procedural and substantive character, for the recourse to reprisals.[20] In Article 4, armed reprisals were declared prohibited in the same circumstances where recourse to war was excluded (whether by virtue of the Briand-Kellogg Pact or in accordance with any other régime that might be adopted in future). The legitimate recourse to non-armed reprisals was made conditional on the previous fulfilment of the State's obligations with regard to procedures of peaceful settlement (Art. 5). Then, the following rules applicable to all peacetime reprisals, whether armed or otherwise, were proclaimed in Article 6:

> "1° Mettre au préalable l'Etat auteur de l'acte illicite en demeure de le faire cesser et d'accorder éventuellement les réparations requises;
>
> 2° Proportionner la contrainte employée à la gravité de l'acte dénoncé comme illicite et à l'importance du dommage subi;
>
> 3° Limiter les effets des représailles à l'Etat contre qui elles sont dirigées, en respectant, dans toute la mesure du possible, tant les droits des particuliers que ceux des Etats tiers;

---

[17] *Ibid.*, p. 1026.

[18] *Ibid.*, p. 1028. Here, the arbitrators apparently relied more on "the general principles of law recognized by civilized nations" (as this source is defined in Art. 38 of the Statute of the International Court of Justice) than on custom; this was in conformity with their earlier announcement that they would bridge possible lacunae of international law "en statuant suivant les principes d'équité, tout en restant dans le sens du droit des gens, appliqué par analogie, et en tenant compte de son évolution"; *ibid.*, p. 1016.

[19] The importance of the award should not be over-rated: the decision was rendered by an ad hoc college of three arbitrators, all of Swiss nationality; hence, neither permanence of the judicial body nor a varied composition representing "the main forms of civilization and the principal legal systems of the world" (Art. 9 of the Statute of the International Court) enhance its value. Due allowance made for these and similar sobering considerations, however, it remains that the award was the outcome of a process of decision-making which in the international community of the time was—as it is today—respected as authoritative.

[20] *Annuaire*, 1934, pp. 692, 708-711.

4° S'abstenir de toute mesure de rigueur qui serait contraire aux lois de l'humanité et aux exigences de la conscience publique;

5° Ne pas détourner les représailles du but qui en a déterminé initialement l'usage; et

6° Cesser les représailles aussitôt qu'il aura été obtenu une satisfaction raisonnable."

Finally, reprisals in reply to legitimate reprisals were expressly excluded (Art. 7).

The *Institut* not being vested with law-making authority, the adoption of the resolution, by a 53 to 3 majority with 6 abstentions, could not bestow force of law on any of its provisions. Evidently, these could nevertheless form part of international law, deriving their force from other sources; on the other hand, they might be *ius constituendum*. On this issue the drafters of the resolution did not provide any enlightenment: they deliberately refrained from indicating where, in their opinion, the line lay between positive law and *ius constituendum*, on the ground that recent developments, particularly in the organization of the international community, had influence on the law of reprisals and that some of the ensuing innovations might still be in the process of hardening into law. In this situation, they considered it an advantage "de laisser dans le vague si les dispositions proposées dans le Règlement sont du droit actuel ou du droit de l'avenir".[21] The preparatory reports and the debates, however, bear witness to the fact that those participating in the drafting consistently kept in mind the need firstly to codify existing law: they merely saw no reason to let the work be hampered by detailed arguments as to its precise scope.

Passing over for the moment the question of the development of norms limiting recourse to belligerent reprisals (which question shall be dealt with in detail in subsequent chapters) the above may be summarized as follows. In the period under consideration, the concept of reprisals as applied in the sphere of international relations has shifted from private reprisals, aiming at the settlement by irregular methods of private claims, to public reprisals. While the latter initially occurred in one form only, viz., the seizure of ships and goods, they have since come to embrace widely different modes of unilateral coercion both in time of peace and war. In contrast with private reprisals, public reprisals did not generally serve to collect certain well-defined debts,[22] but to enforce compliance with claims of a widely varying nature.

---

[21] *Ibid.*, p. 5. This relieved the drafters in particular of the task of taking sides in recent conflicts, such as that around the Corfu incident in 1923; *ibid.*, p. 55.

[22] However, public reprisals could of course be used for that very purpose. Actually, the first conscious attempt to restrict the use in time of peace of armed force for purposes of coercion in interstate relations concerned precisely the resort to armed reprisals against a State which failed to pay a contractual debt: the so-called Porter Convention concluded at the Second Hague Peace Conference in 1907.

At this point it seems opportune to give a somewhat more concrete indication of the place which public reprisals hold in international relations. In that context it may be noted that a State which feels wronged by the internationally unlawful conduct of another State has available a number of widely divergent alternative reactions. To name some of the alternatives (and without prejudice to their legality or illegality): the State can acquiesce, or seek compensation at the expense of third States, or send a note of protest, or start bilateral negotiations with a view to settlement, or appeal to a qualified organ of an international organization, or resort to direct coercion against the other State, and so on. Viewed in the context of this list of alternative policies, the reprisal can be characterized as a decision to act, not acquiesce; to act unilaterally, not by a bilateral or institutional procedure; to apply effective coercion, not mere moral pressure; to resort to limited coercion instead of all-out war; to rely not so much on naked power only as on title and authority as well.

This policy decision rests on a specific reasoning: viz., that the wronged State is not merely impelled, but also somehow or other entitled to have recourse to a mode of acting not normally permitted in interstate relations, but which may serve to coerce the opposing State to act in conformity with international law. It is this reasoning which underlies the development of public reprisals into a widely (though not universally) accepted concept not only in the practice of States, but in the doctrine of international law. Indeed, to deny the status of reprisals as an institution of international law can hardly be correct, in view of the uncommonly high degree of decentralization which characterizes international society to the present day and which must needs be reflected in international law, if only by the recognition for the time being of a legal power of the States, as the decentralized authoritative power units, to act unilaterally in defence of their rights and of the international legal order.

This power, however, is neither arbitrary nor unlimited. Certain more or less definite rules have come to be recognized which govern and limit the recourse to reprisals as an instrument of law. In part, this development is a consequence of the slow but unmistakable growth of institutional structures in international society, in the form of the emerging international organizations. Though this has not so far led to any significant, permanent increase in the recourse by States to arbitration and judicial settlement, as the most sophisticated "legal procedures expediting the settlement of disputes" [23] at their disposal, it seems on the other hand realistic to state that as the new institutions provide States with other effective modes of settling disputes and attaining their legitimate ends, the urge to resort unilaterally to reprisals decreases.

[23] Colbert, *op. cit.* n. 1, p. 13.

10

1.2. REPRISALS IN CONTEMPORARY INTERNATIONAL LAW

The next objective should be to arrive at a more precise assessment of the place and function of reprisals in the international legal order. To that end, a first step will be to state my views on the nature of international law, as a system of norms operating in international society. Next, some remarks will be made about the place of sanctions in that system. A final matter for discussion will be the function and characteristics of reprisals as sanctions of international law.

1.2.1. *International law: its nature*

International law, like other systems of law, is conceived of as a system of norms, or "body of rules". In most general terms, legal norms abstractly prescribe certain modes of conduct for certain particular situations. Essentially, norms are prescriptive, not predictive in character: they do not state what is bound to happen nor what is likely to happen, but what ought to happen. This does not imply that no importance attaches to the degree of conformity of events with preconceived norms: on the contrary, a high degree of effectiveness is the goal of all norms, and a certain minimum effectiveness is a requirement for their very existence. But so long as a norm does in fact exist, its essentially normative character renders it independent of its relative effectiveness; its function is to lay down objectively that a certain type of conduct ought to occur whenever a certain situation arises, whether now or in the future, and irrespective of the personal particularities, desires, etc., of those confronted with the norm.[1]

The norms of international law, taken together, form a system: the international legal order, being the legal order of international society. The norms range from precise and specific rules to the widest general principles. One of the effects of such general principles as objectivity, *bona fides*, and reasonableness, is to strengthen the cohesion among the norms of the system.

There are different views as to which norms form part of the system. According to the Positivists, only those norms can be recognized as legal norms which originate from the formal sources of international law (Kelsen); according to others, the "body of rules" comprises norms of different origin as well: the norms of natural law, being norms inherent in human conscience and reason (Thomas Aquinas) or norms originating in international society as a sort of natural-social growth independent of formal sources (Scelle: *droit objectif*).

The fact that the norms of international law, whether positive or other-

---

[1] Law, and also international law, is only one among several normative orders. However, it is not intended to enter into the similarities and dissimilarities of the various orders.

wise, form a system, is apparent both in their creation and application. Norms do not come into being *in vacuo*, but in the framework of the pre-existing system. Thus, when a treaty is concluded, it need not be stipulated that its provisions shall be binding on the parties. Again, a norm concerning some specific use of the high seas will develop in interdependence with the principle that the high seas are free to all nations; and so on. Needless to say, the system is influenced in its turn by the incorporation of new norms.

Then, application of a norm of international law implies that the norm is considered not in isolation, but as part of the treaty, or of the norms bearing on the same subject-matter, and, in general, as part of the system of international law including the general principles.[2]

The function of norms of international law is as much to serve as a touchstone for the evaluation of past events (provided the norm in question was in force at the time of the event or has been made retroactive to it), as to provide a standard for policy decisions in respect of present or future events (provided the norm is in force at the time of the decision). Thus, application of the norms requires, firstly, an assessment of their force at a particular time. This, again, is a matter of applying certain particular, more or less definite rules governing such issues as the moment when a customary rule has acquired force of law, or when a treaty provision has lost it.

The more specific a norm is, the less uncertainty remains with respect to its precise scope and purport. Application, however, even of a highly specific rule to a particular event is not an entirely mechanical process: some room for interpretation of its contents will usually be left, and on the other hand an analysis of the event must bring to light those of its elements which are deemed relevant to the decision. These interpretative activities are mutually dependent; on the one hand, the selection of relevant facts is influenced by the contents of the rule, and, on the other, the tendency will be to interpret the rule in the light of the concrete event. This leads to the observation that application of a specific rule implies its interpretation in interdependence, not only with the system of international law, but with the concrete situation as well.

The vaguer the norms, the wider the field of their application, but at the same time the less definite their purport. This is most obvious in respect of such principles of international law as proclaim, for instance, that the high seas are free to all nations, or that inhuman conduct is prohibited in warfare. Firstly, these principles are so wide as to have some significance in

---

[2] In the Anglo-Norwegian Fisheries Case, after the International Court of Justice had found that the specific norm providing that the base-line of the territorial sea is the low-water mark did not apply to the Norwegian coast, it continued: "It does not at all follow that, in the absence of rules having the technically precise character alleged by the United Kingdom Government, the delimitation undertaken by the Norwegian Government in 1935 is not subject to certain principles which make it possible to judge as to its validity under international law."; Fisheries Case, Judgment of 18 December 1951: I.C.J. Reports 1951, p. 116, at p. 132.

respect of literally any event that might take place on the high seas or in the course of warfare, respectively. On the other hand, the principles are so vague that they do not say anything definite concerning actual decisions in concrete instances. Moreover, such principles are generally coupled with other principles, stating, for instance, that all nations are entitled to protect their legitimate interests on the high seas, or that belligerents may pursue the legitimate ends of warfare. In consequence, application to concrete events includes a creative interpretation of the complementary principles involved, the finding of a balance between these in the light of the situation, and the determination of their relative impact with regard to the issue. The selection of the facts deemed relevant to the decision is in this case governed much less directly by the contents of the principles.

Notwithstanding the much greater distance between principles and events, in the final analysis it is the principles which determine, *via* a process of interpretation, what ought to happen *in concreto*. From another angle, and doing justice to the creative and intuitive trait inherent in this procedure as well as to the fact that the principles involved may not even be consciously realized by those confronted with the concrete situation (which may be entirely new and unprecedented), the solution found to be "in conformity with international law" may be characterized as a normative concrete decision, or *ius in causa positum*. Characteristically, the opinion will be that such a decision, though arrived at for a particular situation, would be equally valid in respect of other, similar situations. This does justice to the fundamental principle of law, inherent also in international law, that similarities must be treated similarly.

It is evident that application of the norms of international law may lead to different results according to whether this function is performed by one or other of the interested parties, an outsider, or a court of justice or similar disinterested, objective organ of international society. In particular their application by the interested parties may bring to light differences of opinion over the facts of the case or the true purport, or even the existence, of the norm.[3] It is not at all exceptional that either party bases its case on a different norm, at the same time denying the validity or applicability of the norm propounded by the opponent. In the present state of international affairs, such disputes may be resolved in various manners: the parties may reach an agreement[4] or voluntarily submit the issue to judicial or arbitral

[3] See also hereafter, §§ 1.2.6 and 1.3.3.
[4] The law-creating tendency inherent in such agreements is evidenced, for instance, by the Treaty of Washington, 8 May 1871, concluded between Great Britain and the U.S.A. in order to open the way for a settlement of disputes resulting from the Civil War, and which led to the famous Alabama arbitrations. In the Treaty, three rules were formulated which were "agreed upon by the High Contracting Parties as rules to be taken as applicable to the case", while Great Britain made the point explicit "that Her Majesty's Government cannot assent to the foregoing rules as a statement of principles which were in force at the time when the claims mentioned in Art. 1

13

settlement;[5] the intervention of third States or international organizations may effect a compromise; or a resort to force may decide the issue one way or another. It is equally possible, however, that the conflict of opinion and decision remain unresolved, each of the parties adhering to its own decision and applying it in its own jurisdiction. All this is evidence of the decentralized state of international society, resting largely on the principle of the sovereign equality of States. While this evidently has an adverse effect on the proper working of the international legal order, it does not affect its normative character.

While the "body of rules" of the international legal order can be described as a normative system, its interdependence with international society is, on the other hand, manifest. Thus, the principle of the sovereign equality of States is dependent on certain conditions of fact that have not always existed and that can change again at some future time. Such a change in social conditions would obviously entail a radical change in the system of international law.

The interdependence of international law and international society is also evident in respect of individual norms: these are created, exist, and are terminated in the context of society. Both the creation, application, and termination of the norms are achieved by more or less explicit, more or less formal procedures taking place among varying numbers of participants, each holding different positions as regards power and authority, and representing a variety of interests, ideas, and so forth. Viewed from this angle, the procedures referred to are social processes.[6] On the other hand, the primary objects of inquiry for the student of international law are the results, not the social processes as such.

Modification of existing norms may result in particular from the process of application. This is fairly evident as regards customary law: its norms are flexible and adaptable to changing conditions. It is also evident as regards principles: their very vagueness makes these particularly suited to follow social changes. On the other hand, specific treaty provisions may seem most rigid; several methods of adaptation are, however, also available here: viz., interpretation, revision, and, if the latter fails, a resort to the *clausula rebus sic stantibus*. The conclusion is that, while the norms of international

---

arose"; furthermore, the parties agreed "to observe these rules as between themselves in future, and to bring them to the knowledge of other maritime Powers and to invite them to accede to them" (Art. 6). De Martens, *N.R.G.*, Vol. XX, p. 698, at p. 702.

[5] This mode of settling disputes may likewise lead to the virtual creation of new norms. One example out of many is the Anglo-Norwegian Fisheries Case (n. 2, *supra*), where the Court may well be said to have laid down a new general rule relative to straight base-lines for territorial waters (Judgment, p. 129).

[6] The necessity to treat international law as a social process, while not unprecedented, is in present days emphasized in particular by the adherents of the Yale school, founders of which are Harold D. Lasswell and Myres S. McDougal.

14

law may have a significant influence on the course of events in the international society, they are in their turn materially influenced by social events.

This leads to the observation that the abstractness of the norms lies not so much in their nature as in their formulation. Legal norms are expressed in abstract terms, that is, in generalizations rather than references to concrete instances; this is demonstrated with particular clarity in the case of *ius in causa positum*. But the norms are not abstractions in the sense of autonomous entities independent of social reality. In other words: norms are social phenomena existing in the context of the social processes of human society. Nor is this altered by the fact that the legal norms are prescriptive in character: "oughtness" is as much part of social reality as is "being".[7]

In short, while international law in the view developed here is a normative order or "body of rules", it exists in the social context of international society; it is characterized by its normativeness, but this is not something outside reality; and, besides the element of stability inherent in it, it possesses a certain flexibility and adaptibility which enable it to meet the requirements of social change. Its most outstanding characteristic, however, is not so much adaptability as normativity. Accordingly, examination and description of international law will be focused firstly on bringing out the norms, as part of a system, and, secondly, on their interdependence with social processes and events. This can also be formulated in the thesis that the object of inquiry ultimately is the international legal order of "oughtness", not international politics.

1.2.2. *Sanctions of international law*

Besides its normative aspect, a characteristic of the international legal order, like any legal order, lies in the fact that observance of its norms is not simply left to their internal force or to the conscience of those to whom they are addressed: in a certain measure, this is stimulated with the aid of means wielded by persons or entities other than the addressees.

This general statement obviously needs some further amplification, especially as regards such questions as which stimuli are available at what time, and are wielded by whom, in international society. For the sake of

---

[7] This leaves undecided whether "being" is fundamentally different from "oughtness" from a philosophical point of view. The above argument merely serves to defend the view that the norm and the more tangible "thing" are both parts of the same reality.

The view defended in the text is opposite to that held by Kelsen, *Reine Rechtslehre*, 2nd ed., 1960. According to that author, "oughtness" is separated from "being" by an unbridgeable gulf, and as "oughtness" is the most essential characteristic of the legal norm, a legal order is autonomous and rests solely on a hypothetical basic norm providing how the norms of the order ought to be created.

clarity, it should be pointed out that only intentionally given support is envisaged here. This restriction, however, does not imply that a given action may not also serve other purposes: indeed, these may even prevail in the eyes of the actor.

The support contemplated here can take the shape, either, of the positive consequence attached to observance of the norm, or the negative consequence attached to its violation. While the point should be emphasized that law is not only negatively enforced, but also supported with positive means, it stands to reason that the negative form of law enforcement is most frequently discussed as it involves the crucial issue of the use of coercion in protection of the law.

Support, whether of the positive or negative variety, may either be a reaction to an act done, or an anticipatory action. A positive reaction can be described as remuneration, and a negative as retribution, repression, etcetera. A positive anticipation may be termed stimulation, a negative prevention. Actors of the several types of supporting actions may be private persons or groups of persons, or the authorities.

Out of this whole range of conceivable actions, only those which have support of the law as their primary aim are commonly referred to as sanctions.[8] In the widest sense of the term, sanctions may be positive or negative, anticipatory or reactive, official or private.[9] Certain authors, on the other hand, give the term a more restricted meaning, reserving it to the sanctions provided for by (positive) law and hence omitting informal devices like the approval or disapproval by public opinion. Others, again, restrict the term even further and reserve it exclusively to the negative sanctions of positive law (the *Unrechtsfolgen* of the German literature), or, with particular reference to the international sphere, to sanctions initiated by institutional agencies of international society.

Though it is not believed (with Kelsen) that law is a coercive order prescribing certain modes of conduct precisely and solely by attaching negative sanctions to the opposite conduct,[10] nor for any other principal reason, the term "sanctions" shall nonetheless hereafter be used in a

---

[8] Sometimes also self-defence and similar related notions are brought under the term, with the result that it becomes synonymous with support of law. This is done by authors like Kelsen, Verdross and Wengler. See also hereafter, § 1.2.4.

[9] Lasswell and Kaplan, *Power and Society*, 1950, p. 48: "A sanction ... might consist in the manipulation of symbols (praise or censure), or in a redistribution of goods and services, or in the use of violence, or, speaking generally, in reward or punishment by way of any value whatever. The sanction is *positive* whenever it enhances values for the actor to whom it is applied, *negative* when it deprives him of values."

Cf. also Richard Arens and Lasswell, *In Defense of Public Order*, 1961, p. 14: "Sanctions are deprivations or indulgences of individual or group values for the purpose of supporting the primary norms of a public order system."

[10] *Reine Rechtslehre*, p. 26; also: *Collective Security under International Law*, 1954, pp. 6, 101. The negative sanctions consist in forcible deprivations of goods such as life, health, freedom, honour, economic values, and, in general, any values whatso-

restricted sense, namely as: actions particularly (though not necessarily exclusively) aimed at the negative support of a legal order. This is for the purely practical reason that, as indicated above, actions of that category are most likely to give rise to legal questions concerning competence, limitation of permissible use, and so on.

When the above is applied to the international legal order, it is obvious that the term "sanctions", even so defined, embraces a wide variety of actions, ranging from the official démarche of a qualified institutional agency of international society to the unorganized reaction on the part of public opinion. In order to make the notion somewhat more clear, a classification seems appropriate under the following headings: actors, actions within their power, nature of the actions, authority of the actors, legality of the actions.

The actors in the international sanctioning process can be: States, private persons or groups of persons, and international organizations. As the latter categories for the most part are beyond the scope of the present study, it will suffice to make only a few summary remarks concerning each of these.

Private persons or groups of persons may have recourse to sanctions of the following types: (a) disapproval in the independent press, peaceful demonstrations; (b) boycott on the part of private organizations, non-violent obstruction of the freedom of movement of foreign diplomatic missions; (c) privateering, the storming and damaging of foreign embassies. As to their nature, these actions can be divided as follows: the actions under a entail only indirect, moral coercion, those under b entail direct coercion not involving the use of force, and the coercive actions mentioned under c do involve such use of force. No consensus exists as to whether private persons have formal authority, or de facto authority, or no authority at all, to apply such sanctions in support of international law.[11] Another controversial issue is the legality or illegality of the sanctions mentioned. The only undisputed point seems to be that actions like those referred to under c are prohibited. On the other hand, the status of the other sanctions seems uncertain.[12] A final remark concerning this category of international sanctions on the part of private persons is that they are at any rate of

---

ever; the deprivations are not threatened, but *ought* to follow in case of violation of the substantive part of the norms.

[11] The point of view of an author like Kelsen is that no such authority is conferred upon these actors: only States are authorized to have recourse to sanctions which, besides, by definition consist in coercive measures. Scelle, on the other hand, seems to represent the view that private persons have *de facto* authority, at any rate in respect of the actions referred to under *a*: according to this author, "l'opinion publique, l'action de la presse" should be counted among the actions that "font office de sanctions préventives"; *Précis*, p. 59.

[12] It should be emphasized that the mere fact that an unlawful act is committed by

strictly limited and indeed secondary importance in the context of the maintenance of the international legal order.

The spectacular development of international organizations, both as far as numbers and importance are concerned, leaves no room for doubt that these recent international entities have the capacity to play a significant part in the protection of the international legal order, whether on a general and world-wide (or quasi-world-wide) scale like the United Nations, or in the specialized and/or regionally defined spheres of action of other international organizations; and whether in the form of sanctions taken and executed by, or under the authority of, the organizations, or in the form of limitations on the powers of States unilaterally to resort to sanctions against each other. This development, however, has not so far led to anything like the complete take-over of the sanctioning function in international society by the international organizations, nor is it likely that this will come about in the near future. Indeed, it seems a safe assumption that the States will retain their dominant position in this respect for a considerable period of time.

It is fairly evident that the last category of actors mentioned, States, do in fact take sanctions in support of the international legal order. This is a logical result of their position as the principal independent power units in international society, having an interest in the maintenance of its legal order and wielding a variety of means, including military power, all of which can be utilized for sanctioning purposes. According to the strategies employed, the actions resorted to can be categorized as diplomatic, ideological, economic or military, or combinations of these. Then, as explained above, the actions can be preventive or reactive, or, again, a combination of both.

An important aspect of the nature of these actions is the type and degree of coercion involved. Three classes of actions may be distinguished in this respect: those involving only indirect coercion of a moral order (ideological pressure), those involving direct coercion not consisting of the use of armed force (diplomatic and economic actions), and those involving armed force (military actions). The actions involving direct coercion, whether military or otherwise, are generally referred to as enforcement actions.

An issue of major importance is whether States have authority to take sanctions against each other. One might conceive a theoretical view to the effect that formal authority to take sanctions, especially those involving direct coercion, must be reserved to duly qualified supranational organs of the international community applying proper judicial procedures, as only in that manner can a level of sophisticated law enforcement comparable to that in modern States be guaranteed. As by far the greater part of the

---

way of sanction, is not in general sufficient ground for its justification. Thus, the modes of conduct referred to under *c* remain unlawful even though they are applied as sanctions by the actors concerned.

sanctions are noticeably taken not by such organs, but by States, the logical conclusion would be that these have for the time being acquired some sort of *de facto* authority to act as substitutes for the as yet lacking organs. However, in the light of the historical development and actual condition of international society this seems too artificial a construction. Taking into account the extremely decentralized status of international society, in which sovereign States figure as the most important members and at the same time as the most prominent authorities, it seems no more than realistic to accept that the States have formal authority to perform acts in the double capacity of members-authorities, and that this implies, *inter alia*, the power to take sanctions even against each other.

This position of the States is obviously ambiguous. An application of sanctions by one State against another will generally serve its own interests as well as those of society, and it is virtually impossible completely to separate the two aspects. Of course, in particular instances the accent may be noticeably more on one or the other aspect; while the community interest may be expected to be more pronounced where sanctions have a collective rather than individual character, the particular interests will vary with the degree of personal involvement of the States. Thus, the particular interests of a State will probably carry much weight in case of an individual sanction taken in direct reaction to an injury suffered at the hands of another State. On the other hand, the community interest may be assumed to play a pre-dominant part, for instance, when States collectively decide to take sanctions against a State held guilty of a behaviour contrary to the standards of international law, but which brings no direct harm to the particular interests of any of the States concerned. The converse cannot, however, be excluded: a State may feel impelled to apply individual sanctions against another State for the sake of the community interest and while none of its particular interests is endangered by the actions of the latter State; and, in case of collective sanctions, each of the States taking part in their execution may in fact be motivated by the important particular interests which it has at stake in the affair, rather than by the community interest.

It is suggested that the authority of States to take sanctions is not really a matter of doubt in case of collective sanctions decided by a representative majority of States: their individual authoritative position combined with the obvious involvement of the community as such provides sufficient ground for this conclusion. Nor is their authority really doubtful in case of in-dividual sanctions resorted to by the injured State: in that case it is the direct personal involvement of the State concerned which, coupled again with its authoritative position, furnishes the basis for its authority.

Controversy is most likely to arise with respect to the individual sanction against a State guilty of a violation of international law, taken by a State the interests of which are apparently not directly at stake. If in this situation the point is emphasized that the latter State lacks interest and, like the offending State, is no more than a member of international society, the outcome may be that the intervention is characterized as an instance of unauthorized interference in the affairs of a sovereign equal. If, however, primary emphasis is given to the position of the State as a bearer of authority in international society and as a representative of the community interest, the opposite conclusion may be arrived at and the third-party intervention even be qualified as "un devoir, une fonction internationale".[13]

Without pretending to offer anything like a definite solution of this problem, it is submitted that it cannot in any event be decided in a general manner by simply juxtaposing the authority in principle of States to take individual sanctions and the respect due by States to the sovereignty of their equals: either of these principles must be weighed in the light of the concrete situation, that is, the gravity of the international wrong actually committed and the community interest involved in upholding the particular norm of international law violated, as well as the severity of the sanctions.

As regards their legal character, measures taken by States as sanctions against unlawful conduct of other States may be divided into three categories: lawful acts, those acts *prima facie* unlawful but nonetheless justifiable, and irremediably unlawful acts. A further division of the first category would be into acts not infringing any norm of international law and those in fact violating some such norm, but which are nevertheless considered entirely legitimate.

No particular difficulties of a theoretical nature attend the extremes: with respect to both the intrinsically lawful sanctions (which do not infringe any norm) and the irremediably unlawful sanctions the sole problem will be to determine which actions come under these categories.

The two remaining categories have much in common: both in case of a justifiable illegality and of a legitimate encroachment of the law the action taken is neither intrinsically lawful nor ultimately unlawful. What is the difference, if any? First of all this seems a matter of approach: in one case the infringed norm is foremost in the attention, in the other it is the legitimacy of the operation taken as a whole. But this is not all: the difference seems also to reflect a social reality. This is true at any rate in the domestic order of States; sanctions taken by authorized persons (such as police officers) in execution of express provisions of the law are commonly accepted as lawful acts that need no justification, even though the actions might also be construed as infringements of other norms of the legal order. When on the other hand similar acts are performed by persons not expressly appointed as enforcing agents of the law, the acts are often experienced as irregular and in contravention of the law in the first place, and, hence, are deemed to be in need of justification. It should be added

---

[13] Scelle, *Précis*, p. 64.

20

that in the internal order of States the greater part of the sanctions involving direct coercion is taken by authorized persons, and justification of the remaining instances of sanctions is indeed a minor issue.

Is a similar situation found in international society? An author like Kelsen answers this question in the affirmative. According to him, general international law authorizes the individual State to take recourse to sanctions in response to unlawful conduct on the part of another State, and such measures (which of course should not exceed certain limits) are legitimate acts of execution in the international legal order, not acts in need of justification. Consequently, lawful sanctions are equally predominant in international society, and justification is no more a major issue here than in the internal order of States.

This view, however, is far from universally shared. According to a more widespread view, individual sanctions taken by States against other States cannot be compared in all relevant respects with the official sanctions provided by law and taken by especially authorized persons in States internally. Rather, these should be rated as *prima facie* unlawful acts of self-help. In this view the accent is evidently on justification.

The debate between the advocates of these two different conceptions is mainly theoretical in character: it does not seem to lead to different results in practice. For sanctions have to respect the same limits under either view, and the same actions are thus apt to be denounced as definitely unlawful.. The sole remaining difference (leaving aside possible consequences for the onus of proof in international litigation) lies in the legal appreciation of those actions not deemed definitely unlawful: while these are regarded as legitimate in the former view, they are considered only justifiable in the latter. The point should be emphasized, however, that this is not merely a question of words: the issue is influenced by the conception of international society that one has in mind, and the debate cannot therefore be denied a certain fundamental significance.

With respect to this fundamental aspect, it is submitted that the peculiar features of international society make it difficult to maintain a distinction between various "stages of lawfulness" in the same manner as may usefully be done in respect to the internal legal order of States. In the thesis that individual sanctions taken by States are legitimate acts of execution of international law, the suggestion is perhaps too strong that States are "the authorities" in international society and as such would be comparable to the public authorities in the State. On the other hand, the view that such measures are mere acts of self-help may suggest that States would be no more than subjects in international society, and that other institutions would be the real public authorities (or, worse, that these would even be entirely lacking).

To my mind neither suggestion is in accordance with actual social reality. As observed previously, international society is characterized by the

21

ambiguous position of States as member-subjects and authorities at the same time. In this light it is felt that the controversy about legitimacy or justification cannot be satisfactorily resolved with a simple statement that individual sanctions are either acts of execution or mere acts of self-help: in reality, they are an indissoluble mixture of the two elements.

It should be added that an essentially different outcome would be the result of a third imaginable construction, to the effect that individual sanctions taken by States are never lawful nor even justifiable under international law, but always constitute irremediably unlawful acts which are at most tolerated in present international society, because, and for so long as, the means are lacking for their effective prevention or control.[14] However, while such a construction may be evidence of an idealistic conception of the international society as it ought to be, it is certainly a gross misrepresentation of existing international society and of the legal order in force in it. States do actually perform acts of authority in international society: they create and terminate norms of international law, they create international organizations vested with certain public functions, and so on. This being so, it seems wholly unrealistic to deny that they also hold certain legal powers to apply and support international law, that is, to have recourse to sanctions against other States. Any theory, therefore, is untenable if it fails to take into account that *prima facie* unlawful actions taken by individual States might at least be justifiable as sanctions under international law.

1.2.3. *Reprisals as sanctions of international law*

From the historical outline given in the first section of this Chapter, public reprisals emerge as coercive measures taken by one State against another and motivated by an international wrong committed by the latter to the prejudice of the former State. It was moreover pointed out that the decision to select a reprisal action among the available alternatives has the character of a policy decision; it should be added that in taking this decision the interests of the State may safely be assumed to be foremost in the minds of the decision-makers. On the other hand, it may be recalled that their de-

[14] Such a construction seems to underlie the viewpoint of Scelle with regard to reprisals: in "Règles générales du droit de la paix", *R.d.C.* 1933, Vol. IV, p. 331, at p. 672, he explains that *la technique de réciprocité* (which in his opinion includes reprisals) is a phenomenon of classical international law connected with the deficiency, for the time being, of an effective *droit constructif* of the international society. That technique, however, "ne peut avoir, au maximum, qu'une valoir provisoire et relative, comme celle des *compétences de fait* auxquelles elle s'apparente."—*Cf.* also *Précis*, p. 59.

An instance of a merely tolerated action may perhaps be seen in the quarantine of Cuba, in October 1962, by the naval and air forces of the U.S.A., an action which served to prevent the undesirable but not definitely unlawful armament of Cuba with ballistic missiles of Russian origin.

cision rests on the specific reasoning that the wrong suffered at the hands of the offending State gives the victim State not only a motive, but a title of sorts to have recourse to a mode of acting that would not normally be permitted in interstate relations, but that may serve to coerce the offending State to bring its conduct into line with the requirements of international law. These characteristics of the reprisal action bring it under the heading of the sanctions of international law, and specifically of the individual sanctions involving direct coercion or even the use of force.

If this is accepted, the next question is whether reprisals constitute ir-remediably unlawful (though perhaps in some cases tolerated), justifiable, or even entirely lawful acts: the same question as was discussed in the previous sub-section with respect to sanctions in general. Indeed, the debate concerning this issue usually has a bearing on reprisals in particular, rather than on the general problem of sanctions. In this more restricted context, the views advanced in the debate may be summarized as follows: while in the view of authors like Kelsen reprisals constitute legitimate actions in execution of rules of international law (unless they exceed certain limits and thereby become unlawful),[15] according to a more widely accepted view they are a sort of substitute for real acts of execution and, as self-help, are merely justifiable (again on the condition that certain limits are not exceeded).

As was argued in the preceding sub-section, neither of these views is

[15] Cf., e.g., Paul Guggenheim, *Traité de droit international public*, Vol. II, 1954, p. 84. That author expressly rejects the theory that reprisals are justifiable actions, with the following reasoning: "Cette conception a pourtant le défaut de ne pas tenir suffisam-ment compte du fait que les représailles sont une *sanction* (Unrechtsfolge) destinée à remplacer la réparation, lorsque celle-ci n'a pas eu lieu. Les représailles revêtent bien l'apparence d'une violation du droit, mais cela est dû uniquement au caractère primitif du droit international: les sanctions, pour autant qu'il s'agit de mesures d'exécution, sont en réalité des actes d'autoprotection. Etant donné que le droit international coutu-mier ne connaît pas de différenciation des fonctions, c'est là la seule possibilité pour le sujet de droit lésé de réagir contre le tort qui lui est fait. Il n'a pas à sa disposition que des actes qui, s'ils ne constituaient pas une sanction—c'est-à-dire s'ils n'étaient pas l'expression d'une fonction de protection juridique—devraient être considérés comme une violation du droit."

While accepting the main lines of this analysis of the character of reprisals (which, however, according to Guggenheim is merely an *apparence*), I fail to see how this can be reconciled with real legitimacy of the actions constituting reprisals. The word *sanction* cannot be decisive in this respect—unless, that is, one takes it in the signifi-cance accorded to it by Kelsen: viz., of consequences attached to and completing the legal norms and that ought to follow when the substantive part of the norms is not complied with: in that conception, reprisals are lawful acts by definition. But then the question would precisely be whether reprisals come under that narrow definition of sanctions.

See also J.-C. Venezia, "La notion de représailles en droit international public", in *RGDIP*, Vol. 64, 1960, p. 465, who, after a discussion of the controversy of sanction versus justifying fact, arrives at the conclusion that this controversy is highly theore-tical and abstract and of strictly limited importance: at pp. 468-469.

wholly satisfactory. Without repeating the argument developed there, it may suffice to apply the conclusion arrived at for the more general problem to the particular issue of the legal status of reprisals: these should be characterized as acts of "execution-*cum*-self-help", or rather, doing justice to their predominantly unilateral character, as "self-help-*cum*-execution". In short, the fundamental nature of reprisals is that of all individual sanctions in international society: they are imperfect means of supporting international law, in which public authority and private interest are indissolubly united.

This situation, it is submitted, can more accurately be approximated by referring to the justifiability of reprisals than to their legitimacy.

While the basis of the justifiability of reprisals is usually found in their function as sanctions of international law, mention should be made of a completely different theory sometimes advanced in the literature: the theory of reciprocity. According to a typical advocate of this theory, Louis le Fur, reciprocity lies at the root of—and hence is implied in—all international law, whether conventional or customary, and the power of States to take reprisals finds its basis in their ensuing right to consider themselves freed from their legal obligations in respect to other States which have violated the rules underlying those obligations.[16] In this view a reprisal does not need justification: it is the legitimate application of a contractual or quasi-contractual clause inherent in international law.

It is of course conceded that reciprocity plays an important part in international relationships. This fact is also reflected in international law: many international agreements contain an express or implied reciprocity clause,[17] and a similar restriction underlies the scope of certain norms of

---

[16] *Des représailles en temps de guerre*, 1919. The author bases his view on "l'équité et le sens commun" (p. 25), and he defends it with the following reasoning: "... le principe de réciprocité est à la base des conventions entre égaux; sans lui tout contrat serait une duperie et, à proprement parler, il n'y aurait plus même de contrat ni de traité possible" (p. 24); and, with regard to customary law: "Ici comme tout à l'heure, la non réciprocité serait absurdité ou duperie. Si des mesures restrictives quelconques étaient imposées aux Etats en guerre à l'égard même de ceux qui se refusent à les appliquer, ce serait vouloir assurer leur défaite en même temps que celle du droit lui-même; le droit international travaillerait donc à sa propre ruine, ce qui est inadmissible" (p. 26).

Although agreeing with Le Fur that self-destruction of international law is inadmissible, I deny that this consequence would attach to the opinion that norms of international law are binding upon a State even though another State has violated these in respect of the former. What Le Fur deemed inconceivable—viz., that provisions of international law would retain their obligatory force even after their violation—has proved to be precisely the turn which international law has taken: a turn to some extent away from the law of private contracts, which seems to have been very much on Le Fur's mind.

[17] Express clauses of that purport are often included in agreements relating to the

customary law. It is not, however, accepted that the obligatory force of *all* international law is restricted by the condition of reciprocity. On the contrary, it is believed that in the absence of an express or implied reciprocity clause norms of international law continue to be binding upon the State even in respect of a State that has violated such norms to the prejudice of the former State.[18] As Scelle has it: [19]

> "Le fait qu'un sujet de droit viole la règle de droit, n'autorise en aucune façon d'autres sujets de droit, même lésés, à la violer à leur tour. Le droit objectif n'est pas 'contractuel', on l'oublie toujours."

In this *droit objectif* the reprisal cannot simply be explained as an interstate action merely serving to restore the disturbed synallagmatic relationship: its function is (perhaps not always primarily, but in any event also) to enforce the law in international society.

Another objection to the above theory is that reprisals need not affect the same norm as has been violated by the original offender. In fact, in selecting a reprisal action the decision-makers in the State will be guided by considerations of estimated effect rather than reciprocity, and State practice is evidence of the fact that their calculations often result in actions widely different from the offences imputed to the opponent.

A final point of major interest in the present context is whether reprisals belong in the category of anticipatory or reactive sanctions. The consensus seems to be that an action does not constitute a reprisal in the current sense of the term when it is purely anticipatory, that is, motivated not by any prior unlawful conduct on the part of the other State, but merely by the expectation of such conduct at some future time. The historical origin

---

conduct of warfare, armaments, and similar matters of military importance. See, *e.g.*, the *si omnes*-clause in the Hague Conventions of 1899 and 1907.

A peculiar clause, in which reciprocity seems intermingled with the idea of *rebus sic stantibus*, is found in Art. IV of the Treaty Banning Nuclear Weapon Tests in the Atmosphere, in Outer Space and Under Water, signed at Moscow on 5 August 1963. The text runs as follows: "Each Party shall in exercising its national sovereignty have the right to withdraw from the Treaty if it decides that extra-ordinary events, related to the subject matter of this Treaty, have jeopardized the supreme interests of its country. It shall give notice of such withdrawal to all other Parties to the Treaty three months in advance." (U.N.T.S. I : 6964, Vol. 480, p. 43.)

The clause of reciprocity may be deemed to be implied in agreements of a purely synallagmatic character.

[18] Reciprocity has been expressly excluded, *e.g.*, in the Red Cross Conventions of Geneva of 1949. Another instance is presented by the unconditional acceptance by The Netherlands of the prohibition against bacteriological warfare: in ratifying the Protocol of Geneva of 1925 for the Prohibition of the Use in War of Asphyxiating, Poisonous or Other Gases, and of Bacteriological Mehtods of Warfare, reciprocity was stipulated by the Netherlands Government only with respect to the provisions regarding the use of gas, not with respect to bacteriological methods. This example, however, found no imitation on the part of other ratifying Governments.

[19] *Précis*, p. 59.

25

of the concept of reprisals and its development up to the present time leave no doubt concerning this point: only those actions are brought under the heading of reprisals as are taken in reaction to another State's prior action. To this extent, they evidently belong in the category of the reactive sanctions.

This statement, however, does not provide a complete answer to the question put: it does no more than reflect the cause of reprisals, and cannot account for their function. Reactive sanctions can function as means to achieve utterly different goals, ranging from the retrospective punishment-sec and the equally retrospective *restitutio in integrum*, through the repression of continuing wrongful conduct, to the prospective prevention of future law encroachments. It is submitted that reprisals can serve and actually are used to achieve all of these purposes including the prevention of future wrongs,—with the sole exception, that is, of punishment in the narrow sense of revenge pure and simple: if that is the real purpose of a retaliatory action, it does not have the function of coercion characteristic of reprisals.

In this context, two further characteristic features of reprisals are relevant: their indirect operation, and their non-finality. Though reprisals are aimed directly to affect one or other value of the offending State, they are not means of direct execution in the hands of the injured State: their *modus operandi* consists in pressure on the decision-makers in the former State, exercised in the hope that its effect will be to provoke a change of policy on their part.

Nor are reprisals intended to constitute a final settlement of a legal issue. This non-final and in a way subsidiary character comes to light most clearly when the opposing State does not submit to the pressure; for, if in that case the wronged State at a later stage seeks to realize its claim with the aid of other means, it cannot then be warded off with the argument that by taking recourse to a reprisal it has forfeited the right to pursue further its claim.

Summarizing the above, reprisals may be tentatively characterized as: enforcement measures wielded by individual States in their international relations and constituting imperfect, reactive, indirectly operating and non-final sanctions of international law.

1.2.4. *Reprisals and certain related concepts*

The function of reprisals in the international legal order may be clarified somewhat further by considering their relation to certain other concepts, notably to self-defence and retorsion.

Authors are divided on the question of whether acts of self-defence and reprisals belong in the same category.[20] In this respect, it is suggested that

[20] *Cf.* also n. 8.

26

the two concepts differ fundamentally as far as their functions are concerned: while the essence of self-defence is to use armed force directly to ward off a physical danger threatening the State, the function of a reprisal action is to apply coercion with a view to inducing the opponent to change his unlawful and prejudicial policy.[21]

In actual practice, both types of actions can be very close to each other and may even be intermingled. When, for instance, an armed attack of limited proportions is countered not only at the front opened by the attacking State, but by a military operation against another part of its territory as well, it may be hard to decide whether the latter action constitutes an act of self-defence or a reprisal (or, for that matter, a mere unwarranted use of force). It is submitted, however, that this is a question of fact-finding rather than law.

Another current suggestion is that reprisals belong under the same heading as measures of retorsion. The concept of retorsion usually is interpreted to embrace the lawful retort of a State to another State's equally lawful previous conduct. Like the reprisal, the act of retorsion aims at coercing the latter State to discontinue a practice deemed vexatious or harmful. Hence, from a point of view of protection of the particular interests of the State there is reason to bring both reprisals and retorsion under the heading of measures of coercion. From this point of view, it should be added, the enumeration is far from complete, as it ought to encompass the lawful retort to an unlawful action as well,—not to mention the unlawful coercive reaction to a lawful but vexatious action.

It should be noted that Scelle has challenged the very existence of the category of retorsion, principally on the ground that the use of a competence for the purpose of coercion amounts to *abus de droit*, namely *détournement de pouvoir*.[22] Even Scelle himself has recognized, however, that the actual condition of international society does not permit an integral application of the theory of *abus de droit* in the field of international relations.[23] Indeed, it is only realistic to acknowledge that in the present state of affairs the powers of States are often sufficiently discretionary to include being exercised for the purpose of pressure on another State, the actions of which, though vexatious, have not violated international law.[24]

---

[21] This is without prejudice to the question of the justification of armed reprisals.— J.-C. Venezia holds that for want of objective criteria there is no real difference between reprisals and self-defence; *op. cit.* n. 15, at p. 474 ff.

[22] *Op. cit.* n. 14, at p. 671. *Cf.* also *Précis*, p. 16: "c'est en considération des buts que sont conférées les compétences. Si donc il est possible de trouver que le but de l'acte juridique n'est pas conforme à la règle de droit, le pouvoir de vouloir est vicié. Il y a *détournement de compétence*, et l'acte pourra être annulé."

[23] *Op. cit.* n. 14, p. 672.

[24] Thus, if it be true that "[a]ccording to a great principle of Public International Law, the ports of every State must be open to foreign merchant vessels and can only be

While it may therefore be accepted that reprisals and retorsion are treated as related concepts from one point of view, it should be emphasized that the component of law enforcement, essential to the notion of reprisals, is lacking in retorsion. It seems therefore of little value from a legal point of view to class reprisals and measures of retorsion in one category. Rather, while the latter measures are lawful acts at the discretion of States, reprisals, according to their function, belong in the category of the sanctions of international law.

1.2.5. Participants in reprisals

The statement that reprisals are acts of States in retaliation to previous acts of other States, needs some qualification in two respects.

In the first place, it is an obvious fact that the real actors on either side in a reprisal action are individual persons rather than States. These persons may, but need not, hold official positions. Especially as regards the crucial decisions involved in the process, the actors may well be the respective Governments; but it should be stressed that this is not an absolute requirement: the sole condition is that the actual decision-makers can, in the given situation, be considered to engage the responsibility of the State.

Similarly, the interests affected by the reprisal should be connected in one way or other with the State. To this end, it will be sufficient that these are interests of nationals of the State, or of inhabitants of its territory, or, obviously, of the State itself. Whether this condition is fulfilled, will again have to be assessed in the light of the actual circumstances of the case.

A second qualification to the above statement is that even in the formal sense States are not the only conceivable participants in reprisal actions. Other possible participants, either on the active or passive side, include those territorially defined though non-sovereign entities (such as non-self-governing territories, or the component parts of a federation) which possess a greater or lesser measure of autonomy in their international relations.

Another extension of the category of actors arises from the emergence and rapid development of international organizations. These, too, can have recourse to—or be the victims of—retaliatory actions bearing all the characteristics of reprisals.

In the light of these considerations, a definition of reprisals should in-

---

closed when the vital interests of the State so require (Arbitral Tribunal, in Saudi Arabia v. Arabian American Oil Company, Award of 23 August 1958, *International Law Reports*, Vol. 27, 1963, p. 117, at p. 212), a closure for another purpose, such as coercion, would be an abuse of power and hence unlawful. If, on the other hand, it is indeed "the general expectation . . . that the coastal state has comprehensive competence over access to ports in the absence of agreement" (McDougal and Burke, *The Public Order of the Oceans*, 1962, p. 114), even a closure for purposes of coercion would be within the competence of the State and hence lawful.

clude among the possible participants those entities other than States, which play a sufficiently autonomous part in international society to be accorded a measure of legal personality.

1.2.6. *Reprisals and the standard of objectivity*

Reprisals are a legal concept in the international legal order; characteristically, they consist of the intentional violation of a rule of international law in reaction to an act equally violative of such a norm. Their justifiability likewise depends on international law. This necessarily implies the applicability of certain objective standards, bearing on their justification in particular. To deny the existence of such standards virtually amounts to a denial of the existence of international law itself: States would be left free to turn unilaterally and authoritatively any unlawful act whatsoever into a justifiable reprisal, and thereby to suspend at will any norm of international law. When this is realized, the conclusion is obvious that the contention that interested States would be alone competent to characterize certain of their acts as reprisals under international law, properly belongs to the realm of politics, not law.[25]

While it is therefore evident that the mere arbitrary labeling of an unlawful action as a reprisal cannot of itself justify it in law, it certainly can achieve other purposes. With the aid of the propaganda apparatus of the State, the true facts surrounding the alleged reprisal action may be distorted or concealed and, while the other State is accused of the gravest crimes against the law of nations, the action may be depicted as a legitimate recourse to reprisals and, indeed, a chivalrous act in defence of law and morals in international society. Such allegations may arouse the collective passions in the State and induce the population to demand, or give its support to, aggressive modes of action that it might not have been prepared to approve if better informed and less incited. Likewise, the propaganda may induce the outside world to acquiesce in a mode of acting that might otherwise have been denounced as a threat to the peace. Such propaganda

[25] For a comparable argument, reference may be made to: Admission of a State to the United Nations (Charter, Art. 4), Advisory Opinion: I.C.J. Reports 1948, p. 57. It had been contended before the Court that the enumeration of criteria for admission in Art. 4, para. 4, did not prevent Member States from basing their votes on political considerations not included in the enumeration. The Court argued that "[t]o determine the meaning of a treaty provision—to determine, as in this case, the character (exhaustive or otherwise) of the conditions for admission stated therein—is a problem of interpretation and consequently a legal question" (p. 61), and that an interpretation to the effect that political considerations could be superimposed upon the conditions enumerated in the Article, "would lead to conferring upon Members an indefinite and practically unlimited power of discretion in the imposition of new conditions. Such a condition would be inconsistent with the very character of paragraph 1 of Article 4 which . . . clearly constitutes a legal regulation of the question of the admission of new States" (p. 63).

successes are, however, in no way equal to legal justification of the actions concerned.

The opposite of a power of arbitrary decision vested in the interested State would be absolute objectivity in assessing and deciding upon the justification of alleged reprisals. While absolute objectivity is probably an unattainable goal even in the most favourable circumstances, the closest possible approximation of that goal would in any event require the issue to be completely detached from the subjective views and allegations of the States parties to the dispute. Ideally, this would mean that the task of ascertaining both the facts and the law would have to fall to an independent, impartial authoritative body. However, international institutions vested both with the authority and the power necessary to perform the indicated functions even in the face of non-co-operation on the part of the States concerned, are virtually non-existent in contemporary international society; as pointed out before, this deficiency is undoubtedly one of the factors at the root of the very development and subsistence to the present day of public reprisals.[26] Consequently, objective and authoritative appraisal of alleged reprisals by an independent body is a rare occurrence indeed: [27] normally the function of assessing the justification of certain acts as reprisals is left precisely to the States parties to the dispute.

In this situation, the standard of objectivity cannot be maintained with such rigidity as to make the validity of the judgment arrived at by the decision-makers in the State dependent on whether any other person in possession of all the facts would have arrived at exactly the same conclusion. It is submitted that the decision-makers cannot be denied a certain, though not unlimited, discretionary power to assess both the facts and the law. The scope of their discretion may be appreciated by starting from the premiss that they are obliged in good faith to respect the normative, that is the essentially objective character of the elements constituting a reprisal; in other words, they will be under an obligation to aim at objectifying within the bounds of the feasible their—initially necessarily subjective—views.[28] As far as the facts are concerned, this implies that they must base their ultimate decision on the most accurate approximation of objective truth within their power (and not, to be sure, on mere suppositions or wilful distortions).

[26] Cf. § 1, supra.

[27] An outstanding exception is of course the Naulilaa arbitration between Portugal and Germany, mentioned supra, p. 7. The greater part of judicial decisions involving the validity of claims of reprisals are found in litigation where not States but individual persons were the defendants, viz., the war crimes trials conducted after the Second World War.

[28] In the Naulilaa case, the reproach that the German reprisal had not been preceded by a request to remedy the alleged injury can be understood to express the idea, not only of subsidiarity, but also that Germany had been obliged—and had failed—to seek objectivity.

30

The question of the objective appraisal of the legal aspects gives rise to more complicated problems. These concern, firstly, the legal character of the act provoking the retaliatory action. While here in particular a rule might be deemed desirable to the effect that any recourse to reprisals can only be justified when the unlawfulness of the preceding act is not open to any doubt whatever, this seems nonetheless an untenable position. The international legal order is a dynamic order in a changing international society, and its norms range from fixed specific rules through flexible general rules and even wider principles to *ius in causa positum*.[29] In this light, it will at times be a sheer impracticability for States contemplating a resort to reprisals to acquire the required absolute certainty about the state of the law. This must needs lead to the conclusion that the decision-makers in the State also possess a certain margin of discretion in assessing the legal character of their opponent's preceding act; a margin that can be approximated by stating that they must have been reasonably convinced of its unlawfulness.

When can they be held to have been so convinced? In this respect, it should be borne in mind that the decision-makers, in planning a recourse to reprisals, contemplate an intentional infraction of a norm of international law. The implication is that in assessing the legal nature of the other State's act they may be required to take utmost care to avoid *error iuris*, for instance by a clear statement of their views and a careful consideration of any arguments made public on the part of the other State, by probing how much support their view receives on the part of third States and in appropriate organs of international organizations, and so on. Obviously, in all these considerations the issue will not only be whether the incriminated act can be said to have violated international law: it will be necessary to take into account that the act may even then be justified in one way or another. The latter consideration will be important especially if the opposing State has actually claimed its action was a reprisal, as in that case it may be said to enjoy a (rebuttable) presumption of justification.

The purport of the above is that if the State has in good faith used the means at its disposal to obtain the required clarification, and if no common view of the applicable law has emerged in the process, the State is entitled to act in accordance with its considered view of the law, notwithstanding the contrasting opinion held, perhaps in equally good faith, by the opposing State.

The problems attending the legal appreciation of the retaliatory act itself will vary according to whether the retaliating State does or does not recognize its *prima facie* unlawful character. In the first supposition, the crucial question will be whether the act does not exceed the objective limits

[29] See *supra*, p. 13.

set on justifiable reprisals. That such limits exist and that States have no completely arbitrary power of decision in this respect, cannot seriously be denied. As was held by the arbitrators in the Naulilaa case: even if international law were admitted not to require close proportionality between reprisal and original offence, this could certainly not prevent a reprisal out of all proportion to the act provoking it having to be considered excessive and hence unjustifiable.[30]

It is equally clear, however, that the limits at issue may be more or less vague or even of contested validity. This must lead to the recognition that a rigid application of the standard of objectivity is out of the question and that a reasonable discretion should here also be left to the States.[31]

Slightly different problems arise if the retaliating State is not ready to concede that its action is *prima facie* unlawful and, hence, in need of justification. In that situation, the action cannot be said to constitute a reprisal in the technical sense of the term.

The most important legal question here concerns the margin of error left to the retaliating State in considering its action not to be contrary to international law. Here, again, the standard of reasonableness may provide the answer. On the substantive side (and irrespective of the procedural requirements mentioned above) this would mean, *inter alia*, that the more crucial the potentially infringed norm (such as a rule outlawing unilateral resort to armed force or prohibiting the killing or maltreatment of innocent war victims), the smaller the margin of error left to the State which unilaterally decides to consider it either invalid or inapplicable. If doubt persists, it seems prudent to announce the action as a reprisal in the first place.

Another question in connection with the above situation is whether the State which originally did not consider its retaliatory action to be contrary to international law, can claim afterwards that it is justifiable as a reprisal. To this, admittedly theoretical, question the equally theoretical answer would be that such a belated invocation of reprisals as a justificatory ground can only be deemed admissible if the action already bore at the

---

[30] See *supra*, p. 8.—In this context it may be useful to note that proportionality between sanction and injury is a principle generally found in legal systems. The practical application of the principle may vary: instances of arithmetical equality between offence and sanction are set against cases of greater or lesser elasticity in this relation. Where the relation is not rigid, other factors will count beside the gravity of the offence; however, the relation to the offence will never be completely abandoned.

Furthermore, it is common knowledge that the identical offence may meet with widely different sanctions in different places and at different times. While, for instance, carrying arms without a warrant amounts to a minor offence in The Netherlands today, it may be punishable with death in other parts of the world.

[31] The principle of proportionality as formulated in the Naulilaa arbitration is a typical instance: no rigid proportionality was required by the arbitrators, but rather the absence of gross disproportionality.

time it was committed all the essential characteristics of a reprisal: in particular, it must have been an evident reaction to the other State's unlawful conduct, and the coercive purpose must have been apparent.

A final question is whether the State victim of such a nondeclared reprisal would be entitled in its turn to have recourse to a reprisal. This, however, amounts to the issue discussed in the first place in the present context.

1.2.7. *Definition of reprisals*

After the above exposition of certain of the main features of reprisals, the results may be summarized in the following description.

An act in the field of international relations constitutes a reprisal when, firstly, both the actor and the addressee of the act are States or other entities enjoying a degree of international personality.

The act must be a retort to a previous act on the part of the addressee which has adversely affected or continues so to affect the interests of the actor and which the latter can reasonably consider a violation of international law. It must, moreover, itself amount to a violation either of the identical or of another norm of international law.

The *prima facie* unlawful act is not authorized by any previous authoritative community decision. Neither is it an act of self-defence, as its aim is not directly to ward off the blow of the addressee's preceding act.

Its purpose is to coerce the addressee to change its policy and bring it into line with the requirements of international law, be it in respect of the past, the present or the future. This function of law enforcement qualifies the act as a sanction under international law.

The act, finally, must respect the conditions and limits laid down in international law for justifiable recourse to reprisals; that is, first of all, objectivity, subsidiarity, and proportionality.

1.3. BELLIGERENT REPRISALS

After the above exposition of the main characteristics of public reprisals and their function in the international legal order, it seems appropriate to round off this introductory chapter with some preliminary observations concerning belligerent reprisals in particular. The purpose of these remarks will be to give a somewhat more precise indication of their scope and purport in the context of armed conflict.

1.3.1. *Armed conflict*

It seems a foregone conclusion that belligerent reprisals presuppose a state of *bellum,* or "war". This, however, is a far from unequivocal statement, because it leaves undecided what is meant by "war". Indeed, that term can have widely different significances, such as, *inter alia,* the special legal relationship between States which arises from a declaration of war or similar formal act, only to end with the equally formal conclusion of peace; a period of violent conflict involving major military operations and continuing so long as these operations are more than incidental; a state of heightened tension among States contending for supremacy in a given political arena; the class struggle between the oppressed and the oppressor; etcetera.[1]

Most, though not all, of these and similar definitions of "war" have this much in common in that they include (or at least presuppose) the actual use of armed force. True, it is equally possible to envisage an even wider definition, embracing "cold war" as well (*i.e.* the struggle waged with political, economic, ideological and other available means of coercion, probably even including the threat of armed force, but not its actual use). The term shall not, however, be given such an extended significance here. For, while it is not denied that the employment of coercive means other than armed force may lead to levels of coercion being attained not significantly inferior to those involved in actual use of such force, it is not the various means and methods of coercion which are at issue here, so much as the problems attending the unilateral enforcement of international law. These problems assume particular acuteness and even dimensions of their own in the event of armed conflict, involving the applicability (in whole or in part) of the law of war.[2] True, that body of law has developed precisely for situations of armed conflict; but it is obvious that their inherently violent character makes these situations not particularly favourable to considerations of "oughtness". In addition, the sheer number of those taking an active part in the hostilities (and whose actions may hence encroach on the law of war) will probably be immeasurably greater than in any other comparable situation of confrontation. For these reasons, the notion of "war" will be used in the present study in the limited sense of "hot war" or "armed conflict".

On the other hand, in referring to "war" and "armed conflict" it is not

---

[1] The various significances attached to the notion of "war" are discussed by L. Kotzsch, *The Concept of War in Contemporary History and International Law,* 1956. See also G. Schwarzenberger, *International Law as applied by International Courts and Tribunals,* Vol. II: *The Law of Armed Conflict,* 1968, pp. 1-2 and 59 ff.

[2] The most significant difference in this respect is that between international armed conflicts and those not having an international character. While it may be contended that the fundamental principles of the law of war are applicable in either case, and while in any event the principles enumerated in Art. 3 common to the Geneva Conventions of 1949 apply in non-international armed conflicts, the applicability *ipso iure* of the more detailed rules of the law of war is restricted to international armed conflicts.

our intention to exclude the category of non-international armed conflicts.[3] From a point of view of strategies and methods used these need not differ from international wars; indeed, the distinction is not dichotomous: a continuous gradation runs from the purely internal war (without any outside interference or other internationalizing element) to the purely international war (without so much as a trace of internal struggle within the territory of one or other of the belligerents). Moreover, internal war nowadays is often as much a matter of common interest to international society as is interstate armed conflict. These mutually reinforcing considerations lead to the conclusion that it would be altogether too arbitrary to restrict the present study to international wars in the classical sense. Hence, the terms "war" or "armed conflict" shall be used to connote any conflict involving actual use of armed force on a scale sufficiently large to distinguish the international armed conflict from the mere incident, the internal rising from the riot.

The latter criterion obviously is far from exact. However, while for other purposes a more precise criterion may be desirable and perhaps even to a certain degree attainable (by making reference to factors such as the aims sought, the number of troops involved, the type and calibre of weapons used, the relative territorial expansion of operations, and so on),[4] the above vague and imprecise criterion is already sufficient to indicate the scope of the present study. It will be clear that the decisive element here is a certain type of factual situation, the occurrence of which may be attended by—but is not dependent on—certain formalities such as a declaration of war or express recognition of a state of war, a formal statement by an international

---

[3] For a discussion of the two types or armed conflicts, see: J. Siotis, *Le droit de la guerre et les conflits armés d'un caractère non-international*, 1958.

[4] See in particular J. Siotis, *op. cit.* n. 3. In 1962, a committee of experts convened by the ICRC gave the following definition of the non-international armed conflict in the sense of Art. 3 of the Geneva Conventions of 1949: "De l'avis de la Commission, l'existence d'un conflit armé, au sens de l'article 3, ne peut être niée si l'action hostile, dirigée contre un gouvernement légal, présente un caractère collectif et un minimum d'organisation. A cet égard, et sans que ces circonstances soient nécessairement cumulatives, il y a lieu de tenir compte d'éléments tels que la durée du conflit, le nombre et l'encadrement des groupes rebelles, leur installation ou leur action sur une partie du territoire, le degré d'insécurité, l'existence de victimes, les moyens mis en œuvre par le gouvernement légal pour rétablir l'ordre, etc." See: "L'aide humanitaire aux victimes des conflits internes", report of meeting of experts in October 1962, published in *RICR*, Vol. 45, 1963, p. 76, at pp. 79-80.—Obviously, this definition bears in particular on the distinction between non-international armed conflicts and lesser disturbances; it does not provide a criterion for distinguishing non-international and international armed conflicts. In a more recent report of the ICRC, the endeavours are recorded of another expert meeting, held in February 1969, and which attempted to elaborate criteria for the latter distinction; see: "Réaffirmation et développement des lois et coutumes applicables dans les conflits armés", report to the XXIst International Conference of the Red Cross, 1969, pp. 114-118.

body such as the Security Council of the United Nations, the departure of diplomatic representatives, the recognition of the adversary as a belligerent, and so on. In another respect as well the notion of war as envisaged here is purely factual, as no distinction is made between "just" and "unjust" wars, aggressive war and legitimate self-defence, or wars fought by regular combatant forces or (entirely or in part) by irregular armed bands: the sole criterion is the sufficently widespread, sufficiently large-scale use of armed force.

1.3.2. *Participants in belligerent reprisals*

The question of whether retaliatory actions in the context of armed conflict constitute belligerent reprisals will, to a far greater extent than is the case with respect to peacetime reprisals, depend on the status of the parties to such actions, that is on whether these can be regarded as a State or similar autonomous entity. This is already apparent in the event of civil war, where the concept of belligerent reprisals can only find application to the extent that the insurgents have succeeded in establishing themselves as an essentially autonomous party, for instance by bringing part of the territory under their effective control.

The question assumes greatest importance, however, in the event of retaliatory actions against an occupied population, though not in the same measure in all conceivable situations. Thus, no particular problems of the kind envisaged here arise when the action is in retaliation against acts of warfare of the enemy armed forces not in any way connected with the occupation: in that case it is not open to question that the action constitutes a reprisal against the enemy.

This is not so unquestionably self-evident when the immediate cause of a retaliatory measure against the occupied population lies in activities of members of the population itself. In that case, it will depend on the further circumstances of the situation whether the measures can be brought under the heading of reprisals.

Thus, it may be that the Government of the enemy State, though obviously not in a position directly to exercise its authority in the occupied territory, takes an active part in the events by inciting the inhabitants to commit acts of resistance and by supporting and directing such activities with the means at its disposal. If that occurs it may well be that the occupying Power holds the enemy Government directly accountable for illegal acts of resistance and that a retaliatory measure, though having its immediate effect on the population itself, would in reality be aimed against the enemy State.

This may also be stated in more general terms: retaliatory actions against the population in occupied territory may be taken to constitute reprisals against the enemy State, not only when they are directed against unlawful acts of warfare on the part of the enemy armed forces, but also when their evident aim is to coerce the enemy Government to revise a certain, allegedly unlawful policy in respect of certain activities of the occupied population.

What if that purpose is evidently lacking and a retaliatory action against the occupied population can only be deemed to intend pressure on the population itself? With respect to this, it should be borne in mind that characteristically the immediate aim of a reprisal as defined previously is not the punishment of past illegalities nor even the prevention of future illegal acts on the part of individual members of the population (although in particular the latter effect may well be the ultimate goal), so much as to effect a change in the policy of the authorities.[5] A prerequisite for a reprisal is therefore the existence of such authorities, having the capacity in relative autonomy to decide and carry into effect their own policy in respect of certain activities of the community or individual members thereof. It is not hard to realize that this is not a very probable situation in the event of an occupation; on the other hand, it is not absolutely inconceivable either.

Thus, the situation in occupied territory may be characterized by the existence of a strong resistance movement, which has developed into a body hardly distinguishable from a regular army and perhaps has even gained supremacy in part of the territory.[6] In such a factual situation the occupying Power may want to retaliate against unlawful acts of warfare on the part of the resistance army; and, while the retaliatory measures may of course be aimed directly against the resistance army, it is equally imaginable that the occupant, acting on the assumption that strong ties connect the peaceful, non-combatant part of the population with the resistance fighters, inflicts the measures on that part of the population firmly in his grip, in the belief that this may be an effective method of exerting pressure on the authorities in command of the resistance forces. In either case the measures may constitute genuine reprisals, provided at any rate that the ties connecting population and resistance army are so close as to allow their being regarded as a single, sufficiently coherent political entity.

Another possibility might be construed as follows. A situation is conceivable where an occupied community has retained a sufficient degree of coherence and organization and where, despite the fact of the occupation, the ordinary local authorities continue to exercise effective power over the population and to take policy decisions concerning the maintenance of law and order. In this situation, the occupant may at a given moment find a particular policy line, pursued by the authorities concerned, to be detrimental to his position as an occupant; and one might imagine that he, rather than take the maintenance of law and order and the suppression of acts of

[5] See §§ 1.1 and 1.2.3.
[6] For instances of this situation, see Chapter V.

sabotage and similar undesirable acts in his own hands, would prefer to retaliate against the population so as to coerce the authorities to change their policy in this respect. In these conditions, too, the action could be said to constitute a true reprisal.

Admittedly, however, the latter combination of facts seems highly theoretical. The normal case will be that the occupant takes the necessary steps himself to maintain "occupation order" and to repress acts of resistance, and the rôle left to the local community organs in this respect will be anything but autonomous. In that (normal) situation a recourse to retaliatory measures against the population, in so far as it is not just an act of "retaliation" in the sense of blind revenge, can only be understood as a punitive or deterrent action against the members of the population as individual persons. This is true even if a specific measure would be imposed through the intermediary of the local community organs, as will probably be the case with collective fines: while in that case the authorities concerned have the evident freedom to choose whether or not to co-operate in the execution of the measure, the fine itself is intended to affect the individual members of the population, rather than being a means of bringing about a change in the policy pursued by the local authorities.

Obviously, such punitive or deterrent actions do not constitute reprisals in the sense of measures directed against the authorities of a distinct political entity. It should at once be conceded, however, that both in legal debate and in the practice of belligerents the term "reprisals" often has been and is being used without much discrimination to indicate this type of action as well.[7] It seems reasonable to accommodate to this usage, and, in view of the narrow connections between reprisals in the proper sense of the term and punitive or deterrent measures against an occupied population, to include the latter "quasi-reprisals" among the belligerent reprisals examined in this study.

This makes it necessary, however, to enter into some aspects of the measures indicated here as "quasi-reprisals" in somewhat greater detail. A particularly important question is whether a distinction should be re-

---

[7] For the earlier discussions, see Chapters II and III. During the Second World War, the term "reprisals" was used with gruesome frequency to indicate a policy of indiscriminate retaliation in occupied territories, embracing acts which could at best be regarded as instances of collective punishment (as defined in Art. 50 of the Hague Regulations on Land Warfare) and, at worst, as acts of terrorism not distinguishable from plain murder; see Chapter V. As to the post-war period, Art. 33 of the Geneva Convention of 1949 relative to the Protection of Civilian Persons in Time of War, prohibiting "collective penalties and likewise all measures of intimidation or of terrorism" as well as "reprisals against protected persons and their property", bears witness to the fact that some distinction was envisaged between the several categories even at this time; the absence of any precise definition of the terms seems rather less of a shortcoming here, as the various modalities of retaliation are prohibited alike; see Chapter VI, § 6.2.1.

cognized between two types of actions: those with a punitive, and those with a deterrent, character. It might be imagined that measures aimed against the collectivity of the population of a town, village or other locality, and based on the collective responsibility of the population for a hostile act committed in or near the locality, would, as "collective punishment", be regarded as one category, close to (though not identical with) penal punishment. Another category, more closely related to reprisals, would consist of measures intentionally taken against innocents (such as hostages), with a view to deterring those unknown members of the population who might feel inclined in future to commit hostile acts.

It is submitted that this distinction is more apparent than real. True, the possibility cannot be excluded of an occupant resorting to a measure of collective punishment for the mere fact that a hostile act has been committed. Normally, however, his purpose will also (or even primarily) be to deter "the population" (that is, those of its members who might be possible perpetrators of future hostile acts) from continuing on that course. On the other hand, while collective responsibility cannot be alleged to be at the root of a measure against evidently innocent persons, such a measure is equally taken because a hostile act has been committed.

It seems, therefore, that the difference between the two categories boils down to the presumed presence or absence of the element of collective responsibility. It should be emphasized, however, that "collective responsibility" as understood in this context is something widely different from real responsibility for an act committed: usually, it will amount to nothing else but a passive attitude and a lack of co-operation in tracing the perpetrators of the act. In any event, it will be a long way off what would constitute a minimum for criminal or civil responsibility; in actual fact, it more closely resembles joint liability of the members of a community, based on the idea of group solidarity, than on anything like responsibility in the proper sense of the term. Exactly the same idea of group solidarity, however, also underlies the retaliatory measures against innocents.

This leads to the conclusion that there is no real difference between "punitive" and "deterrent" retaliatory measures against (members of) an occupied population. Both varieties will, therefore, be indiscriminately indicated as "collective punishment" or "quasi-reprisals".

A final remark concerns the basis of "quasi-reprisals" as seen from the side of the occupant. Viewed from that angle, it should be noted that such retaliatory measures against an occupied population not aiming to effect a change of policy of responsible authorities do not, like reprisals properly speaking, act as sanctions in the international legal order. Rather, their object will be (in the most favourable case) to protect the vital interests of the occupant, and the occupation régime which is the juridical expression of these interests, against potentially harmful activities on the part of unknown members of the population. This is to say that the basis of such measures can only be sought in the principle of military necessity: the same principle, that is, which lies at the root not only of the other means at the disposal of an occupant for the maintenance of the occupation régime (such as punishment of the actual perpetrators of hostile acts, and internment of suspected persons), but indeed of the whole of the occupant's powers in respect of the occupied territory and its inhabitants. In other words, a requirement for such measures would be that the occupant could with reasonable certainty expect the measure to have a deterrent effect on those unknown individuals likely to commit further infractions of the occupation régime. This is tantamount to saying that there must exist a definite relationship between those individual persons (and their activities) and the population as a collectivity—the same relation of "collective responsibility", in fact, as discussed above from the angle of responsibility for acts already committed.[8]

1.3.3. *Law involved in belligerent reprisals*

Application of the concept of belligerent reprisals does not give rise to any particular difficulties when the law involved in the act underlying the reprisal is the law of war. Other sets of norms may be involved as well, however, especially in situations of internal war and belligerent occupation. Thus, in the event of occupation of (part of) the territory of a belligerent by the forces of the enemy, the conduct of the population vis-à-vis the occupant is governed by the following sets of norms: the law of war, the regulations laid down by the occupant, and the ordinary law of the land. Actions, for instance, such as the theft of goods belonging to the occupant, or a fraud in connection with the supply of goods to that party, will constitute violations of the ordinary penal law in the first place; violation of a curfew, or clandestine possession of arms, may be contraventions of occupation regulations; and the treacherous assassination of a member of the occupying forces may well constitute an infringement of the law of war.

Two comments are necessary. Firstly, it may already be evident from the above examples that one single act may readily fall under more than one set of norms. Thus, the assassination can also be brought under the head of murder, an ordinary crime; and the clandestine possession of arms may be equally punishable under the penal law in force in the territory; and these examples can be multiplied. Secondly, in so far as the different sets of norms have a bearing on the conduct of individual persons in relation to the interests of the occupant, these—and particularly the occupation regulations

---

[8] The issue of the distinction between collective punishment and (other) instances of "quasi-reprisals" assumes particular importance with respect to the text and drafting history of Article 50 of the Hague Regulations on Land Warfare. See *infra*, Chapter II, § 2.3.

and the law of war proper—will hardly be distinguished as separate categories either by the population or by the occupation authorities.

On these grounds, it seems altogether too artificial to make the question of whether a particular retaliatory action constitutes a belligerent reprisal (or "quasi-reprisal") dependent on whether the norms violated are part of the law of war or of another set of norms.

There is yet another side to the issue of the law involved in belligerent reprisals. It is one thing to state that violations of the law of war can give rise to reprisals and that the reprisals themselves consist of acts violative of the law of war as well: but it is another thing to decide which acts actually are such violations. True, the validity of a number of rules of warfare cannot reasonably be denied; but other rules are of doubtful validity and, while wholeheartedly accepted by some, are just as emphatically rejected by others (for instance: rules on contraband, on air warfare, on the use of nuclear weapons, and so on). Taking into account the, indeed highly probable, absence of an independent authority empowered to decide then and there whether a rule alleged to govern a certain situation is actually binding on the parties and applicable in the case at issue, it is apparent that whenever belligerents find themselves in such a situation of uncertainty as to the law in force, the argument developed earlier [9] applies with particular force: either of the parties is entitled to act on the ground of its own reasonable conception of the law governing the actions of both sides. In the long run the respective viewpoints may contribute one way or another to the establishment of a definite rule regarding the issue: but in the meantime it must be accepted that probably neither the action of one belligerent nor the reprisal taken against it by the other can with any certainty be classed as unlawful.

In this unsatisfactory situation, it is imaginable that a reprisal taken against a belligerent on account of a certain mode of conduct would make him realize his error as to the law. It is at least as probable, however, that the reprisal fails to produce that effect, and in that case the (rebuttable) presumption of justification of an action announced as a reprisal cannot prevent the belligerent from feeling justified in considering the alleged reprisal as a mere illegal act. This, in turn, may lead to a counter-reprisal on his part. In this manner, different views concerning the law in force can lead to a sequence of reprisals followed by further reprisals.

This undesirable phenomenon can also come about in a different manner: the belligerents may differ as to the facts underlying the reprisal. In that case, an objective appraisal of the facts must needs lead to the conclusion that one or other of the parties is wrong; but in the absence of such an appraisal, and on the strength of the information available to it, the party

[9] *Supra*, § 1.2.6.

41

concerned may be justified nonetheless in maintaining its (objectively erroneous) view of the situation.[10]

Evidently, therefore, even justifiable belligerent reprisals have a tendency to cause further reprisals and, the object of each new reprisal being to discourage the enemy from his policy as that appears from the latest reprisal on his part, the actions tend to grow harsher in the process (in modern terms: they tend to escalate). It is obvious that this tendency contributes heavily both to the ill fame of belligerent reprisals and to the urge towards their prohibition or at least limitation.

1.3.4. Special features of belligerent reprisals

While some effects of belligerent reprisals have already been referred to in the foregoing, certain other aspects deserve to be treated separately.

For one thing, it is a conspicuous feature of belligerent reprisals that these, even when technically aimed against the State, almost certainly will have their direct impact on individuals who, as likely as not, are innocent of the wrong provoking the reprisal. It should be added, of course, that the same is true of peacetime reprisals: [11] an economic reprisal, for instance, is likely to affect the interests of private persons in the first place; and an action like the Italian occupation of Corfu, in 1923, was neither intended nor suited to act as a direct sanction against the culprits, who were the murderers of the Italian members of the international border commission, nor did it directly affect the members of the Greek Government. Why then the need to broach this issue as a problem of belligerent reprisals in particular?

The answer to this question seems to lie in a complex of considerations. Firstly, the number of individuals, both civilians and soldiers, who in the course of past wars have fallen victims to (alleged) belligerent reprisals and in the process have sustained grievous and often fatal injury, is immeasurably greater than has ever been caused by reprisals in time of peace.

Then, the *de facto* power which a belligerent may temporarily hold over large groups of enemy subjects, not only as a result of occupation of enemy territory, but also in consequence of capturing enemy civilians and soldiers, makes these groups easy victims of retaliatory measures against the enemy State. In this respect, the thesis is sometimes advanced that recourse to reprisals against members of these groups would be out of the question merely on the strength of the argument that they are not in a position to stop the wrong which is being committed by their side. This

[10] It need hardly be added that counter-reprisals can equally be a manifest case of bad faith on the part of the counter-retaliating State. This case is of no interest from a juridical point of view, however, as here the counter-reprisal evidently is a mere illegal act not qualifying for any form of justification.

[11] *Cf.* H. F. van Panhuys, *The Rôle of Nationality in International Law*, p. 109.

argument need not always be correct, particularly where the inhabitants of occupied territory are concerned. But irrespective of this, the argument is in reality immaterial: what matters is whether the suffering inflicted on these persons may be instrumental in inducing the decision-makers of the enemy to effect a change of policy. In this light, however, the position of subjection in which the members of the aforementioned groups find themselves and the relative ease with which measures of constraint can be applied to them by the retaliating State, must needs give rise to the feeling that such reprisals are profoundly unjust.

A third factor is the idea that in warfare a distinction ought to be maintained between the combatant armed forces and the non-combatant civil population, and that the latter category ought to be spared as far as possible the hardships of war. From this principle the thesis may be distilled that the civil population ought not to be made to suffer for the infringements of law committed by the combatants in the course of warfare.[12] It should be noted that this argument, if accepted, would militate solely in favour of the civil population and specifically of those civilians taking no part whatsoever in the hostilities.

From these considerations it may be apparent that a strong case can be made out in favour of the idea that certain categories of persons deserve to be protected against the impact of belligerent reprisals,—a protection that might be achieved by the creation of express prohibitions to that effect.

Another remark is that belligerent reprisals will obviously tend to be in conflict with elementary humanitarian considerations. A number of rules of the law of war have a marginal character, in that their purpose is not so much the realization of some kind of ideally chivalrous combat as the prevention of what is generally felt to be below the standard of what can be tolerated from the viewpoint of humanity, even in the context of warfare. Consequently, a reprisal transgressing such a marginal norm is bound to constitute an inherently inhuman act. In this light, particular importance attaches to the question of whether a rule might have developed to the effect that such sub-marginal acts would be prohibited even by way of reprisals.

Notwithstanding these grave problems evidently attending the concept of belligerent reprisals, it ought to be realized that its emergence as a legal concept has represented a significant step forward in the context of the relations between belligerents: belligerent reprisals could never have become an issue were it not for the fact that warfare had developed into a form of human activity which, once started, was governed by legal norms. In this context it may be appropriate to quote an author, Henri Brocher,

[12] *Op. cit.* n. 11, p. 115.

43

who nearly a century ago expressed his views regarding belligerent reprisals in the following terms: [13]

> "Les représailles étaient, dans le principe, un moyen terme entre la paix et la guerre, un procédé employé pour obtenir satisfaction sans recourir à des hostilités en règle. Aujourd'hui elles sont en outre un intermédiaire entre la guerre que est régulière et celle qui ne l'est pas; ou, si on le préfère, un moyen d'empêcher la guerre de devenir tout-à-fait barbare. Dans le principe, les représailles étaient inconnues, une fois que les hostilités avaient commencé, parce qu'alors le droit de la guerre autorisait ce qui aujourd'hui n'est possible que dans des conditions particulières. Elles sont donc le symptome d'un progrès, bien que de nouveaux progrès doivent amener leur diminution, peut-être même leur disparition."

The present inquiry will centre upon the question as to how much progress has since been made on the road towards the partial or even complete abolition of belligerent reprisals.

---

[13] Henri Brocher, "Les principes naturels du droit de la guerre", in *RDILC,* Vol. V, 1873, p. 349.

CHAPTER II

Evolution of the Law
as to Belligerent Reprisals in the Period
prior to the First World War

2.1. THE CONFERENCE OF BRUSSELS OF 1874

The story of the deliberate attempts on the international level to codify the law with respect to belligerent reprisals is part of the wider history of the codification of the international law of war, and of the law of land warfare in particular. The starting-point of this historical development is the Brussels Conference of 1874, a date which may conveniently serve also as the point of departure for the present survey: for it seems unavoidable to go back to such an early date to gain some understanding of the gradual development of the law as to belligerent reprisals and its application and interpretation (or contestation, as the case may be) in time of war.

Before turning to that significant date, however, it seems necessary to go one step further back and to make mention of a document which, though not itself international, is very much at the root of all subsequent international developments in this field: viz., the *Instructions for the Government of Armies of the United States in the Field*.[1] The Instructions, published pursuant to a presidential order on 24 April 1863, during the War of Secession, and which, after their author, are generally referred to as the Lieber Code, were formally no more than part of the internal legislation of the United States. Yet, they have acquired a significance far exceeding the national level: they have come to be regarded as "the first codification of International Articles of War", uniting "the spirit of humanity, which spirit recognizes as fellow-beings, with lawful rights, our very enemies, and which forbids our visiting upon them unnecessary injury, cruelty, or destruction" with the awareness "that in time of war, it is absolutely necessary to provide for the safety of armies and for the successful conduct of a campaign".[2] These qualities of the Instructions may well serve to

---

[1] Published as General Orders No. 100 of the War Department, Adjutant General's Office. The text has been reproduced in full in *Contributions to political science, including lectures on the Constitution of the United States and other papers. By Francis Lieber, LL.D.*, edited in 1881, after Lieber's death, as Vol. II of his miscellaneous writings, at p. 245.

[2] Quoted from the introduction by Prof. J. C. Bluntschli to the collected papers quoted in n. 1 to this §, at p. 12.

explain their influence on the minds of those who shortly afterwards, in Brussels, undertook the task of codifying the law of land warfare on the international level; an influence which was explicitly recognized by the chairman of the Conference, the Russian first delegate Baron Jomini, when he pointed out "que l'idée du Projet de Convention a été suggéré par ce qui s'est passé aux Etats-Unis lors de la guerre de la sécession. Le règlement du président Lincoln pour adoucir les souffrances de la guerre est présent à tous les souvenirs." [3]

For the purpose of this survey it is important to note that the Lieber Code contains several references to retaliation; among these, two articles deal with the general aspects of reprisals, setting limits to the recourse to retaliation in the conduct of warfare.[4] This express and detailed treatment of the issue of reprisals—which, as Lieber was evidently aware, is of paramount importance both because of its apparent indispensability to belligerents and of its destructive potentialities with respect to the substantive part of the law of war—is evidence of his uncompromising thoroughness in dealing with the recalcitrant subject-matter of the law of war.[5]

In 1874, on the initiative of the Czar, the Conference of Government representatives met in Brussels, "pour régler les lois et coutumes de la

[3] Acts of the Conference, p. 15. See hereafter, n. 6 to this §.
[4] Art. 27: "The law of war can no more wholly dispense with retaliation than can the law of nations, of which it is a branch. Yet civilized nations acknowledge retaliation as the sternest feature of war. A reckless enemy often leaves to his opponent no other means of securing himself against the repetition of barbarous outrage."
Art. 28: "Retaliation will, therefore, never be resorted to as a measure of pure revenge, but merely as a means of protective retribution, and, moreover, cautiously and unavoidably; that is to say, retaliation shall only be resorted to after careful inquiry into the real occurrence, and the character of the misdeeds that may demand retaliation.
"Unjust or inconsiderate retaliation removes the belligerents farther and farther from the mitigating rules of a regular war, and by rapid steps leads them nearer to the internecine wars of savages."
[5] In a letter to General Halleck, written some time after the issue of General Order No. 100, Lieber came back once again to the question of reprisals and in particular to the requirement of proportionality. The passage (quoted by G. B. Davis, "Doctor Francis Lieber's Instructions", in *AJIL*, Vol. 1, 1907, p. 13, at p. 21) runs as follows: "Is the threat of General Burnside true, that he would hang ten Confederate officers for every Union officer hung by the Confederates? Whether true or not, you are aware that this is the spirit which generally shows itself when a barbarous outrage is committed, but which it is very necessary promptly to stop. The wanton insolence of our enemy has been growing so fast, and is so provoking, that I am plainly and simply for quick retaliation; but in retaliation it is necessary strictly to adhere to sections twenty-seven and twenty-eight of General Order 100, to the elementary principle which prevails all the world over—*tit for tat*, or eye for eye—and not to adopt ten eyes for one eye. If one belligerent hangs ten men for one, the other will hang ten times ten for the ten; and what a dreadful geometrical progression of skulls and crossbones we should have."

guerre".[6] Actually, the Conference had no mandate to conclude a convention: its task was merely to prepare a text for the consideration of the Governments, which would thereupon decide whether to sign a convention on the basis of the proposed text or to reopen the deliberations.[7] The Conference duly fulfilled the assigned task and produced a project, which has become known as the Declaration of Brussels.[8] With that, however, matters came to a standstill: notwithstanding efforts on the diplomatic level, no convention was brought about embodying, or conferring binding force on, the proposed text.[9] Yet, the importance of the Declaration for the further development of the law of war is unmistakable, as it has served as a basis both for the subsequent endeavours in this field of the *Institut de droit international* [10] and for the work of the Peace Conference of 1899.[11]

The issue of reprisals was already broached in the first draft text of a Convention relative to the laws and usages of war introduced by the Russian Government: [12] it was referred to in one (the 5th) of the introductory Articles stating general principles, and the entire section IV of the main part was devoted exclusively to the regulation and limitation of the recourse to reprisals. The introductory Article broached the principal aspect of the question, in the following terms:

"Dans le cas où l'ennemi n'observerait pas les lois et coutumes de la guerre, telles qu'elles sont définies par la présente Convention, la partie adverse peut recourir à des représailles, mais seulement comme un mal inévitable et sans jamais perdre de vue les devoirs de l'humanité."

This Article, together with the other statements of principles, disappeared from the project without so much as having been mentioned once in the discussions of the Committee set up for the examination of the project.[13] The gist of it, however, turned up again in a modified version of section IV, introduced by the Russian delegate, Baron Jomini, when that section came up for discussion: [14] under the heading "Des violations des lois et

---

[6] Conference of Brussels, 27 July-27 August 1874. Fifteen States took part. Acts of the Conference: De Martens, N.R.G. 2nd Series, Vol. IV, p. 1.
[7] This merely deliberative task of the Conference was underlined on many occasions in the debates; and see the final protocol, Acts, p. 227.
[8] Acts, pp. 219-226.
[9] On the abortive attempts undertaken in the years following on the Brussels Conference to achieve this transformation of the Declaration into a binding instrument, see the report by G. Moynier to the *Institut's* Brussels session of 1879; *Annuaire* III & IV (1879-1880), Vol. I, at p. 312.
[10] *Infra*, § 2.2.
[11] *Infra*, § 2.3.
[12] Acts, p. 6.
[13] *Ibid.*, pp. 16-19.
[14] Meeting of 20 August; p. 139. This was already a second modified version: an earlier version, introduced in the meeting of 7 August, never came up for discussion; see pp. 57, 207.

47

coutumes de la guerre" the proposed Article now opened with a paragraph running as follows:

> "Les violations des lois et coutumes de la guerre par l'une des parties belligérantes dispensant l'autre partie de leur observation, la justice et l'humanité exigent qu'il soit mis des limites aux représailles."

The Committee showed considerable reluctance to engage in any thorough discussion of the issue; after a few more or less perfunctory observations by some members, the end came in the first round: the Belgian delegate, Baron Lambermont, argued that "le principe des représailles a par lui-même un caractère odieux" and that, as any drafting of rules bearing on reprisals must necessarily embody that odious principle, it seemed wise not to attempt to turn the proposed Article into conventional law at this stage.[15] He therefore proposed "de sacrifier l'article tel qu'il est sur l'autel de l'humanité". This proposal was accepted unanimously.

Both the Russian proposal and the Belgian retort are easily criticised. The draft text in its final version was obviously unfortunate: how could any great enthusiasm be expected for a proposed regulation of reprisals opening with the redundant and dogmatically questionable contention that violations of the law of war by one party dispense the other party from its obligations under it, at a time when the Franco-German war with its mutual accusations of illegal acts had only just come to a close! And the rebuff was hardly less unfortunate: how could dodging the issue promote the cause of humanity?

Notwithstanding this criticism, the discussion is important because it illustrates the two basic attitudes which can be adopted with regard to the issue of express regulation of reprisals. The Russian delegate, in a closing remark after the rejection of the proposed text, accentuated that "l'intention du Gouvernement russe a été de limiter les représailles, non de les consacrer"; a statement in which the recognition was implicit that belligerent reprisals were not completely excluded under existing law and that they should therefore be regulated in order to prevent future abuse.[16] The words of the Belgian representative, on the other hand, betray the fear that a formal regulation would tend to fix the unsatisfactory status quo—which was that belligerent reprisals were not completely excluded under existing law. The difference between the two attitudes lies in which policy is considered best suited to gain control of the resort to belligerent reprisals,

---

[15] "Pourquoi ... ne laisserait-on pas cette matière dans le domaine du droit non écrit, sous la sanction de la conscience publique, en attendant que les progrès de la science et de la civilisation apportent une solution complètement satisfaisante?" (p. 139).

[16] "Je regrette ... de voir rester dans le vague du silence une des plus dures nécessités de la guerre. Si l'on supprimerait la chose en s'abstenant de prononcer le mot, je ne pourrais qu'y applaudir; mais si la chose doit rester dans les nécessités de la guerre, je crains que ce silence et cette obscurité n'en effacent les limites." (loc. cit.)

rather than in the opinions as to the admissibility in principle of reprisals in the absence of any positive prohibition.

In the light of the attitude adopted by the Conference of leaving reprisals alone, the Russian propositions concerning specific limitations of their use never stood any chance of even being brought up for discussion. The great importance attached by their authors to the issue was evidenced, however, by the fact that not only had the original draft already contained such detailed rules,[17] but even a first[18] and second[19] modified version were produced while the Conference was in progress. And further proof of the (justifiable) fears of the Russian delegation for a concept of reprisals left undefined and hence without express limitations, may be seen in the rather too forcedly optimistic concluding words of the Russian first delegate, to the effect that, however much it could not be denied that no legal limitation of reprisals had been effected, the Conference's exertions had at least resulted in a moral limitation of the highest authority.[20]

In addition to these express, though ultimately abortive, attempts at laying down fixed rules concerning the recourse to reprisals, the records of the Brussels Conference contain a few incidental references to reprisals, which, however, are of a nature to throw some additional light on the views held by the Conference in this respect. The incidents occurred in the context of a discussion of the relations existing in occupied territory between the civil population and the occupying Power, and particularly of two distinct issues: armed resistance on the part of the population, and the infliction of collective fines by the occupant.

The first-mentioned issue was discussed under the following aspects: the right of defence of a population, the conditions under which it might

[17] Paras. 69-71; Acts, p. 14. The text of para. 69 read as follows: "Les représailles ne sont admises que dans les cas extrêmes, en observant, autant que possible, les lois de l'humanité quand il sera irrécusablement prouvé que les lois et coutumes de la guerre ont été violées par l'ennemi et qu'il a recours à des moyens réprouvés par le droit des gens." Para. 70 contained the principle of proportionality, and para. 71 laid down the rule that only the commander in chief could authorize a recourse to reprisals.

[18] Para. 60; Acts, p. 207. This version as well contained the principle of proportionality and the requirement of authorization by the commander in chief.

[19] Following immediately after the paragraph quoted in the text at n. 14, *supra*, this version contained very much the same principles as the preceding ones. The formulation of the principle of proportionality ("Elles ne devront jamais dépasser l'infraction commise") was remarkable in that it seemed to suggest the possibility of a strict rather than a marginal test.

[20] "Toutefois je crois que la constatation même dans nos protocoles que la Commission après avoir cherché à régler, à adoucir, à restreindre les représailles, a reculé devant sa tâche et devant la répugnance universelle qu'inspire ce droit extrême de la guerre, je crois que cette constatation aura une portée morale des plus sérieuses. C'est peut-être la meilleure limite que nous ayons pu tracer à l'exercice de ce droit et surtout à l'usage qui en pourra être fait à l'avenir" (p. 140).

acquire combatant status, and its fate when it fails to secure that status.[21] Obviously the connection with reprisals (though more likely than not in the form of quasi-reprisals) lies in the latter aspect: it is only a slight step from denying combatant status to members of the population committing acts of belligerency, to considering those acts illegal. There is no need to examine here the complicated discussions devoted by the Committee to the problems of right of defence and combatant status: but it should be put on record that both the Russian and the German delegates explicitly pointed to the incontestable if regrettable probability of reprisals against the civil population in situations where this would, in their opinion, not be entitled to combatant status.[22]

The infliction of collective fines (*amendes*) was broached as part of the question of the requisitions and contributions which an occupant might exact from the population.[23] Again leaving aside the manner in which that question was dealt with in its entirety, it should merely be noted that several delegates took pains to point out the connection between collective fines and reprisals.[24]

---

[21] Articles 9, 10, and 45-47 of the original project; Acts, pp. 95-106, 110-119.

[22] The Russian delegate, Baron Jomini, observed that "le seul remède que l'on puisse trouver pour parer aux inconvénients que l'on vient de signaler [viz., those concerning the position of a population rising in arms against the occupying forces] est de se tenir de part et d'autre dans les limites d'une guerre régulière. Une population ne tentera de s'insurger que si elle se croit en état de repousser l'ennemi; si elle parvient à son but, l'occupation cessera. Mais si elle a trop présumé de ses forces, elle subira les dures conséquences de son insurrection. Ces représailles auxquelles elle s'expose devront lui faire comprendre que ce n'est pas servir son pays que de tenter de secouer un joug auquel on ne peut se soustraire" (p. 116).

The German representative, General Voigts-Rhetz, who stressed the necessity of a distinguishing mark for the members of a civil population who engage in combat, continued (p. 117): "Mais si l'on n'astreint pas les populations à cette mesure toute de prudence, et qu'on leur dit simplement de respecter les lois et coutumes de la guerre, on les met à la merci de l'ennemi qui pourra toujours déclarer qu'elles ne se sont pas conduites honnêtement et loyalement. Il en résultera dans la continuation de la guerre des épisodes sauvages suivis de cruelles et sanglantes représailles."

[23] Articles 52-54 of the project; pp. 121-138.

[24] "M. le comte Lanza dit que, selon lui, les amendes devraient constituer le seul moyen formellement reconnu pour punir les violations des lois et coutumes de la guerre. Il ne se dissimule pas que d'autres peines seront, en fait, infligées sous forme de représailles; mais il est permis d'espérer que si l'on ne peut pas empêcher d'une manière absolue le recours à ces autres mesures de rigueur, la Conférence ne voudra consacrer en principe que le moyen de châtiment proposé, lequel n'est pas repoussé par le sentiment public. Le silence serait préférable" (p. 133).

"M. de Lansberge demande la suppression des mots 'à titre d'amende' qui figurent au premier alinéa du § 53. Ou bien, dit M. le Délégué des Pays-Bas, une amende sera le résultat d'une infraction prévue par le droit pénal, et alors il est inutile de mentionner spécialement ce cas isolé, ou bien ce sera une représaille et alors il paraît désirable de ne pas plus indiquer ce cas de représailles que les autres mesures excessives et dures qui peuvent être la conséquence de la guerre, mais que tout le monde répugne à sanctionner" (p. 137).

The outcome of the debate on this issue was the inclusion of a reference to collective fines in the article on contributions; in its final version, the Article read as follows: [25]

> "L'ennemi prélevant des contributions soit comme équivalent pour des impôts (v. art. 5) ou pour des prestations qui devraient être faites en nature, soit à titre d'amende, n'y procédera, autant que possible, que d'après les règles de la répartition et de l'assiette des impôts en vigueur dans le territoire occupé."

In conclusion, the same inference can be drawn both from the passages expressly dealing with reprisals in their general aspects and from the scattered casual references to that concept: in the eyes of those taking part in the discussions, the fact had to be recognized that belligerent reprisals constituted an accepted feature of the law of war and that their absolute prohibition for the time being was unattainable. Furthermore, far from undertaking to lay down rules to restrict the legitimate use of these apparently indispensable reprisals, the Brussels Conference had deliberately chosen to exclude any express reference to reprisals from the project of rules which it ultimately laid before the Governments.

Another fact stands out with particular clarity: viz., that the delegates did not make any visible effort to distinguish between belligerent reprisals in a strict sense, as measures aimed against a distinct political entity as such, and quasi-reprisals as measures against the population in occupied territory. This loose use of the term probably accounts for much of the reluctance and even repugnance which many of the delegates displayed in approaching the issue of reprisals.

2.2. THE OXFORD MANUAL

It did not take long before the subject of the codification of the law of war was taken up again, this time however by a non-governmental institution: the *Institut de droit international*. This Institute, bearing in mind that among its aims was the promotion of the observance of the law of war,[1] in 1875 charged a Committee with the task of scrutinizing the Declaration of Brussels.[2] The rapporteur of the Committee opened the proceedings with a questionnaire, in which the question was raised *inter alia* what view should be taken of the suppression, in Brussels, of the proposed section on reprisals. The members of the Committee were quasi-unanimous in their

---

[25] Art. 41; p. 224.
[1] Art. 1, para. 2, 5° of the Articles of Association dating from 1873, the year the *Institut* was founded.
[2] *RDILC*, Vol. VII, 1875, p. 438; rapporteur of the Committee was G. Rolin-Jacque-myns.

opinion that that decision was to be regretted;[3] a general feeling voiced by the rapporteur when he pointed in his report to the urgent need for a definition and regulation of belligerent reprisals, so long as their complete prohibition was unattainable.[4] The *Institut* endorsed this view in the plenary session of 1875 by voting in favour of the relevant passage of the draft conclusions of the Committee.[5]

This position was not altered in the course of the further proceedings which ultimately resulted in the adoption, in the *Institut*'s Oxford session of 1880, of the *Manuel des lois de la guerre sur terre*, or Oxford Manual.[6] As the Manual was intended to be acceptable to Governments, no absolute prohibition of reprisals was envisaged, much as the lack of such a prohibition and, with that, the justifiability in principle of reprisals were regretted.[7] On the other hand, the drafters of the Manual had not, like

[3] One dissenting member even saw fit to rely for his opinion on St. Augustine, who was quoted to the effect that the *lex talionis* is *justitia injustorum*.

[4] "Nous sommes très décidément d'avis que plus le droit des représailles est terrible, plus il convient de le réglementer. Si l'on peut le supprimer, il faut le faire. Mais si, comme nous le croyons, cela est impossible, il vaut mieux le définir en le limitant, que de lui laisser libre carrière en obéissant à un sentiment exagéré d'humanité et de délicatesse. Comme le dit fort bien M. Moynier, si ce scrupule serait fondé, il s'appliquerait à tout ce qui concerne le droit de la guerre" (pp. 509-510).

[5] *Annuaire*, Vol. I, 1877, p. 136: conclusion IX: "Les représailles sont une exception douloureuse, mais inévitable dans certains cas, au principe général d'équité, d'après lequel un innocent ne doit pas souffrir pour un coupable. Du moment où l'on ne peut les prohiber complètement, il serait à désirer que, conformément au projet russe primitif, on les comprit dans la déclaration pour avoir l'occasion de les limiter."

[6] *Annuaire*, Vol. V, 1882, p. 149-174; the Committee which, starting from the conclusions adopted in 1875, prepared the set of rules on land warfare, had as its rapporteur G. Moynier, chairman of the then *Comité international de secours aux militaires blessés*, which later became the International Committee of the Red Cross.

The *Institut* had meanwhile abandoned the original idea of preparing a draft convention, as the moment for such an undertaking was not considered propitious. Instead it had decided to provide the Governments with a manual suitable to be put into the hands of soldiers, and therefore not dry like a legislative document, but fashioned in a rather more popular manner; *cf. Annuaire*, Vols. III & IV, 1879-1880, part I, p. 326; Vol. V, 1882, p. 154.

[7] Regarding this attitude the rapporteur's communications are illuminating (*Annuaire*, Vol. V, 1882, p. 153): "Si elle [viz., the preparatory Committee] ne s'était tenue en garde contre l'écueil d'une philanthropie exagérée, elle aurait mis bien plus d'entraves à la liberté d'action des belligérants; mais, en multipliant ainsi ses *veto*, elle n'aurait pas fait suffisamment,—elle le croit du moins,—la part des nécessités militaires, et, en demandant plus qu'on ne peut lui accorder, elle aurait risqué de compromettre le crédit moral de l'Institut. Du moment que nous ne réclamions pas l'utopie de la paix perpétuelle, mais seulement un frein à l'emploi de la force, nous devions éviter de formuler des exigences auxquelles les intéressés auraient pu opposer, avec raison, celles de la guerre elle-même."

The same thought is repeated in the foreword to the Manual (p. 158): "On n'y trouvera pas, au surplus, de téméraires hardiesses. L'Institut, en le rédigeant, n'a pas cherché à innover; il s'est borné à préciser, dans la mesure de ce qui lui a paru admissible et pratique, les idées reçues de notre temps et à les codifier."

their predecessors at Brussels, simply omitted all reference to reprisals: on the contrary, the possibility of a recourse to reprisals was expressly recognized.[8] In Chapter III, devoted to punishment of infractions of the law of war, individual penal responsibility was put first and foremost.[9] However, the text continued:

"Mais ce mode de répression n'est applicable que lorsqu'on peut atteindre le coupable. Dans le cas contraire la loi pénale est impuissante, et, si la partie lésée juge le méfait assez grave pour qu'il soit urgent de rappeler l'ennemi au respect du droit, il ne lui reste d'autre ressource que d'user de représailles à son égard.

"Les représailles sont une exception douloureuse au principe général d'équité d'après lequel un innocent ne doit pas souffrir pour un coupable, et à celui qui veut que chaque belligérant se conforme aux lois de la guerre, même sans réciprocité de la part de l'ennemi."

This open recognition of the possibility and, indeed, indispensability in certain circumstances, of belligerent reprisals had as a matter of course to be followed by a definition of the rules limiting their use. A first attempt in that direction had already been made at an early stage in the deliberations of the Committee: G. Moynier had, in replying to the original questionnaire, annexed a project of rules on land warfare, which contained a provision to the effect that reprisals may only be exercised to the extent necessary to obtain the termination by the enemy of his unlawful conduct or to prevent further infractions of the violated rule, and that reprisals may only be ordered by the commanding officer of the army.[10] This was not an entirely satisfactory formula, as its first part in particular was extremely wide and could easily be interpreted so as to result in hardly any limitation.

A narrower and more precise limitation of reprisals was found in the conclusions accepted in the plenary session of the *Institut* in 1875. The limits outlined there [11] were subsequently included without material change

---

[8] *Annuaire*, Vol. V, 1882, p. 174.

[9] "Si des infractions aux règles qui précèdent ont été commises, les coupables doivent être punis, après jugement contradictoire, par celui des belligérants au pouvoir duquel ils se trouvent. Donc ... les violateurs des lois de la guerre sont passibles des châtiments spécifiés dans la loi pénale."

[10] *RDILC*, Vol. VII, 1875, p. 519: art. 44.

[11] The text of conclusion IX, quoted partly in n. 5 to this §, continues to enumerate the following principles limiting the resort to reprisals:

"1° leur mode d'exercice et leur étendue ne devraient pas dépasser le degré de l'infraction commise par l'ennemi;

2° elles seraient formellement interdites dans le cas où l'infraction dont on a lieu de se plaindre aurait été réparée;

3° elles ne pourraient s'exercer qu'avec l'autorisation du commandant en chef;

4° elles respecteraient, dans tous les cas, les lois sacrées de l'humanité et de la morale."

The original version of no. 1, as adopted by the committee, read "... seraient proportionnés au degré ..." As a result of an amendment introduced in the plenary

in the text which eventually became the Oxford Manual; in their final version they read as follows: [12]

"Les représailles sont formellement interdites, dans le cas où le dommage dont on a lieu de se plaindre a été réparé.

"Dans les cas graves où des représailles apparaissent comme une nécessité impérieuse, leur mode d'exercice et leur étendue ne doivent jamais dépasser le degré d'infraction commise par l'ennemi.

"Elles ne peuvent s'exercer qu'avec l'autorisation du commandant en chef.

"Elles doivent respecter, dans tous les cas, les lois de l'humanité et de la morale."

Two comments impose themselves. One is that the second paragraph expressed clearly the principles of subsidiarity and proportionality as requirements for justifiable recourse to belligerent reprisals. The other is that the requirement of respect in all circumstances, formulated in the last-quoted paragraph, was much stricter and left less scope to the discretion of belligerents than the passage, embodied in the original Russian proposal to the Brussels Conference, to the effect that reprisals ought to respect the laws of humanity as far as practicable.[13] According to the authors of the Manual, a belligerent would, in resorting to reprisals, be bound to respect the laws of humanity, whatever their contents at any given time; if, for instance, the act of killing prisoners of war would now, but not in the past, be considered an act contrary to the laws of humanity, such killing would be prohibited even by way of reprisal, from the moment that the new rule were accepted. The consequence would be that, as the laws of humanity gain ground and also find more accurate definition, the scope left to belligerents for recourse to reprisals would shrink proportionally.

It is precisely on account of this consequence that some hesitation seems justified with respect to the rule stated in the Manual as part of the positive law of that era. Obviously it was a highly desirable rule, and it may even be that the Manual accurately reflected the trend of learned opinion prevailing at the time; but it seems a bold step to exclude completely that States, in subscribing to new rules of warfare of a primarily humanitarian character, would feel entitled to make the mental reservation that the rules could be put aside by way of reprisal. Of course this hesitation would disappear, either, when a specific humanitarian norm would clearly be intended to

---

session by Sir Travers Twiss these words were replaced by the quoted text ("... ne devraient pas dépasser le degré ..."). Although no motives were given for the amendment (which resulted in a text resembling that of the final Russian proposal in Brussels, see n. 19 to § 2.1), the implication seems to be that, whereas the upper limit of a reprisal would be the severeness of the prior infraction, it might stay below that limit.
[12] *Annuaire*, Vol. V, 1882, p. 174: paras. 85, 86.
[13] See n. 17 to § 2.1. The rule expressed in para. 69 was not repeated in the later versions of the Russian draft.

limit the freedom of action of States even to the extent of prohibiting its violation by way of reprisals, or if the general attitude of States, as apparent from discussions on the diplomatic level, would provide incontestable corroboration of such a trend of opinion and, hence, of the rule under discussion.

In view of these objections, it will be of particular interest to see whether later events have confirmed the correctness of the view expressed in the Oxford Manual as regards the relation between the law of reprisals and the laws of humanity.

This account of the exertions of the *Institut de droit international* concerning belligerent reprisals would not be complete without reference to a discussion which took place in its meeting of 1896, in the context of deliberations concerning bombardment by a naval force. The rapporteurs of the Commission seized of the matter, Holland and Den Beer Poortugael, had in their report dealt with the question of the circumstances justifying bombardment of an open city, and in that connection they had made reference to the bombardment of Dieppe and Le Havre carried out by the English fleet in 1694, an event which, in the terms of the report, "a dû être justifié, même en 1694, comme acte de représailles pour des actes du grand roi". They had concluded that bombing an open city would be permissible, *inter alia*, "[a]ux fins de punir, par voie de représailles, des infractions aux lois de la guerre de la part de l'ennemi".

When during the 1896 session the debate in the Commission turned to this part of the proposed resolution, it became apparent that no consensus existed among the members as to the purport of the notion of reprisals as used in the text. While one member (Gabba) wanted to replace the words "de la part de l'ennemi" by the expression "de la part de la population elle-même", thereby transforming the proposed rule into a permission to bomb by way of collective punishment or quasi-reprisals, another member (Perels) understood the rule solely to envisage reprisals for acts committed by the enemy army, not by the population.

This point was left undecided, however, as were the merits of the proposal. For, after a third member, Lord Reay, had intervened to state that he could not agree to admitting "ce droit de représailles, qui est la négation même du droit, puisqu'il permet de punir des innocents au lieu et place des coupables", the Commission followed his suggestion to delete the entire paragraph. In so doing, the Commission departed radically from the stand taken by the *Institut* in 1875 and affirmed in the text of the Oxford Manual, that "plus le droit des représailles est terrible, plus il convient de le réglementer": [14] this time, even the *Institut* preferred to play ostrich on the issue of reprisals. [15]

[14] n. 4 to this §.
[15] See for this episode: *Annuaire*, Vol. XV, 1896, pp. 146 ff., 311-312.

55

2.3. THE PEACE CONFERENCE OF 1899

Passing over in silence the Military Ibero-American Congress held in 1892 in Madrid,[1] the next mile-stone in the development of the law of war was the Peace Conference which, again on the initiative of the Czar, convened at the Hague in 1899.[2] One of the main items on the agenda was the reconsideration and, where necessary, revision of the Declaration of Brussels: it was a disappointing state of affairs that the Declaration had remained a non-binding instrument and that no convention on land warfare had since come into force, and it was hoped that this time the Conference would be able to reach agreement on a text that would prove acceptable to the Governments.[3]

As the Declaration of Brussels in its final version did not contain any express reference to the issue of belligerent reprisals, that problem was not explicitly laid before the Conference. Nor did the Sub-Committee set up to examine the text of the Declaration[4] voluntarily add reprisals to its burdens: no proposal was advanced even to discuss such problems as the influence of reprisals on the law of war or the general admissibility of belligerent reprisals, let alone to seek agreement on express rules governing these issues. This example was later followed, successively, by the Second Committee of the Conference when it discussed the report of the Sub-Committee, and by the plenary session when it took note of the final report of the Second Committee.

Despite this manifest reserve with respect to the general aspects of belligerent reprisals, these were bound sooner or later to enter into the discussions. The first occasion arose in the Sub-Committee, in the context of a discussion of the relations between occupying Power and occupied population and in particular of those provisions of the Brussels Declaration

---

[1] This Congress elaborated a project for the codification of the law of war (that is both land and sea warfare) which, however, never became a convention. Although the project borrowed much from the Oxford Manual, it did not so much as refer to reprisals; instead, it contained some valuable specific rules of a humanitarian character (such as: prohibition against condemning civilians to death in a war zone except in consequence of a sentence rendered in accordance with penal law—Art. 5 of Ch. III; prohibition against taking hostages—Art. 12 of the same Chapter). A French translation of the project has been published in *RDILC*, Vol. XXV, 1893, pp. 321-337.

[2] *Conférence internationale de la paix*, 18 May-29 July 1899; twenty-six States took part. Reports of the proceedings were published by the Netherlands Ministry for Foreign Affairs, 1899.

[3] This hope was fulfilled when the Conference adopted a Convention on the Laws and Usages of Land Warfare, with an annex containing an equally binding, detailed set of rules, the Regulations on Land Warfare. As to the binding character of the Regulations, see the remarks by Renault, rapporteur of the *Comité de rédaction de l'Acte Final*; Proceedings, Vol. I, p. 196: plenary session of 27 July.

[4] The second Sub-Committee of the Second Committee, both of which were under the chairmanship of the Russian delegate, De Martens.

bearing on the levying of contributions and requisitions by the occupation authorities. One of these articles, it may be recalled, contained a reference to collective fines.[5] With respect to this, several members of the Sub-Committee already expressed in the first round of the debate their view that such a reference ought to be maintained in the revised text.[6]

When hereupon a Drafting Committee[7] had elaborated such a revised text,[8] collective fines had indeed been maintained; more than that, these were now dealt with in a separate Article, reading as follows:

"Aucune peine collective, pécuniaire ou autre, ne pourra être édictée contre les populations à raison de faits individuels dont elles ne pourraient être considérées comme solidairement responsables."

The change was considerable: from a mere detail in the context of pecuniary contributions, collective punishment had developed into a separate issue which no longer was restricted to pecuniary measures. Notwithstanding this substantial change, however, the newly proposed Article was carried unanimously and without having evoked so much as a word of comment.[9]

The discussions concerning contributions and requisitions having thus come to a successful end, the Swiss delegate, Odier, now put forward a proposal[10] with the following text:

"Il ne pourra être exercé de représailles sur la population du territoire occupé pour avoir pris ouvertement les armes contre l'envahisseur."

As no explanatory statement went with the proposal, it remains unknown how the author saw its relation to the preceding articles and notably to that on collective punishment. That such a relation existed is, however, abundantly clear: supposing that acts of armed resistance are committed in occupied territory by "the population", that is, by members of the population, their activities may well engage the collective responsibility of the population; and an interpretation to the effect that in this case "reprisals" (or, rather, quasi-reprisals) would be prohibited (the Swiss proposal) whereas collective punishment would be permitted (the Article agreed on in the Sub-Committee), simply does not make sense. Therefore the proposed text can have only one significance: namely, that in the given situation all

---

[5] *Supra*, p. 51.
[6] Proceedings, Vol. III, pp. 134 (Van Karnebeek), 136 (Odier), 137 (Bourgeois); session of 12 June.
[7] *Ibid.*, pp. 138-139; the Committee was set up because the debates in the Sub-Committee had failed to bring agreement as to the revision of the articles under consideration.
[8] p. 141; session of the Sub-Committee of 17 June.
[9] p. 143. As regards the reasons for these radical modifications of the text, some information is procured in Rolin's report to the Main Committee, which will be reverted to later in this §.
[10] p. 145.

57

reprisals would be prohibited, including those referred to as collective punishment.

The proposal was obviously also connected with those other topics which already in Brussels had brought reprisals into the discussion: to wit, the combatant status of members of the civil population taking part in armed actions. It is therefore not surprising to find that, on a suggestion from the chair, consideration of the proposal was deferred to the discussion of amendments to the articles on combatant status and *levée en masse*.[11]

The debate on these issues opened with a statement by the chairman, De Martens,[12] which was to prove so important that eventually the greater part of it would be inserted in the preamble to the Convention on the Laws and Usages of Land Warfare.[13] In the statement, the point was stressed that it could never be the intention to deprive the population of its right of defence; on the other hand, a completely satisfactory codification of the law in this respect was out of the question for the moment; therefore, the adoption was suggested of a declaration which, after recognizing this evident impracticability "de concerter dès maintenant des stipulations s'étendant à tous les cas qui se présentent dans la pratique", would continue:

> "D'autre part, il n'a pu entrer dans les intentions de la Conférence que les cas non-prévus fussent, faute de stipulation écrite, laissés à l'appréciation de ceux qui dirigent les armées.
>
> "En attendant qu'un code tout-à-fait complet des lois de la guerre puisse être édicté, la Conférence juge opportun de constater que dans les cas non compris dans l'arrangement de ce jour, les populations et les belligérents restent sous la sauvegarde et sous l'empire des principes du droit des gens, tels qu'ils résultent des usages établis entre nations civilisées, des lois de l'humanité, et des exigences de la conscience publique.
>
> "C'est dans ce sens que doivent s'entendre notamment les articles 9 et 10 adoptés par la Conférence."

This declaration met with warm approval on the part of the delegates, who thereupon without further difficulties adopted Articles 9 and 10 under consideration. This left two proposals on the table:[14] the Swiss text, and an English proposition introduced in the meantime and which ran as follows:

> "Rien dans ce chapitre ne doit être considéré comme tendant à amoindrir ou à supprimer le droit qui appartient à la population d'un pays envahi de remplir son devoir d'opposer aux envahisseurs, par tous les moyens licites, la résistance patriotique la plus énergique."

---

[11] *Loc. cit.*; Articles 9 and 10 of the Declaration of Brussels.
[12] p. 152; session of 20 June.
[13] *Cf.* p. 30 (session of the 2nd Committee, 5 July) and Vol. I, pp. 195-196 (plenary session of 27 July).
[14] Vol. III, p. 154; session of the Sub-Committee of 20 June.

This text could not be intended to refer to the *levée en masse* [which] had already been dealt with in Article 10 where the combata[nts as] participants had found recognition. So, the proposal evide[ntly raised] the identical issue as had been broached in the Swiss pro[posal, the] position of the inhabitants of an occupied territory taking u[p arms against] the occupant. The situation was soon simplified, however, [when the Swiss] delegation dropped its own amendment in favour of the English proposal.[15] When thereupon the point was pressed whether the English text should be inserted in the Convention as a separate Article, it became apparent that this was not considered opportune by the Sub-Committee: the majority was of the opinion that the view expressed in it had already found adequate expression in the declaration proposed by the chair,[16] and on the other hand strong opposition was raised by some members against the very purport of the proposed Article.[17] When thereupon the declaration was adopted as an official act of the Sub-Committee destined to be inserted in the final protocol of the Conference,[18] the English proposition was withdrawn upon the understanding that it would be recorded in the proceedings.[19] The end of it was that the declaration of the chairman, as cited above, was embodied in the preamble to the Convention, whereas text and discussion of the English proposal were summarized in the report to the Second Committee.[20]

What do the above discussions in the Sub-Committee bring to light as regards the ideas held in the Peace Conference with respect to belligerent reprisals? Nothing very definite, it is feared: the mere fact that no separate debate was devoted to reprisals, or to sanctions, or even to collective fines, results in uncertainty as to the implications of the insufficiently explained references, recorded above, to these and similar items. Was it the feeling of the Conference that "collective fines, pecuniary or otherwise" would to a certain extent coincide with reprisals, so that the provision concerning collective fines would be relevant in a discussion of reprisals? Or were they held to be something different, belonging in the sphere of penal law? Was "reprisals" merely used as another word for brutal vengeance, for the unlawful killing of innocents,—or in the sense of justifiable reprisals? With respect to such obvious questions the records remain singularly silent. Indeed, the introduction and subsequent withdrawal of the one proposal containing an express reference to reprisals, viz., the Swiss proposal quoted

[15] *Ibid.*, pp. 154-156 (Colonel Künzli), 157.
[16] p. 158: "Le Président consulte la Sous-Commission sur le sort qui doit être fait à sa déclaration. Elle a le même sens que la proposition de Sir John Ardagh mais avec cette différence qu'elle implique l'impossibilité de prévoir tous les cas."
[17] pp. 156-157.
[18] p. 158.
[19] p. 159.
[20] p. 36.

59

above, without so much as a word in elucidation of the proposed text,[21] merely added to the confusion and could even produce a negative effect, as it could leave the false impression that retaliatory reactions to armed resistance of the population would not be covered by the rule on collective punishment adopted by the Sub-Committee.

In this confusion, some enlightenment may be drawn from the paragraphs bearing on collective punishment, contained in the report submitted to the Second Committee by the rapporteur of the Sub-Committee, H. Rolin.[22] In this report the reasons were set forth why the Drafting Committee had adopted a completely new text on collective punishment instead of maintaining the original reference to collective fines as a mere aspect of the financial relations between occupant and occupied population. The term *amende*, the report stated, was apt to lead to confusion in view of the close similarity to notions of penal law. However, what the Sub-Committee had in mind was "une forme déterminée des contributions extraordinaires, consistant dans la perception de sommes d'argent par l'occupant à titre de répression pour des actes hostiles", a mode of repression which ought only to be applied "à la suite d'actes répréhensibles ou hostiles commis par la collectivité ou du moins que celle-ci a laissé commettre."

Hence, no collective repression for strictly individual acts: "il faut que la répression s'exerçant sur la collectivité ait pour fondement *la responsabilité tout au moins passive* de cette collectivité." And the report continued:

> "Mais, une fois entré dans cette voie, le Comité de Rédaction d'abord et la Sous-Commission ensuite, ont cru pouvoir aller plus loin et, sans rien préjuger quant aux représailles, faire déclarer que la règle susdite est vraie, non seulement pour les amendes, mais pour toute peine, pécuniaire ou non, que l'on prétend infliger à l'ensemble de la population."

Evidently, collective punishment was envisaged as something different from penal sanctions, namely as a measure inflicted on the community by way of repression for hostile acts on the part of (members of) the population; evidently, too, its application ought to be restricted to instances of reprehensible or hostile acts committed by the collectivity as such or which the collectivity had at least passively let be committed. Thus, the report may be interpreted confirming that collective punishment was conceived

---

[21] In withdrawing the proposal, Colonel Künzli made no reference whatsoever to the construction applied in his colleague's earlier proposition. All he said was in support of the English proposal; the core of his appeal is found in these words: "Je ne vous demande qu'une seule innovation: Ne punissez pas l'amour de la patrie, ne prenez pas des mesures rigoureuses contre les peuples qui se lèvent en masse pour la défence de leur sol" (p. 155). This comes very near to a plea for amending the collective punishment rule—but the consequence was not drawn.

[22] p. 46.

as nothing very different from reprisals. But how then can one explain the words in the last-quoted paragraph: "sans rien préjuger quant aux représailles"?

The logically most satisfactory explanation seems to be this. The power of collective punishment was seen as a restricted one: it could be used solely in cases of established active or passive collective responsibility for reprehensible or hostile acts. To the extent that reprisals (including quasi-reprisals) and collective punishment actually were synonymous, this restriction would be valid for reprisals as well. The concept of reprisals, however, was wider and embraced measures not identical with collective punishment; those measures could have a bearing on events occurring within or outside occupied territory, and they could be directed against the civil population in occupied territory or otherwise. In so far as these wider aspects were concerned, the reservation was intended to underline that the Conference did not venture to express any opinion on the problems connected with belligerent reprisals as a general concept.

On the other hand, it may well be that the reservation formulated by Rolin was in fact inspired by the terms of the Swiss amendment and that what he had in mind was primarily the issue of (quasi-)reprisals against a civil population, resorted to on account of acts of armed resistance committed in occupied territory. For that and similar situations, the Sub-Committee had accepted the formula proposed by De Martens, to the effect that no express rules could be given yet, but that "les populations et les belligérants restent sous la sauvegarde et sous l'empire des principes du droit des gens, tels qu'ils résultent des usages établis entre nations civilisées, des lois de l'humanité, et des exigences de la conscience publique". In this light, the express reservation as to reprisals may have been no more than an implicit reference to those words: an excuse that the work was incomplete and simultaneously a reminder that principles did already exist which covered the situations which the Conference had failed to solve.

The above considerations assume particular significance with respect to an issue which later was to prove of crucial importance: viz., the question of whether an occupying Power can be justified in resorting to the execution of innocent civilians in retaliation for reprehensible or hostile acts committed by members of the population. At the time, the practice of shooting hostages was only too well known; yet, not a single express reference to it is found in the records of the Conference. But it does not seem open to doubt that in any event the article on collective punishment—Article 50 in the definitive version of the Regulations—has a bearing on the issue. This is borne out by the text of the Article itself, by the observations in Rolin's report, as well as indirectly by an earlier passage in the debates: [23] when

[23] p. 79.

61

the German representative, Colonel de Gross de Schwarzhoff, had proposed to amend the prevision that "[l']honneur et les droits de la famille, la vie et la propriété des individus, ainsi que leurs convictions réligieuses et l'exercice de leur culte doivent être respectés" with the restriction "pour autant que les nécessités militaires le permettent", he was asked by Rolin to renounce his amendment. For, Rolin explained:

> "l'article ... pose le principe général du respect de l'honneur, de la vie des individus et de la propriété privée. Il ne faut pas énerver le principe en lui donnant la forme d'une déclaration dubitative. Les restrictions nécessaires sont indiquées dans d'autres articles, notamment en ce qui concerne les réquisitions."

When one of the provisions bearing on requisitions of private property, namely by way of *amende*, was subsequently elaborated into the separate Article 50 dealing with all forms of collective punishment, this must needs have the effect of extending its operation to the general principle of respect for the lives of individual members of the civil population as well. In other words, the justification of executing innocents by way of collective punishment could only arise in case of collective responsibility of the population, —that is, "sans rien préjuger quant aux représailles".

It is precisely in this context that great importance could attach to the Martens clause: while the Conference had not expressly so stated, it might be contended that the shooting of innocent members of an occupied population, whether by way of collective punishment or as reprisals, must be regarded as a mode of acting contrary to the principles of international law as these derive from, *inter alia*, the laws of humanity and the exigencies of the public conscience. The point should be emphasized, however, that not only are the records of the discussions concerning the treatment of a resisting population silent on this particular issue, but the words actually recorded are even hardly suggestive of a consensus in this respect among the delegates.

However this may be, the conclusion must be that the debates of the Conference of 1899 recorded in the present section have not brought any decisive elucidation of the problems connected with belligerent reprisals. For the sake of completeness, it should be added that neither in the Sub-Committee's second reading of the draft text [24] nor in the discussion of its report in the Second Committee,[25] nor again in the plenary session,[26] is any further indication found as to the views of the Conference regarding the subject at issue.

[24] pp. 160-163; session of 1 July.
[25] pp. 26-29; session of 5 July.
[26] Vol. I, pp. 42-46; session of 5 July.

2.4. THE SECOND PEACE CONFERENCE OF 1907

As far as the law of land warfare was concerned, the activities of the Second Peace Conference,[1] convened at The Hague in 1907, were confined to a reconsideration of those provisions of the 1899 Hague Regulations on Land Warfare to which amendments were proposed in the competent Sub-Committee.[2] As no amendments were tabled with respect to those provisions which on previous occasions had brought reprisals into the discussions, it is small wonder that references to reprisals proved even rarer in 1907 than they had been in 1899.

The almost complete silence regarding reprisals was momentarily broken when the Sub-Committee discussed a German amendment to the Article concerning the *levée en masse*. In the version as agreed on in 1899,[3] this Article provided that civilians taking up arms spontaneously on the approach of an invading enemy army would be recognized as legitimate combatants on the sole condition that they comply with the laws and usages of warfare. The German amendment[4] wanted to add that they must carry arms openly, on the grounds that this would facilitate their identification as combatants. In the debate, a member of the Russian delegation expressed the fear that insertion of this express condition might lead to those civilians not carrying arms at all being unjustly suspected and hence exposed to reprisals.[5] The chairman replied that that risk did not exist, and another member of the Sub-Committee expressed his opinion that the sole effect of the amendment would be to state more accurately what was already implied in the text as adopted in 1899.[6]

The intervention by the Russian delegate does not appear to make very much sense; for it is not clear how a rule expressly stating that in the event of a *levée en masse* those civilians taking an active part in the fighting must carry arms openly, could in itself have the effect that those members of the civil population who meet the enemy without arms in hands, would be

---

[1] *Deuxième Conférence internationale de la paix*, 15 June-18 October 1907; the number of States taking part had again increased significantly, the Conference being attended by fourty-four States. Reports of the proceedings and documents, published by the Netherlands Ministry for Foreign Affairs, 1907.

[2] The first Sub-Committee of the Second Committee (Reports, Vol. III, pp. 101-148); its report (pp. 19-31) was discussed in the 2nd Committee (pp. 8-15; session of 14 August) and finally in the plenary session of 17 August (Vol. I, pp. 85-87).

[3] Art. 2 of the Regulations; in the debates of 1899, prior to the final drafting of the Articles, this was Art. 10 (*supra*, p. 58).

[4] Reports, Vol. III, p. 106.

[5] *Loc. cit.*: "Le colonel Michelson demande comment sera considérée la partie de la population qui ne porte pas d'armes et si aux termes de l'amendement proposé, elle ne courra pas le danger d'être soupçonnée injustement et d'être exposée de ce fait à des représailles."

[6] *Loc. cit.*: Beernaert (Belgium, chairman), Colonel Borel (Switzerland).

turned into suspected persons: any suspicion regarding them could only arise as a consequence of their behaviour in other respects.

Neither is the intervention any great contribution to the evolution of the doctrine of reprisals. Could the mere suspicion indicated by the Russian delegate be sufficient cause for a recourse to reprisals? What would their purpose be: to coerce the non-participants to take up arms nevertheless? or to demonstrate their non-participation in such a manner that the suspicions even of the most distrustful enemy would be allayed? Did he mean to imply that such reprisals would be justifiable? It seems hardly conceivable. Rather, there is a strong suggestion that he had in mind the probability of so-called reprisals, in the sense of harsh measures of repression and intimidation taken against a civil population without regard for their justification.

If this presumption is correct, at least this much can be said in favour of the ill-considered intervention, that it seemed once again to give expression to the often-felt feelings of regret and repugnance at the possibility of such "reprisals" against innocent members of the civil population.

The records of the discussions in the Sub-Committee contain only one further explicit reference to reprisals, and one of greater moment than the more or less casual reference given above. This occurred at the very end of the debates, in a statement delivered by the Dutch representative, Den Beer Poortugael, which, as far as relevant, runs as follows: [7]

"J'avais eu l'intention de proposer une addition à l'article 5 portant que les prisonniers de guerre ne peuvent être mis à mort:
1° qu'en cas de résistance ou de tentative d'évasion;
2° qu'après une sentence pour des crimes ou des actes punis de mort en vertu des lois civiles ou militaires du pays qui les a fait prisonniers.

"Mais comme l'article 4 prescrit qu'ils doivent être traités avec humanité et que ce serait dérisoire que de vouloir soutenir qu'on peut les fusiller avec humanité, soit pour un cas de représailles soit qu'on les trouve embarrassants, j'ai cru que l'interdiction renouvelée était totalement superflue et que vous seriez d'accord avec moi."

None of the other members of the Sub-Committee offered any comment. Does it follow that they all agreed with the quoted words, or even that they realized their importance for the issue of belligerent reprisals? For it is perfectly obvious that Den Beer Poortugael assumed the validity of a norm to the effect that reprisals in time of war must respect the laws of humanity in all circumstances; was it the Sub-Committee's *communis opinio* that this norm was in fact valid?

It is of course impossible to decide with any certainty what went on in

[7] p. 148.

the minds of those present at the debate. However, an indication may be derived from another observable fact: more than once in the debates, members of the Sub-Committee had shown remarkable confidence that rules would find strict interpretation and application by the States and that, moreover, it sufficed for the Sub-Committee to reach agreement on an interpretation designed to exclude a certain mode of acting, to make the States feel no longer entitled to adopt that particular line of action. Cases in point are: the withdrawal of a proposed article which would have precluded the execution of civilian persons in occupied territory without previous sentence by a court-martial, after it had been pointed out to its author that according to the principles already established in 1899 "la vie des habitants doit toujours être respectée"; [8] and the withdrawal, after prolonged discussions, of a Japanese amendment envisaging the express prohibition of internment of enemy civilians resident in the territory of a belligerent, save in case of necessity arising from the exigencies of the war; the latter amendment was actually dropped only after repeated assurances that Article 5 of the Regulations, providing the internment of prisoners of war, implied that prisoners of war were the only category of enemy persons who could be interned. [9]

These instances of reliance in the force and integrity of the law can possibly serve to explain the statement by the Dutch representative, Den Beer Poortugael. It seems to say: I was afraid that prisoners of war might be killed by way of reprisal; but the existing rule that they must be treated humanely is taken by me (and, I presume, by all of us) to have precedence over the right to reprisals; a separate provision precluding such retaliatory killing of prisoners of war would therefore be superfluous.

Was the speaker right in thus assuming the precedence of the laws of humanity over the law of reprisals? The previous history hardly provides sufficient ground to consider the assumption proved beyond reasonable doubt; at any rate, it would have been preferable if an attempt had been made at this occasion to ascertain the validity of the presumed rule. Instead, however, we note the belief expressed by a single member that the rule existed and "que vous seriez d'accord avec moi",—and the answer is silence. It is of course conceivable that a certain number of delegates did in fact hold the same view. But it seems equally probable that other members (whose minds were focused on the substantive aspects of the subject-matter under discussion rather than on general issues, such as the doctrine of reprisals, which might influence its realization in practice) did not give a thought to reprisals and hence missed the point in the quoted statement. Other members, again, may have been aware of the problems posed by reprisals, but may have preferred to keep a mental reservation with respect

[8] Session of 13 July of the Committee of Examination established by the 1st Sub-Committee; p. 132. The proposal had been introduced by Den Beer Poortugael.
[9] pp. 109-110, 114-118, 128-129.

to that subject: a reservation which they may have refrained from bringing into the open either on the ground that the law of reprisals, as part of general international law, was outside the mandate of the Conference, or because they felt that their Governments would not be prepared to confer binding force on any rules the Conference might see fit to formulate concerning reprisals.

It may be evident from the above that the Conference of 1907 has made even less of a contribution to the further clarification of the issue of belligerent reprisals, be it in the sense of reprisals proper or of collective punishment, than its predecessor of 1899.

As far as certain specific aspects of the issue are concerned, two further concluding remarks seem permissible: firstly, that in particular the Russian intervention demonstrated once again the likelihood of the term "reprisals" being used for situations only remotely resembling reprisals in the proper sense of the term; and, secondly, that both the statement of Den Beer Poortugael and certain other interventions furnish convincing evidence—not of an existing consensus that the laws of humanity prevailed over the law of reprisals, but—of a far from negligible trend of opinion in that direction.

2.5. CONCLUSIONS

On the basis of the information recorded in the preceding sections of the present Chapter, it seems possible to arrive at certain conclusions regarding the attitude adopted prior to World War I with respect to belligerent reprisals.[1]

As far as the official governmental activities concerning the law of war were concerned, it has become apparent that only the authors of the American Instructions of 1863 and of the Russian projects for the Conference of Brussels of 1874 had not shrunk from dealing openly with reprisals, thereby acknowledging the reality of their existence, but simultaneously creating the possibility of their regulation. The same attitude was taken by the non-governmental *Institut de droit international* when it prepared and adopted the Oxford Manual of 1880.

In contrast, the governmental Conferences of 1874, 1899 and 1907 (and the *Institut* in 1896) refrained from thus openly dealing with reprisals. Yet, as is apparent from the discussions, the reality of reprisals could not be denied either. Neither may the conspicuous absence of express and comprehensive treatment of reprisals lead to the conclusion that no rules limiting

[1] As for State practice in the period preceding the First World War, see in particular J. M. Spaight, *War Rights on Land*, 1911, p. 462 ff.

their use would have been recognized at the time: such a conclusion is barred by the observable fact that on more than one occasion in the debates the view was expressed that the law in force prohibited reprisals in this or that situation. Indeed, the policy of maintaining silence on the issue of reprisals in its fundamental aspects was solely motivated by the fear that express regulation might be interpreted as a legitimation of their use.

It must be stressed again that that policy was both shortsighted and harmful. Shortsigned, because it disregarded the fact that reprisals constituted a recognized institution of international law, which could not be deprived of such justifiability as it might possess by surrounding the concept with silence. And it was harmful, as it has obstructed the achievement of explicit, written agreement on rules restricting the justifiable recourse to reprisals, rules that had the support of learned opinion and that, to the extent that they did not already form part of customary law or of the principles of law, did at any rate fit in with the trend of the developing law of war.

Defining and restricting the right to apply reprisals would obviously have been no light task, especially not in respect to the law of warfare *stricto sensu*: the rules of combat proper. But it is a severe charge against the governmental Conferences convened to codify and develop the law of war, that they did not even make an attempt in this direction and confined themselves to formulating rules without offering any indication in what circumstances and to what extent those rules could justifiably be set aside by way of reprisals.[2]

This attitude finds a partial explanation in the circumstance, repeatedly pointed out in the foregoing, that no sufficient distinction was made at the time between genuine reprisals, quasi-reprisals as coercive measures of a superior occupant against a civil population at his mercy, and modes of acting merely styled "reprisals" but in reality constituting cruel, inhuman measures against such a population that had better not be mentioned at all, because, among other reasons, public opinion was hostile to them.

Can it be said that at least the rule that reprisals cannot justifiably encroach upon the norms of humanitarian character had gained unequivocal recognition? The first Russian project of 1874 contained a rule tending in this direction; the Oxford Manual of 1880 proposed the validity of the rule; and Den Beer Poortugael assumed in 1907 that all those present were agreed on it. These are strong indications, but not strong enough to be entirely convincing: while they unmistakably point to a trend of opinion in favour of acceptance of the rule, it is submitted that a consensus to that effect had not at the time come about.[3]

[2] Significantly, when in 1913 the *Institut de droit international* elaborated another Oxford Manual, this time dealing with maritime warfare, the new paper did not once refer to reprisals. Evidently the *Institut* had taken the lesson to heart.

[3] For the sake of completeness it is pointed out that the Red Cross Conventions which

In this Chapter the focus was constantly on the law of land warfare, and for a very good reason: for, while it is true that several steps were taken in this period towards a codification of the law of sea warfare,[4] these steps never went so far as to bring about a discussion of reprisals.

All in all, the conclusion seems warranted that on the eve of the First World War almost nothing had been done with respect to the codification of the law of belligerent reprisals.

saw the light in this period (Geneva Conventions of 1864 and 1906 dealing with the victims of land warfare, Conventions of The Hague of 1899 and 1907 relative to sea warfare) do not contain a prohibition of reprisals on humanitarian grounds. Lieber, who in his Code had devoted numerous articles to questions with a humanitarian aspect, such as the treatment of prisoners of war, even stated explicitly that "All prisoners of war are liable to the infliction of retaliatory measures." (Art. 59, para. 2).
[4] Prior to 1907, the attempts at regulating sea warfare were directed towards specific issues only: principles of prize law (Declaration of Paris, 1856), treatment of war victims (abortive attempt of 1868 to extend the principles of the 1864 Geneva Convention to naval warfare; Convention of 1899). In 1907, a wider range of subjects relative to sea warfare were dealt with in treaties (Conventions Nos. VI-XIII concerning such divergent matters as naval bombardment, use of contact mines, grace for enemy merchantmen at the outbreak of war), while in 1908-1909 an attempt at codifying the law of prize resulted in the adoption of the (ultimately unratified) Declaration of London of 1909.

None of these efforts went so far as the Hague Regulations did with respect to land warfare, viz., to provide a complete regulation embracing all aspects of warfare; cf. n. 2 to § 3.1, infra. Indeed, the Second Peace Conference of 1907 had expressed as its 4th voeu that the next Peace Conference should undertake the elaboration of such a regulation for sea warfare (Reports, Vol. I, p. 700). In 1912, when the time for that Conference drew near, the Institut de droit international started deliberations of the subject which resulted in the adoption, in 1913, of the project referred to in n. 2 to this § (Annuaire, Vols. XXV and XXVI, 1912, 1913). The project failed to reach the conference table, as the projected Third Peace Conference was never held.

CHAPTER III

The Period between the First and Second World Wars

3.1. PRELUDE TO THE CONFERENCE OF 1929

3.1.1. The ICRC and the Red Cross Conference of 1921

The outbreak of the First World War marked the end of a period of conscientious attempts to codify and develop the law of war. The task had been performed under conditions of peace, though fresh memories of more than one war had been in the minds of many a delegate. Now the new war put the outcome of their endeavours to the test, exposing several weak spots in the process. Among these was the lack of definite rules on reprisals, a lacuna which placed the belligerents of both sides in a position to label as reprisals such highly dubious and often indeed inhuman modes of acting as the refusal to give quarter, the killing of hostages, unrestricted submarine warfare, and economic blockade.[1]

Of particular interest to the issue of belligerent reprisals proved the bringing about, in the course of the war, of bilateral agreements relative to the treatment of prisoners of war and interned civilians. True, the Hague Regulations of 1907 contained a régime for prisoners of war, embodied in the second Chapter of Part I ("Des belligérants"); but these provisions (Articles 4-20) proved inadequate on two grounds: the provisions were too summary, and they did not include any rules for their enforcement. As to the category of the civilians interned in enemy territory, the Hague Regulations were completely silent.[2]

The insufficiency in these respects of the Hague Regulations having

---

[1] Concerning these instances of (real or alleged) reprisals, see, e.g.: Oppenheim's *International Law*, Vol. II, 7th ed. by H. Lauterpacht, p. 562 ff.; E. S. Colbert, *Retaliation in International Law*, 1948; C. John Colombos, *The International Law of the Sea*, 6th revised ed., 1967, p. 740 ff.; J. M. Spaight, *Air Power and War Rights*, 3rd ed., 1947, p. 49 ff.

[2] It bears pointing out that the Hague Regulations were destined to cover the entire terrain of land warfare: the participants (and their condition upon capture), the conduct of hostilities, the occupation; sole exception was the régime regarding the sick and wounded of the armies in the field, as this had already been made the object of a special convention, the Convention for the Amelioration of the Condition of Soldiers Wounded in Armies in the Field, originally of 1864.

come to light at an early stage, the International Committee of the Red Cross (or ICRC) set to work with a view to improving the condition of these war victims. The first rewards of its unyielding endeavours were gained towards the end of the war, when several of the belligerents entered into agreements [3] containing somewhat more detailed rules concerning the treatment of prisoners. For present purposes, the main interest of these agreements lies in that they provided that reprisals against prisoners of war and civilian internees could only be resorted to on the expiration of a fixed term following their notification. Here, at last, were express rules, embodied in international agreements, concerning the recourse to reprisals.

In a report written after the war and presented to the Xth International Conference of the Red Cross,[4] the ICRC criticized these wartime agreements on three scores: they came too late, they were based on reciprocity rather than justice, and they were composed on casuistic lines rather than establishing general principles suited to govern decisions in specific instances.[5] The disadvantages of this casuistic, enumerative method were expounded: the danger of lacunae on the one hand, and of insufficiently precise definitions on the other; and, in case of a dispute over the application of the agreement, the risk that the absence of any governing principles expressly stated in the text would leave the detaining Power virtually free to decide the issue arbitrarily.[6] This led the ICRC to state the necessity of elaborating a separate code embodying the principles that should in future govern the treatment of prisoners of war.[7]

The importance of this step lies in this. Obviously, the chapter on prisoners of war was not the only part of the Hague Regulations in need of revision. On the other hand, the diversity of subjects covered by the Regulations was so great as to make the success of any attempt at achieving their integral revision highly problematical. In this situation, the fact that the ICRC did not propose such an integral revision, but instead suggested making the treatment of prisoners of war the subject of a special code, had the effect of disconnecting the prisoners of war régime from the diverse problems attending the Hague Regulations and their revision. In this manner it became possible henceforth to develop that régime on its own

---

[3] Some of these are reproduced in De Martens, N.R.G. 3rd series, Vol. XI; Germany —Great Britain (pp. 13, 61), Germany—France (pp. 31, 46), Germany—U.S.A. (p. 80; the most detailed of these agreements).

[4] "Le code du prisonnier de guerre. Rapport présenté par le Comité international à la Xme Conférence", in *RICR*, Vol. III, 1921, p. 102.

[5] *Ibid.*, pp. 104-105.

[6] p. 105.

[7] As was pointed out in the report (*loc. cit.*), any endeavours in this field should be realistic as well as humanitarian: "nous voudrions rappeler que, tout en défendant les principes de l'humanité, il faut poser des règles qui puissent être acceptables et exécutables en temps de guerre, donc en un temps où la haine est déchaînée et où, trop souvent, la force tend à primer le droit."

merits, not only as to its substantive side, but also as to the aspects of supervision and enforcement.

The issue of reprisals against prisoners of war was broached by the ICRC in a part of its report devoted specifically to the problems of supervision and sanctions. In eloquent words, the practice of taking reprisals against this category of war victims was exposed: the relative ease of application of such measures, their character as punishment inflicted on innocent individuals, their inhumanity, their lack of effectiveness.[8] This led the ICRC to a compelling conclusion: from now on, reprisals against prisoners of war should be expressly and categorically prohibited.[9]

This was a statement of the utmost importance, and one which in fact marked a turning-point in the development of the law of belligerent reprisals. The traditional treatment of the issue of belligerent reprisals as something indivisible had so far prevented any progress towards its solution, as the mere mention of the subject was enough to evoke a multitude of conflicting ideas and feelings. Thus, belligerent reprisals might on the one hand consist in measures having their direct impact on the course of the war, and the consequences of any attempts to lay down express rules concerning such reprisals seemed so hard to calculate that States could not be expected to demonstrate any great eagerness at the idea of voluntarily tying their hand by express arrangements to that effect. On the other hand, belligerent reprisals could equally consist in measures the direct effect of which lay outside the sphere of actual warfare, but, for instance, in the prisoners of war camps; and the repugnance which the mere idea of reprisals against such defenceless persons was apt to evoke, combined with the uneasy feeling that such reprisals were nevertheless indispensable, led

---

[8] *Ibid.*, pp. 121-123: "C'est là, sans doute, un moyen de pression commode et de facile emploi pour arracher un avantage à l'adversaire. Les prisonniers sont là, sous la main en quelque sorte, et tenus à merci. On n'a qu'à frapper sur eux pour contraindre leur patrie à se soumettre. Mais tant du point de vue du droit que de celui de l'humanité, ce procédé doit être flétri ... C'est une mesure qui prend ouvertement le caractère d'une pénalité. Or, une peine ne peut atteindre qu'un coupable et les prisonniers n'ont personnellement rien fait pour la mériter. Ils se voient frappés à l'improviste, sans faute aucune de leur part. Ils sont frappés alors qu'ils sont pour rien dans les actes reprochés à leur gouvernement, actes que souvent même ils ignorent, alors qu'ils ne peuvent rien pour amener ce gouvernement à modifier son attitude. Bref, ce sont des innocents qu'on condamne, qu'on sacrifie parfois, tout en les sachant tels, et ce qui porte au comble l'odieux de la représaille, c'est que la décision qui frappe le captif est prise froidement, que souvent le sort du prisonnier devient l'enjeu d'une partie diplomatique ou économique jouée entre deux Etats, sans compter que représaille appelle représaille, que les Etats se piquent au jeu et joutent à qui inventera les procédés de souffrances les plus efficaces. En sorte que l'état de guerre se rouvre au détriment du prisonnier sans défense ... Ajoutons que l'emploi des représailles a en réalité eu peu d'effets pratiques, sauf celui d'aggraver la situation générale des prisonniers et d'énerver l'opinion publique."
[9] *Ibid.*, p. 122.

71

to the avoidance as far as possible of any reference to the issue. Such feelings and considerations could lead to a situation where the idea of a prohibition of certain reprisals would be frustrated by the incalculability of the effects of regulating the right of reprisals and, on the other hand, any attempt at such regulation might be shipwrecked because a repugnant institution such as reprisals should be prohibited, not regulated.

In this predicament, the presentation of the conclusion that reprisals against prisoners of war must be prohibited as part of the development of the prisoners of war régime, and not as a *lex specialis* of the law of belligerent reprisals, amounted to nothing less than a brilliant piece of surgery: the issue, cut loose from its original environment, could henceforth be treated as a separate matter which no longer needed to be governed by such implicit feelings as set forth above.

There is, of course, another side to the question of prohibiting reprisals against prisoners of war. It is one thing to declare that such reprisals ought to be prohibited, but another to fill in the gap and provide for other, more effective and more equitable means suited to take over their function. The ICRC in its report also entered into this aspect of the matter. First of all, it put forward the system adopted for the wartime agreements: notification of a contemplated reprisal to the protecting Power, inquiry by neutral delegates into the justifiability of the underlying grievance, decision whether or not to carry the reprisal into effect taken on the basis of the report of the delegates and preferably by an impartial arbitrator. This system, the ICRC pointed out, had not been tested as to its practicability, as the agreements in question had been concluded only a short time before the end of the hostilities. But the ICRC did not leave it at that: it also protested "contre cette réglementation qui paraît légitimer une pratique éminemment injuste et inhumaine".[10] And indeed, the system adopted for those agreements amounted to a mere suspension of contemplated reprisals, rather than their replacement by better means. Hence, the ICRC proposed to complete the prohibition of reprisals against prisoners of war with an improved system of supervision and enforcement: supervision by neutral delegates of the observance of the agreed prisoners of war régime, and, if that would prove insufficient, the application of pressure in the form of the moral force of public opinion, effective sanctions by a non-involved institution such as the League of Nations, and the individual responsibility of those violating the rules.[11]

[10] *Loc.cit.*
[11] pp. 123-125.

When the Xth International Conference of the Red Cross met in Geneva in 1921,[12] the Committee set up to revise the prisoners of war régime [13] had little difficulty in concurring with the ICRC on the main issues. The *voeu* in which the Committee laid down its views and which was subsequently adopted as Resolution XV by the plenary session of the Conference,[14] in its first section demanded that the Governments would at an early date conclude a Convention relative to the treatment of prisoners of war; it moreover enumerated a number of principles that ought to underlie such a Convention. Among the principles enumerated, one (n⁰ 8) referred to reprisals, in the following terms:

"Les représailles contre les prisonniers sont strictement défendues. L'Etat qui les instituerait serait considéré comme commettant une violation; il ne pourrait invoquer des circonstances atténuantes et donnerait lieu aux sanctions indiquées au chiffre 14."

Under n⁰ 14 the system of guarantees that had been conceived by the Committee and adopted by the Conference was set out. It was an elaborate system, conspicuous for the careful balance between the interests and honour of the belligerents and the need for an ultimately effective result. The means envisaged were varied: punishment of the actual perpetrators of a violation, appeal to public conscience, appeal to the Council of the League of Nations, appeal to the Permanent Court of International Justice; —an ambitious enumeration indeed.[15]

---

[12] 30 March-7 April; report of the proceedings: *Dixième conférence internationale de la Croix-Rouge*, Geneva, 1921.

[13] This was the Second Committee.

[14] Session of 6 April; report, pp. 164-170, 173-177; text of Resolution XV: pp. 218-221; in section II thereof the ICRC was invited to prepare a draft code on the basis, *inter alia*, of the principles formulated in section I.

[15] In case of a suspected violation, the injured belligerent could request the ICRC to verify the facts. If the opponent refuse to agree to the investigation, both the request and the refusal would be made public by the ICRC. Otherwise the ICRC would duly investigate the facts, report the results of its inquiry to the responsible belligerent, and request the latter to apply the necessary punishment to those guilty of the violation. In case of non-compliance with this request, the ICRC would be empowered to refer the matter to the League Council. It was moreover expressly stated in the Resolution that the perpetrators of war crimes against prisoners of war would be individually responsible; if either the legislation of the State concerned or the penalties actually inflicted in a given case would seem insufficient, the matter could be brought before the Permanent Court: "Au cas où les mesures législatives prévues ou les peines appliquées par l'Etat ne paraîtraient pas suffisantes, il pourra en être appelé contre lui à la Cour permanente de Justice internationale". It was even suggested that the power to bring such matters before the Court would primarily lie with the ICRC; as Mr Cederkrantz of the Swedish Red Cross had it: "Le Comité international pourra dans certains cas en référer à la Société des Nations; finalement, il pourra en appeler à la Cour permanente de justice internationale; tout cela est bien clair"; and he only wondered whether the injured belligerent would have a similar power. See Report of the Conference, pp. 176-177. This misconception of the jurisdiction of the Court bore witness to its novelty, as well as to the high hopes which its creation inspired.

3.1.2. *The draft code of the International Law Association*

In the same year, 1921, another code for the treatment of prisoners of war was elaborated by the International Law Association.[16] In the draft text, prepared by a Committee under the chairmanship of Lord Justice Younger, the matter of reprisals was dealt with in Article 13, reading as follows: [17]

"All reprisals, as such, on prisoners of war are deprecated. Wherever reprisals have been taken or threatened, it shall be the duty of the captor State to make forthwith to the protecting Power intimation of the fact with a statement of the jusification therefor.

"It shall thereupon be the duty of the protecting Power to endeavour to eliminate the reasons for the reprisals so intimated, either by arranging a personal discussion between delegates of the belligerent Powers concerned in the presence of a representative of its own, or in such other manner as may seem to it in the circumstances appropriate.

"Prisoners of war shall in no case be subjected to reprisals except in retaliation for acts committed or sanctioned by their own Governments in connection with the treatment of prisoners of war."

This proposal, it is obvious, differed fundamentally from the text proposed by the ICRC. True, it contained both a moral condemnation of reprisals against prisoners of war and a slight restriction of their use, but this was a far cry from their total prohibition. The motives for this completely different attitude were explained by Lord Younger in his introduction to the report of the Committee: while the practice of reprisals against prisoners of war was abhorrent, their prohibition could never be relied on as effective as no army "could reasonably be expected to renounce in war so effective and powerful a weapon for the redress or cessation of supposed intolerable wrong upon its own nationals at the hand of the enemy as immediate or threatened reprisal on enemy units in its own hands".[18]

Why then had the Committee preferred not to propose other means that might be suited to replace reprisals? The answer to this question was given when Article 13 came up for discussion in the Conference and a proposal was introduced by Mr Aubert, delegate of the Swiss Red Cross, to create a neutral supervisory body.[19] The chairman warned the Committee against this idea; his main argument was that "[t]he real solution for the reprisal question is to be found in meetings between the belligerents while the war is going on" and that moreover the Governments would receive with suspicion

[16] 30th Conference, The Hague, 30 August-3 September 1921. Proceedings concerning the P.O.W. code: Report of the Conference, Vol. I, pp. 188-246; this contained *inter alia* the preliminary report of the Treatment of Prisoners of War Committee, referred to in the text above; pp. 188-205.
[17] *Ibid.*, p. 202.
[18] *Ibid.*, p. 191.
[19] *Ibid.*, pp. 231-232.

any proposal to introduce new machinery for this purpose in peacetime.[20]

The idea of Mr Aubert was thereupon rejected by the Conference and Article 13, together with the other Articles of the draft code, were carried without further difficulties.

It is clear where the fundamental difference of opinion lay: the ICRC believed that reprisals against prisoners of war could be done away with completely, provided the necessary machinery were created to replace the traditional method of retaliation. The International Law Association, on the other hand, did not believe that a prohibition of reprisals could ever be effective, and it doubted that new machinery could be created to take the place of reprisals. Furthermore, whereas in the view of the Association a meeting of the belligerents in the midst of the war was likely to yield precisely those desirable results which were unattainable in time of peace, the ICRC felt that at any rate the results gained in that manner in the First World War were insufficient even then, and that now, if ever, was the time to seek agreement among the States as regarded the principal side of the matter.

It seems that in this controversy the ICRC held the better opinion. The International Law Association, like the ICRC, abhorred reprisals against prisoners of war; but it thought it necessary nevertheless to retain the possibility of such reprisals by an army in retaliation for unlawful treatment of its members who had fallen in enemy hands. In this respect, it should be observed that it is of course a psychological fact that the urge to retaliate will be strong in those circumstances; but this is not equal to saying that to yield to the urge ought to be considered legitimate. On the contrary, the thesis could be defended that only the proven impossibility of creating other suitable means might justify the express retention of reprisals for the situation under consideration. In this light, an attempt to

---

[20] The rather amazing statement of Lord Younger continued after the words quoted in the text above: "We had grave difficulties with regard to prisoners and reprisals on prisoners as between the German and British Commands during the war, and until the Hague agreements of 1917 there seemed to be no real way out of them. But when the delegates came together in 1917, and the matter was again discussed in 1918 in the Netherlands, an agreement was come to which, I think for the future, during that war eliminated all further difficulty in regard to reprisals. In other words, when the question had to be dealt with as an existing difficulty, of course the belligerents were prepared to a far more elaborate agreement than you could ever have committed them to in advance; and I think therefore the real answer to the difficulty in connection with Article 13, that has been so strongly pointed out, will be found in this, that if you were to endeavour to introduce new machinery for this purpose only, Article 13 would be received with suspicion by the Powers who are asked to agree to it. On the other hand, any difficulty will be got over if both parties are anxious it should be got over by the machinery provided by Article 21."—Report, pp. 232-233; the Article 21 mentioned by the speaker dealt with the function of the protecting Powers.

bring about the absolute prohibition of reprisals against prisoners of war certainly was worth attempting.

3.1.3. Further preparations for the 1929 Conference

The next move was for the ICRC. As requested by the Xth Red Cross Conference, the task of elaborating the principles adopted by the Conference into a complete code was laid in the hands of a "Diplomatic Committee", which spent a good many meetings on drafting a set of rules suited to form a basis of discussion for the future Diplomatic Conference. This Committee took due cognizance of the draft code adopted by the International Law Association, as well as of the observations forwarded by some Governments; at the last moment a complete draft code for the treatment of prisoners of war was even handed in by the Russian Red Cross, which, however, did not according to the ICRC differ materially from its own project.[21]

As a result of these labours the ICRC was able to put an *Avant-projet de Convention internationale relative au traitement des prisonniers de guerre* before the XIth International Conference of the Red Cross, held at Geneva in 1923.[22] The prohibition of reprisals against prisoners of war had been retained in the project: it was now embodied in Article 2, paragraph 3. As to the sanctions destined to take their place, the draft Convention was much more modest than Resolution XV of the Xth International Red Cross Conference; instead of the elaborate procedures provided in the Resolution, section II of Title VIII (General and Final Dispositions) merely empowered the ICRC to install itinerant committees composed of nationals of neutral States and who would be charged with supervising the observation of the rules regarding the treatment of prisoners of war; the committees would report to the ICRC and this, in its turn, would communicate the reports to the belligerents and then publish them. The belligerents would be bound to remedy the defects indicated in the reports.[23]

The motives for this drastic simplification were given in the report of the Diplomatic Committee: it had been realized that both the appeal to the League and to the Permanent Court of International Justice were open solely to States. Furthermore, the ICRC considered that impartiality was one of its greatest assets and, hence, it did not want to find itself involved in complications of an international character. The ICRC therefore "a préféré s'abstenir de suivre ici les voeux de la Xme Conférence et n'a pas cru

---

[21] The Diplomatic Committee held 19 meetings between October 1922 and the end of March 1923. The report of the Committee, which was endorsed by the ICRC, is reproduced in *RICR*, Vol. V, 1923, pp. 771-786.

[22] *Ibid.*, pp. 786-814; also reprinted in the Acts of the 1929 Diplomatic Conference, pp. 21-34; see hereafter, § 3.2, n. 1.

[23] Articles 97-99.

devoir examiner les moyens d'obtenir les compétences extrèmement étendues qu'on avait désiré lui confier. Il apprécie hautement la preuve extraordinaire de confiance qui lui avait été donnée par la Xme Conférence, mais il croit aussi que, pour pouvoir persévérer avec succès dans la tâche humanitaire qui est la sienne, il doit tenir plus que jamais à sa complète indépendance." It was further pointed out that under existing law States were free to have recourse to the diplomatic intervention of the protecting Powers or to appeal to the League or again (provided the conditions of the Statute were fulfilled) to the Court.[24]

On consideration, even this less sweeping form of the plan for the replacement of reprisals by other suitable means seemed sound. Apart from the means which, in the assumption of the ICRC, would be at the disposal of the belligerent States, the ICRC would itself have the employment of supervisory bodies, in the form of itinerant committees. These means and methods taken together could not of course give a foolproof guarantee that the rules would be observed in practice, but they could be regarded at least as effective as reprisals and, in contrast with the latter, conciliatory rather than provocative in character.

The XIth International Conference of the Red Cross, meeting at Geneva from 28 August-1 September 1923, discussed the general lines of the draft Convention and adopted it without any change. Not a word was said regarding the prohibition of reprisals. As to the proposed itinerant committees, one delegate pointed out that it was imperative that the belligerents would agree with the choice of neutral States from which the members would be selected.[25] Another delegate made the point that in more than one place in the draft Convention the text did not itself provide a solution, but rather exhorted the belligerents to enter into agreements during the war; in this context he inquired whether for the question at issue preference should not be given to the system adopted by the International Law Association, to the effect that on questions regarding the treatment of prisoners of war it would be incumbent on the protecting Powers to seek to secure contact between the belligerents.[26]

No vote was taken on these and other observations: they were simply put on record so that they, together with the draft code, would constitute (in the words of the chairman) "un dossier contenant toutes les opinions émises ici".[27]

With this, the preliminary work was done and the stage set for the next act: the Diplomatic Conference.

---

[24] *Op. cit.* n. 20, pp. 784-786.
[25] Report, pp. 161-162; Lt.-Gen. Wilmaers (Belgium).
[26] *Ibid.*, pp. 147-148; Collette (Netherlands).
[27] *Ibid.*, p. 163.

3.2. THE DIPLOMATIC CONFERENCE OF GENEVA OF 1929

Two main items were on the agenda of the Diplomatic Conference which met from 1-27 July 1929 in Geneva: [1] the revision of the Convention of Geneva of 1906 for the Amelioration of the Condition of the Sick and Wounded of the Armies in the Field, and the creation of a new Convention relative to the treatment of prisoners of war. A committee was set up for each of these subjects. The Second Committee, dealing with the prisoners of war régime, held its discussions on the basis of the draft code prepared by the ICRC. It soon decided to divide into two sub-committees, dealing with administrative and sanitary matters and with diplomatic and legal matters, respectively.[2] The deliberations in these sub-committees resulted in radical modifications of the text in more than one place. The reasons for these modifications remain in the dark, as the summary records of the proceedings have not been published.[3] When the sub-committees had finished their work, the Second Committee resumed its deliberations; these ended with the approbation of a definitive text of a draft Convention.[4] This text was finally adopted without dispute by the Conference in its plenary session of 26 July: [5] a first Convention relative to the Treatment of Prisoners of War had been brought into being.

The issue of reprisals was broached at an early stage in the proceedings of the Conference, when the Second Committee opened the discussion on the proposed Article 2, whose paragraph 3 contained the rule that reprisals against prisoners of war would be prohibited. A majority of the delegates

---

[1] The Conference, convened by the Swiss Government, was attended by 47 States and dependent territories, as well as by the League of Nations, the Maltese Order and the ICRC. It bears pointing out that in 1874 the predecessor of the ICRC, the *Comité international de secours aux militaires blessés,* had vainly applied for admittance; and also the Hague Peace Conferences had been strictly State Conferences. Another conspicuous feature was the absence of the U.S.S.R.: all three earlier conferences, of 1874, 1899 and 1907, had been convened on Russian initiative.

Secretary-General of the Conference of 1929 was P. des Gouttes, formerly a member of the "Diplomatic Committee" which had prepared the 1923 draft code (*cf.* § 3.1.3, text and n. 21); another member of that Committee, G. Werner, now figured as the first representative of the ICRC.

Records of the Conference published by the Swiss Government, 1930.

[2] 1st-4th meetings of the 2nd Committee, 2-5 July; Records, pp. 427-470.

[3] *Cf. La Convention de Genève du 27 juillet 1929, commentaire par Paul des Gouttes,* published by the ICRC in 1930, p. 5: "La Commission II, du Code des prisonniers de guerre, se sectionna très vite en deux sous-commissions, l'un juridique, l'autre administrative et sanitaire, se répartissant les problèmes à étudier, sans que leurs délibérations fussent consignées autrement que dans des procès-verbaux fort sommaires et non destinés à être publiés."

[4] 5th-10th meetings, 20-24 July; Records, pp. 471-560.

[5] *Ibid.,* pp. 631-641; rapporteur of the 2nd Committee was G. Werner (*cf.* n. 1 to this §).

who expressed themselves on the point were in favour of that prohibition.[6] Two delegates took a different stand. The Turkish delegate [7] argued that reprisals ought to be maintained, as reciprocity is at the root of the law of treaties and as on principle it seemed difficult to deny the belligerents a right to take reprisals, even against prisoners of war. But he sustained the argument only half-heartedly: in the same breath he stressed the humanitarian point of view, which made it difficult to accept reprisals against innocent and defenceless persons for wrongful acts committed by their Governments; and the speaker hastened to add that, if the debate were to show a majority for the proposed prohibition, the Turkish delegation was ready to join it.

Another and a more dangerous attack was launched by the British representative, Sir Horace Humbold. In his opinion, the proposed prohibition was bound to be violated, and it seemed therefore preferable "de légaliser la position de tous les belligérants qui pourraient être tentés de se venger d'un acte quelconque commis contre leurs ressortissants".[8] This was of course the view as it had been adopted in 1923 by the International Law Association. That Sir Horace did in fact voice that view, was even more apparent from the text of the proposal which he now introduced, to replace the proposed paragraph by the following text: [9]

"Toute mesure de représailles à l'égard des prisonniers de guerre est condamnée.

"Les prisonniers de guerre ne doivent en aucune instance subir des représailles, sauf dans le cas d'actes illicites commis ou sanctionnés par leur propre Gouvernement en rapport avec le traitement des prisonniers de guerre. Lorsque des représailles de cette nature sont envisagées, la Puissance captrice sera tenue d'envoyer sans retard à la Puissance neutre chargée des intérêts des belligérants—appelée ci-après Puissance protectrice—une notification constatant le fait, accompagnée d'un exposé justifiant la mesure, en donnant dans chaque cas le pré-avis aussitôt que possible. La Puissance protectrice sera tenue par cette démarche d'essayer d'éliminer les causes des représailles ainsi notifiées, soit en provoquant une discussion personnelle entre les délégués des Puissances belligérantes en présence d'un re-

---

[6] Lt.-Col. Mandola (Finland), Wilson (U.S.A.), Sottile (Nicaragua; only as between the contracting parties), Ackermann (Dominican Republic), Col. Babecki (Poland), Schindler (Switzerland); pp. 448-452.

[7] Hassan Bey; p. 448.

[8] Ibid., pp. 450-451. The quoted words were followed by this statement: "Il serait bon aussi de montrer clairement à tous les belligérants que tout acte de représailles de sa part pourra être légitimement repris par son adversaire." This was a dangerous misconception, deriving from notions of reciprocity rather than from a correct understanding of the concept of reprisals.

[9] Ibid., p. 451.

présentant de son propre Gouvernement, soit de toute autre manière qu'elle estimerait plus appropriée dans les circonstances."

Thus, the Conference had before it both opposing views which also in the preparatory phase had been defended with respect to the issue of reprisals against prisoners of war: it was now up to the Conference to make its choice. This did not take long: Article 2, along with the rest of the first Title, having been referred to a legal sub-committee,[10] its rapporteur, G. Werner, was able to report in the next session of the Second Committee that the text as proposed by the ICRC had soon found unanimous support in the sub-committee. He added: [11]

> "L'heure est venue de l'inscrire [*i.e.* the prohibition of reprisals against prisoners of war] dans un texte fondamental du droit des gens. Le prisonnier est un être sans défense; l'humanité ne permet pas de s'en prendre à lui."

True; but it would have been even more interesting to learn which arguments made Sir Horace abandon his own (and the International Law Association's) ideas and join the majority.

When Article 2 came up for a second reading,[12] the text of paragraph 3 appeared to have undergone a change: it now merely said that "Les mesures de représailles sont interdites". As was pointed out by one delegate, however, the Conference was not in a position to formulate a general prohibition of reprisals: the most it could achieve was to prohibit reprisals against prisoners of war. This view was accepted unanimously; and, as the text now before the Committee could indeed be interpreted as a general prohibition, the original text was restored: "Les mesures de représailles à leur égard sont interdites."

The Conference in plenary session, taking cognizance of the results of the endeavours of the two main Committees, did not enter into any further discussion over the issue of reprisals. The importance of the achieved prohibition was underlined once again, however, in the words of G. Werner, reporting on behalf of the Second Committee: [14] "Ce texte [*i.e.* of the new Convention] ne contiendrait-il que cela, vous ne vous seriez pas réunis en vain!"

This may seem somewhat exaggerated. On the other hand, reprisals had done uncounted harm to prisoners of war, and although it was obvious that not even the formal ratification of the prohibition by all States could have the effect of preventing all future reprisals against such persons, at any rate the illegality of such actions would be incontestable; and, more important, the frequency of such reprisals would certainly diminish consider-

---

[10] *Ibid.*, p. 452; this Sub-Committee preceded those mentioned *supra* n. 2.
[11] *Ibid.*, p. 464.
[12] *Ibid.*, pp. 530-532; 8th session of the 2nd Committee, 23 July.
[13] M. de Ruelle (Belgium).
[14] *Ibid.*, p. 634.

ably through the sheer force of the rule. In this light, the words of the rapporteur were not so much of an exaggeration after all.

It remains to be seen how the Diplomatic Conference dealt with the other side of the problem: viz., the means and methods destined to take the place of reprisals. This part of the project (section II of Title VIII) came up for discussion in the Second Committee at a relatively late stage of the proceedings [15] and only after the legal and diplomatic sub-committee had worked on it. The changes were considerable. Thus, the itinerant committees proposed by the ICRC had been discarded. The gist of the proposal, however, had been the express recognition that the ICRC would, with the agreement of the belligerents, be entitled to display its humanitarian activities in favour of the prisoners of war; activities that might readily take the form of inspection and supervision, by delegates specially sent for that purpose, of the manner in which the rules would be observed. This principle had in fact been maintained; it now found expression in the proposed Article 86.[16]

Whereas, on the other hand, the ICRC had not considered it necessary to lay down express rules regarding the functions of protecting Powers (while certainly not intending to deprive these of their functions), it was precisely this aspect of the matter which was now elaborated in the draft Articles 86 and 87; this was in accordance with the wish expressed by those States which during the First World War had performed this task, that the rôle of protecting Powers would be clearly defined and their functions exactly determined in the new Convention.[17]

The Second Committee discussed the proposed Articles at length [18] and finally reached agreement on a definitive text, which was divided into two parts: the functions and powers of protecting Powers as a guarantee of the regular application of the Convention,[19] and their rôle in the event of a

---

[15] Session of 22 July.

[16] "Les dispositions qui précèdent ne font pas obstacle à l'activité humanitaire que le Comité international de la Croix-Rouge pourra déployer pour la protection des prisonniers de guerre, moyennant l'agrément des belligérants intéressés."

[17] Information provided by the rapporteur of the 2nd Committee in the 4th plenary session of the Conference, 26 July; Records, p. 637.

[18] Ibid., pp. 512-520, 544-552.

[19] Art. 86: "Les Hautes Parties Contractantes reconnaissent que l'application régulière de la présente Convention trouvera une garantie dans la possibilité de collaboration des Puissances protectrices chargées de sauvegarder les intérêts des belligérants; à cet égard, les Puissances protectrices pourront, en dehors de leur personnel diplomatique, désigner des délégués parmi leurs propres ressortissants ou parmi les ressortissants d'autres Puissances neutres. Ces délégués devront être soumis à l'agrément du belligérant auprès duquel ils exerceront leur mission.

"Les représentants de la Puissance protectrice ou les délégués agréés seront autorisés à se rendre dans toutes les localités, sans aucune exception, où sont internés des prisonniers de guerre. Ils auront accès dans tous les locaux occupés par des prisonniers

dispute over its application.[20] On balance, it may be said that the definitive version of the text adequately determined the function of the protecting Powers both in its supervisory and in its conciliatory aspects, and that it gave official support to the ICRC in its humanitarian activities. Taking into account, moreover, that Articles 86-88 were not isolated, but were connected with other provisions (such as Articles 8 and 77 dealing with the detaining Power's duties of registration and information, and Article 42 dealing with the right of prisoners to address complaints to the authorities), it may be finally concluded that the system of supervision and enforcement as provided in 1929 stood a far better chance of being effective in practice than the now prohibited recourse to reprisals ever had.

Curiously, the Sick and Wounded Convention elaborated by the Diplomatic Conference of 1929 (though by a different committee) was much more modest in providing guarantees for its application and enforcement. No supervision by a neutral authority was provided; and the sole provision relative to the treatment of alleged violations left everything to the willingness of the belligerents to contribute to the solution of such matters.[21] In conformity with this apparent tendency to rely on the good faith of the parties in the first place, the Sick and Wounded Convention was completely silent on the question of the admissibility or non-admissibility of reprisals. This silence presented a striking contrast with the prominent place which the prohibition of reprisals occupied in its twin, the Prisoners of War Convention.[22]

---

et pourront s'entretenir avec ceux-ci, en règle générale sans témoin, personnellement ou par l'intermédiaire d'interprètes.

"Les belligérants faciliteront dans la plus large mesure du possible la tâche des représentants ou des délégués agréés de la Puissance protectrice. Les autorités militaires seront informés de leur visite.

"Les belligérants pourront s'entendre pour admettre que des personnes de la propre nationalité des prisonniers soient admises à participer aux voyages d'inspection."

[20] Art. 87: "En cas de désaccord entre les belligérants sur l'application des dispositions de la présente Convention, les Puissances protectrices devront, dans la mesure du possible, prêter leurs bons offices aux fins de règlement du différend.

"A cet effet, chacune des Puissances protectrices pourra, notamment, proposer aux belligérants intéressés une réunion de représentants de ceux-ci, éventuellement sur un territoire neutre convenablement choisi. Les belligérants seront tenus de donner suite aux propositions qui leur seront faites dans ce sens. La Puissance protectrice pourra, le cas échéant, soumettre à l'agrément des Puissances en cause une personnalité appartenant à une Puissance neutre ou une personnalité déléguée par le Comité international de la Croix-Rouge, qui sera appelée à participer à cette réunion."

[21] Art. 30: "A la demande d'un belligérant, une enquête devra être ouverte, selon le mode à fixer entre les parties intéressées, au sujet de toute violation alléguée de la Convention; une fois la violation constatée, les belligérants y mettront fin et la réprimeront le plus promptement possible."

[22] Significantly, the commentary to the Geneva Convention mentioned in n. 3 to this § does not contain a single reference to reprisals.

3.3. THE TOKYO PROJECT OF 1934

The attempts undertaken during the First World War to achieve an amelioration in the condition of prisoners had not been confined to prisoners of war in the technical sense of the term, but had embraced interned enemy civilians as well. Thus, the agreements concluded between the belligerents towards the end of the war applied to both categories of war victims.[1]

In its report to the Xth International Red Cross Conference, the ICRC paid attention to the issue of the internment of enemy civilians; in the recent war, it pointed out, internment of members of this category had been common practice, and a drastic restriction of the powers of belligerents in this respect seemed urgently required.[2] The Conference evidently shared this view: the relevant Resolution (XV) did not even distinguish between the position of military and civilian persons in enemy hands, the Governments being invited to conclude at the earliest possible moment a convention (in one breath) "sur les prisonniers de guerre, les déportés, les évacués et les réfugiés".[3]

The "Diplomatic Committee" set up by the ICRC to prepare the requested draft Convention, rapidly came to the conclusion that a division of the subject-matter was preferable,[4] and it confined its own efforts to an examination of the position of prisoners of war *stricto sensu*, leaving aside all questions regarding the civilians not entering into that category. The latter questions were taken up, however, by the chairman of the Committee and member of the ICRC, Dr. F. Ferrière. In a separate report drawn up for the XIth International Red Cross Conference [5] he discussed the position of civilians in enemy or enemy occupied territory in the light of existing law, practice, and the agreements concluded between the belligerents during the World War, and he wound up by giving a list of the subjects which in his view should be covered in a "code des civils". In the latter part of his report he touched upon the matter of reprisals: he endorsed the principle, accepted by the Xth Conference, that reprisals against prisoners should be strictly prohibited, and he considered that the operation of that

---

[1] *Supra*, p. 70.

[2] "Le code du prisonnier de guerre", *op. cit.* n. 4 to § 3.1, pp. 106-108.

[3] *Supra*, p. 73.

[4] Report of the "Diplomatic Committee" (*supra*, p. 76), pp. 774-776. The Committee argued (p. 776): "Ce problème [*i.e.* that of the treatment of enemy civilians], dont l'étude approfondie est hautement à souhaiter, est d'une portée considérable et d'une complexité extrême. Il implique, en somme, une révision générale des usages de la guerre et l'on peut admettre que sa solution nécessitera l'établissement de règles juridiques nouvelles et plus précises que celles qui ont été posées jusqu'ici. La Commission estime qu'il devrait faire l'objet d'une Convention internationale spéciale et croit qu'il serait désirable d'envisager de plus près l'éventualité de négociations internationales à cet effet."

[5] "Projet d'une Convention internationale réglant la situation juridique des civils tombés à la guerre au pouvoir de l'ennemi", in *RICR*, Vol. V, 1923, p. 560.

principle should be extended to civilians interned in enemy territory.[6] As for the situation in occupied territory, he preferred an equally strict prohibition; but if that could not be attained yet, he demanded "qu'au moins les représailles ne portent pas sur des civils, surtout pas sur des femmes, et n'entrent en vigueur qu'après un avertissement préalable suffisant pour permettre l'aboutissement des négociations entamées".[7]

In 1923, the XIth International Conference of the Red Cross considered the problem of the treatment of civilians on the basis of Dr. Ferrière's report. As was realized by the Conference, the ICRC would have preferred it to evolve a series of neatly formulated principles, that could serve as a basis for a draft convention to be elaborated by the ICRC: the same procedure, in fact, as was being followed with regard to the prisoners of war régime. It was also realized, however, that this subject-matter, and in particular the condition of the population in occupied territory, was much more narrowly connected with the actual conduct of warfare, and, hence, with political and military considerations, than was the prisoners of war régime. It was therefore deemed wise not to formulate any specific principles and merely to give some general indications in a vaguely worded *voeu*. The result of the debate was the unanimous adoption of a resolution which gave expression to the desire that a convention should be concluded relative to the condition of civilians in the power of the enemy, and that such a convention take into consideration "[l]es principes d'humanité tels que ceux qui ont inspiré les conventions spéciales conclues en pareille matière au cours de la dernière guerre"; furthermore, the ICRC was requested "de prendre toutes mesures et toutes initiatives qu'il jugera utiles pour arriver à la réalisation des voeux ci-dessus".[8]

The ICRC did not immediately take up the matter, as it considered that priority ought to be given to the subjects which were deemed ripe for consideration by a diplomatic conference: the revision of the Wounded and Sick Convention of 1906, and the conclusion of a Convention relative to the treatment of prisoners of war. Consequently, the issue of the treatment of enemy civilians was not on the agenda of the Diplomatic Conference of 1929. Nevertheless, both committees of the Conference found occasion to formulate a *voeu* relative to the subject; after the two proposed texts had been merged, the final version appeared as *voeu* n° VI in the Final Act: [9]

"La Conférence, faisant siennes les résolutions unanimes de ses deux Commissions, exprime le voeu que des études approfondies soient

[6] *Ibid.*, p. 583.
[7] *Ibid.*, pp. 584-585.
[8] Records of the XIth International Red Cross Conference, pp. 184-185.
[9] Discussion in the 1st Commission: 17th meeting, 19 July (pp. 369-374, 378), 19th and 20th meetings, 24 July (pp. 417, 420). Discussion in the 2nd Commission: 10th meeting, 24 July (pp. 555-559). Adoption by the plenary session: 4th meeting, 26 July (p. 641). The text is reproduced at p. 732.

entreprises en vue de la conclusion d'une Convention internationale concernant la condition et la protection des civils de nationalité ennemie qui se trouvent sur le territoire d'un belligérant ou sur un territoire occupé par lui."

With this backing the ICRC resumed its efforts and in the ensuing years elaborated the text of a draft Convention relative to the protection of civilians in enemy or enemy occupied territory.[10] The draft Convention was thereupon, as a first step, introduced to the XVth International Conference of the Red Cross which met in Tokyo in 1934. The Conference duly accepted the projet without any great difficulties;[11] in the Resolution expressing this acceptance, the Governments were invited to pay careful attention to the project, and the ICRC was requested, this time, "de faire toutes démarches utiles pour faire aboutir une Convention dans le plus bref délai possible".

The prospects for such an undertaking were, however, far from propitious. By that time, the League of Nations had demonstrated its inability to solve the problems, both political and economic, of the post-war period; the League Disarmament Conference had ended in obvious failure;[12] Germany had left both the League and the Disarmament Conference, and, while the Hitler régime was already beginning to show its true face, re-armament was in progress. In this atmosphere of latent aggression, fear and insecurity it would be a hard task to bring the States around the conference table for a discussion of the problems connected with the protection of civilians against the hardships of war.

Notwithstanding these unfavourable prospects, the ICRC started the normal procedure, and in August 1935 transmitted the text of the draft Convention to the Swiss Government: this considered that 1937 might be a suitable time for a diplomatic conference.[13] When, however, the XVIth International Conference of the Red Cross met in June 1938 in London, the representative of the ICRC in reporting on the activities of the ICRC during the past few years was obliged to admit that no progress had been made.[14] When, soon thereafter, in 1939, the Second World War broke out,

[10] *RICR*, Vol. XVI, 1934, p. 657; the draft is preceded by a commentary by Paul des Gouttes, *ibid.*, p. 649.
[11] Records of the XVth Conference, pp. 202-209. Text of Resolution XXXIX: p. 262.
[12] *Infra*, p. 90 n. 2.
[13] Information provided by the ICRC to the national Red Cross societies, 31 July 1936; *RICR*, Vol. XVIII, 1936, p. 671.
[14] "Il ne faut pas se dissimuler que dans ces divers domaines les progrès sont lents à réaliser. ... [L]a convocation d'une conférence diplomatique qui doit en discuter se heurte parfois à des difficultés dont le Comité international n'est pas responsable. C'est le cas pour le projet de *Convention sur l'adaptation à la guerre aérienne des principes de la Convention de Genève* et pour le *Projet de Convention concernant la condition et la protection des civils de nationalité ennemie*. Le Comité international a fait tous ses efforts pour que ces deux projets, acceptés l'un par la XIVe, l'autre par la XVe Conférence puissent, avant la Conférence actuelle, passer devant une con-

no change had occurred in the situation: notwithstanding its strenuous efforts, the ICRC had failed to obtain the adoption *tempore utili* of a Convention providing a legal basis for the protection of civilians in enemy hands.

After this résumé of the history of the Tokyo project, some information about its contents is required. The text consisted of four parts, containing respectively: (1) a definition of the concept of "enemy civilian", (2) provisions concerning enemy civilians in the territory of a belligerent, (3) provisions relating to enemy civilians in territory occupied by a belligerent, and (4) rules on the application and execution of the proposed convention, the supervision of its observance, and final provisions.

The division of the substantive part of the Convention over two chapters, depending on whether the enemy civilians find themselves in the territory of a belligerent or in territory occupied by it, was self-evident for more than one reason: notwithstanding a certain superficial similarity between the two situations, consisting in the fact that in either case civilians were in the power of the enemy, differences both of an historical and a factual order stood out. Historically, the situation of the non-combatant population in occupied territory had been in the limelight since the Conference of Brussels of 1874, and the Hague Regulations of 1899 had contained a section (III) entitled "De l'autorité militaire sur le territoire de l'Etat ennemi". The treatment of civilians of enemy nationality in the territory of a belligerent, on the other hand, had never before the Forst World War given rise to such serious difficulties as had arisen in the course of that war as a consequence of the large-scale internments of such civilians, women and children not excluded; therefore, no specific rules had so far been laid down or even contemplated concerning their condition.

As to the factual aspect, the position of the occupying Power exercising its *de facto* authority in enemy territory and amidst a more often than not hostile population presents problems of control and security and of military government of a kind radically different from the security problems which a belligerent is likely to meet in its own territory, even in relation to the enemy civilians found there.

In the project, an endeavour was made to meet these different aspects. A completely new and detailed set of rules had been elaborated for the protection of civilians in the territory of a belligerent (Title II). On the other hand, the section concerning occupied territory (Title III) was confined to a mere two Articles, one (Article 18) containing an undertaking to observe the rules provided in section III of the Hague Regulations,[15] and

férence diplomatique, qui était envisagée pour 1937; mais celle-ci n'a pas pu avoir lieu."—*RICR*, Vol. XX, 1938, p. 622.

[15] The ICRC evidently expected that a number of States which had not ratified the

the other (Article 19) adding some important though not revolutionary obligations of a humanitarian character to the burden of the occupant.[16]

What had become of the ideas regarding reprisals, expressed by Dr. Ferrière in his project of 1923? As far as civilians in enemy territory were concerned, his views had been followed: in terms identical to those used in Article 2, paragraph 3, of the Prisoners of War Convention of 1929, Article 10 of the project provided that "[l]es mesures de représailles à leur égard sont interdites." [17] The section concerning occupied territory, on the other hand, did not contain a single express reference to reprisals; yet, the possibility of a justifiable recourse to reprisals (or quasi-reprisals, for that matter) was restricted in one important respect: a prohibition on killing hostages or punishing them corporeally had been incorporated.[18] Clearly, the ICRC had shrunk from also proposing a total prohibition of reprisals against the category of the civilians in occupied territory.

As regarded the other side of the problem, viz., the means designed to render the recourse to reprisals superfluous, Title IV of the project contained a set of rules which did not materially differ from those incorporated in the Prisoners of War Convention. Thus, the co-operation of protecting Powers was provided, as well as the power of their representatives or special delegates to visit all localities where civilians might be interned.[19] In the system of the project, the latter power was of limited significance, as the internment of civilians was solely referred to in the context of the treatment of civilians in enemy territory. Nonetheless, the obvious lack of hesitation on the part of the ICRC in embodying this system of supervision and enforcement in the draft Convention for the protection of civilians was in sharp contrast to the reticence which it displayed in proposing new rules for the treatment of the population in occupied territory, especially as reprisals were concerned.

In assessing these features of the Tokyo project, the circumstances prevailing at the time must of course be borne in mind. Caution was obviously the password for anybody desirous to avoid the risk of early failure for any project dealing with a subject-matter so touchy as the

---

Hague Convention on Land Warfare, either that of 1899 or 1907, would become a party to the proposed Convention and that this would nullify in their respect the effect of the *si omnes* clause contained in Article 2 of those Conventions, at any rate as far as the provisions regarding occupied territory were concerned.

[16] The obligations were: (1) to treat hostages humanely if, in exceptional circumstances, the occupant could not dispense with taking them, and never to kill them or punish them corporeally; (2) to abstain from deportations unless these were necessary for the security of the inhabitants in view of the military operations; (3) to allow the exchange of information and the receipt of relief, and (4) to allow the activities of relief societies.

[17] Art. 11 adds that also the taking of hostages would be prohibited.

[18] *Cf.* n. 16.

[19] Arts. 20 ff., particularly Art. 23.

occupation régime; and caution was evidently observed by the ICRC. Indeed, it did itself regard the draft text as a mere first attempt, as was apparent from the commentary accompanying it: "Tel qu'il est et tel que le Comité international de la Croix-Rouge le présente à la XVᵉ Conférence, ce projet d'une Convention relative aux civils ennemis ne constituera peut-être qu'une première étape".[20]

Caution had been especially observed with respect to the issue of reprisals in occupied territory. Was the complete silence on the general aspects of reprisals in conformity with the law in force at the time? True, the draft text did contain an express prohibition with regard to the killing or maltreatment of hostages, a mode of acting that could very well be resorted to by way of reprisals: was it believed by the ICRC that that prohibition was a sufficient means to cope with the evil of reprisals in occupied territory? As far as the latter question was concerned, it should be kept in mind that the practice of killing or maltreating hostages had actually constituted a major problem confronting the ICRC in the First World War. On the other hand, it had by no means been the only form of reprisals against civilians; and the belief expressed by Dr. Ferrière that reprisals against the inhabitants of occupied territory ought to be prohibited without exception, or, at least, should respect civilians and especially women and should only become operative after the lapse of a period of waiting, was evidently based on very realistic considerations.

Taking into account, moreover, that already at the time of the First World War the inhumanity of reprisals against defenceless war victims had been acknowledged by the belligerents, who towards the end of the war had agreed to a drastic restriction of their powers in that respect; that the Diplomatic Conference of 1929 had condemned and outlawed reprisals against prisoners of war on account of their inhuman character; and that there was a definite tendency to consider this prohibition not restricted to prisoners of war but applicable to other categories of war victims as well, —the conclusion seems warranted that the omission in the Tokyo project of a prohibition in one form or another of reprisals against the civil population in occupied territory, while not openly in conflict with the law in force at the time (as the omission evidently was neither intended as, nor had it the effect of, an abrogation), certainly amounted to a serious lacuna in the attempted codification of the law as to belligerent occupation.

In this context it is worth mentioning that in 1937, when the ICRC convened a Committee of Experts to examine the question of the revision of the Wounded and Sick Convention of 1929, the ICRC itself expressed the view that that Convention ought to be completed with an express prohibition of reprisals.[21] And the Committee, while of the opinion "que le

[20] *RICR*, Vol. XVI, 1934, p. 656.
[21] Paul des Gouttes, "Projet de revision de la Convention de Genève du 27 juillet 1929 présenté aux Sociétés nationales de la Croix-Rouge par le Comité international de la

droit des gens prohibe déjà des mesures de représailles ou de réciprocité qui iraient à l'encontre des principes de l'humanité", nevertheless agreed that an express provision to that effect ought to be inserted in the Convention.[22]

In view of these considerations, it is submitted that the ICRC in drafting Title III of the Tokyo project had for once demonstrated too much caution. At an earlier occasion [23] it had taken care to point out that it could not afford to neglect in its legislative activities the realities of warfare for the humanitarian interests: this time, however, it had paid altogether too much heed to the acceptability and practicability of the proposed text from the point of view of the supposed military necessities. The objection to this overcautious attitude is that as a result the Tokyo project could be interpreted as authoritative support for the contention that, according to the law in force prior to the Second World War, reprisals against civilians in occupied territory were not prohibited and, hence, legitimate.

That the ICRC had never intended its project to have that effect goes without saying, and is moreover evident from a letter which it addressed to the Governments of Germany, Great Britain, France and Poland as soon as the Second World War had been declared: this contained a final, urgent appeal to the belligerents to treat civilians humanely, and not to resort to reprisals against them contrary to the humanitarian principles forming part of the law.[24]

Croix-Rouge", in *RICR*, Vol. XIX, 1937, p. 645, at p. 647: "après l'article 5, devrait s'intercaler un article sur les *représailles*. L'expérience en a révélé la nécessité."

[22] *Rapport relatif à l'interprétation, la revision et l'extension de la Convention de Genève du 27 juillet 1929*, presented by the ICRC to the XVIth International Red Cross Conference, 1938; *RICR*, Vol. XX, 1938, p. 193, at p. 223.

[23] *Supra*, n. 7 to § 3.1.

[24] Letter of 13 September 1939 regarding the protection of the civil populations and the observance of the Conventions; *RICR*, Vol. XXI, 1939, p. 760. The letter reads in part: "Le Comité international de la Croix-Rouge saisit cette occasion pour exprimer tout le prix qu'il attache aux déclarations par lesquelles les Parties belligérantes ont récemment manifesté leur intention de respecter les règles du droit des gens et des Conventions en vigueur, en particulier en ce qui concerne la prohibition de certaines moyens de guerre et la protection des populations civiles. Le Comité international de la Croix-Rouge ose exprimer l'espoir que ce respect des règles du droit n'en vienne pas à être altéré par des actes de représailles au cas où une Puissance croirait pouvoir invoquer une violation d'une de ces règles. De toute façon, même dans le cas où des représailles ou des mesures de rétorsion—qui pourraient être considérées comme légitimes par le Gouvernement intéressé—seraient décidées, le Comité international de la Croix-Rouge croit devoir insister de manière particulièrement puissante pour que ces représailles ou mesures de rétorsion demeurent dans les limites des principes humanitaires mis en évidence notamment dans le Préambule de la Convention de la Haye du 18 octobre 1907 concernant les lois et coutumes de la guerre sur terre, et qu'en aucun cas elles n'atteignent les personnes, objets ou établissements protégés par l'emblême distinctif de la Croix-Rouge."

3.4. THE DISARMAMENT CONFERENCE OF 1932-1934

As was related in the foregoing, the efforts initiated by the ICRC in the period following after the First World War, *inter alia*, to do away with reprisals, had purposely been restricted to one aspect of the issue only, namely the prohibition or limitation, on humanitarian grounds, of reprisals against certain categories of war victims: [1] indeed, it was precisely this division of the problem which enabled the ICRC to gain its most note-worthy result in this respect, consisting in the unconditional prohibition of reprisals against prisoners of war.

There was, of course, the other side of the problem: the possibility of reprisals resorted to in the context of the conduct of warfare proper. The crucial importance of that issue, as well as the seemingly insuperable difficulties attending any attempt to solve it, came to light in the same period in the course of the League of Nations Conference for the Reduction and Limitation of Armaments, held at Geneva from 1932 to 1934,[2] in the

---

[1] *Supra*, p. 70.

[2] Article 8 of the Covenant of the League of Nations expressed "that the maintenance of peace requires the reduction of armaments to the lowest point consistent with national safety and the enforcement by common action of international obligations." The efforts to implement this provision ultimately led to the convening, on 2 February 1932, of the above Conference which was attended by 61 States. It met at gradually longer intervals until it finally lapsed dismally in November 1934.

The Conference started in February 1932 with a series of plenary meetings (Records, Series A—Verbatim Records of Plenary Meetings); simultaneously, the two main bodies of the Conference began their work: the General Commission, on which all the delegations were represented (Records, Series B—Minutes of the General Commission), and the Bureau which consisted of the President of the Conference, the Vice-Presidents, and the chairmen of those commissions on which all the delegations were represented (Records, Series C—Minutes of the Bureau; until 21 September 1932 the meetings of the Bureau were private and no minutes were kept; *ibid.*, p. III). In the ensuing months the work was carried on by the General Commission and the Bureau. In July 1932 another plenary meeting was held in which the first phase of the Conference (the phase of general declarations and discussions) was concluded. In the second phase, the Bureau, and the General Commission whenever it was convened by the Bureau, struggled on through the mass of theoretical and practical problems posed by the disarmament issue. Finally, in November 1934, the Conference broke down through the force of political events in Europe; the crisis foreboding the ultimate failure happened when, in October 1933, Germany abandoned the League as well as the Disarmament Conference.

President of the Conference was Mr. Arthur Henderson (United Kingdom), who also held the chair of the General Commission and of the Bureau. A survey of the work of the Conference, composed by Henderson, has seen the light under the title "Preliminary report on the work of the Conference, prepared by the President, Mr. Arthur Henderson"; Conf.D. 171(1), Geneva, July 1936. From this document it appears that after the last meeting of the Bureau, on 20 November 1934, some technical work has been done in various committees in the period of February to April 1935; but this did not lead to results warranting a meeting of the Bureau (p. 34).

context of the fascinating discussion which arose in that Conference concerning the prohibition of the use of chemical, incendiary and bacterial weapons and methods of warfare.

The subject of the prohibition of such weapons was not entirely new: the use of poison and poisoned weapons had already been prohibited in Article 23 (a) of the Hague Regulations on Land Warfare; and a declaration had been signed at the first Peace Conference to the effect that the contracting Parties "s'interdisent l'emploi de projectiles qui ont pour but unique de répandre des gaz asphyxiants ou délétères".[3] Similar provisions had been incorporated in the Treaty of Versailles [4] and in the non-ratified Treaty of Washington relating to the Use of Submarines and Noxious Gases in Warfare, signed 6 February 1922.[5]

When it is further noted that in 1925 the Conference on the Trade in Arms, held under the auspices of the League of Nations, had produced a Protocol renewing, in terms practically identical to those used in the Washington Treaty, the undertaking to forgo "the use in war of asphyxiating, poisonous or other gases, and all analogous liquids, materials or devices" and extending it to the use of bacteriological methods of warfare,[6] the conclusion seems safe that by that time the principle of the prohibition of these weapons and methods had been definitely accepted. But this was not to say that all the consequences of the prohibition would already have been thought out: not by far, and it would not take long before this became apparent.[7]

[3] Proceedings, Vol. I, p. 254.
[4] Art. 171: "The use of asphyxiating, poisonous or other gases and all analogous liquids, materials or devices being prohibited, their manufacture and importation are strictly forbidden in Germany. The same applies to materials specially intended for the manufacture, storage and use of the said products or devices."
[5] Art. 5: "The use in war of asphyxiating, poisonous or other gases, and all analogous liquids, materials or devices, having been justly condemned by the general opinion of the civilized world and a prohibition of such use having been declared in treaties to which a majority of the civilized Powers are parties, the Signatory Powers, to the end that this prohibition shall be universally accepted as a part of international law binding alike the conscience and practice of nations, declare their assent to such prohibition, agree to be bound thereby as between themselves and invite the other civilized nations to adhere thereto."
[6] League of Nations Treaty Series, Vol. XCIV, p. 65. The Protocol, signed at Geneva, 17 June 1925 and in force as from 8 February 1928, was merely a by-product of the conference; its main product, the Convention on Supervision of International Trade in Arms and Ammunition and in Implements of War, signed at the same date, did not acquire sufficient ratifications to enter into force.
[7] A first indication of the problems to come lay in the fact that number of States, in accepting the Protocol, made the reservation that it would cease to be binding for them as soon as the army or allies of their opponents in a future war would have started to use the prohibited weapons. This in fact reduced the Protocol to a mere no-first-use declaration.

The Preparatory Commission for the Disarmament Conference, constituted by resolution of the League Council of 12 December 1925,[8] prepared a draft Convention [9] which in Part V—Chemical Arms, contained only one Article:

> "The High Contracting Parties undertake, subject to reciprocity, to abstain from the use in war of asphyxiating, poisonous or similar gases, and of all analogous liquids, substances or processes.
>
> "They undertake unreservedly to abstain from the use of all bacteriological methods of warfare."

In a commentary, the Preparatory Commission justified the distinction between the two categories of weapons with the argument that several Governments had made their acceptance of the Protocol of 1925 subject to the condition of reciprocity as far as chemical weapons were concerned; [10] and it seemed reasonable to accept that normally speaking the undertaking to abstain from the use of those weapons could only be observed subject to reciprocity.[11] The consequence of this view was obviously that the question of reprisals could not rise in connection with the use of chemical weapons, the violation by one party completely releasing the other party from its obligations. This would be different, however, for the bacteriological methods of warfare, reciprocity not being made a condition for their prohibition. These aspects of the proposal were not however developed by the Preparatory Commission.[12]

The Disarmament Conference, once convened, soon touched upon the subject of chemical and similar weapons, as part of the problem of qualitative disarmament, "*i.e.* the selection of certain classes or descriptions of weapons the possession or use of which should be absolutely prohibited to all States or internationalised by means of a general Convention".[13] The

---

[8] See Records, Series A, Vol. I, pp. 4, 5.

[9] League of Nations Document C.687.M.288.1930.IX; Geneva, 9 December 1930.

[10] *Cf.* n. 7 to this §.

[11] Report by the Preparatory Commission for the Disarmament Conference, C.690. M.289.1930.IX; Geneva, 9 December 1930; paras. 216-231, in particular para. 221.

[12] Different ideas concerning the retaliatory use of chemical weapons existed at the time in the ICRC. This was equally concerned with the issue, though from a different point of view: viz., the protection of the civil population against the consequences of warfare. In an article bearing on this problem, and especially on the protection against air and chemical warfare, Sidney H. Brown, member of the secretariat of the ICRC, pointed to the difficulties inherent in it, among these the danger of reprisals: "Un très grave danger pour la réalisation et l'observation d'un accord international en matière de guerre aéro-chimique consiste dans l'emploi abusif du principe autorisant les représailles. Pour écarter cet abus, les représailles devraient être exclues *expressis verbis* d'une convention de ce genre."—"La protection de la population civile contre les dangers de la guerre aéro-chimique par des instruments diplomatiques", in *RICR*, Vol. XIII, 1931, p. 668, at p. 705.

[13] Records, Series B, Vol. I, p. 113; 16th meeting, 22 April 1932.

General Commission, confronted with that wide issue, resolved that "the range of land, sea and air armaments should be examined by the competent Special Commissions with a view to selecting those weapons whose character is the most specifically offensive or those most efficacious against national defence or most threatening to civilians";[14] and, as the question of chemical and bacteriological weapons was felt to be common to land, sea and air armaments, a Special Committee was set up to deal with those weapons, apart from the "competent Special Commissions" referred to in the Resolution (being the Land, Sea and Air Commissions).[15]

The Special Committee experienced no great difficulties in finding that three classes of weapons and methods of warfare were of a character as indicated in the Resolution: chemical weapons, bacteriological weapons, and (a newly added group) incendiary projectiles and flame projectors. It even went one step further and gave careful definitions of the weapons and methods coming under these heads and the exceptions that should be recognized.[16]

When, on 23 July 1932, the first phase of the Conference came to an end, matters had not been brought any further. The Rapporteur of the General Commission, Beneš, included in the relevant part of the Resolution submitted to the Commission [17] (Part II—Conclusions of the First Phase of the Conference) the following declaration:

"Chemical, bacteriological and incendiary warfare shall be prohibited under the conditions unanimously recommended by the Special Committee."

That this was merely a first step was evident from the text of the paragraph on violations contained in Part III of the Resolution (Preparation of the Second Phase of the Conference; para. 5):

"Rules of international law shall be formulated in connection with the provisions relating to the prohibition of the use of chemical, bacteriological and incendiary weapons and bombing from the air, and shall be supplemented by special measures dealing with infringement of these provisions."

In summary, the first round of discussions had clarified the issue to the extent that the weapons and methods of warfare which should be included in a prohibition of chemical and bacteriological warfare had been carefully selected and defined by an expert Committee. But the question of whether

---

[14] *Ibid.*, p. 116.

[15] *Ibid.*, p. 120; 18th meeting, 10 May 1932.

[16] Chemical and bacteriological weapons: Special Committee; Report to the General Commission, Conf.D. 120, Geneva, 31 May 1932.

[17] The draft Resolution was adopted after prolonged discussions; Records, Series B, Vol. I, pp. 153-205, 23rd-27th meetings, 20-23 July 1932. Text of the Resolution in its final form: Conf.D. 136(I), Geneva, 22 July 1932.

such a prohibition should be absolute or subject to reciprocity had not even been considered yet, and neither had attention been paid to systems of prevention and sanctions.

The Bureau, taking up the matter along with the other issues referred to it by the General Commission, put on record the agreement in principle concerning the prohibition of chemical warfare, as well as the fact that the reaction to violations of that prohibition remained a controversial issue.[18] As an expert opinion seemed desirable at this juncture, the matter was now put in the hands of the Italian delegate, Pilotti, chairman of the Special Committee.[19] This expert duly produced a report,[20] in which the problem was for the first time set out in all its complexity: prohibition of chemical warfare should entail the prohibition of preparations made in time of peace for this kind of warfare; this would in turn give rise to a demand for supervision of the observance of that prohibition; last not least, there was the question of the consequences that ought to be attached to a violation, in time of war, of the prohibition to use chemical weapons.

To begin with, the rapporteur chose in favour of an absolute prohibition, not only of bacteriological warfare, but also of chemical and incendiary weapons: otherwise States would be inclined to make preparations for the eventuality that such weapons might be used by their adversaries in a future war, and any attempt to prohibit peace-time preparations would thus be made illusory. Next, he favoured a prohibition of preparations and supervision of that prohibition by a special section of the Permanent Disarmament Commission.[21] Finally, as concerned sanctions for the event of the use of chemical, incendiary or bacteriological weapons, the rapporteur emphasized in the first place that the establishment of the fact of an infringement should be entrusted to a neutral authority; in this respect, a part should be assigned to some neutral person in the territory of the injured State, such as the doyen of the Diplomatic Corps; and it should be the charge of the Permanent Disarmament Commission to decide and openly to state whether or not a violation had been committed. Once the fact of infringement had thus been established, the question of sanctions would arise; for this issue the rapporteur presented the following threefold solution: (1) individual pressure by third States; (2) consultation among third States to determine what steps should be taken in order to put a stop to the

---

[18] Records, Series C, Vol. I, pp. 7, 8; 14th meeting, 21 September 1932.

[19] Ibid., p. 20; 17th meeting, 22 September 1932.

[20] Conf.D. 142, Geneva, 25 October 1932. The document consists of two parts: the Report proper, and Conclusions.

[21] The creation of a Permanent Disarmament Commission had already been foreseen by the Preparatory Commission, and the idea that a supervisory commission of the League of Nations should be set up when a Convention on disarmament might become operative was not abandoned during the entire Conference.

infringement and to assist the victim State, and (3) a right of retaliation for the injured State, formulated in the following words: [22]

"The State against which chemical, incendiary or bacteriological weapons have been employed shall have the right to retaliate by the use of chemical and incendiary weapons and to make other reprisals, subject to the condition that such reprisals shall not be made outside the fighting area.

"It is understood that the Permanent Commission and the meeting of States in consultation shall have the right to recommend expressly to the State in question that it shall refrain from specified measures of retaliation or reprisal."

The right of retaliation, the rapporteur considered, could not be dispensed with: it might take some time before the assistance by third States would be forthcoming and in the meantime the victim State "might be crushed or suffer great injury. In no case could a State which has honourably fulfilled its obligations under the Convention be allowed to be placed in a position of inferiority." [23] It should be emphasized, however, that this right of retaliation was, like the other sanctions, made dependent on the previous establishment of the fact of infringement by the Permanent Disarmament Commission.

The Bureau provisionally accepted the idea of absolute prohibition as expressed in Pilotti's report; at the same time, however, there was agreement that the definitive acceptance of the prohibition must depend on satisfactory solutions being found for the problems of supervision and sanctions. [24] As the issues of the prohibition of preparations for chemical, incendiary and bacteriological warfare and of the supervision of such a prohibition proved insoluble for the Bureau without prior expert investigation into such questions as the technical possibility of supervising and preventing such preparations and the desirability of including defensive material (such as gas masks and shelters) in the prohibition, these matters were referred to the Special Committee. [25]

As to the crucial issue of sanctions, a broad discussion developed in the Bureau which centred around the retaliatory use of chemical and incendiary weapons. [26] It soon emerged that nearly all the members of the Bureau were opposed to the recognition of a right to retaliate; in fact, the rapporteur himself, when introducing the subject, observed that he "had no great sympathy for the idea of retaliation, and he had endeavoured to reduce this possibility to a minimum. He wished to submit to the Bureau the question whether it was possible to go still further and to abolish

[22] Conclusions, 4-II (3).
[23] Report, Chapter IV, Section II (2).
[24] Records, Series C, Vol. I, pp. 56-59; 23rd and 24th meetings, 8, 9 November 1932.
[25] *Ibid.*, pp. 59-64, 75-78; 24th and 26th meetings, 9, 11 November 1932.
[26] *Ibid.*, pp. 64-75; 25th and 26th meetings, 10, 11 November 1932.

completely any right of retaliation. There would be this advantage in such a decision, that it would bring out still more plainly the anti-social character of gas warfare." [27] An important argument in favour of deleting the passage conferring a right of reprisals was advanced by the Chairman, who pointed out that "[i]f, after first stating that all preparation of chemical warfare was prohibited, the right of retaliation were admitted, it went without saying that States would have to prepare for the exercise of that right—that was to say, for chemical warfare, by manufacturing poison gases, getting ready the necessary appliance, training personnel, etc. The only result would be to facilitate the perpetration of an act which had been declared an international crime." [28]

At the end of the debate the rapporteur introduced an alternative text for the section of his report dealing with sanctions; [29] this new proposal opened with an explicit prohibition of reprisals:

"The State against which chemical, incendiary or bacteriological weapons have been employed shall *in no circumstances* retaliate by the use of the same weapon."

The Bureau thereupon referred the matter to a drafting committee. [30]

In the next meeting of the Bureau [31] the chairman of the Drafting Committee, Politis (Greece), reported on its work: the Committee had agreed on a new text concerning sanctions; this embodied the prohibition of reprisals, couched in terms identical to those used in the final proposal of Pilotti. This prohibition had been accepted wholeheartedly: "The Drafting Committee was unanimous in proposing that the power to retaliate by the same weapons should be prohibited, and that there should be a formal statement of such prohibition." [32]

The Drafting Committee had furthermore realized "that the absolute prohibition of reprisals had its justification in the system of sanctions described in the three preceding paragraphs" [33] and that, hence, those sanctions must be effective. They were of three kinds: individual sanctions (pressure by third States), general collective sanctions (consultation regarding joint steps and "joint punitive action of every description"), and, if so desired by the States concerned, regional collective sanctions ("severe punitive action", creation beforehand of a joint police force). The system had been carefully elaborated; even a detail like the voting procedure on

[27] *Ibid.*, p. 66.
[28] *Ibid.*, p. 68. The rapporteur had conceived a different solution for this problem: in his view, preparations for the use of chemical or incendiary weapons would only become lawful in the event of the adversary having had recourse to the prohibited weapons; Report, Chapter II.
[29] *Ibid.*, p. 74.
[30] *Ibid.*, p. 75; chairman of the Committee was Politis (Greece).
[31] *Ibid.*, pp. 78-82; 27th meeting, 12 November 1932.
[32] *Ibid.*, p. 79.
[33] *Loc. cit.* n. 32.

the occasion of a consultation had been foreseen. On the other hand, the draft text was evidently a compromise between divergent tendencies, one group of delegates desiring automatic sanctions, while the other preferred the idea of consultation and decision *ad hoc.*

Two things emerged from the subsequent discussion in the Bureau: the compromise in the Drafting Committee had not succeeded in reconciling the divergent tendencies,[34] and in the eyes of some important delegations the whole discussion of the problem of sanctions had assumed proportions that had not originally been anticipated, so that they felt obliged to consult their Governments.[35] The Chairman drew the only possible conclusion, and adjourned the discussion until such time as the report of the Special Committee was received and the respective delegations had consulted their Governments.

The detailed and technical report [36] of the Special Committee on Chemical, Bacterial and Incendiary Weapons made one thing abundantly clear: while a prohibition on the preparation of warfare with these weapons might have moral value, it would be largely illusory from a practical point of view, as the research and production in this field could neither be distinguished nor separated from peaceful processes in the chemical industry and as, hence, supervision of the prohibition in peace-time would be impracticable.[37] This brought the whole focus on the problems of establishing the fact of use in wartime of chemical or similar weapons and on the penalties for such use. As to this, the Special Committee report elaborated in great detail a system for the speedy establishment of the fact of a violation; it did not even over-look such details as the transport (by aeroplane, boat, railway or motor-car) of the members of a Commission for Urgent Initial Investigation, and their diplomatic immunity.[38] As regards penalties, the report observed that the Special Committee was in an unfavourable position as the subject was primarily political in character and as the basic political questions had not yet been solved by the competent body. On the other hand, the Committee had realized that the political and technical aspects of sanctions were inter-dependent; it therefore put forward its technical suggestions on the subject, "in the hope that they may afford some measure of assistance to the Bureau

[34] Pilotti (Italy) declined the idea of prepared regional action; Massigli (France) thought that the proposed text was inadequate as it did not provide for automatic sanctions: "Could the right of reprisal be abolished without giving the State victim of the unlawful action the moral certainty that it would have the collective support of the other States?" (p. 82).
[35] Wilson (U.S.A.), Eden (United Kingdom), Dovgaleski (U.S.S.R.).
[36] Conf.D. 152, Geneva, 13 December 1932; rapporteur was Prof. V. H. Rutgers (Netherlands).
[37] General Conclusions, sub B.
[38] Head II, Part I, Chapter III, Section E.

in its consideration of this question".[39] It set out its observations under four heads,[40] and went on to give an estimate of their practical value while remaining (as it took care to emphasize) within the bounds of its purely technical task.[41] It considered that the suggestions regarding assistance of a scientific, medical or technical nature to a State victim of a chemical, incendiary or bacteriological attack might be of genuine technical efficacy. On the other hand, a measure such as the stoppage of external supplies necessary for chemical or incendiary weapons would only have a very limited effect on the guilty State and would in any case be belated. As, finally, concerned the issue of reprisals, the Special Committee had reached the following technical conclusions:

"(a) The recognition of the right of individual reprisals would compromise the prohibition to make preparations for chemical or incendiary warfare, unless, on the one hand, the preparation of such reprisals was made conditional on the previous establishment of the fact of infringement, and, on the other hand, the victim State was assured of concrete assistance from other States in making the said preparations, in order to compensate for its technical inferiority.

"(b) There can be no doubt that the transgressor State would necessarily be in a position of technical inferiority if the countries not directly concerned agreed to exert collective reprisals by means of chemical or incendiary weapons.

"(c) In the event of the Convention excluding all reprisals, even collective reprisals, it cannot be asserted that the transgressor State would always be assured of final superiority, but its position would be considerably strengthened. It could derive very important advantages from the use of chemical weapons. The temptation for such a State to have recourse to forbidden weapons would be much greater if it knew that it was safe from any individual or collective retaliation." [42]

[39] Head III, Chapter I (General Considerations).
[40] Head III, Chapters II (Technical measures of assistance to the State attacked, with a view to protection), III (Technical measures, the object of which is to make the guilty State unable or unwilling to continue to use the illicit weapon), IV (Technical aspect of reprisals), V (Suggestion with a view to hastening the practical application of penalties as soon as the fact of a breach has been established).
[41] Head III, Chapter VI (Conclusions regarding penalties).
[42] In the General Conclusions of the report, the Special Committee returned once again to the issue of sanctions. As regards reprisals, it recalled that it was "not called upon to state whether individual or collective reprisals should be permitted or forbidden"; however, from the technical point of view, the Committee had "realised the extreme gravity of the question in view of the very considerable and possibly even decisive advantages that the use of chemical or incendiary weapons would give to the offender as against an adversary or adversaries who were forbidden to use the same weapons, even by way of reprisals. These advantages would be purely temporary and might even disappear entirely if the use of chemical or incendiary weapons were permitted by way of reprisals under certain rigid conditions." (etc.)

98

To this analysis of the problem the Committee added the observation that "[f]rom every point of view, it would be desirable for the Permanent Disarmament Commission and the States signatories of the Convention to avail themselves of the short period elapsing between the submission of a complaint by a State and the establishment of the fact of a breach to make preparations with a view to the possible application of penalties."

It is obvious that the Special Committee had made a very strong case for the retention in one way or another of reprisals, for the event of the illicit use of chemical, incendiary or bacteriological weapons.

When the report was brought under discussion in the Bureau, it was accompanied by Draft Conclusions drawn up by the rapporteur of the Special Committee, Rutgers.[43] In these Conclusions the problem of reprisals was not dealt with from an exclusively technical point of view: the rapporteur had evidently tried to give a political solution, taking into account the technical arguments advanced by the Special Committee. The solution which he proposed was as follows: [44]

"The Permanent Disarmament Commission shall decide by a simple majority whether chemical and incendiary weapons may be employed in retaliation against the State which has resorted thereto. It is understood that they may not be so used before the decision of the Permanent Disarmament Commission, and that even preparations for their use shall not be allowed until after the Permanent Disarmament Commission's declaration that chemical, incendiary or bacterial weapons have been employed."

The Bureau started its discussion of the report and annexed Draft Conclusions by successively adopting (subject to drafting alterations) the chapters devoted to the prohibition of chemical and similar weapons, the prohibition of preparations, the supervision of the observance of the prohibition, and the establishment of the fact of use of chemical, incendiary or bacterial weapons.[45] When the discussion was then opened on the subject of penalties,[46] much attention was paid to the problem of reprisals and widely divergent opinions were once again defended in that respect: that the use of chemical and similar weapons ought to be prohibited absolutely and completely, even in the form of reprisals; [47] that the prohibition of their retaliatory use would be unrealistic; [48] that their retaliatory

---

[43] Conf.D./Bureau 41; Geneva, 24 January 1933.
[44] Ch. V (3).
[45] Records, Series C, Vol. I, pp. 129-136; 35th meeting, 25 January 1933.
[46] *Ibid.*, pp. 136-142; 36th meeting, 30 January 1933.
[47] Nadolny (Germany).
[48] Eden (United Kingdom); he said, *inter alia*: "It was essential in considering this question to remain within the limits of what was possible and not to ask more of human nature than human nature could bear. There was no country which, when sub-

use must be restricted, within the limits set out by the rapporteur.[49] The discussion did not, however, lead to any definite conclusion on this point, nor, indeed, on any other point of the problem of sanctions in case of chemical warfare, as a majority was ultimately of the opinion that the problem would have to be solved in conjunction with the wider issue of the sanctions to be attached to violations of the other parts of the Convention on Disarmament.[50] This was somewhat of a volte-face, bearing in mind that the General Commission had resolved that the issue of penalties in case of chemical warfare should be dealt with as a special problem. However, the Bureau tried to save its face by acknowledging the special character of the issue under discussion, while simultaneously postponing its solution; a resolution to that effect was adopted by the Bureau.[51]

A curious situation! Time and again the point had been emphasized in the discussions that the absolute prohibition of the use of chemical and similar weapons hinged upon the development of an effective system of sanctions, and that this presented a special problem. Now the Bureau had adopted the entire report of the Special Committee and the Draft Conclusions submitted by its rapporteur, with the sole exception of the chapter concerning sanctions. As concerned the issue of reprisals, the situation was most confusing. As the Greek delegate, Politis, put it: "In November 1932, the whole problem had been concentrated on the point whether or not it was intended to recognise the right of retaliation, and all the delegations admitted that the recognition of that right must involve an increase in the

---

jected to chemical attack, would agree to wait for authority before exercising its right of reprisals. Public opinion would not accept such a limitation."

[49] This standpoint was defended by the rapporteur himself, he advanced two arguments: (1) the risk that a merely unilateral investigation might lead to reprisals while the illicit weapons had not been used in fact, and (2) the consideration that immediate reprisals might not be needed: "The use by a State of the chemical weapon would certainly have an enormous moral effect throughout the world and might be expected to produce a strong reaction, a reaction which might be felt even in the State using the prohibited arm and might bring about a change of Government there. Other States, moreover, would probably hasten to require the guilty State, not only to promise not to resort again to that kind of warfare, but also to give pledges ensuring that that promise would be kept. Lastly, it might be expected that every effort would be made by third States to bring about the cessation of that kind of warfare, and to take measures of conciliation, and in certain cases immediate reprisals would be not merely useless but even harmful."—This analysis has certainly not been borne out by subsequent events, see *infra*, p. 104.

[50] Nadolny (Germany), Stein (U.S.S.R.), Wilson (U.S.A.), Eden (United Kingdom), Meli di Soragna (Italy).

[51] "The Bureau agrees to the principle of special measures being taken in the case of a violation of the prohibition of the use of chemical, incendiary and bacterial weapons. It decides to elaborate the relevant articles with regard to such special measures after the general penalties for the case of the violation of the Convention have been examined by the Conference."

severity of sanctions. At the present meeting, the whole question had been raised anew, and the Bureau seemed no longer inclined to accept the prohibition of the right of retaliation."

The complete deadlock with respect to the issue of sanctions finally found dramatic expression when a Drafting Committee of the Bureau[52] consolidated the results obtained so far in draft Articles.[53] Chapter VI of the draft text (Penalties for the Use of Chemical, Incendiary or Bacterial Weapons) consisted of only one word: "(Reserved)".

The issues of chemical and bacteriological warfare and, in that context, of the retaliatory use of chemical, incendiary and bacterial weapons confronted the Disarmament Conference once again on the occasion of the discussion of a comprehensive draft Convention on disarmament, introduced in March 1933 by the delegation of the United Kingdom.[54] In the words of the British Prime Minister, Ramsay MacDonald, who introduced the proposal in the General Commission,[55] the authors had tried "to fit into the framework of the draft disarmament convention prepared by the Preparatory Commission the solution which a thorough examination of all questions by the Conference had led it to believe would represent a just basis for negotiation, and which would result in a settlement of the problem".

Among the subjects thus treated was the issue of chemical warfare: an entire chapter was devoted to it. This followed the pattern familiar from earlier reports: separate sections dealt with the prohibition of chemical warfare and of preparations therefor, with supervision, and with the establishment of the fact of use of forbidden weapons. A section concerning sanctions was lacking; instead, the Article opening the chapter (47) contained a reference to reprisals:

"The following provision is accepted as an established rule of International Law:

"The use of chemical, incendiary or bacterial weapons as against any State, whether or not a Party to the present Convention, and in any war, whatever its character, is prohibited.

"This provision does not, however, deprive any Party which has been the victim of the illegal use of chemical or incendiary weapons of the right to retaliate, subject to such conditions as may hereafter be agreed." (etc.)

The task of establishing the fact of use was also in this project entrusted to the Permanent Disarmament Commission (Art. 61). However, no consequences whatsoever were attached to its decision in that respect for the

[52] Records, Series C, Vol. I, p. 142.
[53] Conf.D./Bureau 45; Geneva, 7 March 1933.
[54] Conf.D. 157(1); Geneva, 16 March 1933.
[55] Records, Series B, Vol. II, pp. 352-357; 45th meeting, 16 March 1933.

rights and duties of, either, the victim State, the offender, or third States. Evidently the United Kingdom delegation had not seen fit to seek a really adequate solution for the "special problem" of sanctions in connection with chemical warfare; on the other hand, it had not gone to the other extreme either, that of making the prohibition of chemical and incendiary weapons conditional on reciprocity; steering a middle course, it had merely fallen back on the traditional concept of reprisals, leaving it to the Conference to restrict its application by means of "such conditions as may hereafter be agreed".

The discussion in the General Commission regarding the proposed articles on chemical warfare was brief and rather insignificant.[56] Hardly any observations were made concerning the prohibition of chemical warfare and of the preparations therefor, the problem of supervision, and the establishment of the fact of use. The sole matter which received some attention was the issue of reprisals. One or two delegates availed themselves of the opportunity to repeat that in their view the prohibition of the use of chemical and incendiary weapons, like that of bacterial weapons, ought to be comprehensive and should include the retaliatory use of such weapons.[57] The general tendency was, however, to hold the question over until the second reading of the draft Convention.[58] And the matter rested there, in this discussion and thereafter, as no second reading was ever held. The last sign of life was the publication, in September 1933, of a provisional text of the draft Convention "prepared in the light of the modifications adopted in first reading and of the amendments presented by the delegations".[59] Article 47 as proposed by the British delegation was recorded in the text, as well as an amendment which had meanwhile been introduced by the delegations of the Petite Entente,[60] proposing to delete the paragraph on reprisals. It could not have been made more explicit than by this juxta-

---

[56] *Ibid.*, pp. 568-570; 71st meeting, 30 May 1933.
[57] Nadolny (Germany), Fotitch (Yugoslavia, speaking on behalf of the Petite Entente), Paul-Boncour (France; he only accepted collective sanctions).
[58] The following exchange between Rutgers (Netherlands) and Eden (United Kingdom) was illuminating. Rutgers reminded the General Commission that the Bureau had decided to adjourn all discussion regarding sanctions, including the discussion of the question of reprisals; and the Special Committee had definitely taken the view that, if a right to retaliate should be retained, its exercise must be conditional on the fact of use of the chemical or similar weapons by the adversary having been previously established beyond any doubt and this not merely by the victim State. Eden, however, "seemed to remember that an argument had been put forward in the Bureau against M. Rutgers' proposal concerning the establishment of the 'fact of use' by the adversary on the grounds that it might involve considerable delay, that much would depend upon the method employed, and so forth"; so, he said, the delegates ought to refresh their memories on this point, so that they might come to a decision—at the second reading.
[59] Conf.D. 163(1); Geneva, 22 September 1933.
[60] Conf.D./C.G. 123.

position of proposal and amendment, that the issue of the retaliatory use of chemical and incendiary weapons had been left unresolved by the Conference.

The above record of the discussions in the Conference for the Reduction and Limitation of Armaments leads to the following conclusions. First and foremost, it is noteworthy that the discussions have been held at all. In 1874, when the delegates at the Brussels Conference were confronted with a Russian proposal to regulate and limit the recourse to belligerent reprisals, they had agreed "de sacrifier l'article tel qu'il est sur l'autel de l'humanité".[61] After the First World War, part of the question was severed from the main body and dealt with separately: viz., the issue of reprisals against war victims and notably against prisoners of war.[62] In 1932 and 1933, the other half of the question was explicitly raised, narrowed down to a single concrete question: whether the use of chemical and incendiary weapons by way of reprisals ought to be prohibited or not. This time the discussion was not shirked, but pursued tenaciously; and, although no success was ultimately obtained, this much had in any event emerged: the issue could be discussed and agreement was not completely out of the question. It had also emerged that its solution was narrowly connected with the creation of other adequate (and more satisfactory) sanctions.

The use of chemical and incendiary weapons was universally regarded as inhuman, and this was a strong argument for the prohibition of their retaliatory use as well. But the argument was not sufficiently strong to carry the unanimous acceptance of such a prohibition in the teeth of the important counter-arguments of a military and political nature which were raised in the debate. The contest ended in a draw. These points, however, are beyond question:
(1) at no time was it proposed to allow the retaliatory use of bacterial warfare;
(2) at no time was it proposed to allow the retaliatory use of chemical or incendiary weapons on account of any violation of the law of war other than a breach of the prohibition against chemical, incendiary or bacterial weapons;
(3) none of the proposals aiming at retaining retaliation by means of chemical or incendiary weapons meant that the right to be conferred on belligerents should be unlimited; on the contrary, in one form or another all the proposals restricted the right, by, *inter alia*, preventing preparations, or making the right conditional on a previous decision by a neutral authority. In short, the inhuman and anti-social character of chemical, incendiary and bacterial warfare was universally accepted as a sufficient ground to restrict the possible solutions of the issue of reprisals to, either,

[61] *Supra*, p. 48.
[62] *Supra*, p. 72.

total prohibition even of the retaliatory use of the weapons concerned, or a severely curtailed right of reprisals. Between these possibilities the opinions wavered.

The present section would not be complete without a reference to a discussion about the use of gas in warfare, which arose in the context of the debate held on 20 April 1936, in the same rooms where the Disarmament Conference had met, in the 91st (extraordinary) session of the Council of the League of Nations.[63] The debate concerned the report, dated 18 April 1936, of the Committee of Thirteen which, upon the instructions of the Council, had attempted to effect a conciliation between Italy and Ethiopia, both Members of the League, and one of which (Italy) had in October 1935 started a military campaign against the territory of the other. The report [64] was the story of a failure. Besides, however, it contained a great deal of material relating to mutual accusations of violations of the laws of war: the Ethiopians were charged with using dum-dum bullets, maltreatment and killing of wounded soldiers and prisoners of war, and abuse of the Red Cross (Red Crescent) sign; the chief (and well-founded) accusation against Italy was that it made use of poison gas.

The Chairman of the Committee of Thirteen had on 9 April appealed to both parties to observe the laws of war.[65] The Italian Government, replying to this on 11 April, had declared its willingness to do so, but, it observed: [66] "The observance of these laws must be bilateral. The Italian military authorities cannot do otherwise than punish every inhuman atrocity committed by its adversary in contempt of every principle of law and morality." This reply had induced the Committee to state, in a communication of 18 April,[67] that "... the observation in the final sentence cannot justify the use of asphyxiating, poisonous or similar gases".

In the Council meeting of 20 April, the Italian representative, Baron Aloisi, took exception to that statement. By it, he said, the Committee had set itself up "as a judge, giving an interpretation of perhaps the most delicate and complex point covered by the Protocol of June 17th, 1925, which contains no provision prohibiting, in derogation of the general principles, the exercise of the right of reprisal for atrocities such as those of which Italian soldiers have been the victims, and evidence of which has been brought to the notice of all the Members of the League of Nations." [68] But other delegates strongly condemned the use of gas by Italy and were not prepared to accept that this was justified by the alleged atrocities on the

[63] League of Nations *Official Journal*, 1936, p. 357.
[64] C.176.M.122.1936.VII.
[65] League of Nations *Official Journal*, 1936, p. 464.
[66] *Ibid.*, p. 475.
[67] *Ibid.*, p. 373.
[68] *Ibid.*, p. 375.

Ethiopian side;[69] and a Resolution was proposed, reminding the parties to the conflict of their obligations under the Protocol of 1925.[70] It was only after a protest by Baron Aloisi[71] that the text was completed with a reference to other express rules of warfare, so that ultimately it ran as follows:[72]

"Recalls that Italy and Ethiopia are bound by the Protocol of June 17th, 1925, on the use of asphyxiating, poisonous or other gases, and by the Conventions regarding the conduct of warfare to which these two States are parties, and emphasises the importance which has been attached to these instruments by all the contracting States."

This text was adopted with quasi-unanimity, only Italy casting its vote against.

It bears pointing out that in the debate the Italian representative had not in so many words taken the stand that the use of gas by his country was justified as a reprisal on account of Ethiopian atrocities. On the other hand, his express statement to the effect that the Protocol of 1925 did not preclude the right of reprisals in the event of such atrocities, can hardly be understood as anything but a plea of reprisals.[73] In this light it should be recalled that in the discussions in the Disarmament Conference none of the delegates had at any time been heard to contend that the use of poison gas could be justified as a reprisal against any violation of the laws of war other than an infringement of that very prohibition to use gas.

The treatment of the Italian affair in the organs of the League of Nations was also unequivocal in this respect: while the Committee of Thirteen had explicitly rejected that the alleged Ethiopian atrocities could justify the Italian use of gas, the debate in the Council as well as the Resolution adopted at the close of it could likewise only be understood as a rejection of the Italian contention that the gas warfare to which it had resorted in contravention of the Gas Protocol of Geneva of 1925, could be justified as a reprisal.[74]

The Conference of 1932-1934 had, as related above, spent much of its time on the issue of sanctions with respect to violations of the prohibition of gas warfare: it had declared that this constituted a special problem, it

[69] *Ibid.*, p. 378: Eden (United Kingdom); p. 382: De Vasconcellos (Portugal); p. 386: Bruce (Australia).

[70] *Ibid.*, p. 387.

[71] *Ibid.*, p. 389.

[72] *Ibid.*, pp. 392-393.

[73] The Italian Government developed this theme at some greater length in a letter dated 30 April 1936 and addressed to the Chairman of the Committee of Thirteen; *ibid.*, p. 579.

[74] Erroneously, J.-C. Venezia writes that "durant le conflit italo-éthiopien, le Conseil de la Société des Nations n'avait admis la légitimité de l'emploi des gaz toxiques qu'à titre de représailles contre des actes de barbarie (Résolution du 20 avril 1936)."—"La notion de représailles en droit international public", in *RGDIP*, Vol. 64, 1960, p. 465, at p. 488.

had developed proposals for its solution, but ultimately it had failed to reach agreement on any of the solutions proposed. In the debate in the Council of 20 April 1936, it may finally be observed, one representative did explicitly point to the fact that the Ethiopians, victims of gas attacks, were "themselves utterly unprovided with any means of defence against this method of warfare".[75] But not a word was on that occasion said about organized attempts to assist the victim State; and complete silence was also maintained with respect to the question of special sanctions against the malefactor, Italy. In fact, the Council merely succeeded in maintaining the economic sanctions which it had previously recommended against Italy on account of its aggression. For the rest, the Council confined itself to reminding the parties of their obligations under the law in force; and it is perfectly obvious that none of the Members of the League represented on the Council was at the time willing to run the risk of driving Italy into the German camp by intensifying the sanctions in answer to the "menace to humanity and civilisation"[76] of which Italy had become guilty by its recourse to gas warfare. The application of sanctions, it is evident, had very much remained a matter for decision *ad hoc*.

3.5. CONCLUSIONS

The period between the two World Wars, considered in this Chapter, stands in marked contrast to the pre-1914 period firstly in that, unlike the Conferences of Brussels of 1874 and of The Hague of 1899 and 1907, both the Diplomatic Conference of Geneva of 1929 and the Disarmament Conference of 1932-1934 gave express attention to the problems posed by belligerent reprisals. This in itself constituted a major improvement over the atmosphere of taboo which the earlier conferences, in the name of humanity, had maintained with regard to the subject.

At the root of this changed attitude lay the initiative, taken by the ICRC, to detach the prisoners of war régime from the Hague Regulations on Land Warfare and to make it the subject of a separate convention, thus turning it into a part of the "law of Geneva".[1] As a result of that manoeuvre, the humanitarian aspects of this régime stood out far more clearly; and as, moreover, a reasonably reliable system of supervision and enforcement could be brought about, it now proved feasible—though not without struggle—to lay down in the Prisoners of War Convention of 1929 that reprisals against prisoners of war are categorically prohibited. The significance of this achievement is twofold: firstly, this was the very first time that

---

[75] Eden, n. 69, *supra*.
[76] Bruce, *ibid.*
[1] *i.e.*, the law concerning the treatment and condition of war victims, as distinct from the law of warfare proper, or "law of The Hague".

106

a prohibition of reprisals was embodied in a multilateral treaty; in the second place, it constituted a decisive step towards the division of the issue of belligerent reprisals into two parts, according as to whether the reprisal actions were aimed against protected persons and other war victims in the broadest sense, or, alternatively, were resorted to in the context of warfare proper.[2]

As it was just mentioned, the prohibition of reprisals against prisoners of war was the first—and, for the time being, the only—positive result of the new approach. This prohibition certainly did not have the character of a mere codification of existing law: indeed, prior to 1929 widely divergent opinions were defended in this respect. Thus, the International Law Association was found to have opted for a mitigated right of reprisals against prisoners of war, rather than for its total abolition. And an author like Garner condemned the "practice of resorting to reprisals against prisoners of war who are innocent of any offence" as "detestable", but he added that "the threat to resort to it, in many cases had the effect of securing better treatment of prisoners by the enemy".[3] Other authors, again, sought to resolve the issue by a selective approach, stating, for instance, that the rules in the Hague Regulations concerning the conditions and remuneration of labour by prisoners could be set aside by way of reprisals,[4] or that, whereas the execution of a proportionate number of recently made prisoners would be a legitimate reprisal for similar executions on the part of the enemy, the systematic neglect of prisoners resulting in their ultimate death could not be so justified.[5]

With the coming into existence of the Convention of 1929, the commentaries generally took the line of recording the new rule (either approvingly or without comment).[6] Acceptance of the prohibition was not unanimous, however. Thus. one German author, Renken, not only advanced the argument that reprisals had in the past been the only means to save many German prisoners from an increasingly unfavourable treatment, but he went so far as to assert that the only limit to reprisals, as an instance of self-defence, consisted in effectiveness, not humanity.[7] It is even more

[2] It should be pointed out that the authors writing in the period under discussion do not appear to have been particularly aware of the importance of the distinction thus introduced.

[3] J. W. Garner, *International Law and the World War*, 1920, Vol. II, p. 53.

[4] Y. de la Brière, "Evolution de la doctrine et de la pratique en matière de représailles", *R.d.C.* 1928, Vol. II, p. 264.

[5] L. le Fur, *Des représailles en temps de guerre*, 1919, p. 69.

[6] *E.g.*: J. P. A. François, *Handboek van het volkenrecht*, Vol. II, 1933, p. 423; L. Oppenheim, *International Law*, Vol. II, 5th ed. by H. Lauterpacht, 1935, p. 304; J. Spiropoulos, *Traité théorique et pratique du droit international public*, 1933, p. 375; A. von Verdross, *Völkerrecht*, 1937, p. 299.

[7] K.-W. Renken, *Die völkerrechtliche Stellung der Kriegsgefangenen nach dem "Abkommen über die Behandlung der Kriegsgefangenen vom 27. Juli 1929"*, 1934, p. 25.

amazing to find that Canneman, a Dutch author, as late as 1936 treated the issue as a matter of *ius constituendum* and, without so much as a word about the Convention of 1929, flatly rejected as unrealistic the very idea of a prohibition of reprisals against prisoners of war.[8] These rare exceptions could not however undo the general acceptance of the newly created prohibition.

No express prohibition of reprisals was contained in the Sick and Wounded Convention of 1929: it was only on the eve of the Second World War, on the occasion of the (abortive) attempt at bringing about its revision, that it was stated that violation of this Convention by way of reprisal would be contrary to the principle of humanity and, hence, prohibited. It may be added that in the literature of the period scant attention was given to this particular possibility: in fact, only two authors were found to refer to it at all.

One of these, Le Fur, took care to reject explicitly that the act of intentionally killing wounded or shipwrecked enemies could ever be justified as a reprisal.[9] On the other hand, both that author [10] and De la Brière [11] regarded as a legitimate reprisal the detention of members of the enemy medical corps if the enemy were without valid cause to fail to return the medical personnel in his hands. While this may seem a relatively mild form of reprisals, the fact should not be overlooked that the immunity of the medical personnel was one of the key provisions already in the Convention of Geneva of 1864, as the certainty of their imprisonment had previously given cause to the abandonment of the wounded on the battlefield, or, equally injurious, their precipitate transportation.[12]

In the period under consideration, the issue of reprisals (and quasi-reprisals) against civilians was broached by the ICRC in the Tokyo project, in which it ventured to give more adequate rules for the treatment of enemy civilians in the territory of a belligerent or in territory occupied by it. This project, however, was introduced at a time when the political situation in Europe was no longer propitious. Probably for that very reason the project was only mildly progressive: as regards reprisals, a prohibition was proposed of such measures against enemy civilians in the territory of a belligerent; but with respect to the much more crucial issue of the condition of the population in occupied territory, the sole suggestion was to prohibit the killing or maltreatment of hostages, with the project remaining silent

[8] B. R. Canneman, *Represailles*, 1936, p. 77.
[9] *Op. cit.* n. 5, p. 72.
[10] *Ibid.*, p. 73.
[11] *Op. et loc. cit.* n. 4.
[12] *Cf.* P. Boissier, *Histoire du Comité international de la Croix-Rouge: De Solférino à Tsoushima*, 1963, p. 188 ff.

on the general aspects of retaliatory action on the side of the occupying Power. In the light of previous State practice the proposed rule as to hostages obviously was of eminent importance. It is submitted, however, that it would not have been too daring a step even then to propose a rule to the effect that all reprisals against the inhabitants of occupied territory would in view of their inhuman character be categorically prohibited.

As for the literature, while some authors did in fact reject all reprisals against an occupied population,[13] this was certainly not the majority view.[14] The majority opinion did not, however, necessarily include that putting hostages to death was also accepted as legitimate: indeed, while Vanzelow did accept that practice,[15] Hall for one considered that it was prohibited by usage.[16] And François also emphatically rejected the idea that the act of killing hostages would be justifiable: such a crude application of the principle of collective responsibility was not, he said, accepted even in the law of war.[17]

In this respect, mention should be made of the stand taken by the Commission of Responsibilities of the Conference of Paris, which in 1919 included the act of putting hostages to death among the acts which it considered as war crimes. This decision was apparently inspired by reports of large-scale hostage killings in the Balkans. As, however, the report of the Commission was not reasoned and in particular did not state whether decisive importance had been attributed to the probable disproportionality and, indeed, ruthlessness of the acts reported or to the mere fact that hostages had been killed, it cannot be considered to constitute sufficient authority to have dispelled all doubts which existed with respect to that specific issue.[18]

The other half of the issue of belligerent reprisals, viz., reprisals resorted to in the context of warfare proper, was taken up in the most express manner

[13] P. Fauchille, *Traité de droit international public*, Part II, 1921, p. 29; L. le Fur, *Précis de droit international public*, 3rd ed., 1937, p. 549.
[14] W. E. Hall, *A Treatise on International Law*, 8th ed. by A. Pearce Higgins, 1924, p. 90; A. Hold-Ferneck, *Lehrbuch des Völkerrechts*, Vol. II, 1932, p. 284; F. von Liszt, *Das Völkerrecht systematisch dargestellt*, 12th ed. by M. Fleischmann, 1925, p. 457; Oppenheim, *op.cit.* n. 6, pp. 353, 451, 463; E. C. Stowell, *International Law: A Restatement of Principles in Conformity with Actual Practice*, 1931, p. 519; E. Vanzelow, *Völkerrecht, Einführung in die Praxis der Staaten*, 1931, p. 240; Wheaton's *Elements of International Law*, 6th English ed. by A. Berriedale Keith, Vol. II, 1929, p. 810.
[15] *Loc. cit.* n. 14.
[16] *Op. cit.* n. 14, pp. 500, 565.
[17] *Op. cit.* n. 6, p. 359.
[18] Violation of the Laws and Customs of War: Report of Majority and Dissenting Reports of American and Japanese Members of the Commission of Responsibilities, Conference of Paris, 1919; published as Pamphlet N° 32 by the Carnegie Endowment for International Peace, Division of International Law.

by the Disarmament Conference of 1932-1934, in the framework of the discussion on the prohibition of the use of poisonous and asphyxiating gases, incendiary weapons and bacteriological means of warfare. The preference which was soon apparent for an absolute prohibition rather than one subject to reciprocity gave rise to questions not only of prevention (prohibition of preparation, supervision), but of repression as well (establishment of the fact of infringement, sanctions).

In the latter context the problem had to be faced whether the contemplated prohibition should and could imply a prohibition of retaliatory use in case of a breach on the part of the enemy. It appeared that a strong tendency was in favour of a ban on such retaliatory use as well, both on account of the inhuman character of any use of the weapons in question, even if this constituted an instance of retaliation in kind, and because the admission of a right to such reprisals would mean that States might be expected to prepare for such an eventuality, so that any attempt at outlawing peacetime preparations would be made largely illusory. On the other hand, however, the prohibition even of retaliation in kind could have the effect of depriving the victim State of what, according to some, was its most efficacious, and according to others even its only effective answer to the unlawful attack. At any rate, and whether reprisals were banned or not, it was realized that agreement upon a system of enforcement was absolutely essential to the effectiveness of the proposed ban on the means and weapons at issue.

At this point two questions had to be answered: ought special sanctions be introduced for the enforcement of this particular section of the draft convention, or would it be sufficiently protected by the general system of sanctions to be developed for the entire convention? Further: must a strict system of sanctions be introduced, automatically taking effect in the event of an established (or even an alleged) infringement, or was a system preferable that would leave the States free to decide according to circumstances? In point of fact, these questions boiled down to this: were the States or were they not prepared to agree to a really effective enforcement system? The answer to this question is implied in the outcome of the debate: while at times the solution of the issue seemed near, no agreement was ultimately obtained. The conclusion cannot therefore be avoided that in the final analysis the States taking part in the Conference shrank from committing themselves to definitive legal consequences being attached to the violation of the contemplated prohibition.

In this debate on sanctions the issue of reprisals occupied an important place. In this respect is was argued, either, that the envisaged adoption of other effective sanctions would make reprisals superfluous so that these could be banished, or that they ought to be retained, albeit limited by appropriate regulations and under strict control, as an integrated part of the system of sanctions. In the contest between these contrasting opinions

110

the balance was now in favour of the first, now of the other view, without a decisive advantage being obtained by either: in fact, towards the end of the Conference the discussions had resulted in a complete deadlock.

The proposal introduced by the British delegation at that juncture in the discussions amounted to a return to the classical conception: the prohibition against the use of the weapons concerned would be without reserve, but it would not be strengthened by any special and adequate sanctions; silence would also be maintained on the general problem of enforcement of the proposed prohibition, except for an express reference to the right, uncontrolled in principle, for the State to make use of the prohibited weapons for the purpose of retaliation.[19]

The British proposal was never put to the vote. Its reception was not however such as to suggest that it was in fact in accordance with the general opinion: indeed, the debate concerning the admissibility of reprisals was still completely open, and it was only the untimely breaking-off of the discussions which prevented its continuation. It may even be ventured to suggest that, in the supposition of a continued debate, the proposal of the British delegation would have stood the least chance of being accepted: the conviction was too strong that the means of warfare under discussion were inhuman to such a degree that their retaliatory use ought to be prohibited and could at most be tolerated under the most severe limitations and guarantees.

A final remark on the work of the Conference in this field is that the discussion, notwithstanding its ultimately negative result, was of great value for the development of the law of reprisals, owing to the thorough and deep-probing investigation, preceding the final failure, into the problems connected with the prohibition of reprisals in the sphere of warfare proper: for the first time it had been convincingly demonstrated that the issue was capable of being discussed on an international level. At the same time, however, it had become abundantly clear that any attempts to prohibit, or to restrict by regulation, the recourse to reprisals, in this field of the law of warfare proper like in that of the protection of war victims, are narrowly connected with—and indeed form an inseparable part of—the endeavours to effectuate an improved sanctions system of the law of war.

---

[19] "The real argument [*i.e.* in favour of the justification of reprisals] is practical rather than legal. It is that no belligerent can be compelled to fight at a disadvantage, and that if one belligerent disregards the restrictions of the law for his own ends it must be open to the other belligerent to claim the same freedom."—Sir Erle Richards, in defence of the methods of economic warfare at sea as applied by Great Britain in the First World War, as quoted by C. C. Hyde, *International Law chiefly as interpreted and applied by the United States*, Vol. II, 1922, p. 32.

In the light of the foregoing, there can be little doubt that the view was widely shared that reprisals, to the extent that they were not completely prohibited, must respect certain limits. One of these, the principle of proportionality, while not expressly confirmed in the governmental conferences of the period, was considered valid by a majority of the authors, generally in the form of a requirement of absence of obvious disproportionality.[20] Only few authors held a different view. Thus, according to Strupp a rule of proportionality to the act retaliated against would be desirable *de lege ferenda*, but it could not be considered to form part of positive international law.[21] Canneman went one step further, asserting that such a rule would even be inconsistent with the very character of reprisals, as it would deprive the States of the possibility effectively to maintain their rights in the face of opposition on the part of the adversary; the only proportionality which he was prepared to accept, was between the retaliatory act and the object which it aimed to achieve.[22]

In contrast with the requirement of proportionality, the principle of humanity was time and again invoked both in the Diplomatic Conference of 1929 and in the Disarmament Conference of 1932-1934. Does this lead to the conclusion that a rule had by that time found recognition to the effect that no act can be justified as a reprisal if it runs counter to the laws of humanity?

A number of authors did in fact assert that that was a valid rule of international law.[23] At the same time, however, the view was widespread that reprisals against the civilian population are permissible in principle:[24] a fundamentally different stand was only taken by Fauchille, according to whom there existed a rule prohibiting such reprisals irrespective of whether the original wrong had been committed by the military or by members of

[20] *E.g.*: G. Balladore Pallieri, *Diritto internazionale pubblico*, 2nd ed., 1938, p. 341; De la Brière, *op. cit.* n. 4, p. 270; Fauchille, *op. cit.* n. 13, p. 28; François, *op. cit.* n. 6, p. 304; Le Fur, *op. cit.* n. 5, pp. 33, 63; Hall, *op. cit.* n. 14, p. 436; T. E. Holland, *Lectures on International Law*, ed. 1933, p. 379; Von Liszt, *op. cit.* n. 14, p. 440; Oppenheim, *op. cit.* n. 6, p. 120; Spiropoulos, *op. cit.* n. 6, p. 289; Vanzelow, *op. cit.* n. 14, p. 85; Verdross, *op. cit.* n. 6, p. 279; Wheaton, *op. cit.* n. 14, pp. 622, 710.
[21] K. Strupp, "Das Repressalienrecht", in *Wörterbuch des Völkerrechts und der Diplomatie*, Vol. II, 1925, p. 351; the same view in *Grundzüge des positiven Völkerrechts*, 5th ed., 1932, p. 199. However, according to Strupp the issue was governed by the principle of *Treu und Glauben* which he considered to form part of international law.
[22] *Op. cit.* n. 8, p. 29 ff. *Cf.* also F. Castberg, *Folkerett*, 1937, p. 193; and Hold-Ferneck, *op. cit.* n. 14, p. 212.
[23] *E.g.*: Balladore Pallieri, *op. cit.* n. 20, p. 341; De la Brière, *op. cit.* n. 4, p. 267; Fauchille, *op. cit.* n. 13, p. 27; François, *op. cit.* n. 6, p. 359; Hold-Ferneck, *op. cit.* n. 14, p. 213; Holland, *op. cit.* n. 20, p. 379; Strupp, "Das Repressalienrecht", *op. cit.* n. 21, p. 351; Verdross, *op. cit.* n. 6, p. 299.
[24] A. Cavaglieri, *Corso di diritto internazionale*, 3rd ed., 1934, p. 553; C. G. Fenwick, *International Law*, 2nd ed., 1934, p. 496; Hall, *op. cit.* n. 14, pp. 90, 495; Vanzelow, *op. cit.* n. 14, p. 202.

the civil population.[25] This rule, posited by Fauchille as "une loi absolue", did not however prevent him from holding aerial bombardment of undefended towns under certain conditions justifiable as a reprisal.[26] Likewise, several other authors regarded such bombardments as justifiable retaliatory measures.[27] Spaight, while accepting this view as a correct statement of the law in force, added that *de lege ferenda* the prohibition of such reprisals was as urgently needed as was a strict regulation of air bombardment.[28]

The validity of a rule prohibiting reprisals in violation of the laws of humanity was categorically denied by a few authors, namely by Vanzelow (by implication)[29] and Canneman. The latter argued that the sole effective means to cope with an inhuman practice on the part of the adversary would be likewise to have recourse to such practices, and that moreover a prohibition of inhuman reprisals would leave the more unscrupulous belligerents at liberty to disregard the requirements of humanity, as their opponents would have been denied the remedy against their inhuman acts.[30]

A middle course, finally, was steered by an author like Le Fur, who held that the principle of humanity was not in itself decisive in every instance, but had to be balanced with the principle of justice requiring exemplary repression of illicit acts; in his view, however, the rules of moral law (as distinct from mere humanitarian rules) did in fact have absolute force.[31] Similarly, De la Brière held that not all reprisals against the non-combatant civil population were prohibited on account of their inhumanity, but only those violent and cruel acts affecting members of the population and notably women and children individually.[32] Such views, it may be added as a concluding remark, while less contradictory in themselves than the sweeping statements made by the first-mentioned category of authors, came

[25] *Op. cit.* n. 13, p. 28. A comparable view was expressed by Le Fur, *op. cit.* n. 5, p. 84 ff.

[26] *Op. cit.* n. 13, p. 618.

[27] Von Liszt, *op. cit.* n. 14, p. 457; Spiropoulos, *op. cit.* n. 6, p. 289; Spaight, see hereafter n. 28.

[28] J. M. Spaight, *Air Power and War Rights*, 2nd ed., 1933, p. 45. The following passage is especially illuminating: "In truth the question of reprisals and of the restriction of air bombardment are so closely interlocked that it is of little use to lay down rules regulating bombardment unless reprisals by air raids are banned, and it is of less use to prohibit such reprisals so long as the rules governing bombardment are so loose and unsatisfactory that they can be stretched to cover veiled reprisals."

[29] *Op. cit.* n. 14, p. 201: "Auf dem Wege der Kriegsrepressalie kann das ganze Kriegsrecht illusorisch gemacht werden, da es nicht rechtswidrig ist, auf dem Repressalienwege beliebige Rechtssätze im Verhältnis mit dem Gegner für unanwendbar zu erklären."

[30] *Op. cit.* n. 8, p. 33. The argument advanced by Renken, *op.cit.* n. 7, likewise amounted to a denial of the validity of the principle in question.

[31] *Op. cit.* n. 5, p. 65.

[32] *Op. cit.* n. 4, p. 265.

closest to the feelings prevalent in the governmental Conferences recorded in this Chapter: the declarations made there to the effect that reprisals against prisoners of war, or the retaliatory use of certain inhuman weapons, ought to be expressly prohibited because they ran counter to the principle of humanity, should in truth be understood as the recognition that on balance, and taking account of all the relevant facts, the inhumanity of the measures under consideration outweighed their possible usefulness as reprisals.

CHAPTER IV

Reprisals in the Second World War-I: British Reprisals Orders, 1939-1940

4.1. DESCRIPTION OF THE BRITISH MEASURES

Among the actions which in the course of the Second World War were qualified as "reprisals" by the respective belligerents, the Reprisals Orders issued in 1939 and 1940 by the British Government stand out both in duration and scope. They were moreover the first measures so described in that war.

They were resorted to at an early stage of the war, when the war on land could still be called the "phoney" war. The sea was, however, already the scene of operations that were far from "phoney". They were of two kinds: military engagements between the opposing naval and air forces, and economic warfare. The latter in particular was from the very outset a matter of primary concern to both Great Britain and Germany, which were concerned both to protect their own shipping interests and to damage those of the enemy.

4.1.1. *Orders in Council establishing control over enemy exports, November 1939-July 1940*

Among the rules of sea warfare which had developed in the past was the rule, embodied in the Declaration of Paris of 1856, that privately owned enemy exports were not as such subject to seizure. Exported goods, whether enemy- or neutral-owned, would no more be subject to seizure when carried in a neutral vessel than neutral-owned exports carried in an enemy merchantman. Although this rule was not in conformity with earlier British practice, the United Kingdom had in 1856 formally accepted it as a contribution to the establishment of "a uniform doctrine on so important a point" as "maritime law in time of war", which, if left undecided, would "[give] rise to differences of opinion between neutrals and belligerents which [might] occasion serious difficulties, and even conflicts".[1]

Great Britain had experienced considerable difficulty in living up to the

---

[1] Preamble to the Declaration of Paris of 1856 "establishing some Rules of Maritime Law in Times of War". *Cf.* C. John Colombos, *The International Law of the Sea*, 6th revised ed., 1967, p. 621.

new norm, which to British eyes was far from axiomatic. In the course of the First World War, the British Government had in 1917 felt impelled to derogate from it, justifying its step as retaliation for the unrestricted submarine warfare which Germany was waging.[2]

Nevertheless, the official standpoint had remained an unchanged adherence to the rules embodied in the Declaration of Paris. Thus, when another war with Germany became a serious possibility and preparations for such an event began to be made, it was taken as established that in principle privately-owned enemy exports carried in neutral ships would have to be left alone, no matter how great their importance to the enemy economy or however great the desire of those responsible for planning Britain's economic warfare to obtain some control over enemy exports. This situation would be altered only if the enemy, by his manner of conducting the war, gave cause for a resort to reprisals. In such circumstances it was envisaged that the reprisals might, once again, take the form of control over enemy exports. It was realized that such a measure would be subject to a twofold condition: it must be justifiable by the standards applied by the British Prize Courts, and neutral States must not be overly or inopportunely offended by the measure, which obviously could severely affect their interests.[3]

When war broke out in September 1939, the question was therefore whether Germany would act in contravention of the law of war to a degree sufficient to warrant the retaliatory establishment of control over enemy exports, and how the neutral States would react to such a measure if it were imposed.

According to the United Kingdom, Germany committed unlawful acts of war from the outset. At sea several instances of German sinkings of belligerent and neutral merchant vessels were reported; by 4 November, more than fifty ships had been reported sunk by enemy action.[4] It also became

---

[2] As regards these retaliatory measures, see, *e.g.*, Colombos, *op. cit.* n. 1, p. 738 ff.; Colbert, *Retaliation in International Law*, 1948, p. 168 ff.

[3] The history of these preparations as well as the subsequent conduct of economic warfare has found authoritative and detailed description in W. N. Medlicott, *The Economic Blockade*, Vol. I, 1952, and Vol. II, 1959. The work forms part of the History of the Second World War, United Kingdom Civil Series, edited by W. K. Hancock. With reference to the text above, see in particular Vol. I, pp. 16-40 and 112-113.

[4] A Committee, convened by the Ministry of Economic Warfare to examine the factual and legal aspects of the situation, reported on 14 November "that between the outbreak of war and 4th November, thirty-two British and three Allied ships had been sunk illegally and in some cases in circumstances of great inhumanity; as many as thirty-three neutral ships had been attacked and at least sixteen sunk in circumstances which led to the conclusion that the sinking had been illegal. Apart from other illegalities, the German policy appeared to have no regard to the nature, ownership, or destinations of the cargo. The report pointed out that the main consideration in applying reprisals was the importance attached in international law to

116

clear that, while part of these sinkings had been caused by enemy submarines, others were to be ascribed to mines, and in particular to magnetic mines, a type of mine unknown in 1907 when the Second Peace Conference adopted Hague Convention No. VIII "relative to the Laying of Automatic Submarine Contact Mines". These mines could be laid by aircraft as well as by ship and instances of this were reported.[5] All in all, "it became apparent early in November 1939 that the ruthless attacks on shipping would soon compel resort to retaliatory measures".[6]

In the period from 4 to 18 November, some six more merchant ships were sunk; and on the last-mentioned date the Dutch liner *Simon Bolivar* was sunk, apparently by a magnetic mine, some 14 miles off the English coast near Harwich.[7] These events finally clinched matters: the next day the Minister of Economic Warfare sent a recommendation to the War Cabinet that action should be taken.[8] It did not take the War Cabinet long to decide: on 21 November the Prime Minister, Mr. Chamberlain, announced in the House of Commons that the Government had decided to impose export control in retaliation to the German methods, and that an Order in Council to that effect would be issued shortly.[9, 10]

---

the frequency, as well as to the enormity, of the original wrongs in considering the reasonableness of injuries to be inflicted on neutrals as a result of reprisals. This had been brought out clearly in the judgment of the Privy Council in the *Stigstad* case during the 1914-18 war."—Medlicott I, p. 113.

[5] *Cf.* also S. W. Roskill, *The War at Sea, 1939-1945*, Vol. I, p. 98 ff. The book is part of the History of the Second World War, United Kingdom Military Series.

[6] *Loc. cit.* n. 4.

[7] The Netherlands Government, in notes to the German and British Ministers for Foreign Affairs of 19 and 21 December 1939, respectively, protested against the sinking and against the indiscriminate use of mines which was apparent from this and similar instances, and it reserved its rights regarding the damage done. The notes, together with the answers received and further notes sent, were published in April 1940 by the Netherlands Government in *Overzicht van de voornaamste in verband met den oorlogstoestand door het ministerie van buitenlandse zaken behandelde en voor openbaarmaking geschikte aangelegenheden* (i.e., Survey of the most important affairs dealt with by the Foreign Ministry in connection with the state of war and suitable for publication).

[8] Medlicott I, *loc. cit.* n. 4.

[9] Parliamentary Debates, 353 H.C. DEB. 55, col. 1033/4: House of Commons, 21 November 1939.

[10] Retaliation by export control was not the only method considered: in *The Second World War*, Vol. I (*The Gathering Storm*), pp. 456-458, Winston Churchill relates that on 19 November he had sent notes to his colleagues in the War Cabinet concerning a retaliatory action with fluvial mines against the traffic on the Rhine. According to his account, "The War Cabinet liked this plan. It seemed to them only right and proper that when the Germans were using the magnetic mine to waylay and destroy all traffic, Allied or neutral, entering British ports we should strike back by paralyzing, as we might well do, the whole of their vast traffic on the Rhine." It is worth noting that Churchill does not make any reference to the measure of export

Even before the Order in Council was actually issued, a number of neutral Governments had protested.[11] Notwithstanding this, the Order was duly issued on 27 November 1939.[12], [13] It did not come into effect immediately: control of German exports would commence with respect to merchant vessels leaving port after 4 December 1939. Ships sailing from enemy ports (including ports in territory under enemy occupation or control) would "be required to discharge in a British or Allied port any goods on board laden in such enemy port" (Art. 1), and ships sailing from other ports would be required to discharge, again in a British or Allied port, goods of enemy origin or which were enemy property (Art. 2). The implication was that all enemy exports, whether carried directly from enemy ports or, after transportation, from neutral ports, would be liable to seizure. Evidently the interests that would be directly hurt by the measure were, besides the interests of the German *Reich*, those of neutral shipping.

The Order in Council also gave indications regarding the fate of goods discharged (Art. 3): these would be detained under the auspices of the Prize Court, or sold and the proceeds paid into Court; but provision was also made for the requisitioning of goods. On the conclusion of peace the goods detained or their proceeds would "be dealt with in such a manner as the Court [might] in the circumstances deem just"; however, release of goods or payment out of Court of proceeds would be possible at any time, "(*a*) if it be shown to the satisfaction of the Court that the goods had become neutral property before the date of this order, or (*b*) with the consent of the

---

control, which, in contradistinction to the Rhine minelaying operation proposed by him, had actually been accepted by the War Cabinet.

[11] *The Times,* 23 November: Dutch protest; 27 November: survey of the representations made by neutral ambassadors and Governments. The Dutch protest, together with the British reply and the further Dutch note on the subject, have been published in the survey referred to in n. 7. See also hereafter, p. 142.

[12] Order in Council Restricting Further the Commerce of Germany, S.R. & O. 1939 n° 1709. On the same date, the French authorities, acting in concert with the British Ministry of Economic Warfare, issued a similar order: *Décret concernant l'embargo sur les exportations allemandes,* published in the *Journal Officiel* of 27 November 1939.

[13] In the House of Commons, in the Debate on the Address of 28 November 1939, the Under-Secretary of State for Foreign Affairs, Mr. Butler, delivered the following statement: "We are, of course, in receipt of evidence of the extent to which neutral interests have felt themselves threatened by this new Order-in-Council. Such protests as we have received are now being given the close attention of my Noble Friend. We have also had ample evidence of the desire of the neutrals to understand the reasons for our decision and to appreciate the radical difference between the German policy and our own. It has, after all, been the German method to sink by every illegal means British and other ships around our coasts. But we shall continue to use the normal method of search and examination which we have already applied in the exercise of our contraband control. I feel sure that neutral Governments recognize this vital difference between our actions and those of the German Government."—355 H.C. DEB. 55 col. 305/6.

118

proper officer of the Crown". While the exception provided under *a* was limited in time, appeals under *b* were obviously apt to be numerous.

Also after the issue of the Order some neutral Governments commented unfavourably on the British measure,[14] and the German Government made known its opinion that the establishment of export control was a clear breach of international law and of the Declaration of Paris in particular, and reserved the right to take counter-measures.[15]

The Order was put into effect only gradually, and control was not too effective in the beginning. Nevertheless, bitter complaints were raised by neutral exporters who saw important interests threatened; in the meantime, however, they accommodated themselves to the new situation and took care to ship only such goods as were covered by certificates of origin or export passes issued by British or Allied consular officers. As for the reaction of neutral Governments, "[i]n spite of [the] diplomatic protests there were no serious attempts by neutral governments to force the Allies to abandon the control; there were, however, continued and vain attempts to evade it".[16] Thus, the conclusion seems justified that the measure had not offended the friendly neutrals to such a degree as to endanger the political, and in particular the economic, relations between those States and Great Britain. As for the not so friendly neutrals, foremost among which were Italy and Japan, it is improbable that the Reprisals Order of November 1939 had any material influence on their ultimate decision to join the enemy.[17]

On the other hand, the Order proved a fairly effective measure of economic warfare: in April 1940 it was estimated by the Director-General of the Ministry of Economic Warfare "that German overseas export trade had probably been reduced by eighty per cent. of its normal value"; he added that in his opinion it would be "a mistake to press for 100 per cent. completeness of control if this would create a disproportionate loss of goodwill in neutral countries". The latter problem soon lost most of its significance, however, when Germany successively occupied Denmark, Norway, The Netherlands, Belgium and the greater part of France, and Italy entered into the war on the side of Germany: by June 1940, the issue of the control of enemy exports *via* neutral States on the European continent had virtually ceased to exist.[18]

---

[14] U.S. Department of State Bulletin, 1939, p. 651: text of the note of protest delivered on 8 December 1939. Cmd. 6191, 1940: Correspondence between the Italian and British Governments, commencing with an Italian note dated 3 March 1940.
[15] *The Times*, 30 November 1939.
[16] Medlicott I, p. 118 ff.; the quoted text is on p. 121.
[17] This nothwithstanding the statement in para. 9 of the Italian note of protest of 3 March 1940, that "the measure taken by the British Government [was] calculated to disturb and compromise the economic and political relations between Italy and Great Britain, as established by the agreements of the 16th April, 1938". Cmd. 6191, 1940.
[18] Medlicott I, p. 121 ff.; the quoted text is on p. 124.

As related above, another condition which in the opinion of the Ministry of Economic Warfare a reprisals order establishing export control had to fulfil, was that it must be justified according to the standards set by the British Prize Courts. It is noteworthy that not a single reference to the Reprisals Order of 1939 has been found in the published judgments of Prize Courts. In part this was probably because during the war demands for the release of goods were dealt with not by the Prize Courts, but by the Enemy Exports Committee or (when political questions were involved) the Exemptions Committee.[19] Also, the Reprisals Order may have been deemed so unassailable before a British Prize Court that no interested party thought it worth while to raise the issue of its justification.[20]

The entry into the war of Italy, in June 1940, necessitated the extension of the Reprisals Order to that State: otherwise a gap would arise in the system of enemy export control, as Italy was neither neutral nor under German occupation. The British Government did not hesitate long: by Order in Council of 11 June 1940 the régime established by the Order of November 1939 was declared applicable to the commerce of Italy as well.[21] The grounds for this retaliatory measure were found, not in any illegalities committed by Italy itself, but in that the illegalities by Germany had not ceased and evidently were part of its settled method of waging war, and that Italy by associating itself with Germany had made itself a party to the methods applied by that State.[22]

Another gap in the system was filled in July 1940: an Order in Council of 17 July extended the scope of the original Order of November 1939 to goods transported by civil aircraft.[23]

---

[19] *Ibid.*, p. 115; the Enemy Exports Committee, "under the chairmanship of Lord Justice Du Parcq, included representatives of the Foreign Office, Admiralty, Board of Trade, Colonial Office, Ministry of Shipping, the Procurator-General, the French Mission, and the Prize, Legal, Intelligence, Financial Pressure, and Foreign Relations Departments of the Ministry" (of Economic Warfare); the Exemptions Committee "had a membership broadly the same as that of the Enemy Exports Committee".

[20] "The basis on which the legality of retaliatory orders rests before the Prize Courts, namely, that they should not impose on neutrals more inconvenience or prejudice than is reasonably necessary, does not in practice afford adequate protection. Prize Courts are bound by the recitals in the Order enforcing reprisals, and those recitals are certain to allege a case sufficient to justify any action they enjoin."—C. John Colombos, *A Treatise on the Law of Prize*, 2nd ed., 1940, p. 256.

[21] Order in Council applying the Order in Council of November 27, 1939, to Italy; S.R. & O. 1940 n° 979.

[22] A similar Order in Council was issued upon the entry into the war of Japan: Order of 12 December 1941, S.R. & O. 1941 n° 2136. Later, the system was extended to Finland, Hungary, Rumania and Bulgaria: Order of 22 January 1942, S.R. & O. 1942 n° 482.

[23] Order in Council as to Aircraft and Goods Carried Therein; S.R. & O. 1940 n° 1324.

4.1.2. *Order in Council establishing Compulsory Navicerting,*
31 July 1940

While the Orders in Council referred to so far had as their main objective the control of enemy exports, another, and even the primary, target of economic warfare consisted in imports from overseas that might reach the enemy either directly or through neutral countries. In order to prevent such imports, the British and Allied fleets were from the beginning of the war charged with intercepting ships at sea and sending them into the ports that had been appointed as contraband bases: there, and not on the high seas, the ships and their cargoes were inspected and, either, released, or seized as prize.[24]

The effectiveness of this control system could be significantly increased, however, by shifting its centre of gravity to the source of the goods shipped, that is, to the neutral ports of lading. To that end, the system of navicerts was introduced in December 1939: the consular authorities in the neutral countries were authorized to issue certificates stating that, according to the available information, the certified goods did not have an enemy destination (cargo navicerts) or the ships did not carry any goods with enemy destination (ship navicerts). Navicerts were not however made compulsory: while ships sailing without such documents risked the inconvenience of being detained at the contraband bases until sufficient information had been gathered, and while the absence of the documents might add to any suspicion as to the ultimate destination of their cargoes, the ships did not on this sole ground run the risk of being seized in prize. It was realized at the time that navicerting, in order to be really effective, must be universal and therefore compulsory; but for the time being American opposition stood in the way of achieving that objective.[25]

After the Chiefs of Staff Committee had pointed out as early as June 1940 in a note to the War Cabinet the necessity of increased control at source, the Minister of Economic Warfare on 13 July laid a memorandum before the War Cabinet proposing that navicerts should be made compulsory. The Minister was aware that this use of the navicert system was unprecedented, but he was "glad to say that the Attorney-General, the Procurator-General, and [his] own legal adviser [were] agreed that, in present circumstances, the new system can be justified". What was more, it had meanwhile become clear that the American opposition to the system had turned into support on the part of the State Department. Thus, it seemed that both conditions for a new measure were once again fulfilled: justification before the Prize Courts, and probable acquiescence on the part of the most powerful friendly neutral. Hence, the proposed system that

---

[24] *Cf.* Roskill, *op. cit.* n. 5, p. 43.
[25] Medlicott I, p. 431.

121

same day received the approval in principle of the War Cabinet.[26], [27]

The details of the navicert scheme were now elaborated. The intention was that navicerts would be compulsory not only for cargoes but for ships as well: in the last port of lading the ship would have to acquire a certificate stating that it did not carry unnavicerted cargo. A merchant ship sailing in European waters without being covered by a ship navicert would be liable to seizure in prize. The State Department was informed of the scheme, and on 29 July the British Ambassador reported that "their attitude was co-operative, and 'while not disposed to issue direct instructions to American shipowners that they should not sail without a ship navicert, the State Department are eividently concerned that none should in practice do so'." [28] The way was now clear for an announcement of the new rules: on 30 July the Ministers of Economic warfare and of Shipping explained the decisions taken to the House of Commons, and on 31 July the new Reprisals Order in Council was published.[29]

The aim of the Order was to achieve control both of enemy import and export ("enemy" again being taken to comprise territory under enemy occupation or control; Art. 1); in so far as exports were concerned, the Order built on the principle of export control established in the November Order and subsequent Orders, dealt with above. So as to realize the

---

[26] *Ibid.*, pp. 431-432. The proposal included also that the few remaining neutrals on the European continent, and in particular Spain and Portugal, should be rationed.

[27] Another proposal originated from the Admiralty. Even under the proposed system of compulsory navicerting (resulting in the liability of ships and cargoes to be seized in prize when not covered by navicerts), control on the high seas would still be necessary to catch ships attempting to run the blockade. As the number of warships available for the exercise of control was limited and as considerable danger threatened the warships involved in the performance of that task, the Admiralty proposed that the control would be given a stronger deterrent character by the establishment of a war zone off the west coast of Europe and the north-west of Africa, extending to some 300 miles west of the coasts (the range of the German dive-bombers), and within which merchant ships without navicerts would be liable to be sunk.

With respect to this Admiralty proposal the legal advisers to the Ministry of Economic Warfare and the Foreign Office pointed out that "a plain announcement that ships without navicerts would be liable to be sunk would not be justified under existing principles or any admissible extension of these". The advisers offered an apt solution, however: "If it were announced that ships without navicerts 'would be liable after seizure to be sent in or sunk according to circumstances', this would not necessarily involve action outside international law." But the report continues: "The War Cabinet decided, however, on 23rd July, that the Royal Navy should not adopt a policy of sinking neutral vessels. It was agreed, on the other hand, that the area in question should be declared a war zone, and that the Ministers of Economic Warfare and Shipping should announce respectively the forthcoming adoption of compulsory ship navicerts and ship warrants."—Medlicott I, pp. 433-434.

[28] *Ibid.*, p. 434.

[29] *Ibid.*, pp. 434-436. Order in Council Regulating a System of Passes for Approved Cargoes and Ships, S.R. & O. 1940 n° 1436.

objective of the new Order, passes were made compulsory for ships and goods alike: "any vessel on her way to or from a port through which goods might reach or come from enemy territory or the enemy armed forces" must be provided with a valid ship navicert; "goods consigned to any port or place from which they might reach enemy territory or the enemy armed forces" must be covered by a valid cargo navicert, and "goods shipped from any port from which goods of enemy origin or ownership might have been shipped" by a valid certificate of origin and interest. In case of lack or invalidity of any of the required certificates, the sanction was that the goods would "be deemed to have an enemy destination" or "to be of enemy origin or ownership", respectively, while the ship would "be deemed to be carrying contraband or goods of enemy origin or ownership", all this "until the contrary is established" (Arts. 2, 3).

If the interested party failed to produce sufficient counter-evidence and thus refute the presumption against him, the consequences would be as follows: goods "of enemy origin or ownership" as well as the vessel carrying these would be liable to condemnation (Arts. 4, 5). Goods having "an enemy destination" might be contraband or otherwise; when contraband (as would be the normal case), the vessel would be liable to condemnation (Art. 5; no special provision was made for the goods, but their liability to condemnation followed from the general rules of prize law); with respect to goods not constituting contraband and the vessels carrying these, the Order was silent: here, too, the general rules and practices could be supposed to be applicable [30] (no condemnation, probably requisitioning as far as the goods were concerned).

Evidently the presence of a certificate, whether ship or cargo navicert or certificate of origin and interest, was not sufficient guarantee against seizure and condemnation: the certificate must be "valid", and navicerts in particular were so framed as to lose their validity on non-observance of any condition or directive to which the documents were subject (Art. 6; a condition specifically made in the Article was that vessels after obtaining a ship navicert must not call "at an enemy port or (unless otherwise indicated in the Navicert) at any other port than a declared port of destination").

The Order, finally, would only be applicable to those ships leaving their last port of departure on or after 1 August, "on [their] way to or from a port through which goods might reach or come from enemy territory or the enemy armed forces", and to the goods carried by such ships (Art. 7).

All in all, the Order meant a further decisive step towards the control of enemy import and export. Its most striking feature was that in respect of goods and vessels coming under the Order presumption replaced the showing of reasonable suspicion whenever the certificates required were lacking or invalid. According to previous practice in the British Prize

[30] But see hereafter, pp. 145-146.

Courts with respect to contraband, it was incumbent upon the captor to show that there was reasonable suspicion that goods being of their nature contraband were destined for the enemy country, and that goods being of their nature conditional contraband were destined for the enemy Government or armed forces; the goods would be condemned when in the eyes of the Court the evidence was sufficient to uphold the suspicion. If the interested neutral party wished to prevent condemnation, it was incumbent upon that party "to show that there was no reasonable suspicion justifying the measure, or to displace such reasonable suspicion as in fact exist[ed]".[31] The effect of the Order, with respect to enemy imports and exports alike, was that whenever the required certificates were lacking or invalid the captor need not even show the existence of reasonable suspicion as to actual destination, origin or ownership of the goods concerned, and neither need the Court be convinced of the existence of such reasonable suspicion: the reasonable (that is: well-founded) suspicion as to actual destination, origin or ownership of the goods themselves was replaced by the presumption that goods "consigned to any port or place from which they *might* reach enemy territory or the enemy armed forces" did in fact have an enemy destination; that goods "shipped from any port from which goods of enemy origin or ownership *might* have been shipped" actually were of enemy origin or ownership, and that vessels on their way "to or from a port through which goods *might* reach or come from enemy territory or the enemy armed forces" were indeed carrying contraband or enemy export goods, all this failing evidence to the contrary.

A further point was of special interest for enemy exports. While the original exports Order in Council of November 1939 had been vague as to the ultimate fate of goods discharged under it (on the conclusion of peace, the goods or their proceeds would be dealt with by the Prize Court "in such a manner as the Court may in the circumstances deem just"), it was now expressly provided that goods "of enemy origin or ownership" (being goods not covered by a valid certificate of origin and interest and not exonerated by sufficient evidence disproving the presumption against them) would be liable to condemnation.

Indeed, under the new Order in Council of 31 July 1940 the position of uncertified ships and goods had become so disadvantageous that it could truly be said that ship and cargo navicerts and certificates of origin and ownership had been made compulsory. Notwithstanding this, the issue and subsequent application of the Order did not cause any political difficulties in the relations between Great Britain and the neutral States. The effects of the Order on neutral trade were, however, by no means negligible;[32] in

---

[31] Judicial Committee of the Privy Council (in Prize), in the *Louisiana*, 1 February 1918, 5 Ll.P.C. 248 at p. 252.

[32] "The introduction of the 'compulsory' navicert system made possible the establishment of a much tighter control. ... European neutrals were strictly rationed in the

fact, it had such a strong deterrent character that relatively little room was left for enforcement. This is evidenced, *inter alia*, by the almost complete lack of references to the Order in the prize proceedings reported so far. Actually, only two cases have been published in which the Order was so much as referred to by the Judicial Committee of the Privy Council (in Prize).[33] Both times, the reference merely served to show that the decision was not founded on the Order and that, hence, "Their Lordships [need not] consider questions which might be raised as to the validity and effect of the Order in Council"; [34] both cases were concerned with probable contraband, shipped from one Spanish port and consigned to another Spanish port, and in both cases the classical method of reasonable suspicion of enemy destination was employed.[35]

---

more important commodities and quotas were fixed for quarterly periods. When these quotas were filled or the ration for the particular period was 'nil', navicerts were refused. They would also be refused if any suspicion attached to the consigner, consignee or forwarding agent, or if the applicant or consignee were on the Statutory List. . . . Navicerts for non-contraband goods which were known, or suspected, to have enemy destination were refused and the goods were therefore rarely shipped, as shipping companies would not risk incurring the penalties which would result from their carrying unnavicerted cargo."—Medlicott I, p. 437. This statement does not bear out the opinion expressed by Fitzmaurice that already prior to the issue of the Order of 31 July 1940 the navicert system had by the voluntary co-operation of neutral shippers become "general for all shipments to European destinations" and that the new system really was instituted in the best interests of neutral traders themselves, so as to protect them from the perils involved in "the process of intercepting vessels and diverting them into port for contraband control"; G. G. Fitzmaurice, "Some Aspects of Modern Contraband Control and the Law of Prize", in *BYIL*, Vol. XXII, 1945, p. 73, at pp. 85-86.

[33] The *Monte Contes*, 22 July 1943, 1 Ll.P.C. (2nd) 147, concerning a shipment of tinned sardines in the Spanish steamship *Monte Contes* from Vigo (Spain) and consigned to Barcelona; the cargo had been held to be open to suspicion of enemy destination and condemned as contraband by the Gibraltar Prize Court, and on appeal the decree of condemnation was upheld.

The *Sidi Ifni*, 30 May 1945, 1 Ll.P.C. (2nd) 200, concerning a cargo of lemons carried in the Spanish steamship *Sidi Ifni* from Malaga and consigned to Valencia; this time, both the vessel and the cargo had been condemned by the Gibraltar Prize Court, and on appeal by the shipowners the decree concerning the vessel was upheld as the facts provided reasonable ground for the suspicion of enemy destination of the cargo and, as regards the shipowners, of knowledge on their part.

[34] The *Monte Contes*, *loc. cit.* n. 33, at p. 151.

[35] According to Rowson, the rules contained in the Order of 31 July 1940 were procedural rather than substantive in character. That author therefore doubts "whether the doctrine of retaliation constitutes a proper basis of the Order": in his eyes, "[a] more adequate foundation seems to be the inherent right of every state to issue legislation governing the procedure of its own prize courts."—S. W. D. Rowson, "Prize Law during the Second World War", in *BYIL*, Vol. XXIV. 1947, p. 160, at p. 197. However, far from being mainly of procedural concern to British Prize Courts, the Order unmistakably was primarily substantive in character and materially contributed to the further perfection of the system preventing the shipment of undesirable cargoes

This record of the factual aspects of the Reprisals Orders in Council of 27 November 1939 and subsequent dates establishing enemy export control, and of 31 July 1940 establishing compulsory navicerting, should not be concluded without once again emphasizing that the measures contained in these Orders formed part of an intricate system of actions and measures which together constituted the "economic blockade" of Germany and its allies. For this blockade as a whole the same conclusion applies as was arrived at with respect to the specific measures examined in the present section: it proved a fairly effective means of doing damage to the enemy cause. In the words of Medlicott: [36]

> "At no stage of the war was Germany decisively weakened by short-ages due to the blockade alone. That it was not a negligible factor in the Allied war effort is equally certain."

4.2. LEGAL ASPECTS OF THE GERMAN CONDUCT OF WARFARE, 1939-1940

When, after the above account of the factual aspects of the British Reprisals Orders, the question is posed of whether the measures embodied in the Orders did in fact constitute justifiable measures of reprisal, one must first answer the specific point whether the British authorities had been right in assuming that the enemy had by his conduct of warfare given occasion to a recourse to reprisals. In this section an attempt shall be made to answer this question for the successive orders concerned.

4.2.1. German actions prior to the Order in Council of 27 November 1939

In the preamble to the Order in Council of 27 November 1939, the British authorities gave a list of the charges against Germany which in their eyes warranted a recourse to reprisals.[1] According to the legal issues involved,

---

in neutral vessels. In so doing, it significantly affected the interests not only of neutral shipping and trade, but of the enemy first of all.

[36] Medlicott II, p. 631. The author goes on to analyze the effects of the blockade on German strategy, on civilian morale (an effect which he does not want to overrate), on transport and manpower, and on German political influence in Europe; and he concludes (p. 633): "Undoubtedly the most important result of the blockade was the automatic and almost complete severance of Germany's contacts with the overseas market, a severance which was achieved in the first weeks of war and which continued to the end. Of the remaining links, that through Vladivostok ended in June 1941 and through Marseilles in November 1942. After November 1939 her export trade was also prohibited, and had been reduced by 80 per cent. of its normal value within a few months."

[1] "... whereas German forces have in numerous cases sunk merchant vessels, British,

these charges can be classed under the following heads: the sinking by
German forces and especially by submarines of belligerent merchant vessels,
the sinking by such forces of neutral merchant vessels, and the indiscriminate use of mines.

The issue of the sinking of belligerent merchantmen was, like that of the
sinking of neutral traders, governed in principle by the Protocol of London
of 1936, which provides that submarines operating against merchant ships
must conform to the rules of international law to which surface vessels are
subject, and in particular to that prohibiting the sinking of such vessels
save in certain well-defined factual situations.

It is an established fact, however, that the position of the belligerent (and
in practice this meant the British) merchant vessels in the period under
consideration was peculiar. The ships had even prior to the outbreak of the
Second World War been placed under the control of the Admiralty, and
they were at the earliest possible moment equipped with guns [2] and in some
instances even with depth charges.[3] Moreover, the attitude of British
merchant vessels towards enemy submarines was from the outset hostile
and even aggressive, rather than non-combatant and defensive: not only
were the ships required to report the nature and position of any enemy
sighted and did the Defence of Merchant Shipping Handbook of 1938
provide that "[n]o British merchant vessel should ever tamely surrender to
a submarine, but should do her utmost to escape"; but if a surfaced submarine clearly intended to effect a capture and were to approach so close
as to endanger the chances of escape, the merchant vessel was to open fire
to keep it at a distance. And if the enemy were known to torpedo ships
without warning, a merchant vessel sighting the periscope of a submerged
submarine would, on the assumption that the submarine was attacking with

Allied, and neutral, in violation of the rules contained in the Submarine Protocol,
1936, to which Germany is a party:
"And whereas merchant vessels, British, Allied, and neutral, have been sunk by mines
laid by German forces indiscriminately and without notification, in contravention of
the obligations of humanity and the provisions of the Hague Convention No. VIII of
1907 to which Germany is a party:
"And whereas the sinking of these vessels has been effected without regard to their
nationality or destination or to the nature, ownership or destination of their cargoes:
"And whereas these acts have already resulted in grave loss of non-combatant life,
British, Allied and neutral:
"And whereas it is manifest that the German Government have deliberately embarked
on a policy of endeavouring to destroy all seaborne trade between the Allied and
other countries by a ruthless use of the forces at their disposal, contrary to the laws
and customs of war, the rights of neutrals and the obligations of humanity" (etc.).
[2] As Churchill has it: "The men of the Merchant Navy faced the unknown future with
determination. Not content with a passive rôle, they demanded weapons." Op. cit.
n. 10 to § 4.1; and see Roskill, op. cit. n. 5 to § 4.1, p. 21 ff.
[3] Note dated 14 September 1939 of the Director of Trade Division of the Admiralty;
see: I.M.T. Vol. XL, p. 91 (in Document Dönitz-67).

torpedoes, have to increase to full speed and, if the periscope were sighted before the beam, turn towards the periscope,—in other words, attempt to ram the submarine.[4] In fact, the Admiralty announced on 1 October 1939 that British merchant vessels had been ordered to ram submarines if possible;[5] but even before that date, instances had become known in Germany of attacks made by armed merchantmen on German submarines.[6]

Churchill describes the effects of the British practice in the following words:[7]

> "To force the U-boat to attack submerged and not merely by gunfire on the surface not only gave a greater chance for a ship to escape, but caused the attacker to expend his precious torpedoes more lavishly and often fruitlessly."

Quite so; but nothing in this language betrays that merchant vessels and not warships were the actors. Indeed, it is fairly evident—and the British authorities must have been aware [8]—that the protection of merchant vessels provided in the Protocol of London of 1936 could not extend to such warshiplike merchantmen and that the German submarines could not reasonably be expected to attempt to stop and capture the ships without the use of force. Thus, in so far as belligerent merchant vessels were concerned, no charge of illegal conduct could be raised against the German submarines when under an order of the Naval Operations Staff of 4 October 1939 [9] they started sinking these ships at sight.[10]

The situation was different as concerned neutral merchant vessels: in the period under consideration, these ships generally took care to avoid such modes of acting as might constitute a violation of their neutral position (such as: actively resisting capture, reporting the position of warships, or seeking the protection of belligerent escorts). In consequence, there was no valid ground to abandon radically the rules protecting neutral vessels sailing on the high seas against arbitrary acts of belligerents and in particular

---

[4] Defence of Merchant Shipping Handbook, 1938; I.M.T. Vol. XL, pp. 88-90.

[5] I.M.T. Vol. XXII p. 558: Judgment dealing with Dönitz.

[6] Note of a discussion held on 25 September 1939 by representatives, *inter alia*, of the German Foreign Office and the supreme command of the navy; Doc. 852-D, I.M.T. Vol. XXXV p. 548 at p. 550.

[7] *Op. et loc. cit.* n. 2.

[8] The Deputy Chief Prosecutor for the United Kingdom of Great Britain and Northern Ireland, Sir David Maxwell-Fyfe, can hardly have been serious when in cross-examining Dönitz he put this question to the defendant: "Why didn't you give these ships the opportunity of abstaining from resistance or of stopping?"—I.M.T. Vol. XIII p. 361.

[9] I.M.T. Vol. XL p. 86, Doc. Dönitz-65.

[10] "In the actual circumstances of this case, the Tribunal is not prepared to hold Dönitz guilty for his conduct of submarine warfare against British armed merchant ships."—I.M.T., Judgment, *loc. cit.* n. 5. And see the detailed and thorough exposition of this theme in the Final Pleading of Counsel for Defendant Dönitz, Kranzbühler; I.M.T. Vol. XVIII pp. 314-323.

against unjustified sinkings. In this light, the question is particularly important whether, and, if so, to what extent, the German submarines had infringed these rules prior to the issue of the Order in Council of 27 November 1939.[11]

This question was discussed at some length in the Nuremberg trial of the major German war criminals and of Dönitz in particular. In the assertion of the prosecution, "[f]rom the very early days of the war, merchant ships, both Allied and neutral, were sunk without warning";[12] and it was moreover suggested that the Germans had at first attempted to conceal this mode of conducting warfare at sea by restricting it to those areas "where there was a reasonable prospect of being able to do so without discovery",[13] that is, where the real cause of the sinking (either mine or submarine) might remain undetected. The prosecution sought to corroborate its thesis by producing a British Foreign Office report of October 1940 containing facts and figures about losses in the first year of the war, and which concluded that notwithstanding incompleteness of available information "it [was] possible to say that a 'prima facie' case of illegality might be made out in at least fifty cases of attacks by submarines" for that period; that the illegal sinkings had started on 30 September 1939 (the Danish vessel *Vendia*), and that "[by] November submarines were beginning to sink neutral vessels without warning as a regular thing".[14]

The defence interpreted these facts differently. As regards the *Vendia*, it was maintained "that this ship was stopped in a regular way and was torpedoed and sunk only when it prepared to ram the German submarine".[15] And more in general the thesis of counsel for the defence was that prior to January 1940 German submarines had been empowered to attack without warning only those neutral merchant vessels "which conducted themselves in a suspicious or hostile manner", being, "above all, those vessels which sailed blacked-out in the war area".[16] The order to attack blacked-out ships had been issued first for the Channel area;[17] next,

---

[11] Another question is obviously whether such infringements, if established, gave Great Britain a right of retaliation. That question is examined below in this sub-section, at p. 138.

[12] Presentation of Prosecution's Case against Dönitz; I.M.T. Vol. V, p. 208.

[13] *Ibid.*, p. 215.

[14] Doc. 641-D; I.M.T. Vol. XXXV, pp. 247-248.

[15] Final Pleading, I.M.T. Vol. XVIII, p. 326. The defence relied on the war diary of the *U 3*, being the submarine which had sunk the *Vendia*; Doc. Dönitz-83, I.M.T. Vol. XL, pp. 95-96.

[16] Final Pleading, *loc. cit.* n. 15.

[17] In a note of the Naval Operations Staff of 22 September 1939, concerning the request by the commanding officer submarines (Dönitz) to be permitted to sink without warning vessels which would be blacked out or which would take up radio communications after having been stopped by a submarine, it is stated that: "Inzwischen haben die U-Boote im englischen Kanal die Weisung enthalten, alle abgeblendeten

on 2 October it had been extended to cover a wide zone around the British coast;[18] however, already towards the end of September the neutrals had been informed of the risks involved in any suspicious conduct on the part of neutral vessels, "such as changes in course and the use of wireless upon sighting German naval forces, blacking out, noncompliance with the request to stop, *et cetera*".[19] This led the defence to the following conclusion:[20]

> "If therefore, as a result of suspicious or hostile conduct, neutral ships were treated like enemy ships, they [had] only themselves to blame for it. The German submarines were not allowed to attack any one who as a neutral maintained a correct attitude during the war, and there are hundreds of examples to prove that such attacks never did occur."

As regards the practice of carrying out attacks without warning in areas "where there was a reasonable prospect of being able to do so without discovery", the defence showed that this policy had only been followed in the period between January and August 1940 and then only in specially defined operational areas off the British coast, which did not form the whole of the danger area notified on 24 November 1939.[21] Thus, this practice, whether legitimate or otherwise, had at any rate occurred only after the issue of the Order in Council of 27 November 1939.

The Tribunal, it should be mentioned, did not pronounce on the legality or illegality of the various German actions against neutral merchant vessels in the period prior to 27 November.

For an evaluation of the events it is of particular interest to note that the

---

Fahrzeuge anzugreifen. Diese Weisung ist vom Ob.d.M. [the supreme command of the navy] am 21.9 gebilligt." Doc. 191-C, I.M.T. Vol. XXXIV, p. 777.

[18] As was related in the note referred to in n. 17, the commanding officer submarines had requested permission to sink blacked-out ships "im Gebiet nördlich der Breite 48°30′ N (Brest), östlich der Länge 20° W und westlich der Länge 3° Ost; also einschl. Kanalgebiet. Im Norden ist das Gebiet durch die Breite 62° N (Faroer) zu begrenzen." In the presentation of documents, counsel for the defendant Dönitz, Kranzbühler, submitted a document Dönitz-64 (not reprinted in the official edition of the I.M.T. documents) which contained an order of the *Seekriegsleitung* of 2 October to the effect that "Inasmuch as it must be assumed that blacked-out vessels encountered on the English and French coasts are warships or auxiliary warships, full armed action is authorized against blacked-out vessels" in an area around the British coast, presumably identical to that requested by Dönitz; I.M.T. Vol. XIII, p. 410.

[19] Final Pleading, I.M.T. Vol. XVIII, p. 327. *Cf.* Doc. 853-D, I.M.T. Vol. XXXV, p. 551: note dated 27 September 1939 of a discussion between the German Foreign Office and the *Seekriegsleitung* concerning a note to be sent to the neutrals on the next day; in it, the point was made explicit that "Die Notifikation soll nicht die Torpedierung in Aussicht stellen, sondern nur eine Warnung, dass die Schiffe sich durch entsprechendes Verhalten Gefahren aussetzen."

[20] Final Pleading, *loc. cit.* n. 19.

[21] *Ibid.*; *cf.* also the evidence given by Admiral Wagner, I.M.T. Vol. XIII, pp. 451-452.

prosecution in the Nuremberg trial in fact failed to establish that in the period under discussion the sinking without warning of neutral merchant ships had been the official policy for the German submarines, or even that it had become common practice. It seems fairly evident, however, that instances of unjustified sinkings had nonetheless occurred; in other instances the facts may have been insufficiently known (as was probably the case with the *Vendia*) and in those cases the available information may have been such as to warrant a strong suspicion that the sinkings were unlawful.

The third question, and the most complicated one, was the use of mines. This had already in the first few months of the war seriously affected Great Britain: summarizing the period of 3 September until 31 December 1939, Roskill states that "the enemy had caused us substantial losses in the first four months of war totalling seventy-nine merchant ships of 262,697 tons, and had dislocated the flow of our coastal shipping very seriously".[22] Likewise, the official British Foreign Office report of October 1940 concerning German attacks on merchant shipping in the first year of the war stated that a large number of neutral ships had in that period been sunk by mines, and it continued: [23]

> "The great majority of neutral ships which were mined were sunk in the main highways of British trade, and close to places where British ships either had been or were to be sunk. It does not, therefore, seem likely that the mines which sunk them were British."

From both statements it is evident that the German minelaying operations had made "the main highways of British trade" very dangerous indeed, and this not only for British armed ships, but for neutral merchant vessels as well. As was related in the previous section, the danger had become manifest for instance when on 18 November 1939 the *Simon Bolivar* struck a mine some 14 miles off the British coast near Harwich. At the time, the mine danger had not been warned against: while in September and October repeated warnings had been issued against sailing under British escort, blacking-out, and similar, in German eyes unneutral or suspicious, modes of acting, a first warning that a particular area (and in particular an immensely wide area around the British Isles and near the French coast) was dangerous to shipping, was not issued before 24 November; and even then the warning did not explicitly notify that the area, or parts of it, were mined.[24] In other words, prior to the issue of the British Reprisals Order in

---

[22] *Op. cit.* n. 5 to § 4.1, p. 102.

[23] Doc. 641-D, I.M.T. Vol. XXXV p. 246, at p. 248.

[24] The warning of 24 November was conspicuous for its wide scope and vagueness: it merely stated that in view of the increasingly frequent engagements in the waters surrounding the British Isles and near the French coast and which involved all means of modern warfare, the safety of neutral ships sailing those waters could no longer be

Council of 27 November 1939 the neutrals had not been officially warned of the existence and precise location of German minefields.

This point was emphasized by the Dutch Government in its notes to the German and British Ministers for Foreign Affairs of 19 and 21 December 1939, respectively.[25] The German note in reply, of 2 February 1940, stated the point of view of Germany with respect to the question of notification: [26] belligerents were only required to notify minefields when military considerations so permitted, and this condition was not fulfilled in the case at issue as the harbours on the eastern coast of Great Britain served as bases for the British naval forces and any premature notification of measures taken by Germany against the British forces in these waters would prevent their success.

The reasoning in the German reply was evidently false in so far as it suggested that such minefields as had been laid by the German forces had been intended exclusively against the British naval forces: in truth, the

---

taken for granted; and neutrals were recommended to follow the example set by the United States (which had forbidden its ships to sail in a well-defined area covering the waters referred to), and in particular to have their ships take the route south and east of the German-proclaimed danger zone whenever these ships should want to cross the North Sea. Doc. Dönitz-73, I.T.M. Vol. XL p. 92. In German eyes this oblique warning amounted to a notification of a danger zone coinciding with the zone proclaimed by the U.S.A. See also the interrogation of Dönitz by his counsel, Vol. XIII pp. 259-261, and the cross-examination by Sir David Maxwell-Fyfe, pp. 364-368.

[25] Cf. n. 7 to § 4.1. The note to the German Government contains the following paragraph: "Als Ursache des Unterganges des genannten Schiffes sind nach aller Wahrscheinlichkeit an Ort und Stelle vorhandene Minen anzusehen. Der Umstand, dass verschiedene Handelsschiffe ungefähr in den gleichen Regionen gesunken sind, lässt stark vermuten, dass dort Minen gelegt waren ohne Beachtung der Rechte des neutralen Handels und der neutralen Schiffahrt, ohne Warnung vor den Gefahren, denen das Leben der Seefahrenden ausgesetzt wurde und im Widerspruch mit den Bestimmungen des 8. Haager Vertrages von 1907 und mit den Prinzipien, die diesem zu Grunde liegen. Auch wenn man den Haager Vertrag erachten muss, die hier begangene Handlung nicht ausdrücklich zu treffen, kann daraus nicht gefolgert werden, dass die Freiheit zu dieser Handlung besteht. Die Deutsche Regierung hat der Niederländischen Regierung nicht mitgeteilt, dass an der genannten Stelle durch deutsche Streitkräfte Minen gelegt waren."

[26] "Der in der Note der Königlich Niederländischen Gesandtschaft enthaltene Hinweis, dass die Deutsche Regierung der Niederländischen nicht mitgeteilt habe, dass an der Stelle, wo der Dampfer *Simon Bolivar* unterging, durch deutsche Seestreitkräfte Minen gelegt worden seien, erscheint völkerrechtlich nicht begründet. Das Völkerrecht macht die Bekanntgabe von Minenfeldern durch die kriegführenden Mächte nur soweit zur Pflicht, als es die militärischen Rücksichten gestatten. Die Häfen der englischen Ostküste dienen aber bekanntlich der englischen Kriegsflotte als Stützpunkt. Eine vorzeitige Bekanntgabe der von deutscher Seite getroffenen Massnahmen gegen englische Seestreitkräfte in diesen Gebieten würde jeden militärischen Erfolg von vornherein ausschliessen. Die Reichsregierung ist daher leider auch jetzt nicht in der Lage, die von der Königlich Niederländischen Gesandtschaft gestellte Frage, ob am Ort des Untergangs des *Simon Bolivar* deutsche Minen gelegt waren, zu beantworten."

disruption of British trade had been at least an equally important aim of the minelaying operations. The Dutch Government, however, in its rejoinder of 18 March 1940 did not enter into this aspect of the matter, but instead argued from basic principles that belligerents lacked the right to pursue their war aims by the indiscriminate laying of mines in the waters of the high seas.[27]

The above discussion between the Dutch and German Governments is particularly illustrative of the wide gap that could separate the standpoints of belligerents and neutrals with respect to the legal questions involved in the use of mines on the high seas. The essentials of the neutral point of view as expressed in the Dutch notes may be summarized as follows: (1) the existence of rules restricting the rights of belligerents in respect of matters such as blockade, contraband control and submarine warfare, of necessity implies that likewise the use of mines on the high seas cannot be completely free and must be subject to certain principles; (2) a basic principle is that the belligerents lack the right to prevent entirely all navigation on the high seas: the use of mines in particular must be restricted in extent and duration, and even then the neutrals must be warned beforehand. In contrast, the standpoint of the belligerent as represented by Germany was in essence that (1) the mining of sea areas is a permissible method of warfare and need only be notified to neutrals in so far as military considerations permit, and (2) these considerations do not so permit when the success of the minelaying operation depends on secrecy and the resulting element of surprise and uncertainty on the part of the enemy.

In this controversy, the Hague Convention n° VIII of 1907 relative to the Laying of Automatic Submarine Contact Mines was of little avail. Firstly,

---

[27] The note emphasized that the principle of freedom of the high seas as a rule put a ban on minelaying on the high seas; and it continued: "Der Umstand, dass es bisher nicht gelungen ist, diese Materie vertragsmässig konkret zu regeln, bringt es keineswegs mit sich, dass jetzt das Minenlegen unbeschränkt erlaubt sei. Die Niederländische Regierung hat insbesondere ernste Bedenken bezüglich der Auffassung, dass militärische Gründe die kriegführenden Mächte unter allen Umständen der Verpflichtung, Minenfeldern bekanntzugeben, entheben würden. Die völkerrechtswidrige Tendenz dieser Auffassung, die auch schon in Bezug auf das Minenlegen in den eigenen oder den gegnerischen Hoheitsgewässern unannehmbar ist, tritt besonders klar zutage, wenn es sich um das Minenlegen in freier See handelt. Denn, während im Hinblick auf die Rechte der neutralen Schiffahrt—deren Respektierung auf hoher See einen Grundsatz des Völkerrechts bildet—die Rechte der kriegführenden Staaten in Bezug auf Blockade, Banngutkontrolle und Gebrauch von Unterseebooten bestimmten Beschränkungen unterworfen ist, unterläge, nach Auffassung der Deutschen Regierung, das für die neutrale Schiffahrt so äusserst gefährliche Vernichtungsinstrument der Minen keiner anderen Beschränkung als derjenigen, die die Auffassung der kriegführenden Staaten angesichts der militärischen Notwendigkeit bedingen würde. Dies würde einem Freibrief für die kriegführenden Mächte gleichkommen, die Schiffahrtswege des Weltverkehrs, und zwar sogar ohne Warnung, unbefahrbar zu machen. Dies ist vollkommen unannehmbar."

its terms referred so exclusively to contact mines that the Convention could well be denied any significance for mines of the influence type, such as the magnetic mines which Germany started to use in 1939. In the second place, even the use of contact mines was far from absolutely prohibited by the Convention, but merely subjected to certain, none too precise, limitations; as far as the indeed crucial issue of the notification of minefields was concerned, Article 3 merely provided that, should anchored mines cease to be under surveillance, the belligerents would be obliged to notify the danger zones as soon as military exigencies would permit.[28] This was hardly a solution of the problem at issue: as is evident from the foregoing, Germany laid its mines in places where they immediately ceased to be under surveillance, and nevertheless military exigencies stood in the way of notification until the minefields were deprived of their military value by the development of the military situation. Thus, Germany could even profess that its activities were in conformity with the literal text of the Convention.

This highly unsatisfactory character of the Mines Convention was not due to developments after its conclusion: it was an inborn defect. In 1907, all the attempts to arrive at a more conclusive text had failed; the outcome of the debates was that the Convention did not contain any restriction as to sea areas where mines might be employed;[29] a proposal to restrict the use of mines in enemy waters to those areas where the belligerent laying the mines would exercise effective control,[30] had been dismissed[31] without it

[28] Art. 3 reads: "When anchored automatic contact mines are employed, every possible precaution must be taken for the security of peaceful shipping. The belligerents undertake to do their utmost to render these mines harmless within a limited time, and, should they cease to be under surveillance, to notify the danger zones as soon as military exigencies permit, by a notice addressed to ship owners, which must also be communicated to the Governments through the diplomatic channel."

[29] The original British draft Convention which served as a basis of discussion for the 1st Sub-Committee of the 3rd Committee, had already contained the provision that the use of mines would be restricted to the territorial waters of the belligerents, with an extension to ten miles off enemy ports; *Actes*, Vol. III, p. 660. The provisions which ultimately were before the 3rd Committee (Arts. 2-4) failed to obtain an absolute majority of the votes (5th session, 17 September; *ibid.*, pp. 390-393) and hence were suppressed from the text by the Chairman (7th session, 26 September; p. 446).

[30] A Spanish amendment had proposed to supplement the draft Art. 4 with the words in italics (*ibid.*, p. 663): "Les belligérants ne pourront se servir de mines sous-marines de contact que dans leurs eaux territoriales ou dans celles de leurs ennemis *quand ils y exercent un pouvoir effectif*."

[31] In the 3rd session of the 1st Sub-Committee (11 July) the Dutch delegate, Vice-Admiral Röell, said: "Quant au second point [*i.e.* of effective control] il me semble que le principe n'en saurait être accepté. Une guerre maritime a pour but de causer le plus de mal possible aux navires ennemis pour terminer la guerre dans le plus bref délai. Un des principaux moyens est de gêner les navires ennemis dans leur [*sic*] manœuvres par exemple en les empêchant de sortir de leur port en posant des mines et par là même de donner plus de liberté de mouvement à ses propres bâtiments. Si on limite la pose de mines aux zones maritimes où il est exercé un pouvoir effectif, on nuira certainement aux opérations de nature offensive sur le théatre de la guerre,

clearly being realized that this implied that the requirement of notification of minefields so soon as military exigencies would permit, lost virtually all its significance with respect to mines in enemy waters; and a provision to the effect that mines used outside the territorial waters of the belligerents must become harmless within two hours after having been abandoned,[32] had been rejected on account of its blatant impracticability.[33] The result was a text so wide and vague as to be unsatisfactory to all the parties concerned. Indeed, both the British representative, Sir Ernest Satow, and Von Bieberstein, the representative of the major opposing Power, Germany, gave voice to their feelings of dissatisfaction. From their interventions, one thing stands out with absolute clarity: viz., that each side held to his point of view even after the Convention was concluded; this was possible because the text which the parties had compromised upon was so meaningless as to leave undecided all the more important problems attending the use of mines.[34]

In these circumstances, it was perfectly true that (as the British delegate at the Peace Conference had observed and as the Dutch Government later repeated in its first note to the German Minister of Foreign Affairs) the absence of rules prohibiting or restricting certain specific methods of using mines could not be construed as a legal permission for the belligerents to

---

mais on dépassera le but de la proposition espagnole qui a seulement pour objet la sauvegarde des navires neutres, sans gêner toutefois les opérations des belligérants." (*Ibid.*, p. 531).

[32] The *Comité d'examen* charged with the preparation of a definitive text that would be laid before the 3rd Committee, inserted in its proposal an Article 5 reading as follows:
"Dans la sphère de leur activité immédiate, les belligérants ont de même le droit de placer des mines automatiques de contact en dehors des limites fixées par les articles 2-4 du présent Règlement.
"Les mines employées en dehors des limites fixées par les articles 2-4 doivent être construites de façon qu'elles soient rendues inoffensives dans un délai maximum de deux heures, après que le poseur les a abandonnées."

[33] 3rd Committee, 5th session, 17 September; *ibid.*, p. 394.

[34] Sir Ernest Satow underlined that the arrangement could not be regarded as a definitive solution of the issue, as both the interests of the neutrals and the humanitarian side of the matter had insufficiently been taken into account; and he predicted that the lack of any restrictions as concerned the areas where mines might be laid, would needs entail "que la navigation neutre courra de gros risques en temps de guerre navale et pourra subir bien des désastres". Von Bieberstein, for his part, considered that "[u]n belligérant qui pose des mines, assume une responsabilité très lourde envers les neutres et la navigation pacifique" and that "[p]ersonne n'aura recours à ce moyen sans des raisons militaires absolument urgentes"; guarantees against abuse had to be found, not only in the precepts of international law, but also in "la conscience, le bon sens et le sentiment des devoirs imposés par les principes de l'humanité"; for the rest, the creation of rules of warfare was only worth while if their application in time of war would be militarily practicable; in that respect, the matter of the employment of mines was not sufficiently crystallized, and he therefore considered the Convention as a mere temporary arrangement.—8th plenary session, 9 October: *Actes*, Vol. I, p. 281.

apply such methods. In other words, in order to assess the legal character of the minelaying operations carried out by Germany in 1939 in the waters surrounding the British Isles and without notification to the neutrals, it is not sufficient to take account of the Hague Convention n° VIII of 1907: it is also necessary to have recourse to the underlying principles governing the relations between belligerents and neutrals in sea warfare.

Basically, these relations are governed by two complementary principles, which actually found clear expression in the respective notes of the German and Dutch Governments mentioned above: on the one hand, belligerents have power to wage war on the seas; on the other hand, neutrals have the right to navigate the seas despite the war. Any definite solution found or advocated for a particular instance of the impact of sea warfare on neutral navigation can be reduced to a balancing of—and, hence, a compromise between—these complementary principles.

An appreciation of the German minelaying operations in the light of these principles leads first of all to the consideration that the object pursued by Germany was in itself a legitimate one. Belligerents are allowed to apply military means against the enemy military forces at sea. They may also attempt to disrupt the enemy economic overseas relations, if necessary with military means. In so doing, their actions may effect a dislocation of neutral trade: belligerents are not obliged strictly to respect neutral commerce and shipping; on the contrary, they are entitled to prevent goods useful to the enemy war effort (contraband) from reaching their enemy destination, and to encourage neutral trade to operate for their own benefit.

The German minelaying operations, however, were carried out without adequate warning in areas where traffic of neutral merchantmen was particularly heavy. This involved that, while the destruction of enemy warships and the disruption of commercial shipping under enemy flag might be asserted to be the primary purpose of the operations, the foundering of a number of neutral ships was at least a calculated risk and could even be considered to amount to a deliberate effect. In this respect, it should once again be emphasized that neutral vessels do not enjoy anything like absolute immunity from the risks of warfare at sea, and that even the sinking of those vessels may in certain exceptional situations be reckoned with: if their own conduct renders this inevitable, if they have been properly warned, or, perhaps, even without warning if a particular military operation can be assumed to entail only slight risks for neutral shipping (as in the case of a minelaying operation in waters rarely navigated by merchant vessels). But this cannot evade the point that at the root is their fundamental right to safe navigation; in fact, the German representative to the 1907 Peace Conference had been perfectly right when he observed that "Un belligérant qui pose des mines, assume une responsabilité très lourde envers les neutres et la navigation pacifique". In assessing this responsibility for a

136

particular minelaying operation, the humanitarian aspect, and particularly the number of casualties caused among the sailors and passengers on board, is at least as weighty a factor as is the economic side of the loss caused to neutral shipping.

In the light of the above considerations, the conclusion seems justified that in the conditions prevailing at the time the German minelaying operations were unlawful, either on the ground that they intentionally, without previous warning and without sufficient justification damaged neutral interests and caused death and hardships to neutral seafarers, or on account of the manifest disproportionality between the net military profit to the belligerent and the harm to human and economic values on the side of neutrals.[35] This implies that the British Government could with some right regard the actions as a grave breach of the law of naval warfare.[36]

The point cannot be too strongly emphasized, however, that either belligerent's assessment of the admissibility or inadmissibility of these, as of other, military actions was profoundly influenced by their subjective expectations as to the effect of the actions on their war effort. Thus, in the course of the war, in situations where such a line of conduct seemed indicated, Great Britain and her allies apparently felt entitled to employ mines in ways not different from the incriminated German practice. It is a striking feature that, while in the preamble to the Reprisals Order in Council of 27 November 1939 the preceding minelaying operations had figured high on the list of offences imputed to Germany, at the Nuremberg trial, in the indictment against Dönitz and Raeder, the unlawful use of mines was not so much as referred to, nor was it in any other manner given an independent place in the subsequent proceedings. Obviously counsel for the defendant Dönitz, Kranzbühler, was not far off the mark when he surmised that "this reticence may be explained by the fact that the use of these combat means on the British side differed in no way from that on the German side".[37] This cannot, however, alter the fact that in November

[35] But it is an inadmissible oversimplification to suggest, as Roskill does, that the mere fact that mines had been laid in undeclared areas constituted a violation of the Hague Convention n° VIII of 1907 and hence entailed the illegality of the actions concerned; op. cit. n. 5 to § 4.1, at p. 98.

[36] Cf. the recital to the Reprisals Order in Council of 27 November 1939, quoted in n. 1 to this §.

[37] I.M.T. Vol. XVIII, p. 313. The subject of minelaying was broached now and again in the course of the proceedings, in the context of the discussion of the practice followed by the German submarines during part of 1940 to sink without warning neutral merchant vessels only in those areas where mine hits could be declared. See in particular the testimony of Admiral Wagner, witness for the defence, I.M.T. Vol. XIII, p. 451: when asked to which depth the operational zones set up from 6 January 1940 onwards within the much wider danger area notified to the neutrals on 24 November 1939 extended, the witness answered that this was perhaps as far as the 200 metre line, as anchored mines could without any difficulty be used up to that depth.—Cf. also n. 3 to this §.

1939 the British Government were still in a position to denounce the German indiscriminate use of mines as unlawful.

In summary, it may be said that in the period preceding the announcement, in November 1939, of the British intention to take reprisals, the German conduct of naval warfare had not been unlawful as against British merchant vessels; some actions of submarines against neutral merchant vessels had been of dubious character and could be interpreted as unlawful, and the use of mines could without very much reserve be qualified as unlawful in respect of neutral merchant vessels.

This leaves the question of whether the British Government were entitled, not only to expose the German violations of the law of naval warfare, but also to take recourse to reprisals. Evidently, the German actions, in so far as unlawful, had been directly prejudicial to neutral rights. They were, however, acts of warfare, part of a systematic operation aimed at damaging the British position at sea and its vital economic overseas relations; like the actions against British ships, the actions against neutral merchant vessels had been both intended and suited to further that objective. In other words, there is no question but that they were also prejudicial to the British war effort, so that Great Britain could consider herself an interested party and on that account entitled to resort to reprisals.

The above reasoning finds support in the drafting history both of the Mines Convention of 1907 and of the Protocol of London of 1936, which confirms that the purpose of the rules laid down in those instruments was not confined to protecting neutral rights: clearly, they were also intended as a guarantee for Great Britain, as the major maritime Power which was moreover most dependent on its overseas relations, that her vital interests in that respect would not be infringed with impunity.

4.2.2. German actions between 27 November 1939 and 31 July 1940

The preamble to the Order in Council of 31 July 1940 informs us that the German illegalities mentioned in the earlier Orders had "continued in an aggravated form" and that a new element had emerged in the form of "air attacks on merchant and other non-combatant shipping, resulting in grave loss of civilian life". And this was not all: it was further recited that "neutral countries [had] been subjected to unprovoked attack and to invasion and occupation by Germany, in gross violation of their neutrality and for the sole purpose of prosecuting the War against His Majesty and His Majesty's Allies".

These accusations rested on the following facts. On 24 November 1939 Germany had issued the aforementioned unspecified warning to the effect that a wide area around the British Isles was dangerous to shipping.[38] In

[38] *Supra*, p. 131.

the area, minelaying operations had continued, without notification of the precise location of the mines laid. As from January 1940, the German submarines were instructed to sink without warning any neutral vessels sailing alone in certain combat zones successively designated within the danger area, whenever the sinking could be ascribed to a mine hit; these zones were not specifically notified to the neutrals.[39] Furthermore, by the early summer of 1940 the occupation of a large part of the European continent had brought the German airforce in a position where it could take a more effective part in the actions against shipping in the waters along the European coasts, notably by the bombing of merchant vessels.[40]

On the other hand, neutral merchant vessels on their way to or from Great Britain in this period gradually took to sailing in convoys under the protection of the British navy and airforce.[41] Attacks on such escorted vessels could not be considered unlawful: by the voluntary acceptance of direct armed protection of one of the belligerents, the vessels in question assumed the character of legitimate objectives for the armed attacks of the other belligerent.

The position was different for unarmed neutral vessels crossing the dangerous sea area without such escort: to these vessels, even if sailing under British charter or otherwise culpable of unneutral service, the principle applied of the Protocol of London of 1936 stating that they could not be sunk other than under certain conditions set forth in the Protocol: virtual certainty that the ship was good and lawful prize, operational necessity of the sinking, and guaranteed safety for the crew and passengers and the ship's papers and mail prior to the destruction of the ship. It was evident that the practice of sinking on sight, either by submarine or aircraft, did not respect these conditions.

The non-observance of the rules of the Protocol could be explained with the help of military considerations: impossibility for the aircraft to act in conformity with the rules, impossibility for the German surface warships to penetrate into and effectively control the waters surrounding the British Isles, and, as far as submarines were concerned, the unacceptable risk involved in the procedure of surfacing, ascertaining the character of

---

[39] See in particular the testimony of Admiral Wagner, *loc. cit.* n. 37.

[40] See Roskill, *op. cit.* n. 5 to § 4.1, pp. 137 ff.

[41] *Ibid.* at p. 95: "One of the difficulties encountered in these early days was to persuade neutral shipping to sail in our convoys. This problem also came before the Cabinet, and in November [1939] the First Lord suggested that we might get control of all free neutral shipping by charter or other means, and so extend the advantages of convoy to such shipping. At the end of November the First Lord pointed out that, whereas our own losses were steadily decreasing, those suffered by neutrals were rising. But this problem was not finally solved until virtually all European neutral shipping was eliminated by Hitler's 1940 land campaigns. Thereafter arrangements were made to control much of the shipping of occupied countries and so include it in our convoys."

ship and cargo, ordering the ship to be abandoned and waiting until the order was carried out and those on board as well as the papers and mail were safe in the ship's boats, in an area where the superior enemy forces, warned with the aid of technical devices like radio and radar or by air reconnaissance, could arrive on the scene in very little time.

These arguments of military necessity had to be weighed, however, against the humanitarian values at stake. In this respect, it would probably be going too far to regard the neutral seamen as innocent sailors peacefully navigating the free seas; indeed, there may have been more than a little truth in Raeder's remark that the neutrals sailing to Great Britain were acting "for egotistical reasons" as they wanted "to make money" and "received large premiums for exposing themselves" to the risk of being sunk. On the other hand, it was too simple just to conclude from this, as Reader did, that neutrals entering the dangerous area "must pay the bill if they die"; [42] or, as Dönitz had it: "If [the neutrals] entered the combat zones, they had to run the risk of suffering damage, or else stay away. That is what war is ... Strict neutrality would require the avoidance of combat areas. Whoever enters a combat area must take the consequences." [43]

This really is turning matters upside down. True, a neutral merchant vessel may in certain circumstances be seized in prize, and this may even take the form of destruction of the ship, provided the conditions therefor are fulfilled. Furthermore, the exercise by a belligerent of his right to seize neutral ships in sea areas where the enemy puts up a vigorous and alert defence of his overseas trading interests may result in frequent engagements between the armed forces of the opposing belligerents, and this may in turn lead to the notification of such an area as a danger zone or combat area. It remains obscure, however, how one could jump from this observation to the conclusion that the mere fact of entering such an area would render the neutral vessel guilty of dangerous or bellicose behaviour warranting its being made the object of direct, unprovoked attack. Neither could this consequence be attached to the "large premiums" earned by the seamen sailing the dangerous waters: the fact that one receives a princely reward for exposing one's life, does not convey upon the would-be killer a right to take it.

The crucial question here is this: did the conditions prevailing at the time and in the area concerned warrant, not only that unprotected neutral vessels and their cargoes were effectively prevented from sailing to or from British ports, but also that those on board were intentionally and without previous warning killed or at any rate exposed to the danger of loss of life or health? The answer to this question, it is submitted, is that the practical impossibility for the German forces operating in the area to act in conformity with the classical procedure of seizure does not provide sufficient

[42] Cross-examination of Raeder by Sir David Maxwell-Fyfe; I.M.T. Vol. XIV, p. 206.
[43] Cross-examination of Dönitz by Sir David Maxwell-Fyfe; I.M.T. Vol. XIII, p. 365.

ground to incline the balance to the side of the military requirements, as the value of the life and health of the men on board, who did not in any normal sense of the term take an active part in the hostilities, outweighed the military profit that Germany could hope to gain by her methods. In other words: in the existing situation Germany ought to have abstained from attempting to cut off also that part of the overseas trade of the enemy which was carried in neutral, unarmed and unescorted merchant vessels sailing the indicated area, and ought to have accepted the resultant disadvantage, so long as her navy and airforce lacked the capacity to carry out their operations in conformity with the rules of the Protocol of London of 1936. For it is precisely one of the functions of the law of war to point out to the belligerents the actions that are admissible and those that, all things considered, are not.[44]

In summary, the policy pursued by Germany in relation to neutral merchant vessels had retained its, in certain respects, illegal character. Moreover, certain recently introduced practices constituted additional violations of the law of war: namely, the bombing of merchant vessels from the air, and the sinking on sight those unarmed neutral merchant vessels sailing without escort in certain undeclared combat zones designated within the danger area surrounding the British Isles. These aspects of the German conduct of sea warfare could with good reason be characterized, as was done in the preamble to the Order in Council of 31 July 1940, as a continuation of the illegalities "in aggravated form". Needless to say, the German practices had also continued materially to affect the interests of Great Britain as well as those of the neutrals.

As mentioned previously, the Order also cited the gross violation of the neutrality of numerous countries in Europe, "for the sole purpose of prosecuting the War against His Majesty and His Majesty's Allies". There cannot of course be the slightest doubt that the invasion and occupation of a whole series of neutral countries constituted a flagrant violation of the norm prohibiting armed aggression.[45] The question may be left aside whether it was a realistic appraisal to state that the actions against the neutrals had been undertaken for the sole purpose of prosecuting the war against Great Britain and her Allies: in any event, the actions had served that purpose as well and in effect had considerably strengthened the strategic position of Germany in respect to her enemies. To that extent,

---

[44] The British Government in its reply to the Italian Government's note relative to the Order in Council of 27 November 1939 pointed out that continued strict observance of the laws of war would place Great Britain at a disadvantage as against her unscrupulous opponent. However, the note continued: "This disadvantage is one to which His Majesty's Government are prepared to submit as far as humanitarian considerations are concerned."—Cmd. 6191, 1940; cf. n. 14 to § 4.1.

[45] I.M.T., Judgment; Vol. XXII, pp. 459-465.

the invasion and occupation of the European neutrals could be regarded as an illegality adversely affecting the British interests as well.[46]

In view of the above considerations, the conclusion seems justified that the facts underlying the Order in Council of 31 July 1940 indeed constituted a sufficiently significant aggravation of the German illegal practices to warrant a further reprisal on the part of Great Britain.

4.3. LEGAL NATURE OF THE BRITISH MEASURES

The conclusion that both in November 1939 and in July 1940 the British Government had good reason to qualify as illegal certain aspects of the German conduct of warfare and hence could feel entitled to have recourse to reprisals, leads to the next question: that is, whether the measures selected for that purpose did in fact present the characteristics of reprisals and, first of all, whether they constituted *prima facie* violations of international law.

4.3.1. *The Order in Council of 27 November 1939*

As is apparent from the foregoing, the British authorities had recognized that the establishment of a system of enemy export control probably was unlawful and, hence, needed to be justified especially in respect to the neutral Governments and the British Prize Courts, as these, more than the enemy, were in a position to involve the British Government in difficulties of a legal or political order. The German Government, for their part, did not leave any doubt that they regarded the measure as decidedly unlawful (and, obviously, as lacking justification, as they reserved for themselves the right to take counter-measures).

The view that export control constituted a violation of international law was likewise put forward by several neutral Governments. They naturally took the position that, irrespective of whether the measure was unlawful in respect to Germany, at any rate it infringed the rights of neutral States. Thus, the first Dutch note on the subject, dated 22 November 1939, pointed out that the Declaration of Paris of 1856 permitted neutrals "de transporter librement des marchandises destinées à des pays tiers alors même que ces marchandises seraient d'origine allemande".[1] The same point was made in the Italian note of 3 March 1940.[2]

---

[46] This is without prejudice to the question of whether the repeated violation of the norm of *ius ad bellum* prohibiting armed aggression could justify recourse to a reprisal consisting in an infringement of a rule of *ius in bello*. As to this, see *infra*, p. 157.

[1] *Oranjeboek*, April 1940, p. 33; see n. 7 to § 4.1.

[2] Cmd. 6191, 1940, p. 3.

The British reply to both notes was identical: the Government "reserve[d] their attitude as to the extent to which Article 2 of the Declaration [could] be regarded in existing circumstances as covering German exports carried in neutral ships".[3] Nevertheless, the note to the Dutch envoy continued: "the main basis of their actions is admittedly the right of retaliation the essence of which is a departure from the ordinary rules as reprisal for illegal action by the enemy".[4]

This reasoning strengthens the impression that the idea of the British Government was to keep on the safe side and, rather than to rely on an argument to the effect that under existing conditions control of German exports did not amount to a violation of the rules in force, to start from the assumption that the measure was probably unlawful or, at any rate, of questionable legality.

Hesitation with respect to the legal aspects of the situation could arise from the fact that in Germany in 1939 the export trade was in large measure a Government-controlled affair: it could be argued with some force that the rule according to which enemy goods carried in neutral vessels, with the exception of contraband, were exempt from seizure, only protected private interests (both of enemy exporters and neutral shipowners), and that the same protection need to be granted to the public interests of the enemy State. In support of this thesis the argument could be advanced that Government-owned or Government-controlled exports directly contributed to the economy of the enemy and hence to his war potential, and that no belligerent could be required to tolerate such activities contributing to the enemy war effort and which it would be within his power to interfere with.

Obviously, however, such reasoning was not entirely convincing: even in a time of Government control of the export trade it could still be maintained that the real interests at stake were those of the private persons constituting the population; and, the other way round, even an uncontrolled private export trade contributes to the war effort, as its revenues are part of the national product which provides the basis of the power to wage war under such a régime as well. It was not, therefore, at all an unfounded thesis that insufficient arguments were available for making a distinction between private and Government-owned or -controlled enemy exports.[5]

[3] Note of 14 December 1939 to the Dutch envoy, para. 9; *Oranjeboek* (see n. 1), p. 38. Note of 19 March 1940 to the Italian Government, para. 5; Cmd. 6191, 1940, p. 5.
[4] *Loc. cit.* n. 3.
[5] The neutrals lacked the power to submit this and similar issues arising out of the war to pacific settlement, whether judicial or otherwise: in successive letters to the Secretary-General of the League of Nations, the British Government had excluded disputes arising out of events occurring during the war from the participation of Great Britain in the General Act for the Pacific Settlement of International Disputes, Geneva, 26 September 1928 (letter dated 13 February 1939, Cmd. 5947, 1939) and from her acceptance of the Optional Clause of the Statute of the Permanent Court of

This leads to the conclusion that the measure taken by Great Britain in November 1939 as a reprisal against certain German illegalities, either, did in fact constitute a *prima facie* infringement of the law of warfare, or was at any rate regarded as a breach of international law by the enemy and the interested neutrals and as a probable breach by the Government taking the measure. Thus, the establishment of export control could reasonably be maintained to satisfy the essential characteristic of a reprisal that the measure at first sight was in contravention of a rule of international law.[6]

4.3.2. *The Order in Council of 31 July 1940*

Even less unequivocal from a juridical point of view was the measure contained in the Order in Council of 31 July 1940. The view has been expressed that compulsory navicerting was really in the best interests of neutral shipping and moreover amounted to little more than a confirmation of a situation that had developed in practice as a result of the *bona fides* of neutral shippers.[7] Another explanation was that the scope of the Order did not exceed the regulation of the procedure in the British Prize Courts and that the Order could therefore be deemed to be founded on "the inherent right of every state to issue legislation governing the procedure of its own prize courts".[8] Either view, if accepted, could lead to the conclusion that the system of compulsory navicerting as contained in the Order did not infringe any rule of international law and hence need not be justified by an appeal to the right of reprisals.[9] However, neither of these views does sufficient justice to the factual aspects of the situation as set forth in the foregoing.[10]

Taking into account all the facts, the measure can in my submission be most accurately characterized as an attempt effectively to deter neutral shippers and shipowners from the shipment of any unapproved cargoes

---

International Justice (letters dated 7 September 1939 and 28 February 1940, Cmd. 6108, 1939, and Cmd. 6185, 1940, respectively). As for the reasons for these steps, see *infra*, p. 153.

[6] *Cf.* the definition of reprisals in Chapter I, § 1.2.7.

[7] G. G. Fitzmaurice; see § 4.1.2, n. 32.

[8] S. W. D. Rowson; see § 4.1.2, n. 35.

[9] However, Fitzmaurice had some misgivings on this point, as is apparent from the following passage: "Even so, it may be doubtful whether these factors, taken by themselves, would have afforded legal justification for pursuing a policy of making the absence of a navicert a formal ground *per se* for a seizure in Prize; though the authorities might well have decided to adopt such a policy and pursue it unless and until challenged in, and declared to be unwarranted by, the Prize Court. It so happened however that fresh and recent illegalities on the part of the enemy occurred, not only adding to but different in kind from those which had led to the issue of the original Reprisals Order of November 1939. These were held clearly to justify further Reprisals against the enemy's commerce;" ... (etc.; *loc. cit.* n. 32 to § 4.1.2).

[10] See § 4.1.2.

to or from the enemy. Actually, it constituted a direct interference with the freedom of action of the neutral parties concerned and specifically with their freedom to maintain trade relations with the partners of their own choice. It moreover affected the opportunities available to the enemy to maintain a certain import and export trade. To the extent that the measure was illegal, it could therefore be stated to possess that character in relation both to the enemy and to neutrals.

As to the legality or illegality of the system chosen, three different issues can be discerned, according to its effect on contraband goods, non-contraband enemy imports, or enemy exports.

Belligerents have power to seize contraband goods and in certain cases the merchant vessels carrying the goods as well, on the high seas, or, after diversion of the vessel, in their own ports. The existence of this right of itself tends to deter neutrals from the shipment of contraband; but, of course, the neutrals remain free to go on shipping contraband goods and to take the risk of seizure.

In the period under consideration, however, it was not in reality within the power of neutral vessels to leave port freely and with the mere risk, equal for all ships irrespective of their cargoes, of being intercepted on the high seas: Great Britain and her Allies mantained extensive economic information services in every country of sufficient interest from a point of view of economic warfare and where the organization of such a service had proved feasible; in consequence, the real destination of a vessel and the character and ultimate destination of its cargo would more often than not be known to the belligerents.

This being so, it could be regarded as a matter of expediency and of simple co-operation on the part of neutral shippers and shipowners to have the British consular authorities issue navicerts for all cargoes and vessels the sailing of which to a non-enemy destination was voluntarily notified. And it was but one step further to perfect this system by the introduction of a powerful incentive in the form of the prospect that ships leaving port without a valid ship's navicert would be identified with vessels carrying contraband. On the other hand, this entire reasoning is based on a situation of fact (to wit, the existence of economic information centres of the belligerents in neutral countries) which perhaps in itself constituted an unwarranted disturbance of the balance between neutral shipping interests and the exercise of belligerent rights.

Apart from this, however, compulsory navicerting could hardly be regarded as objectionable in so far as it applied to probable contraband goods.

The situation was different with respect to non-contraband goods having an enemy destination. Under the law as it stood, belligerents did not have power to condemn such goods as prize. Neither did any express provision

145

of the Order warrant the conclusion that the law had been abandoned in this respect. As is, however, apparent from the account given by Medlicott,[11] navicerts were also refused for this category of goods. The effect of this was that in a British Prize Court the position of a vessel carrying such unnavicerted goods (rather than of the goods themselves) would be highly unfavourable: under the Order, it would be incumbent upon the owners of the vessel to procure affirmative evidence in rebuttal of the presumption that the vessel, sailing as it did without a valid ship's navicert, was carrying contraband and hence was subject to condemnation as good and lawful prize.

As stated previously, however, more important than the application of the Order in Council by the Prize Courts was its application by the consular authorities charged with the issue of navicerts. Here there is little room for hesitation: the practice of refusing navicerts for non-contraband goods with enemy destination, with the evident purpose of preventing the shipment of such cargoes as effectively as that of contraband goods, amounted to an abuse of power and hence was an unlawful method of waging economic warfare.

The third aspect of the application of the Order concerned enemy exports. It was concluded earlier in this section that the establishment of enemy export control was unlawful under international law. The Order of 31 July 1940 added a compulsory character to the certificates of origin and interest, and removed any uncertainty that might have subsisted with respect to the ultimate fate of uncertified export goods. This, however, merely aggravated the unlawfulness of the system of enemy export control, without adding any new legal aspects.

As was noted in passing in the foregoing, the very presence of the economic information services in neutral countries could perhaps be regarded as an unwarranted situation in itself. Indeed, it seems hard to deny that in the whole system of import and export control as set up by the British and their Allies the information services played a crucial part: it was these services that made possible the system of navicerts and certificates of origin and interest (whether voluntary or compulsory). The activities of the services could certainly not be regarded as a simple performance of the consular functions: on the contrary, in view of their perfection and high degree of effectiveness in the collection and use of information of evident importance for the conduct of the war, the view might well be defended that the economic information services in reality had the character of bases for the conduct of operations of warfare (albeit merely of the economic type), and that this character ought to have prevented the neutrals from tolerating the functioning of the services within their territories.

[11] See § 4.1.2, n. 32.

146

Without going into this at any greater length, it may for present purposes suffice to note that it is a moot point whether the maintenance by the belligerents of economic information services in neutral countries amounted to a violation of the neutrality of the countries concerned, and whether on that very ground the entire navicert system as a means of cutting off neutral trade with the enemy was unlawful as well.

It may be concluded that the establishment of compulsory navicerting in July 1940 was, either, an unlawful method of waging war on the ground that it violated the neutrality of those neutral countries where the system was functioning, or was unlawful in so far as it was applied to non-contraband goods with enemy destination or enemy exports.

4.4. APPRAISAL OF THE GROUNDS ADVANCED IN JUSTIFICATION OF THE BRITISH MEASURES

It having been established so far that Germany had committed violations of the law of war to the prejudice of British rights, and that Great Britain had taken retaliatory measures which were at first sight unlawful, the final question is whether the measures in retaliation were justified as reprisals.

4.4.1. *The Order in Council of 27 November 1939*

The first question is whether the Order in Council of 27 November 1939 establishing enemy export control in fact had the character of a sanction serving the purpose of coercing the enemy to conform to the requirements of international law.[1]

An obvious purpose of the measure was of course to contribute to the achievement of a certain economic objective in the context of the general conduct of the war. As such, it was moreover a premeditated measure: the desirability of enemy export control as an element in the economic warfare against Germany had been recognized by the planners even before the war; it was only the starting date which had been made dependent on a certain condition being fulfilled: viz., the committing by Germany of a sufficient number of violations of the law of war.

This need not however lead to the conclusion that the measure did not constitute a reprisal. Indeed, there is no reason why a reprisal might not be a premeditated measure: on the contrary, premeditation offers the definite advantage of careful assessment of the measure in all its aspects. Furthermore, the unmistakable fact that one of the purposes of the measure consisted in the promotion of the British cause need not prevent one accepting

[1] See Chapter I, § 1.2.2.

that it might also have had the purpose of coercing the enemy to abandon his illegal practices and to conform to the law of war: as observed before, it is of the essence of a reprisal that it is an individual sanction, and it is no more than obvious that it will be selected so as to be to the advantage of the party taking the reprisal.[2]

Thus the question is whether law enforcement really was among the purposes of the measure under discussion. This question is not easily answered, either in a positive or negative sense. A clear indication might have been available if the action had induced the enemy to discontinue his unlawful activities: in that event the subsequent revocation of the Order in Council by the British Government would have been sufficient indication for a positive answer; a failure to revoke the Order, on the other hand, would have been evidence of the opposite. The measure having failed to achieve that effect, however, it is a matter of pure speculation whether the British authorities would or would not have been prepared to revoke the Order if the enemy had changed his policy in response to the reprisal.

Indications are not however completely lacking as to the views of the British Government with regard to the nature and purpose of the action resorted to, and some of these seem to point in a direction other than law enforcement. A first such indication is found in the preamble of the Order in Council, where, after the enumeration of the German misdeeds resulting in the statement that "it [was] manifest that the German Government [had] deliberately embarked on a policy of endeavouring to destroy all seaborne trade between the Allied and other countries by a ruthless use of the forces at their disposal, contrary to the laws and customs of war, the rights of neutrals and the obligations of humanity", it was concluded that "this action on the part of the German Government [gave] to His Majesty an unquestionable right of retaliation". This construction, while not incompatible with the idea that the establishment of export control was for the purpose of law enforcement, is equally suggestive of a different concept: that is, of reciprocity.

The suggestion that reciprocity had played no slight part in the decision to resort to export control is strengthened by a passage in the first British note to the Dutch Government.[3] In another note, this time to the Italian

---

[2] See Chapter I, §§ 1.2.2 and 1.2.3.

[3] "In point of fact, the action against German commerce to which His Majesty's Government have decided to resort is exactly appropriate to the illegal action by Germany which has necessitated it. The German campaign has as its avowed object the stoppage of all seaborne trade with the United Kingdom, without distinction between exports and imports, or between ships of belligerents and those of neutrals. In imposing an embargo upon German exports, in addition to the contraband control which they are already exercising, His Majesty's Government are thus adopting measures whose object is to impose in [sic] German commerce restrictions similar to those which the German Government are attempting to impose on commerce with this country."—Para. 8 of the note, *Oranjeboek* (*op. cit.* n. 7 to § 4.1), p. 38.

Government, the emphasis was more particularly on the related concept of military necessity.[4] In this light, one possible explanation of the idea behind the British retaliatory measure is that the British authorities, realizing that the German practices had a marked effect on the course of the war, saw themselves confronted with the need to counterbalance these practices, an objective that could best be achieved by a measure which in its effects (though not in its humanitarian aspects) was reciprocal to the German actions.

This, however, is not the only interpretation conceivable. It is equally possible that the British Government in their note to the Dutch authorities intended to convey the definite idea that the establishment of export control was a reprisal and as such singularly well attuned to the illegalities giving rise to it. And the passage in the note to the Italian authorities may be explained perhaps even more satisfactorily as an exposition of British self-interest rather than as a statement of the one and only purpose of the measure resorted to.

In other words, the texts of the notes all confirm that the recourse to retaliation had on the British side been prompted by the need to protect British interests and to promote the Allied cause first and foremost. Taken in this sense, the notes are merely illustrative of the individual element inherent in any reprisal action, and it cannot be maintained that they provide a positive indication that the purpose of law enforcement was lacking from the action.

An indication that the measure, besides being in the British interest, was also envisaged by the British authorities as a sanction, is found in the said British note to the Dutch Government. That Government had in its first note of protest raised the question "pourquoi le Gouvernement britannique n'[avait] pas cru devoir recourir, conformément aux règles de la morale et aux principes supérieurs du droit, à une mise en demeure publique de l'Allemagne dénonçant les faits dont le Gouvernement britannique a cru devoir se plaindre, afin d'ouvrir la possibilité—dans le cas où ces faits

---

[4] "His Majesty's Government would point out that in the consideration of the application of principles of international law in present circumstances account must be taken of the fact that they are fighting against an enemy who has on repeated occasions flagrantly disregarded these principles and even the common precepts of humanity. The Italian Government will appreciate that if on the one hand the enemy are to be free to pursue with impunity practices in total disregard of the restraints imposed by international law and moral principles and yet, at the same time, His Majesty's Government are expected at all times scrupulously to observe them, His Majesty's Government are placed at a marked disadvantage in their conduct of the war. This disadvantage is one to which His Majesty's Government are prepared to submit so far as humanitarian considerations are concerned. ... But they are unable to accept the disabilities that would result for them were they to refrain from the full exercise of [their belligerent] rights, and, in particular, of the undoubted right to retaliate to which the policy of the enemy gives rise."—Cmd. 6191, 1940, p. 4.

seraient prouvés—d'une cessation des pratiques incriminées".[5] The answer to this question[6] suggests that in the eyes of the British Government recourse to a retaliatory action was better suited to achieve the purpose of diverting Germany from her illegal course than a "mere expression of disapproval by world opinion" had proved to be. This would imply that coercing Germany to change her policy was among the purposes of the action.

While none of the above arguments seem entirely conclusive one way or another, another factor which must be taken into account is the conduct of naval warfare on the British side. It is not disputed that in the first half of 1940, within a few months after the Order in Council of 27 November 1939 had been issued, Great Britain had without any attempt at justification, either as a reprisal or with the aid of the doctrine of reciprocity adopted some of the very methods of sea warfare that it had so strongly condemned in Germany: in certain sea areas under the control of the German forces, the activities of British aircraft and submarines came to include such practices as the bombing of merchant vessels, the method of "sink at sight" applied by submarines penetrating into the areas, and the employment of mines. The British methods could not be completely identified with those applied by the German forces: in particular, minelaying usually took place in previously declared areas. In essence, however, the methods were the same, and so were the underlying motives: the realization that practices such as the laying of mines in waters under enemy control, bombing, and "sink at sight", could achieve a far more effective disturbance of the enemy overseas trade relations than could ever be hoped to be achieved without such ruthless methods of destruction applied against merchant vessels, enemy and neutral alike.[7]

[5] Note dated 22 November 1939; *Oranjeboek* (*op. cit.* n. 7 to § 4.1), p. 33.
[6] "His Majesty's Government cannot believe ... that any such action as regards German methods of warfare would be more effective than it has been in regard to the methods which Germany has adopted during the past few years in the conduct of her relations with other States. The opinion of the civilised world has expressed itself with no uncertain voice as regards the frequent disregard by Germany of the rights of her weaker neighbours to a free and undisturbed existence, but this has had singularly little effect in diverting Germany from the course of action which she has mapped out for herself and is still pursuing. So long as the German Government consider that they can derive some national advantage from a callous disregard of the rights of others and the law of nations, no mere expression of disapproval by world opinion is likely to have the slightest deterrent effect."—Note of 14 December 1939, *Oranjeboek* (*op. cit.* n. 7 to § 4.1), p. 38.
[7] *Cf.* Roskill, *op. cit.* n. 5 to § 4.1, pp. 123 ff., 144-145, 171-172, 337-338. See also the evidence of Admiral Wagner, who as witness for the defence in the Nuremberg trial provided detailed information about the methods applied by the British armed forces in the German-controlled areas of the Baltic, the eastern part of the North Sea, around Skagerrak and, later, in the Norwegian and French waters, and concerning the merchant traffic, both German and neutral, going on in those areas; I.M.T. Vol. XIII,

It is submitted that when a State enacts a measure as a reprisal against certain illegalities allegedly committed or being committed by another State, it cannot validly claim that the measure serves the purpose of law enforcement when it is or becomes itself culpable without justification of the very infringements of the law that it imputes to the opponent.[8] Applied to the situation under discussion, this means that in any event as from the time when in 1940 the British conduct of naval warfare assumed much the same features as the incriminated German practices, the ground fell away on which the measure of enemy export control could be justified as a reprisal.

This need not, however, lead to the further conclusion that the measure had from the very beginning lacked the purpose of law enforcement. Possibly, the British authorities originally intended to maintain a standard of conduct in conformity with the rules of sea warfare, and in particular to refrain from any unwarranted employment of force against merchant vessels. Another possibility is that they had as early as November 1939 realized and accepted that sooner or later situations might develop where the requirements of effective warfare would impel the British forces to follow the pattern set by Germany, notwithstanding the fact that this would result in not following the same rules of warfare at sea, particularly in respect of merchant shipping, as were being violated by the German forces. In either supposition, however, the November Order in Council could have had the aim of coercing Germany to respect the rules in question; it should be emphasized in particular that the purpose of law enforcement attached to a certain coercive action need not lose its credibility by the reflection that in another situation (namely when the law-enforcing action fails to bring about the desired result) the one-time law-enforcer may feel impelled to commit the same offence in his turn: indeed, this possibility is inherent in the very structure of the international community as it stands and in the dual role played by its principal actors, the States.

The above leads to the following conclusion. In the contention of the British authorities, the establishment of export control constituted a reprisal. In order to find justification as such, the measure ought to fulfil the

---

pp. 453-455.—It should be emphasized that the methods referred to were not resorted to by way of reprisals: they were offensive operations, serving no other purpose than to contest with the enemy the use of the sea even in areas under his control.

[8] The above reasoning is similar to that applied by the Permanent Court of International Justice in its judgment in *The Diversion of Water from the Meuse*, Series A/B 70, p. 25; the Court argued that the fact that The Netherlands had constructed and were operating a lock discharging its lock-water into the Zuid-Willemsvaart in the same manner as the Belgian lock complained of by the Dutch Government, made it "difficult to admit that the Netherlands are now warranted in complaining of the construction and operation of a lock of which they themselves set an example in the past."

requirement that its purpose was to coerce Germany to adopt a line of conduct in conformity with the law of sea warfare. An examination of the available evidence shows that certain indications support the thesis that the required purpose was actually present in this case, while other indications militate against that thesis. A definite finding, therefore, either in a positive or negative sense seems out of the question. This conclusion implies that the possibility cannot be ruled out that the British assertion was correct and that the measure did in fact derive the necessary justification from its characteristics as a reprisal. Even then, however, the measure lost its justification when in the first half of 1940 the British naval and air forces reverted to modes of acting in certain sea areas under enemy control which were not essentially different from the incriminated German practices.

This appraisal of the Order in Council of 27 November 1939 would not be complete without attention being paid to an argument that seems of major significance for a just evaluation of the British motives behind the recourse to export control, and that is found in the note of 14 December 1939 of the British Government to the Dutch Government. In this note, the British Government dealt with the characterization which the Dutch Government had given of the measures as "possessing an 'odious character' in that they affect[ed] the interests of neutrals as well as those of Germany". That Government was reminded "that the members of the League of Nations accepted the obligation, in the case of aggression against a member of the League ..., to cease, and if necessary to prevent, all trade, financial relations or intercourse with the aggressor"; and, as the note pointed out, "compliance with this obligation would involve far more drastic interference with enemy trade, and far more injury to the commercial interests of the countries concerned, than [could] possibly result from the measures which His Majesty's Government have decided to take." [9]

In other words: while the League of Nations system of collective sanctions by all Members against an aggressor was not strictly applicable

[9] The note went on to state that the British Government "are, of course, aware of the attitude towards those obligations of the Covenant which has been adopted in recent years by the Netherlands and other countries, and they are not now making any complaint of that attitude; but when they find their own action described as 'odious', they feel justified in reminding the Netherlands Government that far more drastic action was not so long ago regarded by that Government as perfectly legitimate and desirable in the case of aggression and that the Netherlands voluntarily accepted an obligation to take such action in the interests of those principles of liberty and justice which it was the object of the Covenant to uphold. It is in the defence of these principles that His Majesty's Government are engaged in the present war, and they feel that as regards the measures which they have been compelled to take in order to ensure the triumph of these principles, they should be entitled to count upon some measure of sympathy from those countries to whom the ideals of liberty and justice are not less dear than they are to His Majesty's Government."—*Oranjeboek* (*op. cit.* n. 7 to § 4.1), p. 38.

152

in the present conflict, it was the opinion of the British Government that nevertheless the States which considered themselves neutral ought to live up to its spirit, and ought to discriminate between the aggressor and the defendor and accept that their position in respect to the aggressor be made similar to that which would have resulted from the institution of collective sanctions. This in reality was equal to saying that the neutral States ought to abandon their neutrality—a step that they were loath to take voluntarily, as was implicit in the Dutch reply to the British note, handed to the British Foreign Secretary almost a month to the day before the neutrality of The Netherlands was forcibly terminated.[10]

This difference of opinion obviously was of fundamental significance. In sober terms of interests and expectations the matter was simple: while, once the war started, Great Britain as a belligerent could expect the greatest advantage from other States abandoning their neutrality and joining the British cause, the neutrals could still hope that continued strict neutrality would be in their own best interests. In terms of preferable developments the situation was rather less obvious, however: on the one hand, the British point of view was most in conformity with the goal of collective security as a concern of the community of States. On the other hand, the most promising instrument for the realization of that goal, the League of Nations system, had in fact broken down completely. In these circumstances, the British view could be regarded as the most desirable in the long run, but the standpoint of the neutrals had a sound basis in the consideration that a limitation of the number of belligerents might effect a desirable limitation of the scope of the war.

That the views concerning the necessity of collective sanctions had played no slight part on the British side, is apparent from the text of the letter which the British Government on 7 September 1939 addressed to the Secretary-General of the League of Nations, notifying a new reservation to the British acceptance of the optional clause of the Statute of the Permanent Court of International Justice, to the effect that disputes arising out of events occurring during the war would not be covered by that acceptance.[11]

The reasons for this step were as follows: the original acceptance without this reservation, in 1930, had rested on the consideration "that by the building up of a new international system based on the Covenant of the

---

[10] "It must be evident that the Netherland [sic] Government cannot follow the British Government in this contention [i.e. that the British measures against German exports were in substance the same measures which the Dutch Government had been prepared to carry out in a joint action in the League period], as they will no doubt admit that from a legal point of view a joint action in accordance with the stipulations of the Covenant of the League cannot be compared with a war which was started without recourse to the procedure of the League."—Note dated 8 April 1940, *Oranjeboek* (*op. cit.* n. 7 to § 4.1), p. 42.
[11] See n. 5 to § 4.3.

League of Nations and the Pact of Paris a fundamental change had been brought about in regard to the whole question of belligerent and neutral rights", to the effect that in the event of Great Britain becoming involved in war "the other Members of the League, so far from being in the position of neutrals with a right to trade with our enemy, would be bound under Article 16 of the Covenant to sever all relations with him". This excluded the possibility of a "justiciable dispute between the United Kingdom as a belligerent and another Member of the League as a neutral", "since the other Members of the League would either fulfil their obligations under Article 16 of the Covenant, or, if they did not, would have no ground on which to protest against the measures which His Majesty's Government might take to prevent action on their part which was inconsistent with these obligations."

These considerations, however, had lost their validity since at the League Assembly of 1938 it had "become evident that many of the Members of the League no longer consider[ed] themselves bound to take action of any kind under the Covenant against an aggressor State", as in their opinion "sanctions against an aggressor under the terms of the Covenant could not be regarded as obligatory." As a result, the original system of the Covenant had been reduced to "a general understanding that members should consult one another in the event of aggression against another member, and that such aggression could not be treated with indifference." And, the letter added, even this limited understanding had remained without effect in the present crisis: no action had been taken under Articles 16 or 17 of the Covenant, and several Member States had even prior to the outbreak of hostilities "announced their intention of maintaining strict neutrality as between the two belligerents."

As is apparent from the above language, Great Britain had entertained a definite expectation with respect to the sanctions system embodied in the League Covenant: in future wars the effective conduct of economic warfare (an essential element in British strategic thinking) would not be hampered by the right of neutrals to go on trading with the partner or partners of their own choice. However, when the Second World War broke out the League sanctions system had broken down, neutrality had recovered the lost ground, and in consequence the legal issues attending the relations between neutrals and belligerents had revived. In these circumstances it was a logical step for the British Government to exclude disputes arising out of the war from their acceptance of the optional clause.

There is an obvious connection between this limitation of the previous acceptance of the optional clause and the Reprisals Order in Council of 27 November 1939. For, while the establishment of export control was a typical instance of a measure which under the sanctions system of the League would according to British expectations have been covered by the collective severance of economic relations with the enemy, it was equally obvious that under the traditional system of neutral rights this measure might involve Great Britain in legal disputes with neutrals. In this situation, the reservation had the effect of precluding injured neutrals from challenging the measure before the Permanent Court of International Justice and thus involving Great Britain in a doubtful procedure that might prove far more cumbersome than the ordinary diplomatic handling of disputes with neutrals.

The connection between reservation and subsequent action can also be interpreted in a less favourable way: starting from the assumption that the British authorities intended to establish enemy export control in any event, and that they were aware of the illegality of such a measure and of its lack of justification in respect to neutrals, it might be suggested that the reservation to the acceptance of the optional clause served to prevent a public exposure of the legal defects of the measure, while the announcement of the measure as a reprisal was primarily intended to provide the authorities with an ostensible justification in the diplomatic discussions with neutrals. In this respect, it may suffice to observe that the desire to avoid legal proceedings before the Permanent Court concerning this and similar issues arising out of the war evidently was instrumental in the decision to make the reservation; for the rest, however, no indications have been found of *mala fides* on the British side which would warrant so malevolent an interpretation of the British step.

To my mind, a fair appraisal of all the available information leads to the following conclusions:

(1) In British eyes the severance of economic relations with the aggressor State was an essential and even a self-evident element of the system of collective sanctions of the League of Nations.

(2) That system having broken down in fact, the severance of the economic relations of the enemy remained nevertheless an essential element of warfare, and, in so far as particular actions forming part of that operation might be in contravention of traditional international law, those actions would have first consideration when the occasion would arise for a resort to sanctions (which in the existing conditions needs would be individual sanctions and hence be prompted firstly by the British interests).

(3) The establishment of enemy export control was such an unlawful action; thus, it was duly announced as a reprisal.

(4) While it cannot be definitely affirmed that the measure had the purpose, characteristic of a belligerent reprisal, of coercing the enemy to conform to the law of warfare, neither can the possibility be excluded that it had that purpose; so, to the extent that export control violated the law of war, it was probably justified as a reprisal, at any rate until such time as the subsequent British actions against enemy shipping interests in sea areas under enemy control brought this justification to an end.

155

4.4.2. *Extension of export control to other enemy States*

After the above discussion of some of the main questions arising out of the Order of 27 November 1939, a few brief remarks may suffice with regard to the later Orders in Council extending the scope of the original Order to the States taking the German side. At first sight it seems an unjustifiable step, to begin with, to order a reprisal against a belligerent who has only just entered into the war and has not even had time to commit unlawful acts of warfare. On the other hand, the change from neutral to belligerent did not come about unexpectedly and without preparation: indeed, Italy had in the period preceding its entry into the war become increasingly committed the German cause. On that ground the British contention in the preamble to the Order in Council of 11 June 1940, that Italy, by joining the war on the side of Germany, had "made herself a party to the method of waging war adopted by Germany and [would] share in any advantages derived therefrom", could not be simply dismissed as obviously and totally unfounded.

This does not however seem to be the real point with regard to this group of Orders in Council. Actually, none of these Orders contained independent reprisal actions, carried by their own motivations and justifications: they were mere sequels to the Order of 27 November 1939, constituting necessary extensions of the system of enemy export control that otherwise would be deprived of its efficacy.

By the time these extensions were successively proclaimed, the November Order had, as argued above, lost such justification as it might originally have had. This leads to the conclusion that the Orders in Council extending the system of export control to the new enemies completely failed to find justification as reprisals.

4.4.3. *The Order in Council of 31 July 1940*

Like the establishment of enemy export control, the Order in Council of 31 July 1940 proclaiming compulsory navicerting also served primarily to promote the interests of Great Britain and particularly to improve the British chances of war by doing effective damage to the economic position of the enemy. Again, the question is whether the measure had the purpose of law enforcement as well.

According to its preamble, the Order was motivated first of all by the continuance in an aggravated form of the illegal acts forming part of the German conduct of sea warfare; and, as set forth previously, there were sufficient facts supporting this contention to provide ground for a further reprisal on the part of Great Britain. However, the argument developed in the foregoing concerning the impact of the British conduct of sea warfare on the continued justification of the November Order applies *a fortiori* to the Order of 31 July 1940, which was issued only after the British forces had taken to using practices similar to those of which Germany was accused.

Neither is the Order saved by the second ground advanced in the preamble: the invasion and occupation of the territory of a number of European States. For one thing, even if it were accepted that those actions had been undertaken "for the sole purpose of prosecuting the War against His Majesty and His Majesty's Allies", they nonetheless formed part of a policy of systematic, unprovoked aggression against peaceful States and as such amounted to gross violations of the norm of general international law prohibiting armed aggression. In other words, the actions might be retaliated against by declaring war on the aggressor (or, in the case of the victims, by putting on record that a state of war had come to exist), and a war so declared would be legitimate,—but in the war so started the retaliating belligerent would not be entitled to disregard the laws of war on the sole ground that the adversary was guilty of aggression: belligerents are bound to observe the law of war irrespective of whether one of them can be stigmatized as the aggressor. Thus, the establishment of compulsory navicerting contrary to the existing law of warfare could not validly be defended as a reprisal against the invasion and occupation of the European neutrals.[12]

Further, even apart from the above reasoning it seems evident that in the prevailing circumstances the resort to compulsory navicerting was particularly unsuited to achieve the purpose of coercing the enemy to change his policy in regard, either, of the former, or of the remaining neutral States. This is not to say that on this ground the measure could not have been intended to have the required purpose; its futility in that respect does imply, however, that such a contention would possess singularly little credibility.

All in all, the available indications seem overwhelmingly against the contention that the Order of 31 July 1940 establishing a system of compulsory navicerting really would have had the purpose of coercing Germany to conform to the law of war. This leads to the conclusion that the measure, rather than being justifiable as a sanction under international law, merely constituted a belligerent action serving to promote the British cause in the war and which, to the extent that it violated the law of war, was and remained unlawful.

---

[12] But *cf.* the argument rendered in § 4.4.1, to the effect that in British eyes a measure such as export control would have been justified under the League system of collective sanctions, and that in the present conflict Great Britain was entitled to continue that system on a unilateral basis; *supra*, p. 152.

4.5. CONCLUSIONS

The British measures dealt with in this chapter were part of a complicated system of economic blockade applied against Germany and her Allies in the Second World War and embracing such other elements as pre-emption on the neutral markets, pressure on and arrangements with neutral Governments and shipowners, and, on the military level, actions such as the diversion, inspection and seizure of merchant vessels or the sinking of such vessels on the high seas by mines, aircraft and submarines.[1] The measures under discussion played a substantial part in achieving the significant results which must be ascribed to the economic blockade as a whole and which, though never decisive for the outcome of the war, contributed heavily to the ultimate defeat of Germany.

While some of the methods of economic warfare were hardly questionable from the point of view of the law of war, the measures of enemy export control and compulsory navicerting, embodied mainly in the Orders in Council of 27 November 1939 and 31 July 1940, constituted infringements of the law in force; not, to be sure, infringements of the most reprehensible variety, as the measures did not directly entail the inescapable and needless death or misery of human persons: but infringements nonetheless, both in relation to the neutrals and the enemy. Neither had the probable illegality of the measures escaped the British authorities: it was precisely that element which motivated their attempts to justify the actions as reprisals.

On close inspection, these attempts at justification are only partially successful. On the one hand, there is sufficient evidence that the high seas were the scene of unlawful acts of warfare being committed by the German armed forces. An important restriction here is that no such illegality attached to the actions against British merchant vessels, as the armament and offensive attitude of these vessels had from the outset turned these into virtual combatant ships in favour of which no particular consideration could be claimed or expected. Subject to this restriction, it may be stated that the gravest infringement of the law of sea warfare committed by Germany in the early months of the war consisted in the indiscriminate use of mines, both of the magnetic and contact types; the illegality of that practice arose, not so much from its being in direct contravention of the text of Hague Convention n° VIII of 1907, as from its violating the basic principles of sea warfare interpreted in the light of all relevant aspects of the situation. Some further unlawful actions, though more of an incidental nature, had to be put on the account of German submarines.

As from January 1940, two aspects betrayed a tendency on the part of

---

[1] Medlicott, *op. cit.* n. 3 to § 4.1, gives a full account of the entire range of these activities.

the German authorities to intensify the conduct of warfare against commercial shipping: the policy of "sink at sight", applied when mine hits could be claimed by submarines operating in undeclared combat areas designated within the wide danger zone declared around the British Isles, and the attacks on merchant vessels by land-based German aircraft. Either method must be deemed unlawful in respect to those unarmed neutral merchant vessels not sailing in British or allied convoys. At any rate it was evident that a much more systematic and ruthless policy of destruction of merchant shipping had been launched, irrespective of whether the ships victims of that policy were of enemy or neutral nationality.

The above practices were unlawful primarily in respect to the neutrals. The practices were, however, part of a policy of economic warfare conducted against Great Britain and her Allies and directly affecting the war effort of those belligerents. For that reason, the German practices could be regarded as unlawful acts of war in respect to Great Britain and her Allies as well.

The British Government in the Order in Council of 31 July 1940 also invoked the invasion and occupation of the greater part of the European neutrals. This incontestably amounted to a major violation, though of the norm of general international law prohibiting aggression rather than of the law of war, and so was not suited to be retaliated against with a mere belligerent reprisal.

Even irrespective of this, it seems doubtful whether the measures taken by the British Government, allegedly in retaliation to the above illegalities, met the requirements of reprisals. The Order in Council of 27 November 1939 may indeed have constituted a true reprisal, although some doubt persists as to its initial purpose. When, however, in the first half of 1940 Great Britain resorted to offensive methods of sea warfare in areas under enemy control similar to those applied by Germany, the British Government did not seek to justify this with the aid of any legal argument (such as reciprocity, or reprisals). This leads to the conclusion that as from that time it could no longer be maintained that the purpose of the Order was to enforce the law of sea warfare against Germany. This defect equally vitiates the attempts to justify both the later Orders in Council extending the system of export control to new enemy States, and the Order in Council of 31 July 1940 rendering navicerts compulsory.

Thus, the final conclusion is that, all things considered, only the Order in Council of 27 November 1939 probably passes the test for justifiable reprisals, and then for a limited period of time only.

Perhaps the most remarkable element in the reasoning on which the British Government relied in defence of their retaliatory measures, consists in the thesis that the measures did not significantly differ from the economic sanctions which the Members of the League of Nations would not so long ago have been both prepared and obliged to apply collectively, and that on

159

that account the States which had hastened to announce their neutrality in the present conflict ought not to complain too loudly of the relatively modest impact which the British actions inevitably must have on their interests. Leaving aside whether the first half of this argument was an entirely correct assessment of the League system, the conclusion drawn from it was in any event far from compelling,—unless one would be ready to accept that neutrality had become an obsolete concept.

From a point of view of general international law, however, neutrality was not dead at all, and the virtual dissolution of the League of Nations had evidently restored its vitality. It could moreover be argued with some force that States, by not taking sides in the conflict, could contribute to the containment of the war within the narrowest possible bounds. Against this, it could be advanced in defence of the British thesis that the interest of world order would be served best by openly taking sides against a manifest aggressor.

The fact that these two divergent lines of argument could be brought into play, was evidence not only of the contrasting interests of Great Britain and the neutral States respectively, but also of the peculiar state of international relations prevailing at the time and characterized, on the one hand, by the concept of independent States having the power to determine as sovereign bodies their national policy (and, hence, their belligerency or neutrality with respect to armed conflicts in which they were not immediately involved), and on the other hand by the creation and initially fruitful activity of the League of Nations, the first major attempt at organized co-operation among States with a view to maintaining international peace and security, if need be with the aid of co-ordinated enforcement action on the ground of a community decision.

However this may be, the fact of the existence of the League of Nations with its one-time promising system of collective sanctions cannot alter the above final conclusion concerning the measures taken unilaterally by Great Britain at a time when the League was no longer capable of effective action.

CHAPTER V

Reprisals in the Second World War - II

5.1. GERMAN REPRISAL BOMBARDMENT OF LONDON, SEPTEMBER-NOVEMBER 1940

5.1.1. *The facts*

In the first phase of the air war in the West, from September 1939 to April 1940, neither Germany nor Great Britain (nor France, for that matter) bombed objectives in enemy territory. This reticence was explained in part by the undertaking, given voluntarily by each of the belligerents in response to an appeal by the President of the United States of America,[1] that they would refrain from unrestricted air warfare.[2] It was, moreover, a

---

[1] The appeal, addressed on 1 September 1939 to the Governments of Great Britain, France, Italy, Germany and Poland, and published in the Department of State Bulletin, Vol. I, 1939, at p. 181, read in part: "If resort is had to this form of inhuman barbarism [*i.e.*, "the ruthless bombing from the air of civilians in unfortified centers of population"] during the period of the tragic conflagration with which the world is now confronted, hundreds of thousands of innocent human beings who have no responsibility for, and who are not even remotely participating in, the hostilities which have now broken out, will lose their lives. I am therefore addressing this urgent appeal to every government which may be engaged in hostilities publicly to affirm its determination that its armed forces shall in no event, and under no circumstances, undertake the bombardment from the air of civilian populations or of unfortified cities, upon the understanding that these same rules of warfare will be scrupulously observed by all of their opponents."

The appeal followed the example set by the statement relating to air bombardment delivered by the British Prime Minister, Charberlain, on 21 June 1938 in connection with certain events in the Spanish Civil War and the Sino-Japanese War, and the Resolution concerning the same issue passed by the Assembly of the League of Nations on 30 September 1938.

[2] The British reply of 2 September, published in the same volume of the Department of State Bulletin at p. 182, welcomed the appeal and went on to state that "it was already the settled policy of His Majesty's Government should they become involved in hostilities . . . to confine bombardment to strictly military objectives upon the understanding that those same rules will be scrupulously observed by all their opponents. They had already concerted with certain other governments the rules that in such an event they would impose upon themselves and make publicly known."

In a joint statement of the same date, the British and French Governments not only publicly expressed their firm intention to respect the civil populations, but also made

matter of expediency for both parties: on the strength of military considerations (such as the number and capabilities of available bombers, and the
expected effect of enemy defence) neither Germany nor Great Britain
considered herself capable of launching immediately a reasonably effective
bombing offensive against the enemy territory, and they were therefore
equally desirous to postpone this extension of air warfare until such time
as the prospects would be more propitious.[3] In the meantime both belligerents were busily engaged on building up an adequate bomber force and
on elaborating plans for its employment against objectives in enemy
territory.

For, despite their voluntary undertakings, neither of the belligerents had
the intention to refrain from bombing enemy territory for the duration of
the war. As for the British, they had never after the First World War
abandoned the idea that in case of a war between Great Britain and a
continental Power the British bomber force would be destined to play a
major and independent part in the conduct of the war, in particular by
doing direct damage to the productive capacity and morale of the enemy
nation.[4] And while on the German side the pre-war preparations had not
been aimed at the timely development of a long-range bomber force, Hitler
had meanwhile come to realize the important part which the German air
force would have to play in the war against the Power which had unmistakably become his main opponent, Great Britain.[5]

---

known that they had already issued pertinent instructions to their respective headquarters that only strictly military objectives, in the narrowest sense of the term,
could be bombed either from the air or by artillery (naval or land-based). The Governments once again pointed out, however, that this and the further undertakings
embodied in their joint declaration would be observed only on the basis of reciprocity.
A French version of the declaration is reproduced in *RICR*, Vol. XXI, 1939, at p. 733.

The reply dated 1 September of the *Führer* read in part (Department of State Bulletin, Vol. I, 1939, at p. 183): "The view expressed in the message of President Roosevelt that it is a humanitarian principle to refrain from the bombing of non-military
objectives under all circumstances in connection with military operations, corresponds
completely with my own point of view and has been advocated by me before. ... I
already gave notice in my Reichstag speech of today that the German air force had
received the order to restrict its operations to military objectives. It is a self-under-
stood prerequisite for the maintenance of this order that opposing air forces adhere
to the same rule."

See further, *e.g.*, J. R. M. Butler, *Grand Strategy*, Vol. II (1957), pp. 567-568; the
work forms part of the History of the Second World War, United Kingdom Military
Series.

[3] C. Webster and N. Frankland, *The Strategic Air Offensive against Germany, 1939-
1945*, Vol. I (1961), pp. 134-135; published in the same series.—K. Klee, *Die Luftschlacht um England 1940*, in: *Entscheidungsschlachten des zweiten Weltkrieges*, ed.
by H.-A. Jacobsen and J. Rohwer (1963), pp. 63-67.

[4] Webster and Frankland, *op. cit.* n. 3, pp. 52 ff., 134-143.

[5] In a memorandum dated 9 October 1939 to his top military commanders, Hitler
pointed out the rôle assigned to the air force: "The ruthless employment of the

This period of "the lull before the storm" [6] came to an end in May 1940. On 10 May the German armies opened the offensive against the Low Countries and France, and among the immediate reactions of the British Government was the announcement that "they reserved to themselves the right to take action which they considered 'appropriate in the event of bombing by the enemy of civil populations, whether in the United Kingdom, France or in countries assisted by the United Kingdom'." [7] On 14 May the Germans bombed Rotterdam, and although "[t]his attack caused far less damage and death than was at the time reported, ... it was obvious that the gloves were off".[8] It was also obvious that the strategic situation was changing rapidly, thus necessitating an immediate decision about the putting into action of the British bomber force. In fact, as early as October 1939 the War Cabinet had accepted that "when German operations looked like 'being decisive' Bomber Command would be launched on a full-scale daylight assault against the Ruhr, which was believed to contain about sixty per cent of all Germany's vital industry and a population 'which might be expected to crack under intensive air attack'." [9] It seemed that the moment for such an assault had now arrived. Thus, on 15 May, after further lengthy discussions, "the War Cabinet authorized Bomber Command to attack East of the Rhine, and that night ninety-nine bombers were despatched to attack oil and railway targets in the Ruhr": [10] the strategic air offensive against Germany had begun.

Another event, of a rather more trivial nature, took place at about the same time: in the afternoon of 10 May bombs fell on the German town of Freiburg, and in the *Wehrmacht* communiqué this incident was duly announced as an enemy attack; falsely, however: the truth of the matter

---

Luftwaffe against the heart of the British will-to-resist can and will follow at the given moment."—Memo. to Brauchitsch, Raeder, Göring and Keitel, as quoted by Webster and Frankland, *op. cit.* n. 3, p. 137 n. 2.

In his *Weisung* n° 9, dated 29 November 1939, Hitler underlined that Great Britain must be considered the main opponent and that in combating that nation economic warfare would take an important place: "Im Krieg gegen die Westmächte ist England der Träger des Kampfwillens und die führende Macht der Feinde. England niederzuringen ist die Voraussetzung für den Endsieg. Das wirksamste Mittel hierzu ist, die englische Wirtschaft durch Störung an entscheidenden Punkten lahmzulegen."—See also Klee, *op. et loc. cit.* n. 3.

[6] As is the title of section 1, Ch. III of the book by Webster and Frankland, *op. cit.* n. 3.

[7] Butler, *op. cit.* n. 2, p. 182.

[8] Webster and Frankland, *op. cit.* n. 3, p. 144.

[9] *Ibid.* p. 136, quoting a memorandum prepared by the British Chiefs of Staff and approved by the War Cabinet on 21 October 1939. The memorandum pointed out that heavy casualties would be inevitable among the civil population, and that the bombing would therefore "have to be justified by some previous German behaviour of a similar kind, such as the unrestricted bombing of France or Britain, or the infliction of numerous casualties during an invasion of Belgium"; p. 137.

[10] *Ibid.* p. 144. Butler, *op. cit.* n. 2, p. 182.

was that some German aircraft had unloaded their bombs in the belief that they had arrived above their targets near Dijon, in France. However, the German propaganda made use of the incident and issued the warning that henceforward retaliation would take place.[11]

It was quite some time after this incident and, for that matter, after the opening of the bombing offensive by Great Britain, before the German air force in its turn started actions against objectives in England.[12] This is not surprising, taking into account that for the time being the German forces, not excluding the air force, were fully occupied with the large-scale operations which eventually resulted in the occupation of Holland, Belgium, and part of France, and the armistice with the French régime in the other, unoccupied part. It was only after all this had been brought to a satisfactory end, that Germany could turn to the next goal, "die endgültige Nieder-ringung Englands".[13]

In order to attain this goal, the German air force on 1 August 1940 received the order to destroy the British air force, and in particular to attack the enemy aircraft, their ground and maintenance organization, and the aviation and anti-aircraft industry. The civil population as such was not made an object of attack: Hitler's *Weisung* n⁰ 17 stated expressly that "Terrorangriffe als Vergeltung" were reserved to the *Führer*. In the *Weisung* it was further laid down that the intensified air warfare against Great Britain could start as from 5 August. Actually it was not before 13 August that the offensive against the British air defence system was seriously launched and the Battle of Britain began.

The objectives sought by the German air force in the first phase of the Battle of Britain were definitely legitimate military objectives in the stricter sense of the term: the main accent lay on attacks on enemy aircraft and ground stations, with a view to gaining superiority in the air; in addition, some attacks were made on the industrial targets mentioned above. An incident which occurred in this phase and which suggested a different policy, was the more or less indiscriminate bombing of London by indi-

[11] E. Hampe, *Der zivile Luftschutz im Zweiten Weltkriege* (1963), p. 112.
[12] In the *Wehrmacht* communiqué of 20 June 1940 reference was made once again to the "attack" of 10 May, and it was announced that retaliation had now started: "Seit 10. Mai haben feindliche, und zwar vorwiegend britische, Flugzeuge fortgesetzt in der Nacht offene deutsche Städte angegriffen. Auch in der vergangenen Nacht fielen diesen Angriffen wieder acht Zivilpersonen zum Opfer. Die deutsche Luftwaffe had nunmehr mit der Vergeltung gegen England begonnen".—See *Dokumente über die Alleinschuld Englands am Bombenkrieg gegen die Zivilbevölkerung*, issued by the German *Auswärtiges Amt* in 1943, p. 146.
As is pointed out by E. Murawski, *Der deutsche Wehrmachtbericht 1939-1945* (1962) p. 104, this announcement (which was not in conformity with the facts) served "als moralische Stütze für die Einleitung der grossen deutschen Luftoffensive gegen England und insbesondere London".
[13] *Weisung Nr. 17 für die Führung des Luft- und Seekrieges gegen England*, issued by Hitler on 1 August 1940.

vidual aircraft on the day and night of 24 August. The suggestion of another policy was wrong, however: as happens so often in war, "these bombs on London were dropped against orders by enemy crews who supposed themselves to be elsewhere".[14] The British reaction was prompt: on the night of 25 August British bombers made an attack on Berlin, where industrial targets were the intended objectives (though it is doubtful that these were hit in any significant measure).[15] Further attacks on the German capital fellowed on later nights.

While up to this time attacks on London had been expressly excluded from the objects of attack which Hitler had authorized, this policy was now drastically reversed and for some time London would even be the main object of the German air raids. From the available data the following chronology may be construed of this change in policy.

A first reference to preparations for a major attack on London is found in a report dated 1 September of the high command of the *Luftwaffe*.[16] On the next day, the Air Ministry issued orders for the new phase of the battle.[17] On 4 September, Hitler delivered a speech in which he pointed to the harm which the German population was made to suffer from the British night bombing raids, and he announced that London would by way of reprisal be made the object of German attacks in turn.[18] On 5 September, a *Führer* directive was issued whereby the planned attacks on London were formally authorized.[19] On that same day Hitler's order concerning the retaliatory bombing of London was mentioned in a broadcast by Göring.[20] After these preparatory orders, activities and statements, attacks were carried out on a relatively small scale on the nights of 5 and 6 September; and the raids were started with full intensity in the afternoon and night of 7 September.[21]

[14] T. H. O'Brien, *Civil Defence* (1955) p. 385, text and n. 2. The book is part of the History of the Second World War, United Kingdom Civil Series.
[15] Webster and Frankland, *op. cit.* n. 3, pp. 152, 215. And *cf.* Butler, *op. cit.* n. 22, p. 410: "It was in reprisal for (the dropping of bombs on London) that a few British bombers were sent to Berlin the following night. The Cabinet took credit for an intention to bomb military targets only (though in such a case the distinction could not possibly be observed)".—It may be pointed out that this bombing action did not in any event constitute a reprisal in the juridical sense of the term: it may be that the War Cabinet took its decision with a view to retaliation, but this intention was not made manifest in any way.
[16] Klee, *op. cit.* n. 3, p. 80. That author assumes that Hitler had approved the new policy even before that date.
[17] B. Collier, *The Defence of the United Kingdom* (1957), p. 234; published in the History of the Second World War, United Kingdom Military Series.
[18] M. Czesany, *Nie wieder Krieg gegen die Zivilbevölkerung* (1961), p. 92; Collier, *op. et loc. cit.* n. 17.
[19] Butler, *op. cit.* n. 2, p. 410; Collier, *loc. cit.* n. 17.
[20] Butler, *loc. cit.* n. 19.
[21] Klee, *op. cit.* n. 3, p. 81; Czesany, *loc. cit.* n. 18; H. G. Dahms, *Der Zweite Weltkrieg* (1960), p. 140; Collier, *loc. cit.* n. 17.

In the *Wehrmacht* communiqués, a first indication of the new policy was only given on 7 September. The communiqué of that date did not even then state in so many words that the raids on London were meant as a reprisal for earlier British actions; but a retaliatory intention could be inferred from the announcement, after the report that British bombers had carried out another night raid on Berlin, that "[d]ie deutsche Luftwaffe ist *daher* dazu übergegangen, nunmehr auch London mit starken Kräften anzugreifen".[22] Next day's communiqué made the point explicit: "Diese Angriffe [*i.e.* on the British capital] *sind die Vergeltung* für die von London begonnenen und in den letzten Wochen gesteigert geführten Nachtangriffe auf Wohnviertel und andere nichtmilitärische Ziele im Reichsgebiet."[23] This position was reiterated in a semi-official commentary on the raids issued in Berlin on 9 September, where it was stated "that they were 'a well-deserved reprisal for Britain's crimes against the German civilian population'."[24]

From 7 September the attack on London was pursued with full force for a fortnight, with large groups of heavy bombers carrying out raids virtually every day and night. The attacks first appeared to be directed primarily against the dockyard areas and other objectives of military value; but also the city and the residential districts suffered heavily, in particular from the night raids: while perhaps the German bombers flying night missions had orders to concentrate on the docks and similar objectives, the actual damage did not bear out any intention of aiming at such objectives in particular, but was instead suggestive of a policy of indiscriminate bombing. Soon, all pretence at bombing only militarily important objectives was abandoned and both the day and night bombardments assumed the character of actions indiscriminately directed against the London area as a whole.[25]

From 20 September a further change occurred in the pattern of the operations: while the night raids of the bombers continued in force, the daylight attacks were no longer carried out by massive groups of heavy bombers, but by smaller groups of fighter-bombers (which combined the bombing of objectives in London with the contest for air superiority with the British fighters). Also this phase, and, with that, the period of the concentrated "reprisal attack" on London came to an end when on the night of 14 November a heavy bombing raid was carried out on Coventry: from

[22] Text of the communiqué quoted in *Dokumente über die Alleinschuld Englands* (etc.), *op. cit.* n. 12; italics added.
[23] Quoted in Murawski, *op. cit.* n. 12, p. 104; italics added. See also Czesany, *loc. cit.* n. 18; that author adds that the retaliatory character of the actions had also been pointed out in leaflets dropped by German aircraft over English territory.
[24] Spaight, *Air Power and War Rights*, 3rd ed. (1947) p. 53, quoting The Times of 10 September 1940.
[25] *Cf.* Butler, *op. cit.* n. 2, at p. 410; Klee, *op. cit.* n. 3, p. 81 ff.; Czesany, *op. cit.* n. 18, p. 90 ff.

166

that time, the attacks by the German bombers were directed against industrial and other economic targets throughout the country, including—but with no special accent on—the London area.[26]

5.1.2. *Legal character of the British and German bombing actions, May-November 1940*

The issue of whether the bombing raids carried out by the *Luftwaffe* on London in the period from 5 September-14 November 1940 could be justified as reprisals or in any other manner, would be easily decided if one accepts as correct the suggestion created by the text of the appeal by the President of the United States and the replies received thereto on the part of the belligerents,[27] namely, that the obligation to refrain from bombing the civil populations was nothing but the result of the voluntary undertakings embodied in these declarations and, by their very wording, subject to reciprocity. For it could not be denied that at least part of the British raids over German territory had in effect amounted to attacks on the population, so that the obligation for Germany to refrain from bombing the civil population would thereby have come to an end and the raids on London could not be regarded as contravening an obligation which had ceased to exist.

This suggestion was, however, incorrect. Admittedly, the fact that the rules of warfare formulated at the Hague Peace Conferences of 1899 and 1907 had never since been adapted to the development of the air arm into a branch of the armed forces capable of operating independently of the other branches and of penetrating deeply into the enemy air space, resulted in uncertainty as to the law in respect of air warfare and especially aerial bombardment. But it could not be denied that there were certain rules and principles governing air warfare and that these were valid irrespective of the willingness of belligerents to reach an understanding in the matter or to enter into unilateral undertakings.

Central among these rules and principles stood the distinction between military and non-military objectives,[28] the former category embracing those

---

[26] Klee, *op. cit.* n. 3, pp. 81-83; Czesany, *op. cit.* n. 18, pp. 92-93; Collier, *op. cit.* n. 17, p. 234 ff.; O'Brien, *op. cit.* n. 14, p. 385 ff.

[27] See notes 1 and 2 to this §.

[28] This distinction was implicit already in the text of the Regulations on Land Warfare (1907, Art. 27) and it was clearly expressed in the Convention concerning Bombardment by Naval Forces in Time of War (1907, Arts. 1 and 2). It had been elaborated further by the Commission of Jurists which in 1922-23, at the instigation of the Governments of the United States, Great Britain, France, Italy, Japan and The Netherlands, had produced a set of draft Rules bearing on some new aspects of warfare (the control of radio in time of war, and air warfare).—For an extensive discussion of the state of the law with respect to aerial bombardment at the time of the outbreak of World War II, see: K. H. Kunzmann, *Die Fortentwicklung des Kriegsrechts auf den Gebieten des Schutzes der Verwundeten und der Beschiessung von Wohnorten* (1960), in particular the Chapter headed *Das Luftbombardement* (p. 147 ff.).

objects the elimination of which constitutes a legitimate goal as the military importance of their elimination outweighs the detriment to human values inherent in such an action. The category of the non-military objectives, on the other hand, is made up of those objects in respect of which the balance of military interest and human values tips the other way, so that their elimination cannot be considered a legitimate goal. This distinction, while simple in essence, could of course easily lead to disagreement in practice, as in many instances the dividing-line between the two categories would be unclear.[29] However, the core of either notion was so evident as to be free from such differences of opinion: it was not open to doubt that military installations such as gun emplacements, anti-aircraft batteries, naval ports and so on were military objectives, while the civil population as such provided the clearest example of a non-military objective.

In the light of these considerations, it is not hard to decide that the British air raids carried out over German territory in the period preceding the bombardment of London presented certain characteristics incompatible with the law as it stood. True, the orders for the British bombers were to drop their bombs on certain well-defined and identified objectives which on account of their importance for the war effort could be characterized as military objectives. The actions were, however, carried out as night raids, and, notwithstanding the often enthusiastic reports brought home by the crews, the accuracy of their navigation, target identification and bomb aiming generally was very low. This already led to the result that a majority of the raids brought indiscriminate (though not generally extensive) damage to the locations actually struck and to the civil populations living there.

These unfavourable results were unquestionably worsened by the activities of the German air defence and especially by the anti-aircraft fire: at times this caused so much confusion among the British bombers that these were diverted from their set course and, for want of adequate means

---

[29] The ICRC in a memorandum of 12 March 1940 recognized this aspect of the matter: "In the absence of any recent Convention formally and specifically regulating aerial warfare, and taking into account the changes that have occurred in the conduct of hostilities, an idea common to all civilized nations has nevertheless made its appearance: military objectives alone can be permissibly attacked. ... The statement of a principle is, however, not sufficient in itself, since the notion of 'military objectives' remains lacking in precision, and because difficulties arise from the fact that military objectives are sometimes close to harmless inhabited areas, or are more or less mixed up with them."—"Appeal of the International Committee of the Red Cross of 12th March, 1940, to the High Contracting Parties signatory to the Geneva Convention for the Relief of the Wounded and Sick in Armies in the Field, and to the Fourth Hague Convention of 1907 respecting the Laws and Customs of War on Land" (extract), in: *Draft Rules for the Limitation of the Dangers incurred by the Civilian Population in Time of War*, published by the ICRC, 2nd ed., 1958, p. 154, at p. 155.

of checking their position, ultimately discharged their bombloads at places miles distant from—but believed to be—the original goals. This is not sufficient argument, however, to excuse the in fact indiscriminate character of the bombing, which must be considered unlawful precisely to the extent that it proved indiscriminate.[30]

Neither is this conclusion shaken by the reflection that even prior to the opening in May 1940 of the British air offensive German bombs had been dropped on members of the civil population in more than one country. At most this could provide the British authorities with a reason for feeling no longer bound by their voluntary undertaking of 1 September 1939;[31] but it was decidedly not sufficient in itself to release them from the obligation to respect the existing rules of air warfare. Neither did the British authorities in this instance seek to justify their action by an appeal to the doctrine of reprisals.

Similar considerations apply with respect to the question of the legal character of the bombing raids carried out by the *Luftwaffe* on the London area in the period from September to November 1940. The area in question was built up of a variety of objects, ranging from purely military installations (like anti-aircraft batteries), through the docks and similar objects of immediate significance for the war effort, to such non-military objectives as churches and hospitals, and the residential districts of the civil population. No reasonable doubt could therefore exist that whole districts of the London area constituted non-military objectives that could not lawfully be made the object of express attack. But neither could it be seriously contested that an area like the harbour district could in its entirety be considered a military objective.

This leads to the conclusion that, according to the standards stated above, part of the bombing raids could by themselves be considered legitimate: viz., those raids which were clearly directed against a complex of military objectives such as the harbour area. As related before, such raids occurred particularly in the first phase of the action, and then in day-time only. For the rest, the bombardment of London had an indiscriminate character, the German bombers unloading their bombs without any apparent regard for the nature of the targets. Obviously, even thus damage was sometimes done to objects that could be classed as military objectives; but this cannot modify the intrinsically unlawful character of this mode of bombardment which was in contravention, not only of the undertaking of 1 September 1939, but of the rules governing air warfare.

[30] With respect to this episode *cf.* Webster and Frankland, *op. cit.* n. 3 to § 5.1, at pp. 144, 152, 215 ff., 299.
[31] For the question of whether the earlier German actions were indeed entirely comparable to the British bombing raids over Germany, and, for that matter, to the German bombardment of London, see *infra*, p. 170.

On account of the factually indiscriminate character of the early night raids, and of the open abandonment of any attempt at discrimination either at night or by day soon thereafter, it seems safe to conclude that the bombardment of London, taken as a single operation, was *prima facie* unlawful according to the law of air warfare in force at the time; a conclusion which is not diminished in the least by the consideration that certain individual raids forming part of the action may have lacked this unlawful character.

5.1.3. *Appraisal of the alleged character as a reprisal of the bombardment of London*

In view of the conclusion that both the British bombing actions against German territory and the bombardment of London constituted violations of the law of air warfare, the question arises next whether the action undertaken by the Germans could find justification as a reprisal.

A first consideration is that German bombers had, even prior to the commencement of the British air offensive, in May 1940, unloaded their bombs on the houses of the civil population and similar targets in several of the countries which successively had become the victims of German aggression. While this certainly did not strengthen the German position in respect of the bombardment of London and its allegedly retaliatory character, neither was it sufficient ground to conclude that Germany was precluded from complaining of the British bombing raids over its territory. For, irrespective of how one might assess the early German bombardments from a humanitarian point of view, there was at least the significant difference that those bombardments had been carried out in the context of military operations envisaging (and resulting in) the occupation of the countries concerned. It could therefore be argued that those bombardments were governed more especially by the text of Article 27 of the Hague Regulations on Land Warfare, which for the event of an occupation bombardment merely provides that certain specific objects (such as churches, museums and hospitals) should be spared as much as possible, but which does not provide a general protection for the civil population in a besieged place.

The bombing raids over German territory, on the other hand, did, like the bombardment of London, belong in the category of destruction bombardments: bombing actions against targets in regions the occupation of which is not in progress nor immediately envisaged. The principle that only military objectives can be legitimate objects of attack, and that the civil population does not constitute such an objective, had been recognized in particular with a view to destruction bombardment. There might therefore be more than a little ground for the contention that the earlier German bombardments were so essentially different from a legal point of view from the British raids over Germany, that that State had not by its own earlier actions lost the right to complain of—and to retaliate against—those raids in so far as these were illegitimate.[32] In any event the argument derived from the earlier German actions is too disputable to consider the matter of the justification of the bombardment of London as settled. It is therefore necessary to examine the further arguments relevant to that issue.

First to mention among these arguments is the objection that the attempt to characterize the action as a reprisal was merely a matter of propaganda, as it had been planned some considerable time in advance.[33] This does not however appear a really decisive argument. As argued before,[34] there is no need why the sole fact that an action is premeditated should disqualify it as a reprisal; neither does it justify the conclusion that the qualification of the action as a reprisal is nothing but a propagandistic stunt. Indeed, in the given instance a certain measure of propagandistic support would be indispensable in order to ensure the realization of the purpose which the action, as a reprisal, would be destined to serve. Another question is, however, whether other indications urge the conclusion that in this case the qualification as a reprisal was in reality a mere propagandistic abuse of the term, serving to conceal the true nature of an action that was neither intended as, nor met the requirements of, a reprisal; this hypothesis will be examined below.

Narrowly connected with the above argument is the consideration that the action had not only been planned some time in advance, but was clearly destined to contribute to the realization of the military aims of the German air offensive against Great Britain. Actually, its purpose in this respect was threefold: to gain the air superiority over the British Isles which the operations carried out so far had failed to secure (and which would be indispensable if ever the idea of an invasion were to be carried into effect); to inflict damage on the British economy; and to break the will to resist of the British people.[35]

The unsatisfactory results of the actions which the *Luftwaffe* had carried out in August, had been mainly due to the tactics of the British fighters, who whenever possible had dodged engagements with superior numbers of German fighters and instead had concentrated on the bombers. By so doing

[32] The situation, in other words, was radically different from the one discussed by the Permanent Court of International Justice in its judgment in *The Diversion of Water from the Meuse; supra,* p. 151 n. 8.

[33] Murawski, *op. cit.* n. 12 to § 5.1, at p. 104, refers to the *Wehrmacht* communiqué of 8 September 1940 which characterized the attacks on London as *Vergeltung,* and he continues: "Auch in den dann folgenden WB [*i.e.* the armed forces bulletins] werden diese an und für sich schon lange eingeplanten Luftangriffe immer wieder als Vergeltungsangriffe bezeichnet."

[34] *Supra,* p. 147.

[35] Concerning these purposes of the German action, see in particular: Klee, *op. cit.* n.3 to § 5.1, p. 80 ff.

they had managed to avert unbearable losses on their own side and to inflict appreciable losses to the enemy. Now, the idea on the German side was that the attack on an object like London, which on account of its paramount importance would have to be defended at all costs, might force the British fighters into abandoning these evasive tactics. And to a certain extent this prognosis was borne out by the events: from the beginning of the attack on London the British fighters kept on a vigorous defence, and their losses were correspondingly high. Not so high, however, as to lead to the virtual elimination of their fighter force; indeed, time and again the fighters managed to revert to their earlier tactics and to inflict considerable losses on the attacking German bombers after these had been separated from the accompanying fighters. It was precisely this experience which led to the next change in the pattern of the German actions: as related previously, from 20 September the daylight raids were carried out by fighter-bombers, the idea being that thus the British fighters would finally be precluded from pursuing their favoured tactics and would be forced to face the destructive powers of this new type of German planes. This change once again proved a dangerous threat to the British fighter force; but, again, it proved not decisive, and the attempt to gain rapidly the superiority in the air was abandoned soon thereafter (together with the idea of an invasion, for that matter), in favour of the other purposes of the action.

The attempt to force Great Britain onto her knees by an attack from the air on the vulnerable parts of her economic system was in fact inaugurated with the start of the bombardment of London: the harbour district, against which the early daylight raids were directed, constituted an important link in the system of overseas trade communications. And even when soon thereafter the bombing took on completely indiscriminate features, this did not imply that the policy of doing damage to the economically important parts of the London area had been abandoned: the infliction of such damage remained a major aim of the attacks throughout.

The third purpose of the bombardment of London (and one which had already been present in the earliest German air operations against British territory) was to break the morale of the civil population (and hence, it was hoped, of the Government). The idea was that, when the British people would find itself confronted with the reality that the London area had itself become the object of direct attack by the German bombers, it would rapidly come to the conclusion that to continue the war would serve no worth-while ends. In this idea, indiscriminate attacks were believed to be best suited to contribute to the realization of this purpose.

So, both the design of the bombardment of London and the various stages of its execution demonstrate that it fitted into the strategic and tactical considerations at the time governing the German military operations against Great Britain. In other words: whatever other purposes the action might have had besides, it was in any event launched and sustained with a view to promoting the realization of the main war aim of that period, namely the ultimate defeat of Great Britain.

The conclusion is that, if it were found to be true that the bombardment of London constituted a reprisal, the action would once again afford clear evidence of the peculiar feature of reprisals that these, while functioning as sanctions in the international legal order, at the same time are usually chosen with a view to promoting the interests of the State having recourse to them.

There remains the question of how much truth there is in the contention that the bombardment of London, besides being motivated by the German interests, was also a reprisal, that is: a reaction to the illegal aspects of the preceding British bombing raids, resorted to for the purpose of coercing the British authorities to change their policy and henceforth to abstain from bombing German territory in a manner reprehensible on account of its indiscriminate effects.

Indications to the effect that the action actually was intended to serve as a reprisal may be seen in the repeated references by responsible authorities in Germany to the illegal aspects of the British attacks and in the deliberate use of the term *Vergeltung* with respect to the ensuing actions against London. And, indeed, at first sight one might perhaps be prepared to attach credence to the assertion that the harm done to his people had moved Hitler to order reprisals, so as to protect the people from further undeserved injury.[36]

Other indications are to the contrary, however. As was related previously, Hitler had already in October 1939 informed his closest military co-operators that "[t]he ruthless employment of the *Luftwaffe* against the heart of the British will-to-resist can and will follow at the given moment".[37] True, this is not an entirely unequivocal statement: in particular the reference to the "heart of the British will-to-resist" can be understood in more than one way, the most favourable being that the idea was to destroy Great Britain's economic viability.[38] On the other hand, a rather less lenient interpretation—and one that finds support in the use of the term „ruthless"—is that the actions envisaged for the *Luftwaffe* would have as their aim the breaking of the morale of the British people and that, no matter which particular part of British society might be selected to figure as the main objective of such actions, these would in any event be carried out without any consideration for the civil population, and, more probably, with the additional intention to terrorize it. The action started in September 1940

---

[36] As is suggested in particular by Czesany, *op. cit.* n. 18, p. 92; *cf.* also Klee, *op. cit.* n. 3, p. 80, and Dahms, *op. cit.* n. 21, p. 139.
[37] See note 5.
[38] In this respect *cf.* the passage from *Weisung* Nr. 9, quoted in note 5.

against London would undoubtedly fit into the latter train of thought.

Moreover, in the period preceding September 1940 the British raids had not yet caused really extensive damage, either to industrial targets or to the civil population in Germany. While this does not alter the in effect indiscriminate character of those raids, it does have a bearing on the appreciation of the subsequent large-scale assault on London and of the grounds advanced for its justification. Here a statement made on 7 September 1940 by the German Minister for Propaganda, Goebbels, provides us with a particularly valuable piece of information. It gave expression to his disappointment at the fact that the raid on Berlin of the preceding night had only been on a relatively minor scale, and he went on to express the hope that soon another British raid would provide the necessary excuse with which to justify the enormous scale of the attacks on London.[39]

These words, it should be realized, were uttered in the context of a discussion about the propagandistic aspects of the situation and thus are likely to have been prompted by the requirements of propaganda first of all. However, making every allowance for this side of the quoted passage, the fact remains that at a time when Germany was launching a large-scale operation which those in authority had chosen to announce as a reprisal against Great Britain, one of those authorities overtly expressed the hope that the unlawful mode of acting allegedly at the root of the reprisal action would be continued in an aggravated form. This flatly contradicted the character of the action as a reprisal. It seems therefore justified to interpret Goebbels' statement as another strong indication against the contention that the bombardment of London was meant to constitute a reprisal in the legal sense of the term, and in favour of the thesis that the announcement of the bombardment as an act of *Vergeltung* was in reality nothing but a propagandistic abuse of the notion of reprisals.[40]

[39] "Der Minister unterrichtet darüber, dass der Fliegerangriff der letzten Nacht in Berlin entgegen den Erwartungen nicht die Auswirkungen gehabt hat, die nötig sind, um der Welt genenüber mit einem Schrei der Empörung eine gewaltige Steigerung unserer Angriffe auf London zu rechtfertigen. Man müsse sich darüber klar sein, dass die Vernichtung Londons wohl die grösste Menschheitskatastrophe der Geschichte darstellen würde, so dass diese Massnahme auch vor der Welt irgendwie gerechtfertigt erscheinen müsse. Man müsse also hoffen, dass eine derartige Möglichkeit durch einen der englischen Fliegerangriffe möglichst bald gegeben werde."—Minutes of the meeting held on 7 September 1940 in the Ministry for Propaganda under the chairmanship of the Minister; in: *Kriegspropaganda 1939-1941, Geheime Ministerkonferenzen im Reichspropagandaministerium*, ed. by Willi A. Boelcke (1966), p. 493.

[40] This interpretation is borne out by remarks made by Goebbels on subsequent occasions. Thus, on 9 September he gave order that "Der englische Angriff auf Hamburg soll so ausgeschlachtet werden, dass er vor der Weltöffentlichkeit mit als Unterlage für die Fortsetzung unserer Vergeltungsangriffe gegen London gilt". And at the next meeting, on 10 September, he not only ordered that "Die Fliegerangriffe auf Berlin und Hamburg in der Nacht zum Dienstag sollen unter möglichster Aufbauschung aller Einzelheiten so aufgemacht werden, dass sie vor der Welt die Berechtigung unserer Vergeltungsmassnahmen weiter untermauern", but he also gave instruction once again

On the strength of the above mutually corroborative indications I am disinclined to place any credence in the contention that the action against London, carried out by the *Luftwaffe* in the period from 5 September to 14 November 1940, had the purpose of coercing the enemy to observe the law of war. In my view the action was prompted solely by the motives of national interest given previously, and above all by the hope of the *Führer* that the massive assault on the heart of British society would be sufficient to break the will to resist of the British people and of its Government and that he would thus succeed in realizing the predominant goal of his policy of the time: to drive Great Britain out of the war.[41]

The above leads strongly to the conclusion that the bombardment of London cannot find justification as a reprisal. As, however, the evidentiary value of Goebbels' statement is not beyond all doubt, there is perhaps some room left for a different appreciation of the German intention. It seems therefore necessary to enter into some further aspects of the action under consideration, and in the first place into the question of its proportionality.

It seems evident from the foregoing, and in particular from the statement by Goebbels, that even the German authorities realized at the time that proportionality was not the most conspicuous feature of the action: rather, the idea seems to have been that the scale of the action was grossly disproportionate to the raids carried out so far by the British bomber force. This is in conformity with what has since become known about the scale of the German action and of the preceding, rather ineffectual British raids. It is therefore submitted that even without further detailed enquiry the conclusion is warranted that the bombardment of London failed to meet the standard of proportionality to the act retaliated against.

It is worth while to mention here the attempt which another author, Czesany, has made to assess the justification and, in that context, the proportionality of the retaliatory bombing actions carried out by the German airforce.[42] His enquiry is not confined to the bombardment of London, but embraces the entire period of the German bombing offensive against Great Britain, which lasted from May 1940 to May 1941. It is of

---

to go over the earlier British raids so as to extract from these the maximum amount of propagandistic profit: "Ferner soll das Material der letzten Monaten mehr ausgewertet werden als bisher, um auch auf diese Weise die Berechtigung unserer Massnahme zu verdeutlichen." (*Ibid.*, at pp. 497, 498).

[41] In so far as one might be inclined to attach value to the information that Hitler's personal indignation, roused by the first British raid on Berlin on the night of 25 August 1940, would have played a part in the decision to lift the ban on bombing London, it may be observed that this element of personal emotion is best explained as at most a mere addition to the official motives of the bombardment expounded in the text above; at any rate it would not of itself have been sufficient to transform the action into a reprisal: rather it would confer upon it the quality of an act of revenge.
[42] *Op. cit.* n. 18, pp. 95-97.

particular interest to observe how that author, on the basis of the extensive information available,[43] endeavours to give a quantitative appraisal of the British actions and the German counter-actions and to establish the ratio between these. About half-way through his study he finds "dass die Luftwaffe in der fraglichen Zeit auf englischen Boden etwa zwei- bis dreimal soviel Bomben abgeworfen hat als die RAF auf deutschen Boden",[44] and this difference in bombloads dropped leads him to a tentative conclusion of disproportionality of the German actions. He then proceeds to diminish the significance of his finding (and the rigidity and narrowness of the standard applied) by advancing other relevant factors beside the quantity of bombs dropped: daylight versus night attacks, aims pursued, objects actually hit; some of these factors seem to reduce the disproportionality of the German actions, while other factors have the opposite effect. Without however attempting to quantify these further factors in his equation, Csezany next posits his final conclusion: "Trotzdem kann jedoch als wahrscheinlich angenommen werden, dass es während der Luftschlacht um England zu einem Repressalienexzess von seiten Deutschlands gekommen ist." [45]

Thus, the attempt at quantitative appraisal undertaken by Csezany was only half-hearted and not sustained to the end. The difficulties which he encountered in the course of his enquiry are, however, typical of what anyone should expect who after the conclusion of a war endeavours to appraise the proportionality of an alleged reprisal action consisting in a somewhat extensive military operation, such as the bombardments on the British Isles which extended over a year. The problem is not so much the absence of all information: it is rather that for a really exact appraisal of operations of the scale as discussed here, it will be necessary to quantify all such varied and hard-to-weigh factors as the precise extent of the damage to military, industrial and other objects, the number and seriousness of casualties among combatants and non-combatants, and so on,—an operation the magnitude of which is not easily overrated. Moreover, even assuming for a moment that that manoeuvre could be brought to a successful end, the next question would be what standard should be applied to compare the results. One thing seems certain: that standard cannot be a rigid one, as the belligerents themselves could never be expected nor required to apply it *durante bello*; indeed, to ascertain the facts with the degree of accuracy required for such an appraisal would be an absolute impracticability for them. Accordingly, the only standard applicable seems

---

[43] There was no lack of information in this instance: fairly accurate data were available about the sorties flown, the bombloads transported, the number, location and duration of airraid warnings, the number and size of fires started, etcetera. In fact, it is amazing how much detailed information was put on record in the course of the war.
[44] *Op. cit.* n. 18, p. 96.
[45] *Ibid.*, p. 97.

the marginal test according to which an action cannot be justified as a reprisal when it is so obviously and grossly disproportionate to the illegalities giving rise to it, that the belligerent having resort to it cannot reasonably have deemed it an appropriate reaction.[46]

However this may be, it is a particularly fortunate circumstance that the minutes of Goebbels' ministerial utterances have provided the postwar world with the certain knowledge that even on the German side the gross disproportionality of the contemplated action against London had been fully realized in time.

A final aspect of the case under discussion concerns the norms violated by the German action. While the primary aim of the act of dropping a variety of high explosive and incendiary bombs on a built-up area may be assumed to be the destruction of the buildings, it was certain that human beings were living in the London area; and, as most of the bombing was intentionally indiscriminate, it was equally certain that numerous civilians would be among the persons hit. It may therefore be assumed that the intention on the German side was *inter alia* to kill or injure civilians who where not taking part in the war in any normal sense of the term. The conclusion is that among the norms violated by the German action was the prohibition wilfully to kill or injure enemy non-combatants, a rule the primarily humanitarian character of which is beyond dispute.

In earlier chapters the question has been examined of whether in the period preceding the Second World War a rule had emerged prohibiting reprisals against the non-combatant civil population.[47] It may be recalled that several of the authors who wrote at the time, expressly discussed the case of the retaliatory air bombardment; and it was found that a majority among them were of the opinion that, while as a general rule reprisals were not allowed to violate the elementary principles of humanity, no rule existed prohibiting retaliatory bombardment under all circumstances.[48] Spaight, for one, had added that a prohibition to that effect was urgently needed *de lege ferenda*.[49] The bombardment of London, even though in my submission only a pretended reprisal and in any event not justified as a reprisal on account of gross disproportionality, provides a striking example underlining the correctness of his opinion and the urgency of the desired provision.

Summarizing the above, the bombardment of London carried out in the period of 7 September to 14 November 1940 cannot be said to have constituted a reprisal in the proper sense of the term, as it lacked the purpose required for such an action. Alternatively, it failed to find justifi-

---

[46] *Supra*, p. 32.
[47] Chapters II and III.
[48] *Supra*, pp. 112-113.
[49] *Supra*, p. 113.

cation as a reprisal at it was obviously and grossly disproportionate to the actions purportedly giving rise to it. Finally it should be noted that the action constituted an infringement of the laws of humanity; but it cannot be maintained with certainty that this provided a separate ground standing in the way of its justification.

Further instances of bombardments characterized as retaliatory actions have occurred at later stages of the Second World War.[50] As, however, both parties in the war had by then resorted to indiscriminate bombing on too many occassions for an attempt to justify a particular instance as a reprisal to be taken seriously any longer, there is no need to enter into those instances here.

5.2. REPRISALS AGAINST PRISONERS OF WAR

The period between the two World Wars had, as related in Chapter III, yielded only one express conventional provision concerning belligerent reprisals: the prohibition, laid down in Article 2 of the Geneva Prisoners of War Convention of 1929, to take reprisals against prisoners of war. That prohibition, together with the Convention in its entirety, was put to the test of actual large-scale warfare in the course of the Second World War. Not all the belligerents participating in that war were parties to the Convention (notable exceptions being the U.S.S.R. and Japan); but it had been ratified by the States figuring as actors in the present section: Germany, Great Britain, Canada, and France.

The prohibition in fact proved incapable of preventing all reprisals against prisoners of war. Indeed, the International Committee of the Red Cross (or ICRC) devoted a whole chapter of the report covering its activities during the Second World War to this issue, relating several instances of reprisals or threatened reprisals against prisoners of war that had come to its knowledge and given rise to an intervention on its part.[1] The most serious cases among these were the affair of the shackling of prisoners, and the killing of German prisoners held by the French Forces of the Interior. An instance not mentioned in the report of the ICRC, but which is worth examining if only on account of its horrific character, is the notorious Commando Order.

5.2.1. The shackling of prisoners of war

The first major amphibious operation by Allied forces against the European mainland was the raid on Dieppe, carried out on 19 August 1942 by

[50] For an inventory of such allegedly retaliatory bombardments, see in particular Spaight, op. cit. n. 24, pp. 53-54, 286-287.
[1] Report of the International Committee of the Red Cross on its activities during the Second World War, Vol. I, pp. 365-372.

Canadian and British landing forces.[2] In the course of that operation a number of German soldiers who fell into the hands of the attacking forces, were tied by their captors. This mode of acting apparently was in execution of instructions issued for the raid.[3] When the German discovered this from documents captured on prisoners taken at Dieppe, they raised a sharp protest and on 2 September

"...threatened to place in chains all the prisoners taken at Dieppe. The War Office then announced that if an order for tying prisoners was found to have been issued as stated, it would be 'cancelled'. On 3 September the Germans cancelled the proposed reprisals. On 7 October, however, they issued a second order, stated to be the result of further investigation concerning Dieppe and of an incident at Sark on 4 October, when German prisoners taken in a very minor raid were reported to have been tied. British and Canadian prisoners were tied on 8 October; later, handcuffs replaced the ropes." [4]

Confronted with this measure, the British Government (and in their wake, but reluctantly, the Canadian Government) decided to apply the same treatment to an equivalent number of German prisoners. Apparently the British Government via the Protecting Power notified the German authorities of their decision, as well as of their view that the tying of prisoners as practised at Dieppe was not unlawful, as it was necessitated by the conditions prevailing in the zone of operations and as the Geneva Convention of 1929 was not applicable so long as the prisoners were still on the battlefield.[5] In any event, on 10 October the decision was carried into effect and a number of German prisoners were handcuffed in certain British and Canadian camps.[6]

Meanwhile, the developing situation had led the ICRC to intervene: in a telegraphic message of 9 October 1942 it offered its good offices to the parties concerned. As the German Government failed to reply, the offer was renewed in a telegram dated 22 October, and, according to the account given by the ICRC, this time it came within an inch of being accepted by

[2] A very comprehensive and detailed account of the raid on Dieppe is found in: Colonel C. P. Stacey, *Six Years of War—The Army in Canada, Britain and the Pacific* (1955), being Vol. I of the Official History of the Canadian Army in the Second World War.
[3] The order being that "Wherever possible, prisoners' hands will be tied to prevent destruction of their documents"; Stacey, *op. cit.* n. 2, p. 396.
[4] *Loc. cit.* n. 3.
[5] *Report, op. cit.* n. 1, p. 368. See also *Commentary on the 1949 Convention relative to the treatment of prisoners of war* (1960), p. 73 n. 1, where it is further alleged that the German prisoners would have been handcuffed at Dieppe "in order to prevent any escape"; but see n. 3, *supra*.
[6] Stacey, *op. cit.* n. 2, p. 397. The measure did not fail to provoke some resistance; as Stacey relates: "There was resistance in certain Canadian camps; in Camp 30, at Bowmanville, Ontario, the guard had to fire a few shots, although nobody was killed."

179

the German authorities. The acceptance failed to come about, however, and in consequence the shackling was continued on both sides.[7]

No change occurred in this unpleasant situation until 12 December 1942. On that date, the German prisoners in British and Canadian hands were unshackled. The enemy, however, failed to follow this step: [8]

"It appeared that he was still demanding guarantees against the issuance of further orders of the type he objected to. After discussion between the United Kingdom and Canada, the former issued an Army Council Instruction and the latter a Canadian Army Routine Order forbidding the binding of prisoners of war except in case of operational necessity on the field of battle. The Germans objected to this reservation, and the Canadian and British prisoners remained shackled until 22 November 1943, when, following conversations between Dr. Burckhardt of the International Red Cross Committee and the German authorities, the latter, without formally rescinding the order, stopped all shackling."

In contrast with the instances of belligerent reprisals examined so far, in this case it seems not hard to decide that both the German measure and the British-Canadian counter-measure were *prima facie* unlawful. The measures were taken against prisoners of war interned in fixed P.O.W. camps far from any field of operations, and, while no provision in the 1929 Convention expressly prohibited the shackling of the inmates of such camps, the system of the Convention could not leave the slightest doubt that the internment of the prisoners was the maximum permissible deprivation of liberty and that—apart from the application of disciplinary or penal sanctions—no further restraints were allowed in their regard. Thus, to shackle prisoners confined in camps was indubitably in contravention of the Convention. Neither did it make any difference whether the measure was carried into effect by tying the prisoners' hands with ropes (as the Germans did at the outset) or by applying handcuffs (as they did later, and the British and Canadians right from the start).

Could at least the original German measure derive a semblance of justification from the practice demonstrated by the Canadian and British troops at Dieppe? In other words: was it unlawful to tie prisoners in battle-field-conditions, and in particular in conditions such as those prevailing in the assault zone at Dieppe? The answer to this question is not so easily given. It may be recalled that the motive of the tying as given in the official order [9] was: "to prevent destruction of their documents". This would mean that the practice formed part of the endeavours on the part of capturing

[7] *Report, op. cit.* n. 1, pp. 368-369.
[8] Stacey, *loc. cit.* n. 6. See also, in particular with respect to the rôle played by the ICRC, *Report, op. cit.* n. 1, p. 370.
[9] See n. 3 to this §.

forces to extract a maximum of information from the captured enemies.

Under the 1929 Convention a prisoner of war was not obliged to provide information, and neither was coercion allowed with a view to extracting any information which he was not ready to give voluntarily.[10] On the other hand, the capturing forces were fully entitled to seize as booty any State-owned articles found in the possession of prisoners (with the exceptions enumerated in the Convention),[11] and among these articles particular importance would attach to any documents, such as orders, communications, and so on, that might reveal information to the captors. So, it is understandable that they were anxious to secure as many documents as possible.

One could equally understand the idea that, while in ordinary battle conditions a simple measure such as ordering the prisoners to keep their hands up, combined with a close guard, might suffice to prevent the destruction of documents by prisoners, in the circumstances of a hit-and-run raid such as the one carried out at Dieppe such undesirable activities on the part of the prisoners could only be prevented with the aid of special precautions. In this train of thought, the tying of the prisoners' hands might be envisaged as a reasonably effective and only moderately vexatious specimen of such a special precaution. And against the contention that the measure would run counter to the letter of the prohibition to use coercion with a view to extracting information,[12] it could be advanced that, if this were the correct interpretation of that provision, it would be equally applicable to the common practice of ordering hands up. Indeed, it seems a more reasonable interpretation that this prohibition was only applicable to such coercion as might be applied against a prisoner who, upon questioning, demonstrated his unwillingness to give away any information which it was within his power to conceal; and documents, it is submitted, are not among this kind of information as they can be taken from the person of the prisoner without his co-operation and even against his will.

There is however a final consideration. The prisoners in British and Canadian hands at Dieppe were far from being out of danger: on the contrary, they were as much exposed to the immediate dangers of the battlefield as were the members of the raiding force. In these circumstances to tie the prisoners' hands might well be equal to depriving them of the necessary freedom of movement in a situation where that freedom could prove an essential prerequisite to saving one's life. Viewed thus, the practice as demonstrated in the raid on Dieppe might be held to run

---

[10] Art. 5 of the Convention of 1929.
[11] Art. 6.
[12] Art. 5; the text of para. 3 of the Article runs as follows: "No pressure shall be exerted on prisoners to obtain information regarding the situation in their armed forces or their country. Prisoners who refuse to reply may not be threatened, insulted, or exposed to unpleasantness or disadvantages of any kind whatsoever."

counter to the letter and spirit of the rule providing that "prisoners shall not be unnecessarily exposed to danger while awaiting evacuation from a fighting zone",[13] a rule which could be deemed to elaborate the fundamental principle of respect for the prisoner's life and, even more fundamentally, of humane treatment of prisoners of war.[14]

It is submitted that the last-mentioned consideration decides the issue, to the effect that the shackling of prisoners of war as practised during the raid on Dieppe was unlawful. As for the ground advanced by the British Government that the measure was necessitated by the conditions prevailing in the zone of operations, it should be noted that Article 1 of the Convention of 1929 provided an exception of that purport only for the case of capture in the course of operations of sea or aerial warfare, making such deviations from the Convention permissible as might be rendered inevitable by the circumstances of the arrest. The British reliance in the above ground seems hardly reconcilable with the express restriction of the relative exception to sea and air warfare. And a further, even more fundamental objection to the British argument is that the deviation at issue was neither inevitable nor did it result from the circumstances of the arrest as such; it was a measure deliberately decided upon by the capturing Power for the purposes of his intelligence interests. So, the appeal to exceptional circumstances fails, and the conclusion stands that it was an unlawful practice to tie prisoners of war in the operations zone so as to secure the documents in their possession.

It follows that the reprisal ordered by the German authorities could find a semblance of justification in the illegality of the practice giving rise to it. Furthermore, the measure unmistakably had the purpose of coercing the opponents to abandon the illegal practice: as appears from the account of the episode given above, the German authorities took the definitive decision to resort to the shackling of prisoners in their power only after— and because—evidence had come into their possession that the British authorities also after Dieppe intended to maintain the incriminated order that raiding parties should tie their prisoners' hands in order to prevent destruction of documents.

All this cannot however alter the fact that the German measure was only apparently justified, full justification inevitably being frustrated by the express prohibition of reprisals against prisoners of war laid down in Article 2, paragraph 3, of the Convention of 1929.[15]

[13] Art. 7, para. 3 of the Convention of 1929.
[14] Art. 2, para. 2.
[15] According to Wengler, the German measure would have constituted a typical instance of a disproportionate reprisal. That author refers to "die Fesselung einer grossen Anzahl kanadischer Kriegsgefangener ... als Repressalie gegen die Fesselung einzelner deutscher Kriegsgefangener" (*Völkerrecht*, Vol. I (1964), p. 519 n. 4). However, the number of prisoners made by the attacking forces at Dieppe was not so negligible at all: while only a few (37) prisoners were ultimately evacuated from the area, a considerable number of Germans had been held as prisoners for some time

182

After the above considerations it is not hard to conclude that the British/ Canadian measure taken in response to the German action was equally unlawful: it may suffice to note that it was in contravention of the same rule prohibiting reprisals against prisoners of war.

Had perhaps the prior German violation of that rule liberated the British and Canadian authorities from their obligation to respect it? The answer to this question is that nothing in the Convention of 1929 warrants the suggestion that reciprocal observance of the prohibition of reprisals would be a condition for its continued validity between belligerents. The rule had been adopted solely on the strength of humanitarian considerations, and particularly the desire to safeguard the prisoners against inhumane treatment as a reaction to violations of the law of war (as, for instance, of the Convention of 1929) on the part of the enemy.

It was no more than a token of realism on the part of the British and Canadian authorities that they rescinded the retaliatory order after a relatively short lapse of time. The German authorities, on the other hand, maintained the measure for a considerable length of time afterwards. In this respect it should be borne in mind that, while it was true that the British/Canadian counter-reprisal had been discontinued, it was equally true that the original cause of the German measure, being the standing order for the treatment of prisoners by raiding units, had not been removed: when ultimately a modification was introduced into the text of the order, the new text could hardly be deemed satisfactory from the German point of view, as the order to tie the hands of prisoners had merely been replaced by the order not to tie their hands except for the case of "operational necessity"—a term sufficiently imprecise as not to be reassuring.

In this light it is understandable that the attempt on the part of the German authorities to bring about a more complete change in the policy of their opponents with respect to this point was continued for such a considerable time. On the other hand, it is also evident that when the reprisal order was finally rescinded it had, like the counter-reprisal of the opponents, failed to bring about the desired result: even the quasi-justification arising from effectiveness was denied these illegitimate reprisals.

---

during the raid; *cf.* Stacey, *op. cit.* n. 2, at p. 390. Furthermore, in this instance proportionality would not be a question of mere numbers, as also the conditions of the respective groups of prisoners had to be taken into account. In this respect it seems evident that the shackling of prisoners in combat conditions, like these prevailed in the zone of operations during the raid on Dieppe, constituted a more severe measure than the shackling of some thousand prisoners in the comparative safety of a prisoner-of-war camp.

5.2.2. The Commando Order

The *Führer* issued the directive commonly referred to as the *Kommando Befehl*, or Commando Order, on 18 October 1942, a mere eleven days after the issue of the order to shackle British and Canadian prisoners. And neither was the time of issue the only connection between the two orders: another connecting point was their immediate cause. For, while the shackling order had been provoked by a particular clause in the standing orders for British and Canadian soldiers taking part in raids, the commando order was a reaction to those raids themselves and, in a wider sense, to the activities of those small bands of commandos and similar troops (such as parachutists and other special forces), who, after landing by sea or from the air, by all kinds of actions did damage to the enemy in territory under his control. With this, however, the similarity between the orders ends: for, whereas the order to shackle British and Canadian prisoners of war was openly announced, the Commando Order was—except for a none too clear hint given prior to its issue—kept completely secret. Moreover, it was in a different class of gravity when compared with the relatively innocent shackling affair.

A description of the facts of the case may appropriately begin with the text of the aforementioned "hint", which consisted in a paragraph added to the *Wehrmacht* communiqué of 7 October 1942 of the following content: [16]

> "In Zukunft werden sämtliche Terror- und Sabotagetrupps der Briten und ihrer Helfershelfer, die sich nicht wie Soldaten, sondern wie Banditen benehmen, von den deutschen Truppen auch als solche behandelt und, wo sie auch auftreten, rücksichtslos in Kampf niedergemacht werden."

Although it was not stated in so many words, the text was evidently meant to convey the suggestion that in future quarter would be refused Allied soldiers belonging to "terror and sabotage bands" who moreover "behave like bandits". The "bandits" who had irritated the Germans to the point where these threatened their ruthless extermination "im Kampf", were the commandos employed on the above-mentioned missions in German-controlled territory. Widely though their missions might vary, these generally had in common that their aim was not so much to engage the armed forces of the enemy as to damage his cause by some specific act, such as the demolition of a military installation or a vital industrial plant, or the destruction of a warship lying in harbour, or alternatively, by intelligence activities or support to partisan groups (although the latter duties were normally performed by special forces rather than by ordinary commandos). Sometimes the soldiers could, upon completion of their

[16] See: I.M.T. Vol. XXVII, in Doc. 1266-PS.

mission, be picked up again, by a submarine, a small surface craft, or an airplane. Usually, however, the only way to save their lives would be to escape to neutral territory or, more probably, to surrender to the superior enemy forces which, when all had gone well, would arrive on the scene only after the mission had been completed. And the commandos were desirous to save their lives: they were not suicide troops.

Was this mode of acting in itself the "banditry" referred to in the *Wehrmacht* communiqué—or would only those members of the indicated forces qualify for the announced treatment who fulfilled the additional condition that they were guilty of some specific violation of the laws of war (such as operating in enemy uniforms, or killing prisoners)? Another vital question arising from the quoted text was whether the ruthless slaughtering would be restricted to the battlefield or would also be put into practice when individual men happened to fall alive into enemy hands (for instance, because they were arrested by the police).

The answer to these questions appears to have been unclear even to the authorities in the *Oberkommando der Wehrmacht* who, after the broadcast of 7 October, were set to work to translate the threat into a directive for the German forces.[17] Further grounds for hesitation on their part lay, firstly, in the consideration that the contemplated measure could hardly be called chivalrous; secondly, and more important, they realized that a literal interpretation and application of the threat would most certainly result in the loss of valuable information that might otherwise be obtained from living prisoners; and, finally, there was the fear that similar treatment might be given to members of German sabotage groups operating within reach of the enemy and particularly of Russia. The several draft orders circulated and discussed among the authorities concerned reflect these perturbations.

The most serious attempt to restrict the scope of the projected order was made by Admiral Canaris, Chief of the Counter-intelligence Service. In his view, the order could be applicable only to those members of sabotage units detected while wearing either civilian clothes or German uniforms, as they would be guilty of a violation of the rules of warfare that characterized them as francs-tireurs. Members of sabotage groups wearing their proper uniforms but suspected of some other discreditable or unlawful mode of acting, would have to be made prisoners. The latter individuals, however, would have to be kept separate from other prisoners, and their further treatment would depend on instructions to be given for each individual case by the responsible authorities, including those of the counter-intelligence.[18]

---

[17] *Loc. cit.* n. 16; the departments of the High Command involved in the drafting of the directive were: the Armed Forces Operations Staff, the Counter-intelligence Service, and the Legal Department.
[18] I.M.T. Vol. XXVII, in Docs. 1263-PS and 1265-PS.

Lehmann, Head of the Legal Department of the *Oberkommando der Wehrmacht*, shared in principle the idea that a division should be made between a category of commandos who would be ruthlessly killed and another category who would be made prisoners. However, he continued, the prohibition to refuse quarter laid down in Article 23 *c* of the Hague Regulations on Land Warfare had been drafted at a time when modern methods of warfare, and especially air warfare, were still unknown; a case in point was the employment of parachutists for sabotage purposes. Accordingly, it might be contended that the soldier who performs an act of sabotage with the intention to surrender afterwards without putting up a fight, would not behave like an honourable warrior and hence could be held guilty of an abuse of the right conveyed by Article 23 *c*. This would mean that the order ought to be made applicable to all commandos on sabotage missions, irrespective of whether clad in their proper uniforms or otherwise. Significantly, Lehmann added that to maintain without reserve this idea of the unlawful character of sabotage commandos as such would require that it be respected on the German side as well.[19]

Lehmann moreover suggested that the order ought to be suited for publication and that it ought to make explicit the non-applicability of Article 23 *c*.[20] The Operations Staff dismissed the latter submission with the argument that publication of the definitive order was not necessary, as the intention to proceed to the discussed mode of acting had been made sufficiently known with the communiqué broadcast on 7 October.[21] The Operations Staff did however accept the view that no distinction ought to be made between properly uniformed and other commandos: according to the draft text as it ultimately emerged from this department, the order would be applicable to all "terror and sabotage groups", whether soldiers or otherwise and whether or not properly uniformed, who accomplish acts deemed contrary to the fundamental principles of warfare and thereby place themselves outside the protection of the law of war.[22]

Hitler evidently shared the latter view,[23] which accordingly was laid down in the definitive *Führer* directive[24] as well as in the explanatory order accompanying it.[25] In the directive, the text bearing on this crucial point runs as follows:[26]

[19] *Ibid.*, in Doc. 1265-PS.
[20] *Ibid.*, in Doc. 1266-PS.
[21] *Ibid.*, in Doc. 1263-PS.
[22] *Loc. cit.* n. 21.
[23] I.M.T. Vol. XXVII, in Doc. 1266-PS: note of a telephone conversation between General Jodl, Chief of the Operations Staff, and Lehmann.
[24] I.M.T. Vol. XXVI, Doc. 498-PS: directive of 18 October 1942.
[25] *Ibid.*, Doc. 503-PS: order of the same date, passed on by General Jodl, Chief of the Armed Forces Operations Staff, by order of 19 October.
[26] Para. 3 of the directive.

"Von jetzt ab sind alle bei sogenannten Kommandounternehmungen in Europa oder in Afrika von deutschen Truppen gestellte Gegner, auch wenn es sich äusserlich um Soldaten in Uniform oder Zerstörertrupps mit und ohne Waffen handelt, im Kampf oder auf der Flucht bis auf den letzten Mann niederzumachen. Es ist dabei ganz gleich, ob sie zu ihren Aktionen durch Schiffe und Flugzeuge angelandet werden oder mittels Fallschirmen abspringen. Selbst wenn diese Subjekte bei ihrer Auffindung scheinbar Anstalten machen sollten, sich gefangen zu geben, ist ihnen grundsätzlich jeder Pardon zu verweigern. Hierüber ist in jedem Einzelfall zur Bekanntgabe im Wehrmachtbericht eine eingehende Meldung an das O.K.W. zu erstatten."

Another main question indicated above was whether the order to kill without mercy would only apply in the course of action, or would equally have to be applied to commandos who for some reason or other might have been taken alive. Evidently, this was not merely a humanitarian problem: first and foremost it was connected with the conflict between the projected measure and the interests of the counter-intelligence service. The interrogation of enemy soldiers such as the commandos, who might hold vital information, was essential for the purposes of the latter service. This meant that they would have to be kept alive, if only temporarily.

For the Chief of the Counter-intelligence Service, Admiral Canaris, the problem here was restricted to those commandos who, not being clad in their proper uniforms, were in his view francs-tireurs and hence not entitled to treatment as prisoners of war. The members of this category who on account of military interests were taken alive in the course of action, would have to be dealt with in the same manner as the men who fall into German hands not in the course of action: they would be interrogated first, and thereafter their fate would have to be decided *standgerichtlich*, that is, by a drumhead courtmartial composed of a lieutenant and other ranks deciding summarily.[27] Taking into account that Canaris considered the men of this category as francs-tireurs, the outcome of the proceedings which he suggested would probably be the death sentence. In any event, however, he made an endeavour to institute something like decent proceedings in the matter.

Thoughts in the Armed Forces Operations Staff did not go towards working out such a respectable solution. On the one hand, it was never made a matter of doubt that interrogation would have to take the place of instant killing whenever the first alternative would be in the captor's interests. On the other hand, even the first Staff notes on the subject solved the problem of the treatment following interrogation by stating that the persons concerned were "dem SD zuzuführen",[28] without any indication

[27] I.M.T. Vol. XXVII, in Docs. 1263-PS and 1265-PS.
[28] *Ibid.*, in Doc. 1266-PS.

being given of what the Security Police and SD were expected to do with them. The final draft directive upheld this view, and it stressed the point that the men should on no account be interned in prisoners of war camps.[29]

While both the Chief of the Counter-intelligence Service and the officers in the Operations Staff had given attention to the issue of the counter-intelligence interests, the definitive *Führer* directive did not make any express provision concerning this point. On the other hand, the directive did refer to the case of individual commandos who fall into the hands of the armed forces as a result, not of the activities of those forces, but of some other body, such as the local police in occupied territory. In such cases the armed forces were ordered to hand the commandos over to the Security Police and SD without delay, and they were reminded that the internment of such persons in prisoners of war camps was "strengstens verboten".[30]

In so far as the directive might have left the impression that the *Führer* had neglected the impact of the measure on the intelligence interests, the explanatory order made it clear that he had not really lost sight of the interests of the Counter-intelligence Service. Indeed, this document treated the subject with rare frankness: [31]

> "Sollte sich die Zweckmässigkeit ergeben, aus Vernehmungsgründen einen oder zwei Mann zunächst noch auszusparen, so sind diese nach ihrer Vernehmung sofort zu erschiessen."

In the light of this unequivocal and brutal order, the quoted paragraph of the directive takes on a new and sinister significance where it provides that the commandos would have to be finished off "im Kampf *oder auf der Flucht*". The italicised words were evidently intended to connote the same idea here as in other instances of treatment of prisoners: to wit, that they would be murdered in cold blood, the official cause of death being: shot while attempting to escape.

The questions formulated above with respect to the *Wehrmacht* communiqué of 7 October 1942 had thus been authoritatively answered. The *Kommando Befehl* was applicable to all commandos on special missions outside the actual theatre of war, not merely to those who could be accused of some particular war crime. And application of the order would mean the killing of the commandos immediately and to the last man, unless it would seem advisable temporarily to spare "einen oder zwei Mann" (or complete units, for that matter) for the purposes of interrogation. This, however, should not be interpreted as an indication that the commandos concerned were given quarter; on the contrary, they would have to be shot forthwith upon the completion of the interrogation.

[29] *Ibid.*, in Doc. 1263-PS.
[30] Para. 4 of the directive.
[31] Final paragraph of the explanatory order.

For present purposes, it is not necessary to give a full account of the instances where the *Kommando Befehl* was actually brought into practice, nor of the times it was disobeyed, nor again to examine who were responsible for its application or exonerated by its non-application in any given instance. It may suffice to note that the directive has without doubt been carried into effect in a number of cases,[32] and that it remained in force virtually till the end of the war.[33]

The question at issue here is whether the measure contained in the Order constituted a reprisal under international law. This question can be sub-divided into the following specific questions: did the commandos by their mode of acting violate the law of war? was the Commando Order *prima facie* unlawful? was it justified as a reprisal?

As for the character of the commandos and their mode of acting, a first and obvious remark is that they were members of the armed forces and hence in principle entitled to combatant status according to Article 1 of the Hague Regulations on Land Warfare. They were moreover usually recognizable as such, at any rate until such time as they had completed their missions, by the uniforms which they wore. It was only upon completion of their mission that they might try to improve their chances of escape by changing their uniforms for civilian clothes; a mode of acting that could not in reason be regarded as treacherous, let alone disqualify as combatants the commandos as a group.

Were they perhaps so disqualified by other aspects of their *modus operandi*? This in fact was the thesis advanced by Lehmann in the preparatory phase; and it was upheld in the explanatory order of 18 October 1942, where the theme was elaborated in a paragraph [34] asserting that the com-

---

[32] For instances of application see: I.M.T. Vol. XXVI, Docs. 508-PS, 509-PS, 512-PS. The first-mentioned document (a note made in the Operations Staff concerning a landing in Norway of two British airplanes and the capture and subsequent shooting of 17 uniformed men of the passengers and crew) records that after the event the theatre commander had issued instructions that in such cases, where thorough interrogation by the proper authorities might be important, the prisoners should not be shot too speedily (in this case: after one day) but should be handed over to those authorities.

[33] *Ibid.*, e.g.: Docs. 551-PS (express order of 25 June 1944 that the Commando Order remained in force also after the Allied landings in Normandy, except for the actual theatre of operations) and 537-PS (directive of the *OKW* dated 30 July 1944 regarding application of the Commando Order to Allied soldiers captured in the course of actions against partisan groups to which they were evidently attached as members of Allied military missions).

[34] "Dabei ist diese Art von Krieg für den Gegner gänzlich gefahrlos. Denn indem er seine Sabotagetrupps in Uniform absetzt und andererseits aber auch Zivilkleidung mitgibt, können sie je nach Bedarf als Soldaten oder als Zivilisten in Erscheinung treten. Während sie selbst den Auftrag besitzen, ihnen hinderliche deutsche Soldaten oder sogar Landeseinwohner rücksichtslos zu beseitigen, laufen sie keinerlei Gefahr, bei ihrem Treiben wirklich ernsthafte Verluste zu erleiden, da sie ja schlimmstenfalls

mandos, while themselves criminals in part and in any event without mercy for soldiers and civilians alike, took no risks for themselves and in case of detection surrendered immediately, in the belief that the Prisoners of War Convention would protect them. But this, the paragraph hastened to add, constituted a grave abuse of that Convention.

The argument in the quoted paragraph was far from sound. For, apart from the evident irrelevance of the reference to the alleged criminal case histories of individual commandos, it was simply untrue that the commandos were in the habit of surrendering immediately whenever they were surprised in the execution of their mission. And even if it had been true, there is no ground for the assertion that this constituted an abuse of the Prisoners of War Convention. Basically, the tactics which the commandos applied (stealthy approach, surprise attack, and attempt to escape) were indicated for any small unit venturing into enemy-controlled terrain. In the case of the commandos, an additional factor was that normally the road back to the own positions was cut off and that they were surrounded by vastly superior enemy forces. In these circumstances the options for these men were few: to fight to the last man (certainly glorious, but hardly economical as they were not defending any strategic positions, and in any event not required by international law), to escape (the ideal way out, but not always practicable even with the aid of civilian clothes), or, when an attempt to escape would fail: to surrender.

In fact, neither the surprise character of their attacks nor the fact that the commandos would after the attack probably attempt to escape or else surrender, warranted the conclusion that their tactics were treacherous or even unsoldierly. Nor could it be maintained that the fact that forces were sent on such missions at all was in itself sufficient ground to disqualify the actors. In particular could this not be based (as Lehmann had ventured to suggest) on the truism that at the time of the Hague Peace Conferences the method of dropping parachutists had not yet been developed: nothing in the new methods warranted the suggestion that the makers of the Regulations on Land Warfare would have refused parachuted soldiers the status of legitimate combatants, any more than to any other small body of men penetrating deep into the enemy positions.

In short, neither the fact that the commandos were despatched on missions of the type described above, nor the tactics which they employed, could justify the conclusion that they were not entitled to be treated as combatants. Indeed, these factors could not even be construed as consti-

---

gestellt, sich augenblicklich ergeben und damit theoretisch unter die Bestimmungen der Genfer Konvention zu fallen glauben. Es gibt keinen Zweifel, dass dies aber einen Missbrauch der Genfer Abmachungen schlimmster Art darstellt umsomehr, als es sich bei diesen Elementen zu einem Teil sogar um Verbrecher handelt, die, aus Gefängnissen befreit, durch solche Aktionen ihre Rehabilitation erreichen können."

tuting violations of the law of war for which the commandos, in spite of their combatant status, might be held accountable as a group.

But were the commandos perhaps guilty of other, more specific war crimes? It may be recalled that already the communiqué of 7 October 1942 had accused the commandos of behaving "like bandits". This theme was elaborated in the text of the Commando Order, where it was asserted that for some time past the enemy had been using methods of warfare in contravention of the Geneva Conventions and that in particular the commandos behaved "besonders brutal und hinterhältig". Furthermore, the text continued, it had come to light from captured orders that the instruction of the commandos was, not only to shackle prisoners, but to kill them whenever that were deemed expedient.[35] On the other hand, the allegation was not that commandos had actually committed any particular atrocities,[36] let alone that they were guilty as a group of killing prisoners and similar inhuman practices. Therefore, the allegation of wholesale banditry seems to have been more in the character of an insinuation than of a definite charge.

This leads back to the legal nature of the measure laid down in the Commando Order. Upon analysis, this is seen to consist of two distinct elements. Firstly, the ruthless slaughtering to the last man of commandos in the course of combat—that is: the refusal to give quarter, as prohibited by Article 23 c of the Regulations on Land Warfare. Secondly, and in a way in flat contradiction with the first part of the new policy: the capture of commandos, their interrogation for the purposes of counter-intelligence, and finally their merciless execution—that is: the cold-blooded murder of prisoners without previous trial. The latter mode of acting was absolutely prohibited by the Prisoners of War Convention of 1929 with respect to those enemies having the status of prisoners of war, and for the rest it was in contravention of the principle that every person caught alive by the enemy and suspected of a crime has a right to be tried prior to being executed. This principle, expressed in Article 30 of the Regulations with respect to persons suspected of spying, is with regard to other persons im-

[35] Para. 1 of the directive; the text runs as follows: "Schon seit längerer Zeit bedienen sich unsere Gegner in ihrer Kriegführung Methoden, die ausserhalb der internationalen Abmachungen von Genf stehen. Besonders brutal und hinterhältig benehmen sich die Angehörigen der sogenannten Kommandos, die sich selbst, wie feststeht, teilweise sogar aus Kreisen von in den Feindländern freigelassenen kriminellen Verbrechern rekrutieren. Aus erbeuteten Befehlen geht hervor, dass sie beauftragt sind, nicht nur Gefangene zu fesseln, sondern auch wehrlose Gefangene kurzerhand zu töten im Moment, in dem sie glauben, dass diese bei der weiteren Verfolgung ihrer Zwecke als Gefangene einen Ballast darstellen oder sonst ein Hindernis sein könnten. Es sind endlich Befehle gefunden, in denen grundsätzlich die Tötung der Gefangene verlangt worden ist."
[36] As they may well have done. But when in 1944 the *Führer* wanted to stage a trial in order to demonstrate that commandos had been guilty of war crimes, Admiral Canaris had great difficulty in finding more than a very few instances where such crimes could be established. See I.M.T. Vol. XXXIX, Doc. 057-UK.

plicit in the Martens-clause embodied in the preamble to the Convention on the laws and usages of land warfare, of 1899, declaring that in cases not covered in the Regulations the populations and the belligerents would remain under the protection and the rule of the principles of international law deducible from the usages established between civilized nations, the laws of humanity and the requirements of the public conscience.[37]

Thus, leaving aside whether it might perhaps be excusable to refuse quarter in combat to persons lacking the status of legitimate combatants, it was in any event unlawful in respect of the commandos. And application of the second part of the policy outlined in the order, that is, the execution after interrogation, must be deemed grossly unlawful in all events.

From the foregoing it already follows that the measures ordered in the Commando Order could not be justified as a reprisal. In fact, the explanatory order of 18 October 1942 did not continue the attempts to establish the character of the Order as a reprisal, in the sense of a measure resorted to on account of illegalities committed by the opponent. The greater part of the order was devoted to a lengthy demonstration of how necessary the policy was from a military point of view: sabotage bands were apt to cause great damage, as had become apparent on the Russian front, and the same risk was threatening in the West; the only effective method of fighting the bands was to slaughter them to the last man; as the German soldier was not by nature inclined to conduct war in such a ruthless manner, he was now ordered to do so, both in his own and in his country's interests. In short, the aim of the measure was not so much to prevent illegalities on the part of the commandos as their actions as such.[38]

In summary, the *Wehrmacht* communiqué of 7 October 1942 had implicitly suggested that the commando operations amounted to unlawful methods of warfare warranting a reprisal in the form of the merciless killing of the members of the units concerned. This suggestion of the retaliatory character of the measure at issue was maintained both in the opinions expressed by those taking part in the drafting of the directive, and in certain passages of the directive in its final version and of the explanatory order accompanying it. On closer inspection, however, it is evident that the facts of the situation did not furnish anything like an adequate justification of the

[37] *Supra*, p. 58.

[38] This aim had already found more succinct expression in the following note of a telephone conversation of 14 October 1942 between the Chief of the Operations Staff, General Jodl, and Lehmann, the Head of the Legal Department: "[The Chief Operations Staff] hat geäussert, dass es das Ziel des Führers bei der Aktion sei, diese Art der Kampfweise (Abwurf von kleinen Trupps, die grossen Schaden durch Sprengungen usw. ausrichten und sich dann zur Festnahme stellen) zu verhindern. Auf die letzte deutsche Veröffentlichung [*i.e.* the communiqué of 7 October] sei bereits ein Fortschritt in dieser Richtung zu verzeichnen."—I.M.T. Vol. XXVII, Doc. 1266-PS.

measure as a reprisal, and it is even evident that the measure, far from having been intended as a true reprisal, was nothing but a means of fighting the commandos that was resorted to because their activities threatened to cause great damage to the German war effort. In this context, the suggestion of "banditry" and of a consequent right of reprisals had merely served, internally, to salve the consciences of those who would be charged with the execution of the directive, and externally as an added psychological incentive intended—in combination with the prospect of being ruthlessly killed—to deter the commandos from continuing their sabotage activities.

This leads to the conclusion that the Commando Order was an instance of a flagrant violation of the laws of war committed for reasons of military expediency. That its illegality had been realized on the German side is evidenced by the fact that after the vague hint in the communiqué every effort was made to keep the directive a secret, instead of its being published as a reprisals order designed to come to the knowledge of the enemy and thus to effect a change of policy on his part. This secrecy, it may be added, may well have been intended especially to cover the fact that death would not always be inflicted immediately in the course of combat, but might (and in practice often would) follow only after the victim had been kept alive and a prisoner for some time for the purposes of interrogation; an aspect of the case that makes it all the more gruesome and that at the same time provides the ground to treat it under the heading of reprisals against prisoners of war.

5.2.3. The killing of German prisoners of war held by the French Forces of the Interior

While the incident of the shackling of prisoners of war arose out of a primarily tactical (and presumably unlawful) aspect of the treatment immediately upon capture of enemies whose combatant status was not in any way at issue, and while in the affair of the Commando Order the combatant status of the commandos had, like the legality of their actions, been put at issue merely as a pretext serving to conceal the true purport of the Order, the retaliatory action that shall be discussed in this paragraph had its origin in a grave issue of fundamental concern: the question of whether certain units of French resistance fighters operating in French occupied territory had a right to be recognized as legitimate combatants.[39] This question had arisen at an early stage of the war, as soon as bands of

[39] For a French exposé of the affair, see: René Hostacher, *Le conseil national de résistance* (1958), p. 421 ff.; the book forms part of the series *Esprit de la résistance*. A German view may be found in: Hans Luther, *Der französische Widerstand gegen die deutsche Besatzungsmacht und seine Bekämpfung* (1957), published in the series *Studien des Instituts für Besatzungsfragen in Tübingen zu den deutschen Besatzungen im 2. Weltkrieg.*

maquisards had formed that could be said to conform to the conditions for legitimate combatancy as enumerated in Article 1 of the Regulations of Land Warfare. Already in 1943, a request by the resistance movement for an opinion gave the well-known French international lawyer, Basdevant, occasion to state as his view that [40]

> "... en vertu de la généralité des termes de cet article, les lois, droits et devoirs de la guerre s'appliquent aux milices et corps de volontaires réunissant ces conditions même si ces milices et corps de volontaires ont été constitués en territoire occupé."

This opinion dealt with one aspect of the situation developing in France: the question of whether a body of volunteers constituted in occupied territory could be brought under the terms of Article 1 of the Regulations on Land Warfare. Another problem lay in Article 10 of the Franco-German armistice agreement of 1940, providing that all French nationals who, after the conclusion of the agreement would continue to resist the German forces, would be regarded as francs-tireurs. It was of course a moot point whether this armistice agreement, and therefore Article 10, could still be invoked after the French Provisional Government was set up in London and co-operated with the Allied Powers, and French troops, organized outside France and clad in French uniforms, had begun to take an active part in the Allied operations against the Axis Powers; in actual fact, and in contrast with alarming rumours circulating at the outset, the Germans did not apply the provision of Article 10 to members of these French forces falling into their hands.[41]

This did not however necessarily imply that the German authorities in occupied France would be equally inclined to recognize under certain conditions the combatant status of the members of resistance groups operating in the territory and to grant them treatment as prisoners of war. In fact, their negative attitude in that respect was evidenced by their practice of executing such prisoners.[42] This was of course a grave issue, which assumed a particularly urgent character with the Allied invasion of Normandy, in June 1944. The resistance fighters, by then organized in the French Forces of the Interior (or FFI), took part in the operations by such actions as attacks on the German forces in the rear, thus endangering their positions significantly. In reaction to this situation, the German Army commander in Western Europe issued a declaration stating explicitly that "persons taking part in movements of rebellion directed against the rear of the forces of the occupying Power, have no right whatever to the protection which may be claimed by regular combatants"; and, after a reference to the terms of the armistice agreement of 1940, the declaration

[40] As quoted in Hostacher, *op. cit.* n. 39, p. 422.
[41] With respect to this issue and the dealings which the ICRC had with it, see: *Report, op. cit.* n. 1 to this §, pp. 519-520.
[42] Hostacher, *op. cit.* n. 39, pp. 421-423.

194

announced that "such rebels will not be regarded as prisoners of war, but executed in accordance with martial law".[43]

This statement of policy evoked vehement objections on the part of the FFI, and on their request the Provisional Government, which by that time had its seat at Algiers, formulated a sharp protest transmitted to the German Government by the ICRC. The protest took the position, firstly, that the Germans could not invoke "the terms of a pseudo-armistice", and, secondly, that the FFI formed part of the French Army and also in all other respects conformed to the conditions for legitimate combatancy. Finally, the Provisional Government warned that it would contemplate reprisals if the policy announced by the German commanding officer were carried into effect.[44] Messages of similar purport were sent to the Allied authorities, who were requested likewise to consider reprisals; no such action, however, ensued on their part.[45]

As for the German authorities, they not merely rejected the protest, but they declared it null and void, alleging that they had no knowledge of the existence of any Provisional Government at Algiers.[46] As moreover the practice of executing captured members of the FFI was continued, the FFI urged the Provisional Government to carry the threatened reprisals into execution. That Government did not however hasten to satisfy this request. In view of this hesitating attitude, the leaders of the FFI in France thereupon decided to take retaliatory action themselves.[47]

An opportunity for such action arose when the FFI in August 1944 captured a large number of German officers and men, chiefly in the Haute-Savoie where some 3000 Germans were made prisoners, more than 1000 of them as a result of the capitulation of Annecy alone.[48] The decision of the FFI command to take reprisals did not however imply that all these Germans were immediately threatened with extermination; on the contrary, it was publicly announced that they would be treated as prisoners of war in conformity with the Convention of 1929.[49] When, however, it became subsequently known that the Germans had again executed eighty French prisoners and that further executions were imminent, the FFI command at Annecy decided that eighty of the prisoners in their hands would in turn be shot.[50]

The ICRC, which already in an earlier stage had reminded the parties to the dispute of the express prohibition of reprisals against prisoners of war,[51]

[43] The quoted text in *Report, op. cit.* n. 1, at p. 520.
[44] *Ibid.*, p. 421.
[45] Hostacher, *op. cit.* n. 39, pp. 424-426.
[46] *Report, op. cit.* n. 1, p. 522.
[47] Hostacher, *loc. cit.* n. 45.
[48] Hostacher, *op. cit.* n. 39, at p. 426.
[49] ICRC, *Report, op. cit.* n. 1, p. 522.
[50] *Report, loc. cit.* n. 49; Hostacher, *op. cit.* n. 39, p. 427.
[51] ICRC, *Report, op. cit.* n. 1, p. 521.

now intervened in an attempt to avert the execution of the eighty Germans; the ICRC "laid stress upon the consequences, immediate and remote, affecting large numbers of PW, that would be likely to ensue from such reprisals".[52] In response to this intervention,

"the FFI Command consented to postpone the execution for several days, to enable the ICRC to make urgent representations in Berlin. The aim of these steps was to secure an undertaking from the German Government not to proceed with the execution of French civilian internees and further to ensure for all French partisans captured the benefit of PW treatment. The German prisoners in FFI hands in Haute-Savoie were, moreover, visited by ICRC delegates, and favourable reports were sent to Berlin, as also the distinctive badge worn by the FFI. Six days having elapsed without the German Government having replied, the eighty German prisoners were executed."[53]

In the light of these facts it is not hard to decide that the reprisal shooting was a *prima facie* unlawful action, in flagrant contravention of one of the basic principles underlying the régime of prisoners of war, viz., that of humane treatment and respect for their lives. Slightly more complicated is the question of whether the German executions giving rise to the reprisal had been unlawful as well. A first complication arises from the uncertainty which prevails over the precise circumstances of the shooting that was the immediate cause of the reprisal.[54] This, however, does not constitute a really serious obstacle, as in reality the reprisal was not so much motivated by that particular instance of shooting alone as by the general practice of the German occupation forces, summarily to execute members of the resistance movement whenever they thought fit, and by their threat that this practice would be carried on even at this stage of the war and in respect of an openly operating armed force like the FFI. The question to be answered is therefore whether it was lawful for the German occupation authorities in France to execute members of the resistance movement who were organized under a responsible command, wore a distinctive badge, wore arms openly and on the whole observed the law of war in their conduct of military operations, all this at a time when the Allied armies had established a bridge-head on French territory and were rapidly extending the area liberated from the German occupation.

[52] *Ibid.*, p. 522.
[53] *Ibid.*, pp. 522-523. And see Luther, *op. cit.* n. 39, p. 79, who furnishes further details regarding the executions which according to his account took place on 2 September 1944.
[54] In the version of the ICRC, the victims were "political hostages in the Montluc prison at Lyons". According to Hostacher, it was the rumour that "les Allemands commencent à fusiller les prisonniers du fort Montluc (au nombre de 1200)" which gave rise to the announcement that "80 prisonniers allemands seront exécutés, répondant de la vie de 80 prisonniers français abattus à Saint-Genis-Laval".

Under the prevailing circumstances, the German authorities could no longer venture to justify their mode of acting by simply relying on the clause in the armistice agreement of 1940, under the terms of which French nationals resisting the German forces were to be treated as francs-tireurs: by that time, the armistice had in fact ceased to exist. Moreover, even if it were to be assumed that the agreement of 1940 was still operative, that could hardly imply a power for the German authorities to treat persons as francs-tireurs who according to the general law of war had to be considered as legitimate combatants (or, in other words, to commit what under any other view would amount to simple murder). The question of whether in the conditions prevailing at the time the members of the FFI could be treated as francs-tireurs or, alternatively, were entitled to treatment as legitimate combatants, cannot therefore be decided by a mere reference to the provision of Article 10 of the 1940 armistice agreement: other considerations, of a more general nature, have to be taken into account.

It seems a moot point whether at the time of the Second World War the law was as Basdevant stated it to be in his opinion of 1943: viz., that members of resistance groups operating in occupied territory had combatant status provided they met the requirements outlined for the militias and volunteer corps in Article 1 of the Hague Regulations on Land Warfare.[55] There is, however, no need to answer this question in general, as at the time of the reprisal, that is, in the second half of 1944, the activities and *modus operandi* of the FFI were no longer those of a resistance movement in the strict sense of the term; by that time the FFI had assumed the character of a regular army and it behaved accordingly. Thus, many of its actions (such as: occupation of territory, fighting full-scale battles with the German armed forces, conquest of localities, et cetera) presented the characteristics of regular warfare. Obviously, however, certain of its activities still had the features of guerrilla warfare.

Moreover, the operations of the FFI were no longer the actions of resistance fighters in a territory under effective enemy occupation and isolated from the actual theatre of war. Since the Allied invasion, the French territory had itself become the scene of the most important military operations going on at the time. On the one hand, it was precisely that situation of fact which allowed the FFI to conduct its operations in the way it did. On the other hand, the connection between the Allied operations and those of the FFI strengthened the argument that the FFI was now engaged in regular warfare. In this context it should be pointed out that the German commanding officer was completely wrong and guilty of an inadmissible understatement when he suggested that the activities of the FFI could be

---

[55] In 1949 this issue was settled in so far as granting prisoner of war status to such persons was concerned, by the insertion of an express clause to that effect in Art. 4, A (2) of Geneva Convention n° III relative to the treatment of prisoners of war, of 12 August 1949.

characterized as "movements of rebellion against the rear of the forces of the occupying Power". In other words, assuming for a moment that "execution in accordance with martial law" of "rebels" who were also francs-tireurs might be justified in certain cases, it by no means follows that the German authorities could be justified in extending this "rebel treatment" to all members of the FFI who might fall into their hands in the course of the current operations.

In point of fact, one is confronted here with the case of an army irregular in origin, but meanwhile meeting the requirements enumerated in the Regulations on Land Warfare; an army that in a previous stage might have been engaged in activities the aim of which could not go beyond prejudicing the effectiveness of an otherwise unassailable occupation, but the actions of which now constituted an element in the operations designed to expel the enemy and to liberate France. It is submitted that in these circumstances of fact to deny the members of this fighting army the status of legitimate combatants was unjustifiable under the law as it then stood, either on the ground that such a denial would be in direct contravention of the express rule granting combatant status to the members of militias and volunteer corps (if this rule is held directly applicable to the situation at issue) or because it infringed a norm which, although not laid down in any written rule, could be derived from the written law by analogy, and according to which combatant status could not be refused the members of a "corps of volunteers" operating in occupied territory (and hence technically under the scope of the occupation régime) but in such conditions of fact as to make it virtually indistinguishable from any other army. Under this submission, those members of the FFI who fell into the hands of the enemy were entitled to be treated as prisoners of war and in any event could not be summarily executed as "rebels".

Even if the above submission were incorrect, it is still maintained that the execution of members of the FFI was an act not merely unwarranted, but positively prohibited by the law in force. For, no matter what might be said of the proposition that these persons were entitled to full combatant status, it cannot be seriously contested that they were under the protection of the fundamental norm, embodied in Article 2 of the Prisoners of War Convention of 1929 but also valid independently of that treaty provision, of respect for the life of the respectable enemy.

It is therefore concluded that the execution of members of the FFI as provided in the proclamation of the German commanding officer and as apparently carried into effect in a number of instances, was unlawful and amounted to wilful murder.

Did the refusal on the part of the German authorities to apply the Convention of 1929 to captured members of the FFI have any effect on the obligation of the French authorities—and notably of the command of the

FFI—to apply its provisions to the German prisoners in their hands? Actually, this is an academic question, as the FFI command had itself made known its decision to apply the Convention; but the matter is not without some interest from a theoretical point of view. It is not open to doubt that Germany, being like France a party to the Convention, was bound by its provisions in her relations with France. Likewise, it is an established fact that the German authorities generally applied the Convention to French prisoners. In other words, the refusal to apply its terms to a certain group of French nationals, viz., the members of the FFI, constituted a violation of the Convention if—as is believed to be the case—that group was entitled to treatment as prisoners of war. The refusal might accordingly give rise to various reactions, as had also happened in actual practice: protest, intervention by the ICRC, and so on. One possible reaction was however forbidden the French authorities by the express terms of the Convention: to take recourse to a reprisal against German prisoners of war. And it is clear that a refusal to apply the Convention to German prisoners in turn, would amount to precisely that. This leads to the conclusion that the French authorities, the command of the FFI included, continued to be bound by the Convention of 1929 and were obliged to apply its provisions even in relation to German prisoners of war, irrespective of the open refusal on the part of the German authorities to apply it to members of the FFI.

A final aspect of the action discussed here concerns the question of responsibility. As related above, the leaders of the FFI had requested the Provisional Government at Algiers to take reprisals against Germany, but this had not been prepared to do so. The FFI leaders had thereupon themselves taken the decision in principle to resort to reprisals, and the military command of the FFI had finally converted this decision in principle into a specific decision to execute a given number of German prisoners. This sequence of events might give rise to the question as to whether the reprisal shooting ultimately carried out without the express approval of the Provisional Government could be imputed to France—or, in other words, whether the action really was a reprisal.[56]

One may observe that the Provisional Government had in an earlier stage of the proceedings itself contemplated the possibility of a resort to reprisals; it had even given a warning to that effect to the German Government. Further, while the Provisional Government did not actually take a reprisal, it did nothing to remove the impression that it was ready to do so; and even after the FFI had carried out the reprisal shooting, the Provisional Government failed to denounce the action as one not covered by its authority and hence taken under the exclusive responsibility of the FFI.

[56] *Supra*, p. 28.

By this attitude the Provisional Government may be said to have taken the action as its own. It seems therefore impossible to maintain that the action would not have been imputable to France.

Moreover, France would have been accountable for the shooting even irrespective of this attitude of the Provisional Government. For, while the FFI had originated from scattered, small resistance groups operating individually, on their own initiative and for their own risk, it had developed into an organized army operating under the direction and authority of the Provisional Government, that is, as an organ of the State.

Did this reprisal, though unjustifiable, at least prove effective? It appears that after the reprisal the Germans discontinued the executions of French prisoners.[57] But was this attributable to the reprisal? It should be borne in mind that at the time the situation was rapidly deteriorating for the Germans; in those circumstances, a variety of motives may have influenced their attitude towards the French prisoners. In any event, it cannot be stated with certainty that in this case *post* was also *propter*; but neither can causality be definitely excluded.

In summary, the retaliatory action discussed in this sub-section is an example of an action taken by a military (or para-military) authority on a lower echelon, but imputable to the State. The action was designed to coerce the enemy to discontinue the illegal execution of captured members of the FFI, and it may or may not contributed to the realization of that goal. However, no matter how much the action may in the light of the German practices appear understandable from a psychological point of view, it was irreparably unlawful nonetheless on account of the strict prohibition of reprisals in the Convention of 1929, the applicability of which to the Germans in their hands, the FFI command had only just expressly reaffirmed.

5.3. REPRISALS AGAINST THE CIVIL POPULATION IN OCCUPIED TERRITORY

As is only too well-known, of all the retaliatory measures taken during the Second World War by far the greatest number was directed against the populations in the territories under German occupation. In a way, this is nothing but a reflection of the development of active resistance movements in many of the occupied countries. But the outcome, both in numbers and in severity of the retaliatory measures taken, has obviously been influenced

---

[57] Somewhat vaguely, Hostacher informs us that "[l]a violence répondant à la violence, le massacre s'arrêtera et les portes de Montluc seront ouvertes aux rescapés."—*Op. cit.* n. 39, p. 427.

for the worse by the fact that from an early stage of the war the central authorities in Germany had consciously opted for a hard policy of retaliation and saw to it that this line was pursued on the lower levels of command as well.

No attempt will be made here to catalogue all the individual cases—indeed, in view of their overwhelming number that would be a sheer impracticability—nor even to compile a list of the gravest instances. Rather, it is precisely the fact of the centrally directed policy which urges treatment of the issue as a whole.

The facts may be sketched briefly as follows. In the course of the war, the Germans saw themselves increasingly confronted with acts of resistance committed by members of the civil population in a number of occupied countries. The activities of these persons varied widely, from the comparatively harmless, spontaneous deception of German soldiers asking for the road, to organized obstruction of the occupying Power's administration; and, on the level of violence, from isolated instances of assassination of single Germans by members of the civil population acting on their own, to sabotage raids and even full-scale armed attacks on positions of the occupying forces carried out by organized bands of resistance fighters. Wherever the resistance assumed such proportions as to be no longer completely negligible, the occupants resorted to counter-actions which more often than not were not restricted to the punishment of actual or probable culprits, but which came to embrace such measures as the execution of members of the population who did not themselves bear any direct responsibility for the acts retaliated against (and who might or might not have been apprehended as hostages beforehand), the random destruction of houses and even of entire villages, and so on.

Numerous documents and testimonies have revealed the rôle which the central authorities in Germany have played in setting and pursuing this policy. In many instances where acts of resistance entailed the death or injury of military or civil members of the occupation apparatus, the ensuing order to execute a certain number of inhabitants in retaliation for every German killed or wounded emanated directly from the *Führer*'s headquarters and was signed either by the *Führer* himself or by one of his close collaborators. The general policy in this respect was outlined in a directive issued on 16 September 1941 by Fieldmarshal Keitel, Chief of the High Command of the Armed Forces, relating to the forcible suppression of resistance in occupied countries.[1]

The directive, which took the position that the resistance movements generally were of communist origin and directed from Moscow, stated that their activities increasingly endangered the German war effort.[2] According-

[1] I.M.T. Vol. XXV, Doc. 389-PS.
[2] Para. 1 of the directive (emphasis as in the original): "Seit Beginn des Feldzuges gegen Sowjetrussland sind in den von Deutschland besetzten Gebieten allenthalben

ly, and as earlier measures had proved inadequate, the *Führer* now ordered the severest repression,[3] indicating as a standard that to avenge the life of a single German soldier the summary execution of 50 to 100 communists would be appropriate.[4]

This prescribed ratio of 50-100 : 1 was of course exceptionally severe. It may be added right away that in many instances where the policy was brought into effect, a rather more "lenient" ratio, for instance of 10 : 1 (or, for wounded Germans, 5 : 1) was maintained. However, the point that deserves primary emphasis here is not the at first sight questionable proportionality, nor other particulars of the directive, so much as the fact that the directive provides decisive evidence of the existence of a centrally directed policy of ruthless retaliation.

In order to ascertain the legal nature of this policy, it is first of all necessary to clarify the character of the acts retaliated against. This appears to hinge on the status of the perpetrators of the acts in the first place: were they, or were they not, legitimate combatants?

If one attempted to decide this question on the basis of the rules laid down in the Hague Regulations, it would soon be apparent that no generally valid answer can be given for the different periods of the war and for all the

---

kommunistische Aufstandsbewegungen ausgebrochen. Die Formen des Vorgehens steigern sich von propagandistischen Massnahmen und Anschlägen gegen einzelne Wehrmachtsangehörige bis zu offenem Aufruhr und verbreitetem Bandenkrieg. Es ist festzustellen, dass es sich hierbei um eine von Moskau *einheitlich geleitete Massenbewegung* handelt, der auch die geringfügig erscheinende Einzelvorfälle in bisher sonst ruhigen Gebieten zur Last zu legen sind. Angesichts der vielfachen politischen und wirtschaftlichen Spannungen in den besetzten Gebieten muss ausserdem damit gerechnet werden, dass *nationalistische und andere Kreise* diese Gelegenheit ausnützen, um durch Anschluss an den kommunistischen Aufruhr Schwierigkeiten für die deutsche Besatzungsmacht hervorzurufen. Auf diese Weise entsteht in zunehmendem Masse eine *Gefahr für die deutsche Kriegführung*, die sich zunächst in einer allgemeinen Unsicherheit für die Besatzungstruppe zeigt und auch bereits zum Abzug von Kräften nach den hauptsächlichen Unruheherden geführt hat."

[3] Para. 2 reads in part (emphasis as in the original): "Der Führer hat nunmehr angeordnet, dass *überall mit den schärfsten Mitteln* einzugreifen ist, um die Bewegung in kürzester Zeit niederzuschlagen. Nur auf diese Weise, die in der Geschichte der Machterweiterung grosser Völker immer mit Erfolg angewandt worden ist, kann die Ruhe wieder hergestellt werden."

[4] Para. 3(b) (emphasis as in the original): "Um die Umtriebe im Keime zu ersticken, sind *beim ersten Anlass* unverzüglich die schärfsten Mittel anzuwenden, um die Autorität der Besatzungsmacht durchzusetzen und einem weiteren Umsichgreifen vorzubeugen. Dabei ist zu bedenken, dass ein Menschenleben in den betroffenen Ländern vielfach nichts gilt und eine abschreckende Wirkung nur durch ungewöhnliche Härte erreicht werden kann. Als Sühne für ein deutsches Soldatenleben muss in diesen Fällen im allgemeinen die Todesstrafe für 50-100 Kommunisten als angemessen gelten. Die Art der Vollstreckung muss die abschreckende Wirkung noch erhöhen" (etcetera).

widely divergent situations that arose in the various occupied countries. As stated previously,[5] the point could be attained where even according to the said rules combatant status could no longer reasonably be denied the forces of a resistance movement, as these were organized, wore uniforms or distinctive signs, wore arms openly and generally respected the laws of war. Below that point, many modalities could be imagined where strong arguments would militate in favour of the recognition of combatant status, while other factors would be indications to the contrary. Finally, it is not open to doubt that in many other instances, and particularly (though not exclusively) in the early stages of development of resistance movements, no serious arguments could be advanced in support of recognition of the resistance fighters as legitimate combatants in the classical sense.

Taking into account that the line of the German policy of retaliation was set in the early stages of the war, at a time when many acts of resistance were committed by persons or groups of persons who were undoubtedly precluded from claiming combatant status even under the most liberal interpretation of the rules in force, the issue may be simplified by postulating the least favourable situation, to wit, that the acts retaliated against were hostile acts committed by members of the civil population who under the classical rules as embodied in the Hague Regulations could not be considered legitimate combatants.

It should be immediately added, however, that the rules of the Hague Regulations specifically bearing on the distinction between combatants and non-combatants could not be the final word in the matter. The issue ought to be examined in the wider context of the relationship between an occupying Power and the inhabitants of the occupied territory.

As related previously, the Hague Peace Conference of 1899 had dealt with that relationship and, in that context, with the issue of a possible recognition of a right to resist of the occupied population. And, while it had not seen its way expressly to grant such a right of resistance, the Conference had not seen fit to deny it either.[6] What the Conference did lay down, however, was the duty of an occupant to respect a series of fundamental rights of the inhabitants: their lives, honour, family life, property, and so on (Articles 44 ff.). In laying down this fundamental duty of the occupant, the assumption was that the population would generally conform to a normal standard of peaceful behaviour. Incidental departures from the normal pattern of peace and order could be met by the occupying authorities: they would be entitled to maintain order (Article 43), to punish individual offenders, or even, exceptionally, to inflict collective punishment whenever the actual offenders remained unknown and the local population could be held collectively responsible (Article 50).

---

[5] *Supra*, pp. 197-198.
[6] *Supra*, p. 57 ff.

It was finally recognized by the Conference that such powers as the occupant might possess to take reprisals against the population were not impeded by the rules regarding collective punishment.

Unquestionably, however, this whole structure of rules regulating the relationship between a belligerent occupying a territory and the inhabitants of the territory, rested on a further premise of primordial importance, namely, that the occupying Power himself behave like a "respectable occupant". This is not to say that he could be expected always and without exception to observe all the rules. It does mean, however, that he would be expected not to behave in a manner fundamentally in discord with the very essence of the concept of belligerent occupation.[7]

In view of this consideration, it becomes opportune briefly to enter into the character of the German occupation régime as displayed not in one country in particular, but in all the countries occupied in the course of the Second World War. This can be characterized in few words: territorial expansion of Germany, germanization and nazification of the conquered territories.[8] It was evidenced by such measures as the systematic plunder of materials and products, including basic foodstuffs needed for the local population; forced labour of the populations, both in the occupied territories and, after deportation, in Germany; introduction of Nazi legislation; terrorization of the population; and, most horrific of all, the extermination of entire groups of the populations, the Jews in the first place. The occupation régime, in short, was monstrously dissimilar to anything the makers of the Hague Regulations could ever have envisaged.[9]

In the light of these extreme conditions of fact, all the previous discussions relating to the recognition or non-recognition of a right to resist seem to lose their relevance, and only one conclusion seems acceptable, viz., that in face of such a perverted occupation régime the populations had acquired a positive right of resistance, based on the fundamental right of self-defence of communities immediately threatened as to their very existence.[10] This implies that the traditional rules restricting the recognition of combatant status could not be maintained here: it might be said that an extraordinary combatant status fell to those taking part in the resistance

---

[7] In the same sense: *e.g.*, T. J. Jansma, *Het bezettingsrecht in de praktijk van de Tweede Wereldoorlog* (*i.e.*, Occupation law in the practice of the Second World War) (1953), p. 47.

[8] *Cf.* also Jansma, *op. cit.* n. 7, p. 18.

[9] In the same sense, *e.g.*: Oscar M. Uhler, *Der völkerrechtliche Schutz der Bevölkerung eines besetzten Gebiets gegen Massnahmen der Okkupationsmacht* (1950) at pp. 96, 132, 155, 176.

[10] This view was expressed already in 1944 by Ellen Hammer and Marina Salvin, "The Taking of Hostages in Theory and Practice", in *AJIL* 1944 (XXXVIII) p. 20, at p. 27: "The Germans have violated every duty of the occupying power to the civilian population. Automatically then the oppressed populations are released from any obligation of obedience: they cannot be denied the right of self-defence."

activities. In any event, the mere fact that members of the civil population committed hostile acts could not suffice to make the acts illegal.

Admittedly, individual military or civil occupation authorities may have been justified in believing that all acts of resistance (and especially acts of a violent nature) were unlawful *per se*. The possible *bona fides* of individual lower officials is, however, immaterial for a legal appreciation of the events in their totality.

The above conclusion does not imply that every single act of resistance was justified. True, the situation of the resistance fighters in respect of the occupying forces differed markedly from that of opposing armed forces in the traditional sense, if only because they in general were the very opposite of a regularly organized, uniformly clad army distinctly separate from the pupulation. Even so, however, there is no reason why they should not have been obliged to respect certain essential principles of the law of war, such as the prohibition of wanton cruelty and of treacherous acts. In other words, acts such as the torture of prisoners, abuse of the enemy uniform, or treacherous assassination of enemy soldiers could even in the abnormal situation envisaged here be considered illegitimate acts of resistance which, hence, could give rise to justifiable acts of retaliation. But it seems only probable that such inherently illegitimate acts of resistance will have represented a minority of the acts committed.

It should be added that neither does the above conclusion imply that the occupying forces were as a matter of law obliged to tolerate the resistance activities: they were obviously entitled to defend their positions and to fight the resistance with all permissible means.

The next question is evidently whether the measures taken in execution of the German policy of ruthless retaliation were among these permissible means. While this policy encompassed a wide variety of measures, it shall only be discussed here in its most extreme form: viz., the execution of members of the civil population. Among the persons so executed, a certain number may have borne direct responsibility for the particular acts retaliated against. On the other hand, the question of personal responsibility was wholly immaterial in most instances. It seems therefore justified to neglect this complicating factor of a possible element of personal retribution. This narrows down the issue to the execution of innocent civilians.

One thing seems clear: as the executions at issue did not constitute lawful executions of death penalties, nor, for that matter, legitimate acts of belligerency, they were *prima facie* unlawful acts, and particularly grave ones at that, as the norm infringed was the fundamental principle of respect for human life.

The acts were retaliatory measures. As such, they could come under the head, either, of reprisals, or of collective punishment. They would be reprisals if their purpose was the bringing about of a change of policy on the

205

part of opposing authorities—be they the Government in exile, the local civil authorities, or the leaders of a resistance army. Those measures, on the other hand, which had as their aim the direct coercion of the population to abstain from acts of resistance and similar undesirable activities, had to be characterized as collective punishment.[11]

It would require a detailed investigation into the facts of each individual case to determine under which of the above two heads it came. Certain facts are, however, so well-known as to warrant certain generalities even without entering into such a detailed exposition of individual cases. Thus, the German occupation apparatus in the several occupied countries, far from being weak or otherwise dependent on positive support on the part of local civil authorities, was singularly well equipped to maintain and, where necessary, to restore order. Consequently, the chances that the purpose of particular retaliatory measures against the population would ever have been the bringing about of a change in the policy pursued by the local authorities, seem so slight as to be negligible.

Again, while it is an unquestionable fact that several Governments in exile have stimulated resistance activities in their respective territories and contributed to their development, there are no indications that any significant number of the retaliatory acts committed against the population in these countries had the specific purpose of bringing pressure to bear on the Government in question.

It appears therefore that, in the conditions as these actually existed in the occupied countries, only one among the conceivable modalities of retaliatory actions against the population constituting reprisals by virtue of their purpose stood a chance of being realized more than incidentally, namely, actions having the purpose of exerting pressure on the leaders of an organized resistance army. True, such armies did not exist in all the occupied countries. But where they existed (*e.g.* in Yugoslavia, France and Norway, where their activities ranged from guerrilla to open warfare), retaliatory measures against the population may conceivably have had the aim of coercing the authorities in command of the army to conform to the law of war.

On the other hand, even in that situation—and *a fortiori* in countries where no such resistance armies had come into being—it is equally possible that the purpose of the measures was not the one referred to, but to put direct pressure on the civil population as such, with a view to inducing it (that is, its members as individual persons) to withhold support from, or refrain from taking an active part in, the resistance activities going on in the territory. In that supposition, however, the measures would have the character of collective punishment, or even of acts of terror, rather than of reprisals.

[11] *Supra*, p. 36 ff.

The Keitel directive furnishes some further support for the above appraisal. Admittedly, the policy outlined in the directive was apparently based on the theory that the resistance movements were all directed by Moscow, and this might perhaps suggest that the aim of the retaliatory measures was to bring about a change in the policy pursued by Moscow-based international communism. However, as is evident from the rest of the text, the purpose of acts committed in execution of the policy would be to prostrate the local resistance movements and to deter the local populations from joining in or supporting their activities.[12]

In view of the above considerations, the issue of the justification of the retaliatory executions in German-occupied countries is narrowed down to the question of whether their purpose was to bring pressure to bear on the leaders of a resistance army with a view to maintaining the law of war—so that the executions would come under the head of reprisals and their justification would depend on the further conditions therefor being fulfilled—or whether, in the absence of that specific purpose, the shootings possessed the characteristics of an act of collective punishment (or, in other words, rested on the collective responsibility of the population for acts retaliated against) and for the rest fulfilled the further conditions governing the justification of that mode of punishment.

No attempt shall be made here to answer this question with reference to specific instances. Rather, attention is once again focused on the Keitel directive, the text of which does not provide the slightest indication that concepts like law enforcement in respect of a resistance army, or collective responsibility of a population for particular acts of resistance, would play any part whatsoever in the decision to retaliate.[13] This is to say that, in any event so far as the central policy of retaliation was concerned, the issue of justification evidently has carried little weight, if any. It also implies that the risk was obviously taken that individual measures implementing the directive would be mere acts of terror—a risk which has materialized in a number of ill-famed instances, for instance, Putten in Holland, Lidice in

---

[12] *Supra*, notes 2-4; para. 3(c) of the directive explains that "[e]s ist ... zu bedenken und auch propagandistisch herauszustellen, dass scharfes Eingreifen auch die einheimische Bevölkerung von den kommunistischen Verbrechern befreit und ihr damit selbst zugutekommt. Eine geschickte Propaganda dieser Art wird infolgedessen auch nicht dazu führen, dass sich nun aus den scharfen Massnahmen gegen die Kommunisten unerwünschte Rückwirkungen in den gutgesinnten Teilen der Bevölkerung ergeben."

[13] On the contrary, para. 3(e) of the directive emphasized that "kriegsgerichtliche Verfahren in Verbindung mit kommunistischem Aufruhr oder mit sonstigen Verstössen gegen die deutsche Besatzungsmacht" should only exceptionally be resorted to, and that in such cases the severest punishment was required: "Ein wirkliches Mittel der Abschreckung kann hierbei nur die Todesstrafe sein. Insbesondere müssen Spionagehandlungen, Sabotageakte und Versuche, in eine fremde Wehrmacht einzutreten, grundsätzlich mit dem Tode bestraft werden. Auch bei Fällen des unerlaubten Waffenbesitzes ist im allgemeinen die Todesstrafe zu verhängen."

Czechoslovakia, the *Cave ardeatine* in Rome, to name only a few out of many.

It remains to be examined whether the occupation authorities could be justified in selecting the execution of innocent persons as their means of retaliation even in the most favourable supposition, that is, if the act retaliated against were an act of resistance illegitimate even in the prevailing conditions (which gave the populations a right to resist) and if the retaliatory action could either be brought under the head of collective punishment or, by its purpose, of reprisals.

Two issues should be distinguished here: the question of whether the killing of innocent civilians for acts presumably committed by other members of the population must be deemed prohibited according to the law as it stood, and the question of proportionality, both qualitative and quantitative, between the incriminated acts and the ensuing executions.

The former of these questions has been broached in previous chapters. There it was found that, on the one hand, in the literature of the period preceding the outbreak of the Second World War the view was defended with some force that an action consisting in the violation of one of the fundamental humanitarian norms could never be justified as a reprisal. Moreover, the trend of opinion was strongly towards a prohibition of reprisals against the population in occupied territory in general, and of killing hostages in particular; the last-mentioned prohibition was even expressly propounded in the Tokyo project elaborated by the ICRC. On the other hand, the broad view concerning violations of humanitarian norms had obviously not hardened into a rule accepted as law by the States, and both the general prohibition of reprisals against an occupied population and the specific prohibition to execute hostages, while accepted as valid by some commentators, were denied legal force by others; and the Tokyo project had remained what the name indicated: a project.[14]

In the light of these considerations, it cannot be maintained with certainty that under the law in force at the time of the outbreak of the Second World War an occupying Power was unquestionably precluded from executing hostages and similar innocent persons: the doubts persisting in that regard appear to stand in the way of such a definite conclusion. But neither could these doubts be interpreted as a licence to proceed to such executions without so much as a second thought. Indeed, such a conclusion would be clearly incompatible with the idea, expressed in the Martens-clause in the preamble to the Hague Convention on Land Warfare of 1899, that even in situations where no specific rules govern the relations between belligerents and civil populations, the belligerents would be obliged to pay due heed to humanitarian considerations.

[14] *Supra*, Chapter III, §§ 3.3 and 3.5.

It need hardly be added that the Keitel directive was in flagrant contradiction with the above considerations, in that it indiscriminately prescribed immediate use of the sharpest means of retaliation, including the execution of "communists". In this respect, the directive evidently laboured under a total lack of elementary carefulness.

It was already stated above—and it need hardly be reiterated—that also the ratio prescribed in the directive was disproportionate to such a degree as to pass all comprehension, in any event if one still had in mind the idea of justification of otherwise unlawful measures. True, the ratio prescribed remained unapplied in many instances; on the other hand, it has been applied in certain cases. The point is not, however, whether it was brought into practice or not, but that it could be prescribed at all. This provides another indication of the complete disregard which those laying down the policy had for the justifiability of acts implementing it, be it as reprisals or measures of collective punishment. It also betrays the real nature of the policy of retaliation, the terrorization of the populations in the occupied countries, so as to deter them from any activities contrary to the interests of the German *Reich* and the policy pursued by its leaders.[15]

In summary, the possibility cannot be excluded that specific instances of retaliatory executions of innocent members of the population in occupied territory met the norms governing recourse to reprisals or collective punishment and, hence, could be considered justified under international law. This would have required, first of all, that the act retaliated against was unlawful; and, as the Germans had by their policy in respect of the occupied countries themselves provided the populations with a right to resist, this unlawfulness would not already result from the mere fact that the act retaliated against was an act of resistance.

Secondly, the execution must either have had the purpose, characteristic of a reprisal, of law enforcement—and in the circumstances prevailing in

---

[15] As early as 25 October 1941, President Roosevelt issued the following statement sharply disapproving the German practices: "The practice of executing scores of innocent hostages in reprisal for isolated attacks on Germans in countries temporarily under the Nazi heel revolts a world already inured to suffering and brutality.

"Civilised peoples long ago adopted the basic principle that no man should be punished for the deed of another. Unable to apprehend the persons involved in these attacks, the Nazis characteristically slaughter 50 or 100 innocent persons.

"Those who would 'collaborate' with Hitler or try to appease him cannot ignore this ghastly warning. The Nazis might have learned from the last war the impossibility of breaking men's spirit by terrorism. Instead they develop their *Lebensraum* and a 'New Order' by depths of frightfulness which even they have never approached before. "These are acts of desperate men who in their hearts know they cannot win. Frightfulness can never bring peace to Europe. It only sows seeds of hatred which will one day bring a fearful retribution."—*Punishment for War Crimes*, issued by the Inter-Allied Information Committee, London, Vol. I [Inter-Allied Declaration signed at St. James's Palace, 13 January 1942], p. 15.

the occupied territories this was tantamount to saying that it must have had the purpose of bringing pressure to bear on the leaders of a resistance army of the Tito variety—or it must have rested on the established collective responsibility of the population for the act retaliated against, so that the execution could be brought under the head of collective punishment.

Then, the retaliatory execution of innocents being very nearly prohibited according to the trend of the law prevailing at the time, the necessity of that course of action in the given instance must have been very carefully weighed.

Finally, the number of persons executed must have been proportionate to the gravity of the act retaliated against; and, while some doubt might persist as to whether a ratio of one person executed for every German killed was the absolute maximum tolerable, it is not open to doubt that the ratio of 50 or 100 to 1 was shockingly disproportionate in any circumstances.

This list of requirements makes it abundantly clear that only a minority of the executions actually performed in the course of the war can have met the conditions for justification of such acts. For the rest, the executions had the same character as was evidenced by the policy directive of September 1941: they were acts of terror, not justified by any norm of international law.

Besides being unjustified, the policy of sharp retaliation has not proved an effective method of determent either. Obviously, it will have deterred a certain number of individual persons from joining in resistance activities. But in the long run, and taken as a whole, it had the opposite effect to the one envisaged: together with the other elements of terror inherent in the German occupation régime it engendered so much hate among the occupied populations so as to stimulate strongly the further development of resistance activities in all forms, from sabotage to guerrilla and other forms of warfare.[16]

5.4. CONCLUSIONS

Discounting for a moment the great number of retaliatory actions in German-occupied countries (which, however, were all the outcome of a single policy), few instances of alleged reprisals have been reported in the last two Chapters. Even rarer proved the instances where such alleged reprisals had the purpose of law enforcement, characteristic of true reprisals, and the number of reprisal actions justifiable in all respects appears to be exactly nil.

Instances of acts of warfare alleged to constitute reprisals were the air

[16] Some specific instances of so-called reprisal shootings shall be dealt with hereafter, in Chapter VI, § 6.1.

bombardment of London in 1940, and, in the economic sphere, the measures against the German import and export taken from November 1939 onwards.

As regards the latter measures, embodied in the Reprisal Orders in Council of 1939 and 1940, their justification as reprisals was highly dubious from the outset, and their continued application at a time when the Allied forces had taken recourse to methods of sea warfare hardly distinguishable from the earlier German practices was not justifiable at all. The measures were certainly effective, that is, as powerful means of economic warfare. However, in so far as law enforcement may have been their objective, they proved wholly ineffective.

As for the bombardment of London, the assertion that that action would have constituted a reprisal proved ill-founded, as it lacked the purpose of law enforcement. It was not a mere military operation either, at any rate according to the intentions of some of the authorities behind it: in Hitler's eyes it primarily had a political objective in that it would serve to bring the British people to their knees in a very short time. However, this political end was not achieved, and also from a military point of view the value of the action was less than expected: it did not break down the British defence system, and the bombs dropped on non-military objectives in the London area achieved no useful end whatsoever. On the contrary, the indications are that the action enhanced the will to resist of the British people.

An instance of a retaliatory action only partly belonging in the sphere of warfare proper was the ruthless extermination of commandos in combat, as ordered in the Commando Order. Viewed from the other aspect, that measure belonged under the head of the treatment of prisoners, as the order also included that commandos would be made prisoners first and killed only after interrogation. As the accent in practice lay heavily on the latter part of the policy ordered, the issue shall be reverted to below, under the head of alleged reprisals not consisting in acts of warfare proper.

In the latter category of alleged reprisals, the records show several instances of measures against prisoners of war. Among these, the shackling of prisoners as applied by the Germans subsequent to the raid on Dieppe and in retaliation to certain practices applied by the raiding forces on that and other occasions, can without doubt be regarded as a genuine reprisal: it evidently had the purpose of coercing the enemy to bring his policy into line with the law of war. The measure cannot even be denied a certain effectiveness in that respect, as the British authorities brought some modifications to the standing instructions of commandos engaged in raiding operations. However, the shackling of prisoners of war was unjustifiable nonetheless, in view of the express prohibition of reprisals against prisoners of war in the 1929 Prisoners of War Convention.

211

The same applies *a fortiori* to the counter-reprisal taken by the British and Canadian authorities and which equally consisted in the shackling of a number of prisoners in their hands. Their action was doubly unjustifiable, however, as reprisals against reprisals are out of the question. It was, moreover, completely ineffectual.

Another and a more dramatic instance of a reprisal against prisoners of war was the execution of eighty German prisoners in the hands of the French Forces of the Interior, the resistance army operating in French territory in close co-operation with the Allied command. In the light of the German treatment of members of these forces falling into their hands, which was based on the denial that such persons had combatant status and were entitled to be treated as prisoners of war, the act of retaliation was perfectly understandable. Moreover, while there are no indications that the subsequent change in the German policy with regard to these forces was in any way decisively influenced by the action at issue, neither can the possibility be excluded that it would have materially contributed to the change. Once again, however, justification of the measure is frustrated by the aforementioned unequivocal prohibition.

Two alleged reprisal policies remain to be accounted for: the policy laid down in the Commando Order, and the retaliatory policy in occupied territories as evidenced in the Keitel directive. Both of these lines of policy were alleged to be justified on account of grave and dangerous infringements of the law in force, committed respectively by the criminals serving in the commando forces and by communists operating as resistance fighters. However, in either case the true purpose of the measure, far from being the enforcement of the law of war in respect of an opponent violating it, was purely and simply terror, and implementation of the policy—rare exceptions aside—was plain murder.

Has the practice of the Second World War confirmed the validity of a norm to the effect that belligerent reprisals may not violate essential humanitarian norms? This cannot be maintained so far as respect for the life of non-combatant civilians is concerned: both in the bombardment of London and similar actions, and in the German policy of retaliation in occupied territories, the victims belonged primarily to that category. However, neither of these actions was a genuine reprisal, so that for the theory of belligerent reprisals no definite conclusions can be drawn from these particular instances of non-observance of a potential norm. It may be added that none of the belligerents in the Second World War displayed any great respect for the life and property of the enemy civil population, as is evidenced not only by the indiscriminate bombing of enemy towns, but also by a measure such as the economic blockade of Germany and her partners: that blockade, besides being a weapon against the industrial capacity of the

Axis Powers, constituted a threat to the life and health of the populations as well.

More favourable is the picture with respect to prisoners of war: only very few instances were reported of reprisals in respect of them. Thus, it may be concluded that the norm referred to above has been respected fairly well as far as this category of war victims was concerned. It should be added, firstly, that in the Geneva Prisoners of War Convention of 1929 the norm in question had been converted into an express rule prohibiting reprisals against prisoners of war, so that the state of the law was not questionable on this score. Secondly, the need for reprisals against prisoners of war had definitely decreased by virtue of the system of inspections as brought into practice by the ICRC (and accepted by a majority of the belligerents) and, generally, by the unremitting efforts of the ICRC to bring the belligerents to observe the Convention and, in the event of difficulties, to discuss these with the enemy (*via* the ICRC, if required) rather than take recourse to retaliation.

Another essential element in the doctrine of reprisals is the requirement of proportionality: was it respected during the Second World War? Clear instances of evidently proportionate reprisals may be seen in the affair of the shackling of prisoners of war, and in the execution of eighty prisoners of war by the FFI. It should be noted that both cases also presented all other characteristics of genuine reprisals, and that neither of the actions can be denied a measure of effectiveness as such; their justification was, however, excluded by the express prohibition in the Prisoners of War Convention.

Proportionality was hard to assess in a complicated situation such as the economic blockade of the Axis Powers—a measure the truly retaliatory character of which was, for the rest, very much in doubt. And the same obtains for the bombardment of London, although there is evidence that the disproportionality of that action was realized even at the time it was committed.

The requirement of proportionality was most openly disregarded in such directives as the Commando Order and the Keitel directive, outlining the policy to be pursued in respect of commandos and the civil populations in occupied territories, respectively. However, the total absence of proportionality in these instances is merely a reflection of the true nature of the policies in question, which was terrorization, not law enforcement.

It may therefore be submitted that the closer a retaliatory measure came to being a genuine reprisal, the better the requirement of proportionality was observed, and vice versa. This is an indication that proportionality is not only a logical requirement of elementary justice for reprisals as for sanctions generally, but that it also represents a positive element contributing to their effectiveness: the measured reprisal stands a far better chance of achieving the desired effect than the disproportionate policy of terror.

In addition to the above conclusions relating to the instances of alleged reprisals investigated in the foregoing, some observations seem pertinent regarding the fact that these instances were so limited in number.

This fact may be explained, firstly, as an admission of the limited importance in practice of belligerent reprisals. These are in fact virtually useless, for instance, in respect of an enemy who by his whole attitude demonstrates a total disrespect for certain parts of the law of war (as was the case with Germany particularly where occupation law was concerned). They are equally useless when applied in a situation where the interests at stake are so great as to make it utterly improbable that a belligerent would change his policy merely on account of a certain pressure exerted on him by the enemy: instances of such crucial issues were the strategic air bombardment and the unrestricted submarine warfare, practised by either side in the course of the Second World War.[1]

A factor connected with the foregoing, but of distinct and even fundamental significance, may be seen in the decision taken in an early stage of the war by the Allied Powers and formally enacted in the Interallied Declaration on Punishment for War Crimes, signed in London on 13 January 1942.[2] According to that Declaration, the Allied Powers „place[d] among their principal war aims the punishment, through the channel of organised justice, of those guilty of or responsible for" the crimes committed by Germany in the occupied countries, "whether they have ordered them, perpetrated them, or participated in them". In other words, it was decided that the war criminals would be punished individually after the war for their personal guilt. And, while this need not entail the omittal of reprisals *durante bello*,[3] it is evident that the Allied Powers did in fact attach that

---

[1] *Cf.* the argument advanced by the British Government in their discussions with the Netherlands Government concerning the first Reprisals Order in Council: "no mere expression of disapproval by world opinion", it was stated, would be "likely to have the slightest deterrent effect" on the German Government (*supra*, p. 150).

True, the argument was used by the British Government precisely in support of its decision to take a reprisal, on account of allegedly illegal methods of sea warfare. But, then, the British Government were very anxious to take the particular reprisal (viz., establishment of export control), and in any event the measure failed to bring about even the slightest change in the German methods of warfare.

[2] *Punishment for War Crimes, op. cit.* n. 15 to § 5.3.

[3] The opposite view is held by M. W. Mouton, *Oorlogsmisdrijven en het internationale recht* (*i.e.*, War crimes and international law) (1947), according to whom reprisals and the punishment of war criminals are mutually exclusive; p. 442. He quotes in support an opinion of H. Lauterpacht, who has written that "there is room for the view that if the victorious belligerent has himself, in pursuance of reprisals, violated international law in a particular sphere, he cannot properly make such acts on the part of his opponent the subject of prosecution for a war crime" ("The Law of Nations and the

consequence to the policy chosen.[4] It may therefore be concluded that their deliberate choice of another sanctions system has been instrumental in keeping the record of reprisal actions so conspicuously low.

---

punishment of war crimes", in *BYIL*, Vol. XXI, 1944, p. 58, at p. 77). However, the two views are not entirely concordant. For, while in Mouton's eyes individual punishment would be excluded because of the fact of the earlier application of a reprisal (that is, a sanction), Lauterpacht's idea seems to be that the perpetration of a particular law infringement, even if justified as a reprisal, is sufficient ground to deprive the perpetrator of the right to punish an opponent who has infringed the same norm.

[4] The point was made explicit in the third Molotov note on German atrocities, of 27 April 1942, reporting a new series of German crimes against the Russian people and *inter alia* against Soviet prisoners of war. In connection with the latter category of crimes the note stated that "the Soviet Government even in present circumstances does not intend to resort to reprisals against German war prisoners", and it announced that those responsible for the crimes would be punished after the war. The Third Molotov Note on German Atrocities, London, 1942.

CHAPTER VI

Developments after the Second World War

6.1. JUDICIAL DECISIONS RELATING TO THE SECOND WORLD WAR

Unlike in previous periods, the number of judicial decisions dealing with reprisals in one form or another, resulting from the Second World War has been far from negligible. This is explained by a conjunction of circumstances: on the one hand, the decision taken on the Allied side in an early stage of the war to bring to trial the individual perpetrators of war crimes committed by the enemy and particularly in Axis-occupied countries, rather than revert to reprisals;[1] and, on the other hand, the fact that many of the very acts committed in those countries and which were listed as war crimes by the Allied Powers, either had from the outset been announced as reprisals by the enemy,[2] or in any event were alleged to have constituted reprisals by those brought to trial for the acts after the war.

While the range of the reprisals coming to the test of judicial appraisal was thus limited,[3] some of the judgments delivered are of the greatest interest, not only for a better understanding of the complex notion of

---

[1] For a survey of the background of the idea to bring individual war criminals to trial and its elaboration during and after the war, see: *History of the United Nations War Crimes Commission and the Development of the Laws of War*, compiled by the United Nations War Crimes Commission and published in London, 1948.

While the policy of individual punishment was originally formulated in reaction to German atrocities in occupied territories (*supra*, p. 214), it came to embrace other infringements of the laws of war (not to mention the crimes against the peace and against humanity). This led to trials for acts which at the time of their commission had provided the argument for reprisal actions on the Allied side; thus, the British (alleged) reprisals described in Chapter IV were excused with the aid of certain German practices of sea warfare. Significantly, when the International Military Tribunal at Nuremberg, dealing with the charge against Dönitz that he had conducted unrestricted submarine warfare, decided not to mete out punishment to the accused for that particular war crime, the argument was not that it had already led to reprisals, but that the Allied had adopted similar methods of sea warfare; *cf.* the argument about the non-final character of reprisals, *supra*, p. 26.

[2] See § 5.3.

[3] As mentioned in § 4.1 (*supra*, pp. 120, 125), the British reprisals orders of 1939-1940 did not lead to any judicial pronouncements on their justifiability.

216

"reprisals" in occupied territory, but for the general doctrine of belligerent reprisals as well.

6.1.1. *Discussion between prosecution and defence in Trial of Major War Criminals, Nuremberg*

The International Military Tribunal, set up by the Allied Powers for the trial of the German major war criminals,[4] did not itself deal in its judgment with the issue of reprisals, other than by holding that certain modes of conduct (such as the extermination of commandos and the killing of hostages) constituted war crimes and thus implicitly rejecting the plea that these might be justifiable as legitimate reprisals.

However, the issue of reprisals has been the subject of an interesting discussion which took place in the course of the oral proceedings before the Tribunal between Justice Jackson, Chief Prosecutor for the United States of America, and Drs. Stahmer and Exner on the side of the defence. The discussion arose from a remark of the defendant Göring who, being interrogated by his counsel, Dr. Stahmer, about the development of resistance activities in the occupied part of France and the German policy of repression, stated that the resistance fighters had committed atrocities and that this could be proved with the aid of documents. Justice Jackson, interrupting, raised the question of whether these facts, and the documentary evidence relating thereto, could be relevant to the charge of atrocities having been committed in France by Germany. If, he said, the intention of the defence was to rely on the theory of reprisals for the justification of these German atrocities, this would needs imply an admission of the fact of the atrocities in the first place, and, moreover, the defence would have to take into account the conditions governing the justification of acts as reprisals. This led him to set out those conditions as he saw them.

First, the defence would have to relate the plea to acts other than against prisoners of war, as reprisals against those persons were specifically prohibited under the P.O.W. Convention of 1929. Then, any act claimed to be justified as a reprisal "must be related to a specific and continuing violation of international law on the other side"; otherwise international law would have no foundation, as any "casual and incidental violation" on one side would "completely absolve the other from any rules of warfare". Next, the act claimed to constitute a reprisal "must follow within a reasonable time" after the offence, and then only after due notice; and the act "must be related reasonably to the offense which it is sought to prevent. That is,

---

[4] Agreement for the Prosecution and Punishment of the Major War Criminals of the European Axis, with annexed Charter of the International Military Tribunal, signed in London on 8 August 1945; Cmd. 6668, 1945-46. See also History of the U.N.W.C.C., *op. cit.* n. 1.

you cannot by way of reprisal engage in wholesale slaughter in order to vindicate a single murder". A final and most important point was that "a deliberate course of violation of international law cannot be shielded as a reprisal. ... You cannot vindicate a reign of terror under the doctrine of reprisals".[5]

To this statement of conditions governing recourse to reprisals, both Dr. Stahmer and Dr. Exner made objections, and it is interesting to note how each of them approached the subject from a totally different angle. Dr. Stahmer's argument was that the German authorities in France had been confronted with an emergency situation, "caused by conduct violating international law, that is by unleashing guerrilla warfare". And this fact, he said, "justified the army commanders to take general measures in order to remove these conditions brought about illegally." [6]

It may be observed that Dr. Stahmer did not enter upon the points raised by the prosecution concerning the general aspects of reprisals, but restricted his argument to the point at issue of "reprisals" against an occupied population. Another observation is that the ground which he advanced in justification of the measures taken virtually boils down to military necessity.

Dr. Exner took up the general aspects of reprisals and, while conceding that reprisals against prisoners of war were prohibited, denied the existence and validity according to international law of any further rules restricting their use, even the norm of proportionality: that was indeed a desirable norm, but "in existing international law, in the sense that some agreement has been made to that effect or that it has become international legal usage, this is not the case". From this absence of positive rules he concluded that "[i]t will have to be said therefore, on the basis of violations of international law by the other side, that we under no circumstances make a war of reprisals against prisoners of war, every other form of reprisals is, however, admissible." [7]

The Tribunal did not pronounce upon the theoretical questions raised in this discussion. As to the point at issue, namely, the admissibility of certain documentary evidence, it evidently did not hold the objections raised by the prosecution decisive: it ruled the evidence admissible "on the question of reprisals", while reserving for future consideration the weight that it should carry.[8]

In its final judgment, the Tribunal confined itself to putting on record that Article 6 (b) of its Charter,[9] which included the killing of hostages in

[5] I.M.T. Vol. IX: Proceedings, 8-23 March 1946; p. 323.
[6] *Ibid.*, at p. 325.
[7] *Loc. cit.* n. 6.
[8] *Ibid.*, at p. 326.
[9] Charter of the International Military Tribunal, see n. 4. Art. 46 of the Hague Regulations on Land Warfare provides, *inter alia*, that the occupant must respect the life of the inhabitants.

occupied territory among the war crimes, was "[i]n the main ... declaratory of the existing laws of war as expressed by the Hague Convention, Article 46".[10]

The significance of this episode lies not in such qualities as the clarity or perfection of the arguments advanced (and, having regard to the *ad hoc* character of the discussion, this could hardly have been otherwise), so much as in the fact that it is illustrative of the main lines of reasoning that have played an important rôle in all discussions of the period about the subject at issue. These can be summed up as follows: (1) retaliatory measures against an occupied population could only be justified as reprisals in so far as they complied with the general norms restricting the right to take reprisals; (2) such measures were always justified as reprisals, as there are no generally accepted, valid, legal norms restricting the right to take reprisals (with the sole exception of the prohibition of reprisals against prisoners of war); (3) irrespective of whether the measures could be justified under the general doctrine of reprisals, they were in any event measures of reprisal deriving their justification from military necessity.[11]

Thus, even though the International Military Tribunal did not give an express ruling on the validity of any of these viewpoints, the discussion reported here can usefully serve as an introduction to the subsequent judicial decisions of other courts.

6.1.2. *The Hostages Case*

The question of the hostage killings and their possible justification arose in several of the cases tried under Control Council Law No. 10 by United States Military Tribunals, convened at Nuremberg in the American zone of occupation of Germany.[12] In the so-called Hostages Case [13] it even constituted the main issue.

In this case, tried by United States Military Tribunal V, the "murder of hundreds of thousands of persons from the civilian populations of Greece, Yugoslavia, and Albania, by troops of the German armed forces" under

[10] Judgment of the I.M.T., in: I.M.T., Vol. XXII, p. 475.
[11] With respect to the last-mentioned view, *cf.* § 1.3.2 (*supra*, p. 39), where the view was defended that military necessity is the sole *ratio* of measures of collective punishment (or quasi-reprisals). As was emphasized there, this argument does not imply that it would suffice for a measure to be announced as a "reprisal", "collective punishment", or the like, to be justified irrespective of its substance. In particular, it does not in any way decide the question of whether inhabitants of occupied territory can justifiably be killed by way of "reprisal".
[12] See: Trials of Criminals before the Nuernberg Military Tribunals, published by the U.S. Government Printing Office. Basic documents, such as the Charter of the I.M.T. and Control Council Law No. 10, are reproduced at the beginning of each case or group of cases.
[13] Trials (etc.), Vol. XI, p. 757: The United States of America *v.* Wilhelm List *et al.*

the command of the defendants figured as Count One of the indictment. It was related that the victims included two categories of persons: those who were simply "rounded up from the streets, from their houses, or from their places of work, and placed in prison camps and stockades", and those "arbitrarily designated as 'partisans', 'Communists', 'Communist suspects', 'bandits', and 'bandit suspects'"; the victims of both categories were murdered "without benefit of investigation or trial", "in retaliation for attacks by lawfully constituted enemy military forces and attacks by unknown persons against German troops and installations". It was furthermore stated that "these acts of collective punishment were part of a deliberate scheme of terror and intimidation, wholly unwarranted and unjustified by military necessity and in flagrant violation of the laws and customs of war".[14]

In his opening statement, General Taylor, Chief of Counsel for the prosecution, stated that "the concepts of 'hostage' and 'reprisal' both derive from relations between nations, or between their opposing armed forces, and not from the relations between a nation or its armed forces on the one hand and the civilian population of an occupied territory on the other": retaliatory measures against the latter category could indeed constitute reprisals, but only if these were inflicted "for the purpose of persuading the enemy government to discontinue an unlawful course of action, and not for the purpose of punishing the civilian inhabitants themselves".[15] He furthermore suggested to the Tribunal that, while the taking of hostages might be permissible, "the execution of hostages, under the circumstances pertinent to this case, [was] quite definitely and clearly a crime under international law"; for this he did not solely rely on Article II of Control Council Law No. 10,[16] nor on "the weight of authority, however impressive": he sought the main argument in "practical considerations of military necessity". For, he said, while "[t]he fundamental tenet of the laws of war ... is that human life should not be taken unnecessarily", "there is absolutely no footing, either in the authorities or in general practice, for the conclusion that the execution of hostages is ever really necessary." Somewhat surprisingly, he added that "if [such executions are] not [necessary], [these] are in flat contradiction of Article 46 of the Annex to the Hague Convention." [17] The words "if not" seem to imply that in General Taylor's eyes the presence of military necessity would have been sufficient ground to disregard Article 46. This would explain why he thought fit to lay so much stress on the absence of that ground in the actual circumstances of the case. However, it

[14] *Ibid.*, at pp. 765-766.
[15] *Ibid.*, at p. 841.
[16] That the killing of hostages should be treated as a war crime, had been authoritatively decided in Article 6 (*b*) of the Charter of the I.M.T. and in Article II, para. 1 (*b*) of Control Council Law No. 10.
[17] Trials, Vol. XI, at p. 845.

should be added that Mr. Rapp, who delivered the closing statement for the prosecution, stated that "it is the prosecution's contention that the plea of military necessity can never be used as a defense for the taking of an unarmed civilian's life, if he is innocent of any hostile conduct against the occupying power." [18]

General Taylor advanced one further ground for the illegality of the incriminated actions: even irrespective of whether the partisans had been legitimate combatants (as they had certainly been in parts of south-eastern Europe), the peoples in those countries "had every right to rise and defend themselves by armed force because the Germans themselves so flagrantly violated the laws of war. .... If the occupying forces inaugurate a systematic program of criminal terror, they cannot thereafter call the inhabitants to account for taking measures in self defence. This ... nowhere appears in so many words in the Hague Convention, but it is in entire harmony with the purpose of the articles, and I think no one will be heard to deny that this is the only conclusion which is possible in accordance with 'the principles of the law of nations, as they result from the usages established among civilized peoples, from the laws of humanity, and the dictates of the public conscience'." [19]

The closing statement for the prosecution elaborated these arguments somewhat further, and it made the final point that even if the execution of a single hostage were not a crime in itself, the numbers of hostages killed and the ratio of the killings to the numbers of Germans dead or wounded were such as to leave no doubt about the complete disproportionality and vengeful character of the measures taken.[20]

Counsel for the defendant List, Dr. Laternser, in his opening statement developed the theme that the hostage killings had constituted reprisals and were justified as such. Specifically, he denied that reprisals could not obtain in the relations of a nation or its armed forces to the population of an occupied territory; he said: [21]

> "The action according to plan of inciting the civilian population to acts of sabotage and attacks upon members of the German occupation forces and the fight of the partisans in violation of international law in the occupied territories had the result that during the Second World War reprisals had to be resorted to above all against illegal actions of

[18] *Ibid.*, at p. 1162. The latter view seems more in conformity with general opinion about the relation of military necessity to specific rules of warfare.
[19] *Ibid.*, at p. 852. Cf. also § 5.3, where a similar argument was developed.
[20] *Ibid.*, at p. 1170; statement of Mr. Fenstermacher. The ratio referred to was the notorious 50 or 100 : 1 ratio, laid down *inter alia* in the Keitel directive of September 1941; see § 5.3. One of the charges against the defendants was precisely that they had issued, distributed or executed orders of this purport.
[21] *Ibid.*, at p. 867.

221

the civilian population, in order to force the latter to desist from its illegal conduct. It would be absurd to assume that the commanders of the armed forces of a belligerent party had to endure acts of an enemy civilian population in violation of international law, without being able to protect their troops, when necessary, by retaliatory measures."

This piece of reasoning is remarkable in more than one respect. First, by introducing the element of a plan and of the incitement of the population, the problem was shifted from retaliation against a population as such to reprisals against Government-inspired and -directed actions; this line was not however pursued any further: it was merely indicated.

Then, the "fight of the partisans" was qualified as a "violation of international law". This point was maintained tenaciously during the subsequent proceedings. Thus, Dr. Laternser in his closing statement argued at great length that the partisans had lacked combatant status and that hence all their belligerent acts must be considered to have constituted war crimes.[22] And he both sharply denied the correctness of the allegation that prior German violations of the Hague Regulations had prompted resistance in legitimate self-defence of the populations, and declared "more than dubious from the point of view of international law" "the attempt to make the offenses against international law committed by the population appear lawful".[23]

The most remarkable feature of the above quotation is, however, the ease with which Dr. Laternser jumped from "inciting according to plan" and "illegal partisan fighting" to the necessity of reprisals "against illegal actions of the civilian population, in order to force the latter to desist from its illegal conduct". On the one hand, the population is here suddenly transformed into a collectivity, collectively responsible for "its" illegal conduct. On the other hand (and this should be particularly emphasized): notwithstanding the suggestion to the contrary resulting from the repeated reference to "illegal conduct", the real reason for the reprisals appears to be, not so much the protection of international law, as the protection of the occupation forces—that is, military necessity. This point, too, was elaborated at some considerable length in Dr. Laternser's closing statement;[24] he even went so far as to suggest that the German commanders in south-eastern Europe had been confronted with partisan activities "affect[ing] the very existence of the particular belligerent" (i.e. Germany), and, said he, in such a situation "no responsible commander will be able . . . to avoid taking all, even the most stringent measures, in order to suppress such crimes."[25]

---

[22] Ibid., pp. 1188 ff.; this in spite of the fact that the travaux préparatoires of the Hague Regulations clearly indicate that their authors neither accorded nor denied the population a right of defence.

[23] Ibid., at p. 1184.

[24] Ibid., pp. 1210 ff.

[25] Ibid., at p. 1217; even here, in respect to partisan activities allegedly affecting the

He conceded that a rule existed to the effect that members of the civil population, whether or not arrested as hostages beforehand, should not summarily be killed. This rule was expressed in the Charter and Judgment of the International Military Tribunal, as well as in Control Council Law No. 10 which governed the present proceedings. However, he argued, it is precisely the effect of reprisals that they justify otherwise unlawful modes of acting, and this effect was of course not excluded by the aforementioned rule, which had no bearing on the issue of reprisals. Thus, he concluded, the killing of hostages by way of reprisals was specifically justified by the very operation of the doctrine of reprisals. A contrary opinion might be readily understandable "from the point of view of humanitarian principles, but it is also quite certain that it is incorrect from the point of view of the laws of war".[26]

With respect to the question of proportionality, Dr. Laternser denied that a rule had developed to the effect that reprisals have to be proportionate to the gravity of the preceding violation of international law perpetrated by the opposing party. "Naturally", he said, "the reprisals measure must not be excessive; that is, it must not exceed what is necessary. This limitation follows from the general principle of humanity which limits application of power to the necessary extent. The verdict whether or not one is dealing with a military necessity and what is its extent depends on conditions, whatever they may be, and is ordinarily the concern of the military commander who has to make the decision".[27]

Two observations seem pertinent here. Firstly, the "proportionality" professed by Dr. Laternser bears little similarity to the standard of proportionality as it is usually conceived in the doctrine of sanctions, namely as a relation between sanction and preceding act. This strengthens the impression that he did not really envisage reprisals as a sanction in the international legal order. To that extent it merely corroborates the second observation: that the above quotation is the most unequivocal confirmation imaginable of the thesis that military necessity, and military necessity alone, was the basis of the so-called reprisals.[28]

Military Tribunal V in its judgment of 19 February 1948 went to great lengths to explain why it found the hostage killings as practised by the

---

very existence of Germany, the suggestion is maintained that it was the criminality of the activities rather than their dangerous character which would have prompted the counter-measures.

[26] See in particular the closing statement, pp. 1207-1209; the quoted words are at p. 1209.

[27] *Ibid.*, at p. 1217.

[28] For the sake of completeness it is recorded that a final argument was advanced in defence of List, to the effect that he could not at the time have known all the facts and that the legal position was vague, so that the Tribunal ought to allow that he could have felt "justified in ordering the measures he did"; *ibid.*, at p. 1227.

Germans in south-eastern Europe inexcusable, and, hence, the defendants guilty. For the Tribunal ultimately arrived at this conclusion, notwithstanding the fact that it did not consider the execution of hostages *a priori* unjustifiable; its line of reasoning was as follows.

The Tribunal argued that the countries in south-eastern Europe where the acts set out in the indictment were said to have been perpetrated, had become occupied territories (as distinct from a territory where an invasion is in progress); that resistance arose soon and "increased progressively in intensity until it assumed the appearance of a military campaign"; but that, while "certain band units in both Yugoslavia and Greece complied with the requirements of international law entitling them to the status of a lawful belligerent", on the other hand "the greater portion of the partisan bands failed to comply with the rules of war entitling them to be accorded the rights of a lawful belligerent" and, hence, upon capture were liable to be killed as francs-tireurs.[29]

However, the main issue did not arise from the killing of such francs-tireurs for their own acts, but "gravitate[d] around the claimed right of the German armed forces to take hostages from the innocent civilian population to guarantee the peaceful conduct of the whole of the civilian population and its claimed right to execute hostages, members of the civilian population, and captured members of the resistance forces in reprisal for armed attacks by resistance forces, acts of sabotage and injuries committed by unknown persons". The Tribunal observed that hostages can, and may, be taken, *inter alia*, "to insure against unlawful acts by enemy forces or people". In this connection the Tribunal defined hostages as "those persons of the civilian population who are taken into custody for the purpose of guaranteeing with their lives for the future good conduct of the population of the community from which they were taken".[30]

This definition of hostages, as persons taken into custody not for acts committed but as a guarantee for future good conduct, led the Tribunal to observe that another possibility consisted in the seizure and punishment of innocent individuals for past violations of the laws of war; and, said the Tribunal, in that case "no question of hostages is involved", but of reprisals —a question "closely integrated" with that of hostages, however. But notwithstanding this close connection, the Tribunal found it necessary to observe somewhat sternly that "[t]hroughout the evidence in the present case, we find the term hostage applied where a reprisal only was involved".[31]

While the latter quotation is suggestive of a fundamental difference between hostages and the category of "reprisal prisoners" (being, in the words of the Tribunal, "those individuals who are taken from the civilian popu-

[29] *Ibid.*, pp. 1243-1244.
[30] *Ibid.*, pp. 1248-1249.
[31] *Loc. cit.* n. 30.

lation to be killed in retaliation for offenses committed by unknown persons within the occupied area"), it is apparent from the subsequent parts of the judgment that no real difference obtained between the two categories, other than the hardly essential relation of the moment of their arrest to that of the commission of the acts leading to their execution.[32] The Tribunal, it is true, first stated its views as to the killing of hostages and then of reprisal prisoners, but the latter argument is little more than a slightly abbreviated repetition of the first. Therefore, as it is the issue of the killing of these persons rather than their arrest which is at stake here, it seems justified to disregard the distinction between the two categories.

The Tribunal next set out to give its legal appreciation of the retaliatory executions. Its reasoning can be divided into two parts: the grounds why and the conditions under which it considered the taking and killing of hostages exceptionally justifiable, and the reasons why no such justification could obtain in the case at issue.

The Tribunal found the fundamental basis of the right to take and execute hostages in "a theory of collective responsibility" of the inhabitants of an occupied territory, who "owe a duty to carry on their ordinary peaceful pursuits and to refrain from all injurious acts toward the troops or in respect to their military operations." The occupant, upon whom the fact of the occupation confers "the right of control for the period of the occupation within the limitations and prohibitions of international law", "may properly insist upon compliance with regulations necessary for the security of the occupying forces and for the maintenance of law and order. In the accomplishment of this objective, the occupant may only, as a last resort, take and execute hostages." [33]

The Tribunal explained what it understood by "collective responsibility" in its further consideration that it must "be shown that the population generally is a party to the offense, either actively or passively. ... If the act was committed by isolated persons or bands from distant localities without

[32] Not even the Tribunal itself maintained the distinction with any great accuracy. Thus, when the question of the execution of hostages had been brought to an end and that of the execution of reprisal prisoners was broached, the Tribunal referred to "the detention of members of the civilian population for the purpose of using them as the victims of subsequent reprisal measures", and it added that "[t]he most common reason for holding them is for the general purpose of securing the good behavior and obedience of the civil population in occupied territory" (*ibid.*, at p. 1251). This formula is hardly distinguishable from the earlier definition of hostages.

[33] *Ibid.*, at p. 1249. It bears pointing out that the Tribunal neither entered into the argument of the prosecution that previous violations of occupation law on the German side had given the population a right of self-defence (and that, hence, the normal rules restricting legitimate combatancy to certain well-defined categories of persons did not apply), nor did it pay attention to the suggestion, made by the defence, that the resistance movement had in reality been an integral part of the Allied war effort (and, hence, should not be regarded as an affair of the populations only).

the knowledge or approval of the population or public authorities, and which, therefore, neither the authorities nor the population could have prevented, the basis for the taking of hostages, or the shooting of hostages already taken, does not exist." In the opposite supposition, however, hostages could be taken or shot, and "under certain circumstances" (which the Tribunal did not further specify) they could even be selected on the admittedly arbitrary and deplorable, but not unlawful basis of mere "nationality or geographic proximity"—provided always the required connection between population and crime could be shown.[34]

With respect to the other essential element in the Tribunal's reasoning, viz., that the taking and execution of hostages may only be indulged in as a "last resort", the Tribunal emphasized that "[h]ostages may not be taken or executed as a matter of military expediency. The occupant is required to use every available method to secure order and tranquility before resort may be had to the taking and execution of hostages." The weight which the Tribunal attached to this character of *ultimum remedium* is apparent from the pains it took to enumerate measures that could (and, hence, should) be imposed on an occupied population prior to the taking of hostages. Only if all other measures would have failed, that is, "[i]f attacks upon troops and military installations occur regardless of the foregoing precautionary measures and the perpetrators cannot be apprehended", would the taking of hostages become admissible.[35]

---

[34] *Ibid.*, at p. 1250. While in the passage quoted in the text above the crucial element lies in the impossibility for the authorities or the population to have prevented the incriminated act, the Tribunal elsewhere explained the requirement "that the population as a whole is a party to the offense, either actively or passively" by stating that "[i]n other words, members of the population of one community cannot properly be shot in reprisal for an act against the occupation forces committed at some other place. To permit such a practice would conflict with the basic theory that sustains the practice in that there would be no deterrent effect upon the community where the offense was committed." (p. 1252); this time the decisive element was sought in deterrence, that is, of future acts of resistance.

[35] *Ibid.*, pp. 1249-1250. As to the prior measures, the Tribunal observed (*loc. cit.*): "Regulations of all kinds must be imposed to secure peace and tranquility before the shooting of hostages may be indulged. These regulations may include one or more of the following measures: (1) the registration of the inhabitants, (2) the possession of passes or identification certificates, (3) the establishment of restricted areas, (4) limitations of movements, (5) the adoption of curfew regulations, (6) the prohibition of assembly, (7) the detention of suspected persons, (8) restrictions on communication, (9) the imposition of restrictions on food supplies, (10) the evacuation of troublesome areas, (11) the levying of monetary contributions, (12) compulsory labor to repair damage from sabotage, (13) the destruction of property in proximity to the place of the crime, and any other regulation not prohibited by international law that would in all likelihood contribute to the desired result."

This avowedly non-exhaustive enumeration has received a good deal of attention in the literature. Of course, it raises various questions, such as whether the order of the measures mentioned should be observed by an occupant, whether all the measures

A requirement more or less implied in the previous elements taken together, but separately mentioned by the Tribunal, consisted in the impossibility of apprehending the perpetrators of the acts retaliated against (be it by taking hostages, by their execution, or by the taking and execution of reprisal prisoners).[36]

Apart from these essential aspects of the issue, the Tribunal set out some further elements, both of a substantive and of a procedural character. A question of substantive law is evidently whether proportionality must be observed in the execution of hostages. On this point, the judgment is not free from ambiguity: while it states at one place that "[t]he number of hostages shot must not exceed in severity the offenses the shooting is designed to *deter*",[37] elsewhere and namely in the context of the treatment of reprisal prisoners the verdict was that "the shooting of innocent members of the population as a reprisal measure [may not] exceed in severity the unlawful act it is designed to *correct*".[38] Needless to say, the latter standard seems more in conformity with elementary considerations of justice. More concretely, it seems particularly hard to assess the severity of merely potential crimes (which it is even hoped to deter and so prevent their realization) with such arithmetical precision as to allow the definite jugdment that a specific number of hostages shot would "not exceed in severity" those merely hypothetical crimes. It seems therefore a justifiable assumption that the words "to deter" in the first-quoted sentence are a slip of the judicial pen.

Two further requirements, both of a procedural order, were set out by the Tribunal: (1) publication of proclamations notifying the fact that hostages or reprisal prisoners had been taken,[39] and (2) judicial proceedings

---

mentioned come under the heading of "regulations not prohibited by international law", and so on. However, such attention seems hardly profitable from the point of view of the doctrine of reprisals: the only materially important element of the Tribunal's words lies in the idea that "every available method to secure order and tranquility" which is not prohibited by international law must be applied "before resort may be had to the taking and execution of hostages", because the latter mode of acting is illegal *per se* and only justifiable if applied as a last resource. It should be observed, moreover, that not merely the execution, but already the taking of hostages was brought under this restriction.

[36] *Ibid.*, at pp. 1250 (taking of hostages), 1252 (execution of hostages or reprisal prisoners). *Cf.* also pp. 1256-1257, where it is underlined with some force that to take reprisals ". . . is not . . . an exclusive remedy. If it were, the persons responsible would seldom, if ever, be brought to account. The only punishment would fall upon the reprisal victims who are usually innocent of wrongdoing."

[37] *Ibid.*, at p. 1250; emphasis added.

[38] *Ibid.*, at p. 1252; emphasis added.

[39] Proclamation immediately upon the taking of hostages, giving their names and addresses and warning "that upon the recurrence of stated acts of war treason the hostages will be shot" (*ibid.*, at p. 1250); proclamation "that a certain number of reprisal prisoners will be shot if the perpetrators cannot be found" (p. 1252). In the

in order to determine whether the fundamental requirements for the shooting of hostages or reprisal prisoners were met.

As is evident from the judgment, the Tribunal did not conceive the judicial proceedings as anything but a guarantee against "arbitrary, vindictive, or whimsical application of the right to shoot human beings in reprisal" on the part of military commanders. Apparently, such arbitrariness could be expected (or, in any event, had to be feared) from these commanders, and, as "[i]t is a fundamental rule of justice that the lives of persons may not be arbitrarily taken", the Tribunal concluded that a rule of international law existed to the effect "that the lives of persons may not be taken in reprisal in the absence of a judicial finding that the necessary conditions exist and the essential steps have been taken to give validity to such action. . . . We have no hesitancy in holding that the killing of members of the population in reprisal without judicial sanction is itself unlawful."

It was indeed a far-reaching consequence which the Tribunal attached to its (negative) appreciation of the ability of military commanders to take unbiased decisions in matters of life and death and to its (perhaps over-optimistic) assessment of the powers of a judicial body in that respect. The Tribunal itself, it is true, conceded that the chances were "that such judicial proceedings may become ritualistic and superficial when conducted in wartime"; and, after thus having considerably reduced any value its dictum might have had, it added somewhat lamely that in any event the recourse to judicial proceedings "appears to be the best available safeguard against cruelty and injustice." [40]

It is submitted that what the Tribunal considered to be a rule of international law, in reality was its own invention: it is not believed that international law has yet considered the details of the procedure which a military commander ought to follow in order to arrive at a balanced

---

latter instance, the proclamation evidently is conceived as posterior to the act leading to the execution. Curiously, the Tribunal did not require that in the case of hostages having been taken a second proclamation would be issued after "stated acts of war treason" would have recurred and prior to shooting the hostages if the perpetrators could not be found. It is moreover remarkable that the Tribunal envisaged a warning that "the hostages"—and this suggests all of them—would be shot. One would more readily understand a warning that "hostages" would be shot, their number to be determined after the commission of—and in proportionality with—fresh "acts of war treason".

In the light of this criticism, the statement is all the more incomprehensible that "[t]he number of hostages shot must not exceed in severity the offenses the shooting is designed to deter": as in the system of the Tribunal this number would be identical with the number of hostages taken, a commander would be required to make a prognosis of the severity of a potential third wave of acts of resistance, in order to determine the number of hostages he is going to take into custody on account of the first (and for the time being the only actual) wave of such acts.

[40] *Ibid.*, pp. 1252-1253; *cf.* also pp. 1250-1251, where the same argument, though in a less extensive form, is put forward with respect to the killing of hostages.

decision in respect to a contemplated execution of hostages or reprisal prisoners. What remains, of course, is the rule at the root of the Tribunal's reasoning, that "the lives of persons may not be arbitrarily taken".

While the arguments rendered so far had a bearing on the general aspects of the taking and execution of hostages or reprisal prisoners, the Tribunal besides had to deal with the particular features of the German practices as demonstrated in south-eastern Europe in the course of the war. In this respect, the Tribunal did not hesitate one moment in its judicial appreciation. Even in the midst of the discussion of the general legal problems attending the execution of reprisal prisoners, the Tribunal unexpectedly let fly with the exclamation that "[t]he extent to which the practice has been employed by the Germans exceeds the most elementary notions of humanity and justice"; here, moreover, the Tribunal came nearest to acknowledging that the German régime of terror could have given the populations in the occupied territories a right of self-defence: "where legality of action is absent, the shooting of innocent members of the population as a measure of reprisal is not only criminal but it has the effect of destroying the basic relationship between the occupant and the population".[41]

When it finally broached the actual German practices, the Tribunal did not lose itself in theoretical speculation: it merely stated that "[t]he evidence in this case recites a record of killing and destruction seldom exceeded in modern history",[42] and it continued: "Mass shootings of the innocent population, deportations for slave labor, and the indiscriminate destruction of public and private property, not only in Yugoslavia and Greece but in many other countries as well, lend credit to the assertion that terrorism and intimidation was the accepted solution to any and all opposition to the German will."[43] These and similar observations were sufficient ground for the Tribunal to arrive at the conclusion that the acts set out in the indictment and proved in the subsequent proceedings were criminal in character, so that the only task left was the assessment of the personal guilt of each of the defendants.[44]

What is the character of the judgment related here and what value should be attached to it, and in particular to those of the Tribunal's considerations devoted to the general problems inherent in the taking and execution of hostages or reprisal prisoners? It should be pointed out in the first place, that the Tribunal obviously did not find it necessary to go to any great lengths to explain why it found the German practices so totally irreconcilable with the requirements for justifiable executions which it had previously

[41] *Ibid.*, at p. 1252.
[42] *Ibid.*, at p. 1254.
[43] *Ibid.*, at p. 1255.
[44] *Ibid.*, pp. 1257 ff.

set out in such detail. This apparent incongruity and lack of connection suggests the following interpretation. The Tribunal very much desired to give the defendants their due and to leave not even the slightest doubt as regards its willingness to treat the issues inherent in the acts charged with complete open-mindedness and objectivity. Accordingly, it went out of its way to sketch in minute detail its views concerning the requirements of international law for justifiable executions of hostages and reprisal prisoners, while all the time it was *luce clarius* that all this had little bearing, if any, on the practices with which the defendants were charged. It should be admitted that this makes the theoretical considerations appear more or less superfluous: the *dicta* of the Tribunal in this respect are really *obiter*. However, this does not detract from the appreciation one can feel for the attempt which the Tribunal made to give a motivated reply to the question of why it found the defendants guilty.[45]

6.1.3. *The Einsatzgruppen and High Command Cases*

United States Military Tribunals have in two further cases found occasion to revert to the issue of the justification of retaliatory executions. In the first of these, the judgment rendered on 8 April 1948 by Military Tribunal II-A in the Einsatzgruppen Case,[46] the point at issue was not so much the killing of hostages: the main charge against the defendants was that the *Einsatzgruppen* had taken an active part in the extermination programme of the Jews and other groups by liquidating hundreds of thousands of them in the sector of the eastern front. However, certain of these measures had been labelled reprisals either in the German documents recording the events or by defence counsel. This gave the Tribunal occasion to devote a separate section of its judgment to the subject of reprisals.[47]

The Tribunal pointed out that generally the victims of belligerent reprisals will be innocent of the acts retaliated against. However, it said, "there must at least be such close connection between these persons and these acts as to constitute a joint responsibility." In that connection the Tribunal quoted the text of Article 50 of the Hague Regulations, and, recalling an instance where "859 out of 2,100 Jews shot in alleged reprisal for the killing of 21 German soldiers near Topola were taken from con-

---

[45] Strangely, the Tribunal at no place referred to—let alone adopted—the views expressed by the prosecution concerning the true character of reprisals as actions between nations or their armed forces. Neither did the Tribunal find it necessary to mention Article 50 of the Hague Regulations (which deals with collective punishment) in connection with its own theory of collective responsibility. It is suggested that the Tribunal thus missed an opportunity to find a more satisfactory distinction than between "hostages" and "reprisal prisoners", namely, between genuine reprisals and quasi-reprisals or collective punishment.
[46] United States of America *v.* Otto Ohlendorf *et al.*; Trials, Vol. IV, p. 1, at p. 411.
[47] *Ibid.*, pp. 493-494.

centration camps in Yugoslavia, hundreds of miles away", it concluded that in that instance it was "obvious that a flagrant violation of international law occurred and outright murder resulted", evidently because joint responsibility was out of the question there. The Tribunal went on to point out that the gross disproportionality of 2100 killed for 21 deaths "only further magnifie[d] the criminality of this savage and so-called reprisal".

The line of reasoning given here differs from the arguments of the Tribunal in the Hostages Case in an interesting respect. For, while the latter judgment conspicuously avoided so much as a reference to the notion of collective punishment or to Article 50 of the Hague Regulations,[48] that provision was explicitly quoted in the *Einsatzgruppen* judgment. The effect of that quotation was in fact to suggest a complete identification of reprisals and collective punishment, even to the point where the Tribunal seemed to consider the requirement of collective responsibility, embodied in Article 50 for the case of collective punishment of an occupied population, a mere application of a general principle requiring joint responsibility on the part of the victims of any belligerent reprisal for the illegal act retaliated against. However, so sweeping a generalization seems hardly an accurate statement of the law.

Of course, the *Einsatzgruppen* judgment may be interpreted in a different manner, more in conformity with generally accepted views, by assuming that the unqualified reference to "reprisals" was in reality designed to refer to quasi-reprisals (or collective punishment) only. But it should be emphasized that the Tribunal did not itself make any effort to clarify its judgment in that respect.

On the contrary, the Tribunal went on to cause even greater confusion in a passage devoted to the relationship between the German occupation forces and the occupied populations. It had stated earlier that "the first prerequisite to the introduction of this most extraordinary remedy [*i.e.* of reprisals] is proof that the enemy has behaved illegally". It now added that in order to establish the illegality of given acts of resistance in Russia "it would still have to be shown that these acts were not in legitimate defense against wrongs perpetrated upon them by the invader. Under international law, as in domestic law, there can be no reprisal against reprisal. The assassin who is being repulsed by his intended victim may not slay him and then, in turn, plead self-defense."

While one might feel inclined to subscribe to the first part of this statement dealing with the possible character of self-defence of the resistance activities, this inclination rapidly disappears in the face of the next part of

---

[48] Instead, the Tribunal gave its own definition of collective responsibility of the population as a requirement for a recourse to retaliatory measures in occupied territory; *supra*, p. 225.

231

the sentence, where the comparison to the assassin being repulsed by his intended victim creates the impression that what the Tribunal really had in mind was the illegality of the aggression rather than of atrocities ("wrongs") committed against the population; this while illegality of the invasion would not in itself be sufficient ground to give the population, once occupied, a right of armed resistance.

On top of this, the argument bearing on the exclusion of counter-reprisals suggests that the resistance would not have been a matter of legitimate self-defence so much as of reprisals. Presumably, the aim of these "reprisals-in-resistance" would have been to coerce the German occupation authorities in future to abstain from the terrorization of the population, rather than to do damage to the military position of the occupation forces; an improbable construction, to say the least.

All in all, the quoted passage, and in fact the entire section of the *Einsatzgruppen* judgment devoted to reprisals, is perhaps the least satisfactory text about reprisals to be found in any legal document.[49]

A rather more favourable view can be taken with respect to the other judgment in this series expressly dealing with reprisals, viz., the judgment of 28 October 1948, rendered by Military Tribunal V-A in the High Command Case.[50] In this case, the policy of terror murders in occupied territories, examined already in the Hostages Case, was again at issue as the defendants, all members of the German High Command, were charged *inter alia* with having taken part in the formulation of that policy and of the directives elaborating it. Not surprisingly, therefore, the Tribunal

---

[49] In a note on the case in the *Law Reports of Trials of War Criminals*, Vol. VIII, at p. 88, the annotator attempts to reconcile the Hostages and Einsatzgruppen judgments as far as the reference to the norm embodied in Art. 50 was concerned. He saw a possibility to achieve such a reconciliation "if the statement of the former, that the population against whom action is taken must be a party to the offences whose cessation is aimed at, is interpreted strictly, so as to ensure observance of Article 50 of the Hague Regulations". Tribunal V, he felt, had not itself given any conclusive indication "of the degree of connection between the victims of the killings and the original or the feared offences which the Tribunal would have regarded as sufficient to make these victims 'parties' to those offences". Evidently the annotator overlooked the passages in the Hostages judgment where the element of collective responsibility was elaborated as a prerequisite for considering the population "a party to the offense, either actively or passively" (*supra*, p. 225). On the other hand, his own interpretation of "joint responsibility" seems beside the point of Art. 50: in considering that "if persons are jointly responsible for an offence, action may be taken against them irrespective of any laws of reprisals" he obviously substituted a penal concept of complicity for the notion of collective "responsibility" for acts (or feared acts) for which the population carries no responsibility in any normal sense of the term.

[50] United States of America *v.* Wilhelm von Leeb *et al.*; Trials, Vols. X-XI; the judgment is in Vol. XI.

opened the section of its judgment dealing with "hostages and reprisals" [51] with a reference to the judgment in the Hostages Case.[52] It reduced the views developed there to the statement "that under certain very restrictive conditions and subject to certain rather extensive safeguards, hostages may be taken, and after a judicial finding of strict compliance with all pre-conditions and as a last desperate remedy hostages may even be sentenced to death. It was held further that similar drastic safeguards, restrictions, and judicial preconditions apply to so-called 'reprisal prisoners'."

Reference to these holdings of Military Tribunal V was not however tantamount to their integral adoption; indeed, the attitude of Military Tribunal V-A in respect to the views of its predecessor can perhaps best be described as polite scepticism. This is apparent already in the manner in which it juxtaposed the supposition that "so inhumane a measure as the killing of innocent persons for offenses of others, even when drastically safeguarded and limited, [would be] ever permissible under any theory of international law", to the possibility that "killing [would be] not permissible under any circumstances": evidently the sympathies of the Tribunal were not on the side of the former hypothesis.

On the other hand, the Tribunal did not go so far as to openly reject the views expressed in the Hostages judgment: the judges merely put on record that "[i]n the case here presented, we find it unnecessary to approve or disapprove the conclusions of law announced in said judgment as to the permissibility of such killings." For, the Tribunal observed, the killings in the present case were "merely terror murders" under any view of the law, either (in the supposition that international law would exceptionally permit such actions) because they did not even purport to meet "the safeguards and preconditions required to be observed" by the judgment in the Hostages Case, or, in the opposite supposition, by virtue of the very rule prohibiting such killings.

When it is kept in mind that the killings at issue in the High Command Case were by and large the identical instances as those dealt with in the Hostages Case, it is evident that Military Tribunal V-A by stating that "in the case here presented" legal exertions such as had been demonstrated in the Hostages Case were not necessary, very clearly implied that Military Tribunal V giving judgment in the Hostages Case could equally have done without such exertions, or, in more reverent language, that these were *obiter dicta*.

6.1.4. *The Ardeatine Cave Cases*

An event which took place in March 1944 in Rome and which has since

[51] *Ibid.*, Vol. XI, pp. 528-529.
[52] Characteristically, the judgment in the Einsatzgruppen Case, though likewise posterior to the Hostages Case, does not so much as refer to the judgment in that case.

become known as the Ardeatine Cave massacre, has been the subject of three reported judicial proceedings: two before British military Courts in Italy,[53] and one before an Italian military Tribunal.[54] The facts of the case, which were amply described in the reports, can be summarized as follows.[55]

On 23 March 1944, a bomb exploded in the *Via Rasella* in Rome, amidst a marching column of German police; thirty-two German policemen were killed by the explosion and a great number wounded. Hitler, immediately informed of the attack, gave the order to shoot within 24 hours ten Italians for every German policeman killed. This order was communicated to Field Marshal Kesselring, Commander of Army Group "C" in Italy, who passed it on to General Von Mackensen, Commander of the 14th Army in whose sector of operations Rome was situated. The latter telephoned General Maelzer, Military Commander of Rome, to inform him of the order and to find out whether there were enough persons awaiting execution to make up the required number. General Maelzer again passed this question on to Lieutenant-Colonel Kappler, head of the S.D. (*Sicherheitsdienst*, or Security Service) in Rome, who was in charge of the prisons. While it was not established with certainty in the judicial proceedings how Kappler had in fact answered that question, the order was in any event carried into effect on 24 March 1944 and a section of the S.D. under Kappler liquidated 335 prisoners by a shot in the back. The massacre took place in the *Cave ardeatine*, which were blown up after the event.

The issue in this case could be subdivided as follows: of the 335 prisoners executed, 330 were alleged to have been killed in reprisal, namely 320 as ordered for the 32 victims of the attack in the *Via Rasella*, and 10 for another German killed since then; the latter, although not strictly covered by the 10 : 1 order, were alleged to have come under its terms nevertheless. This left five: their execution was an avowed mistake—or, in other terms, plain murder. Thus, the case did not present any particular difficulties as far as the qualification of those five deaths was concerned, and it merely remained to establish the measure of responsibility of each of the accused for that part of the event.[56]

---

[53] Trial of Generals Von Mackensen and Maelzer, British Military Court, Rome, 18-30 November 1945; *Law Reports of Trials of War Criminals*, Vol. VIII, p. 1: Case No. 43.

Trial of Field Marshal Kesselring, British Military Court, Venice, 17 February-6 May 1947; *ibid.*, p. 9: Case No. 44.

[54] Trial of Kappler, Military Tribunal (*Tribunale militare territoriale*) of Rome, 20 July 1948; *Annual Digest*, 1948, p. 471, referring to *Foro Italiano*, 72 (1949) II, p. 160; also in *Annali di Diritto Internazionale*, Vol. VII, 1949, p. 211.

[55] See in particular *Law Reports*, Vol. VIII, pp. 1, 2.

[56] In the proceedings against Kesselring, "[t]he Judge Advocate said in his summing up: 'whatever you may think about International Law and reprisals, clearly five of these 335 Italians were murdered. That was a war crime and you cannot get away

However, it would have been hardly satisfactory to convict the accused merely for that fivefold murder, without so much as attempting to ascertain the legal character of the killing of the other 330 Italians, which by any normal standard constituted the main issue of the case and which does not at first sight impress the observer as an example of a completely regular execution. Accordingly, it is the mass execution and its alleged character as a reprisal which was the main theme in the proceedings before all three Courts called upon to adjudge the affair.

In order to determine whether the execution had indeed constituted a reprisal, it was first of all necessary to establish who had been the perpetrators of the bomb attack in the *Via Rasella*. The reports of the British cases merely record that it had been carried out by "unknown partisans"—that is, by unknown individuals who, moreover, presumably did not possess the capacity of legitimate combatants. Actually, this description of the perpetrators as "unknown partisans" was precisely the assumption at the root of the German retaliatory action. At the time, the German authorities had not waited for the definitive result of the police investigations, opened after the attack in order to discover the responsible persons; even while those investigations were in progress, they had given effect to the Hitler order and caused the executions to be carried out.

The Italian military Tribunal, for its part, went into somewhat greater detail in describing the position of the actual perpetrators in relation to the resistance movement in Italy. The Tribunal related that the attack had been performed by a clandestine, militarily organized volunteer corps, acting in close co-operation with, and under the general directives of, the Military Directorate (*Giunta militare*). It had been among the functions of the *Giunta militare* to give a uniform direction to the activities of the various resistance organizations. Yet, these had not been in a strict sense subordinate to the Directorate: each decided its own activities, merely taking into account the directives issued by the *Giunta militare* through the intermediary of their own leaders. The Tribunal concluded that, although by March 1944 the partisan movement had assumed large proportions and even had acquired a certain moderate organization, it had not acquired all the characteristics required for the status as a legitimate combatant force. Accordingly, the attack in the *Via Rasella* had constituted an unlawful act of warfare.

This being so, the next thing for the Tribunal was to determine the relation, if any, of the perpetrators of the attack to the Italian State; an aspect of the case, incidentally, which the British Courts did not deal with at all. The Italian Tribunal considered that the attackers had formed part

---

from it. There was no Führer order to cover it and it was quite outside the reprisal.' "
(*Ibid.*, at p. 13).

235

of a military organization operating in occupied territory for the cause of the national liberation, in the interests of the legitimate Italian Government. That Government had, as evidenced by numerous manifestations, granted the organization implicit recognition. Moreover, the Italian State had after the war treated as regular combatants those partisans who had actively fought the Germans. From these indications the Tribunal deduced that the resistance organization had figured, at least *de facto*, as an organ of the Italian State.

Did the massacre in the *Cave ardeatine* constitute a true reprisal? One might first remark that the British military Courts did not render a reasoned judgment (nor were they so obliged under their rules of procedure). The only fact known with certainty about their appreciation of the legal side of the affair is therefore that they evidently rejected the thesis of the defence that the mass execution was justified as a reprisal. For the rest it is a matter of pure conjecture which of the various conceivable grounds for that rejection has motivated their stand in the matter.[57] On the other hand, the reports of the British cases put on record certain elements of the positions taken by the prosecution and the defence, as well as by the Judge-Advocate in the Kesselring trial.

The prosecution in both cases appears to have defended the view that the character of the attack in the *Via Rasella* was such as to justify a recourse to reprisals in principle, but that the taking of human lives was not justified as it was not a reasonable reprisal in the given instance; moreover, the 10 : 1 ratio was condemned as disproportionate.[58] The defence, for its part, took the obvious position that the execution was both reasonable and proportionate in view of the circumstances prevailing at the time (great activity of partisans endangering the German position, nearness of the front).[59]

The Judge-Advocate summing up the case in the trial of Field Marshal Kesselring entered into the question of whether the taking of human life in

[57] The annotator in the *Law Reports*, commenting on the trial of Von Mackensen and Maelzer, observes (p. 7): "It cannot be said with certainty whether the Court found that the reprisals were unreasonable (i.e. the taking of lives was not warranted) or that they were excessive (i.e. the ratio 10-1 was not warranted) or that the accused were responsible for the manner in which they were carried out. Any of these three contentions would support the findings."

[58] *Law Reports*, Vol. VIII, pp. 5, 12. The position of the prosecution was "that the German authorities would have been entitled to blow up the houses" in the *Via Rasella*. This brings to mind the enumeration in the Hostages judgment of measures that ought to precede the taking of hostages; under (13), the tribunal mentioned "the destruction of property in proximity to the place of the crime" (see n. 35). Evidently, the British prosecutors would not have subscribed to the view that such measures of destruction belonged in the category of actions "not prohibited by international law" (*ibid.*): otherwise they needed not have characterized these as reprisals.

[59] *Ibid.*, pp. 2, 5-6, 12.

reprisal was ever permissible. International law, he said, bears on the relations of one belligerent State to another. But "what Field Marshal Kesselring had to deal with were not countries which were organised with governments but irresponsible people in the main whom he could not negotiate with, people in respect of whom he could not say to responsible leaders 'You must control your followers.' Therefore I do suggest that if there ever were circumstances in which one would have to resort to reprisals if one failed after proper application to find the real culprit that that is the sort of thing in which a reprisal must have been considered appropriate." And he went on to state that he had arrived at the conclusion "that there is nothing which makes it absolutely clear that in no circumstances and especially in the circumstances which I think are agreed in this case that an innocent person properly taken for the purpose of a reprisal cannot be executed." This doubt as to the law led him to give as his opinion that a deliberate order to shoot one innocent person by way of reprisal would not have been sufficient ground for a conviction of Kesselring for a war crime.[60]

In comment, it may be observed that the statement confirms the view that what Kesselring had had to cope with was not a Government but the incoherent collectivity of "the people". The interesting feature is, however, that precisely that erroneous view of the facts led the Judge-Advocate to consider that here was a situation pre-eminently suited to a recourse to reprisals. This can only be satisfactorily explained, it is submitted, by assuming that what he wanted to convey was the urgency, from a military point of view, of measures of retaliation against the collectivity of an otherwise elusive population the activities of which constituted a real danger for the occupying Power. In other words, his opinion was not a presentation of any theory of reprisals proper: it was a pure reflection of the idea of quasi-reprisals, or collective punishment, based on military necessity. And it should be noted that not only did he evidently appreciate that the taking of human life by way of (quasi-)reprisal could be strongly indicated in such a situation: he even did not feel entitled to say that such taking could not be justified in any circumstances.

The Italian Tribunal examined the thesis of the defence that the shooting in the *Cave ardeatine* had constituted a legitimate reprisal, on the basis of its earlier finding that a relationship had existed between the attackers in the *Via Rasella*, as members of the partisan movement, and the Italian State the organ of which—the Military Directorate—had co-ordinated the partisan activities with the aid of general directives. The Tribunal first gave an exposé of the theory of reprisals, viewed as acts between States, resorted to on account of an act for which the opposite State bears responsibility.

[60] *Ibid.*, pp. 12, 13.

Next, it examined in particular the problem of "whether the occupying State may have recourse to reprisals within the territory subject to military occupation, following an illegal act suffered by it at the hands of the State which has lost the territory or of the civil population which has remained there." [61] The answer to this question, the Tribunal considered, must be found with the aid of the general rules regarding State responsibility.

Such responsibility would be attracted, *inter alia*, by a State violating its obligations recognized under general customary law of prevention or repression in respect of acts of individuals. The Tribunal pointed out that "the duty of prevention and punishment which attracts international responsibility for individual acts is only imposed upon the holder of the sovereign power in a specific territory if he is the sole holder of the powers of government within the territory". In the case of occupation, however, those powers passed, at least *de facto*, to the occupying State, so that the occupied State could not be held responsible for the injurious acts of individuals committed within the occupied territory. Consequently, reprisals would be permissible in occupied territory only "if the violation of international law which took place in territory subject to military occupation is due directly to the intention of the State which has lost the territory." In those circumstances the criterion of insufficient prevention or repression did not apply, as the violation of international law could be directly attributed to the policy of the State itself. [62]

Applying these considerations to the case at issue, the Tribunal concluded from the relationship outlined previously between the partisan movement and the Italian State, that "as a result of the illegal act committed in the *Via Rasella*, the occupying State was entitled to apply reprisals", that is, against the Italian State. [63]

The next question was obvious: had the massacre of 335 persons in the *Cave ardeatine* really constituted a reprisal? The Tribunal did not hesitate to answer this question in the negative. No matter what the character assigned to reprisals in legal theory (and the Tribunal mentioned in this respect the concepts of reprisals as self-help, as sanctions, and as acts of legitimate self-defence), proportionality between the injury suffered and the injury caused in retaliation was a fundamental requirement under any point of view. And the executions in the Ardeatine Caves were grossly disproportionate to the attack in the *Via Rasella*, both from the point of view of the number of victims and of the ensuing injury. This was true even if the Tribunal were to follow the argument of the defence that the injury arising from the attack in the *Via Rasella* must be assessed from the angle of the damage inflicted in the framework of military operations—a framework in which the soldier was alleged to react more sharply than the

[61] *Annual Digest*, 1948, at p. 474.
[62] *Ibid.*, p. 475.
[63] *Loc. cit.* n. 62.

civilian. For, when assessed from that point of view, a disproportionality even more obvious than was implied in the sheer ratio of the numbers, would result from the consideration that among those shot in the *Cave ardeatine* were five generals, eleven senior officers (and among them a colonel who was the head of an important clandestine military organization), twenty-one subalterns and six non-commissioned officers, all of whose ranks and positions were known to the Germans.[64]

In view of this obvious disproportionality between injury suffered and injury caused, the Tribunal concluded that the shooting did not find justification as a reprisal.

Having arrived at this conclusion (which, in view of the facts as exposed by the Tribunal, really had the effect of deciding the case), the Tribunal went on to examine the subsidiary argument of the defence that, if the executions in the *Cave ardeatine* could not be regarded as legitimate reprisals, they were in any event justifiable measures of collective punishment. The Tribunal did this without being obliged to do so: it had found that the shooting came under the definition of a reprisal against the State, and this finding excluded it being at the same time regarded as a measure of collective punishment against the population. However, the Tribunal declared itself willing to take into account that in the period following immediately after the attack the German authorities had had only insufficient information at their disposal about the attackers and their relation to the Italian State. Neither did the Tribunal regard the circumstance that the defence had throughout the proceedings consistently referred to the shooting as a reprisal, as a bar to an examination of the argument of collective punishment; for, the Tribunal observed, "it is well known that in practice the usage has become established to treat measures of collective punishment as reprisals, notwithstanding a clear distinction between the two institutions".[65]

Collective punishment, the Tribunal observed, was dealt with in Article 50 of the Hague Regulations. The expression "collective responsibility", used in that Article, gave the concept a broad scope as it had the effect of introducing a concept of complicity which bore no relation to the principle

---

[64] *Ibid.*, p. 476. The enumeration of particular categories of victims in the Italian judgment differs markedly from the information procured in the report of the trial of Von Mackensen and Maelzer, that "[t]he victims included a boy of fourteen, a man of seventy, one person who had been acquitted by a Court, and fifty-seven Jews who had nothing to do with any partisan activities and some of whom were not even Italians" (*Law Reports*, Vol. VIII, p. 2). This difference shows clearly the different purposes behind the enumerations: while the list in the Italian judgment was intended to demonstrate that the victims of the executions carried more weight even from a military point of view than their numbers indicated, the list in the British account served to underline the inhumane character of the measure.

[65] *Annual Digest*, 1948, p. 477.

of that name in penal law: "In fact, this form of responsibility applies where it is impossible to determine complicity in the meaning of criminal law, inasmuch as the authors of the illegal act could not be detected. It is an exceptional rule which operates in occupied territory when the normal proceedings have not led to positive results. In substance collective responsibility may arise when it has appeared impossible to establish who was or who were the culprits. This can be seen clearly if it is kept in mind that the power envisaged in Article 50 is exceptional as compared with the normal powers granted by Articles 43 ff." [66]

While this did not give a very clear idea of what the Tribunal understood by collective responsibility, other than that this was something fundamentally different from the penal law notion of complicity, its views found further clarification when it went on to set out certain further principles governing the recourse to collective punishment. The Tribunal mentioned in particular that Article 50 could only operate after the occupying Power would have published the criteria that it would apply for determining collective responsibility, and that it did not appear permissible that measures of collective punishment would affect the human person. But even irrespective of this, it had emerged clearly that the occupying State had in the case under review not observed any of the principles governing collective punishment. The retaliatory action had not been preceded by any serious attempt to discover the authors of the attack: the search which had in fact been organized had merely been a secondary action started only when the preparations for the shooting were already in progress. Thus, an essential condition for the recourse to collective punishment had not been met.

Moreover, the Tribunal argued, the majority of the victims of the execution could not be regarded as collectively responsible for the attack. For, while admittedly collective responsibility was a concept much broader than complicity in penal law, it could only arise if there could be established a strict connection, either in respect of location, service, or office, between the authors of the attack and the civil population. Collective solidarity, the Tribunal pointed out, could not be presumed: it must be established in every case by some kind of proceedings, no matter how summary. No such proceedings had taken place; nor, for that matter, had the occupying Power issued a decree stating the criteria that would be applied for determining collective responsibility.

Thus, the Tribunal considered it established that both the plea of reprisals and that of collective punishment were manifestly ill-founded. It followed that the shooting in the *Cave ardeatine* must be qualified as murder.[67]

---

[66] *Ibid.*, p. 478.

[67] *Ibid.*, pp. 478-480. The tribunal subsequently examined an aspect of the case relating to Italian military law, which may be omitted here.

A first comment on the cases of the *Cave ardeatine* bears on the factual side of the affair. As pointed out above, the reports of the British cases give a version of the facts markedly different from the one contained in the judgment of the Italian Tribunal, the *Tribunale militare territoriale di Roma*. In this controversy, I am inclined to accept as true the version given by the Italian Tribunal. For obvious reasonse that court was in a far better position than its British counterparts to ascertain a factual situation such as the status of the resistance movement in Italian territory and the relations of its various component parts to the Italian State.

The acceptance of one or the other version of the facts entails certain consequences for the juridical evaluation of the affair, and in particular for the appreciation of the thesis that the mass executions in the *Cave ardeatine* had constituted a reprisal,—that is, unless one would make no distinction between collective punishment and reprisals and the latter notion were thus made to embrace measures against the unorganized collectivity of an occupied population.

The British military Courts seem to have used the term in this wide and indiscriminate sense. At any rate, there are no indications in the reports that any of the participants in the proceedings made a conscious attempt to differentiate between the two notions. Indeed, the Judge-Advocate in the Kesselring trial, far from concluding that the retaliatory execution, as a measure aimed against the non-responsible people, must be characterized as collective punishment, went so far as to emphasize that this was precisely the type of situation where a recourse to reprisals could be most strongly indicated and most urgently needed. In so doing, he merely continued the usage pointed out by the Italian Tribunal, "to treat measures of collective punishment as reprisals, notwithstanding a clear distinction between the two institutions".

It remained for the Italian Tribunal to point out this clear distinction between reprisals and collective punishment. In the construction of the Tribunal, these concepts are not merely distinct: they even seem mutually exclusive. To retaliate, as it were blindly, against the population (on the basis of an essentially fictitious collective "responsibility") is tantamount to admitting that it has proved impossible properly to localize responsibility for the act retaliated against, while retaliation against the State implies that in any event the State is held responsible for (its part in) the act. On the other hand, it is possible to regard a certain retaliatory measure as aimed against "the population" and at the same time, conditionally, against the State, for the event that its responsibility for the act retaliated against be established.

The Tribunal in its judgment not merely established that in the circumstances of the case a recourse to reprisals would have been open to the German authorities: it explicitly characterized the action actually taken as a reprisal. This seems to imply that the Tribunal construed the German action as being at least conditionally aimed against the Italian State, subject to it being found responsible for the attack in the *Via Rasella*. It is, however, a definite lacuna in the judgment that the Tribunal did not offer a word in explanation of its construction.

Another important feature of the case concerns the norms on which the Italian Tribunal in particular based its judgment that the execution in the *Cave ardeatine* could be justified neither as a reprisal nor as a measure of collective punishment. As regards the reprisal thesis, it sufficed for the Tribunal to consider that the execution was obviously disproportionate and, hence, in open conflict with the standard of proportionality. It should be pointed out, however, that the Tribunal did not so much as refer to another norm which, if applicable, logically would have deserved priority: viz., the humanitarian norm prohibiting the killing of innocent persons for the deeds of others. The silence of the Tribunal on this score suggests that it did not hold that norm applicable in case of genuine reprisals against the State.

As regards collective punishment, the judgment is somewhat vague. The Tribunal noted in passing that there seemed to exist a norm to the effect that measures of collective punishment ought to respect human life. It immediately added, however, that the judgment need not be based on that presumed norm, as the German retaliatory action had violated other fundamental requirements for justifiable recourse to collective punishment, among which were the requirements of subsidiarity and of collective responsibility.

Admittedly, the judgment in its parts dealing with collective punishment bears largely the character of *obiter dictum*. It is therefore not permissible to attach too much consequence to the arguments advanced there. Yet, the point should be emphasized that the Tribunal evidently hesitated to subscribe to the validity of a rule protecting human life against the impact of collective punishment. On this score, the Tribunal did not differ much from the Judge-Advocate in the trial against Kesselring, who, too, did not feel entitled to say that in a situation like the one under consideration the retaliatory taking of human life could in no circumstances be justified.

6.1.5. *The Rauter Case*

A case of paramount importance both for the theory of reprisals and from the point of view of Netherlands interest, is the trial against Rauter, conducted in two instances in 1948 and 1949 before the Special Court in the Hague and the Special Court of Cassation, bodies of the special judicature set up in the Netherlands after the war to adjudicate on the criminal cases arising out of the war.[68]

---

[68] Special Court in The Hague, judgment of 4 May 1948; Special Court of Cassation,

During the occupation of the Netherlands, Rauter had served as Higher S.S. and Police Leader and General Commissioner for Public Safety, functions which had made him only second to Seyss-Inquart who was the Reich Commissioner for the Netherlands. He was held accountable for many aspects of the occupation régime brought into practice in this country, either because these could be directly traced to decisions taken or transmitted by Rauter, or on account of actions of subordinates for which he was held responsible.

Among the crimes (or, rather, the criminal policies) charged against Rauter, Count VII of the indictment referred in particular to measures of retaliation. It was contended that, in retaliation for acts aimed or presumably aimed against the occupying Power, the defendant had systematically applied the following policies: (a) the infliction of collective fines, (b) the removal of furniture from private dwellings, (c) the arrest and detention or abduction of innocent civilians, resulting in the death of many of them, and (d) retaliatory murders. It was further contended that the policy followed by Rauter, as set forth *inter alia* in Count VII, amounted to systematic terrorization of the Dutch people. Therefore, the issue of reprisals and collective punishment in occupied territory could not fail to come up for discussion in this case.

In the trial at first instance, before the Hague Special Court, two issues in particular were raised by the several participants in the proceedings: the question of whether prior illegal modes of acting on the part of the Netherlands Government had given the German occupation authorities the right to retaliate against the population, and the concept of collective responsibility and its implications for a recourse to reprisals.

Throughout the proceedings, Rauter tenaciously defended the thesis that it was the Netherlands Government which had introduced an illegal method of warfare and which had thus given the Germans the right to counter-act; in his submission, the illegal mode of warfare had consisted in the activities of the resistance movement, in contravention of the obligations of the occupied population to behave peacefully, and in the fact that these activities had been incited and, once underway, stimulated and actively supported by the Government, among other things by large-scale weapons droppings. Thus, in his final statement he contended that "this internationally illegal method of warfare" had been the sole cause of the

---

judgment of 12 January 1949. For a report of the case, see: *Annual Digest*, 1949, Case No. 193. See also *Law Reports of Trials of War Criminals*, Vol. XIV, Case No. 88. A full and even nearly completely verbatim record of the proceedings in both instances has been published in Dutch under the title "*Het proces Rauter*" (The Rauter Trial) by the Netherlands State Institute for War Documentation, 1952. The judgment of the Special Court of Cassation has also been published in *Nederlandse Jurisprudentie* (collection of Netherlands judicial decisions) 1949, No. 87.

disturbances of the peace which had come about in occupied Holland, and of the needless bloodshed which had ensued. This had forced the German occupation forces, and especially the police against whom the main thrust of the resistance activities had been aimed, to resort to those means which no occupation Power lightly decides to apply: viz., to "repressive measures" (*Repressivmassnahmen*). It was a complete reversal of the facts to charge those events against the German occupation authorities, who had had to defend their legal and legitimate position in accordance with international law.[69]

It is not clear whether Rauter regarded *Repressivmassnahmen* as something entirely synonymous to reprisals. On the one hand, he repeatedly stated that it was the illegal policy of the Netherlands Government which had necessitated retaliatory action. On the other hand, he did not once contend that the *Repressivmassnahmen* had the purpose of bringing about a change in the incriminated policy of that Government. Indeed, his argument is suggestive of the view that the measures taken, rather than having as their aim the enforcement of the law of war, were simply necessary from a military point of view for the defence of the German position in the irregular warfare initiated by the adversary.

Rauter was strongly supported on this point by his counsel, who in his address for the defence laid much stress on the need to assess the German actions in the context of "total war" and in particular of the systematic endeavours on the part of the Netherlands Government to create anarchy in the occupied territory, endeavours which had preceded by some ten months Rauter's so-called terror policy. Counsel concluded that the occupying Power had done everything within its power to prevent chaos, and, when underground anarchy had nevertheless been brought about, to deter the population from taking an active part in that form of irregular warfare.[70] It ought to be pointed out that counsel's reasoning does not, any more than Rauter's statement, contain any indication that the deterrent actions would have constituted real reprisals in any sense, let alone that these would have been directed against the Netherlands Government.

While the prosecutor in his closing statement did not deal with this

---

[69] *Het proces Rauter*, pp. 276-277. Actually the argument developed by Rauter was more complicated: it was based also and even primarily on the contention that the 1940 capitulation instruments, brought about with the co-operation of the Dutch supreme commander after the Queen and the Cabinet had departed for England, had laid an international obligation on the Netherlands Government to refrain from any activities which might lead to a disturbance of peace and order in occupied Holland; cf. *Annual Digest*, 1949, at p. 530. I feel justified in leaving this issue aside: it raises various specific questions which are of little interest here, and on the other hand it does not materially affect the outcome; for the German occupation authorities were both obliged and entitled to maintain law and order anyhow, with or without express affirmation in an instrument of capitulation.

[70] *Het proces Rauter*, p. 265.

aspect of the case, the Hague Special Court in its judgment gave ample attention to it.[71] The Court conceded that the occupant could have considered the resistance unlawful from his national point of view, because the resistance fighters had not met the conditions laid down in the Hague Regulations for legitimate combatancy; from this point of view, Rauter had been entitled to counter-act. On the other hand, the Court observed, the occupant has only *de facto* authority, and the occupied population is neither ethically nor juridically obliged to obey him; consequently, resistance can be a lawful mode of warfare. The Court saw no contradiction between these two statements: it pointed to the comparable case of espionage which similarly is considered a lawful method of warfare, while at the same time the belligerent who catches a spy is entitled to punish him, even with death.

Then, the Court held that no rules of international law had precluded the Netherlands Government from inciting resistance or from dropping weapons above occupied territory. On this ground Rauter's plea that the attitude of that Government had given him the right to disregard the Hague Regulations was rejected. Moreover, the Court said, resistance had sprung up and gradually spread in the Netherlands as a natural and necessary and, hence, justified reaction to a series of measures on the part of the German occupation authorities which were in flagrant contravention of international law: the actions with regard to the House of Orange, deeply injurious to the Dutch people in their feelings of attachment towards their lawful sovereign; the treatment of the Jews; the deportation of Dutch workers; the ruthless oppression of the population; and, last but not least, the attempted nazification and germanization of this country. As the Court had established in an earlier part of its judgment, these features of the German occupation régime had become manifest a long time before any active resistance had developed.

As to the second main theme mentioned above, to wit, the issue of collective responsibility and its relation to reprisals, the public prosecutor in his closing statement [72] took the position that collective responsibility is at the root of any recourse to belligerent reprisals (including, evidently, quasi-reprisals or collective punishment). He submitted that an occupant may retaliate when confronted with disturbances of peace and order on the part of the occupied population, not only against the perpetrators, but, if the disturbances can be attributed to the collective attitude of the population, against the "responsible circle". Regrettably, neither the notion of a collective attitude nor that of a responsible circle found further elaboration in this statement of the public prosecutor.

In order to determine whether this collective responsibility was present

[71] *Ibid.*, pp. 371-372.
[72] *Ibid.*, pp. 236, 239.

245

in a particular case—he went on—it would be necessary for the occupant to investigate the actual circumstances of the case. Moreover, as reprisals may only be resorted to as a subsidiary means and indeed as an ultimate remedy, a further condition would be that other means should have been attempted first and should have failed to bring about the desired effect. As the German practice of retaliation had disregarded both these requirements and on the contrary had amounted to systematic interference with life and property of the inhabitants, as the standard method of maintaining order, that practice was unjustifiable in its totality. It was this aspect of the case which he had wanted to bring out by including in the charge that Rauter had "systematically" applied the incriminated policies.

Rauter, in his final statement, as in the numerous speeches with which he interlarded his examination, went to great lengths, first, to deny responsibility for particular instances of retaliatory actions, and in the second place to explain that in his eyes collective or group responsibility had indeed existed in many instances.[73] However, his explanations do not serve to shed any further light on the issue of what should be understood by collective responsibility.

---

[73] Thus, when discussing a case of hostage shootings, Rauter simply stated that collective responsibility of the population had without any doubt been a reality in the Dutch region (*ibid.*, p. 277).

It may be appropriate in this context to quote *in originali* part of a statement delivered by Rauter when interrogated about the detention of innocent civilians: not because it is so especially clear, but because it is a good example of Rauter's rambling style of argumentation (*ibid.*, p. 139): "Ich erinnere mich eines Falles, ... wo Fallschirmjäger, die in Europa wirklich heldenhaft gekämpft haben, hier verwundet worden sind im Kampf gegen die Engländer; die Männer wurden im Transportwagen, im Verwundetenwagen zurückgebracht, wurden unterwegs von knokploegen überfallen, wurden zusammengeschossen und dann hat man die Überlebenden noch mit Stricken erwürgt und dann die ganze Sache in die Luft geblasen. Sehen Sie, meine Herren, wenn solche Sachen vorkommen, die wirklich gegen jedes Völkerrecht sind, dürfen Sie sich nicht wundern, wenn in der Wehrmacht, naturgemäss unter solchen Ereignissen unterstützt mich jeder Offizier, eine besondere Erregung herrscht und dass dann zu Massnahmen gegriffen sind, die man eben normalerweise nicht versteht, wenn ich sie nicht im Zusammenhang mit der ganzen Sache schildere. Und diese Dinge, die damals sich abgespielt haben, wo ein Heer von Untertauchern in Holland bestand, wo wirklich ... von London aus der Befehl kam mit Funkspruch, vierzehn führende NSBer abzuschiessen und dafür ... lautlos schiessende Pistolen herüber geschickt worden sind, der Funkspruch wurde im Rahmen des Englandspiels auch gegeben, und wir haben andere Verbindungen mit England auch noch gehabt, wenn die drüben sich so illegal und gegen jedes Völkerrecht benehmen, meine Herren, wenn es da der deutschen Polizei mit legalen Mitteln nicht mehr möglich ist, die Leute hier zu verhaften und gerichtlich zu erforschen, ... dann ist doch der Zustand gegeben, wo internationalrechtlich festgestellt wird, es liegt eine absolute Ablehnung der Bevölkerung vor, es herrscht eine absolute Hilfe der Bevölkerung und der Behörden und Polizeieinrichtungen zu Gunsten dieser Sabotagegruppen, damit ist der Fall gegeben, wo auf Geisel und derartige Massnahmen wie Verhaftungen von Familienangehörigen zurückgegriffen werden kann."

The Special Court discussed the question of collective responsibility in connection with a German regulation which had governed the imposition of collective fines in the occupied Netherlands territory. The Court held that the regulation, as well as the German practice in the matter, were at variance with Article 50 of the Hague Regulations, which lays down in substance that no collective punishment may be inflicted upon the population for individual acts for which it cannot be held collectively responsible. For, the Court said, the imposition of a collective fine for a specific act of resistance could only be justified if it had been previously established with the aid of appropriate investigations that the requirement of collective responsibility was fulfilled in that particular case; and Rauter's complete silence on that point was sufficient ground for the Court to assume that no such investigations had preceded the individual decisions to impose collective fines, nor had these been required by the aforementioned regulation. Moreover, it was generally known that acts like the cutting of telephone cables, which had repeatedly provoked the imposition of a collective fine, usually were the doing of individual persons acting on their own and without much sense of responsibility, and that the population as a whole did not favour such practices. The Court concluded that the imposition of collective fines, on the basis of the regulation referred to, had been illegal,—unless (it added) the measures could find justification as reprisals.[74] The Court mentioned in this connection that Rauter had asserted that several of the acts charged against him had constituted reprisals in accordance with the law of war. This gave the Court occasion to develop its views about the general theory of reprisals.

It is generally accepted, the Court said, that a belligerent is entitled to take reprisals in retaliation for unlawful acts of warfare of the opponent; on the other hand, it is open to doubt whether collective fines may be imposed or innocent civilians killed by way of reprisals. In this predicament, the Court was inclined to adopt the view most favourable to the defendant. This it found in the judgment rendered by United States Military Tribunal V in the Hostages Case, where the killing of innocent civilians was considered, as an exception, justifiable. However, that Tribunal had not confined itself to simply stating this principle: it had also laid down a series of requirements which had to be fulfilled in each concrete instance before the killing of hostages could be held justified.

In the opinion of the Court, the views expressed in the Hostages judgment were a correct reflection of the requirements for a justified recourse to reprisals under international law at the time of the Second World War. Accordingly, the Court went on to test the German practices of retaliation in the light of these requirements. It found that none of these had been observed: the alleged reprisals had not been used solely as an

[74] *Ibid.*, pp. 374 ff.

ultimate remedy, they had not been proportionate to the offence, they had in certain cases continued even after the perpetrator had been caught, and they had not in all instances been carried out or even announced openly. In view of these findings the Court rejected Rauter's claim that the retaliatory actions with which he was charged had constituted justifiable reprisals.

The above summary of the case at first instance brings to light some interesting aspects. In the first place, the parties were apparently divided both on the facts and the law concerning the spreading of resistance in the Netherlands, and on the implications which this, and the attitude of the Netherlands Government in the matter, had for the justification of the German policy. The appreciation of the facts ran from the position defended by Rauter and his counsel that the German policy of retaliation had only been initiated after the resistance movement had assumed unacceptable proportions, and that the origin of this resistance movement must be sought in the policy of incitement and support pursued by the Netherlands Government (and not, apparently, in any previous actions of the occupying Power), to the view held by the Hague Special Court that the development of a resistance movement in the occupied territory and the encouragement and support which the Government in London had given it, had been preceded (and, presumably, caused) by certain illegal features of the attitude and activities of the occupying Power.

Another fundamental difference of opinion between Rauter and his counsel on the one hand, and the public prosecutor and the Court on the other, bears on the legal position of the population in occupied territory and of the Government-in-exile. According to Rauter, the resistance constituted an irregular method of warfare prohibited by international law, as it was a clear violation of the obligation on the population to behave in a peaceful and orderly way and not to thwart the occupying Power in the discharge of his functions. Obviously, incitement to such undesirable activities was to that view equally contrary to international law. The Court, on the other hand, held that no international illegality attached to the policy pursued by the Netherlands Government, nor, for that matter, to the fact of the resistance as such, as international law cannot be said to preclude the population of an occupied territory from resisting the occupant, especially not if the latter is himself guilty of a pattern of conduct violatory of the rules governing military occupation.

It seems that neither Rauter nor the Court were correct in their reasoning. Rauter rightly considered the Netherlands Government responsible for its part in the development of resistance in the Netherlands; but it was a misconception on his part to think that according to international law the resistance had been illegal in all respects: on this count the Court was in the right. A more viable line of defence would have been for Rauter to contend that certain specific acts of resistance had been unlawful, on the double ground that the perpetrators lacked combatant status and that the acts were in contravention of specific rules of warfare, so that the German occupation authorities had been entitled to take reprisals for those acts: reprisals, that is, against the State of the Netherlands, as the Netherlands Government could be held responsible for the illegal acts of resistance as well as for the resistance in its entirety. However, such reprisals would have had to comply with all the requirements set by international law, whereas the German authorities had evidently neither distinguished between resistance activities constituting war crimes and other acts merely obstructing them in the realization of their goals, nor had they given any indication that the measures taken were aimed against the Netherlands Government.

The Court came somewhere near this line of reasoning when it argued that the German authorities had been entitled to take counter-measures because the resistance fighters lacked combatant status. However, its reasoning was fallacious in that it did not distinguish between acts of resistance pure and simple (which obviously could lead to counter-measures on the part of the Germans, without, however, warranting a recourse to reprisals) and those acts of resistance violating specific rules of warfare in addition (and which, hence, could justify a resort to reprisals).

As for the issue of collective responsibility, it was seen that the public prosecutor first contended that this constituted a fundamental requirement for all reprisals; but in his further argument he related it solely to retaliatory measures against an occupied population. The Special Court, for its part, specifically applied the condition of collective responsibility to the imposition of collective fines, as an instance of collective punishment according to Article 50 of the Hague Regulations. In its enumeration of requirements for a recourse to reprisals, on the other hand, the Court did not repeat this condition. Evidently, the Court envisaged two different ways of retaliation in the event of reprehensible acts on the part of an occupied population: collective punishment (governed by the aforementioned Article 50), and reprisals (less definite, but governed as a minimum by the requirements set out in the judgment in the Hostages Case). The judgment does not however make clear what, according to the Court, was the distinguishing mark between collective punishment and reprisals against an occupied population.

For the Special Court of Cassation, the real issue in this case turned around the nature of reprisals and the question of whether the German measures of retaliation could be brought under that head. A first indication of the Court's views in this respect was given when in the course of Rauter's interrogation the President explained to him the difference between belligerent reprisals, as measures against the enemy State on account of violations of the law of war committed on the part of that State, and collective punishment for acts of individual members of an occupied population. The President added that a belligerent could be precluded by his own earlier illegalities from taking reprisals against the enemy State reacting to these. As to collective punishment, he emphasized that this was only permissible when the collectivity of which the perpetrator of the act was a member, could be held responsible for the act, not merely on the ground that the perpetrator happened to live amidst the collectivity, but because there was at least an element of passive involvement on its side.[75]

The question of earlier illegalities on the German side was broached again in the course of a discussion arising between Rauter and one of the members of the Court of Cassation, Professor Verzijl, in connection with the view expressed by Rauter that the Government-in-exile had conducted warfare in a manner contrary to international law. With respect to this, Verzijl asked him whether he had never realized that Germany had been the first to act illegally: that it had started an aggressive war, and that it had applied unlawful methods of warfare right at the beginning of the war, so that it was not Germany which had had a right to take reprisals against the Netherlands, but the Netherlands against Germany? To these questions Rauter merely replied that that was precisely the element in the situation which made it so difficult for him to defend his position.[76]

The issue was also touched upon by the Judge-Advocate General, who once again described how resistance had sprung up in the Netherlands as a result of a series of wrongs experienced at the hands of Germany: the aggressive war, the use of means of warfare contrary to international law, the setting up of a civil administration, the measures aiming at the nazification of the Netherlands, the insults levelled at the House of Orange, and the systematic plundering of this country. Resistance, he said, had sprung up spontaneously, without any influence of the Government in London: that had only at a later stage urged the population to disobey certain German orders, and its exhortations had then had a bearing on the measures taken by Germany in defiance of international law. In short: the resistance had been a product of the German infringements of international law, and Rauter could not now argue that in combating the resistance he had no longer been obliged to observe the norms of international law.[77]

The Special Court of Cassation in its judgment discussed the matter at

[75] *Ibid.*, pp. 398-399.

[76] *Ibid.*, pp. 470-471. Later, Rauter merely repeated the argument that it had been the character of the resistance and the deliberate policy of the Netherlands Government in respect to it which had made nonsense of the traditional laws of warfare and had necessitated the recourse to reprisals (or *Repressivmassnahmen*, he added) on the side of the occupying Power; pp. 483 ff.

[77] *Ibid.*, pp. 543-544. It would seem that the Judge-Advocate General reduced the rôle of the Netherlands Government to altogether too insignificant proportions by merely referring to the official statements broadcast over the radio during the war.

some length.[78] Rauter, the Court said, had failed to take into account the distinction between reprisals properly speaking (being measures contrary to international law, resorted to by a State because the enemy State, acting through one or other of its organs, had commenced to commit acts in violation of international law) and measures in retaliation for hostile acts on the part of the population, or individual members thereof, in occupied territory. Had Germany, the Court questioned, been in a position to take reprisals properly speaking against the population in the occupied Dutch territory? This question would have to receive a positive answer if the Netherlands had been guilty of any previous wrong against Germany. For, as had been expressly recognized in the official commentary on Article 50 of the Hague Regulations, embodied in the report which Rolin had made in 1899,[79] that Article did not prejudice the question of reprisals; and such genuine reprisals could be aimed against any suitable object: the armed forces of the enemy State, its other organs, its territory, merchant navy or property, its nationals wherever they might be found, or their property. In other words, the occupied population could be made the subject of a reprisal, provided certain limitations and a certain proportionality were taken into account.

However, the Court continued, all this was of no avail to Rauter, as there was no question of any previous wrong on the part of the Netherlands. For, as was generally known and as had been convincingly established by the International Military Tribunal at Nuremberg, Germany had commenced an unlawful aggressive war, *inter alia* against the Netherlands, and in so doing had already given the latter State a right to take reprisals. Germany had moreover made use of various treacherous methods of warfare, and also after the short period of actual warfare it had continued to commit number of violations of international law: the failure any longer to recognize the lawful sovereign, the setting up of a civil administration independent of the military commander in the occupied territory, the systematic nazification, the gradually intensified persecution of the Jewish members of the population, the pressing of Dutch workers into the German war and other industries, and so on. The Court concluded that the State of the Netherlands, far from having been a legitimate object for German reprisals, would itself have been entitled to take reprisals against Germany, and the latter State would not in its turn have been justified in taking counter-reprisals against such reprisals taken in conformity with international law.

Having thus rejected the proposition that Rauter's actions would have constituted genuine reprisals, the Court of Cassation next broached the issue of retaliatory measures on account of hostile acts in occupied territory.

[78] *Ibid.*, pp. 577-581.
[79] *Supra*, p. 60.

The Court once again turned to Article 50 of the Hague Regulations: for it was precisely the function of that Article to restrict the recourse to "so-called reprisals", or collective punishment, in response to reprehensible or hostile acts of individual members of an occupied population. Only those measures had not been prohibited as would at least find their basis in a passive co-responsibility of the population, in conformity with the principle evidently at the root of the provision, that an occupant ought, no more than a sovereign in his own realm, punish innocents for the deeds of others. This would, moreover, constitute a mode of conduct which the Court considered was at variance with all principles of justice, and incompatible with the Martens clause contained in the preamble to the Hague Convention on Land Warfare, stating that in cases not provided for in the annexed Regulations the populations would remain under the protection of the principles of international law, as these result from the usages established among civilized nations, from the laws of humanity and from the dictates of the public conscience.

What did the Court understand by "passive responsibility"? This, it explained, could only be assumed in respect to those persons who had had knowledge about certain hostile acts and could have prevented these: it was not sufficient that an attitude of mental resistance against a cruel enemy result in silent approval for such acts after the event.

Having thus reduced to a minimum the freedom to take retaliatory measures against persons other than the actual perpetrators of hostile acts, the Court went on to state that even the remaining freedom lost its justification where the hostile acts had themselves been provoked by internationally illegal acts of the occupant. On these grounds, the Court rejected the thesis that the German actions would have been justified as measures of collective punishment, as it had previously rejected the argument that these would have constituted reprisals properly so-called.

In its principal aspect, the judgment of the Special Court of Cassation can only meet with warm approval: here, like in the judgment of the Italian Tribunal in the Kappler case, a clear distinction was made between reprisals in the proper sense of the term and "so-called reprisals" or measures of collective punishment for reprehensible or hostile acts committed in occupied territory by individual members of the population. However, approval in principle need not stand in the way of certain criticisms regarding specific aspects of the Court's reasoning.

A first such criticism concerns the grounds advanced for the determination that the acts charged against Rauter could not be justified as reprisals. The conclusion of the Court appears to rest on two grounds: (1) Germany having been the first to commit a series of violations of international law in respect of the Netherlands, the latter State could not consequently be charged with any international wrong in respect of Germany; (2) on the contrary, the Netherlands would have been entitled to take reprisals, against which counter-reprisals would not have been permissible.

The first ground seems entirely fallacious: it is evidently based on the argument of reciprocity, which is a false and even dangerous concept when made the overriding principle of the law of war.[80]

The thesis, on the other hand, that counter-reprisals are inadmissible against legitimate reprisals, undoubtedly constitutes a generally accepted and even self-evident rule of international law. The point is, however, that the Netherlands had at no time actually taken reprisals against Germany; in particular, neither the acts of the resistance movement nor the support which the Government in London gave it could be so interpreted. In other words, the rule relating to the inadmissibility of counter-reprisals simply did not apply in the given instance.

In the final analysis, the reasoning on which the Court relied (and which had also found expression in the intervention of its member, Professor Verzijl, in the course of the oral proceedings) amounted to the assertion that a belligerent who is himself guilty of violations of international law cannot justifiably challenge any acts the adversary chooses to perform, even if such acts in their turn constitute infringements of international law. It is submitted that this is not a true statement of the law; the mere fact that illegalities have been or are being committed by a belligerent does not preclude him from taking reprisals on account of illegalities on the part of the adversary,—unless, that is, the illegalities committed on both sides are identical.

It should be noted that the Court did not rely on the same argument when it rejected the thesis that the German retaliatory actions could have found justification as measures of collective punishment: this time its argument was that the resistance had in fact been provoked by the occupant's own illegalities. In other words, the Court did not base its conclusion on this point on a right that the Netherlands could have (but had not) invoked, so much as on the actual sequence of events. It should be added that in so doing it came very near to suggesting that the illegalities committed by the occupant had not merely provoked, but had justified the resistance.

Another critical comment concerns the meaning which the Court attached to the concept of collective responsibility in the context of "so-called reprisals", or collective punishment. It was entirely in conformity with generally accepted views that it interpreted Article 50 of the Hague Regulations to encompass passive responsibility. However, it seems an unduly restrictive interpretation of the notion of passive responsibility to hold it

[80] See *supra*, p. 24, where the argument of reciprocity has been treated at some length.

applicable only to those persons who not only had knowledge of an act, but could have prevented it: so defined, the notion comes very close to ordinary complicity as a concept of criminal law. At any rate, it narrows down the circle of passively responsible persons in two ways: it excludes those persons who must be deemed to have lacked either the authority or the physical strength, or, for that matter, the mere opportunity, to prevent the act, and it equally excludes the persons who after the event gain knowledge of the act as well as of the person of the actor, and who are then unwilling to reveal that information to the occupation authorities.

This whole line of reasoning moreover bears too close a resemblance to criminal law considerations of individualized responsibility, and it fails to appreciate that actually the concept of passive responsibility as envisaged in Article 50 of the Hague Regulations amounts to a more or less fictitious group responsibility attributed to "the population" as a collectivity, for acts the actual perpetrators of which remain unknown and which are not evidently isolated incidents so much as instances of a general pattern of conduct. Obviously, a relatively small number of active members of the population can set the pattern in this respect, provided this minority is supported by the feelings and attitude of a significant part of the population. These are precisely the circumstances of fact where an occupying Power turns to the expedient of retaliatory measures against the collectivity of the population. It is submitted that this character of collective punishment was not fully appreciated in the judgment of the Special Court of Cassation.

It has been pointed out in the literature that a rule emerges from the judgment, to the effect that "offences committed by members of the civilian population of an occupied territory can in no case entitle the occupying Power to kill hostages".[81] This is undoubtedly a correct inference so far as the judgment goes: hostages, being persons whom the occupant has arrested beforehand so as to warn the population against carrying out certain undesirable activities, are by definition innocent of any such acts intervening after their arrest and cannot bear any responsibility therefor, not even in the most passive form imaginable. However, this "emerging rule" is of little avail to persons arrested after the event on account of the passive responsibility then attributed to them by the occupant: in the construction of the Special Court of Cassation, those persons will not be completely innocent of the acts (which they could even have prevented!), and the judgment contains no indication that they might not be killed by way of collective punishment: after all, in 1899 the scope of Article 50 of the Hague Regulations was expressly extended from collective fines to all modalities of collective punishment. In view of this consideration it seems preferable not to place too much reliance in the above argument to prevent

[81] *Law Reports of Trials of War Criminals,* Vol. XIV, at p. 137.

the execution of members of the population other than the actual perpetrators of hostile acts and other directly responsible persons.[82]

6.1.6. *The Falkenhausen Case*

On 9 March 1951 the Military Tribunal in Brussels (2nd Chamber) pronounced sentence in the trial of General Von Falkenhausen and three other
German general officers.[83] Each of the accused had during the war held
high positions in the military occupation apparatus in Belgium, and they
were charged *inter alia* with having been responsible for the murder of
some 240 persons, executed "by way of belligerent reprisals". With respect
to this charge, the judgment sets out the following facts.[84]

The executions had been carried out in retaliation for attacks and acts
of sabotage committed during the occupation by persons unknown at the
time of the executions. The attacks had all been aimed against members of
the occupation forces, or, alternatively, at life or property of Belgian
nationals who collaborated with the enemy; the sabotage actions had been
directed against military installations of the occupant, industrial or mining
facilities operating for his benefit, or means of communication in the
occupied territory. In retaliation for these acts, Von Falkenhausen had
ordered a total of eighteen executions, in the course of which the above
240 persons had been killed. Each of these executions had served as repression for a certain number of attacks and acts of sabotage at a time.

Von Falkenhausen had issued orders to the effect that the victims of the
executions were to be selected from among the group of the political
detainees, being persons suspected of belonging to those circles which he
qualified as terroristic and to which in his eyes the probable perpetrators of
the acts retaliated against were also likely to belong. More particularly, the
victims had to be selected from among those political detainees who, when
brought to trial before a German military court, would be liable to incur
the death penalty, because they had been taken red-handed while com-

---

[82] The Rauter trial was not the only case involving questions of reprisals, hostages
and so on, in the Dutch jurisprudence. Some further instances have been reported in
Annual Digest, 1949 and 1950. It has not however appeared necessary to include
these instances in the present survey.

A somewhat different and, in fact, less clear view of reprisals was expressed in an
unpublished judgment of the First Chamber of the Special Court of Cassation
(Rauter's case, as all cases against German accused, was decided by the Second
Chamber). The First Chamber did not differentiate between reprisals proper and
quasi-reprisals, but instead referred to "the acts in question" [*i.e.*, the hostage kil-
lings] . . . in so far as they constituted reprisals" (etc.). See: B. V. A. Röling, "The
Law of War and the National Jurisdiction since 1945", in *R.d.C.* 1960, Vol. II, p. 423,
n. 77.

[83] *Revue de droit pénal et de criminologie*, Vol. 31, 1950-1951, p. 863.

[84] *Ibid.*, pp. 867-868.

mitting a hostile act, or because they had been found hiding weapons or explosives.

The defendants had been charged with murder under the Belgian criminal code. On the other hand, the Tribunal considered, these murders had also had the character of executions by way of belligerent reprisals, that is to say (it added) of collective punishment, inflicted in time of war upon civilians on account of acts committed by third persons.[85] It was therefore incumbent upon the Tribunal to examine the juridical character of the executions under both aspects.[86]

It took the Tribunal no great effort to establish that the facts charged against the defendants and which neither had been nor could be contested, constituted murders in the sense of the relevant articles of the Belgian criminal code. Therefore, but for the specific character of the acts as war crimes, the defendants must be held guilty.

The Tribunal next considered that while the Hague Convention on Land Warfare of 1907 did no more than the Regulations annexed thereto contain any express provision with respect to hostages, Articles 46 and 50 of the Regulations nonetheless had the effect that their execution was implicitly regarded as a violation of the laws and usages of war. However, it was an established fact that the defendants had acted on the strength of directives and orders issued by their superiors.[87] This meant that under the system of the Belgian criminal code they were entitled to invoke superior orders in justification, unless the incriminated acts could be said to constitute flagrant violations of the law of war.

The Tribunal considered in this respect that executions by way of reprisals were alien to law in general and to international law in particular, the latter only knowing reprisals of State against State. Such executions belonged in the sphere of what was sometimes indicated with such vague terms as "martial law", which in reality stood for the manifestation of military force by penal means and which had no other justification or limit but absolute military necessity in time of war. It was not so much the legality as the necessity of the taking—and, in consequence, the killing—of hostages which was recognized as an ultimate means for ensuring the security of armies in the field or of occupation forces, and then this recognition did not rest on international custom as a source of law, but on the practice of armies.

In the light of this practice of armies, and in view of the formal rules on the subject embodied in the relevant German regulations, the Tribunal held

---

[85] *Ibid.*, p. 868: "Que ces homicides ont, d'ailleurs, le caractère d'exécution par représailles de guerre, c'est-à-dire de châtiment solidaire, infligé en temps de guerre, à des personnes civiles à raison d'actes commis par des tiers."
[86] *Ibid.*, pp. 868-880.
[87] The tribunal cited *inter alia* the Keitel directive of October 1942; see Chapter V, § 5.3.

that, in so far as the reprisal executions ordered by the defendants had kept within the strict limits of military necessity, there was no ground for the view that these would at the time they were ordered have constituted "flagrant" violations of the laws and usages of warfare. The limits of "military necessity", the Tribunal held, included those executions ordered with a view to the repression and prevention both of attacks on the occupation army, its members or the members of its auxiliary services, and of acts of sabotage against military, industrial or other equipment, *materiel* or installations of vital importance for the conduct of the war or for the occupation forces. Within these limits—and only within these limits —was the Tribunal prepared to consider the reprisal executions justified on the ground that the defendants had acted in accordance with formal prescriptions and superior orders.

From these justified reprisal executions the Tribunal distinguished those executions ordered as reprisals without any military necesssity properly speaking and which had merely had the aim to repress and prevent attacks on collaborators of Belgian nationality, their families and their property: the latter category of executions constituted "flagrant" violations of the laws and usages of warfare and were unjustifiable according to the Belgian criminal code.

In view of this division of the reprisal executions into those which could and those which could not be considered justified, the Tribunal next set itself to determine with respect to each separate instance related in the indictment whether the execution had been solely or decisively motivated by attacks on the German occupation forces (etcetera), or by attacks on collaborators of Belgian nationality, or, again, whether doubt persisted as to what had been the determining factor. The first group were declared justified, the second unjustifiable, and with respect to the third group the Tribunal felt obliged to decide in favour of the defendants.

A final paragraph of the part of the judgment dealing with this count of the indictment bears on the issue of proportionality. The Tribunal did not apply proportionality as a determining factor for the justifiability of reprisal executions, but it saw a mitigating factor in the evident care displayed by Von Falkenhausen to limit the executions, both as their number and the number of victims on each separate occasion were concerned. Here, the Tribunal regarded as relevant certain clear facts, only one of which need be mentioned: taking into account the orders which had emanated from Von Falkenhausen's superiors, the number of victims killed had been comparatively moderate.[88]

---

[88] Count II of the indictment concerned the illegal arrest followed by transportation to Germany of hostages and certain other categories (Jews, workers) who in the process had been threatened with death. This charge was so unfortunately formulated that the tribunal could only find that no instance mentioned in the indictment met all the requirements (arrest as hostage, transportation to Germany still in that quality,

257

An important aspect of the judgment in the Falkenhausen case is the manner in which the Tribunal used the term "reprisals", in particular where the acts charged against Von Falkenhausen *et al.* are described as "exécutions by way of belligerent reprisals" (*exécutions par représailles de guerre*). This use of the term is somewhat misleading, in that it might suggest that the Tribunal would have been inclined to regard the hostage killings as reprisals in the true sense of the term. However, the Tribunal made it abundantly clear that it envisaged reprisals as acts of one State against another, and that it regarded the executions "by way of reprisals" charged in the indictment as measures of collective punishment, inflicted upon members of a civil population for acts which they have not themselves committed. It seems worth emphasizing this point, because in so doing the Tribunal ranged itself among the judicial bodies differentiating between reprisals properly so-called and quasi-reprisals, or collective punishment.

Was it sufficient justification for the executions charged against the defendants to have been ordered by way of collective punishment? This the Tribunal categorically denied: reprisal executions were "alien to international law" and could not be justified under that law. The Tribunal did not shut its eyes to the fact that military necessity could prompt recourse to such methods, and it even pointed expressly to the development of a certain practice to that effect. That practice, however, could not have created law as it was merely "the practice of armies". This seems an unfortunate argument: it is difficult to see why armies, as organs of the State, would lack the capacity to put into practice a certain mode of conduct under such conditions as would allow its development into customary law. Obviously, however, what the Tribunal really wanted to convey was precisely that the practice at issue had not become customary law and had remained a mere practice based on military necessity, evidently on the ground that the element of *opinio juris* was lacking.

The Tribunal found support for this view in Articles 46 and 50 of the Hague Regulations, which (it argued) imply a recognition of the unlawfulness of reprisal executions. On the other hand, the text of these Articles was not so completely unambiguous as entirely to exclude the possibility of justifiable error as to the law. Such error could not, however, be justified if the illegal character of the act was "flagrant". For a clear comprehension of this argument, it should be emphasized that the Tribunal wielded the criterion of "flagrant character" only indirectly and within the framework of superior orders: its contention was not that *error juris* was in itself sufficient ground to justify a non-flagrant violation of the law of war: rather, the criterion operated, negatively, to exclude the exculpatory force of

---

threat with death). This charge may hence be left aside here, as no point of interest for present purposes arose out of it.

superior orders in the event of the act ordered by a superior officer constituting a flagrant violation.

This construction was of course conditioned both by the applicable Belgian law as to superior orders and by the circumstance that the defendants had actually ordered the executions in reliance on directives emanating from their superiors. It would seem, on the other hand, that from the point of view of international law the criterion of "flagrant violation" need not be confined within this framework. Many of the rules of warfare are manifestly ambiguous, and those who have to apply them in action will not generally be in the position to seek unbiased and authoritative advice as to their interpretation first. Therefore, it seems no more than reasonable to regard as exculpated even in the absence of superior orders any person who has committed a violation of the law of war in the technical sense, but who in so doing actually did—and reasonably could— err as to the law. The judgment of whether a specific error can be considered reasonable will obviously depend on a variety of factors, among which great importance will attach to the degree to which the act committed infringes fundamental concepts of humanity.[89] In that light it may well be questioned whether the Tribunal was right in assuming a difference between reprisal executions for attacks on the occupation forces and similar executions for attacks on Belgian collaborators: it seems a tenable proposition that the degree of inhumanity inherent in the killing of one member of the civil population for the acts of another did not differ in either instance. On the other hand, the grounds advanced by the Tribunal in support for this distinction (viz., military necessity and previous practice) cannot be denied a certain weight.

Another comment concerns the passage in the judgment where the Tribunal regarded as a mitigating circumstance the fact that the defendants had demonstrated moderation in the number of victims killed in each separate execution, especially when compared with the ratios prescribed in the directives of their superiors. These directives, it should be realized, had variously prescribed ratios of $100:1$ and $10:1$ for every German killed. It is not clear from the judgment which ratio the defendants had applied in practice, but this much is clear, that it had been more than $1:1$ in several instances. To have, say, five persons killed in retaliation for the death of one German would of course remain well below the prescribed ratio; yet, this need not be considered moderate from every point of view. In any event, the Tribunal did not apply the strict standard of proportionality that one man executed was the maximum for every single German killed.

Indeed, the point should be emphasized that the Tribunal did not make proportionality a condition for the justification of the executions—or,

---

[89] *Cf.* also Chapter I, § 1.2.6.

rather, having regard to the construction applied by the Tribunal, for the non-exclusion of the justification resulting from superior orders. Neither did the Tribunal find it necessary to explain why it did not apply this standard.

6.1.7. The Dostler Case

From 8 to 12 October 1945 a case was tried in Rome before a United States Military Commission, which as far as subject-matter is concerned was very different from the cases dealt with so far in this section: the trial of General Dostler.[90] This German General had as commander of the 75th Army Corps on or about 24 March 1944, in the vicinity of La Spezia in Italy, ordered the summary execution of two officers and thirteen men of the United States Army who had been captured by his forces. The order had been carried into effect on 26 March 1944.

The facts were as follows.[91] On the night of 22 March 1944 the American soldiers had landed on the Italian coast, north of La Spezia and some 250 miles behind the front. Their mission was to demolish the railroad tunnel on the mainline between La Spezia and Genoa: this was a *bona fide* military mission, and the men were in uniform. On 24 March the group were captured and brought to La Spezia, where they were interrogated. In the course of the interrogation one of the officers revealed the nature of their mission. A report was made to the 75th Army Corps, and on the morning of 25 March a telegram was received at La Spezia, signed by Dostler, and ordering the immediate execution of the captured American soldiers. After an exchange of some further communications, amongst which another telegram from Dostler ordering that compliance with the execution order should be reported to his headquarters by 7 o'clock on the morning of 26 March, the fifteen Americans were shot early in the morning of that day.

Among the arguments advanced in defence of General Dostler was the plea of superior orders, based *inter alia* on the Commando Order of October 1942.[92] It was alleged that during the war German officers had no alternative but to obey orders emanating from the Führer Headquarters; and, while it was conceded that certain of these orders might have infringed international law, it was further contended that the officers at the front charged with the execution of these orders had been convinced that Hitler would in some way or other inform the enemy Governments of his decisions, so that the officers would not be responsible for the execution of the orders. Moreover, the argument continued (relying on Oppenheim's International Law[93]) "an act otherwise amounting to a war crime might

[90] *Law Reports*, Vol. I, p. 22: Case No. 2.
[91] *Ibid.*, at p. 25.
[92] *Cf.* Chapter V, § 5.2.2.
[93] 6th ed. by Lauterpacht, Vol. II, p. 453.

have been executed in obedience to orders conceived as a measure of re-prisals, and...a Court was bound to take into consideration such a circumstance".[94] As the Commando Order had in fact represented itself as a reprisal order, and as the Geneva Prisoners of War Convention of 1929 recognized retaliation as lawful,[95] General Dostler had "had a perfect right to believe that the order, as a reprisal order, was legitimate".[96]

The prosecution, which did not accept this line of defence, according to the report based its rejection on two arguments: that an illegal order is no defence, and that the shooting in the present case had not been covered by the terms of the Commando Order. Leaving aside the second argument, as a question of appreciation of the facts in the light of the terms of the order, it should be observed that the first-mentioned argument seems hardly sufficient to meet the defence, unless it is interpreted to imply that neither was the Commando Order a legitimate reprisal, nor could it be taken in good faith, even by a German officer during the war, to constitute such a reprisal.

The Military Commission found General Dostler guilty and sentenced him to death.[97] In the absence of a reasoned judgment, it remains unknown whether the decision rested on the argument that the Commando Order did not constitute—or could not *bona fide* be considered to be—a legitimate reprisal, or that the shooting had in fact exceeded the bounds set by the Order.

The issue in this case, so far as related here, was obviously the fundamental right to life of prisoners of war and, as a consequence, their right not to be executed summarily (but only after their liability to the death penalty would be established in a judicial process meeting the requirements of a fair trial). This right to life was hard to deny in principle, and the only lines open to the defence were of course: that the captured men had not been entitled to prisoner of war status—an untenable proposition in view of the established fact that they were members of the United States armed forces and had worn uniform—or that their summary execution was, or could in good faith be held to be, an action in execution of a justifiable measure of reprisal. The latter line of defence, however, was bound to fail as well, in view of the fact that measures of reprisal against prisoners of war were the very instances of reprisals expressly prohibited in a multilateral Convention ratified, *inter alia*, by Germany and the United States of America.

The United States Military Commission, in holding Dostler guilty of the fifteenfold murder charged against him, set the pace for a series of judg-

---

[94] *Law Reports*, Vol. I, at p. 28.
[95] It is difficult to see how this assertion could be made in the face of the express prohibition of reprisals in Art. 2, para. 3, of that Convention.
[96] *Loc. cit.* n. 94.
[97] *Ibid.*, at p. 29.

ments where the identical point was at issue: viz., the lack of justification as a reprisal of the Commando Order.[98]

In a note to the Dostler Case in the *Law Reports of Trials of War Criminals*,[99] a parallel is drawn between this case and the *Dover Castle* case decided in 1921 by the German Supreme Court in Leipzig. In that case, a German naval officer, Neumann, was charged with (and pleaded guilty to) having torpedoed a British hospital ship, the *Dover Castle*, in the Mediterranean in 1917. His plea was that he had acted in accordance with a German Admiralty Order laying down that as from a given date enemy hospital ships would be sunk at sight, unless previously notified. It appeared that this Order corresponded with two memoranda, sent to the enemy Governments in January and March 1917, announcing this line of policy in view of the suspicion that the enemy hospital ships were utilized *inter alia* for military purposes. These memoranda had apparently been known to Neumann, who moreover had received from his colleagues information corroborating the above facts. Accordingly, he had been "of the opinion that the measures taken by the German Admiralty against enemy Hospital Ships were not contrary to International Law, but were legitimate reprisals. His conduct clearly shows that this was his conviction."[100]

According to the annotator in the *Law Reports*, the line of thought of the defence in the Dostler Case was similar to that applied by the German Supreme Court in the *Dover Castle* case: viz., that the accused had had a right to believe that a particular order, as a reprisal order, was legitimate. In the meantime, however, Article 2, paragraph 3, of the Prisoners of War Convention of 1929 had intervened, prohibiting reprisals against prisoners of war. This led him to the following conclusion:[101] "Through the express provision of Art. 2, paragraph 3 of the Geneva Convention, the decision of the German *Reichsgericht* in the 'Dover Castle' case has lost even such little persuasive authority as it may have had at the time it was rendered."

The parallel between the two cases seems not, however, so close as suggested in this annotation. Firstly, while reprisals against prisoners of war were expressly prohibited by 1944, no express conventional prohibition had protected hospital ships against reprisals in 1917. In the second place, the measures ordered in 1917 had been announced openly and in time to the enemy Governments, while the publicity around the Commando Order had been decidedly less. It seems, therefore, that Lieutenant Neumann could have had far more reason to believe that the Admiralty Order was

[98] The question arose, for instance, in the Nuremberg trial of the major war criminals, and in the High Command and Ministry Cases decided by United States Military Tribunals at Nuremberg.
[99] *Law Reports*, Vol. I, at p. 31.
[100] German War Trials. Report of Proceedings before the Supreme Court in Leipzig. Cmd. 1450, 1921, p. 42, at p. 43.
[101] *Loc. cit.* n. 99.

justified as a reprisal, than General Dostler could have in respect to the Commando Order. Leaving aside whether the *Dover Castle* had, or still has, any "persuasive authority" in the matter of the plea of superior orders in connection with reprisals, it should be pointed out that in any event the judgment in the Dostler Case can no more have impaired this than Article 2, paragraph 3, of the Geneva Convention of 1929.

6.2. ATTEMPTS AT CODIFICATION: SUCCESS AND FAILURE

In the years following the conclusion of the Second World War, various aspects of the issue of belligerent reprisals have been the object of more or less successful attempts at codification. These attempts can conveniently be treated under the following headings: (1) the Conventions of Geneva of 1949, (2) the Convention of The Hague of 1954, (3) the *Projet de règles* of the International Committee of the Red Cross, and (4) the Draft Code of Offences Against the Peace and Security of Mankind.

6.2.1. *The Conventions of Geneva of 1949*

Remarkable success has been achieved by the ICRC with its edeavours, started immediately after the war, to renew and adapt and, where feasible, to complete the humanitarian law of war protecting the victims of warfare. The four Conventions signed in Geneva on 12 August 1949, which were the outcome of these efforts, each contain certain provisions which are directly relevant to the issue under discussion: prohibitions of reprisals against the persons protected under the Conventions, and improved provisions regarding their enforcement. Thus, while prior to World War II only the category of the prisoners of war had been afforded express protection against reprisals, the categories so protected now also embrace the wounded and sick coming under the First Geneva Convention, the wounded, sick and shipwrecked falling under the Second Convention, and those civilian persons protected by the Fourth Convention.

While thus the range of the categories legally protected against reprisals has been considerably extended, it is all the more surprising to see how little discussion was needed to achieve these results. As regards the First (Land) and Second (Maritime) Conventions, it was merely considered that the express exclusion of reprisals was a confirmation of an uncontested rule [1] and that already in 1937 the idea had been to introduce the principle into the Conventions in force at the time. [2] And as far as the Third or

---

[1] XVIIth International Conference of the Red Cross, Stockholm, 1948: *Projets de conventions revisées ou nouvelles protégeant les victimes de la guerre*, 2nd ed., p. 28.
[2] *Rapport sur les travaux de la Conférence d'experts gouvernementaux pour l'étude des Conventions protégeant les victimes de la guerre (Genève, 14-26 avril 1947)*, p. 60.

Prisoners of War Convention was concerned, it was never made a matter of doubt that the prohibition of reprisals should be retained: the point was emphasized that the experiences of the last war had reaffirmed the pointlessness of reprisals against prisoners of war.[3]

Slightly more attention was given to the introduction of a prohibition of reprisals into the Fourth or Civilians Convention. The main focus here was on the question of hostages: it was recognized from the outset that in the light of past experience the taking (and, *a fortiori*, the execution) of hostages should be absolutely prohibited, and this not only with respect to enemy civilians within the territory of a belligerent, but with respect to the inhabitants of occupied territory as well.[4] Once accepted, this principle was at no time in the further proceedings challenged in any way.[5]

To this prohibition from taking hostages was coupled, in an equally early stage of the proceedings, the absolute prohibition of reprisals and of all forms of collective punishment. In this connection it is worth noting that there is nowhere in the proceedings so much as the slightest indication of what was understood by those terms, and in particular of what was the difference, if any, between reprisals on the one hand and collective punishment on the other.[6] The point that stands out most clearly from the debates,

---

[3] *Ibid.*, pp. 121-122. The point was particularly brought to the fore by Sir Harold Satow (United Kingdom); see *Procès-verbaux de la Conférence d'experts gouvernementaux* (etcetera), Vol. III, p. 67. This expert also advocated the idea to enumerate certain specific forms of reprisals against prisoners of war in the text of the Article (such as the shackling of prisoners and the withholding of food). This amendment of the Article was not however taken on by the conference of experts, as the existing text was considered sufficient to cover all cases.

[4] To this effect already the *Rapport sur les travaux de la Conférence préliminaire des Sociétés nationales de la Croix-Rouge pour l'étude des Conventions et de divers problèmes ayant trait à la Croix-Rouge (Genève, 26 juillet-3 août 1946)*, pp. 101-102. The prohibition even against the taking of hostages in occupied territory was proposed by the Norwegian Red Cross Society.

[5] *Cf.* the report (p. 291) and the *procès-verbaux* (Vol. IV, p. 64 ff.) of the conference of government experts of 1947, and the *Projets de conventions* (etcetera) of 1948, p. 170. In the *Final Record of the Diplomatic Conference of Geneva, 1949*, the only comment is found in the report of Committee III: "The simplicity of the prohibition to take hostages laid down in Article 31, ensured its passage, undisputed, through the crucibles of Stockholm and Geneva." See *Final Record*, Vol. IIA, p. 823.

[6] Unacceptable is the conclusion arrived at by O. M. Uhler, *Der völkerrechtliche Schutz der Bevölkerung eines besetzten Gebiets gegen Massnahmen der Okkupationsmacht* (1950), according to whom the reference to "reprisals" in Art. 33 would be restricted to "Repressalien im weiteren Sinne", or quasi-reprisals, taken against an occupied population for hostile acts of private persons. He argues (pp. 114-115): "Einmal ergibt sich aus der Gesamtbetrachtung der Zivilkonvention, dass ihr Sinn und Zweck der Schutz der Kriegsopfer ist und dass die Genfer Konferenz eine Neufixierung der Gesetze und Gebräuche des Landkriegs weder durchführen konnte noch wollte ... Aber auch aus der systematischen Stellung von Art. 33 innerhalb der Konvention, im Abschnitt 1 des dritten Titels, ... geht hervor, dass mit dem Ausdruck Repressalie nur die uneigentliche, gegen Zivilpersonen i.w.S. gemeint ist. Diese

is the emphasis laid on the principle of individual responsibility as the sole ground justifying punishment of protected civilians within the territory of a belligerent or in occupied territory. From this principle, expressed in so many words in Article 33 of the Fourth Convention, were derived both the prohibition of "collective punishment and likewise all measures of intimidation or terrorism", and the prohibition of "reprisals against protected persons and their property".[7]

The text of the relevant provisions in the four Conventions runs as follows:
First Convention, Chapter VII (Execution of the Convention), Article 46:
"Reprisals against the wounded, sick, personnel, buildings or equipment protected by the Convention are prohibited."
Second Convention, Chapter VII (Execution of the Convention), Article 47:
"Reprisals against the wounded, sick and shipwrecked persons, the personnel, the vessels or the equipment protected by the Convention are prohibited."
Third Convention, Part II (General Protection of Prisoners of War), Article 13, paragraph 3:
"Measures of reprisal against prisoners of war are prohibited."
Fourth Convention, Part III (Status and Treatment of Protected Persons), Section I (Provisions Common to the Territories of the Parties to the Conflict and to Occupied Territories), Article 33:
"No protected person may be punished for an offence he or she has not personally committed. Collective penalties and likewise all measures of intimidation or of terrorism are prohibited.
"Pillage is prohibited.

Auffassung wird zudem noch bestätigt durch den Wortlaut von Abschnitt 3 des betreffenden Artikels, wo ausdrücklich von Repressalie 'à l'égard des personnes protégées et de leurs biens' die Rede ist."
While it is undoubtedly correct that the Conference of Geneva did not purport to re-codify the law of The Hague, and while it is equally correct that the prohibition of reprisals in Art. 33 is restricted to reprisals against the persons protected under the Convention and their property, there is no conceivable ground why the term "reprisals" would only encompass measures in retaliation for hostile acts of members of the population in their private capacity, and not also measures against the occupied population in retaliation for illegalities, whether committed by members of the population or otherwise, but for which the enemy State is held accountable.
[7] See in particular the *Projets de conventions* (etcetera) of 1948, p. 170. In the Diplomatic Conference of 1949, the proposed rules passed Commission III without so much as a word in comment of the principles laid down therein: the debate in the Commission turned on questions like the destruction of private property by long-range bombing. In so far, it was a foreshadow of subsequent discussions, in Red Cross and other circles, about the implications of the development of nuclear weapons, guided missiles, and so on, for the continued effectiveness of the Geneva Conventions of 1949.

"Reprisals against protected persons and their property are prohibited."

Article 34:

"The taking of hostages is prohibited."

The Articles, it will be observed, have each been given a prominent place in the relevant Convention, so as to guarantee the widest possible effect. On the other hand, it should be noted that the scope of these far-reaching prohibitions is not merely dependent on their place in this or that chapter of the Conventions, but is determined by two further factors: the applicability of the Geneva Conventions, and the definition of the persons protected by each of the Conventions. The latter aspect need not be examined here in any great detail: it may suffice to note that, roughly speaking, the First to Third Conventions protect members of the armed forces and related categories enumerated in the relevant articles,[8] while the Fourth Convention extends its protection to those persons, not protected by the first-mentioned three Conventions, who find themselves within the territory of a belligerent or in occupied territory and who are neither nationals of the belligerent (or occupying Power) nor are excluded by other clauses of the relevant article.[9]

The question of the applicability of the Conventions, on the other hand, is of prime importance here. In this respect, the common Article 2 is unequivocal: the direct applicability of the Conventions is strictly limited to armed conflicts presenting an international character.[10] This is not to say that nothing would have been provided for internal armed conflicts (or, more accurately, armed conflicts not of an international character); on the contrary,—and this inroad into the sphere of domestic jurisdiction is in itself a feat of major importance,—the equally common Article 3 lays down the norms that each party to such a conflict is bound to apply as a minimum. It moreover points out that the parties to the conflict "should further endeavour to bring into force, by means of special agreements, all or part of the other provisions of the present Convention". In the absence of such special agreements, however, the only provisions which the parties are

---

[8] Convention I: Art. 13; Convention II: Art. 13; Convention III: Art. 4.

[9] Convention IV: Art. 4; certain derogations are provided in Art. 5.

[10] According to Article 2, the Conventions "shall apply to all cases of declared war or of any other armed conflict which may arise between two or more of the High Contracting Parties, even if the state of war is not recognized by one of them"; they "shall also apply to all cases of partial or total occupation of the territory of a High Contracting Party, even if the said occupation meets with no armed resistance". Provision is moreover made for the situation where "one of the Powers in conflict may not be a party" to one or more of the Conventions: in that case "the Powers who are parties thereto shall remain bound by it in their mutual relations. They shall furthermore be bound by the Convention in relation to the said Power, if the latter accepts and applies the provisions thereof".

positively bound to apply are those embodied in Article 3; and among these an express prohibition of reprisals is sought in vain.

Does this imply that in internal armed conflicts the resort to reprisals is allowed with respect to those categories of persons who would be protected from reprisals in case of international armed conflict? The answer to this question is definitely not an unqualified "yes": Article 3 prohibits certain specific acts in terms so categorical as to suggest that the commission of those acts cannot be justified even with an appeal to reprisals. The acts in question (which "are and shall remain prohibited at any time and in any place whatsoever") include:

> "(a) violence to life and person, in particular murder of all kinds, mutilation, cruel treatment and torture;
> (b) taking of hostages;
> (c) outrages upon personal dignity, in particular humiliating and degrading treatment;
> (d) the passing of sentences and the carrying out of executions without previous judgment pronounced by a regularly constituted court, affording all the judicial guarantees which are recognized as indispensable by civilized peoples."

If one accepts, with the ICRC's *Commentary* to the Conventions, that "any reprisal which entails one of these acts is prohibited",[11] there will not be much room left for reprisals against the persons protected by Article 3. The scope for reprisals would be even smaller, if the further contention were also accepted that "speaking generally" any reprisal is prohibited which is "incompatible with the 'humane treatment' demanded unconditionally in the first clause of sub-paragraph (1)"[12] (*i.e.*, of Article 3). However, it is precisely this sweeping conclusion which arouses some misgivings as to the claim that reprisals are prohibited by virtue of Article 3. Is it so unmistakably certain that a norm prescribing humane treatment of persons and thus protecting them as human beings, that is, in their individual capacity, excludes recourse to reprisals (or quasi-reprisals) adversely affecting those same persons as members of a community, held responsible for some or other reprehensible activity of other members of the community? To put this question in a slightly different manner: is it certain that a retaliatory action entailing the death of human beings amounts to "murder", or, more generally speaking, to a violation of the norm of humane treatment? It is feared that opinions may vary in this respect. It might well be contended that an act can only reasonably be characterized as murder if it fails to find justification in one way or another. This would imply that the contention that reprisals entailing the death of human beings

---

[11] As is stated in an identical passage in all four volumes of the *Commentary* to the Geneva Conventions of 1949, published under the general editorship of Jean S. Pictet: I, p. 55; II, p. 36; III, p. 40; IV, p. 39.
[12] *Ibid.*

are prohibited because they amount to murder, would merely beg the question.

An additional ground for these misgivings lies in certain elements of the drafting history of the common Articles. At one stage of the proceedings in the Diplomatic Conference of Geneva of 1949, the proposal was that the Article on internal armed conflicts would not itself enumerate particular acts, absolutely prohibited even in case of internal armed conflict, but would refer to a list of such acts in the preamble to the Conventions. That list, according to a text proposed by the French delegation,[13] would have comprised not only the acts enumerated in the present Article 3, but also an express reference to "collective punishment as well as all acts of intimidation and terror". However, even before this proposed text, and in fact the whole idea of having such an elaborate preamble, was finally rejected,[14] a new text entirely different from the one originally proposed was placed before the Committee dealing with the draft article on internal armed conflicts; in this new version, the reference to the preamble had disappeared and instead the proposed article itself contained an enumeration of specifically prohibited acts. That enumeration, however, did not include any express reference to collective punishment, reprisals and so on. The records provide no indication whatsoever of the reasons for this modification.[15]

Then, an alternative text for the same article, proposed by the Russian delegation (and which would in fact have led to different texts for Article 3 in each of the Conventions) contained an express prohibition of reprisals in the text designed to be included in the Fourth Convention. This proposal was, however, rejected as a whole, without any previous detailed discussion of its contents.[16]

Obviously, this entire episode of the drafting history bears two different interpretations. On the one hand, it can be interpreted as implying that a reference to reprisals and collective punishment was finally left out because

[13] This proposal was introduced, and subsequently adopted in a slightly modified version, in an *ad hoc* Working Party of Committee III; see *Final Record*, Vol. IIA, pp. 777-779 (report of the Rapporteur of the Working Party presented in the 45th meeting of Committee III) and Vol. III, pp. 97, 98 (proposed texts).

[14] Committee III, 45th meeting, 9 July 1949; *Final Record*, Vol. IIA, p. 782.

[15] The new draft text, drawn up by the second Working Party of the Special Committee of the Joint Committee (which latter Committee was concerned with the common articles), was submitted to the Special Committee on 17 June 1949. It was discussed in several meetings of the Special Committee, where it ultimately failed to find sufficient support; see 7th Report of the Special Committee, *Final Record*, Vol. IIB, p. 123. The same text was however subsequently adopted by the Plenary Meeting of the Conference; 9th Plenary Meeting, 29 July 1949; *Final Record*, Vol. IIB, p. 339.

[16] The Russian proposal was introduced in, and rejected by, the Special Committee of the Joint Committee; 7th Report of the Special Committee, *Final Record*, Vol. IIB, p. 123.

it was considered superfluous in the light of the strict prohibitions actually embodied in the Article. On the other hand, a diametrically opposite interpretation would be that a prohibition of reprisals and collective punishment was considered unacceptable for internal armed conflicts, and hence was expressly omitted from the text. In the absence of any positive indication in the records in one direction or the other, it must be concluded that the drafting history of Article 3 leaves room for uncertainty with respect to the question raised.

Can the issue be decided by a recourse to fundamental principles? This, in fact, is what the authors of the ICRC's *Commentary* claim to do when they attribute overriding significance to the fundamental requirement of humane treatment and interpret this to entail the exclusion of reprisals against the categories of persons protected under Article 3.[17] But another, perhaps equally fundamental consideration is that the States, in elaborating the text of Article 3, have displayed the greatest caution in signing away any of the powers at their disposal in the case of internal armed conflict; in other words, an implicit waiver of such a power cannot lightly be assumed. Hence, this more fundamental approach does not, any more than the historical line, lead to a really convincing argument in favour of one or the other point of view.

In this situation, the point should be emphasized that the interpretation given by the ICRC obviously deserves the widest possible adherence, as it represents the view most in conformity with humanitarian considerations and in particular with the principle that the innocent ought not to be made to suffer for the deeds of others.[18] On the other hand, equal stress should

---

[17] *Supra*, p. 267.

[18] A Committee of Experts, convened by the ICRC in October 1962, gave as its opinion that "[l']article 3 interdit certainement, de l'avis de la Commission, la mise en œuvre de la 'responsabilité collective'." The Committee quoted the following paragraph from the report of a similar meeting of experts held in 1955: "En ce qui concerne la clause souvent appelée de responsabilité collective, la Commission a été unanime à désapprouver la notion de responsabilité possible d'une personne, par le seul fait qu'elle appartiendrait à une collectivité déterminée, et indépendamment d'actes délictueux commis par cette personne elle-même. On doit strictement condamner l'incarcération et la punition de membres de la famille de la personne impliquée dans des 'troubles intérieurs' et spécialement de ses enfants."

The Committee of 1962 continued to state that "[l']article 3 ... interdit la prise d'otages et prouve par là qu'il condamne toute idée de responsabilité collective. De plus, en cas de poursuites, l'article 3 exige 'un jugement ... assorti des garanties judiciaires reconnues comme indispensables par les peuples civilisés'. Le fait de détenir, de juger et de condamner une personne quelconque pour des faits commis par d'autres qu'elle-même, ou simplement en raison de son appartenance à un groupe particulier, constitue incontestablement une violation de ces dispositions." This reasoning, while not sufficiently cogent to establish beyond a doubt the correctness of the interpretation adopted by the expert Committee, certainly provides a convincing argument for the desirability of a prohibition of reprisals and collective punishment in the event of internal armed conflict.

be placed on the need for Article 3 to be amended at the earliest opportunity with an express reference to that principle, or, preferably, with an express prohibition of reprisals and collective punishment in the case of internal armed conflict.

Reverting once again to the main part of the Geneva Conventions, the provisions applicable in international armed conflicts, mention should be made of the improvements archieved in 1949 in a field narrowly connected with the issue of reprisals, that is, the enforcement of the Conventions by means other than reprisals. The improvements concern in particular the supervision of the application of the Conventions, and the punishment of violations.

The power of supervision is primarily vested in the Protecting Powers. This principle, which in 1929 had only been stated in the Prisoners of War Convention, now finds expression in all four Conventions; moreover, supervision has been made obligatory, and arrangements have been made for the replacement of Protecting Powers when these, no matter for which cause, are no longer able to perform their functions.[19] In the latter supposition, one of the solutions envisaged is that the ICRC, or another impartial humanitarian organization, assumes the humanitarian functions otherwise performed by a Protecting Power; in that case, not all the functions of a Protecting Power would devolve on such organization, but the humanitarian side of the supervisory function would evidently be among the functions taken over.[20]

Supervision of the application of the Conventions by Protecting Powers, while an important means for improving the standard of observance of the Conventions, is not necessarily the ideal solution: conceivably, supervision

[19] Articles 8/8/8/9 and 10/10/10/11 of the First, Second, Third and Fourth Conventions, respectively. See the *Commentary* to the First Convention, pp. 86 ff. and 112 ff.

[20] Art. 10/10/10/11. Principally, the ICRC does not depend for its humanitarian activities on any formal grant of power in the Conventions. In conformity with this, it is recognized in Art. 9/9/9/10 that the provisions of the Conventions "constitute no obstacle to the humanitarian activities which the International Committee of the Red Cross or any other impartial humanitarian organization may, subject to the consent of the Parties to the conflict, undertake" for the protection of war victims and their relief. When this negative formula is compared with the relevant paragraph of Art. 10/10/10/11, it is evident that a much more stringent formula has been applied in the latter Article: "If protection cannot be arranged [according to the preceding paragraphs], the Detaining Power shall request or shall accept, subject to the provisions of this Article, the offer of the services of a humanitarian organization, such as the International Committee of the Red Cross, to assume the humanitarian functions performed by Protecting Powers under the present Convention." The function of this provision is not to invest the ICRC with the formal power to supervise the application of the Conventions in their entirety, but to lay an obligation on the Detaining Power to "request or accept" in the given situation the humanitarian activities offered, *e.g.*, by the ICRC.

by an impartial organization (for instance, a body of independent experts) might achieve a higher degree of efficacy. Thus, it is another step forward that the Conventions of 1949 open the possibility that States Parties to the Conventions "may at any time agree to entrust to an organization which offers all guarantees of impartiality and efficacy the duties incumbent on the Protecting Powers by virtue of [the Conventions]." [21] In that case, not merely the humanitarian functions, but all the duties of Protecting Powers resulting from the Conventions are charged to the organization thus appointed.

Even more impressive are the improvements regarding the punishment of violations. Previously, only the Land and Maritime Conventions contained provisions in this respect, enjoining the Governments of the Contracting States to introduce in their respective legislative bodies the necessary proposals for the repression, in time of war, of all acts contrary to the Conventions. As had become sufficiently clear in the years before the Second World War, this was too weak an obligation. The Prisoners of War Convention, for its part, was even completely silent on the matter.

The present position is that all four Conventions lay a strict obligation on the Contracting States "to enact any legislation necessary to provide effective penal sanctions for persons committing, or ordering to be committed, any of the grave breaches" defined in each of the Conventions. The States are moreover under an obligation to search for, and bring to trial, "persons alleged to have committed, or to have ordered to be committed, such grave breaches".[22] This double obligation seems practically the limit to which the Conventions can go with a view to the repression of grave breaches, short of creating an international criminal jurisdiction.

As regards violations of lesser importance, each of the Conventions provides that the Contracting States "shall take measures necessary for the suppression" of all such acts.[23] This evidently amounts to a much less stringent obligation than the dual obligation accepted for grave breaches. However, this difference seems no more than a reflection of the difference between grave breaches and minor violations of the Conventions.

The point should finally be emphasized that no international machinery has been created either for the task of supervision, or for the punishment of violations: in the last resort, the extent to which the Conventions are actually enforced by means other than reprisals against the persons which they protect, remains dependent on the good will of the States concerned

---

[21] Art. 10/10/10/11.
[22] Art. 49/50/129/146. With respect to the issue of punishment of violations, *cf.* the *Commentary* to the First Convention, pp. 351 ff.
[23] Art. 49/50/129/146, paragraph 3.

and the possibilities at their disposal—and on such salutary influence as such institutions as the ICRC will be able to exert.

6.2.2. The Convention of The Hague of 1954

From 21 April to 14 May 1954 an intergovernmental Conference met at The Hague, under the auspices of UNESCO, for the purpose of elaborating rules for the protection of cultural property in the event of armed conflict. This Conference resulted in the signature, on 14 May 1954, of the following instruments: the Convention for the Protection of Cultural Property in the Event of Armed Conflict, with annexed Regulations for its execution, and a separate Protocol for the Protection of Cultural Property in the Event of Armed Conflict.[24]

The Convention of The Hague of 1954 is not wholly unprecedented; rules bearing on the protection of churches, museums and the like are already found in the Hague Regulations of 1899 and 1907 and in the Hague Convention concerning Naval Bombardment in Time of War, of 1907; and the Washington Pact of 15 April 1935 for the Protection of Artistic and Scientific Institutions and of Historic Monuments (the scope of which was restricted to the Western Hemisphere) was even entirely devoted to the matter at issue.[25] In the period before the Second World War there had even been an attempt to bring about a general treaty for the protection of cultural property: a draft text, drawn up by the International Museums Office, was approved in principle by the Council and the Assembly of the League of Nations in October 1938, and the Netherlands Government was instructed to explore the possibilities for a diplomatic conference that would elaborate a definitive text for a convention. However, nothing came of this as a result of the outbreak of the war in 1939.[26]

While, thus, the Convention of The Hague of 1954 is not a new concept in every respect, it is on the other hand the first comprehensive treaty concerning the protection of cultural property in the event of armed conflict, which is not restricted to a particular region and which provides

---

[24] *Records of the Conference Convened by the United Nations Educational, Scientific and Cultural Organization Held at The Hague from 21 April to 14 May 1954*, published by the Netherlands Government, 1961 (quoted hereafter in this sub-section as *Records*). The Regulations for the execution form an integral part of the Convention; Art. 20. The Protocol bears in particular on the restitution of cultural property, as defined in Art. 1 of the Convention, exported illegally from occupied territory.

[25] The Washington or Roerich Pact, signed by the U.S.A. and a number of Latin American States, was only ratified by a few of these. This limited its scope even further.

[26] Concerning this episode, see *Records*, p. 360 (Historical Note), at p. 362. See also *La protezione del patrimonio storico artistico e culturale nel guerra moderna*, report to the 2nd International Conference of the International Society of Military Law and Law of War, by G. Vedovato; *Recueils de la Société internationale de droit pénal militaire et de droit de la guerre*, Vol. II, 1963, p. 117 ff.

far more effective protection, especially for the most valuable assets of the cultural heritage, than any previous international instrument.[27] Viewed in that light, the 1954 Convention represents an innovation comparable to that brought about by the Civilians Convention of Geneva of 1949.

The Convention of 1954 bears a close resemblance to the Civilians Convention in other respects as well: notably, the provisions regarding the scope and enforcement of the Convention of 1954 are evidently framed on the model of the respective provisions of the Civilians Convention. Thus, the Convention of 1954 is applicable in its entirety in the event of an international armed conflict,[28] while certain fundamental provisions are declared applicable *ipso facto* in the event of an internal armed conflict.[29] Then, a system of supervision has been elaborated in which a dominant part is played by the Protecting Powers as well as by an independent international agency, namely UNESCO.[30] Again, a provision has been included bearing on the punishment of violations of the Convention.[31] Finally, Article 4, paragraph 4 of the Convention expressly provides that the Contracting States "shall refrain from any act directed by way of reprisals against cultural property."

In the context of the present study, prime importance attaches to the last-mentioned provision. It forms part of the general system of protection applicable to all cultural property falling under the Convention, and in

[27] While all cultural property falling under the definition given in Art. 1 of the Convention enjoys a certain, limited degree of protection, Chapter II sets forth a system of special protection (which comes very near to absolute protection) for "a limited number of refuges intended to shelter movable cultural property in the event of armed conflict, of centres containing monuments and other immovable cultural property of very great importance" (Art. 8).

[28] Art. 18 provides that the Convention "shall apply in the event of declared war or any other armed conflict which may arise between two or more of the High Contracting Parties, even if the state of war is not recognized by one or more of them"; it "shall also apply to all cases of partial or total occupation of the territory of a High Contracting Party, even if the said occupation meets with no armed resistance"; finally, provision is made for the case that "one of the Powers in conflict is not a Party" to the Convention, to the effect that the other Powers "remain bound by it in their mutual relations" and shall even be bound by it "in relation to the said Power, if the latter has declared that it accepts the provisions thereof and so long as it applies them".

[29] Art. 19; see *infra*, p. 276.

[30] Arts. 21, 23. The rôle of the Protecting Powers and of UNESCO is elaborated in the Regulations for the execution of the Convention.

[31] Art. 28. This Article merely provides, however, that the States Parties to the Convention "undertake to take, within the framework of their ordinary criminal jurisdiction, all necessary steps to prosecute and impose penal or disciplinary sanctions upon those persons, of whatever nationality, who commit or order to be committed a breach of the present Convention". Evidently this is a less far-reaching undertaking than has been accepted in 1949 with respect to grave breaches of the Red Cross Conventions. On the other hand, the distinction between grave breaches and violations of lesser importance has not been made in the present Convention.

particular of the obligations bearing on respect for such cultural property.[32] The draft text which UNESCO laid before the Conference, already contained the provision that "[c]ultural property shall not by way of reprisals be singled out for attack nor seized".[33] The principle embodied in that text was not challenged by anyone. In fact, in the course of the debates the issue was only touched upon more or less incidentally, when the question was raised whether the proposed prohibition of reprisals was designed to apply to singling out for attack as well as to seizure: while the English text suggested this, the French version was ambiguous.[34] It was replied that both attack and seizure would come under the prohibition; as it was pointed out: "the banning of reprisals arose out of the general obligation to respect", and the proposed paragraph "implied that there could be no deviation from the obligation to respect even in the case of reprisals".[35] The latter statement, it should be noted, was wider and of more fundamental significance than the proposed text.[36]

The representative of Greece then proposed to introduce this more general concept into the text of Article 4. According to this delegate the paragraph in question should read: "The singling out of cultural property by way of reprisals shall be prohibited." In that manner, he said, the banning of reprisals in the cultural field would be absolute, as it was on the human level under the Conventions of Geneva of 1949.[37]

The language finally adopted for Article 4, paragraph 4, is designed to give expression to the general and absolute character of the prohibition.

This general and absolute character is emphasized by a discussion bearing on the related question of whether reciprocity would govern the obligations, laid down in Article 4, paragraph 1, to respect cultural property. That paragraph translates the undertaking of the Contracting States "to respect cultural property situated within their own territory as well as within the territory of other High Contracting Parties" into a double obligation: to refrain from any use of cultural property and its immediate surroundings or of the appliances in use for its protection "for purposes

---

[32] The protection of cultural property is divided into the "safeguarding of and respect for such property" (Art. 2). Safeguarding is primarily the task of States within the territory of which the cultural property is situated (Art. 3), while the principle of respect entails obligations for both parties (Art. 4).

[33] UNESCO draft, Art. 4, para. 3; Document CBS/3, *Records*, p. 374.

[34] Mr. Lazareanu (Rumania); Minutes of the Main Commission, 3rd meeting, nrs. 258, 260; *Records*, p. 139.

[35] Mr. Saba (UNESCO, Secretariat); Minutes of the Main Commission, 3rd meeting, nrs. 259, 261; *Records*, *loc. cit.* n. 34.

[36] It went not so far, however, as the remark made in passing by Mr. Matteucci (Italy), according to whom "theft and reprisals were in any event forbidden under international law"; Minutes of the Main Commission, 4th meeting, nr. 270; *Records*, p. 143.

[37] Mr. Eustathiades (Greece); Minutes of the Main Commission, 6th meeting, nr. 344; *Records*, p. 156.

274

which are likely to expose it to destruction or damage in the event of armed conflict", and to refrain from "any act of hostility directed against such property". The question arose in the course of the debates, whether it would not be necessary to insert a paragraph into Article 4, providing that "if one of the Parties to the conflict violates the obligation laid down in [paragraph 1] and as long as this violation persists, the opposing party shall be released from the obligation to respect the cultural property against which the violation has been committed".[38] This proposed text evidently envisaged the situation where the first-mentioned obligation, not to use cultural property for purposes "likely to expose it to destruction or damage", would be violated by the State within the territory of which the property is situated; and, while it certainly had the effect to permit the destruction or damage of the property in question whenever that could be justified with the argument of military necessity, it even suggested that such destruction or damage would be permissible without any indication of military necessity, as a kind of sanction hardly discernible from reprisals.

At one stage of the debates, the proposed amendment was even adopted by the Main Commission; but at the same time this Commission thought it wise to forward it to the Legal Committee for consideration.[39] In that Committee, no such favourable view was taken of the proposed text. As was reported to the Main Commission: "The majority of the committee had been against the proposal. They had pointed out that paragraph 2 of Article 4 already referred to the possibility of the Parties being freed from their obligation to respect cultural property in the event of imperative military necessity and that it was therefore preferable to make no further provision freeing the Parties from their obligation to respect. That rule would remain applicable except in the case of military necessity, even if the opposing party did not adhere to its undertaking. The minority opinion was that the insertion of the new paragraph was necessary as it would put the Parties on their guard against breaking their engagement." [40] When confronted with this opinion of its Legal Committee, the Main Commission altered its previous vote and rejected the proposed paragraph.[41]

From this episode the conclusion emerges with particular clarity that the obligation to refrain from destroying or damaging cultural property remains, even if the opposing party uses that same property for military purposes, and that it only gives way in the event of imperative military necessity.[42] That ground, expressed in so many words in Article 4, para-

---

[38] Working Group; Document CBS/DR/125; *Records*, p. 376.
[39] Minutes of the Main Commission, 14th meeting, nrs. 1096-1098; *Records*, p. 216.
[40] Report by Mr. Saba (Secretariat) on the work of the Legal Committee; Minutes of the Main Commission, 15th meeting, nr. 1167; *Records*, p. 221.
[41] Minutes of the Main Commission, 15th meeting, nrs. 1168-1169; *Records, loc. cit.* n. 40.
[42] Mr. Saba (Secretariat) even took the precaution to have this interpretation of Art. 4,

graph 2,[43] is indeed the only argument warranting a departure from the otherwise absolute obligation to respect cultural property laid down in the Article.[44] Specifically, no justification for such a departure can be derived from the plea of reprisals, nor from the related argument of reciprocity. In other words, the prohibition of reprisals in this Convention is indeed comprehensive and absolute.

With regard to internal armed conflict, Article 19 provides that "in the event of an armed conflict not of an international character occurring within the territory of one of the High Contracting Parties, each party to the conflict shall be bound to apply, as a minimum, the provisions of the present Convention which relate to respect for cultural property". Does this imply that reprisals against cultural property are prohibited in that event? On the face of it, the answer to this question seems obvious: Article 4 is headed "Respect for cultural property", and this should certainly mean that the provisions which it contains, and with that the prohibition of re-prisals, "relate to respect for cultural property". This would imply that, unlike the Conventions of Geneva of 1949, the Convention of The Hague of 1954 would in this respect be without ambiguity.

However, notwithstanding this apparently unequivocal text, there may be raised some doubt as to the implications of Article 19 for the question at issue. While the UNESCO draft already contained the same reference to "the provisions of the present Convention relating to respect for cultural property" in the Article (then numbered 18) dealing with internal armed conflict, it is arguable that this reference was to Article 2 in the first place: that Article defined the protection of cultural property as consisting, *inter alia*, in "respecting it, by taking appropriate steps on the one hand to avoid the use of the property or the use of its immediate vicinity for purposes which might expose the property to destruction or damage in the event of armed conflict, and, on the other, to spare such property in the course of operations, refraining from any acts of hostility directed against such property". Article 4, on the other hand, then bore a different title ("Obli-gations in respect of cultural property situated within the territory of an-

---

which resulted from the debates, officially recorded; Minutes of the Main Commission, 15th meeting, nr. 1170; *Records*, pp. 221-222.

[43] "The obligations mentioned in paragraph 1 of the present Article may be waived only in cases where military necessity imperatively requires such a waiver."

[44] "Military necessity", and the two specific notions of "imperative military necessity" (Art. 4, para. 2) and "unavoidable military necessity" (Art. 11, para. 2), are key-concepts in the system of protection of cultural property as envisaged in the Convention. Accordingly, an important part of the discussions turned around those concepts, and in particular around the question of whether "military necessity" should be mentioned at all, and around the precise scope of the different notions. See *Records*, Subject Index *sub voce* "military necessity".

other Contracting Party") and only in its first paragraph expressly referred to "respect for cultural property".[45]

On these grounds, and in the absence of indications to the contrary, one might take the view that it was not the intention of the authors of the UNESCO draft that the prohibition of reprisals contained in Article 4, paragraph 4, would be counted among the "provisions relating to respect for cultural property". It could furthermore be contended that this original intention was not modified in the course of the subsequent proceedings, as presumably the possible effect of the shift in emphasis from Article 2 to Article 4 and of the new title for the latter Article was not realized.

Admittedly, the above reasoning is a specimen of a formalistic and consciously restrictive interpretation, in the face of an apparently clear text. However, Governments have often shown a tendency to employ even the most absurdly far-fetched arguments in order to evade unwelcome obligations, and an obligation to refrain from reprisals, even against cultural property situated within their own territory, might be considered an undesirable limitation of their freedom to act in certain situations. It is therefore to be hoped that when such a situation arises the Government in question (or the leaders of the opposing group, for that matter) will allow themselves to be convinced of the untenability of the above reasoning. Two arguments might be adduced to that end: the systematic argument that in the Convention of 1954 the titles of the Articles form part of the definitive text, and the basic argument that "the banning of reprisals arises out of the general obligation to respect".[46]

6.2.3. *The Draft Rules of the International Committee of the Red Cross*

Generally speaking, the Geneva Conventions of 1949 are designed to protect certain well-defined categories of persons in the hands of the enemy against arbitrary action on the part of the latter. The most notable exception to this general rule is Part II of the Fourth or Civilians Convention, as is indicated by its heading: "General Protection of Populations against Certain Consequences of War". According to its opening Article (13) the provisions of this Part "cover the whole of the populations of the countries in conflict, without any adverse distinction based, in particular, on race, nationality, religion or political opinions". However, the scope of this Part is limited in another respect: far from providing the populations with an adequate, general protection against the manifold dangers arising from modern warfare, it merely deals with such matters as, on the one hand, the facultative establishment of various kinds of safety zones in the territories of belligerents, and, on the other hand, the protection of special categories

[45] *Records*, pp. 373-374.
[46] *Supra*, text at n. 35 to this §.

of persons who can be assumed to take no active part in the fighting (children, women, old people, the wounded and the sick).

This is to say that after 1949, for want of any more recent legal instrument governing the matter, the general protection of the civil population against the adverse chances of the war continued to be governed by the relevant rules of the Hague Regulations on Land Warfare of 1899/1907 and the Hague Convention respecting Bombardments by Naval Forces in Time of War, of 1907, and, as these provisions were too dated to bear literal application, by the principles underlying these. However, in particular in the light of the experiences of the Second World War there could be no doubt left that these principles were far from providing clear-cut solutions for the problems involved.[47] Therefore, there was an urgent need for an authoritative elaboration of the principles, adapted to the particularities of modern warfare.

The ICRC, which from an early stage had been aware of the existing lacuna in this field of the law of war, never made a secret of its concern in this respect[48] and of its intention to contribute actively to any efforts at filling the gap. At the same time it realized that in this field the endeavours of a private organization like the ICRC could be no more than preparatory and that it would ultimately depend on the Governments whether the results would ever be converted into binding rules of law. Neither did the ICRC shut its eyes to the fact that the elaboration of rules protecting the civil population against the dangers inherent in the conduct of belligerent operations would amount to laying down rules for warfare proper; and, while the ICRC had always concerned itself with the issue of the protection of the civil population, it had so far refrained from taking the initiative in attempting to codify that part of the law of war which traditionally is referred to as "the law of The Hague", or law of combat.

With these considerations in mind, the ICRC set to work and in 1955 produced a set of "Draft Rules for the Protection of the Civilian Population from the Dangers of Indiscriminate Warfare".[49] The Draft Rules were based on the same principles as had been at the root of the Conventions of 1899 and 1907; a relationship with the past which, while evident from the

[47] Chapter V, § 5.1.1.
[48] Already at an early date after the Diplomatic Conference of 1949 the ICRC expressed its concern at the fate of the civil population in the event of war, in particular in the light of recent armaments developments: in an appeal addressed on 5 April 1950 to the Governments Parties to the Geneva Conventions, it urged them to arrive at an agreement concerning the prohibition of nuclear weapons, and of blind weapons in general. The appeal is reprinted in *Reaffirmation and Development of the Laws and Customs Applicable in Armed Conflicts*, report submitted by the ICRC to the XXIst International Conference of the Red Cross, May 1969, p. 036.
[49] Published as a separate document by the ICRC in June 1955; it consists of an introduction, text, and commentary.

278

text of the five "general principles" which together constituted part I of the draft, was expressed in so many words in the fifth principle.[50] Certain features of modern warfare were, however, alluded to even in this part,[51] and the present prevailed entirely in part II ("Rules of application") where an attempt was made to elaborate adequate solutions for the problems raised by such matters as long-distance bombing, target area bombing, terror bombing, use of nuclear weapons.

For present purposes, particular importance attaches to the final (6th) section of part II, entitled "Execution of the rules". In this section, provision was made for the function of Protecting Powers (Article 14); reciprocity was excluded as a ground for the non-observance of the rules (Article 15); and the principle was expressed that punishment of violations of the rules would follow the lines etablished in the Geneva Conventions of 1949 (Article 16). While this enumeration already shows the care displayed by the authors to provide ways and means for the effective implementation of the rules and thus to take away or in any event diminish the urge to resort to reprisals, the close attention which they had given to the issue of reprisals is manifest from the text of the draft Article 15, reading as follows:

> "Infringements of the present rules shall not dispense the injured Party from his obligation to respect the said rules.
> "Nevertheless, in case of violations which, by their repetition or magnitude, constitute a serious danger for the Party to the conflict who suffers them, the latter shall be bound, should it deem it necessary to resort to the same methods of war, to address, before so doing, an appeal to the Authorities of the adverse Party, inviting them to put an end to such violations. It shall at the same time offer them an opportunity of having the justice of its allegations established by the Protecting Powers concerned.
> "The Protecting Powers concerned, or possibly other neutral States, shall, by offering their good offices to the Parties to the conflict, endeavour to prevent either of such Parties resorting to measures contrary to the present rules."

Evidently this proposed text did not amount to an absolute prohibition of reprisals: it merely attempted to create a procedure by which a contemplated recourse to reprisals would be postponed and its execution perhaps even averted. Equally evidently, the question could be raised whether an absolute prohibition might not be preferable. The ICRC set out its answer

---

[50] "These principles ... have long been proclaimed by public opinion and recognized in international law."
[51] Principle IV reads: "The use of weapons, which, when directed against the enemy armed forces, would, by their nature or effect, cause considerable losses among the civilian population, is therefore excluded."

279

to this question and at the same time the motivation of its choice in the form of another question: [52]

> "Il y a là, évidemment, une question extrêmement importante pour la Croix-Rouge dans les propositions qu'elle va soumettre. Doit-elle s'en tenir à la prohibition générale des représailles inaugurée dans les Conventions de Genève, mais qui peut risquer de rester inopérante, du fait que les Règles du 'Projet' ont des répercussions sur la conduite des hostilités beaucoup plus étendues que n'en ont les Conventions de Genève; ou doit-elle, au contraire, considérant la possibilité de représailles comme une faculté que les Gouvernments veulent se réserver inévitablement dans un tel domaine, essayer tout au moins de les réduire le plus possible ou d'en éviter même la survenance?"

Among the experts which the ICRC consulted in 1956 with a view to the preparation of a second version of the draft rules,[53] these questions initially met with a variety of answers. Some of them disapproved the solution proposed in Article 15, both on grounds of principle [54] and because they deemed it impracticable, as the actual conditions of modern warfare would leave no time for a procedure as envisaged in the Article. Other experts were of the opinion that as reprisals must be recognized as a reality, some sort of solution ought to be found for the problem posed by their occurrence. In that context, the idea was discussed of laying down an express requirement of proportionality. This the experts rejected in the end as impracticable, in view of the difficulty of assessing the relative proportion of concrete instances of belligerent acts.

At this juncture in the discussions, one of the experts returned to the idea underlying the text proposed by the ICRC, which he would regret to see completely abandoned; he admitted, on the other hand, that any formulation given it would have to avoid conveying the impression of a legitimation of reprisals. This view received the support of a military member of the group. To his mind, a distinction ought to be made between the opening phase of hostilities in a modern war, and the later stages of the

---

[52] *Protection juridique des populations civiles—Groupe de travail consultatif composé d'experts délégués par des Sociétés nationales de la Croix-Rouge (Genève, 14/19 mai 1956): Documentation préliminaire,* pp. 24, 25.

[53] *Protection juridique des populations civiles—Groupe de travail consultatif composé d'experts délégués par des Sociétés nationales de la Croix-Rouge (Genève, 14/19 mai 1956): Compte rendu analytique,* pp. 54-56.

[54] "L'un d'eux insiste sur les raisons de principe qui l'amènent à rejeter cette disposition: alors que l'al. 1 pose l'interdiction des représailles, l'al. 2, paraît laisser la possibilité d'y recourir, ce qui n'est guère logique; en outre dans l'état d'imperfection du droit international, il y a malheureusement certains points dont il est préférable de ne pas parler dans un texte juridique, et c'est précisément le cas pour les représailles" (p. 54). This manner of looking at the matter (or, rather, of avoiding to look at it) is reminiscent of the view expressed already in 1874 by the Belgian delegate, Baron Lambermont, at the Brussels Conference; *supra,* p. 48.

war. In the first phase, the rapid succession of retaliatory actions on both sides would leave no room for a procedure as envisaged in Article 15. In the second stage, however, "on peut avoir affaire à une guerre de longue durée et dans laquelle l'efficacité relative des attaques de terrorisation est prise dûment en considération, car alors les belligérants ne peuvent plus se permettre de disperser leurs forces; dans cette dernière situation, la possibilité d'instituer un frein aux représailles est plus grande." [55]

This idea ultimately prevailed in the group of experts, and their majority endorsed the suggestion to retain in any event the third paragraph of Article 15, which then could probably be combined with Article 14.

In the second version of the Draft Rules,[56] which the ICRC published in 1956 as a preparatory document for the XIXth International Red Cross Conference to be held at New Delhi in 1957, the majority opinion of the experts had been followed and the original Articles 14 and 15 were drastically reduced to a single Article (18), the text of which read as follows: [57]

"States not involved in the conflict, and also all appropriate organisations, are invited to co-operate, by lending their good offices, in ensuring the observance of the present rules and preventing either of the Parties to the conflict from resorting to measures contrary to those rules."

In a commentary to the proposed Article 18,[58] the ICRC pointed out that two elements should be distinguished in it: the issue of supervision, and that of violations of the rules. As regarded the first issue, the most notable change was the omission of all reference to Protecting Powers: to charge those Powers with the supervision of the rules would be tantamount to charging them with a task fundamentally different from their traditional functions and which in practice would amount to supervision of the conduct of warfare. The ICRC had therefore preferred to repeat the principle, expressed in the common Article 1 of the Geneva Conventions of 1949, that the contracting States would not merely be obliged themselves to apply the norms, but would also be expected to exert their influence to obtain their universal application. Also "qualified bodies" were invited to contribute their good offices to that end.[59]

---

[55] Op. cit. n. 53, p. 55.
[56] Draft Rules for the Limitation of the Dangers Incurred by the Civilian Population in Time of War, 1956; a second edition of this version was published in 1958; the references are to the 1958 edition.
[57] Ibid., p. 15.
[58] Ibid., pp. 127-134.
[59] In this context, the ICRC broached the question of whether it would itself be such a "qualified body". It observed that in this field of the law of war ("battlefield law") its possibilities would be distinctly less than in the domain of the Conventions of Geneva. On the other hand, if no other body would be in a position to intervene and

As for the question of reactions to violations of the rules, the ICRC, recalling its original, much more elaborate proposal to put a rein on reprisals, explained once again that this had in the first place been designed "to emphasise that it is essential, even after an infringement, for both sides to continue to observe the rules necessary for the safety of the civilian populations as far as they possibly can, and for the Parties not to take justice in their own hands at every turn".[60] Another element in the proposed text had been "the need for appropriate notice being given in case one or other of the Parties might deem it indispensable to take reprisals".[61] While the experts had qualified the latter idea as impracticable in many situations, they had retained the former element and it was this fundamental concept which now found expression in the second half of Article 18. The commentary added that precisely an impartial "qualified body" as envisaged in the Article would be in a good position "to try to prevent infringements by either of the Parties giving rise to similar measures by the adverse party, for such a development would end up by jeopardising the whole application of the present rules".[62]

In a final paragraph, the ICRC once again explained its stand in the matter of reprisals: "The Red Cross is obliged to be realistic and, in that spirit, it could not fail to study the problem of reprisals in preparing the present set of rules. But the only principle which it would like to see unanimously recognised is that of the observance of the present rules in all circumstances as expressing the dictates of humanity." [63] Accordingly, it was certainly not the intention of the ICRC to legitimize reprisals as a legal institution: on the contrary, as is evident from the quoted words, its avowed long-range objective was to achieve their absolute prohibition, even in this particular field of "battlefield law".

The further proceedings with respect to the Draft Rules had not so much the character of a detailed discussion of the merits of the various rules proposed, as of a general debate on the principles involved. This was evident in the XIXth International Conference of the Red Cross, held at New Delhi in 1957, where the debates in the Commission on International Humanitarian Law were conducted on the basis of a draft resolution proposed by the ICRC and couched in very general terms: it confirmed that the elaboration of rules limiting the risks run by the civil population in the event of war was a highly desirable goal, and that the objectives of the

---

notably in the event of armed conflicts not of an international character, the ICRC would not hesitate to consider any initiative that might contribute to the application of the rules under discussion.

[60] *Ibid.*, p. 131.
[61] *Loc. cit.* n. 60.
[62] *Ibid.*, p. 132.
[63] *Loc. cit.* n. 63.

Draft Rules were in conformity with the aspirations of the Red Cross and the requirements of humanity; for the rest, it invited the ICRC to continue its efforts in the matter.[64]

Notwithstanding this general and non-binding character of the debates at New Delhi, several delegates entered into the merits of particular rules. One among them criticized the proposed text of Article 18 as grammatically incorrect and incomprehensible, and he even took the trouble to introduce an amended version designed to make the dual purpose of the Article more explicit. However, as no votes were taken on individual Articles or amendments, this criticism and the proposed amendment were simply reported in the records of the debates.[65]

By that time, the ICRC had lost all hope that the States could in the near future be induced to agree to a detailed set of rules elaborating the idea of protecting the civil population against the evils of war. Accordingly, instead of pursuing its efforts towards the perfection of the Draft Rules, the ICRC in 1961 started consultations with outstanding personalities in various countries, with a view to obtaining their opinions both on the possibility of "limiting the evils of war" and on certain more specific questions relating to the protection of the civil population.[66] The answers which the ICRC obtained [67] were practically unanimous in confirming that acceptance by the States of precise and detailed rules for the protection of the civil populations was for the time being out of the question. At the same time, it became apparent that the majority of the personalities consulted saw some value in a declaration reaffirming and setting out a number of essential principles bearing on the position of the civil population.

[64] See: *XIXe Conférence internationale de la Croix-Rouge, La Nouvelle-Delhi, octobre-novembre 1957: Actes concernant le Projet de Règles limitant les risques courus par la population civile en temps de guerre*, published by the ICRC in 1958, at p. 131; the text of the resolution in its final version (which deviates only in some insignificant details from the text originally proposed) is at p. 151.

[65] This delegate, General J. D. Schepers, of the Netherlands Red Cross, proposed the following text (*ibid.*, p. 73): "Un ou plusieurs Etats non impliqués dans le conflit, ainsi qu'un ou plusieurs organismes qualifiés peuvent, par leur propre initiative ou sur la demande d'une des Parties au conflit: (a) soit attirer l'attention d'une des Parties au conflit sur une infraction aux présentes règles commise par cette Partie; (b) soit faire leur possible pour qu'une Partie au conflit ne recoure pas à des mesures non compatibles avec les présentes règles. L'exercice de ce droit ne peut jamais être considéré par l'une ou l'autre des Parties au conflit comme un acte peu amical."

[66] See: *Centenary Congress of the International Red Cross, Geneva, August 28-September 10, 1963: Council of Delegates: Legal Protection of Civil Populations Against the Dangers of Indiscriminate Warfare; Report presented by the International Committee of the Red Cross*, Geneva, June 1963.

[67] See: *XXth International Conference of the Red Cross, Vienna, October 1965: The Legal Protection of Civilian Populations Against the Dangers of Indiscriminate Warfare; Report submitted by the International Committee of the Red Cross*, Geneva, March 1965.

283

While the details of the questions put by the ICRC and the answers received need not be gone into here, it is worth mentioning that, according to the report drawn up by the ICRC, "the personalities consulted informed the ICRC of the manner in which the major Powers envisaged the fate of the civilian population in the event of war", and that they "noted that the problem of reprisals, given the power of destructive weapons, is of capital importance and that it is the object of no precise conventional ruling".[68] In that context one of the personalities suggested "that the declaration should also treat the question of the proportionality to be observed in the event of reprisals".[69]

Having received these answers, the ICRC entirely abandoned the idea to perfect further the Draft Rules with a view to their subsequent conversion into a convention, and instead proceeded to draft the text of a declaration embodying the fundamental principles governing the position of the civil population in the event of war. A first result of this new approach was the adoption by the XXth International Conference of the Red Cross, held at Vienna in 1965, of Resolution XXVIII [70] which solemnly declared that all governmental and other authorities bearing responsibility for the conduct of hostilities in the event of armed conflict should as a minimum observe the following principles: [71]

> "(a) that the right of the parties to a conflict to adopt means of injuring the enemy is not unlimited;
>
> (b) that it is prohibited to launch attacks against the civilian populations as such;
>
> (c) that distinction must be made at all times between persons taking part in the hostilities and members of the civilian population to the effect that the latter be spared as much as possible;
>
> (d) that the general principles of the law of war apply to nuclear and similar weapons."

As the next step, the ICRC brought the matter to the United Nations, where the General Assembly in its twenty-third session unanimously voted Resolution 2444 containing substantially the same text (omitting only principle d), and in so doing affirmed the continued validity of the

---

[68] *Ibid.*, p. 6.
[69] *Loc. cit.* n. 68.
[70] The text of the resolution has been reprinted in *Reaffirmation and Development, op. cit.* n. 48, p. 034.
[71] The ICRC in a memorandum dated 19 May 1967 brought the text of the resolution, together with a survey of existing rules of international law respecting the protection of the civil population against the dangers of indiscriminate warfare, to the attention of the Governments of the States Parties to the Conventions of Geneva of 1949 and the Hague Convention on Land Warfare of 1907. The text of the memorandum, published in *IRRC*, Vol. VII, 1967, p. 302, has been reprinted in *Reaffirmation and Development, op. cit.* n. 48, p. 049.

principles in question.[72] In the same Resolution, the General Assembly invited the Secretary-General to study, in consultation with the ICRC and other appropriate international organizations, both steps that might lead to a better application of existing humanitarian law in all armed conflicts, and the need for additional legal instruments; this amounted to an acknowledgment on the part of the General Assembly that much remained to be done in this field and that the principles set out in its Resolution 2444 (XXIII) were in themselves insufficient to guarantee the civil population adequate protection in the event of armed conflict. In particular, the point deserves some emphasis that neither the Resolution nor the discussions preceding its adoption had so much as touched upon the issue of reprisals.

While, therefore, the result obtained so far could not be characterized as anything but a first step on the road towards the realization of the goal which the ICRC had set, it was a very important step nevertheless, as it amounted to the authoritative reaffirmation of the fundamental principles underlying the conduct of hostilities in any armed conflict.

The ICRC was not long in taking up the matter again. Subsequent to a meeting of experts, held at Geneva in February 1969, it issued in May of that year a report entitled "Reaffirmation and Development of the Laws and Customs Applicable in Armed Conflicts".[73] In the report, submitted to the XXIst International Conference of the Red Cross (Istanbul, September 1969), the ICRC gave a detailed exposé of the present state of the law of war and of the fields where its development was most urgently needed.

While the report constitutes a most valuable contribution to the develop-

---

[72] Res. 2444 (XXIII), adopted on 19 December 1968 on the report of the Third Committee (A/7433). The omission of the principle bearing on nuclear and similar weapons was due to an amendment introduced by the Soviet Union, based on the argument that the principle was not in conformity with earlier United Nations decisions regarding the prohibition of the use of nuclear weapons. While this argument was not accepted by all representatives, it was agreed that no specific reference to the principle should be made in the resolution. The representative of Sweden, who on behalf of the co-sponsors of the resolution accepted the Soviet amendment, did so on the understanding that the remaining principles were applicable to all armed conflicts regardless of their nature or of the kinds of arms used—another manner of stating the contested principle! See: Report of the Third Committee (A/7433), paras. 52-54.

The issue of the fate of the civil populations (and other threatened categories) had earlier been the subject of a Resolution (XXIII) adopted by the International Conference on Human Rights, held at Teheran from 22 April-13 May 1968. In the operative part of the Resolution, the General Assembly was requested to invite the Secretary-General to study the issues mentioned in the text above. See: Final Act of the Conference (A/CONF.32/41). For the introduction of the proposed resolution in the Second Committee and the (very summary) debate devoted to it, see: A/CONF. 32/C.2/SR.13; adoption by the Plenary Meeting of the Conference: A/CONF.32/ SR.25.

[73] See reference in n. 48, *supra*.

ment of the law of war in its entirety, it may for present purposes suffice to put on record that reprisals were among the questions declared urgent.[74] The ICRC, while premising that it "[could] not but hope to see the complete prohibition of reprisals", had put the question to the experts whether this was a practicable solution. As an alternative, it had mentioned the possibility of setting certain limits to the exercise of reprisals, "in order to reduce their tragic consequences": (a) obligation to offer an opportunity for impartial inquiry prior to resorting to reprisals; (b) proportionality; (c) selection of the reprisal from the same field of law as that of the violation, and (d) respect for the laws of humanity.[75]

The experts, according to the report, had "demonstrated two trends of opinion: Some felt that from the point of view adopted by the meeting—viewing the norms formulated in the fields previously examined as rules designed to protect fundamental human rights—it was no longer possible to authorize resort to reprisals." Hence, these experts stressed, all efforts "should be aimed at the development of procedures and bodies which would enable supervision and ensurance of the application of the proposed rules", if necessary by "the punishment of the culprits". "Other experts, on the contrary, considered that the international community had not yet reached a stage of development where the functioning of the supervisory bodies in question could be guaranteed under all circumstances." The conclusion of those experts was that "[i]n these conditions, total prohibition of reprisals would not only be shutting the eyes to reality but would perhaps have contrary effects".[76]

Notwithstanding this fundamental difference in approach, the experts were "unanimous in considering that efforts should be made to restrain the exercise of reprisals to the largest possible extent". "In this spirit, the experts approved the principle of proportionality... They were more reserved as to... the possibility of limiting reprisals to the same field of law where the violation has been committed. Reprisals can, of course, in no case be exercised in the fields covered by the Geneva Conventions and against the persons protected by these. The principle in (a) was approved, while doubting it would always be possible to apply." [77]

While the ICRC could "only fall into line with the experts who would like to see reprisals totally prohibited, in favour of developing procedures for the investigation of violations", it concluded from their deliberations that "so long as belligerents consider it necessary to resort to reprisals in certain cases" the most promising policy would be to make "efforts... to reduce their harmful effects. To this end, the limits examined earlier, in

[74] Part II, Chapter III, under D, 2; pp. 83 ff.
[75] Ibid., pp. 84, 85.
[76] Ibid., pp. 85-86.
[77] Ibid., pp. 86-87.

286

particular that of proportionality, should be applied." [78] Thus, the sense of reality characteristic of the ICRC had once again forced it to acknowledge that the state of imperfection, not only of the law of war, but of the international community, stood in the way of making the total prohibition of belligerent reprisals anything but a long-range goal.

6.2.4. *The Draft Code of Offences Against the Peace and Security of Mankind*

This section can appropriately be concluded with some few words about a so far abortive attempt at codification in a matter closely related to reprisals, to wit, individual responsibility for, and punishment of, war crimes. While the special provisions on this issue, contained in the Geneva Conventions of 1949 and the Convention of The Hague of 1954,[79] are limited to the subject-matter dealt with in those Conventions, a more general approach is found in the Charter of London of 1945.[80] There, one finds a definition of "war crimes" as well as a list of principles for the punishment of individual perpetrators of such crimes. The applicability of the Charter is however limited in another respect: its provisions apply only to individual war criminals of the Axis Powers, as the former enemies of the Allied Powers in the Second World War. Therefore, there was room for the creation of another instrument, be it convention, resolution or declaration, incorporating these principles and which would not be so restricted.

The General Assembly of the United Nations took up the matter in its first session; at the time, it confined itself to affirming "the principles of international law recognized by the Charter of the Nürnberg Tribunal and the judgment of the Tribunal".[81] In its second session it arrived at the conclusion that a further elaboration of the principles was necessary, and it entrusted this task to the International Law Commission.[82] However, the text of the Resolution in question is not free from a certain ambiguity: while its main element seems to consist in the request to re-draft the principles recognized in the Charter of London, it contained the further request to incorporate the principles into a wider code of offences against the peace and security of mankind. This ambiguity (which, for that matter, had

---

[78] *Ibid.*, p. 87.
[79] *Supra*, §§ 6.2.1 and 6.2.2.
[80] See n. 4 to this §.
[81] Res. 95 (I), adopted on 11 December 1946.
[82] Res. 177 (II), adopted on 21 December 1947. In this Resolution, the General Assembly decided "to entrust the formulation of the principles of international law recognized in the Charter of the Nürnberg Tribunal and in the judgment of the Tribunal to the International Law Commission", and it directed the Commission to formulate those principles and to "prepare a draft code of offences against the peace and security of mankind, indicating clearly the place to be accorded" to the said principles.

been at the root of the Charter of London) would in the end prove an insurmountable obstacle in that it amounted to the intermingling of two entirely different issues: individual responsibility for, and punishment of, "crimes against the peace"—*i.e.*, violations of norms of the *ius ad bellum* —and of "war crimes"—*i.e.*, violations of norms of the *ius in bello*. As was apparent from the language of the request, the authors had given primary attention to the "crimes against the peace". On the other hand, the *ius ad bellum* was precisely the subject-matter where speedy agreement among the Powers was least to be expected: while those Powers might perhaps agree on the abstract principle of the prohibition of aggression and of individual responsibility for and punishment of acts of aggression, it would be quite a different matter for them to reach agreement on anything like a concrete, directly applicable definition of aggression.

The dealings of the International Law Commission with the question were short-lived: in 1950 it produced a text stating the principles recognized in the aforementioned documents,[83] and in 1951 and 1954 it submitted reports concerning the elaboration of a draft code of offences against the peace and security of mankind (embodying the principles of individual responsibility and liability to punishment).[84]

The General Assembly, for its part, never really came to grips with the matter treated in the draft code: on the ground that it was closely related to the question of defining aggression, the Assembly time and again, lastly in 1957, deferred discussion of the draft code until such time as the latter question be clarified—a stage which so far has not been reached.[85]

---

[83] See: *Formulation of Nürnberg Principles*, report by J. Spiropoulos, Special Rapporteur, Doc. A/CN.4/22, in: Yearbook of the International Law Commission, 1950, Vol. II, p. 181, at p. 195. The General Assembly subsequently invited the Governments of Member States to furnish their observations; Res. 488 (V) of 12 December 1950. No further action was taken in the matter.

[84] Yearbooks of the International Law Commission, 1951, Vol. II, p. 43, and 1954, Vol. II, p. 112. In its 1951 report, the International Law Commission disposed of the entire problem of the codification of the law concerning war crimes *stricto sensu* in a single sentence, when after the opening words of Article I of the draft code ("The following acts are offences against the peace and security of mankind. They are crimes under international law for which the responsible individuals shall be punishable.") it mentioned under (10): "Acts committed in violation of the laws or customs of war". In a commentary the Commission put on record that these crimes in reality did not affect the peace and security of mankind, and that the decision to include them in the draft code at all had only been taken on the ground that they figured among the crimes enumerated in the Charter of London. On the other hand, the Commission had decided not to lay down in the code an exhaustive enumeration of all war crimes and merely to include the aforementioned general definition, as that seemed the only practicable way; 1951, Vol. II, at pp. 58, 59.

[85] Yearbooks of the United Nations, 1954, p. 408; 1956, p. 385; 1957, p. 375. Obviously, the real disagreement among the Member States does not so much have a bearing on the technical-juridical problem of finding a definition of aggression, as on fundamental issues concerning their international relations.

Thus, as even the final version of the "Nuremberg principles", as formulated by the International Law Commission in 1950, is a long way from providing a comprehensive code for the individual punishment of war crimes in (or subsequent to) future wars, the fact should be acknowledged that for the time being the codification of the law with respect to this alternative to belligerent reprisals, has proved an unattainable goal.

6.3. BELLIGERENT REPRISALS IN CONTEMPORARY INTERNATIONAL PRACTICE

While in the preceding section the focus was on the extent to which post-war attempts at codification in the field of the law of war have influenced the power of belligerents to take belligerent reprisals, the question to be examined in the present section is whether the practice of belligerents in the period after the Second World War shows any instances of real or alleged belligerent reprisals.

It may be noted at the outset that there has been a frequent use of the term "reprisals" in connection with international incidents involving the use of armed force. In many instances, however, these references fall outside the scope of the present study, either because they had a bearing on situations where no armed conflict was going on, or because they did not concern actions constituting a *prima facie* violation of the law of war. This may be elucidated with the aid of a few examples.

6.3.1. *Armed non-belligerent reprisals*

The first example is taken from the Vietnamese war and specifically from the period when the United States had become involved in it. In the afternoon of 7 February 1965, elements of the United States and South Vietnamese air forces started "reprisal bombardments" on certain objectives situated within the territory of North Vietnam, in response to attacks on air strips and other military installations in use by the United States armed forces in South Vietnam. These attacks had been carried out by Vietcong forces, but, according to the American authorities, upon the orders and under the responsibility of North Vietnam.[1] Similar attacks, again followed by further reprisal bombardments, were carried out on subsequent days, the last reprisal bombardment taking place on 11 February.[2]

Prior to the bombardment of 7 February 1965, the United States armed forces had carried out no significant armed actions against the territory of

---

[1] Department of State Bulletin, Vol. LII, 1965, p. 238.
[2] When the bombing of North Vietnamese territory was resumed in March 1965, the actions were no longer referred to as reprisals.

North Vietnam.[3] The situation as it existed at the time can be explained in two ways: it can be maintained, either, that there was no armed conflict going on between the United States of America and North Vietnam, or that those parties had by that time already become involved in an armed conflict. On the first assumption, the bombing actions would constitute instances of at first sight prohibited use of armed force in a situation of peace, and the actions might or might not be justified as armed reprisals. In fact, the American actions would then come very near to the classical concept of reprisals as measures short of war, that is, actions whereby the actor brings pressure to bear on his opponent while at the same time indicating that it is not his intention to start a war—unless, of course, the opponent would force him so to do. Viewed thus, the fact that the early bombardments of objectives within North Vietnamese territory were characterized as reprisals would from a political point of view have had a definite function in the process of coercion in which the American and North Vietnamese authorities were involved, namely to make it clear to the latter that the American position would escalate to a higher level of coercion, including the use of armed force against North Vietnam, unless the North Vietnamese would make the escalation unnecessary by modifying their policy with respect to the war in South Vietnam.

On the assumption, on the other hand, that an armed conflict was already going on at the time between the parties indicated, the American bombing actions would not in themselves have infringed the law of war. The use of the term "reprisals" would in that supposition have been wholly figurative, indicating that a certain type of belligerent actions which were within the powers of the Americans as belligerents but from which they had so far refrained, would henceforth be included in the conduct of the war, unless, again, the North Vietnamese authorities would modify certain aspects of their conduct of the war.

Thus, in either supposition the real function of the characterization of the actions as reprisals would have been to indicate an impending change in the level of coercion. International law, and in particular the norms bearing on the use of force by States, would have entered into the picture in the first supposition, while no norms of international law would have been so involved in the second view. In any event, in neither supposition could the retaliatory bombardments be regarded as belligerent reprisals, in the sense of actions designed to operate as sanctions of the law of war.

An incidental observation, which, however, may throw some further light on the use of the term "reprisals" by international actors, concerns

[3] The sole exception admitted by the U.S. authorities consists in the actions against North Vietnamese motortorpedoboat bases carried out on the night of 5 August 1964, following the alleged second attack on American warships in the Gulf of Tonkin, which according to the Americans had been carried out on 4 August. See: Department of State Bulletin, Vol. LI, 1964, p. 258.

the different characterization of the American actions by the various American authorities expressing themselves on the issue. The White House in a statement issued on 7 February 1965 duly characterized the bombing actions as reprisals; likewise, Mr. McNamara, Secretary of Defense, in a statement delivered in a press conference held on that day, referred to "retaliatory action".[4] On the other hand, the U.S. representative to the United Nations in a letter of the same date to the President of the Security Council described the action as "prompt defensive action".[5] This difference in approach can best be explained by assuming that different functions were assigned to the various statements: while the White House and Mc-Namara statements (besides being destined for public opinion) were addressed directly to the North Vietnamese authorities, to act as explanatory notes accompanying the bombing actions and emphasizing their purpose of coercion, the communication to the Security Council was a clear attempt to depict the actions as being in accordance with the terms of the United Nations Charter. For, while Article 51 of the Charter recognizes the right of individual or collective self-defence, a recourse to armed reprisals is not so easily reconciled with the provisions of the Charter.[6]

It cannot surprise that the representative of the Union of Socialist Soviet Republics, replying to the American contentions in a letter addressed some days later to the President of the Security Council, denied that the bombardments could be characterized as instances of legitimate self-defence; in his view, the actions amounted to sheer acts of aggression.[7] Irrespective of the merits or demerits of the various positions taken in the exchange of views concerning the actions at issue,[8] the point should be emphasized that nowhere in these discussions was any reference made to their alleged character as reprisals.

Similar considerations apply to the air attack which the British air force

[4] Department of State Bulletin, Vol. LII, 1965, p. 238.
[5] The letter is reproduced in Department of State Bulletin, loc. cit. n. 4.
[6] Cf. J.-C. Venezia, "La notion de représailles en droit international public", in RGDIP, Vol. 64, 1960, p. 465, at p. 466: "Il est exact en effet que les Etats ont à l'heure actuelle accoutumé de ne plus recourir aussi fréquemment que par le passé au vocable de représailles pour justifier certains de leurs comportements. Mais il reste précisément à savoir s'il ne s'agit point là d'un artifice verbal motivé soit par le souci de ne point heurter une opinion publique internationale sensibilisée par la violation au cours du second conflit mondial et sous le couvert des représailles des règles d'humanité les plus communément reçues, soit par un réflexe de prudence élémentaire qui leur commanderait de ne point se mettre en infraction ouverte avec certaines dispositions de la Charte des Nations Unies qui selon d'aucuns prohiberait les représailles."—It would seem that while the concern mentioned in the first place has gradually disappeared (as is evidenced by State practice), the last-mentioned discretion is evident in the instance dealt with in the text above.
[7] Letter dated 9 February 1965, S/6178.
[8] Also other delegations took a part in this exchange of letters; see: S/6185, S/6187, S/6190, S/6201, S/6203, S/6204, S/6206, S/6211, S/6224.

carried out on 28 March 1964 on Harib Fortress, close to the village of that name on the Yemen side of the frontier with Beihan, one of the States of the South Arabian Federation. According to a statement issued after the attack by a spokesman of the British High Commissioner in Aden, this was in retaliation for earlier attacks by Yemenite forces on Beihan.[9] In this instance there was no question of an armed conflict between Great Britain, as the Protecting Power of the Federation, and Yemen; nor, for that matter, did an armed conflict subsequently arise between these parties. Therefore, the contention that the action constituted a reprisal could only be understood in the light of the classical concept of armed reprisals as coercive measures short of war.

As in the previous case, the characterization of the action as a reprisal was not adopted by other parties in the debate, nor was it maintained by the British when the incident was discussed in the Security Council. On that occasion, the British representative qualified the action as a "defensive response".[10] The representative of Yemen (like the representatives of the U.S.S.R. and of various other States) rejected this qualification and asserted that the action constituted "a flagrant act of aggression".[11] This position, it should be added, corresponded with the attitude taken immediately after the attack by the Council of the Arab League.[12]

As a third and last example of this category of non-belligerent reprisals, mention may be made of one of the many incidents which have accompanied the conflict going on in the Middle East between Israel and its Arab neighbours ever since Israel was constituted as an independent State on 14 May 1948. The incident considered here is the reprisal attack which Israeli armour, aircraft and infantry carried out on 13 November 1966 against the village of As Samu, in Jordan. The attack was launched in retaliation for minelaying activities on the territory of Israel, carried out by units of the Arab guerrilla organization Al Fatah operating from Jordanian territory.[13]

At the time, the relationship between the two countries was governed by the armistice agreement signed at Rhodes on 3 April 1949;[14] though often violated, this had never been denounced by either of the parties. The Israeli authorities therefore regarded the activities of Al Fatah as a violation of the armistice on the part of Jordan as the responsible territorial State. On the other hand, the reprisal attack was itself a *prima facie* violation of

[9] The Times, 30 March 1964.
[10] Security Council Official Records, 1106th meeting (2 April 1964), para. 51.
[11] *Ibid.*, para. 16.
[12] The Times, 31 March 1964.
[13] See, *e.g., Israel and the Arab World: The Crisis of 1967*, Adelphi Paper Nr. 41, October 1967, at p. 13.
[14] U.N.T.S., Vol. 42, 1949, p. 303.

the same armistice. Accordingly, the question could arise whether in this instance the retaliatory action should be considered a belligerent reprisal, in the sense of a measure taken in the context of a war and designed to enforce the law of war: for armistice as an institution belongs in the sphere of war rather than peace.

However, while this may be true in principle, it is on the other hand equally evident that the main obligation resulting from an armistice agreement, and the one which was precisely at issue in the present instance, is the obligation to refrain from the use of armed force against the adversary; an obligation, moreover, which especially in case of an indefinite armistice like that between Israel and Jordan coincides with the Charter prohibition of the use of armed force.[15] In this light, the reprisal attack of 3 November 1966 should, like the earlier examples, be characterized as a coercive measure "short of war", this term being used here in the sense of a measure designed forcibly to remind the adversary of his obligation to observe the armistice agreement, while at the same time indicating that it was not the immediate intention of the Israeli Government to reopen the hostilities.

In the Security Council, the views expressed by the representatives of the two States directly concerned followed the usual pattern: while the representative of Jordan denounced the action as a "wanton and reckless act of aggression",[16] the Israeli representative described it as a "defensive action".[17] This time, however, several other delegates taking part in the debate denoted the action as a "retaliatory action" or even as a "military reprisal",[18] and in the Resolution adopted by the Council on 25 November 1966 Israel was censured for the "large-scale military action in violation of the United Nations Charter and of the General Armistice Agreement between Israel and Jordan" and it was emphatically put to Israel "that actions of military reprisal cannot be tolerated".[19] So, contrary to the practice found in the previous instances, the Security Council this time left no doubt that it considered the action at issue as an armed reprisal, incompatible as such with the Charter. It should be stressed that this

---

[15] Even in the view that the situation in the Middle East continued to be one of "war", the armistice agreements between Israel and its Arab adversaries had the effect of depriving the parties to the conflict of their right to carry on armed actions against each other's territories. While this evidently is a special case of the prohibition of use of armed force, it coincides with the general prohibition contained in the Charter of the United Nations, so that a breach of the armistice agreements at the same time constitutes a "breach of the peace".

[16] Security Council, Provisional Verbatim Record of the 1320th meeting, 16 November 1966; S/PV. 1320, pp. 13-15.

[17] Ibid., p. 36.

[18] E.g., ibid. p. 46 (U.K.), p. 52 (U.S.A.); S/PV. 1321, p. 2 (France); S/PV. 1322, p. 3 (Argentina), p. 4 (Japan), p. 7 (New Zealand); S/PV. 1323, p. 7 (Netherlands), pp. 8-10 (China); S/PV. 1324, p. 42 ff. (Uruguay); S/PV. 1327, p. 3 (Nigeria).

[19] S/RES/228 (1966).

qualification implies the recognition that the action constituted a violation of the prohibition to use force, not of the law of war proper.[20]

6.3.2. Reprisals and punishment of war crimes

While the actions discussed so far, though perhaps reprisals in the sense of measures short of war, certainly did not constitute belligerent reprisals in the sense as understood in the present study, the next question to be examined is whether there have occurred in recent armed conflicts other instances of retaliatory actions that did enter into that category.

A preliminary observation concerns the materials to be examined. The complete history of present-day armed conflicts has not yet been written, nor has the present author attempted to make a systematic survey of the available records of all these conflicts. This leads to a twofold reservation. On the one hand, any discussion of specific events stands open to correction in the light of new facts. On the other hand, instances of alleged belligerent reprisals may have escaped my attention—although it should be added that it is of the nature of belligerent reprisals to find a certain publicity.

With these reservations made, it can be stated at the outset that surprisingly few instances of alleged belligerent reprisals have so far been found. True, in each and every armed conflict waged in the period under discussion allegations have been made, generally by all the parties concerned, that violations of the law of war had been committed on the part of the enemy. However, irrespective of the degree of truth in these various accusations, the point of interest is that only rarely were these followed by anything other than a demand for (or a threat with) punishment, as war criminals or otherwise, of those bearing individual responsibility for the alleged acts.

As an example of this tendency we mention the Korean war which began in 1950 with the invasion of South Korea by North Korean troops.[21] In the course of that war, the United Nations forces which, composed mainly of units of the armed forces of the United States, were fighting on the side of

---

[20] For a discussion of another similar incident which took place on the night of 28 December 1968, see: R. A. Falk, "The Beirut Raid and the International Law of Retaliation", in *AJIL*, Vol. 63, 1969, p. 415.

[21] With respect to the law of war aspects of that war, see: J. G. Verplaetse, "The ius in bello and Military Operations in Korea 1950-1953", in *Zeitschrift für ausländisches öffentliches Recht und Völkerrecht*, Vol. 23, 1963, p. 679. One of the crucial (and much debated) issues was in this instance whether a United Nations force could be subject to the law of war, especially so far as this is embodied in conventions concluded among States, such as the Red Cross Conventions. However, for present purposes it may suffice to note that neither side did on this account declare itself entitled to act with complete disregard for the rules of warfare.

South Korea, were accused of waging bacteriological warfare;[22] and atrocities against civilians, wounded and prisoners of war were charged both against United Nations and North Korean forces. However, there has been found no indication that reprisals have been threatened or carried out on this account.

On the other hand, the United Nations Command at one time even announced as its official policy that prisoners of war guilty of war crimes committed prior to capture would be tried,[23] and a war crimes division was set up in the headquarters of the 8th United States Army stationed in Korea.[24] Only a fortnight after the announcement of these steps the United Nations Command was able to report that no new atrocities had come to light,[25] and in subsequent reports there was no further mention made of atrocities. It seems a moot point, however, whether this sudden change should be attributed entirely or even in any significant part to the publicly announced policy with respect to punishment of war criminals: other factors may have played a part, among these the fact that just about that time the Chinese intervention in force on the side of North Korea brought a marked change in the mode in which the war was conducted on that side.[26]

However this may be, it is an established fact that reprisals did not play any part in bringing about this apparent change for the better.

6.3.3. Reprisal executions by the Vietcong

The war in Vietnam provides a first instance of acts announced as reprisals and which undoubtedly had a bearing on the law of war: the execution, on two separate occasions, of American prisoners of war by the Vietcong in reprisal for the execution of Vietcong prisoners by the South Vietnamese authorities. The facts can be summarized as follows.[27]

[22] Yearbook of the United Nations, 1953, p. 152.
[23] 8th Report of the UN Command covering the period of 16 to 31 October 1950; UN document S/1885.
[24] 9th Report of the UN Command, period 1 to 15 November 1950, S/1953. Here some evidence can be seen of the difficulty mentioned in n. 21: the UN Command could not very well take on this job, which eventually might lead to prosecution and trial of suspected war criminals, as it lacked jurisdiction for such matters.
[25] 10th Report of the UN Command, period 16 to 30 November 1950, S/1953.
[26] The Commander of the United Nations force, General MacArthur, in his 10th report in which the Chinese intervention was set forth in detail, mentioned a "marked contrast" as regarded the treatment of war victims by the enemy. This change, he continued, was too small yet "to draw any valid conclusions as to whether the actions taken and publicly announced by the United Nations Command to insure the punishment of war criminals have convinced the enemy of the necessity that all prisoners of war and non-combatants receive the humane treatment required under international law and demanded by modern civilization."—With respect to this episode cf. also I. F. Stone, The Hidden History of the Korean War, 1952, p. 326 ff.
[27] The incidents have been treated by H. S. Levie, "Maltreatment of Prisoners of

295

In April 1965, a South Vietnamese court sentenced a Vietcong prisoner to death. The Vietcong thereupon announced that, if the sentence was carried out, they would shoot a named American aid officer in their hands. Neither of the executions was carried out.[28]

Then, on 22 June of that year, a Vietcong prisoner was executed in Saigon, apparently after having been tried, convicted and sentenced to death by a South Vietnamese special military tribunal.[29] Three days later it was announced by the other side that an American sergeant, held as a prisoner of war by the Vietcong, had been executed in reprisal.[30]

The third and last instance occurred some months later: on 22 September 1965 three Vietcong prisoners were executed in Da Nang, apparently again after they had been tried, convicted and sentenced to death by a South Vietnamese court. The Vietcong retaliated once again: on 26 September the execution in reprisal was announced of two American prisoners of war, a captain and a sergeant.[31]

Since that time, the South Vietnamese authorities have not carried out death sentences on Vietcong prisoners. In November 1967, three prisoners who had been sentenced to death were given a last minute reprieve by the South Vietnamese Premier.[32]

The facts in the present case, as set out above, are simple. On the other hand, they involve some intriguing juridical questions. These can be brought under two headings: did the executions of American prisoners of war by the Vietcong constitute reprisals? and: if so, could they be justified as such?

In order to determine whether the actions resorted to by the Vietcong constituted reprisals, a first question is whether the executions of Vietcong prisoners by the South Vietnamese authorities were illegal, or, in any event, could reasonably be held illegal by the Vietcong. In this respect it has been asserted that "[a]ccording to the newspaper accounts, in each instance the individuals had been tried, convicted and sentenced to death by a South Vietnamese court in accordance with the law of South Vietnam" and that the contention that the executions were illegal nevertheless could only be meant to imply "that it is a crime to try, convict and execute a Vietcong apprehended in the course of committing what was probably a Vietcong approved and ordered act of terrorism".[33] Two comments impose themselves: first, it remains to be seen whether the executions had indeed in

---

War in Vietnam", in *Boston University Law Review*, Vol. 48, 1968, p. 323, at p. 353.
[28] New York Times, 22 June 1965.
[29] *Ibid.*
[30] New York Times, 26 June 1965.
[31] The Times, 28 September 1965.
[32] New York Times, 17 November 1967.
[33] Levie, *supra* n. 27, at pp. 354-355.

each instance been preceded by a trial which was not merely in accordance with the law of South Vietnam, but with generally accepted principles of fair and regular trial; secondly, it seems a debatable point whether the "Vietcong approved and ordered acts of terrorism", for which the accused were said to have been tried, must be considered illegal acts of warfare warranting a death sentence.[34]

As regards the procedural side of the trials, information is scant. However, on the information available it seems open to doubt that these would have been fair and regular. While the first Vietcong executed by the South Vietnamese in Saigon was said to have been tried by a "special military court" and to have confessed prior to being sentenced, the trial—the date of which was not disclosed—had evidently not been public, nor were there any indications that other essential procedural safeguards had been complied with. On the other hand, facts that did become known were that the military group which had taken control in Saigon on 14 June 1965 (the National Leadership Committee under General Nguyen Van Thieu) had "threatened to shoot terrorists and war profiteers without trial when... apprehended with tangible proof of guilt" and had "ordered the setting up of public execution grounds in the country's main centers as a warning to the population that the military government intend[ed] to rule according to what [was] described as revolutionary discipline", and that Air Vice Marshal Nguyen Cao Ky, who took over the duties of Premier the day before the execution, on that occasion said that "an execution would take place shortly".[35] These facts, combined with the lack of information concerning the trial, are hardly reassuring as to its legal character. Indeed, while there are not sufficient indications to conclude that in reality there had been no trial, it seems a safe conclusion that, in so far as a trial had in fact taken place, it had only been as part of a set-up staged to demonstrate the power and determination of the new leaders in Saigon. In other words, the circumstances surrounding the case certainly seem to justify distrust as to the legality of the proceedings.

As far as the presumed trial at Da Nang is concerned, the only information available is a statement by an American spokesman in Saigon, who was reported to have said on 27 September that the execution of the Vietcong prisoners had followed a trial "conducted in accordance with

---

[34] It is assumed here that South Vietnam was bound to observe the law of war in the armed conflict with the National Liberation Front and its military arm, the Vietcong. As the armed character of the conflict could not be denied, the least that it could amount to was an internal armed conflict, so that the minimum requirements of Art. 3 of the 1949 Geneva Conventions would apply in any event. That Article prescribes *inter alia* a fair trial prior to execution of suspected persons.—The issue of whether the Vietcong was equally bound to observe the law of war, is dealt with in the text below.

[35] New York Times, 22 June 1965.

established Vietnamese law and procedure".[36] In view of the doubt raised with respect to the first trial, the quoted summary statement by the American spokesman cannot be considered sufficient guarantee as to the correctness of the proceedings in the Da Nang case. Here, therefore, the same distrust seems justified.

On the substantive side, we are informed that the prisoner in the first case "was accused of having prepared to blow up a United States officers' billet in a suburb of Saigon" and that he had confessed "that he had been trained in demolition techniques and terrorism by the Vietcong".[37] Now, these are precisely circumstances which can give rise to doubt as to his liability to punishment. True, attempts to demolish buildings in the occupation of friendly missions, with the attendant risk for the lives of the inhabitants, are not generally tolerated by the authorities in any reasonably well-organized State. However, in the present instance the act was committed as a belligerent act in the framework of an armed conflict; it was aimed against an object which could without any doubt be regarded as a military objective; and it seems by no means certain that the perpetrator of the act should not be considered a combatant entitled to commit belligerent acts with impunity.[38]

Again, the available information is insufficient to arrive at any definite conclusions, in particular as regards the question of combatant status. But the case which the new South Vietnamese authorities selected for their demonstration can hardly have been the most convincing instance of wanton terrorism in their hands. Perhaps the conclusion is not too far-fetched that the decisive factor in selecting this case among many others was not its illegality, so much as the fact that the intended victims of the attempt had been American officers: the speculation may have been that the execution of this particular prisoner would please the Americans. In any event, even on the little information available it is evident that grave doubt persists as to the correctness of the sentence (if there was one) in the present case. All in all, therefore, it seems that the execution in June had presented the Vietcong with a unique opportunity to retaliate with a semblance of right.

With regard to the execution carried out in September, the only information available concerning the charge is again found in the statement by the American spokesman. Evidently, this official did not want to leave any

[36] The Times, 28 September 1965.
[37] New York Times, 22 June 1965.
[38] According to a report in the New York Times of 26 June 1965, the US Administration had been reluctant to threaten specific reprisals for acts of terrorism, *inter alia* "because it [did] not wish to be in a position of having to respond to the acts of saboteurs who [might] be operating under varying degrees of Vietcong discipline". This seems to imply that even at that time the US authorities were inclined to accept that certain saboteurs, operating under a minimum degree of Vietcong discipline, would have to be granted prisoner of war status.

doubt as to the infamous character of the executed Vietcong and the acts which they had committed: he described them as "three civilian non-uniformed Vietcong agitators" who had been "convinced of fomenting public violence".[39] On the face of it, this seems wholly conclusive: individuals meeting such a description and guilty of such conduct must certainly be considered liable to the death penalty in time of war. On the other hand, in view of the grave doubt resulting from the slightly more complete information concerning the previous instance, it is suggested that the mere statement of the American spokesman is insufficient ground to discard entirely the suspicion that circumstances rather more disadvantageous to a favourable evaluation of the South Vietnamese conduct of the case may have attended the execution in Da Nang as well. In other words, notwithstanding the confident representation of the facts in the quoted statement, the possibility cannot be excluded that in this case, too, the correctness of the death sentence might be open to doubt.

Assuming henceforth that the Vietcong could reasonably regard the executions by the South Vietnamese authorities as unlawful and, hence, as a ground justifying reprisals, the next question is whether the actions actually taken by the Vietcong present the characteristics of reprisals. The actions were indubitably *prima facie* unlawful: the Americans were prisoners of war, and while the Vietcong denied that they were bound by the Conventions of Geneva of 1949,[40] they certainly did not claim the right to kill prisoners at will, nor was there any legal ground why the executed prisoners should have forfeited their lives.[41]

Did the executions (which scrupulously observed the norm of proportionality) serve the purpose of enforcing the law of war? Their primary purpose obviously was to protect the Vietcong prisoners in the hands of the enemy from being executed. However, by its actions the Vietcong claimed at least by implication that the South Vietnamese lacked the right to execute such persons, who as protected persons (be it prisoners of war or arrested civilians) were entitled to respect and protection, unless—and until such time as—their liability to execution would have been established in a fair and regular trial and on the basis of the rules of the law of war in force. In other words, the reprisal actions could be considered as serving the purpose of enforcing the rule of the law of war prohibiting the wanton killing of prisoners of war and other protected persons.[42]

[39] The Times, 28 September 1965.
[40] *IRRC*, Vol. V, 1965, p. 636.
[41] In the same sense: Levie, *op. cit.* n. 27, at p. 354, note 154: "It should be borne in mind that at no time have the Vietcong or the NLF ever contended that the executed Americans had committed any act warranting execution or that their executions were pursuant to the sentences of a court."
[42] This is not to say that the South Vietnamese would in no circumstances have been entitled to sentence to death and execute Vietcong prisoners: it is merely suggested that in the cases at issue the Vietcong was—and could be—convinced that the

While the above arguments seem sufficient ground to regard the executions by the Vietcong as reprisals according to their purpose, it is worth noting that the manner in which the Vietcong had chosen to retaliate proved remarkably effective. In all three instances (that is, the threatened reprisal in April 1965 and the reprisals carried into effect in June and September of that year) the victims were American prisoners. Evidently the Vietcong speculated that the American authorities would take the executions of their soldiers extremely seriously and would find occasion to exert pressure on the South Vietnamese authorities to change their policy. If so, this speculation was not in vain: notwithstanding public statements on the part of the American authorities that the "Communist threats to intimidate, of course, [would] not succeed",[43] it did not remain a secret that United States officials had imparted to the South Vietnamese authorities their concern about the policy pursued by the latter.[44] For want of information, there cannot of course be any certainty which element— American pressure, or the direct impact of the reprisals on the South Vietnamese authorities—has been decisive in bringing about a change in the incriminated policy: but this much is certain, that it was in effect changed, so that the reprisals can be said to have been completely effective.

This leaves the question of their justification. Here the most acute juridical questions are met. Reprisals against prisoners of war are categorically prohibited in Article 13 of the Geneva Prisoners of War Convention of 1949, but this provision is as such only applicable in international armed conflicts; did the Vietnamese war in 1965 constitute an international armed conflict? If it should be considered an armed conflict not of an international character, Article 3 of the Convention would apply; does this contain an equally unequivocal prohibition of reprisals against prisoners of war? Was, in either supposition, the Vietcong bound by the Convention, whether in its entirety or by Article 3 in particular?

It is an obvious truth that the war in Vietnam presented the features of a civil war both in its origin and in the aims sought by the main contending parties (the régimes in Hanoi and Saigon, respectively); nor are matters different when the theatre of the war in South Vietnam is viewed separately

---

executions failed to meet the requirements for justification.—Levie suggests (in another context) that the law with respect to bombing non-military objectives "is certainly sufficiently controversial to preclude unilateral decision by the North Vietnamese with respect thereto" (op. cit. n. 27, at p. 350, note 135). It is submitted, however, that controversiality of an issue (such as the status of Vietcong terrorists) does not preclude a national tribunal from exercising its jurisdiction, even where that implies giving an interpretation of the controversial point of international law.
[43] Department of State Bulletin, Vol. LIII, July-December 1965, p. 55; statement read to news correspondents in Washington on 26 June 1965.
[44] New York Times, 26 June 1965.

(the main parties then being the régime in Saigon on the one hand, and the National Liberation Front with the Vietcong on the other side). However, it is submitted that these factors are not decisive for a juridical appreciation of the situation. In order to determine the legal character of the conflict—that is, in order to determine whether it constituted an international armed conflict, or an armed conflict not having an international character, or not an armed conflict at all in the sense of the law of war—account should be taken of the territorial division of Vietnam into two parts, each constituting an autonomous party to the conflict; of the scope of the conflict going on between these parties, both as regards intensity, means employed, and duration; and of the intervention in force by the United States of America, the air actions of which had even carried the conflict into the territory of North Vietnam. These factors taken together, with the intervention by the United States perhaps as the decisive element, appear to have created a situation where, in the words of the International Committee of the Red Cross,[45] "[t]he hostilities raging at the... time in Viet Nam—both North and South of the 17th parallel—ha[d] assumed such proportions... that there [could] be no doubt they constitute[d] an armed conflict to which the regulations of humanitarian law as a whole should be applied"—in other words, an international armed conflict in the sense of Article 2 of the Geneva Conventions of 1949. This, to my mind, is the only realistic view of the situation as it existed at the time of the events related above.[46]

To put it another way: even though the armed conflict in Vietnam might have to be regarded as a civil war in origin and essence, the characteristics it had assumed in 1965 had the effect of making the law of war applicable in its entirety, whether the parties to the conflict liked it or not.

It follows that the prohibition of reprisals against prisoners of war, embodied in Article 13 of the Prisoners of War Convention of 1949, was applicable in Vietnam in 1965, unless it could be shown that one or other of the parties to the conflict was not bound by that Convention and that neither had its principles, and the prohibition of reprisals in particular, become binding for such party in some other manner.

[45] Appeal, dated 11 June 1965, of the ICRC to the Governments of the Republic of Vietnam, the Democratic Republic of Vietnam and the U.S.A., as well as to the National Liberation Front; *IRRC*, Vol. V, 1965, p. 417.

[46] As Levie points out (*op. cit.* n. 27, at p. 328), the above issue "has been the subject of considerable dispute. It is the official position of the United States that what is taking place in Vietnam is an international armed conflict. This position has received support from unofficial sources. Opponents of United States participation in the Vietnamese hostilities assert that it is a civil war." It is submitted, however, that neither the lawfulness nor the political wisdom of the United States intervention in Vietnam play a part in determining the character of the armed conflict in that country and the applicability of the law of war: those arguments pertain to international (and, not to forget, national) politics, and, as far as international law is concerned, to the law regarding the use of force by States or *ius ad bellum*, not to the *ius in bello*.

With respect to this, the facts are as follows. Of the main contending parties, Vietnam had in 1954, prior to partition, acceded to the Convention; North Vietnam had acceded separately in 1957; and the United States had ratified in 1955.[47] As for the National Liberation Front, this could not accede to the Convention as it did not at the time represent a separate State or Government. On the other hand, it could have declared that it considered itself bound by the Convention. However, in its reply to the appeal of 11 June 1965 by the International Committee of the Red Cross,[48] it took the position that "the NLF was not bound by the international treaties to which others beside itself subscribed".[49] The question is whether this declaration could have the effect of freeing the Front and the Vietcong from the obligation to observe the rules laid down in the Convention.

Technically, the National Liberation Front constituted the political component of the insurgent movement in South Vietnam of which the Vietcong was the military component. That movement, however, was not fighting a war of its own, unconnected in any way with the armed conflict going on between the other parties who had chosen Vietnam as their battling ground: on the contrary, its war effort was closely integrated with, and supported by, the North Vietnamese war effort. In other words, the Front and the Vietcong were a party in the international armed conflict being waged in Vietnam. In that situation, it seems a completely un-acceptable construction to suggest that the NLF and the Vietcong would have been at liberty to decide whether they would or would not consider themselves bound by the Geneva Conventions of 1949. Indeed, in virtue of the above-mentioned accessions these Conventions were applicable throughout the territory (or territories) of Vietnam, and the NLF and the Vietcong lacked the power unilaterally to reject this applicability. The statement concerning this question, while understandable politically, was therefore null and void from a legal point of view.[50]

Even if the above reasoning were not accepted, another argument would be that the principles of the Prisoners of War Convention and notably the prohibition of reprisals against prisoners of war had become part of general

---

[47] See, *e.g.*, Levie, *op. cit.* n. 27, at p. 323 note 4.

[48] *Supra* n. 45.

[49] *IRRC*, Vol. V, 1965, p. 636.

[50] For a discussion of the point at issue starting from the assumption that the armed conflict going on at the time was a civil war being waged in South Vietnam, see: "The Geneva Convention and the Treatment of Prisoners of War in Vietnam", Note in *Harvard Law Review*, Vol. 80, 1966-1967, p. 851, at p. 855 ff., examining various theories that could make Art. 3 of the Conventions binding on an insurgent party in a civil war. The conclusion is that "it does not seem unfair to bind insurgent groups without their consent" and that "no practical reason exists for holding the NLF free from the provisions of Article 3" (p. 858). While these conclusions and the arguments on which they rest seem perfectly acceptable, the underlying thesis that the conflict in Vietnam even in 1965 constituted a civil war, cannot be accepted.

customary international law and, hence, were binding on the parties to the conflict regardless of their acceptance or non-acceptance of the Conventions of 1949. In that connection, it is noteworthy that the very claim of the NLF and Vietcong that the South Vietnamese lacked the power to execute Vietcong prisoners without due process, implicitly recognized the applicability of the principles of the prisoners of war régime and, with that, of the prohibition from taking reprisals against that category of war victims.

Thus, in my submission the norm embodied in Article 13 of the Prisoners of War Convention of 1949 applied in the situation under consideration, and the executions of American prisoners of war carried out by the Vietcong were clear violations of that provision.

In a situation like the above, the argument may be expected that notwithstanding the comprehensive and absolute formulation of the prohibition of reprisals in Article 13, this cannot be meant to deprive the parties to an armed conflict of the right to apply reciprocal treatment to the prisoners of war in their hands, if their adversary treats the prisoners of war in his hands in a manner fundamentally at variance with the Convention. One cannot deny this argument a semblance of reasonableness: how, for instance, can one expect a party to respect and protect the prisoners of war which he captures, when the enemy flatly refuses even to grant quarter to his soldiers?

However, the argument is fallacious nonetheless. There cannot be the slightest doubt that the prohibition of reprisals has been intended to be exactly as categorical as it is formulated, outlawing reprisals on the basis of reciprocity as well as on any other ground. Central to the whole issue is of course the argument that the prohibition precisely aims to prevent controversies about the interpretation and application of the Convention being fought out at the cost of the prisoners of war—a reasoning at least as compelling as the psychologically understandable argument of reciprocity.

As regards the viewpoints of the parties to the conflict, it is not surprising that the United States authorities refused to accept that the executions were justified as reprisals. They denounced these as "acts of brutal murder" and asked the International Committee of the Red Cross "to take all possible action within its competence with respect to these violations of the 1949 Geneva convention".[51] As it was reported laconically by the ICRC:[52] "This protest was forwarded to the NLF which rejected it."

[51] Statement read to news correspondents in Washington on 27 September 1965, Department of State Bulletin, Vol. LIII, July-December 1965, p. 635.
[52] IRRC, Vol. VI, 1966, p. 411. This remarkably curt statement, combined with the absence of a protest by the ICRC itself against the flagrant violation of the prohibition of reprisals, suggests that the ICRC at the time was disinclined to pay too much attention to the incidents. This attitude may have been prompted by the open ill-

Not content with this, the United States raised the point once again, this time in the International Humanitarian Law Commission of the XXth International Conference of the Red Cross, held in Vienna in October 1965. The United States governmental delegate stated there that his Government had been "shocked and deeply saddened by the brutal murder of prisoners as acts of reprisal", and that it was "profoundly concerned that other prisoners [might] be executed in violation of international law".[53] And he proposed a Resolution [54] (which was subsequently adopted in the plenary session by 117 votes to none, with 6 abstentions) the preamble of which stated that "the utilization of prisoners of war as objects of retaliation is inhuman", and recognized that "the international community has consistently demanded humane treatment for prisoners of war . . . and condemned reprisals directed against them".

The appeal contained in the operative part of the Resolution, however, was remarkably less one-sided, in that it called upon "all authorities involved in an armed conflict" "to ensure that every prisoner of war is given the treatment and full measure of protection prescribed by the Geneva Convention of 1949 on the Protection of Prisoners of War, including the judicial safeguards afforded to every prisoner of war charged with any offense". This could equally well be understood as an admonition addressed to the authorities in South Vietnam as to those of the NLF/Vietcong.[55]

In view of the conclusions arrived at in the foregoing, there is no need for me to enter into a discussion of the legal problems that arise when the conflict in (South) Vietnam is considered to constitute an armed conflict not of an international character. It may suffice to note that a variety of arguments have been adduced in support of the thesis that not only were in that situation the parties to the conflict bound to observe the fundamental principles of humanitarian law expressed in the common Article 3 of the Geneva Conventions of 1949, but the Vietcong must be considered bound by that minimum even without its consent.[56]

---

treatment of prisoners of war on the South Vietnamese side, an evil which the ICRC was at the time attempting to suppress (*ibid.*, pp. 404, 405).

[53] Department of State Bulletin, Vol. LIII, July-December 1965, p. 725.

[54] The text of the Resolution is reproduced in the quoted volume of the Department of State Bulletin, at p. 726. The Resolution (Nr. XXIV), together with the other resolutions adopted at the XXth International Red Cross Conference, has been published in *IRRC*, Vol. V, 1965, p. 580, at p. 586.

[55] Even the North Vietnamese could be regarded as addressees of the exhortation, as they refused to admit that the American prisoners in their hands—which they regarded as war criminals—were entitled to prisoner of war status. *Cf., e.g.*, Levie, *op. cit.* n. 27, at p. 342 ff.

[56] See, *e.g.*, the survey of theories in "The Geneva Convention and the Treatment of Prisoners of War in Vietnam", *supra* n. 50, at p. 855 ff.

In an earlier part of the present Chapter,[57] some doubt was raised as to whether Article 3 would have the effect of outlawing reprisals in non-international armed conflicts. It was argued there that neither the text nor the drafting history of the Article were wholly conclusive in this respect, and the fear was expressed that Governments might feel inclined to take the position that their power of retaliation had not been impaired by the Article. It is a curious reflection that the first party since the entering into force of the Geneva Prisoners of War Convention of 1949 [58] to avail itself —not of the above reasoning, but—of the faculty to take reprisals against prisoners of war, was not a Government but an insurgent party, that is, precisely the party to the conflict which Article 3 was primarily intended to protect against the arbitrary acts of those in power. It should be immediately added that none of the parties to the conflict in Vietnam have so much as hinted at the argument that Article 3 would not prohibit reprisals —let alone that they would have relied on it.

6.3.4. The hostages in Stanleyville

An episode involving measures on the part of a belligerent that could at first sight be taken for belligerent reprisals, occurred in 1964 in the Republic of the Congo (Leopoldville). At the time, the central Government under Mr. Tshombé had to face a serious rebellion, led by Mr. Soumialot and Mr. Gbenye, in the eastern part of the country. The scope of the rebellion and the nature of the actions on both sides were such that the situation could without any doubt be classified as an internal armed conflict.

At an early stage of the conflict (which broke out in the month of May 1964, shortly before the departure of the last United Nations forces from the Congo) [59] Mr. Tshombé resorted to the employment of white mercenaries [60] and of bombing aircraft manned by foreign pilots.[61] These

---

[57] Supra, pp. 267-270.

[58] On 21 October 1950, six months after the deposit of the second instrument of ratification, on 21 April 1950, by Yugoslavia. The first State to ratify had been Switzerland, on 31 March 1950.

[59] The last UN forces left on 30 June 1964; see New York Times, 1 July 1964. Cf. also report dated 29 June 1964 of the Secretary-General to the Security Council, S/5784.

[60] See: "Stanleyville: Août-Novembre 1964", analytical account of the occurrences in Chronique de politique étrangère, Vol. XVIII, 1965, p. 471.

[61] New York Times, 23-26 August 1964. While U.S. military aid was contemplated already in the first days of August (New York Times, 7 August 1964), a first shipment of four C-130 "transport planes" was reported in the New York Times of 13 August; these were followed by some B-26 light bombers: New York Times, 18 August. Finally, the New York Times of 27 August reported for the first time that a U.S. plane with an American crew had been hit by rebel fire while dropping leaflets over Uvira, a locality in rebel hands; and two American planes flown by Cuban exiles were reported to have strafed rebels in Ruzizi Valley.

measures—which immeasurably enhanced the effectiveness and fighting power of his armed forces—the rebels sharply denounced. On the other hand, the insurgents (who likewise received outside support) took to holding as hostages the white residents whom they found in the areas under their control.[62] The latter practice assumed alarming proportions in particular in Stanleyville, where some 1600 whites were concentrated at the time the rebels took it on 7 August. On 30 August, the rebels announced that they would hold all the whites as hostages so long as Tshombé would not desist from the use of mercenaries, and they denounced attempts to obtain the evacuation of the whites as manoeuvres calculated to make the bombardment of Stanleyville possible.[63]

In that dramatic situation, the ICRC (which had been asked by several Governments to exert its influence) sent a delegate to the Congo, to see what steps could be taken; and on 18 September it launched an appeal "to all those exercising authority in the Congo", insisting on the respect all parties to the conflict owed to certain fundamental norms: respect of prisoners of war and non-combatants, prohibition against taking hostages and bombing the civil population.[64] On the next day the head of the rebel government,[65] Mr. Gbenye, gave authorization for an ICRC aircraft to land at Stanleyville. The aircraft which, carrying a group of ICRC delegates as well as medicine and other relief supplies, departed immediately from Switzerland, landed on 25 September, and negotiations followed between the delegates and the rebel leaders. According to the report published afterwards by the ICRC, the delegates "noted that those with whom they spoke were ignorant of the provisions of the Geneva Conventions to which they did not consider themselves bound. The two insurgent leaders, however, stated that the evacuation of European residents from Albertville had been followed by bombing. Mr. Gbenye and Mr. Soumialot expressed their fear that a similar evacuation from Stanleyville would have the same consequences." [66] Ultimately the delegates failed to achieve the release of

---

[62] The New York Times reported a first message concerning this practice on 27 August 1964, the same date that the activities of American planes were reported (see previous note).

[63] "Stanleyville: Août-Novembre 1964", *op. cit.* n. 60, at pp. 474-475. New York Times, 4 September 1964. At the same time, the warning was given that any plane would be fired at, and the UNO, the ICRC and WHO were charged with being part of the "imperialist plot" against the rebels.

[64] *IRRC*, Vol. V, 1965, p. 30.

[65] The rebels had proclaimed the Congolese People's Republic, under a government headed by Mr. Gbenye, in the beginning of September; New York Times, 8 September 1964.

[66] *IRRC*, Vol. V, 1965, p. 31. In fact, the bombing of Albertville had been preceded by an ICRC mission into that town, which had obtained the evacuation of the whites. This sequence of events made the rebels suspicious of the ICRC and its intentions. This is probably the reason why no further missions of the ICRC were admitted into Stanleyville after the one reported mission.

the hostages: they only obtained a promise of repatriation for certain groups on humanitarian grounds [67]—a promise which did not have any practical consequences.[68]

In the period following this largely fruitless ICRC mission into Stanleyville, the situation deteriorated further, the rebel government openly threatening the execution of whites held as hostages in the event of towns being bombed by the governmental forces. In this situation, Mr. Kenyatta, Prime Minister of the Government of Kenya and President of the Conciliation Commission which the Organization for African Unity had set up for the Congolese conflict,[69] intervened in Stanleyville on the urgent request of several interested Governments. His step resulted in an assurance on the part of Mr. Gbenye that the lives of the foreigners were not in danger. On the other hand, the ICRC obtained from Mr. Tshombé an undertaking "to restrict the operations of his air forces to purely military objectives, to spare the civilian population and to respect the Geneva Conventions." [70]

Whilst no new factors were brought to the situation at the end of October and early November 1964, anxiety increased nevertheless for the safety of the whites held as hostages in Stanleyville.[71] In these circumstances, the ICRC appealed once again to Mr. Gbenye. "In answer, Stanleyville requested the ICRC to 'ensure first of all the cessation of American and Belgian bombing' to enable the ICRC aircraft to land. Shortly afterwards Mr. Gbenye added that all foreigners would in future be considered as 'prisoners of war'." [72] The Stanleyville authorities specifically justified the

---

[67] *Loc. cit.* n. 66.

[68] The report of the ICRC does not mention any repatriations in consequence of the promise obtained; the survey of events in *Chronique de politique étrangère, supra* n. 60, states (at p. 475) that "personne ne fut autorisé à répartir dans cet avion,—bien que l'autorisation eût été demandée pour des malades et des enfants."

[69] New York Times, 10 September 1964; the Resolution of the 3rd extraordinary session of the Council of Ministers of the OAU, dated 10 September 1964, is reproduced in *Chronique de politique étrangère, supra* n. 60, at p. 504.

[70] *IRRC*, Vol. V, 1965, pp. 31-32. Letter dated 22 October 1964 from Mr. Tshombé to the President of the ICRC, reproduced in *Chronique de politique étrangère, supra* n. 60, at p. 506.

[71] Elements adding to this anxiety could be seen in an intercepted radio message asking the rebel government authority to execute some of the hostages (New York Times, 16 October 1964); the announcement that the American missionary Dr. P. Carlson, whom the rebels had captured in September, would be tried for spying (New York Times, 29 October 1964); the rebel radio broadcast blaming the Americans and Belgians for the air raids and ordering all whites to be placed under house arrest (New York Times, 31 October 1964); Gbenye's threat to apply a "scorched earth policy" if he would not get aid against the American and Belgian bombardments (New York Times, 1 November 1964). Moreover, the operations of the Congolese armed forces (*i.e.*, of the mercenaries in the first place) began to make an attack on Stanleyville possible (New York Times, 31 October 1964).

[72] *IRRC*, Vol. V, 1965, p. 32. The demand of the rebels that US and Belgian participation in the fighting end as a condition for the freeing of some 550 Belgian and

latter step, announced on 5 November, as a measure in retaliation for the bombings carried out by foreigners in areas held by the rebels.[73]

These exchanges were followed by a pause in the military campaign of the Government forces against Stanleyville.[74] However, the pause did not last long: on 20 November the Government troops, led by mercenaries, opened the drive on the rebel capital.[75] This brought matters rapidly to a head. In the following days, urgent negotiations were held between the various parties. The Belgian Government, apprehensive of the reprisals which it expected the rebels to take against the Belgian hostages in their hands if there were any participation of white mercenaries in the final attack on Stanleyville,[76] flew 600 paracommandos to Ascension Island as a precautionary measure[77] and urged Mr. Tshombé to agree to their intervention in Stanleyville.[78] Reportedly, this suggestion was not at first met favourably by Mr. Tshombé.[79] In the meantime, talks were arranged between a representative of the rebel leaders and the United States ambassador in Nairobi, Kenya; but, as in the end the rebel representative did not turn up, nothing came of this.[80] While frenzied diplomatic activity was going on among the Governments concerned with a view to saving the hostages from their apparently imminent doom,[81] and while the Congolese forces were nearing Stanleyville, the rebel radio announced on 21 November that the Belgian and American hostages had been moved from

---

American hostages held in Stanleyville, was also transmitted in a radioed appeal by the Belgian consul in that town (New York Times, 3 November 1964).

[73] *Chronique de politique étrangère, supra* n. 60, at p. 481.

[74] New York Times, 14 November 1964, where this pause in the operations was attributed to fear for the safety of the white hostages. This fear was apparently not taken away by Prime Minister Kenyatta's statement, made on 12 November, that he had appealed once again to the rebels and that these had assured him that no harm would be done to the foreigners (New York Times, 13 November 1964; *cf.* also *IRRC*, Vol. V, 1965, p. 32).

[75] New York Times, 20 November 1964.

[76] The Times, 19 November 1964.

[77] New York Times, 21 November 1964.

[78] New York Times, 22 November 1964.

[79] *Ibid.*; Tshombé, who did not want the world to think that he needed a Belgian intervention in order to reach his goal, even stated that he would regard a landing of paratroopers without his consent as an act of aggression.

[80] New York Times, 21, 22 November 1964.

[81] Thus, the Governments of the U.S.A., Canada, Great Britain and Belgium jointly asked India to use its influence (New York Times, 21 November 1964); and by the action of thirteen Western Governments a radio appeal was broadcast on 21 November from Geneva to the whole world, requesting that the immediate arrival of ICRC staff at Stanleyville be permitted (New York Times, 22 November 1964). See also the letters dated 21 November 1964 from the representatives of Belgium and the U.S.A. to the President of the Security Council, setting forth the various steps taken and preparing the ground in case an urgent session of the Council would prove necessary (S/6055, S/6056); and the report of the ICRC, *IRRC*, Vol. V, 1965, p. 32.

Stanleyville to an undisclosed destination,[82] and the warning was given that if the city were attacked the hostages would be killed.[83] At the same time, a message ostensibly emanating from the Belgian and American consuls in Stanleyville urged the Governments of the countries concerned to exert their influence on Mr. Tshombé to obtain a cease-fire; with no result, however.[84]

On 24 November, the bomb burst. With the consent of the Congolese Government obtained on 21 November,[85] the Belgian paratroopers, flown in United States aircraft, were landed in Stanleyville. In a rapid action, they captured the airport and the town, linking up with the Government forces which moved in from the south soon after the landing. Many white hostages were freed; but when the Belgian commandos drew near, rebels opened fire on a group of hostages in the town, killing some twenty of them.[86]

A similar operation was carried out on 26 November 1964 in Paulis, some 200 miles to the north-east of Stanleyville. Again the para-commandos took possession of the town and freed an important number of white hostages, while some were killed by the rebels.[87]

Soon afterwards, the Belgian paratroops were withdrawn: on 29 November 1964, all of them had left the Congo for Belgium. In the course of their operations, they had freed some 1700 people, for the most part whites; according to reports, another 900, dispersed over the rebel-held area, remained in the hands of the rebels.[88]

It may be evident from the above account that the Congolese hostages affair was complicated and involved a variety of questions. Some of these concerned the Belgian/American armed intervention: these questions, turning around the asserted humanitarian character of the intervention, have been

---

[82] *Chronique de politique étrangère, supra* n. 60, at p. 482. See also New York Times, 22, 23 November 1964. The announcement proved false: while the rebels had indeed attempted to move some 100 of their prisoners to a place outside Stanleyville, they had seen themselves forced to give up this attempt; *cf.* statement by the former Belgian consul, in *Chronique de politique étrangère,* at pp. 498-499.

[83] The Times, 24 November 1964; *Chronique de politique étrangère, supra* n. 60, at pp. 482, 483.

[84] The Times, 23 November 1964.

[85] Letter dated 21 November 1964 from Mr. Tshombé to the Ambassador of Belgium at Leopoldville; annex II to letter dated 24 November 1964 from the Belgian representative to the President of the Security Council, S/6063.

[86] New York Times, 24, 25 November 1964. *Cf.* also *Chronique de politique étrangère, supra* n. 60, at p. 483, and the account by the former Belgian consul, *ibid.,* at p. 500.

[87] New York Times, 26, 27 November 1964.

[88] New York Times, 29 November 1964; letter dated 1 December 1964 from the representative of Belgium to the President of the Security Council, S/6074.

the subject of extensive debate, both in the Security Council [89] and else-where; [90] however, they lie outside the scope of this study. For present purposes, the interest of the affair lies in the character of the acts of the rebels giving rise to so much anxiety and, ultimately, to the intervention: did these constitute belligerent reprisals?

A first question is against which acts or policies of the Leopoldville Government the measures of the rebels were directed. As to this, there is an apparent inconsistency in the arguments advanced on their part. In the initial stage, the taking of hostages was motivated with a reference to the air raids carried out by the enemy and in particular by foreign pilots acting under his orders. However, while this argument (sometimes narrowed down to the bombing of towns) was repeated on various occasions throughout the episode, the motive given in the first place for holding as hostages the whites found in Stanleyville, was the use of mercenaries. And finally the threat of the rebels that the hostages would be killed, was made with a view to preventing the imminent attack on Stanleyville.

Of these diverse arguments, the specific charge that towns were being bombed came nearest to a justification of the taking of hostages as a re-prisal for illegitimate acts of warfare committed on the part of the enemy. For, while much may be uncertain about the law of air warfare, it is generally agreed that bombardments of the civil population as such are prohibited.[91] The accusation made by the rebels could be understood to be based on this norm. In this respect, it should be recalled that the ICRC in its appeal of 18 September 1964 reminded the parties to the conflict of the prohibition against bombing the civil population; and the Prime Minister of the Congolese Government, Mr. Tshombé, in a letter dated 22 October 1964 gave the ICRC the undertaking that air operations would be restricted to purely military objectives and that the civil population would be spared.

While the latter result could only be welcomed, it seems highly dubious that it had been brought about by the policy pursued by the rebels: more probably, it should be attributed to outside influence, of foreign Govern-ments as well as of an organization like the ICRC. However, a more important obstacle to using the above reasoning as a possible justification for the taking of hostages as reprisals, is that it does not account for the other arguments which the rebels adduced in justification of their actions, and thus fails to give a satisfactory explanation of their policy as a whole. It appears that the common denominator of the various arguments on which they successively relied, lies in the element that these were all

[89] The Security Council between 9 and 30 December 1964 devoted 17 meetings to the affair; Official Records, S/PV. 1170-1189.
[90] In the Belgian parliament first of all, but also in the literature. See: A. Gerard, "L'opération Stanleyville-Paulis devant le Parlement belge et les Nations Unies", in *Revue belge de droit international*, 1967, p. 242.
[91] *Supra*, p. 284; *cf.* also p. 168.

310

connected with military actions of the Congolese Government threatening their position: the air operations were together with the actions of the mercenaries the most effective means employed by the Government in its efforts to overcome the rebellion, and the attack on Stanleyville constituted a crucial phase in the operations against the insurgents.

This leads to the conclusion that the taking of hostages, far from serving to enforce the law of war, in reality was designed to exert influence on the progress of the military operations. This conclusion is borne out by the attitude of the rebels, who on several occasions in the course of the conflict made the release of the hostages conditional on the cessation of certain aspects of the operations being conducted against them. The conclusion is furthermore supported by the notable fact that the rebels, notwithstanding their often repeated threats, did not proceed to the execution of hostages when their demands failed to be met: on the contrary, as Mr. Gbenye and other rebel leaders repeatedly assured, the hostages were not in danger— that is, as far as the policy of the leaders was concerned. For that policy consisted precisely in keeping at their disposal a contingent of living hostages, who by their very presence would act as a safeguard for the rebels and who moreover, it was hoped, could be bartered for concessions in the military/political field.[92]

Thus, the policy of keeping hostages as applied by the insurgents in Stanleyville lacked the characteristic feature of a belligerent reprisal: it was not so much a means to enforce the law of war as to guarantee the insurgents a degree of safety and to further their policy objectives.

As such, it was prohibited by the common Article 3 of the Geneva Conventions of 1949, which enumerates the "taking of hostages" among the acts that "are and shall remain prohibited at any time and in any place whatsoever" with respect to, *inter alia*, "persons taking no active part in the hostilities". The applicability of that Article in the given situation was beyond doubt: the fighting unmistakably amounted to an armed conflict not of an international character, and while in 1952 the then colonial sovereign, Belgium, had in ratifying the Conventions expressly extended their application to the territory of the Congo, the Republic of the Congo (Leopoldville), successor to Belgium as the territorial sovereign, had in

---

[92] This conclusion is in conformity with the views expressed by several of the delegates taking part in the debate in the Security Council; see statements by Mr. Spaak (Belgium; S/PV. 1173, para. 16), Mr. Seydoux (France; S/PV. 1176, para. 54), Mr. Usher (Ivory Coast; S/PV. 1177, para. 65), Mr. Sette Camara (Brasil; S/PV. 1177, para. 90) and Mr. Sidi Baba (Morocco; S/PV. 1178, para. 39). Even the representative of Sudan, Mr. Mahgoub, referred to the fact that the rebels had looked upon the hostages "as a bargaining counter"—although he suggested that no "fair-minded person" could "blame the authorities in Stanleyville overmuch" for their attitude, in the light of the "ruthless manoeuvring and the gaining of ends irrespective of means" to which the Government in Leopoldville had in his assertion resorted (S/PV. 1181, para. 44).

1961 removed any such doubt as might perhaps arise as a result of the recently acquired independence by solemnly declaring that it considered itself bound by the Conventions.[93]

But was this sufficient ground to conclude that the rebels were equally bound to observe their terms? It should be recalled that on the occasion of the one and only mission of the ICRC into Stanleyville, on 25 September 1964, its delegates had "noted that those with whom they spoke were ignorant of the provisions of the Geneva Conventions to which they did not consider themselves bound". In this sentence, two distinct elements can be discerned: the ignorance of the rebels as to the provisions of the Conventions, and their denial that they were bound by these.

As to the first element, irrespective of whether the ignorance of the rebels had been real or simulated, such ignorance on the part of pretended authorities could not of course have the effect of releasing them of their international obligations: at most, it might be regarded as a mitigating factor in judging their acts. Moreover, any ignorance which the rebel leaders might have had prior to the visit of the ICRC delegates, was removed on that occasion. From that time ignorance could not therefore serve the rebels as a pretext for acting in contravention of the Conventions.

This leaves the question of whether they were bound by the Conventions, and by Article 3 in particular: the identical question as was met in the context of the Vietnamese war with respect to the position of the Vietcong. However, while on that occasion the situation amounted to an international rather than an internal armed conflict, this time the question arises in the context of a doubtless internal armed conflict, where the only part of the Geneva Conventions applicable without special agreement between the parties was precisely Article 3. In view of this consideration, it seems appropriate to repeat here the adherence, expressed in the preceding part of this section, to the viewpoint that there are really no valid grounds why rebels should not be considered bound by Article 3 irrespective of their consent.

In support of this view, the following argument may be advanced. The norms laid down in the Geneva Conventions are not only binding upon the States which have ratified or acceded to the Conventions,[94] but must be observed by the individual members of their communities, on penalty of becoming liable to individual punishment in case of violation.[95] There is no conceivable ground why rebels would by the mere fact of their rebellion be released of these obligations resting upon them as individual persons. It

---

[93] U.N.T.S. Vol. 139, p. 459; Vol. 392, p. 339.
[94] This is the overwhelming majority of States. In fact, their number is so overwhelming that it may be suggested that those few States which have chosen to refrain from expressly accepting the Conventions, should nonetheless be considered bound at least by the substantive part of the Conventions, and *a fortiori* by Article 3.
[95] *Supra*, p. 271.

may be that different considerations were valid at a time when the law of war was generally conceived as a body of law governing the relations between belligerent States: in that era, great and perhaps overriding importance could be deemed to attach to elements like consent on the part of an insurgent party to be bound under the law of war, or its recognition (be it as insurgents, as belligerents, or even as a government) by the legitimate Government in the first place.[96] However, at the present time—that is, since the war crimes trials held after the Second World War and since the adoption of the Geneva Conventions in 1949—it cannot really be questioned any longer that at any rate the principles of the law of war as embodied in Article 3 of the Conventions are binding on any individual person or group of persons involved in an internal armed conflict, be it as participants or otherwise.[97]

In addition to this fundamental reasoning, other arguments may be adduced, such as the equally fundamental line of thought which takes as its point of departure the necessity to interpret the Geneva Conventions in such a manner that the realization of their purposes is guaranteed to the maximum extent possible in the light of changing conditions and that ambiguities are resolved in favour of the widest possible coverage, and which, taking into account that since 1945 civil war has been the principal form of armed conflict, concludes that it is not unfair to hold insurgent groups bound to the common Article 3 without their consent, as that Article represents an effort to mitigate the excesses of civil war without overlooking other legitimate interests.[98]

[96] For a recent exposition of these concepts, see: E. Castrén, *Civil War*, 1966.—In "The Geneva Convention and the Treatment of Prisoners of War in Vietnam", *op. cit.* n. 50, at p. 857, the following is stated with respect to the view defended in the text above: "The ... theory asserts that 'the rebels are bound because the original adherence of the legitimate government to a convention containing the article binds all its subjects even though some of them later may rebel against that government...' [quoting M. Greenspan, *The Modern Law of Land Warfare, 1959*, p. 623]. This is the basis on which the International Committee of the Red Cross seems to consider the NLF bound. But this theory ... is inconsistent with the traditional view that rebels are not subject to international law until they are accorded belligerent status." It is, however, precisely the validity of the traditional view for the present law of war which is denied in the text above.
[97] The view defended in the text finds support in GA Resolution 2444 (XXIII) (*supra*, p. 284) affirming that the principles which it sets forth must be observed "by all governmental and other authorities responsible for action in armed conflicts".
[98] This is the view defended in "The Geneva Convention and the Treatment of Prisoners of War in Vietnam", *op. cit.* n. 50. The Note argues (p. 854) that "if the Convention is to survive and be effective, it must be treated as having a potential for growth similar to that which has characterized the customary rules of warfare. The object of interpreting the treaty, therefore, must be to determine how its purposes may be best achieved in the light of changing conditions. In particular, the specific purposes of the Geneva Convention demand that ambiguities be resolved in favor of the widest possible coverage. The goals of mitigating the excesses of war and providing

313

Another argument, less basic and more *ad hoc* in character, is that in the discussions in the Security Council none of the delegates ventured to deny the applicability of Article 3. In fact, among the relatively few delegates who expressed an opinion about the legal character of the hostage takings, only one put up an argument in defence of the measures, describing these as the justifiable or at least understandable taking into custody of "all people who, by reason of their nationality—and some of them, certainly, by their activities—could be considered agents of those Powers which sent the arms by which the population of whole areas was being massacred"; [99] an argument which was not supported by anyone else in the debate and which, incidentally, not even the rebels themselves had brought to the fore.

Of the other delegates expressing themselves at all on the point, some merely declared the hostage takings contrary to international law.[100] One delegate took the trouble to enter into the question in somewhat greater detail; he pointed out that obviously "... one cannot say that the Geneva Conventions apply to the activities developing in a campaign such as the one which is taking place in the Congo, which has all the earmarks of internal insurrection. But the general principles which lead us to observe at least a minimum of respect for the human person should be applied, even to the civil war which now engulfs the Congo." [101]

While this was an apposite description of the minimum law that should be observed in an internal armed conflict, it was not an explicit reference to Article 3 of the Geneva Conventions. Such an explicit reference was in fact found in the statement of only one delegate, who referred to "accepted

---

humane treatment for war victims require a broad and flexible construction of the treaty. To some extent, of course, provisions for implementing these ideals reflect a compromise between humanitarian goals and a desire to preserve national sovereignty; the balance should not be upset by a one-sided view of the treaty's purposes. But in many significant disputes such a conflict between legitimate interests is not presented."

Applying this basic reasoning to the question of whether the NLF must be considered bound by Art. 3 of the Convention, the Note continues (p. 857): "Since 1945, civil war has been the principal form of armed conflict, and Article 3 of the Convention represents an effort to mitigate its excesses. ... Probably, no greater protection can be given to the interests of insurgents, short of requiring their consent. By definition, insurgents cannot adhere to a treaty prior to the commencement of hostilities, and if the applicability of Article 3 were made to turn on accession afterwards, there would be too great a risk of nonadherence merely as a short-sighted response to the pressures of the moment. ... Accordingly, it does not seem unfair to bind insurgent groups without their consent."

[99] Mr. Hajec (Czechoslovakia); S/PV. 1181, para. 6.

[100] Mr. Spaak (Belgium), S/PV. 1173, para. 16; Mr. Nielsen (Norway), S/PV. 1183, para. 53.

[101] Mr. Sette Camara (Brasil); S/PV. 1177, para. 91.

314

standards of humanitarian conduct, particularly as they are required by Article 3 of the Geneva Convention".[102]

Obviously, the question of the legal nature of the taking of hostages had by the turn of the events in the Congo become a very minor issue in the eyes of the delegates taking part in the debate in the Security Council: they were mainly concerned with the characterization of the Belgian/American intervention as well as with the solution of the Congolese situation. However, even the few remarks made in the course of the debate condemning as illegal the practice resorted to by the rebels, together with the absence of any significant arguments to the contrary, provide valuable support for the viewpoint that the rebels in the Congo must be considered bound to observe as a minimum the principles of humanitarian law embodied in Article 3 of the Geneva Conventions.

The conclusion is, therefore, that the practice of taking hostages as applied by the rebels constituted a direct violation of Article 3. It should be added that this probably was not the worst instance of violations of the humanitarian law of war committed in the course of that particular armed conflict: reports of wanton cruelty, torture and massacres abound. However, this does not detract from the fact that the taking of hostages constituted a grave breach of the Geneva Conventions. Indeed, the episode may be seen as evidence that the makers of the Conventions were right in laying down a prohibition, not merely of the killing, but even of the taking of hostages. For, while in the given instance the policy of the leaders did not of itself lead to the death of the persons held as hostages, in practice it certainly entailed grave danger for the lives of these innocent persons who were directly exposed (and intentionally so) to the risks ensuing from the military operations conducted against the rebels, as well as to the wanton violence that, notwithstanding the official policy of the leaders, could be feared—and in the end occurred—on the part of the rebels.

6.3.5. *The destruction of houses in Israel-occupied Arab territory*

In the aftermath of the six-day war waged in June 1967 between Israel and its Arab neighbours (Egypt, Jordan and Syria) Israel saw itself increasingly confronted with the activities of Arab guerrillas [103] in the territories conquered on that occasion and which it held occupied since, notably in the

---

[102] Mr. Stevenson (U.S.A.); S/PV. 1174, para. 87.

[103] These were variously referred to as Palestinians, Syrians or other Arab groups, and as "partisans", "resistance fighters", "saboteurs", "terrorists", or "extremists". The term chosen in the text seems sufficiently neutral and wide to cover the whole range of their activities (which ran from the lobbing of handgrenades into cinemas to raids on military installations) without already implying a qualification or disqualification of their activities.—As was mentioned in § 6.3.1 of this Chapter, Israel had prior to the six-day war had to put up with similar activities directed against its territory.

west bank of the Jordan and in the Gaza Strip.[104] The guerrilla organizations, foremost among which was Al Fatah, had their bases in the Arab countries and from there undertook their infiltrations and raids into the occupied territories. They moreover aimed at setting up nuclei of resistance in the various districts and at mobilizing the population into lending active support to their cause.[105]

The Israeli occupation authorities, on their part, did their utmost to fight these tendencies. To that end, they first of all took measures to intercept the greatest possible number of infiltrators and raiders, and to track down those guerrillas who in spite of these measures succeeded in penetrating into the occupied territories. But besides these steps against the guerrillas proper, the Israelis also took measures against those members of the population suspected of being more or less actively involved in the guerrilla activities, by harbouring guerrillas, concealing weapons or explosives, or even participating actively in particular acts of terrorism or sabotage. It is the practice which the Israeli occupation authorities developed in respect of this category of persons that should be put at issue here.

The general policy of the Israelis was to take a tolerant attitude to the doings of the occupied population. On the other hand, this policy of tolerance did not prevent them from taking a firm stand in the event of non-co-operation on the part of the population: in such cases, besides the punishment of individual instigators [106] they did not hesitate to inflict collective measures, such as curfews.[107]

This more stringent policy line found its most acute expression in the practice which they adopted with respect to cases of suspected support to the guerrillas and their activities, and which included the demolition of the houses where the suspects lived. This practice was carried through with great determination, with the result that in March 1968 it was reported that in the Gaza Strip alone already more than a hundred houses had been destroyed "because their owners were thought to have had a hand in terrorism or to have harboured guerrillas or arms".[108] A specific instance

---

[104] *E.g.*: The Times, 25 September 1967 (sharpened Israeli vigilance in the West Bank area), 3 October 1967 (first hit and run raid across the Jordan river), 21 October 1967 (guerrilla band cleaned out in the West Bank), 19 January 1968 (new outbreak of terrorism in Gaza Strip), 29 January 1968 (Arab underground organization uncovered in Gaza Strip).

[105] See, *e.g.*, The Times, 6 March 1968, for a detailed account of the plans.

[106] The Times, 9 August 1967 (three months' imprisonment for the alleged organizers of a general strike in Jerusalem).

[107] For instances of such measures, see, *e.g.*: The Times, 25 September 1967 (curfew from 5 p.m. until 7 a.m. in Nablus), 8 January 1968 (total day-and-night curfew in the Gaza Strip).

[108] The Times, 6 March 1968. On 3 October 1967 that newspaper had already reported that in the period preceding that date "the Israelis ha[d] seized more than 100 suspected members of terrorist bands and destroyed a number of houses where they had been sheltered."

occurred in October of that same year: after an Arab youth aged seventeen had been arrested on suspicion of having thrown a handgrenade at a mosque in Hebron, it was reported that "[s]ecurity forces today blew up three Arab houses in Hebron in reprisal for the grenade attack. One house belonged to the family of the youth who, the police alleged, ha[d] admitted throwing the grenade." [109]

How should this practice of demolishing houses be assessed from a juridical point of view? In particular, did the measures constitute reprisals for violations of the law of war, and, if so, could they be justified as such?

Assuming for a moment that the law of war was applicable in the situation under review, it is evident that some of the activities giving rise to the above repressive measures were in contravention of it; this was notably true of the acts of indiscriminate terrorism against the civil population.[110] On the other hand, activities like the mere harbouring of guerrillas or the concealment of weapons could not be so considered. Of course, the Israeli authorities could regard the latter acts as a danger to security and order in the occupied territories and as such needed no more tolerate those acts than the acts of terrorism. They were therefore justified in taking effective steps against these various forms of support for the guerrillas on the part of the population, irrespective of whether these were in contravention of the law of war or not. In so doing, however, the authorities were themselves obliged to stay within the limits set by the law of war, and by the Fourth Geneva Convention of 1949 in particular—that is, if that was found to be applicable in the given situation.

Could there be any doubt on that point? The facts seem to speak for themselves: while it might be a debatable point whether the situation as it existed after the six-day war, taken on itself, presented the characteristics of an armed conflict between Israel and its neighbours, the six-day war had in any event constituted a clear case of such an armed conflict. It had ended with a mere cease-fire on the one hand, and with the occupation by Israel of considerable portions of the terrritories of Egypt, Jordan and Syria on the other. The inhabitants of these territories were nationals of the Arab States just mentioned, and in any event they were not nationals of Israel. It seems therefore not open to question that all the conditions were fulfilled for the application of the Fourth Convention: (1) an armed conflict that had broken out among four Contracting States (Article 2)[111] and that had re-

---

[109] The Times, 11 October 1968.
[110] The ICRC in a report published in the *IRRC*, Vol. 9, 1969, p. 88, records that "during the course of various discussions which delegates of the ICRC in the Middle East have had with elements of the Palestinian resistance, they clearly drew their attention to respect of the essential humanitarian rules which also applied to acts of resistance, especially as regards respect for the civilian population".
[111] The States involved in the conflict had ratified or acceded to the Fourth Convention on the following dates: Jordan on 29 May 1951 (U.N.T.S. Vol. 91, p. 381); Israel

317

sulted in the occupation of part of the territories of three of these States (Article 2, paragraph 2); and (2) a group of persons (the inhabitants of the occupied territories) who as a result of the belligerent occupation found themselves in the power of an occupying Power of which they were not nationals and who, hence, had the status of protected persons (Article 4).

While it is therefore not open to doubt that the Fourth Convention had become applicable as a result of the six-day war, it should be noted that the application of that Convention is not intended to continue indefinitely: Article 6, paragraph 3, provides expressly that "in the case of occupied territory, the application of the present Convention shall cease one year after the general close of military operations". Assuming for the sake of argument that 10 June 1967 (the day when the last cease-fire, between Israel and Syria, came into effect) would be the date of the "general close of military operations"—and that the infiltrations, raids, harassing attacks, artillery exchanges, bombing actions and strafings which continued to occur regularly in the period following that date did not amount to a continuation of the military operations—the Convention as a whole would therefore have lost its applicability as from 10 June 1968. Even in that supposition, however, all those provisions relevant to the present issue would have retained their applicability, by virtue of paragraph 3 of Article 6 which, after the text quoted above, goes on to provide that "however, the Occupying Power shall be bound, for the duration of the occupation, to the extent that such Power exercises the functions of government in such territory, by the provisions of the ... Articles" enumerated in that paragraph.[112] For an appreciation of the situation under discussion it does not therefore make any difference whether or not 10 June 1967 is considered as the date at which military operations came to a general close.

But has there since the end of the six-day war been any modification to the status of the occupied territories or populations, either by an agreement or similar instrument, or by a unilateral declaration taken by Israel? One thing is certain: in the period under discussion there has been brought about no agreement between the parties to the conflict or other valid international instrument resolving the question of the occupied territories or of their populations, or conferring any greater powers on Israel as an occupying Power than those provided in the Fourth Convention. On the other hand, the position unilaterally adopted by Israel was not so unmistakably clear. At the time, it was already asserted now and again by more or less official sources that never would the occupied territories be restored to the Arab States from whom they had been conquered. But such statements had no more the effect of a definite annexation than had the decision which the

---

on 6 July 1951 (U.N.T.S. Vol. 96, p. 326); Egypt on 10 November 1952 (U.N.T.S. Vol. 150, p. 372), and Syria on 2 November 1953 (U.N.T.S. Vol. 180, p. 304).
[112] Articles 1 to 12, 27, 29 to 34, 47, 49, 51, 52, 53, 59, 61 to 77 and 143.

Israeli Government took on 29 February 1968, to change the status of the occupied territory from "enemy territory" to "militarily occupied territory".[113] Indeed, irrespective of the intentions which the Israeli authorities might have had at the time, and no matter what decisions they might have taken in respect of the territories in question, no unilateral statement or decision on their part could possibly have the effect of modifying the status of the populations inhabiting those territories: such an effect is expressly precluded by Article 47 of the Fourth Convention.[114] The conclusion seems therefore indisputable that there could be found no argument whatsoever that might lead to the non-applicability of that Convention, or in any event of those of its materially significant provisions enumerated in Article 6, paragraph 3.

This was evidently the view of the ICRC as well: in a report of activities published in February 1969 it referred to "persistent ICRC representations to the Israeli authorities stating that the Fourth Convention [was] applicable throughout all the occupied territories".[115] The Israeli authorities, however, were not ready to admit this: as reported by the ICRC, "the Government of Israel has declared that it wished 'to leave open for the time being' the question of the application of the Fourth Geneva Convention, preferring to act on an *ad hoc* basis by granting practical facilities to the ICRC delegates".[116]

The ICRC did not in its report make mention of any specific arguments which the Israeli Government might have advanced for its attitude. While it seems obvious that these must be sought in the political sphere, an additional ground for Israel not to recognize the applicability of the Convention may have been the very issue of the justification of the methods used for the repression of undesirable activities on the part of the civil population, and of the demolition of houses in case of suspected support for the guerrillas and their activities in particular.

The ICRC in its above report made mention of the "acute concern" which its President had expressed to the Israeli authorities "over these demolitions which are contrary to Articles 33 and 53 of the Fourth Geneva

[113] The Times, 1 March 1968. This step, which caused considerable anxiety as to Israel's intentions, was officially explained as a purely internal measure "necessary to correct a legal situation in which visiting or trading with the west bank was technically a contravention of a regulation of the Ministry of the Interior which designated Allenby Bridge, across the Jordan, as a point of exit and entry".

[114] The text of Art. 47 reads as follows: "Protected persons who are in occupied territory shall not be deprived, in any case or in any manner whatsoever, of the benefits of the present Convention by any change introduced, as the result of the occupation of a territory, into the institutions or government of the said territory, nor by any agreement concluded between the authorities of the occupied territory and the Occupying Power, nor by any annexation by the latter of the whole or part of the occupied territory."

[115] *Op. et loc. cit.* n. 110.

[116] *Ibid.*

319

Convention".[117] The last-mentioned Article prohibits the destruction, *inter alia*, of "real or personal property belonging individually or collectively to private persons", "except where such destruction is rendered absolutely necessary by military operations". It needs no argument that in the instances discussed here there was no question of military operations, let alone that these could have made the demolitions absolutely necessary.

The official Israeli view, on the other hand, was that the demolitions represented punitive measures. In this respect it should be noted that the measures, while allegedly aimed primarily against the individual suspects, even in the most favourable supposition (that is, that only the house was destroyed where the suspected person lived or where the weapons or explosives had been concealed) undoubtedly directly affected other persons besides: for it was unlikely that the suspect was the sole inmate of the house.[118] And in a case like the one reported above, where three houses were destroyed apparently for the hostile act of one youth, the character of collective punishment was even more evident. Significantly, the press referred to the latter instance as a measure of reprisal. As it happened, the use of that term was in that case not even completely off the mark, as the act retaliated against apparently constituted an infringement of the law of war.

However, the retaliatory measure could in that instance no more be justified than in the other cases. An attempt to justify the destructions as punitive measures inflicted on the individual suspects is bound to fail, in view of the conspicuous absence of anything like a fair and regular trial preceding the execution of the measures and establishing the liability to punishment of the persons in questions. That such a trial is an absolute prerequisite for the lawful punishment of protected persons in occupied territory, is implicit in the system of the provisions of the Fourth Convention dealing with the legislative and jurisdictional powers in criminal matters of the occupying Power. The point is even made explicit in Article 5, where it is stated that even those protected persons who are detained under "definite suspicion of activity hostile to the security of the Occupying Power" and who then, on account of "absolute military security", are "regarded as having forfeited rights of communication under the present Convention", "shall nevertheless be treated with humanity and, in case of trial, shall not be deprived of the rights of fair and regular trial prescribed by the present Convention".[119]

---

[117] *Op. cit.* n. 110, p. 87.

[118] This factor was stressed by the President of the ICRC in his aforementioned protest to the Israeli authorities: as the report states, he "drew their attention to the particularly difficult situation in which these families found themselves, deprived overnight of a dwelling-place"; *loc. cit.* n. 117.

[119] The point is even more explicit in Art. 3, which enumerates among the acts "prohibited at any time and in any place whatsoever" even in the event of an armed conflict not of an international character: "the passing of sentences and the carrying

On the other hand, the measures could no more be justified as measures of collective punishment or reprisals: an attempt at justification on these lines is frustrated by the clear text of Article 33 (the first Article invoked by the ICRC), prohibiting without any reservation on the one hand "collective penalties and likewise all measures of intimidation or of terrorism" and, on the other, "reprisals against protected persons and their property".

The above leads to the conclusion that, whichever way the matter is considered, the practice adopted by the Israeli occupation authorities of demolishing houses in retaliation for suspected support of the Arab guerrillas and their cause, fails to find justification in the law of war and in the Fourth Convention of Geneva of 1949 in particular.

Another conclusion forces itself upon the observer: to wit, that notwithstanding the official attitude of the Israeli authorities the real purpose of the measures was not so much punishment as the intimidation of the population. As such, the measures were a weapon of questionable efficacy and indeed not without danger for the user, as the demolitions might well evoke a reaction among the population completely opposite to the one envisaged, thus leading to a spread and an increased fierceness of the resistance movement rather than to its suppression.[120]

6.4. CONCLUSIONS

What has been the contribution of the period after the Second World War to the picture of belligerent reprisals, both in their theoretical aspects and in practice?

A first conclusion is that a number of specific prohibitions have been added to the prohibition, already laid down in the Geneva Prisoners of War Convention of 1929, of reprisals against prisoners of war. As a result, reprisals are now unconditionally prohibited in international armed conflicts against all categories of protected persons as enumerated in the four Geneva Conventions of 1949. In the Fourth Convention, this prohibition is supplemented with a prohibition of collective punishment of protected civilians.

Reprisals are equally prohibited against another category of protected

---

out of executions without previous judgment pronounced by a regularly constituted court, affording all the judicial safeguards which are recognized as indispensable by civilized peoples".

[120] The fact stands out that in 1968 and 1969 the populations in the occupied territories were more inclined to offer active resistance to the occupying Power than in the early days of the occupation. *Cf.* also the report dated 5 March 1968 of a correspondent of The Times in Tel Aviv; he writes, *inter alia*: "It is now thought, however, that repression of this kind has been much less effective a curb to extremism than the accurate work of the Israel intelligence service."—The Times, 6 March 1968.

"objects", to wit, cultural property. This prohibition is laid down in the Convention of The Hague of 1954.

Both the Geneva Conventions of 1949 and the Convention of The Hague of 1954 contain articles specifically applicable in the event of internal armed conflict and laying down the minimum rules of conduct to be observed in that event in respect to protected persons and protected property, respectively. It is a regrettable lacuna that these articles do not contain an equally express prohibition of reprisals as is found in the articles applicable in international armed conflicts. This leaves room for the argument that for want of an express prohibition the parties to an internal armed conflict have not been deprived of their power to make protected persons or property the object of reprisals.

However, it should immediately be added that strong arguments militate against such a restrictive interpretation. First, the articles in question should be regarded as condensed versions of the Conventions, which, without going into all the details of the several Conventions, set out their basic principles with a view to achieving as effective a protection of the various categories of protected persons and property as possible: it is definitely not the purport of these articles to exclude the application of this or that specific rule in the event of internal armed conflict. Then, the arguments bearing on the relative usefulness of reprisals as sanctions of the law of war in the hands of belligerents, on the one hand, and on the inherent inhumanity of inflicting reprisals on protected persons, on the other, are no different in respect to international or internal armed conflict; so, there is no cogent reason why a different rule should govern the admissibility of reprisals in one type of armed conflict or the other.

Neither is the lack of any express reference to outside supervision in the articles relating to internal armed conflict sufficient ground for a different conclusion: while it is true that these articles do not attribute any function in this respect to Protecting Powers (as indeed would be hardly conceivable in the event of internal conflict), the articles do provide that organizations like the ICRC, and UNESCO as far as cultural property is concerned, may offer their services to the parties to the conflict; an opening which the ICRC, for one, never fails to utilize, nor is its assistance, which in practice amounts to supervision of the humanitarian rules, often rejected. On the other hand, in the event of an international armed conflict the actual realization of the supervisory function of Protecting Powers or qualified organizations in the territory of one or other belligerent party always remains dependent on that party's approval of the persons designated as delegates by the Powers or organizations indicated. Accordingly, the difference between the two situations is more apparent than real: it lies in the legal basis for the supervisory activities rather than in the realization thereof in practice.

These considerations add up to the conclusion that nothing stands in the way of adopting the interpretation of the articles in question which un-doubtedly is most desirable from the point of view of the humanitarian and cultural interests at stake, to wit, that reprisals against protected persons or protected property are prohibited in internal armed conflicts as well.

A branch of the law of war where so far no conventional prohibition or restriction of reprisals has been brought about (nor, indeed, any up-to-date regulation of the field of law itself) is the law relating to the means and methods of warfare proper ("battlefield law"). This lacuna assumes particular significance in view of the development of weapons with very high destructive power and which may be used either intentionally against the civil population in enemy territory (which is not among the categories protected by the Fourth Geneva Convention of 1949) or in so indiscrimi-nate a manner as to create grave danger for the civil populations.

This problem, which was touched upon in the foregoing in the context of the ICRC's Draft Rules, shall be discussed at some greater length in the final Chapter of the present study.[1]

As for State practice, a first reflection is that neither the existence of the United Nations Organization nor the express prohibition of the use of force in its Charter have resulted in turning the recourse to armed reprisals into a rare occurrence in present-day international relations. This reflects the limited efficacy of the system of collective security as achieved so far. However, as stated above, these armed reprisals are outside the scope of the present study as they do not belong in the category of belligerent re-prisals conceived as sanctions of the law of war.

Armed conflicts have no more become rare than have armed reprisals; indeed, both international and internal armed conflicts have been numer-ous. And, it may be added, there have been countless acts of inhumanity and savagery committed or alleged to be committed in the context of these various conflicts. This is in sharp contrast to the small number of acts, recorded in this Chapter, having the appearance of—or even being re-motely similar to—belligerent reprisals. The record probably is not complete: it may be that later detailed study of the history of these conflicts will yield further instances of occurrences belonging in the same category. Even so, however, the small number of instances that came to the attention of the present author is a strong indication that even a complete list of these occurrences cannot be very long, as it is of the essence of reprisals to be resorted to not in the dark but openly, so as to achieve their intended effect.

It is a conspicuous fact that among the instances recorded none consisted in an express infringement of the law of The Hague, or law of combat:

[1] See Chapter VII, §§ 7.1.3 and 7.1.4.

without exception, they consisted in acts contrary to the Conventions of Geneva. This was true even in respect to those occurrences where the motive for retaliation was sought in alleged use of unlawful means or methods of warfare on the part of the opposite party. It is indeed a curious reflection that belligerent reprisals were only resorted to where they were expressly prohibited, and never where there was at least no express conventional prohibition formally excluding their justification.

A final general observation with respect to contemporary State practice concerns an element common to the three instances related in the previous section of this Chapter: to wit, that in each case a preliminary issue was the applicability or non-applicability of one or other of the Geneva Conventions, or of the common Article 3 in particular. It is apparent (and this not only from the cases indicated here, but from the records of other recent armed conflicts as well) that parties to armed conflicts, whether international or internal, often display a marked reluctance to admit that the Conventions are applicable. A probable cause of this attitude—apart from the evident inconvenience which integral application of the Conventions entails for a belligerent—is a definite tendency on the part of belligerents to approach the question of the applicability as a political issue, with an eye to their supposed interests. If so, this attitude is highly regrettable and the result of a serious misappreciation of the real issues at stake: the overriding and indeed the only consideration ought to be the interests of those human beings whose position and even whose very existence is put in jeopardy by the events of the war.

A somewhat closer look at the three instances of reprisals (or alleged reprisals) indicated above, reveals that the executions of American prisoners of war by the Vietcong bore all the characteristics of reprisals, but were prohibited by virtue of Article 13 of the Prisoners of War Convention of 1949; the taking of hostages by the Stanleyville rebels was not a reprisal at all, but a policy which the rebels introduced with a view to furthering their military and political interests—and which moreover was prohibited by Article 3 of the Civilians Convention; and the demolition of houses in Israel-occupied Arab territory, whether regarded as a form of collective punishment or as intimidation of the population, was prohibited by virtue of Article 33 of that Convention.

The Vietcong incidents bear an interesting resemblance to an instance recorded in an earlier Chapter: the execution of German prisoners of war by the French Forces of the Interior.[2] In both cases identical acts were committed in reprisal, proportionality was rigorously observed, and the suggestion is strong that the reprisals achieved the desired effect. And, more important yet, the parallel is even perceived when the policy re-

[2] Chapter V, § 5.2.3.

taliated against is taken into account: this consisted in either case in the killing of enemy prisoners. True, the grounds for this policy were not at first sight identical in both cases: while in the case of the F.F.I. the Germans had refused to recognize that body as an army the members of which were entitled to prisoner of war status and, hence, had seen fit to proceed to their wholesale execution, the South Vietnamese had taken to executing, allegedly after trial, individual prisoners whose acts they chose to qualify as criminal acts of terrorism. However, the real point at issue in the latter instance as well was the status of the prisoners: were they combatants who should be accorded prisoner of war status, and whose acts should be regarded as legitimate acts of belligerency unless these were at variance with the law of war, or were the South Vietnamese right in denying them this status? Here, the parallel is apparent again: in either case the victims of the executions were persons who had taken part in the hostilities without being unquestionably entitled to combatant status.

In retrospect, it is not hard to arrive at a positive appreciation of the position of the F.F.I.-fighters, if only because as a body they fulfilled all those requirements that from a substantive point of view could be considered essential for a recognition of combatant status; and the only flaw in their image, that they had been organized as a resistance army in occupied territory, was after the war recognized not to be a flaw at all, as in 1949 the members of organized resistance movements were included among the combatants who are entitled to prisoner of war status (Article 4 of the Prisoners of War Convention). In this respect the position of the Vietcong prisoners was decidedly less favourable: they belonged to a movement which to a much lesser degree had the outward appearances of an army in the classical sense, and which evidently counted among its members all sorts of individuals, ranging from disciplined and uniformed full-time fighters to incidental participants in single actions. This is to say that in each individual case the question could be raised with some right whether a particular Vietcong prisoner should be regarded as a regular combatant, or as a mere occasional participant in the hostilities who perhaps needed not be accorded prisoner of war status. However, this is a far cry from calling the lot of them "terrorists" and executing them for activities that perhaps even were lawful acts of belligerency (though in its specific form of guerrilla warfare).[3]

The parallel between the two instances leads to the reflection that even in situations where a belligerent might at first sight be justified in refusing prisoner of war status to certain persons who have participated in the hostilities prior to capture, it is very much to be doubted that their execution

[3] Significantly, the South Vietnamese authorities agreed only in August 1965 (that is, after the first—but prior to the second—execution) "to grant prisoner of war status to National Liberation Front (NLF) fighters taken captive while bearing arms"; *IRRC*, Vol. VI, 1966, p. 404.

during the course of the war on any large scale would be an adequate policy. Indeed, such a policy cannot fail to evoke sharp reactions, probably in kind, unless and to the extent that it be applied under the most stringent guarantees for an absolutely fair decision in each individual instance—a decision, in fact, the fairness of which not even the enemy could reasonably challenge. Needless to say, these are precisely the guarantees required by the Geneva Conventions of 1949 in particular for the infliction of the death penalty on protected persons.

A further reflection bears on the observable fact that in the Vietnamese situation the system of supervision as embodied in the Geneva Conventions operated only very defectively. Neither of the parties to the conflict had nominated a protecting Power, and the ICRC was only gradually and haltingly (and then after the executions had taken place) brought in a position to carry out its humanitarian functions (and then only as far as the prisoners in the hands of the Americans and the South Vietnamese were concerned).[4] This is to say that an important element in the system of the Geneva Conventions, intended *inter alia* to prevent or remove distrust as to the application of the Conventions on the part of the adversary, had not been brought into effect at the time of the executions. The general aspects of this probable connection between the element of supervision and the effective prohibition of reprisals constitute another subject that will be reverted to in the final Chapter.[5]

Two important conclusions arise from the Stanleyville hostages case. In the first place, the whole episode bears evidence to the appropriateness of the total prohibition of taking hostages, as laid down in Article 34 (as well as in Article 3) of the Civilians Convention of 1949. Obviously, the notion of "hostages" is wide and embraces a variety of situations. However, no matter what the motive for taking hostages, the persons brought in that position will always be exposed to considerable danger. This was evident in the situation at issue, where the hostages were in mortal danger even though their (supposed) value to the rebels lay precisely in being alive in their hands.

Secondly, the fact stands out that the speculation on the part of the rebels that the indiscriminate taking and indefinite holding of large quantities of hostages would enable them to secure advantages in the military and political sphere, proved a failure: except for a short pause in the operations against Stanleyville, neither the presence of the hostages nor the threats uttered repeatedly with respect to their persons produced any noticeable effect.

The destruction of Arab houses by the Israeli occupation authorities,

[4] *IRRC*, Vol. V, 1965, p. 477; Vol. VI, 1966, p. 404.
[5] See Chapter VII, § 7.3.4.

finally, could not be regarded as individual punishment of particular persons for their personal guilt, as not even the semblance of a trial preceded the actions.[6] As measures of collective punishment or reprisal, on the other hand, the actions were not only in contravention of a formal prohibition but indeed were inexcusable, as they were carried out despite the fact that in each and every instance the probable perpetrators of the hostile acts had been caught. Moreover, the efficacy in the long run of this policy of intimidation was more than doubtful.

"Judicial decisions", according to Article 38 of the Statute of the International Court of Justice, are among the "subsidiary means for the determination of rules of law". This subsidiary character is the principal reason why in this concluding section of the present Chapter the judicial decisions discussed in the foregoing have been kept to the last. Their treatment in the first section was determined not by legal but by historical considerations: the decisions were all connected with events of the Second World War, and it was only the moment of adjudication that brought the decisions in the present Chapter.

Another reason for giving the judicial decisions a rather less prominent place in the present section lies in their limited value for the development of the law respecting belligerent reprisals: with negligible exceptions, the judgments were all concerned with the peculiarities of the German occupation régime and, hence, had a bearing on occupation law in particular. True, in many cases the judgments contained extensive discussions of the general aspects of reprisals, collective punishment and so on, but these reasonings always had to be understood in the context of the situations and events discussed, that is, in the context of the law concerning belligerent occupation. Other aspects of belligerent reprisals were hardly broached at all, and in the one instance mentioned (to wit, the Dostler case) the point at issue was still the relation of reprisals to the treatment of (a particular category of) war victims. In no instance did a judicial body find occasion to pronounce upon the questions involved in the use of reprisals in the context of belligerent actions proper.

Even so, the judicial decisions recorded in this Chapter are of outstanding importance. First of all, because the very existence of this body of jurisprudence is evidence that the factual and legal questions involved in recourse to belligerent reprisals lend themselves to judicial assessment. Indeed, the judgments demonstrate amply that the judicial process, taking place in conditions of comparative detachment as regards the actual occurrences adjudged, is far better suited to achieve a fair, penetrating and

---

[6] It is an interesting speculation whether the demolition of houses (implying the destruction of essential community values) could be considered a legitimate penalty under any system of law. In this respect, the measure is fundamentally different from mere confiscation, which does not lead to a destruction of community values.

327

sufficiently objective appraisal of the questions at issue than the wartime decisionmaking process of the belligerents can ever be expected to achieve.[7]

Then, this was the first time that judicial bodies saw themselves confronted on such a large scale with the issues involved in the application of reprisals, collective punishment and the like. True, already the Peace Conferences of The Hague of 1899 and 1907 had dealt more or less thoroughly with these issues.[8] But the enormous mass of case material resulting from the Second World War gave the judicial bodies a far better opportunity to arrive at a realistic appraisal of the actual potentialities of these concepts and the consequences of their use.

This led, for one thing, to a fundamental debate concerning the position of resistance movements. The debate arose in the context of what often constituted a preliminary question in the juridical assessment of retaliatory measures which the German occupation authorities had taken against the population in occupied territory: viz., the legality or otherwise of the activities retaliated against. On the German side the thesis was tenaciously defended that active resistance in occupied territory was as such contrary to international law. It should be emphasized that this was an obvious misconception of the law as it had emerged from the Brussels and Hague Conferences: there was no question but that these Conferences had not wanted to outlaw resistance, any more than they had wanted to legalize it. In consequence, resistance belonged in the category of "unprivileged belligerency", where the participants could not count on the protection which the law of war affords legitimate combatants, and had to accept beforehand the risk of the harshest treatment and even death if they would fall into enemy hands.[9] The occupant was, moreover, evidently entitled to take the necessary security measures in defence of his interests. But he could not with good reason take the position that all resistance was an international wrong giving him the right to take reprisals against the occupied population.[10]

On the other hand, resistance movements could develop into centralized, Government controlled organizations, the actions of which could be imputed to the State. In such situations, those of their acts as would violate

---

[7] This emphasizes once again the imperative necessity of a faithful implementation of the provisions concerning outside supervision, embodied in the Geneva Conventions: this can to a certain extent remedy the inherent defectiveness of the subjective appreciation of events, both in their factual and legal aspects, by the belligerents.

[8] See Chapter II, §§ 2.3 and 2.4.

[9] The term "unprivileged belligerency" has been coined by R. R. Baxter, "So-called Unprivileged Belligerency: Spies, Guerrillas and Saboteurs", in *BYIL* Vol. 28, 1951, p. 323.—Under the 1949 Civilians Convention the position of the above category has been modified in so far as it is now no longer open to doubt that the death penalty can only be inflicted after a trial.

[10] In this sense, the judgments in the Kappler Case and in the Rauter Case (both instances).

the laws of war could give rise to measures in reprisal, against the occupied population or otherwise.[11]

An element that played an important rôle in several of the judicial decisions, was the character of the occupation régime maintained by the Germans in many of the occupied countries. It has been amply shown, in the judgment of the International Military Tribunal at Nuremberg first of all, that that régime amounted to a flagrant violation of practically every rule of the law of occupation in force at the time. While this policy of overall lawlessness is of course primarily to be deplored in view of the countless victims which it entailed, a secondary reflection is that it has distorted the picture of belligerent occupation, of the relationship between occupying Power and occupied population, and of the position of resistance movements in occupied territory. For, while the authors of the Hague Regulations had not conferred a right of resistance upon occupied populations, it could hardly be denied that the effect of the German practices was precisely to create such a right for the threatened populations, as a form of legitimate self-defence against the continued attempts on their national existence.[12]

This aspect of the matter was dealt with in several of the judgments recorded in this Chapter; and, while some of the tribunals concerned did not see their way to recognize that such a right of resistance had come about,[13] other tribunals did in fact accept the above argument.[14]

Many of the problems of occupation law to which the events of the Second World War gave rise and that had to be decided on the basis of the all too summary Hague Regulations, have lost their relevance to the future in view of the much more elaborate codification of occupation law embodied in the Fourth Geneva Convention of 1949. The point should however be emphasized that the problem discussed here is fundamental and cannot be disposed of by the simple means of adopting an improved set of conventional rules. In any future war, the situation may arise again where an occupant is seen to abuse his powers to such a degree that this goes to the very root of the system of powers, rights and obligations laid down in the Convention. In that event, the question will once again be whether the occupied population acquires by that fact a right of resistance —and strong arguments will militate in favour of a positive answer. While this answer to a fundamental legal question is in itself a matter of major importance, it should be realized, of course, that it is only part of the issue:

[11] The existence of this situation was assumed in particular by the Rome Military Tribunal in the Kappler Case.
[12] *Supra*, p. 204.
[13] This is implicit in the judgments in the Rauter Case (first instance) and in the Falkenhausen Case.
[14] Judgments in the Hostages Case (implicitly), the Einsatzgruppen Case, and the Rauter Case (second instance).

what remains, is the cruel suffering that such a course of events will unavoidably bring on human beings.

Another question involved in many of the judicial decisions was the nature of reprisals and collective punishment. This led to interesting attempts to establish the distinguishing marks of either of these concepts and their mutual relationship. It even led to the introduction of the notion of "quasi-reprisals", as something distinct from reprisals proper on the one hand, and hardly discernible from collective punishment on the other.

Among the various aspects of the question discussed, mention should be made in particular of the theories of collective responsibility evolved with a view to finding a basis for the justification of repressive measures against an occupied population. This concept of collective responsibility, which derives from Article 50 of the Hague Regulations [15] outlawing the infliction of general penalties "upon the population on account of acts of individuals for which they cannot be regarded as jointly and severally responsible", proved elusive to a degree. Some interpretations had the effect of virtually reducing it to a synonym of complicity in the criminal sense. Others sought the criterion in that members of the punished collectivity, to which the presumable perpetrators of the hostile acts were believed to belong, would have had authority or the opportunity to prevent the act. At other times, again, it seemed to suffice for persons to be considered "jointly and severally responsible" for a given hostile act if they were members of the same population, or lived (or found themselves) in the same locality, district or even country, as the presumable perpetrators.

Neither of these criteria was particularly satisfactory. To interpret collective responsibility as complicity meant to do away with collective punishment as a separate notion and to reduce it to a simple application of the doctrine of complicity according to criminal law; this could hardly be the correct solution of the riddle, if only because complicity in the criminal sense implies an individualized appreciation of each person's mode and degree of responsibility and never can be imputed, as it were blindly, to a collectivity of persons (as is done in the case of collective punishment). The criterion of authority or opportunity to prevent the act, as a faculty in the hands of certain members of the punished collectivity, resulted in making collective punishment largely synonymous to reprisals proper, as measures of retaliation against a more or less organized collectivity for the attitude of those in authority; as such it was evidently wrong, as the drafting history of Article 50 shows clearly that collective punishment was conceived as a concept distinct from reprisals. And the criterion of mere (original or accidental) co-membership of a certain collectivity was not really a criterion

---

[15] *Supra*, p. 57. For a comprehensive review of the theoretical debate around Article 50, see: O. M. Uhler, *op. cit.* n. 6 to § 6.2, p. 84 ff.

at all, as it reduced the requirement of collective responsibility to mere empty words.

In my view, the Rome Military Tribunal was nearest to the mark when it explained [16] that collective punishment rests on an exceptional form of responsibility, designated as collective responsibility and having as its outstanding characteristic that it is not responsibility at all in any ordinary sense of the term, because it consists in holding persons "responsible" for acts the real responsibility for which lies with other, for the time being unknown, persons. In order to avoid that this attribution of "responsibility" amounts to sheer arbitrariness, it is of course necessary to find some point or points of contact between the persons (or group of persons) held collectively responsible and the presumable authors of the act, other than the mere fact of living, or even finding oneself, in the same occupied country. The Italian Tribunal, like other judicial bodies, indicated certain elements that could be taken into account in this respect.

It would be going too far, however, to follow all these various exertions any further, as the effect of Article 33 of the Fourth Geneva Convention of 1949 has been largely to deprive these, like the deliberations and attempts at clarification of the concepts of collective punishment and reprisals in occupied territory in general, of their relevance to the future. Under that Article (which along with the other provisions of principal concern in the Geneva Convention of 1949 can with confidence be attributed the character of general international law) the accurate determination of a particular punitive or enforcement action as a reprisal, collective penalty, measure of intimidation or of terrorism is no longer decisive for an appraisal of the lawfulness or otherwise of the measure in question: it suffices to establish that the measure falls within the scope of these categories viewed as a continuum ranging from reprisals, as the most official and least arbitrary variety at the one end, to measures of intimidation or terrorism at the other extreme.

This is not to say that the determination of specific measures under one or other of the above heads would have lost all its interest: it retains its relevance especially in the context of a theoretical analysis and appreciation of such events.

While thus many of the judicial deliberations and decisions concerning these and similar subjects (as the question of the taking and execution of hostages and "reprisal prisoners") may have lost their relevance for an appreciation of the legal character of future events, their general and lasting interest lies in the conscious efforts on the part of the judicial bodies concerned to do away with arbitrariness and to apply legal standards to the issues before them. This is evidenced not only in the manner in which these

[16] *Supra*, p. 240.

bodies sought to clarify such concepts as collective punishment and reprisals, but at least as clearly in the manner in which they treated the hostages problem. For one thing, none of the tribunals abstained from assessing the legality or illegality of the executions on the argument that this would be a matter left to the discretion of the occupation authorities and not suited to judicial appreciation. Then, while the legal approach to the issue might vary widely (as sometimes became apparent even in respect to one and the same particular sequence of events) [17], it can be seen how the tribunals all came to rely in one way or another on certain fundamental principles, and namely on those of subsidiarity and proportionality; two principles, it should be added, the significance of which is not restricted to the hostages problem but extends to the whole issue of reprisals.

The former of these underlines the exceptional nature of measures in reprisal and implies that these can only justifiedly be resorted to when other, more normal means have failed: when, for instance, in an occupied territory the attempts to find the real authors of a hostile act have remained without success, or when in the context of the relations between belligerents the protests to the authorities of the enemy State have remained ineffectual.[18] Proportionality, on the other hand, emphasizes the character as sanctions inherent in the measures in reprisal; it should correctly be understood as proportionality (that is, absence of obvious disproportionality) to the acts retaliated against.[19]

The point deserves particular emphasis that the principles of subsidiarity and proportionality have been reaffirmed time and again in the judicial decisions rendered after the Second World War, thus contributing authoritative support to the contention that these are valid legal standards for the appreciation of belligerent reprisals.

---

[17] Cf. supra, p. 233, where it was pointed out that the same events were at issue in the Hostages and High Command Cases.

[18] Subsidiarity was made a specific requirement in the judgments in the Hostages Case, the Kappler Case and the Rauter Case (first instance, by implication).

[19] Proportionality was required in the same judgments as mentioned in the previous note. In the Falkenhausen Case the Tribunal did not apply proportionality as a requirement for justification; it merely considered the circumstance that the defendant had remained well below the ratios prescribed by his superiors as a mitigating factor.

CHAPTER VII

Results and Perspectives

7.1. THE LAW IN FORCE CONCERNING BELLIGERENT REPRISALS

At the end of the first Chapter is was recorded how Henri Brocher as early as 1873 expressed the view that the emergence of the concept of belligerent reprisals constituted a step forward in the development of the law of war, but that further steps would have to follow in order to achieve their partial or even complete abolition.[1] How far has this road been travelled in the meantime?

The answer to this question can conveniently be split into two parts, dealing respectively with treaty provisions and customary law; this division coincides with another: express prohibitions, and norms regulating recourse to belligerent reprisals. We shall hereafter examine how the law in force affects two crucial issues, viz., the retaliatory use of NBC weapons, and retaliation against the civil population in unoccupied enemy territory.

7.1.1. Prohibitions in force

Two bold steps have led to the protection against the impact of belligerent reprisals of all persons having the status of protected persons within the meaning of the Geneva Conventions: in 1929, the prohibition of reprisals against prisoners of war (extended in 1949 so as to embrace the wounded, sick and shipwrecked persons and the medical and other personnel protected by the First and Second Geneva Conventions); and, in 1949, the prohibition of reprisals, collective punishment and so on against civilian persons protected by the Fourth Convention.

The first step marked a break-through in the official treatment of the issue of belligerent reprisals: though up to that time the notion of belligerent reprisals had usually been regarded as an indivisible concept which, whilst horrifying, was indispensable, in 1929 a particularly horrifying and perhaps not quite so entirely indispensable specimen of belligerent reprisals was separated from the main body and prohibited outright.[2] This set the

[1] *Supra*, p. 44.
[2] *Cf.* §§ 3.1 and 3.5, *supra*.

333

scene for further development, which led logically to the result achieved in 1949.

The latter step, however, even though logically obvious, was again a remarkable feat in that it meant the outlawry of a form of reprisals which had been widely practised by occupying Powers; a form, moreover, which even the judicial bodies dealing with the war crimes of the Second World War had not only not dismissed as illegal, but in respect of which they had taken great pains to elaborate norms governing their use.[3] Viewed thus, the prohibition achieved in 1949 was a great innovation, which could rightly be characterized as "ein kühnes Experiment, eine Neuerung, die auf keiner Gewohnheit beruht, sondern als Protest gegen die bisherige Praxis geschaffen wurde".[4]

This "protest against the previously existing practice", laid down in the form of an express treaty prohibition of that practice, could not fail to evoke criticism, any more than its 1929 predecessor had escaped this fate.[5] As long ago as 1952, a sharp attack was launched by P. Boissier, who in

[3] See § 6.4; and *cf.* A. R. Albrecht, "War Reprisals in the War Crimes Trials and in the Geneva Conventions of 1949", in *AJIL*, Vol. 47, 1953, p. 590, at p. 611.

[4] P. Urner, *Die Menschenrechte der Zivilpersonen im Krieg gemäss der Genfer Zivilkonvention von 1949*, 1956, p. 88.

[5] *Cf. supra*, p. 107. Even in 1952, a writer criticized the prohibition of reprisals in the 1929 P.O.W. Convention, without so much as hinting at the conclusion of the Convention of 1949: A. von Reding, *Die rechtliche Stellung der Kriegsgefangenen im modernen Völkerrecht.*—In view of the earlier criticism of the 1929 Convention, it is less remarkable than Prof. Dr. H. F. Pfenninger seems to think that the prohibition contained in the Fourth Convention should meet with some theoretical opposition; "Sind persönliche Kriegsrepressalien erlaubt?", in *Schweizerische Juristen-Zeitung*, Vol. 60, 1964, p. 245, at p. 250.

The issue of whether the law in force at the time of the Second World War already prohibited the killing of hostages, has been hotly debated in the literature. An advocate of the idea that such a prohibition did in fact exist, Lord Wright (chairman of the United Nations War Crimes Commission) in an article published in 1948 characterized the killing of hostages as "terroristic murder" and asserted that "[t]he overwhelming balance of law, expressed by the highest authority, condemns without qualification that course." ("The Killing of Hostages as a War Crime", in *BYIL*, Vol. XXV, 1948, p. 296, at p. 301; *cf.* also p. 310). More cautiously, C. Pilloud (of the staff of the ICRC), while equally strongly rejecting the idea "que l'innocent puisse être puni pour le coupable", and while holding that the killing of hostages was incompatible with Articles 46 and 50 of the Hague Regulations, nevertheless deemed it impossible "d'affirmer que le droit international prohibe totalement la prise et la mise à mort d'otages"; a conclusion which he based on the interpretation of the Regulations in the manuals of several major Powers as well as on "le fait que le Projet de Tokio contient des dispositions expresses au sujet des otages, dispositions dont l'utilité resterait incompréhensible si l'on avait estimé qu'il existait déjà des interdictions suffisantes;" (et cetera; "La question des otages et des Conventions de Genève", in *RICR*, Vol. XXXII, 1950, p. 430, at pp. 443-444).—For obvious reasons, the issue has in particular drawn the attention of German authors; *cf.*, *e.g.*, H. A. Schütze, *Die Repressalie unter besonderer Berücksichtigung der Kriegsverbrecherprozesse*, 1950; A. von Knieriem, *Nürnberg—rechtliche und menschliche Probleme*, 1953; E. Trapp, *Die kriegsrechtliche Bedeutung der Nürnberger Urteile*, 1957.

his book *L'épée et la balance* advocated the displacement of the absolute prohibitions contained in Articles 33 and 34 of the Fourth Convention by a regulation, especially of the taking and killing of hostages. For, he considered, whilst recent practice had shown that the complete silence of international law on that issue could only lead to gross disproportionality and abuses on the side of the occupying authorities, the total prohibition would place these authorities in a dilemma: [6] the police measures allowed by the Convention would soon prove insufficient to prevent the security and prestige of the army being endangered by hostile acts on the part of the population, and if they then had recourse to the only remaining effective remedy and took hostages from amongst the population, they would in the event of new hostile acts be obliged to resort to their execution and—a crucial point—this would lead to far graver consequences than in the absence of an absolute prohibition: [7]

> "La réciprocité voulue par le droit étant rompue, l'adversaire, animé d'un courroux que l'opinion publique viendra alimenter avec des arguments tirés de la violation du droit, exécutera, lui aussi, des otages en cas de besoin. Cette pratique redeviendra d'usage courant, accentuée et envenimée par l'idée de 'crime de guerre', impuissante à servir de frein, mais bien propre, au contraire, à provoquer cette surenchère vers le pire qui est la forme diabolique de la réciprocité."

On the other hand, regulation of the taking and execution of hostages— which he considered feasible, for instance by means of an enumeration of requirements drawn up on the basis of the list contained in the judgment in the Hostages Case—would not deprive the occupation authorities of the one effective means at their disposal for combating resistance, and would no longer leave them with the need to improvise (which could only lead to disproportionality and abuse). But, more important, a commander applying such a regulation [8]

> "... ne provoquera pas, de la part de l'adversaire, de retorsions amplifiées, car il ne sera pas un violateur. De ce fait, la réciprocité se trouvera fixée sur un plan relativement acceptable."

However, the advantage of this third possibility over the second (viz., absolute prohibition) was only relative: [9]

> "Cet équilibre, hélas instable, durera jusqu'à ce que l'un des adversaires dépasse, ou paraisse dépasser, la mesure, et ce sera la spirale des surenchères, moins rapidement ascensionnelle cependant que dans le cas d'une interdiction absolue."

This interesting partly legal and partly psychological approach appears to rest on the following basic assumptions: that the taking and execution of

---

[6] *Op. cit.*, p. 122 ff.
[7] *Op. cit.*, p. 125.
[8] *Op. cit.*, p. 127.
[9] *Loc. cit.*

hostages would be an effective—and ultimately the sole effective—means of preventing the recurrence of hostile acts on the part of an occupied population, and that the rule prohibiting this is essentially based on reciprocity.[10] The latter proposition is of course of fundamental concern from a legal point of view. It is submitted, however, that precisely from that point of view it is ill-founded: while admittedly reciprocity is a very basic element in the structure of international law,[11] the prohibition to take (and, hence, to execute) hostages no more rests on a balance of interests, or of rights and obligations, between contracting parties than does the prohibition of reprisals against or collective punishment of protected civilians: fundamentally, it rests on a parallelism of interests of the belligerents and even of the entire international community. Hence, its violation by one side does not provide the other side with anything like a valid argument (let alone a title) for committing a violation in its turn.[12]

There remains the argument of the effectiveness and indeed indispensability of the taking and execution of hostages. In this respect, Boissier is supported by A. R. Albrecht, who concludes an article on the subject of *War Reprisals in the War Crimes Trials and in the Geneva Conventions of 1949* [13] with the observation that whilst experience has shown that "reprisals against prisoners of war are by no means indispensable", "[t]he prohibition of reprisals against 'protected persons' in the Convention on Civilian Persons ... is of more doubtful merit" as it can "create grave difficulties for an occupying Power". "Under circumstances of widespread and active resistance, an occupant may find the prohibition almost impossible to observe, for reprisals or the threat of reprisals against the local civilian population may be a vital measure in maintaining order amongst a hostile civilian population." This leads to a suggestion very similar to that made by Boissier, but formulated even more widely, viz., "that the blanket prohibition of reprisals in the Geneva Convention on Civilian Persons may need to be reconsidered and that the rules which were developed in the war crimes trials may be useful in establishing a sounder basis for the regulation of war reprisals against civilians."

Other writers have opposed this view. The first to do this, O. M. Uhler, published his work, *Der völkerrechtliche Schutz der Bevölkerung eines be-*

---

[10] As the author observes (p. 127): international law "demeure d'essence compromissoire (ce qui ne signifie nullement que ses fins ne soient pas d'entraîner ce que l'on pourrait appeler une économie de mal, mais que ses moyens sont foncièrement différents" (*i.e.*, different from those of municipal law).

[11] See too *supra*, p. 24.

[12] On the other hand, whilst the first violation does provide the enemy with a psychological opportunity, in the absence of a prohibitory rule he would not even need to wait for such an opportunity. For the rest, it seems a matter of pure speculation which will entail graver consequences: a prohibition that is in the end broken, or a regulation that is finally broken too.

[13] *Op. cit.* n. 3, p. 614.

setzten Gebiets gegen Massnahmen der Okkupationsmacht, as long ago as 1950, before the publication of Boissier's book. Uhler rests his case on two arguments. Firstly, collective punishment may be an obvious and simple means for preventing aggressive elements among the population from committing hostile acts, and as such it may even achieve momentary success, but in the long run its effect is quite the reverse, as it engenders embitterment, infuriation and a strengthening of the will to resist; viewed thus, collective punishment is really a double-edged weapon and leads in the end to "ein ungleicher, durch die ganze Besetzungszeit sich hindurch-ziehender circulus vitiosus von gegenseitig an Grausamkeiten sich über-bietenden Gewaltakten." [14] Secondly, it is not true that this intrinsically defective means is indispensable: there is nothing to prevent the occupying Power from prosecuting and punishing the actual perpetrators of hostile acts; it can bring into the occupied territory so many of its police and para-military forces as are necessary for putting a policy of individual punish-ment into effect. [15]

P. Urner, whose book *Die Menschenrechte der Zivilpersonen im Krieg gemäss der Genfer Zivilkonvention von 1949* was published in 1956, did not confine himself to endorsing fully the general view expressed by Uhler,[16] but also entered into the specific issue of hostages raised by Boissier.[17] With respect to this, he showed that it was highly questionable whether a regulation such as the one proposed by the latter would lead to an outcome fundamentally different from the known unfavourable result of a simple silence of the law. He also refuted the argument that execution of hostages in reliance on a regulation would be regarded differently by the opposite party from an execution in violation of an express prohibition: even though the occupant might seek to throw responsibility for the execution on the resistance, as being the result of their activities, the popu-lation would still hold the occupant accountable for an act which in its eyes would be nothing but the unjustifiable murder of innocent people.

The present writer accepts without reservation the correctness of the prohibitions laid down in Articles 33 and 34 of the Fourth Convention, both in their general aspects and as regards the specific issue of the taking and execution of hostages.[18] He is convinced that it would not be possible effectively to regulate the resort to reprisals against protected persons in occupied territory, and these measures are not in his view indispensable to the occupant. Moreover, a consideration of even more fundamental concern is that no matter what name be given to particular retaliatory measures against innocent members of an occupied population, these all amount to—

[14] *Ibid.,* pp. 118, 119.
[15] *Ibid.,* pp. 119, 120.
[16] P. Urner, *op. cit.* n. 4, p. 82.
[17] *Ibid.,* pp. 83-88.
[18] To the same effect, *e.g.*: Pfenninger, *op. cit.* n. 5, at p. 251.

or at any rate are experienced as—terrorism and hence are not only in-effectual in the long run, but are even likely to achieve the opposite of their intended effect. This being so, the end is far too uncertain of achievement to justify the means, a means so inhuman as to render inadmissible any reliance on that highly questionable maxim.

The above view raises an obvious question: what if the hostile activities on the part of the population assume intolerable proportions? Is the occupant then still bound to observe the prohibitions of Articles 33 and 34? This question has been dealt with by Urner, who held that such a development would go to the root of the Convention and would result in a lawless situation between the parties, as the Convention (and, hence, Articles 33 and 34) could only be expected to be applied if both sides showed a certain minimum respect for its provisions.[19]

This seems a dangerous argument and, moreover, one that is hardly in conformity with Urner's general line of reasoning described above: it opens the road to arbitrary overriding of the Convention in general and of Articles 33 and 34 in particular, as an occupant need then only allege that hostile activity on the part of the population has assumed such proportions as to make futile his policy of combating the resistance by dealing with individual perpetrators.

The correct answer to the question, and the only one that does justice to the letter and the spirit of the Convention, it is submitted, is the following: an occupant may, in order to maintain his position, take the necessary security measures with a view to preventing hostile activities; he may use the necessary military force in combating such activities whenever these actually occur, and he may punish the actual perpetrators of any illegal activities on whom he can lay hands. This, and in particular the combating of hostile activities with military means, may assume large proportions and may even develop into actual battles, involving the use of every permissible means of land or air warfare. Where such battles are waged, the civil population *in loco* (which technically is still an occupied population) should be spared as much as possible in so far as it does not take any part in the fighting, but it cannot claim any special immunity on the ground that it is an occupied population. On the other hand, the population outside the zone of operations is fully entitled to the protection offered by the Fourth Convention, including the prohibition of reprisals, collective punishment, and measures of intimidation or of terrorism. The Fourth Convention only ceases to apply when (part of) the territory cannot be regarded as occupied territory any longer, *i.e.*, when the army of occupation has lost the capacity to exercise its "autorité de fait" in the territory in question and cannot regain it without resorting to major military operations amounting to a regular war of conquest.[20]

[19] Urner, *op. cit.* n. 4, p. 87.

[20] As Article 42 of the Hague Regulations has it: "Territory is considered occupied

In other words: no amount of resistance on the part of an occupied population can free the occupying Power of its obligation to observe the provisions of the Fourth Convention, or Articles 33 and 34 in particular: the only factor which can terminate its obligations as an occupant is the termination of the occupation. In this respect, the situation is the exact reverse of that which arises when an occupant disregards the basic principles of the occupation régime so completely as to give the occupied population a right of resistance: in such a situation, too, the members of the population who take up arms against the occupant are still under an obligation to observe the laws of war.[21]

Among prohibitions achieved, mention remains to be made of acts "directed by way of reprisals against cultural property", as provided in Article 4 of the Hague Convention of 1954. This prohibition has not so far given rise to any discussion on its merits, nor is there any reason for opening such a discussion here: while obviously reprisals intentionally aimed against cultural property have not played any significant rôle in the history of belligerent reprisals,[22] their prohibition can only meet with approval. It may be added that no one could even suggest that a regulation of permissible recourse to reprisals would be preferable here.

7.1.2. Norms regulating the recourse to belligerent reprisals

As no general prohibition of belligerent reprisals has so far been achieved, it remains to be seen whether any norms regulate the recourse to such belligerent reprisals as have not been prohibited. The post-war trials of war criminals reveal a definite consensus of opinion regarding the validity of certain norms of this type. Admittedly, however, the specific form of reprisals to which these were applied by the courts (viz., quasi-reprisals in occupied territory) was actually banned in 1949. This gives rise to two questions. Can the norms in question be considered to apply to those other forms of belligerent reprisals which have so far not been expressly prohibited? And what is their precise import?

Regarding the first question, the fact is that the norms applied by the

---

when it is actually placed" (French: "placé de fait") "under the authority of the hostile army. The occupation extends only to the territory where such authority has been established and can be exercised."

[21] As to the latter situation, cf. supra, p. 205.
[22] The exception being the so-called Baedeker raids carried out by the Luftwaffe against certain cultural centres in Great Britain in the course of the Second World War, in alleged reprisal for similar attacks on German centres of culture; cf. Spaight, Air Power and War Rights, 3rd ed. (1947); with respect to the general aspects of the issue of allegedly retaliatory bombardments in the course of the Second World War, cf. Chapter V, § 5.1, supra.

judicial bodies were no newly invented *ad hoc* norms: they had all found support in pre-war literature, as well as in those few relevant decisions that had then been delivered on the matter. Hence, the significance of post-war judicial practice lies in the frequent and authoritative application of the norms to concrete cases, rather than in their formulation. It therefore seems beyond doubt that those norms the validity of which has been corroborated by recent decisions apply to non-prohibited instances of belligerent reprisals.

Among the various norms proposed in the literature, two have almost invariably been applied by the courts, viz., subsidiarity and proportionality.[23] The force of these basic principles of the law of reprisals is evident; they are of the very essence of reprisals. Their precise significance is more difficult to define; the terms "subsidiarity" and "proportionality" are obviously too vague for unqualified application to concrete cases.

The requirement of subsidiarity has generally been taken to mean that recourse to belligerent reprisals is an exceptional measure which must be regarded as an ultimate remedy, after other available means of a less exceptional character have failed. Applying this criterion to inter-State belligerent reprisals (as opposed to State-to-population or quasi-reprisals), it would imply that protests, warnings, appeals to third parties and other suitable means must have remained without effect, or so obviously been doomed to failure that there was no need to attempt them first.[24] Nor is this an unreasonable requirement even in time of war: the practice of belligerents shows a frequent recourse to such comparatively innocent means as protests, appeals to international public opinion, complaints lodged with appropriate international bodies, threats to punish individual war criminals, and so on. Indeed, it would seem that in no instance have belligerent reprisals been taken without previous attempts to obtain satisfaction in other ways, or in any event without its having been considered that these would have been possible.[25] However, on theoretical considerations the possibility cannot be excluded of situations where the fruitlessness of any other remedy but reprisals is apparent from the outset. In such exceptional situations, too, recourse to reprisals can be regarded as an ultimate remedy and, hence, as meeting the requirement of subsidiarity.

While the concept of subsidiarity can thus to a certain extent be clarified, it is nevertheless far from being a clear-cut rule that leaves no room for any freedom of appreciation. The alternative to this situation would be the adoption of specific rules subjecting recourse to reprisals to strict conditions, such as the expiry of a given term, or prior recourse to a given

[23] *Cf. supra*, p. 332.
[24] *Cf.* the discussion between the Dutch and British Governments, *supra*, pp. 149-150.
[25] A frequent objection to German practices in the occupied territories was precisely that purported reprisals were taken in situations where other, lawful, means of repression were open to the occupant.

340

international body. So long as these do not exist, however, there is no alternative but to accept the flexibility and relative vagueness of the requirement of subsidiarity.[26]

Similar difficulties attach to the requirement of proportionality. This requirement, too, can be clarified to a certain degree. In particular, it can confidently be stated that the proportionality envisaged here is proportionality to the preceding illegality, not to such future illegal acts as the reprisal may (or may not) prevent.[27] Expectations with respect to such future events will obviously play a part in the decision-making process; thus, a prognosis that the enemy, unless checked, will commit increasingly grave breaches of the laws of war, will tend to make the reaction to the breaches already committed still more severe. Whilst, however, this psychological mechanism may be of interest from the point of view of theories of escalation, it cannot influence a legal judgment of the retaliatory action, which can take account only of its proportionality to the act against which it constitutes retaliation.

Furthermore, it can be stated with equal confidence that proportionality in this context means the absence of obvious disproportionality, as opposed

---

[26] As Venezia points out, the freedom of decision left to States in this respect can easily lead to arbitrariness on their part; he even imputes to States "une invincible tendance à transformer en arbitraire" their "marge de liberté". See J.-C. Venezia, "La notion de représailles en droit international public", in *RGDIP*, Vol. 64, 1960, p. 465, at p. 491. Whether or not States really are subject to such an irrepressible tendency, however, abuse of their freedom of decision can always be challenged by interested parties or in appropriate bodies of the international community. As Venezia rightly observes: "L'examen de la jurisprudence internationale relative aux conditions d'exercice des représailles n'est pas sans évoquer le contrôle que le juge administratif français exerce sur l'utilisation par l'administration de ses pouvoirs de police" (*ibid.*, p. 485).

[27] With respect to proportionality *cf.* in particular Chapter VI, § 6.4, *supra*. For a contrary opinion, see McDougal and Feliciano, *Law and Minimum World Public Order*, 1961, p. 682: "It may be suggested ... that if reprisals are to signify something more than an adventitious 'survival of *lex talionis*', they should be adapted and related, not so much to the past illegality but rather and primarily to the future purpose sought. It is a common emphasis that the legitimate purpose of reprisals is not the infliction of retribution but the deterrence of future lawlessness. From such emphasis, it would seem to follow that the kind and amount of permissible reprisal violence is that which is reasonably designed so to affect the enemy's expectations about the costs and gains of reiteration or continuation of his initial unlawful act as to induce the termination of and future abstention from such acts. The quantum of permissible reprisal violence, so determined, may under certain circumstances conceivably be greater than that inflicted in the enemy's original unlawful act."—It is submitted that the weight of evidence is against this (seemingly logical) reasoning; it has emerged clearly from the investigation of specific belligerent reprisals in the previous Chapters, that the only instances having a semblance of efficacy were precisely those which strictly observed the requirement of proportionality to the wrong retaliated against. In other words, the "amount of reprisal violence" which is "reasonably designed" to achieve the purpose set forth in the quoted text, is precisely the amount proportionate to "the enemy's original unlawful act."

to strict proportionality. In other words, belligerents are left with a certain freedom of appreciation; a freedom which in law is restricted by the requirement of reasonableness, but which in practice can easily lead to arbitrariness and excessive reactions. One may regret this state of affairs; but, again, in the absence of a more precise rule (which, indeed, would here be hardly conceivable, seeing that reprisals need not be similar in kind and that even where they are their comparative effect on each side may be complicated and hard to assess) there is no alternative but to accept the flexibility and relative vagueness of the requirement of proportionality.[28]

Does "humanity" constitute a third requirement which, like subsidiarity and proportionality, governs recourse to non-prohibited reprisals? If so, this would be an important restriction on the freedom of belligerents to decide on certain measures of reprisal, and one, moreover, that, unlike subsidiarity and proportionality, would not be implicit in the nature of reprisals as sanctions of international law; for even in domestic law the infliction of sanctions often results in encroachments on such essential values as a man's freedom or his life. As has already been pointed out, however,[29] this question is of peculiar importance in the case of belligerent reprisals, as many of the rules of war permit conduct that verges on what is intolerable from a humanitarian point of view, so that their transgression by way of reprisal will soon lead to acts that, from the humanitarian point of view, are in fact intolerable.

Prior to the Second World War, a marked hesitation and divergence of opinion prevailed in this respect. In the literature, the view was widely defended that humanity did in fact constitute a valid norm of the law of reprisals, but at the same time there was decidedly less unanimity concerning the prohibition of the killing of hostages, and air bombardment of enemy territory was even often argued to constitute an acceptable reprisal.[30] Again, when the specific problem of prohibiting certain weapons was discussed in the Disarmament Conference, a strong tendency made

---

[28] Even in instances where at first sight the ratio would seem to be a simple matter of counting the numbers killed on each side (*e.g.*, one American P.O.W. for one Vietcong prisoner), other factors may play a part besides the strictly numerical aspect; *cf.* the judgment of the Rome Military Tribunal in the Kappler case (*supra*, p. 238), where it was pointed out by the Tribunal, in answer to an argument of the defence, that among the numbers executed by the Germans were numerous general officers and other superior officers, whereas the victims of the attack in Rasella Street had been common German soldiers. The opposite argument was advanced by German defendants in, *inter alia*, the Hostages Case, where it was alleged that the value of Germans as compared with Southern Europeans was indeed of the order of 1 : 100 (*supra*, pp. 221, 223). Cf. too p. 175, where there is a description of Czesany's attempts to arrive at a mathematical assessment of German and British aerial bombardments during a given period.

[29] *Supra*, p. 43.

[30] *Supra*, p. 112.

itself felt to exclude the use of the weapons in question even by way of reprisal.[31]

These various tendencies prevailed throughout the Second World War. Air bombardment was resorted to, *inter alia* in alleged reprisal for earlier illegalities on the side of the enemy, and this resulted in great destruction and countless casualties among the civil population.[32] Hostages were executed in large numbers.[33] On the other hand, no instances are known of the retaliatory use of prohibited weapons; though it is true that very few prohibitions of that kind were in existence at the time, the only important one being the prohibition on the use of poisonous gases or similar substances.[34]

After the war, only one aspect of this entire issue was assessed judicially, viz., the execution of hostages. And, despite the outright condemnation of this practice as a war crime in the Charter of London of 1945 and related instruments, judicial bodies were far from unanimous in holding it illegal irrespective of the circumstances of each individual case.[35] As regards retaliatory air bombardment, this was never explicitly submitted to judicial appreciation.[36]

In view of the above considerations, the present writer entertains grave doubts as to the correctness of the statement that "[c']est en effet une règle généralement acceptée que les représailles ne doivent pas comprendre des actes inhumains ou immoraux"[37]—which thesis the author quoted, Veezia, then applies to the issue of the retaliatory use of nuclear weapons. And, of course, it is precisely that issue—and, viewed from a different angle, the issue of the protection of the civil population—which makes most urgent the question discussed here. On account of its overriding

---

[31] *Supra*, p. 103.

[32] Chapter V, § 5.1.

[33] Chapter V, § 5.3.

[34] Hague Regulations, Art. 23 (*a*); Geneva Protocol of 1925.

[35] Chapter VI, § 6.1.

[36] The issue of the bombing of cities with the resultant death of civilians was referred to incidentally in the judgment of the American Tribunal in the Einsatzgruppen Case, in connection with the defence submission "that the defendants must be exonerated from the charge of killing civilian populations since every Allied nation brought about the death of noncombatants through the instrumentality of bombing". The Tribunal rejected this contention on two grounds: (1) Germany had started an aggressive war and had moreover been the first to bomb cities; (2) "even if it were assumed for the purpose of illustration that the Allies bombed German cities without Germans having bombed Allied cities", the fact would remain that "the one and only purpose of the bombing is to effect the surrender of the bombed nation" and, hence, not to kill noncombatants wilfully. The first ground came somewhere near a defence of reprisals; the second was *obiter*—irrespective of its merits (or, rather, demerits). *Trials of War Criminals before the Nuernberg Military Tribunals*, Vol. IV, pp. 466-467.

[37] J.-C. Venezia, *op. cit.* n. 26, at p. 488.

importance, it will be treated separately, in the final paragraph of this section.

As far as the alleged requirement of humanity is concerned, the conclusion of the present writer is that this is not a legal requirement of the law of reprisals, not even a flexible one, that would of itself suffice to render particular retaliatory measures illegal. On the other hand, as is evident from the uncertain practice, it may be considered to constitute a principle of law, which in any particular case should be carefully balanced against other principles, such as necessity and effectiveness.[38] The outcome of this weighing up process may, or may not, be the illegality of certain measures of reprisal.

7.1.3. The retaliatory use of means of warfare: the issue of NBC weapons

As has just been observed, the use in reprisal of specifically prohibited means of warfare has never amounted to much of an issue in the practice of belligerents. The theoretical possibility of such retaliatory use has however in the past occasioned considerable debate. The Disarmament Conference of 1932-34 was a case in point: there, the issues of absolute prohibition, supervision, specific sanctions and reprisals were treated as closely related subjects.[39]

In recent years this theoretical debate has been reopened, primarily in consequence of the introduction of nuclear weapons, although the enhanced potentialities of chemical and biological means of warfare have also played their part in this respect.[40]

Positive (written) law treats nuclear weapons, on the one hand, and biological and chemical means of warfare, on the other, differently in one important respect: whilst the use of the latter means is governed by express conventional provisions (the most recent being the Geneva Protocol of 1925), no international instrument of equal authority has yet come into being with respect to nuclear weapons. In consequence, the issue of the retaliatory use of this last-named category of weapons is dominated by a preliminary question which no longer burdens the debate on biological and chemical means of warfare: [41] is the use of nuclear weapons unlawful even in the absence of a conventional prohibition?

[38] With respect to the part played by principles in international law, see *supra*, p. 12.
[39] Chapter III, § 3.4.
[40] The term "nuclear weapons" is used here to indicate all nuclear and thermo-nuclear weapons. The term "chemical and biological means of warfare" is intended to cover the entire range of asphyxiating, poisonous and other gases and similar substances, as well as bacteriological and biological means of warfare.
[41] So far as chemical and biological means of warfare are concerned the main problem is one of interpretation, as the wording of the Geneva Protocol (particularly the reference to "other gases" and "all analogous liquids, materials or devices" in addition to asphyxiating and poisonous gases, and the equally ambiguous reference to

344

Much energy has been devoted to this important question.[42] For present purposes, however, there is no need to enter into the arguments advanced by the various participants in the debate: as it is the probable use by way of reprisal which is at issue here, it may simply be assumed that the use of nuclear weapons, like that of chemical and biological means of warfare, is prohibited.

Does this imply a prohibition on the use of these weapons in reprisal as well? I shall consider this question first with respect to chemical and biological weapons, and on the basis of the 1925 Geneva Protocol; not because the latter is an example of legal perfection, nor even because it can definitely be said to cover the whole field of presently-known chemical and biological means of warfare, but because it is an existing legal instrument binding a large number of States and at the same time a good example of what the endeavours of States to bring about the express prohibition of an important means of warfare have been able to accomplish.

---

bacteriological "methods" of warfare) gives rise to much uncertainty as to its applicability in respect of particular substances. While the General Assembly has repeatedly reaffirmed the validity of the Protocol (see, lastly, Res. 2454 (XXIII) of 20 December 1968), the issue of amending the legal situation with respect to the above means of warfare has recently been taken up by the Committee on Disarmament, which meets at Geneva under the auspices of the United Nations. See too the report of the Secretary-General on chemical and bacteriological (biological) weapons and the effects of their possible use, transmitted to the Security Council on 1 July 1969 (S/9292).

[42] See, for example, G. Schwarzenberger, *The Legality of Nuclear Weapons*, 1958, and "Report on Self-Defence under the Charter of the United Nations and the Use of Prohibited Weapons", in *International Law Association, Report of the 50th Conference held at Brussels*, 1962, p. 192; N. Singh, *Nuclear Weapons and International Law*, 1959; A. Euler, *Die Atomwaffe im Luftkriegsrecht*, 1960; Baron Von der Heydte, "Le problème que pose l'existence des armes de destruction massive et la distinction entre les objectifs militaires et non militaires en général", reports drawn up for the 5th Commission of the *Institut de droit international* (*Exposé préliminaire*, 1961; *Rapport provisoire*, 1964; *Rapport définitif*, 1967), in *Annuaire*, 1967, Vol. II.

Concerning steps taken by the United Nations to deal with this matter and the text of the resolutions it has adopted (including GA Res. 1653 (XVI) of 24 November 1961, which in one breath declares the use of nuclear weapons unlawful and requests the Secretary-General "to consult the Governments of Member States to ascertain their views on the possibility of convening a special conference for signing a convention on the prohibition of the use" of such weapons), see: *The United Nations and Disarmament 1945-1965*. See too the report of the Secretary-General on the effects of the possible use of nuclear weapons and on the security and economic implications for States of the acquisition and further development of these weapons, transmitted to the General Assembly on 10 October 1967 (A/6858).

Finally, mention should be made of the judgment dated 7 December 1963 of the District Court of Tokyo in *In re Shimoda and others*, an English translation of which has been published in the *Japanese Annual of International Law*, Vol. 8, 1964, p. 212; for an analysis of this case see: R. A. Falk, "The Shimoda Case", in *AJIL*, Vol. 59, 1965, p. 759.

It should be noticed that the Protocol itself is completely silent on the question of reprisals: it neither allows nor precludes them, whether in the form of retaliation in kind or otherwise. The issue of whether the use of gas is only permissible where it constitutes retaliation in kind arose in the League period, however, when in 1936 the Committee of Thirteen and the Council were confronted with the Italian use of gas in the Ethiopian campaign. It is true that the Italian authorities did not in so many words claim that that use was justified as a reprisal on account of atrocities committed by the opposing armed forces, but this was evidently what they wanted the world to believe and accept. And it is deserving of emphasis that the League organs rejected in no uncertain terms this construction and the implied suggestion that violation of norms of warfare other than the Gas Protocol itself could justify the violation of its terms.[43]

This authoritative interpretation of the Protocol must obviously be understood in its context: the crimes of which the Ethiopian forces were accused consisted in the inhuman treatment and killing of prisoners and other similar violations of the humanitarian part of the law of war; in other words, these were not encroachments which were likely to have any great influence on the outcome of the operations in progress. The question may be raised whether the League organs would have adopted the same interpretation if the alleged infringements of the law on the Ethiopian side had consisted, say, in the treacherous conduct of warfare (e.g. use of Italian uniforms and other distinctive signs) on so vast a scale as to threaten significantly to influence the events of the war.

While the answer to such a question cannot be anything but speculative, some greater certainty may perhaps be obtained by taking into account the discussions held on these topics in the Disarmament Conference. There, the issue treated was not the interpretation of the Protocol of 1925, but the effects of various forms of prohibitions proposed to the Conference. And one thing emerged with absolute clarity: the idea was categorically rejected that poison gas and similar prohibited substances might be used for retaliation not in kind, irrespective of the character of the norms violated on the other side and the probable influence of such violations on the course of the war.[44] In view of this attitude at the Disarmament Conference, it seems a safe conclusion that the delegates on the League Council in 1936 would not have arrived at a different result.

The above argument, however, is postulated in the context of the situation as it existed in the 1930s. Since then a new fact of considerable significance has emerged: the introduction of nuclear weapons. It might be suggested that their use on any significant scale is even "worse" than the use of chemical and biological means of warfare: hence, the theoretical argument might be raised that the retaliatory use of the latter means of

[43] See supra, p. 105.
[44] Supra, p. 103.

346

warfare could be justified even though it would technically constitute a measure of retaliation not in kind. The prohibition on the use of chemical or biological means of warfare as retaliation not in kind, would thus not extend so far as to cover retaliation "almost in kind".[45] Before entering upon this argument, however, it seems desirable to examine the case of retaliation in kind.

As was recalled above, the Geneva Protocol contains no indications regarding the lawfulness or unlawfulness of retaliation in kind. It should be added that neither does it provide for special sanctions against belligerents who violate its terms: it is completely silent on the entire issue of sanctions, whether special or general. The Disarmament Conference had in fact considered the question of whether the prohibitions on the use of gas, etc. should not be given "teeth" by means of special sanctions for their breach, and delegates had shown a strong inclination to accept the principle that a belligerent who was the victim of a gas attack would be entitled to retaliate in kind.[46]

The legal situation is even more complicated under the Geneva Protocol of 1925. For while its text may be silent on the question, the reservations made by a number of States are not. According to these reservations, the Protocol "shall cease to be binding" on the reserving States toward any adversary "whose armed forces, or the armed forces of whose allies, fail to respect the prohibitions laid down in the Protocol".[47] This is not merely a reservation of the right to take reprisals in kind, attached to an otherwise absolute prohibition: it amounts to a condition of reciprocity.

The far from negligible difference between these two situations is simply demonstrated. Violation by an enemy of an absolute prohibition on the use of a particular weapon may give a belligerent the right to use the same weapon by way of reprisal. In doing so, however, it is bound to observe not only the rules of the laws of war governing the use of weapons of war (*e.g.* as regards objectives and methods of use), but also the rules of the law of belligerent reprisals. In other words, the belligerent may only use the weapon as an ultimate remedy, other means having remained without effect; and it may only use it proportionately to the prior use made by the enemy; moreover, of course, the use should cease as soon as the enemy ceases using the weapon and gives sufficient guarantees that it will hence-forth refrain from doing so.

On the other hand, violation by one belligerent of a reciprocal prohibition of a given weapon has more far-reaching effects: it restores to the other belligerent its freedom to employ the weapon just as if no prohibition had ever obtained. The latter belligerent need not seek to justify, by asserting a right of reprisal, the use which it might thereafter choose to

[45] As Singh has described the reverse situation; *op. cit.* n. 42, p. 220.
[46] See Chapter III, § 3.4.
[47] As the text of these reservations generally runs.

make of the weapon; it need not ascertain whether other means might be sufficient to induce the enemy to abandon its policy of using the weapon; it need not observe proportionality, nor is it required to discontinue the use of the weapon when the enemy does in fact abandon its policy. The only rules which this belligerent is bound to observe in using the weapon in question are the aforementioned general rules governing the use of weapons of war.

In fact, the condition of reciprocity attached to the prohibition of a particular weapon amounts to a very effective, automatic sanction. Indeed, it is submitted that this is so powerful a sanction as to preclude recourse to any additional reprisals on account of the same violation. In other words, a belligerent which not only uses the same weapon but uses it in a manner or against objectives not permitted by the law of war, cannot justify the latter infringements of the law as being reprisals against the mere use of the prohibited weapon by the enemy.

To revert to the question under discussion, whilst it is true that the Geneva Protocol is not actually drafted so as to make its prohibitions conditional on reciprocity, the large number of States which have made such a reservation in acceding to the Protocol, together with the fact that even belligerents which have not done so can avail themselves of the reservations made by their opponents if the latter are the first to violate its terms, virtually result in reducing the unqualified prohibition laid down in the Protocol to a prohibition on condition of reciprocity.[48] Consequently, a belligerent need not resort to any theory of reprisals should it wish to use chemical or biological weapons in retaliation for their prior use by an enemy: it may simply do so, on the sole (though far from insignificant) condition that its use of them is in conformity with the norms governing the use of weapons in general.

In view of these considerations, it is submitted that it would be both unreasonable and unrealistic to assume that the right of "retaliation almost in kind" referred to above is more restricted. Hence, irrespective of the merits of the case, the conclusion of the present writer is that under the terms of the Protocol and the reservations thereto, and within the limits imposed by the aforementioned general rules, a belligerent is fully entitled to use chemical or biological weapons if the enemy has made use of nuclear weapons.

The next question concerns the use of nuclear weapons in reprisal. This

---

[48] It should be emphasized that in order to restore to the Protocol its original force, it would suffice for the reserving States to abandon their reservations: there would be no need for the cumbrous and risky procedure of amending the Treaty. On the other hand, the result would be limited in scope, as the question would then arise whether the text of the Protocol permits infringements which constitute reprisals in kind.

348

question cannot be dealt with on the basis of an existing treaty text: in attempting to answer it, it will be "necessary to rely much on general principles, and on a train of reasoning, founded on cases in some degree analogous to this".[49]

Relying heavily on one such general principle, namely, the "norm of humanity", Venezia categorically rejects the idea that nuclear weapons could be used in justified reprisal: "L'exigence d'humanité condamne l'emploi de l'arme nucléaire à titre de représailles". The dilemma in which the advocates of the "norm of humanity"-theory find themselves, however, emerges clearly from his next sentence, where he adds an important qualification to his statement of principle: [50]

"Il reste cependant que, si l'on admet que les représailles cruelles et contraires aux lois de l'humanité sont permises dans le cas où elles constituent le seul moyen 'efficace' de mettre fin à des agissements également cruels et contraires aux lois de l'humanité, la question de savoir si des représailles atomiques peuvent être utilisées pour ré- pondre à un acte d'agression perpétré au moyen de l'arme nucléaire, peut être tranchée par l'affirmative."

For a more precise answer to the question, it seems best to start once again with retaliation not in kind. Can such a retaliatory use of nuclear weapons conceivably be in conformity with the law of belligerent reprisals? In the first place, can it meet the condition of proportionality to the wrong committed by the other side? Some writers leave this possibility open. Thus, Lauterpacht writes that "recourse to the atomic weapon may be justified against an enemy who violates rules of the law of war on a scale so vast as to put himself altogether outside the orbit of considerations of humanity and compassion".[51] This argument, it should be noted, is strongly reminiscent of the position taken by the Italian Government with respect to the allegedly retaliatory use of gas in the Ethiopian campaign, when it refused to agree that the Geneva Protocol of 1925 "precludes the exercise of the right of reprisal in punishment of such abominable atrocities as those committed by the Ethiopian forces".[52]

The latter reference is already indicative of a danger inherent in Lauter- pacht's view: it necessarily implies a certain discretion for belligerents to

---

[49] To quote a famous passage from *The Schooner Exchange* v. *McFaddon*, United States Supreme Court (*per* Marshall, C.J.), 1812, 7 Cranch 116.

[50] Venezia, *op.cit.* n. 26, at p. 489. The concession which Venezia feels compelled to make to effectiveness, confirms the view expressed in § 7.1.2 that "humanity" is a principle of the law of reprisals, rather than a directly applicable rule.

[51] *Oppenheim's International Law*, Vol. II, 7th ed., 1952, p. 351. To the same effect: Euler, *op. cit.* n. 42, p. 165: "Die Verwendung von Atomwaffen als Repressalienmittel dürfte in diesen Fällen jedoch nur ausnahmsweise bei besonders schweren Rechtsver- letzungen gerechtfertigt sein."

[52] Letter dated 30 April 1936 to the Chairman of the League Committee of Thirteen; League of Nations *Official Journal*, 1936, p. 580; *supra*, p. 105.

decide that violations of the law of war committed by their opponents are so extremely grave as to make the use of nuclear weapons in reprisal permissible. On this point, Singh argues that "it is always dangerous to leave matters to the discretion of individual States since it would be a question of interpretation as to what constitutes 'gross', 'flagrant', or 'wholesale' violation of the law of war".[53] This argument, however, is not wholly decisive: the danger to which Singh rightly points, is inherent in the concept of belligerent reprisals as measures unilaterally decided by the injured belligerent. It may, on the other hand, readily be conceded that in the situation under discussion the danger assumes particularly grave proportions, in view of the exceptionally noxious nature of the weapons in question.

Indeed, the latter consideration may even lead to the argument that the use of these weapons as a means of retaliation not in kind would be grossly disproportionate in any circumstances. Singh comes near to accepting this view when he argues that the nuclear weapon "is unique and no other weapon is known to cause so much damage", so that "it would normally not be possible to justify the first use of nuclear weapons".[54] However, this statement leaves room for a different outcome in the event of "abnormal" situations. Singh himself admits that one could visualize one such situation: "resort to nuclear arms as a measure of retaliation in the event of the enemy using chemical and bacteriological weapons of war". "This would, however, amount to a measure of retaliation almost in kind", the author hastens to add.[55] This is true in a sense: whilst there is no single prohibition covering the use of chemical and biological means of warfare, on the one hand, and nuclear weapons, on the other, the prohibitions are in the same category, viz., prohibitions on the use of certain specified weapons of war of great military importance. Viewed thus, the retaliation "almost in kind" evoked by Singh might indeed be regarded as an instance of a proportionate retaliatory use of nuclear weapons.

An important factor seems missing, however, in the above line of reasoning. It can hardly be said that "the" use of nuclear weapons is, or is not, proportionate to "the" violation of this or the other norm of the laws of war. The damage caused by the explosion of a single nuclear weapon, of the smallest possible size, above a particular military objective of equally modest proportions, is incomparably less than the damage resulting from the wiping out of the enemy armed forces with the aid of a series of nuclear explosions of varying force. Similarly, chemical or biological weapons may be used in widely different quantities and under totally different conditions; and the same holds good with respect to the

[53] Singh, *op. cit.* n. 42, p. 216.
[54] *Ibid.*, p. 217.
[55] *Ibid.*, p. 220.

350

violation of other rules of war. In other words, the assessment of the proportionality of a particular belligerent reprisal is not merely a matter of comparing the rules that have been infringed, but rather of weighing the actual infractions against each other.

The above reasoning may perhaps give rise to the objection that whilst it might be correct from a purely theoretical point of view, it makes no sense in the case of nuclear weapons, as the slightest use of such weapons might be sufficient to provoke all-out nuclear warfare. This objection, however, is beside the point. What it is sought to establish here, is whether the rule of proportionality would in itself be sufficient to exclude the use of nuclear weapons by way of retaliation not in kind; in this context, such further reactions as their use might or might not provoke are irrelevant.

It is submitted that the use of nuclear weapons as a means of retaliation not in kind may in certain circumstances be proportionate to the wrong against which its retaliation is intended.

There is, however, another and even more fundamental aspect to the matter. The contention that nuclear weapons may be used as a means of reprisal not in kind, would seem to imply that a belligerent against which nuclear weapons are thus justifiably used is not entitled to retaliate in its turn: counter-reprisals are not permitted against legitimate reprisals. But nuclear weapons, even when employed with the greatest possible restraint, are an extremely effective means of warfare, and their use by one belligerent, whether by way of reprisal or otherwise, cannot fail to have a profound influence on the course of the war. Can it seriously be contended that a belligerent would in law be obliged simply to suffer this, because the nuclear explosion which destroyed its soldiers was a justifiable measure of reprisal? To my mind, it would definitely be over-rating the forbearance of States to assume that they could reasonably be expected to accept a system which included such deadly sanctions. In other words, if ever the use of nuclear weapons is prohibited by treaty, it is to be expected—and it seems reasonable—that the use of such weapons as a reprisal not in kind will be prohibited as well. The only exception to this rule might consist in "retaliation almost in kind" against the prior use of chemical or biological weapons; it has already been submitted that the prohibition on their use may be considered as falling into the same category as the prohibition on the use of nuclear weapons.

In a way, the latter remark anticipates our examination of the last remaining aspect of the issue under discussion: viz., the use of nuclear weapons as a reprisal in kind. The view is widely held that such use is permissible.[56] It seems necessary, however, to point out certain conse-

---

[56] Thus, Lauterpacht states without hesitation that "its use [*i.e.* of a nuclear weapon] must be regarded as permissible as a reprisal for its actual prior use by the enemy or his allies"; *loc. cit.* n. 51. See too Singh, *op. cit.* n. 42, p. 222; Euler, *op. cit.* n. 42, p. 166; Venezia, *loc. cit.* n. 50.

quences of this view. If the use of nuclear weapons in response to their prior use by the enemy is really to constitute a reprisal, they must be used in conformity with the law of belligerent reprisals, and in particular with the requirements of subsidiarity and proportionality. Is the mere fact that the enemy has seen fit to be the first to use such weapons a sufficient indication that nuclear weapons alone are capable of inducing it to alter its policy—or must the belligerent who is the victim of such use try the efficacy of protests, appeals to the Security Council of the United Nations and other more normal methods of seeking redress? Is it reasonable to require the belligerent to observe proportionality—and, if so, to what: to the explosive force of the weapons used by the enemy, to the suffering caused, or to the military effect achieved? Is the belligerent bound to discontinue using nuclear weapons as soon as the enemy effectively abandons their use? Is the belligerent even required to have the express aim of coercing the enemy to abandon its policy of using nuclear weapons? To pose these questions is not to suggest that they must all be answered in the negative: my purpose is merely to point out that there is another way of restricting the use of nuclear weapons than by considering their use in reply to the prior use by the enemy as being governed by the rules governing reprisals. This other approach is that of reciprocity.

In the view of the present writer, the possibility cannot be excluded that States would prefer to attach a condition of reciprocity to a prohibition of nuclear weapons by treaty, rather than accept the more limited right of reprisal.[57] It would then be important to prevent such a reciprocity clause from having consequences as drastic as those which, as described above, ensue from the reservations to the Geneva Protocol of 1925. In particular, it seems reasonable to demand that proportionality remain a requirement (notwithstanding the avowed difficulties inherent in that notion). Even with this restriction (which, it should be added, derives its reasonableness from the very nature of nuclear weapons), the condition of reciprocity seems a sufficiently strong sanction for enforcing the prohibition of being the first to use nuclear weapons.

Needless to say, the right of belligerents to retaliate in kind when nuclear weapons are used against them, whether construed as a right of reprisal or as a (mitigated) condition of reciprocity, does not in any way affect their obligation to respect the laws of war governing the use of weapons by belligerents.[58] This bears not so much on the conduct of

---

[57] "It is evident, however, that if one Party, in violation of definite rules, employs weapons or other methods of warfare which give it an immediate, great military advantage, the adversary may, in its own defence, be induced to retort at once with similar measures." *Reaffirmation and Development of the Laws and Customs Applicable in Armed Conflicts*, Report submitted by the ICRC to the XXIst International Conference of the Red Cross, 1969, p. 83.

[58] To the same effect Singh, *op. cit.* n. 42, p. 222: even when the use of nuclear

352

military operations against enemy armed forces, as on the protection of the civil population against the consequences of war. This will be discussed separately below.

Finally, it need hardly be added that the total prohibition of even the retaliatory use of nuclear weapons (and of chemical and biological means of warfare too) would be preferable to either a right of reprisal in kind or a condition of reciprocity. This seems unattainable, however, unless some other effective enforcement system is agreed upon. This too is a separate issue, and will be dealt with in the final section of this Chapter.

7.1.4. *Retaliatory attacks on non-military objectives: the protection of the civil population in enemy territory*

A problem repeatedly encountered in previous parts of this study is the impact on the enemy civil population of armed attacks, whether retaliatory or not, on enemy territory.[59] This issue, which already constituted a grave problem prior to and during the Second World War, assumed new and even more threatening proportions in the period subsequent to that war in consequence of the introduction of nuclear and other weapons of mass destruction.

Any idea of protecting the civil population necessarily implies certain distinctions: between combatants and non-combatants, military and non-military objectives, and so on. Developments in technical capabilities, however, coupled with the tendency towards "total war" apparent in certain recent armed conflicts and notably in the Second World War, have induced in some experts a profound pessimism as to the possibility of maintaining these distinctions.[60] With respect to this, three observations seem called for. Firstly, it is more than doubtful that the belligerents concerned would have contended that the practice of "total war" was either in conformity with existing law or had created new law; it is consequently a moot point whether any recent practices of this nature would amount to an "international custom as evidence of a general practice accepted as law".[61] Secondly, belligerents have, on the contrary,

---

weapons is "admitted as legitimate when resorted to as retaliation in kind", "it should be assured that their use would not amount to reprisals against prohibited categories of persons and property". Singh goes on to consider the situation which arises when the enemy not only uses nuclear weapons, but in so doing "destroys protected persons and property". That situation, however, can best be considered in our next sub-section.

[59] See Chapter VI, § 6.2.3, *supra.*

[60] With respect to this, reference may be made to the reports of Baron Von der Heydte, and in particular to the views given there, of Commission members Brüel and Giraud; *op. cit.* n. 42, *passim.* See too: *Reaffirmation and Development, op. cit.* n. 57, pp. 39-40.

[61] Art. 38, para. 1 (b) of the Statute of the International Court of Justice.

in numerous instances specifically relied on the distinctions mentioned above.[62] Thirdly, irrespective of how individual observers might be inclined to interpret the facts of recent armed conflicts and, in that light, to predict the behaviour of belligerents in future armed conflicts,[63] it is submitted that the issue of whether rules which protect the civil population against certain consequences of war have survived has for the time being been authoritatively decided by the unanimous adoption on 19 December 1968 of General Assembly Resolution 2444 (XXIII):[64] this makes untenable the argument that the law of war must surrender unconditionally to the new realities.[65]

The Resolution reaffirms, firstly, "that it is prohibited to launch attacks against the civilian populations as such". And with respect to the question of whether and to what extent the civil population may be made to suffer the consequences of attacks on military objectives, it states "that distinction must be made at all times between persons taking part in the hostilities and members of the civilian population to the effect that the latter be spared as much as possible".

The obligation to spare the civil population "as much as possible" is necessarily a vague one. Indeed, drawing the line between justifiable and unjustifiable damage to the civil population as a result of attacks on military objectives in enemy territory is one of the major problems of the present-day law of war, to which no definite solution has yet been found.[66] I shall not attempt a solution here. For present purposes, let it suffice to note that attacks on enemy territory may be unjustifiable on account of the damage caused to the civil population, notwithstanding the fact that military targets also suffer. It seems that this will obtain in two situations: unmistakable gross disproportionality between the importance of the military target(s) attacked and the civilian loss caused, and evident complete indifference as to the targets hit. Attacks falling under either of these heads may be termed indiscriminate attacks.

In short, the General Assembly Resolution prohibits (or, rather, re-

---

[62] See Von der Heydte, *Rapport définitif; op. cit.* n. 42, p. 168 f.

[63] Part of the debate concerning the future can even be disregarded as being irrelevant to the present discussion: *i.e.*, the arguments about "counter city" versus "counter force" strategy, "first" and "second strike capability", and so on. For that debate, and the realities underlying it, bear on the coercive or deterrent effect of the mere potential or threatened use of the weapons of mass destruction, as well as on the need to prevent the outbreak of an armed conflict in which they would actually be used. The point at issue in the present discussion, on the other hand, concerns the position of the civil population in the event of an armed conflict already having broken out.

[64] *Supra*, p. 284.

[65] "Le Droit ne doit pas reculer devant la force brutale; il ne doit pas capituler ni abandonner le terrain à l'inhumanité."—Von der Heydte, *Rapport définitif; op. cit.* n. 42, p. 162.

[66] See in particular the reports of Von der Heydte, *op. cit.* n. 42, *passim. Cf.* also *Reaffirmation and Development, op. cit.* n. 57, p. 65 ff.

affirms the already existing prohibition of) armed attacks on enemy territory which are either indiscriminate or directed against the civil population as such.

There remains the question of reprisals. Can attacks on enemy territory with nuclear or other weapons which violate the rules protecting the civil population be justified as reprisals?

A preliminary point is that such attacks would not only violate the above general rules but would also be likely to infringe certain specific rules embodied in the Geneva Conventions of 1949 and the Hague Convention of 1954, which create specially protected objects even in unoccupied enemy territory. These are mainly hospitals, whether military or civilian (Articles 19 of the First and 18 of the Fourth Geneva Conventions), and those objects constituting "cultural property" as defined in Article 1 of the Hague Convention. Article 4 of the latter Convention even expressly precludes belligerents from making cultural property the object of reprisals, and the same obtains for military hospitals by virtue of Article 46 of the First Geneva Convention. The Fourth Convention, on the other hand, is not explicit on this point; [67] but the only reasonable interpretation seems to be that reprisals against civilian hospitals in enemy territory are prohibited, since they would be completely incompatible with the spirit of the Geneva Conventions.

These specific rules protecting particular objects in enemy territory play an important rôle in the arguments of some authors. The most extreme position in this regard is taken by Von der Heydte, who argues that weapons cannot justifiably be used in reprisal if their effect cannot be limited to objects against which reprisals may lawfully be directed.[68] This decides at least part of the issue, as it excludes the retaliatory use of weapons of mass destruction against enemy territory; the question remains, of course, whether retaliation with conventional means of warfare would be permissible.

Singh attaches less far-reaching consequences to the above specific

---

[67] Article 33, containing the prohibition of reprisals against protected persons and their property, is in a different part of the Convention from Article 18 dealing with the protection of civilian hospitals, viz., in Part III, the scope of which is restricted to the status and treatment of protected persons in the territories of the Parties to the conflict and in occupied territories.

[68] Von der Heydte, *Exposé préliminaire, op. cit.* n. 42, p. 89: "A partir du moment où les effets de ces armes ne peuvent pas être limités à des objets qui, juridiquement, sont susceptibles d'être exposés à des représailles, on doit admettre que ces armes ne peuvent pas être utilisées pour des représailles. En conséquence, les représailles ne sauraient constituer une justification de l'emploi des moyens de destruction massive, même s'il y avait proportionnalité entre le dommage causé par les représailles et celui causé par l'acte illicite que ces représailles ont pour but de réprimer."—This opinion is maintained in *Rapport provisoire, ibid.*, p. 53.

rules.[69] Whilst emphasizing that the use of nuclear weapons by way of retaliation in kind should not amount to reprisals against protected persons or property, he argues that a different view may be indicated if the enemy has been the first to attack such persons or property. His argument may be summarized by saying that the use against enemy territory of nuclear and thermo-nuclear weapons is only permissible as retaliation in kind and on the further condition that such use either does not violate the provisions protecting certain categories of persons or property, or, if it does violate them, that the enemy has done so first.

In the opinion of the present writer, both Von der Heydte and Singh attach too much importance to the special rules in question. This is shown by the following example. Among the objects covered by the definition of "cultural property" in Article 1 of the Hague Convention of 1954, are "manuscripts, books and other objects of artistic, historical or archaeological interest". Suppose, now, that certain valuable manuscripts are in the house of a private person situated in a large residential district: could it be seriously contended that, according to the intention of the Contracting Parties, knowledge of this fact by the enemy would be sufficient to preclude him from carrying out a retaliatory attack against the district in question? Or—if an example drawn from the Geneva Conventions is preferred—is it to be believed that the known presence in one of the houses of the district of a wounded person (who, according to Article 16 of the Fourth Convention, "shall be the object of particular protection and respect") would so preclude the enemy?

The actual purport of the Conventions in question, it is submitted, is merely to protect certain named objects from attacks directed specifically against those objects, not to decide *en passant* the entire, much wider, issue of the protection of the civil population.[70] In other words, the above-

---

[69] Singh, *op. cit.* n. 42, p. 222: "However, if the first user of nuclear weapons destroys protected persons and property, there would appear to be justification to retaliate in kind, both as a measure of self-defence and in reprisal, even though the provisions of the Geneva Conventions were being violated. This would appear a warranted conclusion, because, short of surrender to the first user of these prohibited weapons, the victim would have retaliation in kind as the only remedy. As the first user would be clearly guilty of a crime, to allow him the laurels of victory by surrendering to him with a stockpile of nuclear weapons, which cannot be used for fear of violation of the provisions of the Geneva Conventions, would be to encourage the first use of the prohibited weapon. Thus, short of destruction of the human race and the world, the only permissible use of thermo-nuclear weapons would appear to be as retaliation in kind alone."

[70] Significantly, the ICRC in its recent report to the XXIst International Conference of the Red Cross confines the scope of the prohibition on reprisals in the Geneva and Hague Conventions to the persons and objects protected by them; and it puts on record the opinion of experts that "[r]eprisals can, of course, in no case be exercised in the fields covered by the Geneva Conventions and against the persons protected by these"; *Reaffirmation and Development, op. cit.* n. 57, at pp. 84 and 87.

356

mentioned specific rules are largely irrelevant to the question of the justifiability or otherwise of retaliatory attacks on the civil population, whether with weapons of mass destruction or with conventional weapons.[71] Its solution is to be sought only on the basis of the general rules applicable to the issue in its entirety.

It is noteworthy that in the statements of those publicists who take this more general approach and who moreover accept the use of nuclear weapons by way of retaliation in kind, it is usually implied, rather than stated expressly, that this would amount to their retaliatory use against enemy territory and, hence (save in exceptional situations) against the enemy population. This is evident, for instance, in an opinion expressed by Schwarzenberger, to the effect that nuclear weapons "would probably still be legitimate as identical reprisals against an enemy who, by their use, had testified to all the world his own barbaric character";[72] this statement can have no bearing on the use of nuclear weapons in, say, outer space.

It seems both necessary and possible, however, to go more deeply into the problem, starting with the question of the justifiability of retaliatory attacks against the enemy civil population as such. A good starting-point is the reflection that "war reprisals are legal de lege lata, if they correspond to the conditions laid down by the law for the exercise of war reprisals".[73] Secondly, it is clear that there is no express treaty prohibition of reprisals against the enemy civil population, nor can it be maintained that a customary rule to that effect has emerged from the practice of belligerents. Hence, the issue is reduced to an appreciation of whether reprisals against the population as such "correspond to the conditions laid down by the law for the exercise of war reprisals". In this connection, it is submitted, the requirements of subsidiarity and proportionality are of little avail: it is not hard to imagine a situation where even the use of thermo-nuclear weapons against the enemy population could be regarded as a last resort

[71] This is not to say that the specific rules referred to lack all relevance in the present context: e.g., the rules affording special protection to such cultural property as meets the conditions therefor (inter alia, international acceptance of the special status, and registration with UNESCO; Arts. 8-11 of the Convention) exclude any armed attack, whether retaliatory or otherwise, on objects situated near the cultural property and which would be likely to entail damage to the cultural property. Similar reasoning applies if hospital or security zones or localities have been established in enemy territory. However, even here the protection afforded does not cover all war risks. In particular, it has always been realized that the provisions in the Fourth Geneva Convention of 1949 concerning hospital or security zones cannot protect the persons inside those zones from the effects of nuclear explosions in relatively distant regions.
[72] Schwarzenberger, Report, op. cit. n. 42, p. 221. See also: Euler, op. cit. n. 42, pp. 165-166; Venezia, op. cit. n. 26, p. 489.
[73] J. L. Kunz in a letter dated 13 November 1961 to Baron Von der Heydte; Annuaire, op. cit. n. 42, p. 123, at p. 131. Cf. too Reaffirmation and Development, op. cit. n. 57, p. 83: "it is a generally admitted rule that belligerents can resort to [reprisals], except in cases where they are explicitly prohibited."

357

and would, moreover, be proportionate to their previous use by the enemy.

This leaves the principle of humanity, to be weighed against the effectiveness of the measures contemplated. The inhuman and indeed barbarous character of retaliatory armed attacks on the civil population as such need hardly be emphasized: already evident in attacks with conventional weapons, it is even more pronounced if the weapons used are weapons of mass destruction. In the view of such authors as Venezia [74] and Singh,[75] however, this is counter-balanced by the effectiveness of the measures as reprisals. Is this view correct?

The question can be divided in two: the effectiveness of such measures as a matter of objective fact, and the expectations of belligerents in this regard. As far as concerns the objective effectiveness of measures of retaliation against the enemy civil population, the experience of recent armed conflicts, including the Second World War, is decidedly negative: it shows clearly that the short-term effect of such measures is uncertain, and that in the long run they are even likely to produce the opposite effect to the one intended. In other words, the value of a policy of retaliation against—or, which amounts to the same thing, the terrorisation of—the civil population is, to say the least, highly doubtful.[76]

It must be conceded, however, that on the basis of the available facts it cannot unreservedly be stated that the effect of such measures is negligible, or even negative, in all circumstances. Belligerents might accordingly claim that they expect the measures to lead to the outcome they intend; and although the present writer rates the chances of such a successful outcome extremely low, it cannot be denied that this expectation might in certain situations even be a reasonable one.

Weighing this dubious effectiveness against the unquestionable inhumanity of the form of retaliation under consideration leads to a twofold conclusion. On the one hand, retaliatory attacks on the enemy civil popu-

---

[74] See n. 50, *supra.*

[75] See n. 69, *supra.*

[76] "In the event, an obvious lesson was to be drawn from the armed conflicts which had taken place to date, as military experts had declared, thus confirming what the ICRC had learnt in the course of previous consultations: not only did bombardments to terrorize cause great suffering, but they were to a large extent ineffective; they often even strengthened the moral resistance of the enemy and consequently, far from shortening the conflict, prolonged it."—*Reaffirmation and Development, op. cit.* n. 57, p. 68.

The prohibition of terror was already expressed in the Draft Rules of 1956 (Art. 6; *cf.* too the commentary at p. 57 of the 1958 edition); and see Chapter VI, § 6.2.3. See too the draft resolution voted unanimously in September 1967 by the 5th Commission of the *Institut de droit international*, the 6th operative paragraph of which reads as follows: "Sont interdites par le Droit international public en vigueur sans préjuger de la nature de l'arme utilisée, toutes les actions qui, à quelque titre que ce soit, sont destinées à semer la terreur dans la population, soit d'un centre urbain ou rural, soit d'une région, soit d'un pays."—*Annuaire, op. cit.* n. 42, p. 530.

lation as such, irrespective of the weapons with which they are carried out, are so much at variance with the fundamental concepts of the law of reprisals that they can hardly be regarded as anything but highly reprehensible.[77] On the other hand, it seems a moot point whether the law already positively precludes belligerents from seeking to justify such practices as reprisals. This aspect of the matter will be considered further below.

It should be added that the same twofold conclusion applies, *mutatis mutandis*, when the issue is complicated by the presence of military objectives in the region attacked and consequently takes the shape of indiscriminate retaliatory attacks on enemy territory: in such a situation the destruction of military targets is not sufficiently important to outweigh the destruction caused to the civil population.

Belligerents who attack enemy territory in retaliation for earlier attacks on their own territory, may rely on other arguments besides reprisals. Significantly, Singh argues that "if the first user of nuclear weapons destroys protected persons and property, there would appear to be justification to retaliate in kind, both as a measure of self-defence and in reprisal"; and he adds that "short of surrender to the first user of these prohibited weapons, the victim would have retaliation in kind as the only remedy".[78]

The question of whether self-defence would be a sufficient ground for justifying retaliatory attacks on enemy territory, in particular (though not exclusively) with nuclear weapons or other means of mass destruction, lies

---

[77] Substantially the same answer to the question put, in particular with respect to nuclear retaliation, was given in 1965 by Rear-Admiral Sir Anthony Buzzard, former Director of Naval Intelligence in the United Kingdom. He develops his argument with the aid of an analogy: if a thug "threatens to kill my children", it would be justified as a deterrent "to threaten his children". "But", he continues, "supposing the deterrent failed, and despite it the thug killed one of my children. Would I then be justified in implementing my threat and killing one of his innocent children? One's first reaction is, I think, to say: 'No, never'. But on second thought one might, I think, just possibly qualify this and conclude that there might conceivably be one condition in which that child of the thug could be killed, and that might be if the action was likely to stop the thug from killing the rest of my family. For it is, I believe, a basic principle of international law that resort to an illegal means can be justified by way of reprisals for an illegal enemy action, for one purpose only, that of stopping the enemy from so breaking the law. If, however, our reprisals are *not* expected to stop the enemy from breaking the law, or, in fact, *fail* to stop him, then we have no right to go on shooting the rest of the thug's children. *Threatening* enemy cities with nuclear or conventional weapons can, therefore, perhaps be justified, if it is necessary as a deterrent to protect ours. But *destroying* them, if the enemy destroys ours, could only conceivably be justified in the one case of its being likely to stop the enemy from continuing to attack ours."—"Western Unity in Defence and Disarmament", in *Wilton Park Journal*, No. 35, July 1966, p. 21, at p. 23.
[78] *Cf.* n. 69, *supra*.

outside the scope of the present study. I shall accordingly confine myself to some general observations.

Attacks on the civil population as such seem the most inadequate measures of self-defence imaginable; and the same holds good of indiscriminate attacks on the enemy territory. However, irrespective of the adequacy or inadequacy of such attacks as measures of self-defence, it seems necessary to distinguish between the facts and the law. As far as the facts are concerned, it seems only realistic to expect that in the event of an armed conflict between belligerents each of whom possesses nuclear and thermo-nuclear weapons, any large-scale use of these weapons by one side against the territory of the other will automatically lead to their retaliatory use by the latter against the territory of the former.[79]

To admit this, however, is not in the least to admit that the use of these weapons in retaliation for their prior use by the enemy could be justified as an act of self-defence if it contravenes the rule prohibiting indiscriminate attacks on enemy territory. Indeed, the law may well be that such retaliatory attacks, even though to be expected in certain extreme circumstances, would be unjustifiable, whether as reprisals, as acts of self-defence, or otherwise. On the other hand, the above-mentioned element of uncertainty as to what the law is would probably play a part here too.

Finally, it remains for us to consider this uncertain state of the law at greater length. The question, as stated above, is whether retaliatory attacks against the civil population as such, or indiscriminate in character, should be regarded as merely reprehensible or as positively prohibited de lege lata. For obvious reasons, the writer would prefer to endorse the latter view. It would be much the clearer position, and it would moreover accord more fully with the available data and the principles involved. I hesitate, however, to say that this is a statement of the law as it stands. For one thing, a rule to the effect that reprisals against the civil population in unoccupied enemy territory are prohibited would probably not prevent recourse to such reprisals in all circumstances. Indeed, it would certainly be broken in an extreme situation such as all-out nuclear war. As for less extreme situations, it seems impossible to make any reliable prediction of its chances of being observed: much would depend on the degree to which the

---

[79] See § 7.1.3, *supra*, where the view is expressed that a future prohibition of nuclear weapons will probably be accompanied by some sort of reciprocity clause. And *cf.* the letter of J. L. Kunz, *loc. cit.* n. 73, where he states that it would be "wholly unrealistic that a belligerent would be forbidden to exercise nuclear reprisals against an enemy who first has used and is using nuclear weapons in the most illegal way. Such belligerent should be obliged to suffer patiently that his country is wiped off the map, without having the right to retaliate with nuclear weapons? 'Nuclear retaliation' is the declared policy of nuclear Powers."

lesson has been learnt that terror is as ineffective as it is inhuman.[80] These reflections need not, however, in themselves stand in the way of regarding this rule as part of the existing body of law: universal observance is not a characteristic of legal rules.

A more serious difficulty is that the rule, far from being the creation of treaty law or customary law, results from a process of legal reasoning on the basis of certain broadest principles of the law of reprisals. Although this reasoning to my eyes is cogent, it would be presumptuous to contend that it is so absolutely compelling as to leave no room for any other line of argument. Indeed, as is apparent from the foregoing, others have arrived at a different conclusion. It cannot therefore be maintained that the rule posited above is a statement of the law as it stands. The resulting uncertain state of the law, it should be admitted, leaves decision-makers a wide margin of appreciation and decision. It hardly needs emphasizing that this margin is particularly dangerous here and, hence, needs urgently to be reduced as far as possible. To that end, it would be highly desirable that the rule developed in the text above be authoritatively confirmed in one way or another by the international community.

Whether such an authoritative confirmation can reasonably be expected in the near future, is of course a matter of pure speculation. An obvious consideration is that the willingness of States to agree on any solution of the issue of reprisals against the enemy civil population will be distinctly limited so long as other crucial aspects of the fate of the civil population in the event of war and, in that context, of the use of weapons of mass destruction, remain undecided. On the other hand, the adoption of General Assembly Resolution 2444 (XXIII) is an indication that a willingness to consider these problems is not wholly absent. It is therefore to be hoped that efforts such as those of the ICRC will continue and will in the end lead to the adoption of a set of rules appropriate to modern conditions of warfare.[81] The prohibition of attacks against the enemy civil population by way of reprisal would be an essential element of any such set of rules.

---

[80] *Cf.* the opinion of the military expert consulted by the ICRC in 1956, recorded, *supra*, p. 280.

[81] As reported by the ICRC, the experts whom it consulted in February 1969 all stressed the importance of the resolution as "the expression of the legal conception of the international community" and of "the conscience of the peoples" and as a reaffirmation of the existing law. However, it was also stressed by several experts "that, however important, it did not represent an issue but a starting-point" and that "its principles should be developed in the form of more detailed rules". *Reaffirmation and Development, op. cit.* n. 57, at p. 67.

7.2. THE RELATION OF BELLIGERENT REPRISALS TO CERTAIN OTHER CONCEPTS

In the first Chapter of this study some attention was given to the relation between reprisals, on the one hand, and self-defence and retorsion, on the other.[1] In the present closing Chapter, it seems appropriate to consider some other concepts closely related to belligerent reprisals in particular.

7.2.1. Reciprocity

A first such narrowly related concept is reciprocity. It has been suggested that this lies at the root of reprisals, or, in other words, that it provides the basic ground for their justification. One author who takes this position with respect to belligerent reprisals in particular, G. Schwarzenberger, asserts in his book *The Law of Armed Conflict*[2] that "the laws of war constitute a typical illustration of the international law of reciprocity" and that a belligerent when confronted with large-scale breaches of the laws of war on the part of the adversary "may ... prefer to take ... immediate action and, by his reprisals, reverse the operation of the chief working principle behind the laws of war from positive, to negative, reciprocity".

A discussion of the general aspects of this issue in the first Chapter led to the conclusion that the above theory rests on an unwarranted exaggeration of the contractual, synallagmatic element in international law and for the rest does not account for the element of law enforcement which is a characteristic of reprisals;[3] an element the value of which Schwarzenberger himself implicitly acknowledges when he goes on to say that the reprisals to which the belligerent resorts "may involve the disregard of identical or other rules of warfare in order to induce the enemy to comply with his duties under the laws of war".

A slightly different use of the term would be to contend that reciprocity operates in the law of war as a justificatory device comparable to, but distinct from, reprisals. Indeed, this is no more than an obvious truth in respect to those rules of the law of war which are conditioned by an express or implied reciprocity clause. An example of such a rule may be seen in the prohibition to use chemical means of warfare.[4] Likewise, a no-first-use declaration in respect of nuclear weapons would in reality be

---

[1] § 1.2.4, *supra*.
[2] Being Vol. II of his *International Law as Applied by International Courts and Tribunals*, 1968. The quoted words are at pp. 452 and 453. *Cf.* too J. Stone, *Legal Controls of International Conflict*, 2nd ed., 1959, p. 354: "The premise on which retaliation in war proceeds is, indeed, that a belligerent's duty to observe the laws of war is not absolute, but conditional on the enemy's reciprocation."
[3] *Supra*, p. 24.
[4] § 7.1.3, *supra*.

nothing else but a prohibition under the condition of reciprocity.[5] While the basis of such unqualified reciprocity clauses is military necessity (it being unacceptable for a belligerent to be placed in a position of inferiority with respect to his adversary where such highly important means of warfare are concerned),[6] their effect is even more far-reaching than that of an application of the doctrine of reprisals, as the belligerent who avails himself of the reciprocity clause is not obliged to respect the principle of subsidiarity and consider the possibility of other reactions first, nor is he under an obligation to heed the standard of proportionality.

Apart from such express or implied clauses of reciprocity attached to specific rules of the law of war, there is also the rather more exceptional possibility that certain parts of that body of law are as a whole regarded as subject to reciprocity, so that conceivably the non-observance of such a part of the law by one party will have the effect of discharging the other party from its duties under it. This, in fact, is the gist of the argument advanced in an earlier Chapter in support of the thesis that the total disregard of occupation law by Germany had given the occupied populations a right of resistance as a form of self-defence, or, in other words, had freed them of their obligation, fundamental to that part of the law of war, to refrain from hostile activities.[7] The point should, however, be emphasized that here, like in the case of application of a reciprocity clause, reciprocity operates as an autonomous device, not as an instance of (or as a motivating factor behind) reprisals.

To concede the above exceptional possibility is not, however, to admit that reciprocity would be at the root of each and every rule of the law of war. On this point, I am in complete agreement with the opinion of Von der Heydte: [8] "A vrai dire, le droit de la guerre ne saurait admettre un droit absolu de réciprocité."

---

[5] *Ibid.*

[6] To the same effect: *Reaffirmation and Development, op. cit.* n. 57 to § 7.1, p. 83: "It is evident ... that if one Party, in violation of definite rules, employs weapons or other methods of warfare which give it an immediate, great military advantage, the adversary may, in its own defence, be induced to retort at once with similar measures."

[7] *Supra*, p. 204.

[8] *Annuaire, op. cit.* n. 42 to § 7.1, p. 90. *Cf.* also the conclusion formulated by the ICRC (*Reaffirmation and Development, loc. cit.* n. 6): "Reciprocity is a *de facto* element which should not be neglected. It can play an important role in the effective application of the rules concerned. To admit this element, which is more of a sociological order, as a principle of international law in the field considered would however be very dangerous."

In a note, the ICRC mentions that it "often invokes reciprocity when it is a matter of granting advantages to victims over and above the minimum guarantees from which they ought to benefit under international law." In this respect, *cf.* Schwarzenberger, *op. cit.* n. 2, p. 452, who after the quoted passage stating that "the laws of war constitute a typical illustration of the international law of reciprocity" goes on to

7.2.2. *Tu quoque*

Von der Heydte supports his quoted statement on reciprocity with the following argument: [9] "En effet, si l'on acceptait l'application intégrale de la règle *tu quoque*, il suffirait qu'au cours d'une guerre un Etat belligérant viole une norme de Droit international pour que cette norme n'ait plus de valeur durant toute la durée de la guerre." He evidently envisages *tu quoque* as a synonym for reciprocity, that is, as a substantive ground justifying otherwise unlawful modes of behaviour. There is, however, another possible view of *tu quoque*, according to which this does not so much constitute a substantive justificatory ground as an argument of a procedural order, to the effect that a belligerent cannot charge his enemy with a particular form of illegal warfare if he has himself violated the same rule or rules, without this being justified as a reprisal. For this argument, it is not important whether the belligerent was the first to commit that violation, nor even whether he was aware that the enemy was guilty of the same illegal conduct: the contention is that the mere fact of his having infringed the identical norm precludes him from charging that particular illegality against the enemy.

In essence, this is the argument relied upon in the foregoing for holding Great Britain precluded from maintaining its retaliatory measures against alleged illegal conduct of sea warfare by Germany, as from the moment it had itself adopted the same illegal practices as Germany was accused of.[10] The International Military Tribunal at Nuremberg came up against this very question when it had to decide whether Dönitz was guilty of waging indiscriminate submarine warfare, as charged against him under the head of war crimes. The Tribunal distinguished two elements in the practices: the actions against British armed merchant vessels, and the sinking of neutral merchant vessels in operational zones. With respect to the former element, the language used by the Tribunal amounts to a recognition that the sinking without warning of British armed merchant vessels did not constitute a war crime.[11] With respect to the latter of the two issues, however, the Tribunal couched its judgment in words which are strongly suggestive of the argument of *tu quoque*; it said: [12]

---

say that "[i]n particular, those rules of warfare which do not interfere seriously with the necessities of war benefit greatly from this powerful working principle behind the law." Indeed, there cannot be much objection against this effect of what Schwarzenberger styles "positive reciprocity".

[9] *Loc. cit.* n. 8.

[10] *Supra*, p. 151.

[11] "In the actual circumstances of this case, the Tribunal is not prepared to hold Dönitz guilty for his conduct of submarine warfare against British armed merchant ships." I.M.T., Vol. XXII, p. 558.

[12] *Ibid.*, p. 559.

"In view of all the facts proved, and in particular of an order of the British Admiralty announced on 8 May 1940, according to which all vessels should be sunk at night in the Skagerrak, and the answer to interrogatories by Admiral Nimitz that unrestricted submarine warfare was carried on in the Pacific Ocean by the United States from the first day that nation entered the war, the sentence of Dönitz is not assessed on the ground of his breach of the international law of submarine warfare."

While this formula admittedly is not free from ambiguity, the most likely interpretation seems to be that, while the Tribunal held the "breaches of the international law of submarine warfare" not justified in any way, it considered the Allied Powers to be precluded by their own similar practices from charging this *modus operandi* against Germany (or, as a war crime, against Dönitz as one of the individuals bearing direct responsibility for it).[13]

Whether *tu quoque* should be recognized as a valid procedural argument or not, it is not at any rate identical with reprisals. That it is, however, easily confused with reprisals, is demonstrated for example by a report in the International Law Reports,[14] asserting that according to the German *Bundesgerichtshof* the killing, towards the end of the Second World War, of foreign nationals employed in Germany as forced labourers "could not be justified as a legitimate reprisal under international law"; yet, as appears from the rest of the report, the Court in reality said that in the case at issue the accused could not avail himself of the plea of *tu quoque*.[15] Indeed, it seems important to realize that belligerent reprisals and *tu quoque* are as far apart as are sanctions of the law of war and a mere procedural expedient.

7.2.3. *Military necessity*

As belligerent reprisals include both the idea of enforcement of the law of war and the self-interest of the retaliating belligerent,[16] it is obvious that military necessity will often have an important place among the factors motivating the selection of specific reprisals. In respect to quasi-reprisals,

---

[13] To the same effect, *e.g.*: Von Knieriem, *op. cit.* n. 5 to § 7.1, at p. 334.—For a full discussion of the doctrine of *tu quoque*, see, *e.g.*: B. V. A. Röling, "The Law of War and the National Jurisdiction since 1945", in *R.d.C.* 1960, Vol. II, p. 389 ff.

[14] Vol. 32, p. 563; sentence of the *Bundesgerichtshof* of 30 September 1960.

[15] The Court said: "The rule of '*tu quoque*' merely means that no State may accuse another State of violations of international law and exercise criminal jurisdiction over the latter's citizens in respect of such violations if it is itself guilty of similar violations against the other State or its allies. The right and duty of a State to hold its own citizens responsible, in accordance with municipal criminal law, for violations of international law is not affected by this rule." *Ibid.*, p. 564.

[16] *Cf.* Chapter I, § 1.2.3.

or collective punishment, the rôle of military necessity is even more pronounced.[17]

Another matter is whether military necessity also operates as a separate ground justifying violations of the laws of war. This, again, is a much-discussed question. An author who answers it in a positive sense, Von Knieriem, concludes from the preamble to the Hague Convention on Land Warfare of 1899 that the annexed Regulations were no more than a guiding principle that only needed to be taken into account in so far as "military necessities" would permit.[18] This, however, is turning matters upside down; the passage in the preamble (to the effect that the wording of the provisions in the Regulations "a été inspirée par le désir de diminuer les maux de la guerre, autant que les nécessités militaires le permettent") clearly intended to convey that the authors of the Regulations had, in formulating the various rules, taken due account of the element of military necessity and balanced it against the principle of humanity.

Indeed, there is a strong tendency of opinion against the assertion that military necessity constitutes a separate ground justifying deviations from the laws of war. It may suffice to quote, with complete approval, one among many authoritative voices: according to Castrén,[19]

> "This view of the elasticity of the laws of war must be absolutely rejected as it cannot be legally justified and as its practical consequences are most dangerous. It would enable combatants to justify any deviation from the laws of war on the real or supposed ground of military necessity... The laws of war are the result of a compromise between military and humanitarian interests, and the necessities of war had already been sufficiently observed in the framing of those rules."

---

[17] *Supra*, p. 39.

[18] Von Knieriem, *op. cit.* n. 5 to § 7.1, at p. 321: "Die HKLO betrachtete also sich selbst als eine Richtschnur, die befolgt werden sollte, um die Leiden des Krieges zu mildern, aber nur, soweit es die 'militärischen Interessen' gestatteten."

[19] E. Castrén, *The Present Law of War and Neutrality*, 1954 ,p. 66. *Cf.* too Von der Heydte, *op. cit.* n. 42 to § 7.1, at p. 90; that author, whose argument has a bearing on weapons of mass destruction in particular, affirms that "au sein de l'état de nécessite [which is constituted by "la guerre de légitime défense"] il n'y a pas une nécessité supérieure légalisant l'emploi d'armes de destruction massive. Même dans une guerre licite, tout n'est pas permis; sans quoi, toute légalité finirait par disparaître de cette guerre."

For a recent, deep-probing analysis of the issue, see: Schwarzenberger, *op. cit.* n. 2, in particular pp. 128-136; that author, too, holds that "[t]he only legitimate form in which the priority of the necessities of war over international obligations can be secured is by way of reservation in the text of the rule itself" (p. 136, n. 37).

7.3. THE CHARACTER AND FUNCTION OF BELLIGERENT REPRISALS

In this final section, the character and function of belligerent reprisals will be assessed under the following aspects: the relation of belligerent reprisals to change of the laws of war, to international adjudication of disputes arising out of armed conflicts, to individual punishment of war crimes, and to outside supervision during the course of the armed conflict. The section will be concluded with a final appraisal of the merits and demerits of belligerent reprisals in present-day international society.

7.3.1. A misconception: belligerent reprisals as an alleged factor in changing the laws of war

A belligerent reprisal is first of all an act violating one or other rule of the laws of war. This can also be stated in a slightly different manner: an occasion where a belligerent reprisal seems permissible presents the belligerent with an opportunity to violate a rule of the law of war with impunity. It will depend on the circumstances of the case which action and, hence, the violation of which rule the belligerent will select for his purpose. In certain situations, the only practicable way will be to retaliate in kind. If, however, the belligerent has a choice, he may be expected to select that rule (or those rules) which he is most desirous to disregard in the context of the particular armed conflict in which he is involved. This expectation is in conformity with one of the two basic characteristics of a belligerent reprisal: besides being a measure of law enforcement, it also constitutes a measure of self-help.[1]

This feature of belligerent reprisals, combined with the observable fact that in both World Wars the label of "reprisals" has been attached to certain practices constituting deviations from the laws of war and which, once started, were maintained for the duration of the war,[2] has led some authors to conclude that it can be a function of belligerent reprisals to effect a change of the laws of war. Thus, Stone states that the instances which he mentions "require us to recognise that retaliation, which can be an effective sanction of the law of war, may also serve as a powerful instrument for *undermining* or *changing* the law of war"; and he even refers to the "legislative aspect of reprisals".[3]

This theory, however, is ill-founded in all respects. In the first place, it rests on singularly little evidence, both from a quantitative and qualitative point of view. For, while the history of the Second World War yields only

[1] See Chapter I, § 1.2.3, *supra*.
[2] As for the Second World War, see Chapters IV (economic warfare at sea) and V, § 5.1 (aerial bombardment).
[3] Stone, *op. cit.* n. 2 to § 7.2, at pp. 355 and 356.

very few examples of practices of the type described above (the examples usually cited being economic warfare at sea, and the development of aerial bombardment), it is a moot point whether even in those rare instances the law of war was decisively influenced by the practices in question. In particular the development of legal opinion concerning aerial bombardment, which finally resulted in the unanimous adoption of General Assembly Resolution 2444 (XXIII) of 19 December 1968 prohibiting without reserve attacks on the civil population as such, as well as attacks that are indiscriminate in character,[4] seems irreconcilable with the contention that *opinio juris* would have come to accept such practices as lawful. And, while perhaps the state of the law of economic warfare is rather less settled,[5] this is a consequence, not so much of the fact that deviations have been announced as "reprisals", but of the inherent weakness of that body of law which has always rested on a precarious balance of interests between belligerents and neutrals. Moreover, it seems very much to be doubted that in particular the practice of indiscriminate use of mines on the high seas and of sinking merchant vessels at sight, regardless of whether they are belligerent or neutral, armed or unarmed, hostile or peaceful, would have acquired the character (in the terms of Article 38 of the Statute of the International Court of Justice) of "a general practice accepted as law".

While the above criticism has a bearing on the evidentiary value of the precedents underlying the theory of the "legislative" function of belligerent reprisals, an objection of even more principal concern is that the theory is illogical and contradictory. If a belligerent desires to adopt a certain policy despite its probable illegality, and if he then seeks to justify it as a belligerent reprisal, the effect is the strengthening, rather than the undermining, of the legal force of the rule at issue. For, while it may be perhaps too strong to say (as Schwarzenberger does) that "the very resort to reprisals implies the admission of the inherent illegality of the act taken in

---

[4] *Supra*, p. 284.

[5] *Cf.*, *e.g.*, McDougal and Feliciano, *op. cit.* n. 27 to § 7.1, p. 479: "From any perspective that seeks to transcend concern with the syntactic elegance of a 'formal legal analysis' and to relate past experience to probable future decision in comparable contexts, it would seem evident that, despite the disingenuous use by belligerents of technical labels, the traditional law has not remained virginally intact. The embargo measures repetitively applied in the two world wars realistically involve something more than the exceptional, emergency response to a violation of an unquestioned authoritative prescription which the conception of 'reprisals' ordinarily connotes. The nearly universal nonobservance in two global wars of certain nineteenth-century prescriptions which these measures reflect strongly suggest, on the contrary, the clear emergence and crystallization of the particular expectations of uniformities and rightness in decision commonly called law—or, in other words, the growth and development of new patterns of customary law."—As far as "rightness in decision" is concerned, I would draw the line at the more particularly inhumane aspects of the "embargo measures" to which the authors refer: the indiscriminate use of mines, and unrestricted submarine warfare.

368

retaliation",[6] it implies in any event the express recognition of its dubious legality, that is, of its probable illegality. It seems hard to conceive that such a recognition would lead to the exact opposite of what it so clearly suggests.

This leads to the conclusion that it is a misconception to regard belligerent reprisals as an "instrument for undermining or changing the law of war". As Greenspan has it: [7] "Reprisals are illegitimate acts of warfare, not for the purpose of indicating abandonment of the laws of war, but, on the contrary, to force compliance to those laws."

7.3.2. An inconsistency: belligerent reprisals and international adjudication of wartime events

It is characteristic for belligerent reprisals that belligerents claim the right to enforce the law of war in respect to their enemies. In pursuance (or under the pretext) of that claimed right, they have shown themselves prepared to resort to measures that put in jeopardy the life or health of thousands of human beings. In this light, it would be no more than logical that this disposition would also find expression in a readiness on the part of belligerents (or former belligerents) to subject their own and the enemy's conduct of the war to the test of adjudication by qualified international courts or tribunals.

The contrary is the case, however. Not only are war claims rarely adjudicated before such international fora, but even among those States which have voluntarily accepted the compulsory jurisdiction of the International Court of Justice by making a declaration to that effect under Article 36, paragraph 2, of the Statute of the Court, a significant number have expressly excluded disputes arising out of armed conflicts in which they are or have been involved.[8] The effect of these reservations is moreover multiplied by the operation of the principle of reciprocity.

[6] Schwarzenberger, op. cit. n. 2 to § 7.2, at p. 236.
[7] M. Greenspan, The Modern Law of Land Warfare, 1959, p. 408.
[8] A typical instance is furnished by Great Britain, which on 28 February 1940 deposited a declaration of voluntary acceptance in which were excluded "disputes arising out of events occurring at a time when His Majesty's Government in the United Kingdom were involved in hostilities" (Yearbook of the ICJ, 1946-47, p. 212; cf. too supra, p. 153). That State has maintained a similar reservation ever since; since 1955, it is formulated as follows: "disputes arising out of, or having reference to, any hostilities, war, state of war, or belligerent or military occupation in which the Government of the United Kingdom are or have been involved" (Yearbook of the ICJ, 1954-55, p. 188; declaration of 2 June 1955).
As for the United States of America, there is no need to make an express reservation of this purport, so long as the so-called Connally amendment is maintained which excludes "disputes with regard to matters which are essentially within the domestic jurisdiction of the United States of America as determined by the United States of America" (Yearbook of the ICJ, 1946-47, p. 217; declaration of 14 August

369

It is of course hardly consistent for belligerents to set themselves up as judges of their enemies' conduct of warfare and at the same time to refuse expressly to recognize the jurisdiction of the Court with respect to such wartime events in which they are themselves involved. This inconsistency, however, in reality is nothing but a symptom of the high degree of de-centralization which characterizes international society up to the present day,[9] and which leads to an over-emphasis on the powers of States in their capacity as authorities in international society and a corresponding tendency to minimize the effective rôle of existing international organs. While one may already regret having to accept this situation for normal times, it becomes a poignant injustice in its application to times of armed conflict. Needless to say, this consideration profoundly influences the appreciation of the value of belligerent reprisals as a sanction of the laws of war.

7.3.3. An alternative: belligerent reprisals and individual punishment of war crimes

The above reflection automatically leads to the question of whether there is any suitable alternative to belligerent reprisals. In fact, it has been found in the foregoing that belligerents have on several occasions refrained from resorting to reprisals and instead have announced their intention to punish individual perpetrators of war crimes.[10] Is this the alternative sought?

One thing should be stated at the outset: belligerent reprisals and punishment of war crimes are not mutually exclusive. In other words, a belligerent who has retaliated against a particular illegality committed by the enemy, is not thereby precluded from punishing those who bear individual responsibility for it.[11] On the other hand, it is not an un-reasonable expectation that, once a belligerent announces as his set policy that he will pursue the punishment of individual war criminals for their personal guilt, he will not at the same time take recourse to reprisals, which, although in theory directed against the State, in reality affect indi-

---

1946). Significantly, when France in 1959 withdrew its Connally-type reservation, it inserted the following formula instead: "disputes arising out of any war or interna-tional hostilities and disputes arising out of a crisis affecting the national security or out of any measure or action relating thereto" (Yearbook of the ICJ, 1958-59, p. 212; declaration of 10 July 1959).

Out of the 42 States which according to the Yearbook of the ICJ of 1967-68 had by then accepted the compulsory jurisdiction of the Court, 14 had excluded disputes arising out of wartime events.

[9] *Supra*, p. 14.
[10] *Supra*, pp. 214, 294.
[11] *Supra*, pp. 26, 214.

vidual persons and even, more likely than not, persons who are innocent of the crime retaliated against.[12]

Another obvious problem, inherent in particular in post-war punishment of war crimes, arises from the absence of an international tribunal authorized to take cognizance of such cases irrespective of which side has won. As a result, only a belligerent who feels confident that he will win the war can with equal confidence announce his policy to bring the enemy war criminals to trial. If he does not entertain such a definite expectation, his announcement will be a mere empty threat. On the other hand, the possibility of immediate retaliation is open to any belligerent, irrespective of his chances of winning the war. This consideration may lead to a preference for retaliation, unless, of course, the attitude of the enemy makes it clear that that course of action will be equally ineffectual.[13]

This leaves the possibility of punishment of individual war crimes during the course of the war. A first and obvious difficulty of such a policy is that it will in all probability affect only the comparatively insignificant, petty war criminals, as those individuals who can be considered major war criminals are unlikely to expose themselves to the risk of falling into enemy hands during the war. And, on top of this unsatisfactory feature, there is also the fundamental objection that every more than incidental resort to punishment of war crimes during the course of the war cannot fail to evoke a reaction on the part of the enemy and thus will tend to set in motion a chain reaction of retaliatory measures, leading to an increased non-observance of the laws of war and hence to the opposite of the contemplated result.[14]

Viewed in this light, there is little reason why belligerents should prefer punishment of war crimes to belligerent reprisals. Indeed, it seems not too far-fetched to suggest, as Schwarzenberger does, that "[i]t corresponds probably most closely to the evolution of the laws of war to view jurisdiction over war criminals under international customary law as an individualised form of reprisals."[15] On the other hand, from the point of view of desirable development of the law of war there are obvious grounds to prefer the individualized responsibility inherent in individual punishment of war crimes to the collective "responsibility" of innocent, that is, non-responsible, persons which is a characteristic of recourse to belligerent reprisals.

For the development of the idea of individual punishment, it is not enough to lay an obligation on States "to enact any legislation necessary to

[12] *Supra*, p. 42.
[13] *Supra*, p. 214.
[14] P. Boissier describes the idea of punishment of war crimes as "impuissante à servir de frein, mais bien propre, au contraire, à provoquer cette surenchère vers le pire qui est la forme diabolique de la réciprocité"; *L'épée et la balance*, 1952, p. 125.
[15] Schwarzenberger, *op. cit.* n. 2 to § 7.2, p. 453.

provide effective penal sanctions for persons committing, or ordering to be committed, any of the grave breaches" of the laws of war. It is a significant step forward to add the obligation for States either to try or to hand over for trial any persons "alleged to have committed, or to have ordered to be committed, such grave breaches", and this "regardless of their nationality".[16] But practice shows that there is less than little inclination on the part of States to give automatic implementation to such seemingly categorical obligations. The conclusion seems inescapable that the only manner in which this situation might be radically mended, would be by the creation of an international judicature having jurisdiction (and power to bring its jurisdiction to bear) over all, or, at any rate, over the grave, war crimes. It is, however, no less evident that there is for the time being little chance that this idea will be realized.[17]

7.3.4. A substitute: belligerent reprisals and outside supervision

It emerges from the foregoing that belligerent reprisals, though prohibited in a number of situations, have not so far been completely outlawed. In particular, while a strong case can be made out in favour of the contention that application of fundamental principles of the law of reprisals must lead to the outlawry of belligerent reprisals against the enemy civil population, no consensus exists in that respect, nor has an express prohibition to that effect yet been achieved. On the other hand, the possibility of punishment of individual war criminals, though important and deserving of further development, cannot at present be considered as a sufficient alternative for belligerent reprisals in all events.

In these circumstances, is there any prospect of their complete abolition in the near future? With respect to this question, the following considerations seem pertinent. Nearly all the prohibitions achieved so far belong to the sphere of the "law of Geneva" (the only exception being the prohibition

[16] These obligations are found in the Conventions of Geneva of 1949 for grave breaches of their provisions; *supra*, p. 271. For the question of whether these provisions amount to an application of the universality principle, see the discussion between B. V. A. Röling and M. W. Mouton in *Netherlands International Law Review*, Vols. VI, 1959 (special issue: Liber Amicorum J. P. A. François) p. 263, and VII, 1960, pp. 59 and 144.

[17] *Cf.* Chapter VI, § 6.2.4, for a discussion of the dealings of the International Law Commission and the General Assembly of the United Nations with the matter. The ICRC in its report *Reaffirmation and Development* (*op. cit.* n. 57 to § 7.1) concludes that: "The repression of serious violations of the basic rules relating to the conduct of hostilities should certainly be explicitly provided, according to the pattern of a more developed law, while taking into account the particular conditions—combat—under which these violations often occur. It should also be endeavoured to ensure that the repressive bodies are of the most impartial nature possible—although judgment for war crimes subsequent to the close of hostilities (it must be pointed out) was not instituted for the conflicts which occurred after 1945" (p. 93).

of reprisals against cultural property, embodied in the Convention of The Hague of 1954). In that branch of the law of war, "military necessities" play a comparatively modest part. Moreover, all the conventions concerned are conspicuous for their elaborate provisions concerning supervision by a neutral body.[18] Indeed, as has been suggested in an earlier part of this study, this feature, rather than the incorporation of provisions about the punishment of violations, was the determining factor which rendered the effective prohibition of reprisals feasible.[19]

Obviously, the situation is much less favourable in respect to the "law of The Hague". No general system of neutral supervision has so far been provided for that branch of the law of war, nor does it seem at all probable that the introduction of such a system would readily be considered compatible with the requirements of "military necessity". And even if one sets about designing a system of supervision for a specific part of the law of combat, such as the rules prohibiting the use of chemical and biological means of warfare, one will find oneself confronted with great difficulties, as has been amply demonstrated in the Disarmament Conference of 1932-1934; for the participants in that Conference, the difficulties even proved insurmountable.[20]

In this context, it may be useful to make a distinction between the rules prohibiting the use of certain means of warfare (such as dum-dum bullets, or gas) and the rules putting limitations to certain not completely prohibited methods or means of warfare (such as the exclusion of the civil population as a legitimate object of attack, and the requirement to spare the civil population as much as possible in attacking military objectives). As experience shows, the difficulties inherent in any attempt to render prohibitions of the first type both effective and absolute (so that reciprocity and reprisals will be excluded too) are twofold: provision will have to be made for the supervision of their observance during the course of an armed conflict, and there will have to be an effective guarantee that no prohibited preparations are made in time of peace for the use of the means in question in a future armed conflict. In other words, the solution of the riddle presented by an attempt of this kind is narrowly connected, *inter alia*, with the achievement of effective peacetime disarmament measures.

The framing of rules limiting the permissible use of certain methods or means of warfare, on the other hand, is not in this manner entangled with

[18] *Cf.* Chapter VI, §§ 6.2.1 and 6.2.2.
[19] *Supra*, pp. 72, 106, 213.
[20] Chapter III, § 3.3. Similar difficulties are met by the United Nations and the Conference of the Committee on Disarmament (*supra*, n. 41 to § 7.1) in their attempts to bring about a more adequate prohibition of chemical and biological means of warfare. It is of course too early to venture any prediction about the probable outcome of these efforts, let alone of similar efforts that may follow in the future with respect to nuclear weapons.

373

the disarmament issue. Yet, the problems involved in devising a completely effective system of supervision for rules of this type are hardly less difficult to solve. First, such supervision must be on the spot, and the neutral bodies charged with this task must as a minimum be empowered, not only to enter into contact with the authorities of the party they are supervising, but also to exchange information with their colleagues on the other side. Only in this manner can a situation be brought about where the allegations of belligerent parties (one contending that it has attacked and hit a military barracks, and the other maintaining that the object actually hit was a school with innocent children and that there was no military objective in the vicinity) are replaced by, or at least supplemented with, a rather more objective appreciation.

And this is not all: supervision of the observance of this type of rules must not be restricted to *ex post facto* investigation and appreciation, but should preferably also be preventive. This would mean that the supervisory bodies would have power to interfere in the military decision-making process and, whether requested or not, to give their advice as to what would be a permissible course of action in a given situation, and what not. Only when all these conditions are fulfilled, can a system of neutral supervision really be expected to be completely effective. Even then, the possibility remains that a belligerent elects to disregard the admonitions of the supervisors and to transgress the limits. No system of supervision can prevent such a course: it can merely indicate the individuals responsible for the war crime thus committed. In such a case, however, it does not seem at all unreasonable to hold the belligerent who is a victim of the criminal act precluded from taking recourse to a reprisal, as such a measure of law enforcement cannot be expected to achieve any positive result with an adversary who has so openly demonstrated his determination to disregard the law in the face of the world.

The above considerations lead to the conclusion that it does not seem very probable that the difficulties inherent in devising a really foolproof system of supervision for the "law of The Hague" will be overcome within a measurable time. Yet, the need for some measure of supervision as a substitute for reprisals is perhaps even more pronounced here than in respect of the "law of Geneva". For, while considerations of "military necessity" may be expected to urge belligerents to take effective countermeasures against any disturbance of the military power ratio resulting from a breach by the enemy of the laws governing the conduct of warfare, elements like distrust and susceptibility to rumours are likely to enhance the chance that, in the absence of any outside supervision, their reactions to such (actual or alleged) breaches will be disproportionate or even entirely premature.

It seems therefore an urgent task to find, not a completely effective, so much as a reasonably adequate solution for the problem of supervision in

374

this domain of the law of war.[21] A condition for any such solution will be that it does not involve too great a security risk for belligerents. If that condition were met, States might perhaps be ready to agree to such a less than perfect scheme, coupled with the possibility of punishment of war crimes, as a sufficient substitute for belligerent reprisals as a means to enforce the "law of The Hague". If they hesitate, it might be pointed out to them that belligerent reprisals have not generally proved a particularly effective means of law enforcement either.

7.3.5. Final appraisal: merits and demerits of belligerent reprisals in an anachronistic world-order

Belligerent reprisals, though by now prohibited in important fields of the law of war, have not so far come under a total prohibition. The branch where they have not been banned yet, to wit, the law of combat, or "law of The Hague", is precisely the field where recourse to belligerent reprisals can be most damaging to human values. On the other hand, the interests at stake are so great and the issues involved so complicated, that it will be no slight task to achieve an express, reasonably effective prohibition of belligerent reprisals for this part of the law of war too.

In the end, it is submitted, such a total prohibition of belligerent reprisals is the only tenable proposition. However, as was just argued at some length, a prerequisite for the efficacy of any further steps towards that goal is that these are accompanied by the creation of other suitable means providing belligerents with a sufficient guarantee that the laws of war will be respected in their regard. In other words, the power of belligerents to resort to belligerent reprisals can only be effectively abolished to the extent that other adequate means take over their function of law enforcement.

This function, it was stated at the outset, was precisely the chief merit of belligerent reprisals as well as the principal argument in favour of their justification.[22] Indeed, this basic idea of their justifiability as sanctions of the law of war and, hence, as instruments of the international legal order, was maintained throughout the present study. Nor is this peculiar to this

---

[21] Cf. Reaffirmation and Development, op. cit. n. 57 to § 7.1, p. 91, where a similar conclusion is formulated: "The difficulties of the undertaking should not be concealed. The fields of the law of war in question are precisely those where violations may have the most serious consequences and arouse an outburst of passion. Moreover, in these fields, as has been pointed out, belligerents are suspicious in advance of anything which would hamper a freedom of action often considered vital to their very existence. Nevertheless, great as the difficulties may be, the interests of the international community itself and of peace must take priority: these demand that the necessity of submitting to impartial supervision the regular observation of every aspect of humanitarian law applicable in armed conflicts should in future be unanimously admitted."

[22] Chapter I, §§ 1.2.3 and 1.3.4.

study: it has remained usual to the present day to rely on the function of law enforcement attributed to belligerent reprisals to justify their continued existence. Thus, McDougal and Feliciano in their book *Law and Minimum World Public Order* express their view in the following terms: [23]

> "Obviously the doctrine of reprisals, like all authoritative policies, is vulnerable to perversion and abuse. By itself, however, this vulnerability cannot be decisive of the utility or desirability of the reprisals doctrine. In the context of continuing hostilities, and until a comprehensive, centralized, and effective sanctions process is achieved in the world arena, belligerents have to police one another and enforce the laws of war against each other."

There is, however, reason to re-examine this starting-point. A great part of the conceivable applications of belligerent reprisals has been outlawed: can the remaining part still be said to operate as sanctions of the law of war? Two arguments in particular urge a reconsideration of this question. One is of a practical order: neither in the history of the Second World War, nor of subsequent armed conflicts, was there found so much as a single instance of a retaliatory act, resorted to in the sphere of the "law of The Hague", and constituting a genuine belligerent reprisal aiming to enforce the law of war in respect of the enemy. The other argument is that the development of nuclear weapons, guided missiles, and similar additions to the military arsenal has brought about a state of affairs where recourse to belligerent reprisals can entail consequences so disastrous for the enemy civil population and, indeed, for humanity in general, that here the idea of law enforcement has to give way to the sheer inhumanity inherent in such reprisals.

While perhaps neither of these objections is in itself sufficient ground to override the argument that "vulnerability to perversion and abuse cannot be decisive of the utility or desirability of the reprisals doctrine", their combined effect seems to amount to precisely that. The present study has amply shown that there is singularly little left of this utility and desirability, elements which as long ago as 1873 led Henri Brocher to qualify the doctrine of reprisals as "le symptôme d'un progrès".[24] Admittedly, there is always the theoretical possibility for belligerents to resort to retaliatory actions infringing such rules as the prohibition to demolish private property without sufficient necessity, or to use enemy uniforms, and then to claim that the actions constitute justifiable belligerent reprisals. This, however, is indeed no more than a theoretical possibility. The actions that are really considered are the retaliatory use of nuclear weapons and other weapons of mass destruction, the retaliatory resort to indiscriminate aerial bombardment, and similar drastic actions. And, while certain of these may be saved

[23] *Op. cit.,* p. 681.
[24] *Supra,* p. 44.

376

from the verdict of illegality by the operation of a reciprocity clause attached to specific rules, it was argued at some length that the characteristics of this type of actions stand in the way of their being justified as belligerent reprisals and, indeed, render an express prohibition against such reprisals urgently necessary.[25] In this light, the conclusion seems inescapable that the balance of the merits and demerits of belligerent reprisals has now become so entirely negative as no longer to allow of their being regarded as even moderately effective sanctions of the laws of war, and of the "law of The Hague" in particular: in the whole of the international legal order, they have become a complete anachronism.

This ultimately negative judgment about the legal function of what has remained of belligerent reprisals does not, however, lead us to suggest that they should be abolished out of hand and without adequate provision having been made to fill the gap. For, while belligerent reprisals may have lost virtually all credibility as sanctions of the law of war and, hence, as an institution of the international legal order, there can still be another use in belligerents placing reliance in the doctrine and announcing that a certain mode of acting constitutes a "belligerent reprisal". The function envisaged here is not a novelty in any way, and in fact has always been a characteristic of those peacetime reprisals constituting "measures short of war" in the traditional sense: it is to indicate to the adversary that a given step up the ladder of violence is not meant to inaugurate unrestricted warfare, but merely to constitute a measured reaction to a change in the level of violence applied by the adversary, and to hint that further steps up the ladder of escalation will only follow if, and to the extent that, his conduct of warfare necessitates these.[26] Viewed thus, the function of such "belligerent reprisals" is in reality nothing very different from what Henri Brocher described as "un moyen d'empêcher la guerre de devenir tout-à-fait barbare".[27] But it should be realized that the mechanism envisaged here is totally different from that of belligerent reprisals as sanctions of the law of war, the purpose of which was to effect a de-escalation in the level of unlawful violence on the part of the enemy.

In this light, the subsistence to this day, and probably into the foreseeable future, of the remnant of belligerent reprisals, not as a reasonably credible sanction of the laws of war, but as a signal in the military-political power relations between belligerents, is once again a symptom of the imperfect state of affairs in international society. It is an astounding, but no less unmistakable fact that in an era where every imaginable technical achievement seems within the reach of mankind, the possibility can seriously be considered for belligerents to use single nuclear explosions over enemy

[25] This Chapter, §§ 7.1.3 and 7.1.4.
[26] *Cf.* Chapter I, § 1.1. About escalation in peace and war, see: H. Kahn, *On Escalation*, 1965.
[27] *Loc. cit.* n. 24.

territory as an indication of their determination, unless further challenged, not to resort to total nuclear war. It does not appear too exaggerated to qualify this degenerate rôle of the concept of belligerent reprisals, not merely as an anachronism, but as a symptom of an anachronistic world-order.

378

Index of Names[1]

---

[1] Includes authors' names mentioned in footnotes.

Subject Index

prohibited possession of, 32, 40, 207, 316

See also: mines

World Health Organization, 306

wounded, sick and shipwrecked, 69, 104, 108, 263, 265, 333, 356

See also: Geneva Conventions of 1929, 1949; Hague Convention for the Adaptation to Maritime Warfare of the Principles of the Geneva Convention, 1899/1907

Yemen, British air attack on Harib Fortress in, 291-292